TORAH OF THE MOTHERS

TORAH OF THE MOTHERS

Contemporary Jewish Women Read
Classical Jewish Texts

edited by

Ora Wiskind Elper *and* Susan Handelman

URIM PUBLICATIONS
Jerusalem • New York

Torah of the Mothers: Contemporary Jewish Women Read Classical
Jewish Texts
edited by Ora Wiskind Elper and Susan Handelman

About the cover image: Torah cover with the verse from Proverbs 1:8: "Hear,
my child, the instruction of your father, and forsake not the Torah of your
mother." It was designed by Nili Sverdlov and embroidered at the Kuzari
workshop in Jerusalem. The Hebrew lettering and decorations are based upon
the tradition in Silesia during the 17th and 18th centuries of embroidering
Torah binders, or wimples, made from the swaddling clothes of a circumcised
infant. This mantle is used today to cover a Torah scroll which was dedicated
by the children of Joseph V. and Sarah R. Richler of Montreal to the synagogue
of Midrashiyat Amalia in Givat Mordechai, Jerusalem.

Urim Publications, P.O. Box 52287, Jerusalem 91521 Israel

Lambda Publishers Inc.
3709 13th Avenue Brooklyn, New York 11218 U.S.A.
Tel: 718-972-5449 Fax: 718-972-6307
E-mail: mh@ejudaica.com

www.UrimPublications.com

Dedicated, with much love and gratitude, to three women who have taught me by their living example that the deepest meaning and wisdom of *Torat imekha* is *Torat hesed*, the "Torah of lovingkindness": my mother, Miriam (bat Frayda) Handelman, and my dear friends Faige Benjamin and Sara Tzirel Beyer (Aisenfeld). *–S.H.*

and

To Avivah Gottleib Zornberg and to my children, whose love and wisdom have guided my path in learning, in teaching and in mothering. *–O.W.E.*

CONTENTS

PREFACE

"שמע בני מוסר אביך ואל תטש תורת אמך"

**"Hear, my child, the instruction of your father and
forsake not the Torah of your mother."**
(Proverbs 1:8)

This verse, from which we have taken the title of our book, has inspired
and guided us through the long process of its gestation and birth. *Torat
imekha*, the "Torah of your mother," has always been a special part of
Jewish tradition, which often speaks of distinctive maternal and paternal
modes of guidance, of encountering others, of teaching and learning. On
the verse, "Thus shall you say to the house of Jacob and tell the children
of Israel" (Exodus 19:3), describing the giving of the Torah at Sinai, the
well-known midrash says: "'*beit Ya'akov*' (the house of Jacob)—these are
the women; '*benei Yisrael*' (the children of Israel)—these are the men"
(*Mekhilta, Bahodesh* 2). These words teach us that the Torah was given to
the "Mothers" and to the "Fathers"; each was charged to pass on, from
generation to generation, a unique aspect of that divine, eternal message.

We are privileged to be part of an era that has seen an unprecedented
flowering of women's learning and teaching of Torah. This book has
grown out of our desire to bring to a wide audience the insights of many
highly accomplished religious Jewish women teachers of our generation.
For these women, love of Torah—in addition to their intellectual interest
in Hebrew texts—is a central force in their lives. They strive not only to
enhance their students' skills in encountering the sources independently,
but also to inspire that love, aid their human development, and enable
them to draw personal meaning from the texts. Their teaching is analyti-
cally rigorous, but always connected to the spiritual dimensions of our
lives.

And so, too, we intend this to be a book of "Torah teachings," rather than a compilation of academic essays. A book which is meant to be "learned" as well as "read"—its messages slowly imbibed, savored and internalized. The Rabbis themselves likened the Torah to mother's milk: vitally nourishing, ever renewed and available, the understanding and "taste" (*ta'am*) we draw from it is uniquely suited to each of our needs (*Eruvin* 54b).

R. Naftali Tzvi Yehudah Berlin, the "Netziv," in his reflections on the nature of "the instruction of your father" and "Torah of your mother," notes that the Written Torah, or the *Humash* (Five Books of Moshe) is conceived by the Rabbis, in one sense, as a "masculine" entity, emerging directly from God, original and yet incomprehensible on its own. The Oral Torah (beginning with the biblical prophetic books, or *Nevi'im*, in his view) is conceived, by contrast, as "feminine" insofar as it continually transfers its understanding of the Written Torah from one "vessel" to another, each vessel transforming the contents it receives according to its own form. The role of the prophets and later of the Rabbis and, finally, of every teacher is to enable the Divine Word to penetrate, speak to us, be grasped—in all our imperfection, whenever we are ready (*Davar haEmek* on Proverbs 1:8).

In this era of deep spiritual search, when the place and role of the Jewish woman in the synagogue, study hall, family and community are being reexamined, we believe that the teachings of women who have inspired so many, who have forged the path to a new level of Jewish commitment and study, have much to offer. The authors who contributed to this book have advanced educational backgrounds in both the Jewish and secular realms. The majority live in Israel; they teach in Hebrew and English in a variety of settings—*yeshivot*, universities, seminaries, adult education classes— and most have not extensively published their insights. Each speaks in her own distinct voice and takes a distinctive approach. Several of the topics our contributors have chosen deal with women as biblical characters, or "feminine" images and aspects of the Torah; others do not. There are also readings of biblical figures such as Avraham, Ya'akov, Moshe and of midrashic and talmudic passages on subjects such as creation, exile, *teshuvah* (repentance) and redemption. This multiplicity reflects our vision, for "Torah of the Mothers" is not confined to women or women's issues. It extends and breathes a special life into all parts of Torah.

* * *

The essays in this collection fall into four general categories. The first section, "Students and Teachers," contains five articles in which the authors write personally of figures who critically influenced their development and were, in their eyes, true teachers in the traditional Jewish sense. That crucial interaction between *Rav* and *talmid*, or teacher and student, is described extensively in classical Jewish texts, usually on the model of male student and teacher. The new opportunities afforded our generation have enabled women Torah scholars to benefit from and describe such formative relations with their teachers as well. We placed this section first in the conviction that Torah is much more than a text printed on a page; ultimately, it is also an intensely lived interaction within a community of teachers and students, colleagues and friends, parents and children, generation and generation.

In the next section, "Readings of Biblical Texts," we gathered the essays that focus on biblical figures and are based, primarily, on biblical narratives. These articles encompass a range of topics, from the infertility of the biblical matriarchs and the problems posed by infertility today, to the inheritance claims of the daughters of Tzlafchad as a model for navigating the issues of feminism and Orthodox Judaism, to the figures of Deborah and Esther as heroines, to Avraham's relation to non-Jews, to the aging patriarch Ya'akov's reflections on his life.

In the third section, "Readings of Rabbinic Texts," we move to analyses of midrashic and talmudic texts. These essays carefully examine rabbinic views of Creation, images of King and Daughter in midrashic parables, the meaning of self-affliction on Yom Kippur and the process of *teshuvah*, and the significance of Jerusalem. Each article is a close literary and theological reading, seeking a deeper understanding of God's relation to the world, to Israel and to human yearning.

In the final section, we brought together several articles dealing with the great paradigm of "Exile and Redemption" in Jewish, as well as human, experience: essays on Moshe as an adopted child and struggling leader, and the Children of Israel's experiences in Egypt and the wilderness. The approaches taken by the authors and the sources and perspectives they bring vary widely, from linguistics to psychology to classical rabbinic methodology and interpretation, to hasidic readings and kabbalistic symbolism. They reflect the richness of background and approach contemporary religious Jewish women are bringing to Torah study.

The concluding essay leads us "Beyond the Study Hall" into some pressing social issues, and calls us to remember that the tradition of *Torat imekha* is also a tradition urging us to acts of lovingkindness, *hesed*— responding to whomever is vulnerable and in need. For when all is said and done, "Study is not the main thing, but deeds" (*Kiddushin* 40b). We learn, though, from this same text that study is essential nonetheless, because it guides us to proper action.

* * *

In speaking of the biblical Miriam, in whose merit a well was said to have accompanied the Children of Israel in the desert to assuage their thirst (Exodus 20:1–2; *Ta'anit* 9a), R. Kalonymus Kalman Shapira (the Rebbe of Piaseczena and last spiritual leader of the Warsaw ghetto, martyred in the Holocaust) recalled his own departed wife, Rachel Hayyah Miriam. He writes, "She learned Torah every day and was a merciful mother to every despairing soul," and comments that the merit of such righteous women sustained many souls in times of hardship. Their actions were motivated not by external compulsion (commandment), but by a force welling from deep within them. The community was nourished from these "feminine waters" drawn out of love and compassion (*Eish Kodesh*, "Dedication" and "*Hukkat*," 5702/1942, page 183). Our hope is that the essays in this volume, like Miriam's well, will be a source of living waters.

Rav Joseph Dov Soloveitchik also pondered the meaning of the maternal and paternal traditions alluded to in the verse from Proverbs 1:8— *Mussar avikha*, "the instruction of your father" and *Torat imekha*, "the Torah of your mother." Drawing on his own experiences, the Rav said:

> Most of all I learned [from my mother] that Judaism expresses itself
> not only in formal compliance with the law but also in a living experi-
> ence. She taught me that there is a flavor, a scent and warmth to *mitz-*
> *vot*. I learned from her the most important thing in life—to feel the
> presence of the Almighty and the gentle pressure of His hand resting
> upon my frail shoulders. Without her teachings, which quite often
> were transmitted to me in silence, I would have grown up a soul-less
> being, dry and insensitive.
> ("A Tribute to the Rebbetzin of Talne," *Tradition*, Spring 1978,
> pages 73–83)

This sense of "living experience" embodied here in the mother emerges
from the love, understanding and trust she shares with her child. The
relationship between student and teacher, if it is built on the same values,
is equally vital. To imbue words of Torah in the heart of a student, say the
Rabbis, is tantamount to giving birth to that person (*Sanhedrin* 99b).

> R. Elazar said in the name of R. Hanina: "All your children shall be
> taught of the Lord and great shall be the peace of your children"
> (Isaiah 54:13)—do not read "your children" (*bannayikh*) but "your
> builders" (*bonnayikh*).

May this book give birth to many "children," to students blessed with
the strength to build and to spread peace in the world. "May all who love
Your Torah be blessed with peace and may their path not falter."
(*Berakhot* 64a)

Ora Wiskind Elper and Susan Handelman
Jerusalem
Elul, 5760
September, 2000

We gratefully acknowledge the many teachers, friends and colleagues, without whom this work could not have come to fruition. First, our publisher, Tzvi Mauer of Urim Publications, whose unfailing moral support, patience and technical guidance were critical from beginning to end; Sorelle Wachmann, for her devoted attention to the editing and layout of the manuscript; Anne Gordon, whose generous and astute editorial assistance was indispensable; and Emma Corney, for her diligent proofreading.

Next, our teachers: it would be impossible to list all who have so brilliantly and passionately given their Torah to us, illumined our minds and hearts, and made us what we are. Among those who have especially taught us what it means to be a true *talmidat hakham* ("student of the wise," i.e., Torah scholar), we gratefully thank Chana Balanson *z"l*, Nechama Leibowitz *z"l*, Malke Binah, Tamar Ross and Avivah Gottlieb Zornberg. Finally, we give thanks to the One who is mentioned countless times in the pages of this book and to whom we owe the greatest debt of all: *HaKadosh Barukh Hu*, The Holy One Blessed be He.

Students and Teachers

God of My Teachers:
Learning With Rav Soloveitchik

Gilla Ratzersdorfer Rosen

Many years ago, when I was a college freshman, I was approached by a fellow student, eager (it turned out) to convert me. As we sat down on the grass, she asked me how I could relate to a totally male God?

I stared at the poor girl in astonishment. Her question intrigued me. If Judaism had a male God, I hadn't noticed (this was in the *early* 70's). In school, I had been brought up on the God of Maimonides—starkly incorporeal and abstract, omnipresent yet invisible, almost colorless, devoid of anthropomorphic characteristics.

If there was a fault in my education, it was that God was left too abstract for a child—unimaginable, inscrutable, unreachable—approachable only through the set prayers of the Siddur.[1] If the language used to

---

* This essay is based on my personal experience of a *drashah* (Torah lecture) given by Rabbi Joseph Dov Soloveitchik in memory of his wife, on 11th *Adar* 5728/March 10, 1968. It does not represent a comprehensive study of the maternal depiction of God in the Bible (as understood either in midrash or by contemporary feminist thought). Nor is it an attempt to encapsulate the thought of R. Soloveitchik on the subject. Rather, it expresses my own experience of various biblical verses and *midrashim* in light of R. Soloveitchik's approach.

While I was working on this essay, it was brought to my attention that this memorial *drashah* was being prepared for publication within a volume of R. Soloveitchik's lectures. His daughter, Dr. Tovah Lichtenstein was kind enough to make the relevant chapter available to me. The text of the book is based on R. Soloveitchik's manuscripts containing the notes he wrote in preparation for his lectures. Thus, the version in the book differs in certain parts from the lectures as delivered by R. Soloveitchik. The quotations in this chapter are either from a private tape of the lecture delivered by R. Soloveitchik or from the edited version of R. Soloveitchik's manuscript. (In a few instances the two texts are merged.) After this essay was completed, the volume of R. Soloveitchik's lectures was published as *Family Redeemed*, David Shatz and Joel B. Wolowelsky eds. (NY: Toras Harav Foundation, 2000). The lecture to which I will refer appears as the final chapter of the book, entitled "Torah and *Shekhinah*,"

describe God sounded masculine in English translation—in Hebrew it lacked that connotation for me.[2]

Later that day, I sat in class musing about that strange non-meeting of minds on the grass and eventually it dawned upon me that my perception of God was truly different from the expectations of my questioner. I already knew intuitively that truth lay hidden within a kaleidoscopic multiplicity of metaphors. That if God was indeed my father, my shepherd, my king, my beloved, my judge and my craftsman (to name but a few employed in the Bible), then certainly "He" was both all of these and not exactly any of them. One cannot pray on Rosh Hashanah—even as a child—without sensing this.[3]

158–80. I have tried to make it possible for the reader to distinguish between those ideas which R. Soloveitchik explicitly mentioned and my own interpretations, expansions of ideas and dilemmas. For a more comprehensive understanding of R. Soloveitchik's thought, the reader is directed to the above book, or other works by R. Soloveitchik.

[1] This is not intended to be a full portrayal of Maimonides' descriptions of the potential human relationship to God, but rather my understanding at that time. See for example, Maimonides' *Mishneh Torah: Book of Knowledge: Laws of Fundamentals of Torah*, ch. 1 and *Laws of Repentance* ch. 10:3; and *Book of Love: Laws of Prayer*, ch. 1. For an example of this approach to prayer, see *Tanhuma Mikketz* 9, "One is not allowed to pray more than the three prayers every day." See also the description by R. Soloveitchik in *Ish haHalakhah: Galui veNistar*, "Ra'ayanot al haTefillah" (World Zionist Organization, 1974) 243–47.

[2] This may be due to a number of factors. Since Hebrew has no non-gendered personal pronouns (such as "it" or "they") or other non-gendered grammatical forms, the use of the masculine pronoun and verb endings that refer to God does not necessarily connote maleness. (All beings and objects are either "masculine" or "feminine" and a mixed group is generally referred to in the masculine.) Inherent in this situation lies the problem of using a feminine pronoun for God. This may serve to emphasize and even artificially introduce rather than diffuse the issue of gender.

In addition, we learned Torah and prayed in Hebrew, which was a language once removed from our daily experience. Since we were first exposed to the text of the Siddur and the Hebrew language simultaneously at the age of six, our main use of the Hebrew word for "he" was in reference to God and I suspect that the pronoun itself was not totally gendered in my mind.

[3] See for example, the many metaphors in the prayers ״כחומר ביד היוצר״ ״כי אנו עמך״ "Like the clay in the hand of the potter" and "For we are your people..." sung on Rosh Hashanah and Yom Kippur.

Of course, a sense of gender is not just the product of the appellations and pronouns which are used. The dominant image of God gleaned from a relatively superficial reading of the Torah could very well be one of power (with strong male connotations). However, in a reading of Torah mediated by the Sages (in Talmud and midrash), the sense of gender is always denoted as power tempered by lovingkindness: the attribute of justice constantly balanced and even challenged by the attribute of mercy.[4] And that reading of Torah was the only reading I knew, because it is the one Rashi transmitted to us in his commentary on the Torah.[5]

This duality of imagery does not express a duality in God, but rather is a reflection of our inability to see the whole picture. It conveys the insufficiency of any one description or symbol to express something whole about God, or even about God in relation to the world—in effect, the inadequacy of language emerging from the limitations of our minds to comprehend or even imagine God. While a single sustained metaphor might be understood literally in a particularized gendered manner, the duality or even multiplicity of image fosters a deeper comprehension of symbol and metaphor.

Thus the God I knew was not only father, but also mother and possibly more than anything else—maternal. My God was "the God of Abraham and Isaac and Jacob," my mother and my father. "He" was also the God of Maimonides and of Rashi and finally, but probably most compelling for me, He was the God of *the Rav*. For it was the Rav (as the world I grew up in always called Rabbi Soloveitchik) who only a few years earlier had

---

[4] In this understanding, the various names describing God in the Torah portray different ways in which God (as we perceive events) relates to us. Thus the name *Elohim* refers to God's attribute of justice and His presence through the world of nature, whereas the name "the Eternal" refers to God's mercy and immanence as revealed in the potential for relationship between the divine and the human. See Rashi on Genesis 1:1 (last section), based on *Exodus Rabbah* 12.15 and *Exodus Rabbah* 3.6. See also *Mekhilta*, Rashi and Sforno on Exodus 15:3, "The Eternal is a man of war, the Eternal is His name."

[5] Rashi's eleventh century Torah commentary has traditionally been the most popular Jewish one. It is generally the first and principal commentary taught to children and consistently studied by adults. While aiming toward a literal, contextual reading of the Torah, it is simultaneously a virtual window on the thought of the Sages as expressed in the midrash and Talmud.

challenged me to think of these things. And it was the Rav who had taught
me that a deep maternal presence was concealed in the Bible, waiting for
each individual's response.

It wasn't as if I had had the opportunity to be a *talmidah* (student) of
the Rav. It was simply that I had grown up knowing there was a thinker, a
teacher, a *davener* (one who prays) who was, in many ways, central to the
deeper parts of the lives of the adults around me—a teacher in whose
shadow we learned Torah. Then one day, when I was fifteen, in a brilliant
moment of parental nonchalance, I was allowed to join the adults at the
Rav's public lecture in memory of his wife. In one fell swoop, the conventional learning of the classroom was left behind. As I struggled to see
the source sheet shared among a few of us and tried to find space for my
feet, while straining to see the man who almost acted out his words—
language and ideas sharply and brilliantly erupted before me like a
fireworks display. The Rav's lecture was long (so they said), but I was
mesmerized.

The Rav's thesis involved the idea of a maternal presence of God in
the Bible, which drew upon but was not identical to the description of
Shekhinah (Divine Presence) in midrash and mystical literature. It was not
about God as male and/or female, but rather about God-in-relationship in
both a maternal and paternal sense. The Rav showed that intertwined with
the more dominant images of God as father or as a beloved bridegroom, a
maternal theme flows through the Bible like a contrapuntal melody,
changing the music of the whole. Rav Soloveitchik drew upon the classical sources, both halakhic and aggadic, but he moved through them in a
novel, uniquely personal way, making them accessible and newly meaningful.

God as Parent in the Talmud

One of the central texts of the Rav's presentation that night was a section
of the tractate *Kiddushin* which deals with the obligations of parents to
children and children to parents. A *baraita* (tannaitic passage) within that
discussion reads:

It is said *"kaved et avikha ve'et imekha*, Honor thy father and thy mother" (Exodus 20:11) and it is also said *"kaved et Hashem me-honekha*, Honor the Lord with thy substance" (Proverbs 3:9). Thus Scripture compares the honor due to parents to that due to the Omnipresent. (*Kiddushin* 30b)

The common understanding is that this *baraita* increases the gravity of the *mitzvah* of honoring parents. For through the use of precisely the same term, the honor due to parents is compared to and even equated with the honor required toward God.[6]

Rav Soloveitchik, however, read the *baraita* in the reverse direction as well, suggesting that it brought to light God's relationship to us, fulfilling a parental role. The Rav suggested that "the *baraita* wanted to convey to us a very unusual idea. The Torah not only equated, but also identified" honor of parents with honor of God. Thus the *baraita* does not simply read: just as you must have great respect and fear for God, so must you behave with respect and fear toward your parents. Rather (or also) the love and reverence one is obliged to display toward one's parents should be a basis for the learning of love and reverence of God. "By developing proper human relations, the Jew learns how to love, revere and serve God." R. Yohanan ben Zakkai blessed his disciples, "May it be God's will

---

[6] This interpretation is clearly intended in a related *baraita* recorded in the JT *Kiddushin* 2.7 [20b] in the name of R. Shimon bar Yochai: "Great is [the *mitzvah* of] respect for parents, for the Holy One, blessed be He, preferred it to [the *mitzvah* of] respect for Himself. Here it says, 'Respect your father and your mother' and there it says, 'Honor the Lord with your substance'—with what do you pay respect to God? With what you own—you separate the various gifts to the poor in the field and tithes...and you build a Sukkah and [keep the *mitzvot* of] *lulav* and shofar and *tefillin* and *tzitzit* and feed the hungry...if you have [the means] you are obligated in all these [*mitzvot*]; and if you do not have [the means] you are not obligated [to perform] any of them. But when it comes to respect for parents—whether you have [the means] or not [you must] respect (care for) your parents, even if you must seek charity (*me-savev al haPesahim*) [in order to do so]."

Parallel versions of the *baraita* in our text—quoted by R. Soloveitchik—use the phrase *hekish hakatuv* (Scripture parallels, which draws an analogy between the two *mitzvot*) instead of *hishva hakatuv* (Scripture equates, compares) as in our text. See *Sifra* on Leviticus 19:3 and JT *Kiddushin* 1.7.

that the fear of heaven shall be upon you like the fear of flesh and blood" (*Berakhot* 28b).

Furthermore, "when one honors or reveres one's natural parent, one *ipso facto*, honors and reveres God." For if "every phenomenon in nature...the whole cosmic drama, manifests the ceaseless inner quest of creation for the Creator...then the vital powers of man, such as falling in love, reverence, kindness and charity certainly belong to God. In loving father and mother, a person is really in love with God, whose glory shines through two elderly people.... What is transient fatherhood and motherhood if not a reflected beam of light...from beyond the frontiers of the cosmos and what is paternal or maternal concern if not an echo of the great concern of the Almighty?"

"Why," asked Rav Soloveitchik, "does one rise for one's mother and father? Not for the father, but in the presence of the *Shekhinah*. Behind every mother...trails the *Shekhinah* and behind every father...walks the holy King. This is not mysticism. It is *halakhah*."

If we return to the *baraita* and examine it in its entirety, we can see that it can indeed be read in either direction:

> Our Rabbis taught: It is said, "*Honor your father and your mother*" (Exodus 20:12); and it is also said, "*Honor the Lord with your substance*" (Proverb 3:9): thus Scripture compares (identifies) the honor due to parents to that of the Omnipresent. It is said, "*You shall fear every man his father and his mother*"; and it is also said, "*The Lord your God you shall fear and Him you shall serve*" (Deuteronomy 6:13): thus Scripture compares the fear of parents to the fear of God. It is said, "*And he that curses his father, or his mother, shall surely be put to death*" (Exodus 21:17); and it is also said, "*Whosoever curses his God shall bear his sin*" (Leviticus 24:15): thus Scripture compares the blessing of parents to that of the Omnipresent. But in respect of striking, it is certainly impossible. And the comparison is quite logical, since the three (God, father and mother) are partners in creating [the child].

The parental depiction of God is intensified in subsequent passages in the talmudic text:

> Our Rabbis taught: There are three partners in a person: the Holy One, blessed be He, the father and the mother. When a person honors his

father and his mother, the Holy One, blessed be He, says, "ascribe
[merit] to them as though I had dwelt among them and they had honored Me."

When a person vexes his father and his mother, the Holy One,
blessed be He, says, "I did right in not dwelling among them, for had I
dwelt among them, they would have vexed Me." (*Kiddushin* 30b–31a)

God as Both Mother and Father

While the Talmud depicts parents as one unit, it also describes psychological and behavioral differences between them which affect their
children's relationship to them. Rebbe (R. Judah the Prince) said:

> It is revealed and known to *Mi she'Amar veHaya ha'Olam*, He who
> decreed and the world came into existence, that a son loves his mother
> more than his father because she sways him by her tender words.
> Therefore, *HaKadosh Barukh Hu*, the Holy One, blessed be He,
> placed the obligation of love of the father, before that of the mother
> [in Exodus 20:12, "Honor your father and mother"].[7]
>
> And it is revealed and known to *Mi she'Amar veHaya ha'Olam*,
> He who decreed and the world came into existence, that a son fears his
> father more than his mother because he teaches him Torah. Therefore,
> *HaKadosh Barukh Hu*, the Holy One, blessed be He, put the obliga-
> tion of fear of the mother before that of the father [in Leviticus 19:3,
> "You shall fear every man his mother and father"]. (*Kiddushin* 30b)

The Rav argued here that R. Judah the Prince is describing two different
personality types. The father-figure as more distant and restrained, while
the mother-figure as more affectionate and persuasive. A verse in Proverbs characterizes the approach of each parent: "Heed, my child, the
discipline (*Mussar*) of your father and do not forsake the teaching (*Torah*)
of your mother" (Proverbs 1:8). These two forms of relationship do not
just represent successive stages in the child's development, beginning

---

[7] The Rav pointed out in his lecture that in this case, the correct understanding of the
Hebrew phrase "*ben mekhabed*" is that the son **loves** (rather than **respects**) his
mother. He also pointed out that "she sways him by her tender words" was not meant
to imply a competitive play for the child's love, but is an expression of affection for
the child, as in the phrase "*yeled sha'ashuim*"—"a child whom I could play with and
shower with love" (Jeremiah 31:20).

with an intense all-enveloping closeness, which then moves toward independence.

Rather, as the child matures, the archetypal parents move in opposite directions. The archetypal father, in the Rav's analysis, moves toward gradual detachment. The archetypal mother, however, moves toward enhancement and intensification of the bond between herself and the child. She can never totally let go of the child who was once within her, an integral part of her, or divorce herself from her nearly visual image of his or her innocence, even if the child later turns away. As for the child, I understand that he or she needs to experience both parents' forms of movement toward and away from the self as he or she matures.

The Rav suggested that these two different personality types are deep-seated. They reflect "metaphysical, spiritual divergence, an existential distinction." At the same time, the Rav emphasized in his lecture: "and I want you to understand: the *baraita* does not speak of father and mother...[but rather of] father-types and the mother-type. The real father may have some of the characteristics which belong to the mother and the real mother may act like a father. No. The *baraita* speaks of so-called *diokanniot*, prototypes, archetypes."[8]

This distinction was, I believe, crucial to the Rav's thesis and it certainly was crucial in my ability to relate to his ideas, to internalize them and to use them creatively in my own relationship to God. The distinction clarified that in order to work with these divergent forms of being and of relationship, one did not have to come down on any particular side of the feminist dispute. One did not have to argue either for or against radically differing characteristics of actual flesh and blood men and women, although men and women symbolized different forces.

These different forces, these two types of parental roles, are aspects of the image of God embedded in every human being, "reflected beams of light." God acts as both "father" and "mother" to us. He both legislates

---

[8] This distinction between male and female archetypes, on the one hand and living men and women on the other is not as clear in R. Soloveitchik's notes (and hence in the published volume) as it was in the speech as he delivered it. It is the most crucial single difference which I noted between the oral (taped) and written versions. Possibly, although the distinction was obvious to the Rav, he was aware that it needed to be clarified to his listeners lest he be misunderstood.

from heaven and draws us close. He disciplines and "hides His face," and yet never severs the connection. We are unable to understand God's ways and to foresee the way we will experience God's relationship to us in any particular situation.

Following the Rav's analysis, we find that the Bible uses the parental analogy in a number of ways. Moshe describes God's care of the Jewish people during and after the Exodus: "As an eagle that stirs up its nest, hovers over its young, spreads its wings, takes its young and bears them on its pinions" (Deuteronomy 32:11).[9] He exhorts the Jewish people to remember God, "who led you through the great and dreadful wilderness... who brought forth water for you out of the rock (Deuteronomy 8:15)...and afflicted you and caused you to suffer hunger and fed you the manna which you and your father knew not, in order to teach you that not by bread alone does the human being live..." (Deuteronomy 8:3). And as a result of this "You shall know in your heart that as a man disciplines his son, so the Eternal, your God disciplines you" (Deuteronomy 8:5). Moshe points out that although God does "chasten" and lead the Jewish people through difficult and even painful situations—truly like a father—it is in order to train, instruct and improve them. The figure of the father softens here and gives meaning to God's disciplinary behavior. Nevertheless, it is still discipline rather than intimate connection that is being described. God is "*Avinu shebaShamayim*, our father in heaven."

In contrast, the Rav noted, the mother figure comes to the fore when the child—possibly already truly an adult—is needy. Describing the future return to Jerusalem, God promises: "As one whom his mother comforts, so will I comfort you" (Isaiah 66:13).[10] In response, the "child" (here King David) feels: "Lord, my heart is not haughty, nor my eyes lofty. Surely I have pacified and stilled my soul like the suckling infant on its mother's breast, like a suckling my soul is within me. Let Israel wait

---

[9] In the case of the eagle, the male and female share the job of caring for the young. Thus, the eagle presents a non-gendered metaphor for parental power, protection and loving care. (The biblical verse appears in the masculine, because the word eagle *nesher* is masculine in Hebrew.)

[10] This prophecy may be linked to the lines which precede it in which Jerusalem is described as maternal, a common motif. See, for example, Isaiah 40:1–2 and 54.

for the Eternal from this time forth and forever" (Psalms 131:2–3). We "wait" with the faith and unconditional trust "reminiscent of the child's trust in its mother. In fact, God is our mother, the *Shekhinah*."

Why are these two different relationships with God necessary? Of what use are they to the Jewish people as a unit or to the individual? The impact of the Rav's *dvar Torah* stemmed from the connection he created between the text and his own psychological reality: "Let me not refer to *psukim* (biblical verses) but to ourselves; otherwise religious life becomes mechanical...at times we run to the Almighty for advice and encouragement like a confused son who did not perform well, frustrated and disappointed...at times we cling to the *Shekhinah* like a child in utter despair...."

Why do we need the archetypal paternal relationship? For God to legislate, instruct and also to withdraw and create a space in which we can experience free choice and maturity. But "Man is in need not only of Divine law but of Divine help and cooperation as well." When we go astray, we need a parent waiting for our return, enabling us to do *teshuvah* because the parent reaches out with the memory of our past self and our potential. Both the withdrawal and the intimacy are manifestations of God's love.

"Is not Ephraim a dear son to me, a child whom I dandle, for whenever I speak of him, I do remember him?" (Jeremiah 31:20). Isn't the process normally the reverse? Isn't it the memory of someone which stimulates one's own speech about them? "First one recalls an episode and then one discusses it." The Rav claimed that God is speaking here in the maternal mode of relationship to the Jewish people. The discussion about the tribe of Ephraim, in its present sinful state, arouses recollections of Ephraim in a past, innocent state. These are not just inert memories, but stark timeless images which bring Ephraim in his youth back to life. "Therefore my inward parts are moved for him." The metaphorical space within the mother which once held Ephraim stirs for him: "I will surely have mercy on him, says the Lord" (Jeremiah, ibid.).

The images we have described are of course only metaphors, archetypes—not fully embodied by any human mother or father. And so, it seems to me, Isaiah asks "Can a woman forget her sucking child, not have compassion on the child of her womb?" And he answers in the affirmative: "even these may forget." But "I (God) will not forget thee" (Isaiah 49:15). To comprehend God's ways, one must begin with concrete human characteristics, but one must also let the mind stretch to imagine the infinite possibilities of these modes of relationship.

The God of Our Prayers

And so, many years ago when I was asked about the "male God of the Old Testament," I could not locate him. The God I knew anything about was wholly abstract and awesome and He related to the world equally in maternal and paternal modes.

What happened to these maternal and paternal images? Where are they in the Siddur? The maternal seems to be almost totally absent.[11] There may be extrinsic historical reasons for this. But it is possible that (contrary to Rav Soloveitchik's view) the Sages blurred the differentiation (or did not differentiate) between maternal and paternal emotional and spiritual experience and behavior.[12] Thus the Bible's maternal and paternal images may be merged and expressed in the paternal image in the Siddur.[13]

Nevertheless, different modes of relationship are preserved in Jewish prayer in a series of contrasting images. God is our Father and also our King.[14] On Rosh Hashanah we say, "Today all the creatures of the universe are judged. If we are regarded as children," we pray, "have mercy upon us, as a father has mercy on his children; and if as servants, our eyes

---

[11] It is present for instance in Psalm 131 quoted above which is traditionally recited on Shabbat afternoon. Some *piyyutim* (medieval poems) also add dimensions such as descriptions of the matriarchs' relationships to God. (See the service for Rosh Hashanah that falls on Shabbat.)

[12] For a discussion of this issue see Suzanne Last Stone "Justice, Mercy and Gender in Rabbinic Thought" in *Cardozo Studies in Law and Literature*, vol. 8, no. 1, 164–77. In addition, the Siddur as we know it, was compiled over centuries and thus does not reflect the viewpoint of a particular group of sages.

[13] Kabbalah (mystical teaching) even developed a theoretical system in which the quality of *hesed* (lovingkindness) is associated with maleness and *gevurah* (strength) and *din* (justice) are considered female qualities.

[14] For instance, in the prayer "*Avinu Malkeinu*."

are attentively fixed on you until you will be gracious to us and bring forth our judgment as the light, awesome and holy One."[15]

Likewise, there are two blessings recited before the *Shema*. The first is a depiction of God's creation of nature and especially of light and darkness and the movement from one to the other. It is reminiscent of the description of God in the Bible as awesome creator and judge. The second blessing is the story of God's great love for and attachment to the Jewish people, evidenced in His teaching them Torah and reciprocated by the Jewish people in their recital of the *Shema*.[16]

And what a shocking sense of intense closeness is experienced when, after emerging from the awesomeness of Rosh Hashanah, one welcomes Shabbat and sings: "Beloved of the soul, compassionate Father, draw Your servant to Your will...my soul is sick with love for You.... Please reveal yourself and spread upon me, my Beloved, the shelter of Your peace...hasten, show love, for the time has come...."[17]

Torah Study and the Search for God's Presence

I remember, many years ago, being puzzled that night in the subway, on the way home from the Rav's *drashah*. For I felt as if the Rav had spoken directly to me and of issues that mattered to me just at that moment. And yet, the speech had also been highly relevant to the adults around me. In retrospect, it is not at all difficult to understand how my adolescent self

---

[15] From the Rosh Hashanah service. Prayer after the blowing of the shofar.

[16] The midrash understands that although God is awesome at Mount Sinai when he gives the Jewish people the Torah, he also appears to them like an elderly teacher full of compassion. In fact, the experience is so fundamentally different from the experience of the Exodus (described in the blessing after the *Shema*), that it poses a danger. It may fragment the sense of God. "Because He had revealed Himself [to them] at the sea as a mighty warrior and here He revealed Himself as an elder filled with compassion ...[God says]: since I change in appearances do not conclude that there are two [divine] Powers." And He therefore begins the Ten Commandments with the words: "I am the Eternal, thy God, who brought you our of the land of Egypt..." (Exodus 20:1). See Rashi and *Mekhilta*.

[17] Selections from "*Yedid Nefesh*" by Rabbi Eliezer Azikri (sixteenth century), which is traditionally sung on Shabbat. Note here the movement from God as father to God as Beloved—a theme which haunts the works of Hosea, Jeremiah, Ezekiel and of course the Song of Songs.

felt that the Rav had entered her world that night. Firstly, his theme based on the reciprocal relations between parents and children (especially as children grow away from their parents) must have related directly to a teenager's experiences at the time. Secondly, the Rav had suddenly entered a relative vacuum, for my teachers would rarely dare to go "where angels fear to tread" and push us to think about God.

At least as important was the Rav's total personal immersion in the verses of the Torah—his constant movement from the text into the self and back—his attempt to understand the self via the Torah text and the text via the self. The Torah, in all its awesome grandeur, was enmeshed with his psychological reality. His speech, which explored God's relationships to the Jewish people, concluded with the individual encounter with God through Torah.

In the continuation of his *drashah*, the Rav argued that according to Maimonides, the *mitzvah* of "*talmud torah*" does not only involve the learning itself. There is also *kevi'at itim laTorah*—establishing fixed times of study—"a rendezvous with the Torah."[18] Is that encounter, he asked, "an allegory, a mystical vision which recedes with daybreak...? No." For it is truly a rendezvous with the *Shekhinah* who trails behind the Torah. "God, the *Ribbono Shel Olam*, in this case disguised as Mother *Shekhinah*, never separated Herself from Her daughter [the Torah...which] is still *Torat Hashem*, Her word, Her princess."[19] "When two sit together and engage in Torah, God's *Shekhinah* rests upon them" (*Berakhot* 6a). This was not, I came to understand, as an extrinsic gift but naturally,

---

[18] See Rambam, *Mishneh Torah*, Laws of Talmud Torah, Chapter 1.8.

[19] The Rav here takes a halakhic detail from Maimonides' discussion and develops its spiritual and psychological dimensions. Thus, he explores the existential difference between the obligation to study Torah in general and the obligation to create a specific time to study. The setting of a fixed time, suggesting a meeting with someone, becomes an emotionally laden "rendezvous."

R. Soloveitchik's lectures, published in *On Repentance*, are based on this model expounding a text, or a number of conflicting texts in Maimonides' *Mishneh Torah* from an existential perspective.

intrinsically.[20] One may begin studying in search of knowledge but along the way, one falls in love with the *Shekhinah*, with God.[21]

The Rav's Torah learning came through to me as his truth—his one of the "seventy faces of the Torah."[22] It was so deeply grounded in so many parts of Torah—from Scripture to *halakhah* to midrash to Kabbalah that its authenticity was implicit. At the same time, its individual existential quality encouraged the listener to develop his or her own path.

Beyond all of this, however, the aspect of the Rav's teaching that had the greatest impact on me was a sense of shared experience. It was the palpable sense, in an age of doubt, that belief was not some sort of great achievement—something one hopefully acquired by the age of ten, after which one coasted along. Rather, "belief" is a dynamic process. The Rav argued that alongside the *mitzvah* to "believe" in God, *emunah baShem*, there exists another *mitzvah*—to search for God, *bakashat Elokim*.[23] These two *mitzvot* parallel God's two different modes of relating to us. The paternal is satisfied with respect and observance of *mitzvot*—an objective expression of faith. But the maternal, the *Shekhinah*, seeks awareness of Her presence, acknowledgment and affection, closeness and love, *kvi'at itim laTorah*. "The wish of the Mother should not be ignored. One must quest for Her, search for Her. One will finally find Her if the questing is sincere and genuine, if it is done 'with all your heart and with all your soul' (Deuteronomy 4:9)."

---

[20] In *On Repentance*, Pinchas Peli ed. (NJ: Jason Aronson, 1996) 14, R. Soloveitchik describes his personal sense of God's presence when studying Talmud.

[21] The Rav further argued that the *mitzvah* of *"talmud torah"* which is, I understood, part of the relationship with God as Father can be measured in terms of intellectual achievement. But in the *mitzvah* of *kevi'at itim laTorah*—the daily engagement with the *Shekhinah*, it is the effort, sincerity and passion which matter most.

[22] The seventy faces of the Torah refer to the infinite layers of meaning embedded in a single verse which emerge through the study of Torah. See *Deuteronomy Rabbah* 13.14 and *Sanhedrin* 34a and *Shabbat* 88b.

[23] See Deuteronomy 4:29–30 "...from there you will seek the Lord thy God and you shall find Him, if you search after Him with all your heart and with all your soul." The Rav interprets this as a command as well as a prophecy.

A search, by definition, can only make sense in a case when something is absent or missing.[24] Here was someone who at the time seemed almost ancient to me, but yet he was engaging in that very dilemma I thought I was somehow supposed to have solved by the age of fifteen. He spoke of the *mitzvah* not only to acquire belief but also to search actively. If this was so, then doubt, I sensed, had a positive value. The incessant, adolescent questioning, the seething struggles with Torah—so often rejected by the adult world—**they** were my *avodat Hashem*—my soul's service of God. Maybe the search was never-ending. Beyond each sense of encounter with God lay another realm of ontological emptiness and another level of potential awareness of God's presence.[25]

It seemed as if the Rav was describing things he knew "in the flesh"[26]—a search he knew, a need for parenting at different moments in one's life. And although the Rav did not raise it explicitly, there also hovered between the lines the role of the Rebbe, the *melamed*, the teacher or mentor. For to the Sages of the Talmud, there is also another parent in addition to the biological ones: "And you shall teach them to your children" (Deuteronomy 6:7). "These are your students," says the *Sifrei*, "And thus you always find that disciples are called sons...and just as the students are called sons, the teacher is called father...." "Resh Lakish said: He who teaches Torah to his neighbor's child is regarded by Scripture as though he had made him, as it is written, *"and the souls which they [Abraham and Sarah] had made in Haran."* (Genesis 12:5)[27]

---

[24] Having written this, I noticed that these are almost the Rav's own words describing the search for God which is part of the process of *teshuvah*. See *On Repentance*, 129–33.

[25] My impression upon listening to the tape of the Rav's lecture many years later is that the Rav was addressing not so much the issue of doubt as the lack of true awareness of God, of "total religious experience," in daily life. However, the elements of yearning and urgent, continuing and continuous search were definitely present.

[26] In the sense of "from my flesh I see God" (Job 19:26). In the Rav's words: "We are called upon not only to believe in Him...but to find Him with our five senses, to perceive Him the way one perceives light, feel His presence in our midst...."

[27] *Sanhedrin* 99b, see also *Sanhedrin* 19b.

It would seem that the "Rebbe" (the teacher) must be both archetypal father and archetypal mother to his or her students—the stern, almost feared, awesome imparter of truths as well as the "still quiet voice" which calls to the student forever. The Rebbe would be the individual with an unrelenting standard, who nevertheless has faith in the student's potential even when he or she fails—the person whom the student can connect to and in a deep way identify with, in an effort to cleave to God.[28] Can a teacher achieve this? The dilemma awakened in me the question of what it means to be a *talmid* (or *talmidah*), a disciple.

I did not sit for years in the Rav's *shiur* (his daily Talmud class), nor hear him teach the weekly Torah portion every Saturday night, nor care for him in his old age. I do not claim to have "known the Rav." I know only that he taught me things when I needed to learn them, that he bridged for me the intellectual and the emotional, the world of words and the world of being, the cosmic infinite and the microcosm, the learning of Torah and the experience of *Shekhinah*.

The Rav that night intertwined Tanakh and Rambam and midrash and told a story. It was, in part at least, even to a child, a story of personal loneliness and loss, shared with us, his students. But it was also a story of aloneness transcended and turned toward God. It taught me, more possibly than anything, not to fear one's soul's aloneness, for within it reverberates the call of God. May his memory be for a blessing.

---

[28] As in the Rambam's description of the *mitzvah* to "cleave to God" (*devekut*), *Book of Mitzvot*, Positive Commandment # 6, based on the *Sifra*.

Reflections On a Living Torah:
Rabbi Aryeh Kaplan

Yardena Cope-Yossef

In May of 1981, at the age of sixteen, I attended the NCSY (National Conference of Synagogue Youth) National Convention as part of the Chicago delegation. I was a bit shy and not entirely in the know about "who's who" or whom I should be meeting. On Shabbat afternoon I sat down to speak to Rabbi Aryeh Kaplan—but I cannot recall who introduced us or how this conversation began. It turned into a long talk about future plans, colleges, and how one chooses a direction in life. Afterwards, R. Kaplan addressed the entire convention just after the afternoon prayers and I next saw him on Sunday morning, on the last day of the convention. He suggested that I keep in touch. I felt daunted by the prospect of corresponding with a Rabbi who, as I discovered over the course of the convention, was a famous author and lecturer.

Hence, I was quite surprised when I received a letter from R. Kaplan two weeks after the convention:

> I would like to thank you for helping me find a theme for my *devar Torah* after *Minchah* on Shabbos. All Shabbos I was trying to think up a topic that would relate to all the kids at the convention. It would be very easy to relate to the kids who were committed, but what about those who were borderline?.... When you came over to speak to me on Shabbos, I was still struggling with the problem.... After speaking to you, the idea began to jell. Every kid wants to be successful in life. Some kids think that a strong Torah commitment would be an obstacle rather than an asset. Your commitment to Torah and to a difficult career was a paradigm around which I could build....

Rabbi Kaplan's Approach as a Rav

In retrospect, this exchange had certain features that characterized his greatness as a teacher and that seem to be central to an optimal *Rav-talmid* relationship. The first feature was the level of gratitude and reciprocity a teacher can exhibit toward a student. This struck a chord with me. R. Nahman of Bratslav has an extraordinary passage in section nineteen of his *Likkutei Moharan* which illuminates this aspect of the *Rav-talmid* relation. Why, asks R. Nahman, must one travel to see the *tzaddik* in person and hear his teachings directly from him, when one could either hear what he said second-hand, from a fellow hasid who attended the *tzaddik*'s talk, or read what he had to say in a book?

> Because one must purify the face, in order to see oneself mirrored in the face of the other [or *tzaddik*'s] face as in a mirror. Then, without any reprimand or moral rebuke, a person will immediately regret his actions just by virtue of looking into that face. For when one gazes into the other, one's own face is perceived in a mirror and one sees how one's face is buried in darkness.

The answer is surprising. One might expect the claim that a personal interview is better than reading a transcription of the rebbe's teachings. In person, one has the opportunity to ask for clarifications of unclear points or hear the rebbe's most recent teachings, whereas a book leaves much to personal interpretation and error. Instead, though, R. Nahman tries to capture the essence of the very encounter with the rebbe. In effect, the passage may be understood as describing an encounter with any significant mentor or friend.[1]

The encounter changes the entire person. She or he sees herself or himself reflected in the other person's face which is described as a clear, pure vessel. One immediately recognizes that until now he has been wallowing in a darkness not even perceived. Until now, he has gone about his life hidden from others and from himself, and now sees that he has not lived

---

[1] Elsewhere in this article when I refer to a rav or rebbe or to a "*Rav-talmid*" relationship, which technically means "teacher-student" relationship, I have in mind a mentor-disciple relationship. Men and women could fulfill either role.

from his Godly essence but has covered it with the shadow he thought he was. That shadow was not unlike one's true self; it was simply a dimmer and unrefined image of one's underlying strengths and, perhaps, at times a negative portrayal of them. In the reflection, one catches a glimpse of the inner self behind the shadow. This glimpse may also act as a catalyst for change—allowing the Godly essence to emerge and guide one's life.

From R. Nahman's words, I infer that the encounter is not necessarily superior to transcribed teachings as a source of information, although that also might be true. The encounter, however, is considered a much better vehicle for self-refinement than simply reading the rebbe's teachings. For the rebbe's gaze (or that of a significant mentor or friend) is pure, that is, unclouded by self-interest; it is also completely devoted to the momentary encounter. The power of the rebbe's gaze, which allows one to see one's spiritual essence, stems from the greatness of the rebbe's personality, as well as the bond between rebbe and student at the moment of encounter.

In order to serve as a conduit for the student to see herself as she truly is, the teacher allows the student's presence to penetrate the teacher's being, thus reflecting back more than the student originally knew in herself. From the classic sources, this sort of give-and-take seems desirable, but it was eye opening to actually see it practiced to such a degree.[2] This reciprocity, in my opinion, is one aspect of becoming a reflective mirror for one's students. Through R. Kaplan and other mentors, I experienced how fundamental it is to the transformational power of the teacher-student encounter.

Another way I would characterize what R. Kaplan gave his students relates to his style of communication. There was honesty in the letter, not flattery. The reflective mirror R. Kaplan presented throughout our correspondence was not only open and reciprocal—it was also honest. He modeled the value of being honest in communicating with others and respecting the integrity of the other's positions. This became even more of

---

[2] A paradigmatic example is the saying in *Pirkei Avot* (6:3) that one who learns even one letter from someone else should treat that person with respect. The example given is King David calling Ahitofel "My Rav, my general, my advisor" (based on Psalms 54) although Ahitofel was, in general, a wicked person and had taught him a total of two things.

a key issue in subsequent letters, when I not only posed questions or shared information, but challenged his answers on sensitive issues. In keeping with R. Nahman's teaching, the type of influence R. Kaplan had was one of reflecting back to his students their own deepest truth.

Correspondence Excerpts–Examples of His Approach

The correspondence continued over the summer of 1981 when I was preparing to spend a year in Israel, throughout that year and into the next summer. During that period, I saw R. Kaplan only twice. In the fall of 1981, I spent Shabbat with R. Kaplan and his family, and a year later I met him one afternoon while I was studying in New York. By far, though, the most influential part of the connection was our correspondence,[3] which shaped much of my Jewish way of thinking and practice as a young adult—both in content and method.[4] It was composed mainly of three parts—theoretical questions concerning Jewish thought, personal dilemmas about choices that would affect my future, and specific questions stemming from my learning. Sometimes I sought his opinion on ideas I had heard or texts I was studying; other times I asked about something he had written—either in a letter, or in one of his books.

One issue we discussed intermittently was the permissibility of women studying Talmud. He answered:

> The *Perishah*, one of the most important commentaries on the *Tur* in *Yoreh De'ah* 246:14, writes that although it is forbidden to set up an

---

[3] The reader should be aware that the materials quoted in this article represent only a small sample of the advice and *divrei Torah* contained in R. Kaplan's letters to me. Moreover, this correspondence was but one of many such ties R. Kaplan maintained. He corresponded with and taught many other young people in person. One such group was his Sarah Schneirer Seminary class, referred to later. Four undated letters from a correspondence with a boy named "Eric" were published in *Ascent Quarterly* 16 (Tishrei 5750/Fall 1989).

[4] The fact that I am a woman is a detail that needs clarification since R. Kaplan fully considered himself to be part of the ultra-Orthodox world that maintains separation of the sexes in all social settings. I believe that he maintained this correspondence with me, and taught many women and men like myself because he saw a need to reach out and strengthen the Jewish identity of Jews in whatever social or religious milieu they were found.

educational system for girls that includes Gemara in its curriculum, nevertheless, if a girl is motivated on her own to learn it there is nothing wrong with it. I can unequivocally say that there is no major classical *posek* who disputes this ruling. Therefore, if you are motivated to learn Gemara, there's nothing wrong with it.

Had that been all he wrote, I might have interpreted the straightforward halakhic tenor of the answer as a way of dampening my enthusiasm to learn Gemara on my own. Yet, the same letter continued with advice on how to go about learning in order to succeed—which not only signaled to me encouragement to follow my desire, but also was the most practical advice I had received on the subject:

> If you can't get a teacher, a good way to learn is by Torah Tapes [here he included address, prices, etc...]. For example, a good start may be *Berachoth* Chapter 6 and then Chapter 1. The main problem that most people have with Gemara is that they never master the language. And the only way you can do that is by covering ground. If you could do an *amud* (side) a day after you get into it and complete 50–100 pages you will have a good start. Try to memorize all the important new words. Your goal should be to be able to master a page without any outside aids—and it's not as hard as people make it out to be. Once you have mastered the language and style of the Gemara, almost any other *sefer* [book] is easy—including *tosafoth*.

An anecdote from a letter written seven months later confirmed the positive value he placed on Torah learning for all—women and men:

> This past Friday night, we had a double *Sheva Berakhot* at our house—more than 50 people. The *devar Torah* was said by Chaya Korot, a 27-year old talmudic scholar.... She teaches Mishna in Stern [College] and Talmud in Derisha [New York Institute of higher Jewish studies for women].... She was roommates with one of the *Kallot* [brides]. I think having her speak surprised some of the rabbis who were here, but after she finished, she had earned the respect of them all.

A second issue he addressed, in response to my questions on the subject, was Judaism's attitude toward secular education and specifically the desirability of being conversant in secular philosophy:

The difference between Rashi and Rambam in their approaches is
something that I developed in my Seminary (Sarah Schneirer) class.
Rashi is not interested in philosophical categories. There are many
verses in the Bible which Saadia Gaon and the Rambam use to support
various philosophical contentions. Invariably Rashi interprets these
verses so that the philosophical content vanishes. A paradigm might
be the very account of Creation. The philosophical commentaries...write at great length to demonstrate that the account of creation is
"scientific." Rashi, on the other hand, begins his commentary by saying that the entire account of creation is superfluous—if it were not
part of the legal document that deeds the Land of Israel to us...a lesson dealing with Hashem's relationship to Israel and the Torah. My
feeling is that this is the theme of Rashi's entire commentary on Creation. I once explained that the Torah was given through the highest
means possible of revelation, namely the prophecy of Moshe, "the father of all prophets." Would Hashem then use such great revelation to
teach us something that we could figure out with our own intellects
(namely science)? The Rambam, on the other hand, was the philosopher par excellence. Before writing his *Moreh Nebukhim* he made sure
he was the greatest expert on Aristotle in the world...wish those who
deal with science and Judaism would take a cue from the Rambam in
this respect.

From the same letter:

Actually the question regarding how much the secular world has to offer was debated in the time of the Geonim. (See *haKothev* on *Eyn
Yaakov*, *Chagiga* 14b, quoting Hai Gaon at the very end.) It may also
be the dispute between Rabbi Simeon bar Yochai and Rabbi Yehudah.
(*Shabbat* 33b; also see *Tiferet Yisrael* on *Avot* 3:14)

In response to the question of why there still seems to be so much opposition to secular studies in *haredi* (ultra-Orthodox) circles, given that
there were always two schools of thought in classical rabbinic literature,
he wrote:

For an important period of time Sefardic *gedolim* [leading religious
scholars] considered it impossible to be a Torah leader without an
adequate secular education. This also seemed to be Hirsch's philosophy. Of course in Eastern Europe the feeling was the exact opposite.

A third and particularly intense issue was our ongoing debate about the significance of the Land of Israel in *halakhah* and Jewish thought today. This began while I was in Israel studying in a seminary that heavily emphasized the centrality of the Land of Israel to Judaism. We began the parlay with a question I posed about the statement in *Midrash Sifrei Devarim* (*parashat Re'eh* 28) that the *mitzvah* of settling the Land of Israel is equal in weight to all the other *mitzvot*.[5]

R. Kaplan responded with a review of differing opinions about whether or not there is a positive commandment today to settle the Land. We agreed, however, that whether or not this is a formal commandment, the centrality of the role of *Eretz Yisrael* was not in question. This issue, however, became a crucial one for me both on a theoretical and a personal level. I doubted whether one's Jewish life could be fulfilled outside the Land, and was also debating whether to remain in Israel myself and stake my future there.

R. Kaplan shared his insights and dilemmas:

> I guess I have always had a sort of ambivalence about Zionism. On the one hand I do see the current *medinah* [state] as a great gift from Hashem. It is just short of a miracle.... But it is not a manifest miracle—there are many strange coincidences—miraculous ones—but no suspension of the laws of nature. God has given us many hints, but He has not shown His hand manifestly. I feel that until He does, we cannot be sure that it is the "beginning of redemption." That is, it can be the beginning of the redemption, but at this point, it may still be conditional. It all depends on our deeds.

> I feel that Zionist propaganda (and I use that word advisedly) often tends to denigrate the accomplishments of *galuth*.... To make the Land the main focus of Judaism distorts it and discourages many seekers. After all, the central theme of Judaism is God and the Torah,

---

[5] Another seven *mitzvot* are also said to be equivalent to all the other *mitzvot*, each for different reasons. They are: *Tzitzit* (*Shavuot* 29a, *Menahot* 43b, *Nedarim* 25a); *Tzedakah* (*Bava Batra* 9a); Shabbat (*Exodus Rabbah* 25.12, *Deuteronomy Rabbah* 4:4); *Brit Milah* (*Midrash Tehillim* 6:1, *Nedarim* 32a); Not Worshipping Idols (*Mekhilta, Bo* 5); *Lashon Hara* (*Midrash Ecclesiastes Zuta* 9.10, *Tosefta Pe'ah* 1.2); and the Study of Torah (*Mishnah Pe'ah* 1:1, Avot DeRabi Natan 40, *Kiddushin* 40a).

not the Land. We can live without the Land, but not without God and the Torah.

Living in *Eretz Yisrael*, at very best, is only one of the commandments. (According to the Satmar Rebbe, however, it is not even a *mitzvah* to live in *Eretz Yisrael* any more.) Supposing someone would stress the *mitzvah* of *tefillin* to the exclusion of other *mitzvos*. It would not be correct. On the other hand, if a person is careful to keep all the *mitzvos* and then is especially careful to keep the *mitzvah* of *tefillin*, then he is praiseworthy.

This reflects the yeshiva attitude. If most people who were concerned with the *mitzvah* of *yishuv Eretz Yisrael* were also more observant in other ways, there would be no objection. But experience shows that many of the former tend to be lax in other *mitzvos*—not very lax, but lax. It therefore appears that they are emphasizing one *mitzvah* at the expense of others. It then appears that their motivation may be patriotism or nationalism rather than Torah. This is the yeshiva's reason for their apparent (but not necessarily real) opposition.

Since R. Kaplan reassured me several times that he respected our differences of opinion on this topic, I wrote back explaining my reservations. His comments troubled me, since it seemed that the yeshivah world was scrupulous in keeping all *mitzvot*; why single this one out for derision or neglect just because others don't take it as seriously as they should? I was also unsure how his defense of the yeshivah attitude corresponded with his conviction of the importance of *Eretz Yisrael* expressed in his writings and in the letters themselves. He had, for instance, written a small book entitled *Jerusalem: The Eye of the Universe*, emphasizing how all holiness emanates from Jerusalem and the Land of Israel. Also, in the same letters in which he had shared his ambivalence about the current status of the Land he wrote:

One of the main ideas of the Holy Land is that it is the main connection that Jews have with the physical world. Our goal is primarily spiritual and on the spiritual plane, but we must operate on the physical plane. In *Eretz Yisrael* the very food we eat is grown in such a manner that every step involves a *mitzvah*. So our very physical being is totally linked to the spiritual through the Land.

The Torah [in the book of Genesis] is telling [us] how God created that physical world and how the patriarchs functioned and lived in the physical world. But the whole story centers around *Eretz Yisrael*—and Jerusalem…. The *Even haShethiya* [foundation stone] was the focus of creation. Adam was created in the place of the altar in Jerusalem. The Torah does not mention anything about Abraham's early life, beginning with his migration to the Land.

It seemed contradictory not to strive to do one's utmost to live under the direct influence of the Land, regardless of whether or not there is a commandment to do so. Moreover, in case of a doubt, why not adopt a more stringent position and, if at all possible, keep the positive commandment? When I voiced those concerns, R. Kaplan responded:

After reading your letter, I began to look into my own ambivalence regarding Zionism. I am aware of the Ramban [Nachmanides, who maintains in *haShmatot leSefer haMitzvot* 4, that there is a positive commandment to settle the Land of Israel].… I am also aware that sources such as the *Shevilay Emunah* (by a grandson of the Rosh) say that before the Moshiach comes, volunteers will settle the holy land and prepare the way. These are not the words of a modern Zionist, but a midrash quoted in a *sefer* written some 600 years ago. I guess that my ambivalence comes partly from my refusal to pin any labels on myself. I don't want to be labeled a Zionist, nor an anti-Zionist, nor even a non-Zionist. I just want to be a Jew without labels.

There was a time when I had Rabbi Tzvi Kalisher's *Derishat Tzion* and the Satmar Rebbe's *vaYo'el Moshe*, side by side. It was as if to say, "let them fight it out. I don't want to put my head between two mountains." Of course the Rambam at the end of *Melakhim* says that all the messianic prophecies are purposely ambiguous and they won't be understood until they are fulfilled. I like this approach very much.

In a later letter he added:

How is it that Rav Tzvi Kalisher and the Satmar Rebbe looked at the same texts and drew exactly opposite conclusions? They were both honest men, with a wide range of knowledge. But the ambiguity must somehow be built into the system. So the question: Why did Hashem build ambiguity into the Torah? It must be because He wanted it. Perhaps even more than Zionists and anti-Zionists, He wanted the polarity and tension between them. This polarity itself creates energy. If the energy is not dissipated in *machloketh* [dispute], then it has its positive aspects…this may also be true of other difficult areas of Torah: the position of women, our relations with the Gentiles, the question of secular education…perhaps the ambiguity is built into the system. Perhaps more than anything else Hashem wants the tension. Somehow I feel this is related to the concept of *Elu ve'Elu Divrey Elokim Chaim* ["these and these are the words of the Living God," *Gittin* 6b, *Eruvin* 13b].… It also explains why Hashem did not give the unambiguous *Shulkhan Arukh* instead of the Torah, which is subject to so many variant interpretations. Maybe He wanted a certain amount of variety and interchange….

One of the final letters on this point dealt with the personal decision of many great Rabbis today to remain outside the Land and by implication, why R. Kaplan himself, after expressing such passion about the importance of Israel, remained in the United States. This question often arises when discussing contemporary rabbinic personalities, and a variety of answers are offered. Many of them entered my mind when, with a great deal of trepidation, I wrote to R. Kaplan and articulated my question.

He answered on a theoretical level and also addressed his choice to remain in America. More than the actual answer itself (which was neither mystical nor secretive), a passage in one of R. Kaplan's final letters to me made a profound impression. He conveyed yet again the reciprocity of the *Rav-talmid* relationship, especially with regard to this heated dialogue about Israel:

> In shul on Tisha B'Av I was reading (and leading) Rabbi Yehuda HaLevi's *"Tzion ha-lo tishali"* about his love for the Land and I was crying. I realized how much I miss *Eretz Yisrael*—and how much I would like to visit—or live there again—and how much situations hold me back. I usually push the thought aside—…but this time it came to the fore. And I thought of… how much you want to go back and how (from your last letter) things are preventing you. And how uncertain the future is for all concerned.

Reflections on His Methodology

What unique aspects of R. Kaplan's "Torah" did I glean from his letters? Not only did his writings, teachings and letters embrace a wide range of topics, they invariably moved from one topic to another with no hint of a separation between *kodesh* (the sacred) and *hol* (the mundane). No subject was too removed from the sacred to be undeserving of a considered Jewish view on it. Often R. Kaplan addressed topics other shied away from, such as extra-terrestrial life or a Jewish view of draft resistance. He did so with the intention of uncovering how they can be understood through Jewish lenses, and how we can apply classical sources to modern concerns. Guiding his words was a consciousness that all things have a share in the divine. "Every person has his hour and every thing has its place" (*Avot* 4:3).

An introduction by Y. Elkins to the posthumous collection of R. Kaplan's essays entitled *Facets and Faces* closely echoes my thoughts:

> One warm summer Sabbath afternoon, R. Kaplan began to discuss the Torah portion, *Mattos*, which deals with the concept of *nedarim*. This is a technical subject, dealing with intricate *halakhot*, the laws of vows and oaths.... With visible excitement R. Kaplan declared this to be the weekly portion which demonstrates the Torah's infinite scope. In this chapter, he explained, we see how everything in the universe can be brought under the umbrella of Halachah. That is, any individual who makes a vow concerning any object, or any activity, whether to use it or perform, or even abstain from it, automatically brings it into the realm of applied Torah...any Jew can, through this *mitzvah*, activate the latent applications of the Torah to everything in the universe. Nothing exists which could not be enveloped in the holiness of the Torah. The idea clearly gave R. Kaplan great *simhah*, tremendous joy.
>
> This idea was typically Rabbi Kaplan—typical in its striking originality, but perhaps also a metaphor for all of Rabbi Kaplan's thought. For him, the world was a unity. Torah, Judaism, science, the physical and the spiritual world, this life and the afterlife, religious and non-religious, Jew and non-Jew—all were pieces of a whole, a puzzle which he strove to complete. It was this worldview which gave R. Kaplan the extraordinary breadth and depth for which he was famous, the ability to glide between seemingly contradictory or incompatible subjects within a single talk.... The midrash could illuminate the laws

of relativity and developments in bio-genetics could explain Messianic prophecies.[6]

How then could one characterize his methodology in studying these sources and arriving at his conclusions? I will only mention in passing the aspect of R. Kaplan's life work for which he is best known. These are the anthologies and lucid booklets on basic topics in Judaism. He collected, categorized and summarized Jewish sources on myriad Jewish topics, including Shabbat, Jerusalem, Maimonides' Thirteen Principles, prayer, hasidic thought and more.[7] Embedded in these apparently basic summaries, and in his other books and translations, are layers of research and syntheses of concepts. I will attempt to highlight aspects of his methodology based on our correspondence and on my reading of his writings.

Characteristic of R. Kaplan's writings is his insistence that one's informed Torah opinion on a subject be both firmly grounded in Torah sources and carefully understood before declaring Judaism says "X" on this subject. Two assumptions underlie this insistence. First, that "Judaism" does not have a monolithic way of thinking about matters of history or Jewish thought. Unlike halakhic disputes where a halakhic decision is necessary—regarding disagreements about philosophical or historical questions, R. Kaplan maintained that Judaism does not require a conclusive resolution of a dispute.

This is not an original position. It is based on Maimonides' commentary on the Mishnah in several places, including, inter alia, Sanhedrin 10:3. R. Kaplan highlighted the legitimacy of a plurality of opinions with regard to questions of hashkafah (Jewish philosophic outlook). In this vein, he explained the differences between the various contexts in the Talmud in which the phrase "these and these are the words of the living God" is used. In the historical dispute between R. Evyatar and R. Yonatan (Gittin 6b) as to what caused the pilegesh baGiv'ah incident, the dispute concludes, "these and these are the words of the living God," and continues by saying that both opinions can be maintained. By contrast, in the halakhic dispute between beit Shammai and beit Hillel in Eruvin 13b, a

---

[6] Y. Elkins, Facets and Faces.

[7] See appendix to this article for a list of R. Kaplan's works.

heavenly voice decrees, "these and these are the words of the living God and the law is like *beit* Hillel." This, concluded R. Kaplan, was further proof of the principle that in the non-halakhic realm one does not have to reach a conclusive Torah decision.[8]

The second assumption is that people often form opinions on a particular subject based on a limited number of easily accessible sources. Numerous references are overlooked because they are only found in oblique kabbalistic references or rare manuscripts. R. Kaplan studied massive numbers of sources on a particular subject before issuing his opinion about what "Judaism" had to say. His view would often be based on one or more lines of thinking among the ancient or modern Rabbis on this subject. Like a handful of scholars of our generation, his ability to master materials, and his openness to a wide range of Jewish sources from plain-text Tanakh to halakhic monographs to esoteric mystical sources sometimes led him to ideas not widely held in the Orthodox community. His conviction, however, was that if one could anchor one's ideas in authentic Jewish sources, when it came to matters of philosophy or history one was not bound to accept the majority view. He stressed time and again, however, that with regard to *halakhah*, no such latitude is allowed.[9]

Anchoring answers in sources and not inventing them merely to solve the problem is a mainstay of the methodology he stressed on several occasions. There is simply nothing apologetic about uncovering an eleventh century kabbalistic source that suggests the possibility of the universe being fifteen billion years old. That opinion, predating the problem by 900 years, was clearly not invented to resolve the quandary posed by scientific findings. It was, however, uncovered by R. Kaplan and applied to the problem at hand.[10]

His approach to learning might be characterized as a search for "scientific truth." He did not argue his case like a lawyer would, who has made

---

[8] See transcription of the keynote address R. Kaplan gave at the Midwinter Conference of the Association of Orthodox Jewish Scientists, Feb. 18, 1979 entitled, "Kabbalah and the Age of the Universe."

[9] Among other places: R. Kaplan, "The Structure of Jewish Law," *The Aryeh Kaplan Reader* (Artscroll Mesorah, 1983).

[10] In the aforementioned transcript, see note 8.

up his mind whom he must defend and does his best to justify a certain position. Like other facets of his methodology, his background in physics most likely influenced this approach.

R. Kaplan's passion for objective proof, coupled with his reverence and love for Torah writings, motivated him to search for ancient manuscripts.[11] When I visited the Kaplan home, I was privileged to see some of the ancient volumes and fragments he had collected. When he showed them to me and explained the process of preserving them, the sparkle in his eyes conveyed both awe and delight about having uncovered "the real thing." He studied original manuscripts, those he owned and those housed in research libraries, with the care and thoroughness usually confined to academic studies. This included deciphering handwriting, decoding terminology (often in kabbalistic texts), utilizing various techniques to date manuscripts and cross-referencing for accuracy.

This scientific approach also meant that he would discard "neat" answers in favor of "difficult" ones, if they corresponded to his findings. He preferred the tension of a dialectical answer encompassing two contradictory theories (which were both true in some provable way) to one non-contradictory yet incomplete or shallow answer. R. Kaplan saw in competing spiritual axioms a source of strength, not weakness. As we saw above, he viewed conflicts between the Zionists and the non-(or anti-) Zionists as competing spiritual forces. The same phenomenon exists, in his eyes, in philosophical and anti-philosophical streams of Jewish thought.[12]

He applied fundamental spiritual principles—those that explain existence in a comprehensive way—to a variety of phenomena. Just as energy is a concept that permeates the way we understand the physical universe, so too *hesed* (lovingkindness) for example, is a concept that describes aspects of spiritual existence in all spheres. His weekly *shiurim* on Kabbalah, the transcriptions of which were later worked into a book—*Inner*

---

[11] He devoted two articles to this subject, "Gateway to the Past," and "Treasures," which were published in the posthumous collection of essays, *The Aryeh Kaplan Reader* (Artscroll Mesorah, 1983).

[12] See *Waters of Eden* (National Council of Synagogue Youth and Orthodox Union, 1976) 54.

Space—were another example. R. Kaplan neither studied nor taught Kabbalah as a closed, esoteric system but as a window to understanding all of spiritual existence. In his lectures, he often gave analogies or presented possible implications of a theory he was expounding that were drawn from disparate realms such as science, art or family relationships. The editors of the book told me how challenging it was to edit a book that would reflect R. Kaplan's authentic voice while not diverging from the main topics of each chapter. Two examples they chose to include give us an indication of how imaginative was his elucidation of kabbalistic concepts:

Divine Providence

A computer system can provide us with an analogy to the constant interplay between the spiritual and the physical. The programmer sitting at the console corresponds to the "Man" of *Atzilut*. The CPU, Central Processing Unit, is the brain and memory bank of the computer, corresponding to *Beriyah*, the world of thought. Suppose that the computer is programmed to control traffic lights throughout a large metropolitan area. Transmission lines would then be coming out of the CPU, connecting it to traffic lights all over the city. These transmission lines correspond to the universe of *Yetzirah*. The traffic lights…correspond to the world of *Asiyah*, controlling traffic in the physical world.

We mentioned that the relationship between the physical world and the spiritual is always dynamic. Accordingly, God's providential direction of the universe never ceases. He is always acting in the world, guiding events based on our actions.

It is always a two-way process. Let us say we are driving into a large city like Manhattan. If the sensors are detecting the possibility of a massive traffic jam in midtown Manhattan, the computer may close off all bridges leading into the city. Thousands of cars and trucks will be prevented from crossing these bridges and will consider it a terrible catastrophe…. Yet, unless they get a special report on their radios, they will not realize that drastic measures had to be taken in order to divert the possibility of an inner city gridlock….

Sometimes, then, to prevent a greater tragedy, the computer might have to take unpleasant measures…. (*Inner Space*, 34–35)

Tiferet is usually translated as "beauty," but it does not carry the usual connotation of beauty. *Tiferet*-Beauty is like harmony, a harmonic beauty. Take pure white and pure black. Pure white would be *Hesed*-Love and pure black would be *Gevurah*-Restraint. There is no harmony or beauty in each one by itself, but as soon as I take black and white and mix them together I can make all kinds of beautiful pictures, not by merging, which would just give grey, but by a blending of the two. Again with pure *Hesed*, you can take a whole pail of paint and just pour it on the canvas. With pure *Gevurah* you hold a brush in your hand and you are unable to touch the canvas. *Tiferet* means you are able to harmonize and blend these two extremes.
(*Inner Space*, 62–63)

As a translator, R. Kaplan also offered much more than a technical rendering of words into English. His translations added so many levels of meaning that some of his works are being converted back into Hebrew for the benefit of speakers of the Holy Tongue![13] In his introduction to *The Living Torah* (his translation of the Five Books of Moshe) he explicitly stated this goal:

...the philosophy of this translation has been to treat the Torah as a living document.... Our Sages teach that "every day the Torah should be as new." This...also implies that archaic or obsolete language must not be used when translating the Torah, because this language gives the impression of the Torah being old, not new....

More important is the use of idiomatic language in the Torah. The greatest mistake any translator could make would be to translate an idiom literally.... The Talmud itself warns of this. In one of the most important teachings regarding translation the Talmud states, "One who translates a verse literally is misrepresenting the text. But one who adds anything of his own is a blasphemer."

...This places great responsibility on the translator. When one translates literally...ambiguities in the original may be preserved, if not aggravated. But if the translator must understand the text, he also has the responsibility to interpret it. To do so correctly, he must not

---

[13] Translations into Hebrew of R. Kaplan's works include *Memei Gan Eden* (*Waters of Eden*), Emanuel Raabad trans. (*haMercaz ha'Artzi leMa'an Taharat haMishpahah*) and *Meditatziah Yehudit* (*Jewish Meditation: A Practical Guide*) (*Hokhmat haLev*).

only analyze the text very carefully, but he must also study all the works that interpret it.

Teaching and Prayer: Living His Torah

The influence our correspondence had on me is due, to a certain extent, to the way the relationship was characterized at the outset. The two features I noted—the elements of reciprocity and of honesty—became a living guide in developing fundamental aspects of my Jewish identity. This included the embracing of increased women's learning in Judaism twenty years before it became acceptable and widespread in Orthodox circles. It has also included *aliyah* to Israel and a career change from lawyer to Talmud and Jewish Law teacher.

These elements informed the part of me that chose to become a teacher. All teachers who open themselves to the input of their students and interaction with them can probably identify with the words of Rabbi Judah the Prince: "Much I have learned from my teachers, and from my friends more than my teachers, and from my students most of all" (*Makkot* 10a). Often, students offer insights or pose original questions that challenge the teacher to deeper levels of understanding—even an off-hand comment may trigger a profound lesson.

The key, though, is the dynamic begun by the teacher's receptivity to the student's input. Many teachers are uncomfortable with the vulnerability of such a position. They refrain from sharing doubts, questions or personal experiences unless the "exposure" is calculated to induce a specific didactic response in the students.

In my experience, however, truly great teachers often choose to share their own questions or experiences, in the belief that as leaders, the interaction with students will lead to more expansive answers. R. Kaplan's letters often shared personal stories or dilemmas, and on one level I believe he meant to teach an outright lesson to a beginning student in a very subtle and non-threatening way. On another level, the stories opened the pathways of communication and in no way lessened R. Kaplan's stature in my eyes. Quite the opposite. His greatness to me was measured by the way in which he showed me how he dealt with those questions or situations.

In one instance, he shared a story about how spontaneous prayer affected the course of his life:

> ...I guess I began having my own conversations with God when I was
> around 10 or 11. It is still something I do when I am faced with a major
> crisis.... Let me give you a case in point.... When I came to New
> York ten years ago I worked as.... I wasn't used to the backbiting in
> the city and at the end of the year, I was politely asked to leave. I
> spent all summer looking for something else, but I couldn't find a
> thing. That was in the middle of a recession year when everyone was
> getting rid of personnel. Then I went to the cemetery to my mother's
> grave. I began to speak to Hashem and ask him to help me. I recall
> that I was weeping.... This occurred on a Sunday. The next day I got a
> call from....

The story ends with a job that materialized in a completely new direction which led R. Kaplan to writing and publishing, especially for unaffiliated Jewish youth. Certainly the story carried a message. But it was the way in which it was communicated that affected me, as much as the message itself. The tone was not, "see how I solved this problem in the right way," but "see how I too have faced difficulties. Can you relate to this way of solving the problem?" John Holt calls this the hallmark of a leader: "Charismatic leaders make us think, 'Oh if only I could do that, be like that.' True leaders make us think, 'If they can do that, then...I can too.'"

An echo of this message can be heard in the talmudic saying often cited by another of my teachers, Chana Balanson *z"l* (of blessed memory), who also embodied these characteristics of reciprocity and openness with respect to her students.[14] "More than the calf wants to suckle, the cow wants to give milk," said R. Akiva from his jail cell to his student, R. Yohanan. By way of a parable he explained to his student why, even though he desired to teach R. Yohanan more than R. Yohanan imagined, he was afraid to endanger the latter's life.[15] "The message," R. Kaplan taught, "was that more than the disciple wanted to learn, the teacher

---

[14] See articles in this collection on and by Chana Balanson. I was privileged to study with her at MaTaN–The Women's Institute for Torah Studies in Jerusalem from 1989 until her passing in 1992.

[15] *Pesahim* 112a. The background to the story is found in *Berakhot* 62b where R. Akiva is imprisoned and later executed for teaching Torah.

wanted to impart. This is the idea of the *Netzah-Hod* relationship. It is
something that I give, but a giving from which I receive" (*Inner Space*,
65). This image implies other meanings as well. The dynamic of teaching
and learning is as natural as the process of nursing and, as in the natural
realm, the cow needs the calf suckling to draw forth the milk.

The process of suckling has more implications in the human realm than
it does in the animal kingdom. Whereas the animal suckles from the
mother's underside, the human baby sucks *en face* thereby seeing her
reflection in her mother's face. The mother's milk not only helps to build
bones and muscles, her face also acts as a mirror—helping the baby form
a perception of itself and the outside world.[16]

As a result of my encounter with R. Kaplan, I seek more interactive
teacher-student relationships. As a teacher, this means a constant awareness of when I serve as leader and guide—and when I am in the receiving
mode—growing and learning from a student. It entails an ongoing
evaluation of whether I am meeting the requirement of serving as a
reflective mirror, and allowing students to gain their own insights from
my teaching.

R. Kaplan encouraged me to strive to make a unique contribution to
the Jewish people at a time when clearly that belief had nothing to do with
my own personal achievements. Rather, it reflected his way of seeing the
potential behind the individual Jew. His advice took the following form:

> Of course, the question of whether or not to...can be one of the most
> important decisions in your life. Whichever decision you make it will
> affect you for the rest of your life. You really have to look deep into
> your psyche and see what are your deepest values. Pray to Hashem
> that He should help you make the right decision. Hirsch [nine-
> teenth-century German Rabbi Samson Raphael Hirsch] writes that
> *hithpalel* ["to pray"] (from the word *p'l'l* "to judge") is
> self-judgment. Sometimes when a person prays for something, he is

---

[16] I would like to thank R. Daniel Epstein for this idea taught at MaTaN in 1989,
citing psychologist D.W. Winnicott's *Playing And Reality* as a source for this view of
human nursing. In the lesson, R. Epstein reminded the listeners that our Sages took
note of the grace of God in situating woman's breasts, *beMakom bina*—close to the
place of understanding—*Berakhot* 10a. I thank Susan Handelman for pointing out
that a classic statement of this idea can also be found in the French psychoanalyst
Jacques Lacan's "The Mirror Stage" (Paris: *Écrits*, 1966).

able to uncover his own deepest motives. Try it and tell me what happens.

R. Kaplan's views on prayer, and his willingness to write openly about his own experience of prayer, was one of the most important lessons he conveyed in his letters. He taught that sincere prayer is more than understanding the words of the prayer services—more than singing inspiring tunes to accompany the prayers. R. Kaplan at once brought prayer down to the most understandable levels and elevated it to extraordinary heights. Prayer is communication with God. This idea, found mostly in Bratslav teaching,[17] was enhanced by the descriptions of how prayer had helped him formulate important decisions in life. R. Kaplan showed how to view prayer as a real experience and not as a synagogue ritual needing explanation.

He also wrote about prayer as a form of meditation. At that time, in mainstream Jewish circles, the very word "meditation" had far-eastern non-Jewish associations and stigmas. Today, his writings on this subject are very much in demand, and address the deep spiritual yearnings found in even the most mainstream congregations. By translating kabbalistic understandings of meditation and the prayer service into modern terminology, R. Kaplan recaptured the meaning of prayer for the early *hasidim* and saints. He reacquainted us with deep communication with Hashem as a modern possibility. This was an issue only for fringe groups in the 1970's, when he first began writing. It is now clear how much R. Kaplan pre-dated the current trend and wrote some of the most accessible insights on prayer.[18]

Final Reflections

I began with the advantage of the personal over the teachings found in books. I am very grateful for the tremendous amount of time R. Kaplan

---

[17] R. Kaplan translated many of the writings of R. Nahman of Bratslav, wrote a commentary on *Sippurei Ma'asiyot* and a biography of R. Nahman, all commissioned by the Bratslav community in Jerusalem. He quotes R. Nahman often in his books, especially those on meditation.

[18] I recommend to the reader R. Kaplan's *Jewish Meditation* as an excellent source to discover how to pray with more *kavanah*—intention.

invested in me and other students like myself with whom he corresponded. The relationship unfolded over time—and the insights continue to unfold. Paradoxically, most of it unfolded in writing.

Writings have an advantage over the immediacy of personal experience; we are able to reflect over and over on the written word, discovering new levels of meaning. In a sense, one could be accused of finding levels of meaning unfaithful to the original, yet this is precisely what authors leave us as a legacy. This is so poignantly expressed in stories about Moshe's "visit" to R. Akiva's *Beit Midrash* and Moshe's inability to comprehend the discussion that was attributed to his own name, or Choni Hama'agel visiting his own *Beit Midrash* after having slept for seventy years.[19] Their students can no longer ask them for the interpretation of their own teachings, but rather must produce interpretations of their own, pertinent to their generation.

There is certainly a tragic and wistful tone to those stories. I often wish I could consult R. Kaplan now on what he meant in certain places in his letters or writings. This is not only impossible but also undesirable. The responsibility has now been transferred to us, the students and readers, to find the meanings and solve the unsolved problems. I deliberately use the word "responsibility," for it conveys my concern about how delicately and judiciously we must treat the teachings of our Sages and teachers, not simply using them as a banner on which to pin our own ideas. And yet, we are responsible for their interpretation and application to our generation, which requires our own insight and innovation.

Thankfully, R. Kaplan has left us all a prolific legacy of writings to explore—"*ve'idakh zil g'mor*" ("and the rest, go and learn").

---

[19] *Menahot* 29b, *Ta'anit* 23a.

Appendix I

ABOUT RABBI ARYEH KAPLAN

Rabbi Aryeh Kaplan's meteoric rise as one of the most effective, persuasive, scholarly and prolific exponents of Judaism in the English language came to an abrupt end on January 28 1983, with his sudden death at the age of 48.

Rabbi Kaplan was a multi-faceted, uniquely creative and talented author. In the course of a writing career spanning only twelve years, Aryeh Kaplan became known to Jewish youth and adult readers for such books as *Waters of Eden: The Mystery of the Mikvah*; *Sabbath: Day of Eternity*; *The Handbook of Jewish Thought* and *Jewish Meditation: A Practical Guide*. He translated many classics into English, including *The Living Torah*, a clear, contemporary translation of the Five Books of Moses; the *Me'am Loez* commentary, and writings of Rabbi Nahman of Bratslav.

Rabbi Kaplan was born in New York City and was educated in the Torah Voda'as and Mir Yeshivot in Brooklyn. After years of study at Jerusalem's Mir Yeshiva, he was ordained by some of Israel's foremost rabbinic authorities. He also earned a Master's degree in physics and was listed in *Who's Who in Physics* in the United States.

Aryeh Kaplan's unusual warmth, sincerity and total dedication to Torah were an inspiration to the thousands he reached personally. In the process of bringing Torah to the Jewish world, Rabbi Kaplan revealed much of what was previously hidden. His mind contained libraries of books, waiting to be put into writing.

(Adapted, with permission, from the Union of Orthodox Synagogues.)

Appendix II

A List of Rabbi Aryeh Kaplan's Works
(compiled by Sara-Lea Nebenzahl)

KABBALAH
Translation: *Derekh haShem* by Luzzatto, Moses Hayyim, 1974
The Bahir, 1979
Sefer Yetzirah, 1990
Encounters, 1990
Inner Space: Introduction to Kabbalah, Meditation and Prophecy, 1991
Immortality, Resurrection and the Age of the Universe: A Kabbalistic View, 1993
Facets and Faces, 1993

MEDITATION
Meditation and the Bible, 1978
Meditation and Kabbalah, 1982
Jewish Meditation: A Practical Guide, 1985

MAHSHAVAH **(Jewish Thought)**
Love Means Reaching Out (on *kiruv*), 1974
The Handbook of Jewish Thought: vol. 1, 1979
Made in Heaven (on marriage), 1983
A Call to the Infinite (on prayer), 1986
The Handbook of Jewish Thought: vol. 2, 1992
Moreh Or (only book to appear originally in Hebrew), 1992

The Aryeh Kaplan Anthology Vol. 1:
Maimonides' Principles: The Fundamentals of Jewish Faith, 1973
The Real Messiah: A Jewish Response to Missionaries, 1973
The Infinite Light: A Book About God
If You Were God, 1983

The Aryeh Kaplan Anthology Vol. 2:
God, Man and Tefillin, 1973
Sabbath: Day of Eternity, 1974
Waters of Eden: The Mystery of the Mikvah, 1976
Jerusalem: The Eye of the Universe, 1976
(also appeared as a full color picture album: *Jerusalem: The Eye of the Universe–A Pictorial Tour of Jerusalem*, 1993)
Tzitzith: A Thread of Light, 1984

The Aryeh Kaplan Reader: a collection of dozens of booklets and articles (1983)

HASSIDUT
Translation: *Rabbi Nachman's Wisdom*, 1973 (the first book to be published)
Translation: *Rabbi Nachman's Tikun* [excerpt], 1973
Translation: *Outpouring of the Soul*, 1980
Translation: *Gems of Rabbi Nachman* [excerpt], 1980
The Light Beyond: Adventures in Chassidic Thought, 1981
Translation: *Rabbi Nachman's Stories*, 1983 (1987)
The Chassidic Masters: History, Biography and Thought, 1984 (1991)
Until the Mashiach (a biography of Rabbi Nachman), 1985

TORAH and HALAKHAH TRANSLATIONS
The Torah Anthology–Me'am Loez series (16 volumes of Torah, Esther, *Pirke Avoth*, Sefaradi Haggadah, and Tisha Be'Av), 1977–1983
The Laws of Chanukah from the Shulkhan Arukh, 1977
The Living Torah (translation and commentary on the Torah), 1981
The Basic Haggadah [Ashkenazi], 1982
The Yom Kippur Service, 1982

Words on Fire: Then and Now –
In Memory of Nechama Leibowitz

Joy Rochwarger

Nechama, the Person

Nechama Leibowitz *z"l* (of blessed memory), was my teacher, my mentor and my confidante. I first began attending her *shiurim* (lectures) in 1984, during a post high school year of study in Israel. For the next five years I participated in a Tisha be'Av *shiur* that she gave every summer. It was when I made *aliyah* in 1990 that our relationship took on a radically different form. At the urging of a close friend, I began to participate in Nechama's famous Thursday night *shiur* that had been meeting for more than twenty years. Nechama was then eighty-three years old. I was the youngest student there and definitely the least knowledgeable. Most of the other participants were either Israeli or had been living in Israel and studying with Nechama for many years, which put me at a distinct disadvantage. In addition, Nechama's style of teaching was different from any I had ever experienced. Although examples of her teaching technique can be found throughout this essay, her *Studies in...* (the five books of the Torah) best portray her methodology and should be consulted for further reference.

Nechama would begin the *shiur* by asking for quiet, and only when there was complete silence would she begin. The text to be studied that evening would be introduced with a brief explanation. Nechama would then ask a question concerning a seeming discrepancy or contradiction in the text, or compare two or three of the commentaries on a specific verse. Her request for a response from us would be very specific, for example, a three-word answer. Any other possibility was decisively wrong. She would hand out small pieces of paper and pencils and wait for everyone to hand in their answers before continuing with the lesson. If your answer contained five words, or was not phrased in exactly the format that Nechama had designated, it was returned with instructions to think it over and try again. Nechama always modified her remarks for the individual student, relative to his or her needs, holding fast to the dictum, "Train a child according to his way [i.e., his unique path]" (Proverbs 22:6). To an old-timer, she would say that he should know better than to submit such an answer; to a newcomer, she would always be encouraging and provide hints to the correct solution. Having achieved the status of a "regular," I was always anxious that Nechama might call on me. Having witnessed the discomfiture of others who had not responded precisely in accordance with Nechama's concept of the correct answer, I strategically established my *makom kavuah* to be a seat that was comfortably out of her range of vision. During one of our many conversations, I once off-handedly remarked that many people were intimidated by her. Nechama was astonished and couldn't understand what she might be doing that would instill fear in her students. Her sole intention was to spark and inspire within each student the will to learn, and to encourage incisive thinking.

Occasionally, during the week, Nechama would ask for volunteers to help her assemble the leaflets (*gilyonot*) that lined her walls. There were thirty years of these study sheets, each week's *parashah* kept in a separate folder. When a set was ordered, the sheets would have to be collated according to the request—one year, five years and sometimes, all thirty years. Someone would have to painstakingly pull out one *gilayon* from each folder, taking note of which folders were empty or running low. One day after class, I asked Nechama if she would need my help that week. It was the first and last time that I ever volunteered for this task. My back hurt for two days from reaching up to the top rows and bending down to the bottom ones to withdraw the *gilyonot*. However, I still felt a responsibility to give back something in return for everything that Nechama was giving to me. (No payment was ever requested for the Thursday night *shiur*.) The next time I was there, I asked Nechama if there was anything *else* that I could do for her, stipulating, "in addition to the *gilyonot*." She informed me that her doctor allowed her to participate in all activities, but warned her against falling. Would I walk with her Friday mornings when she would go out to do her weekly shopping and thus allay her doctor's fears? I readily accepted and it was from that moment that our relationship took on added and deeper dimensions.

For six years, I spent almost every Friday morning with Nechama, accompanying her on errands to the bank and the local supermarket. Afterwards, I would sit with her in the apartment and discuss issues of varying concerns over a cup of tea and a bar of chocolate. Nechama had an insatiable curiosity for what was going on in the world around her. She wondered about the life style of the Orthodox Jew in the modern American world, and whether or not men there wore *kippot* to work. She was astounded to hear that there are numerous *minyanim* for *Minhah* in law firms and businesses throughout New York City, and that many men wake up two hours early to attend not only a *Shaharit minyan*, but also a *Daf Yomi shiur*. She asked me to describe some of the current women's styles and fashions and was curious as to how much such clothes cost. I once told her that I was having three dresses made to order, in honor of the weddings of three of my siblings. I explained that each wedding had a different color scheme and, therefore, I was expected to appear in a different gown at each affair. I also let her know the price of each gown, and that in all probability each would only be worn that one time. Nechama was dumbstruck by the apparent wastefulness and proudly informed me that not only was her own wedding dress inexpensive, but that she had continued to wear it for over fifty years!

Nechama, the Teacher

Nechama was a teacher of thousands, yet she was able to give each student the feeling that he or she was of singular importance. She made time to discuss ideas for a *shiur*, to review a page of sources recently put together, or to discuss matters of personal concern.

Before I made *aliyah*, I invariably looked forward to my summers in Jerusalem, knowing that one of the most significant mourning periods in Jewish history, the three weeks between the 17th of *Tammuz* and Tisha be'Av, would be made more meaningful and spiritual since they included a visit with Nechama. The *shiur* that Nechama gave on Tisha be'Av was a combination of text-study and discussion concerning the gravity of the day. Her energy was contagious, and while sitting in Nechama's presence it was easy to forget that one was fasting. In her later years, as Nechama grew older, her daytime activities tended to tire her out. Yet sometimes she would begin a *shiur* at 8:30 at night and visibly grow stronger and more determined as the hour grew late. At 10:30, she would abruptly stop and announce that it was time for everyone to go home since they were surely worn out. Frequently, I and two or three others would remain afterwards to discuss specific points of interest with Nechama. The following day, as we walked, Nechama would remark on how impressed she was that the participants in the *shiur* were able to stay up so late, especially the women who had the added concern of finishing their preparations for Shabbat.

Nechama's love for Torah clearly served as the source of her vitality, and gave her wellsprings of strength that allowed her to enable others to partake in and benefit from her fervor. Moreover, as one who took very seriously the responsibility of educating teachers, Nechama strove to impart one simple rule that would serve as the overriding standard: the teacher should always remember that the purpose of our function in the school is not to disseminate large quantities of information; and it's not within our grasp to produce erudite scholars who are proficient in all areas of the Torah. Rather, our purpose is to propagate love for the Torah so that the words of the Torah will be loved and cherished by the student. This (love) will enable her or him to see the great light that radiates forth from our commentators and illuminates the verses so that the hearts of our students are warmed by their light.[1] Nechama embodied this principle and showed, by personal example, how it could be implemented.

Nechama's methodology in teaching biblical exegesis is a commonly discussed topic among her students and those familiar with her work. It is not an exaggeration to state that once one is familiar with her approach, one never reads or teaches Tanakh in quite the same way again. Nechama defined her approach as eliciting the literal meaning of the text by using

---

* This article is based on a lecture given by the author at Shalhevet Torah Institute for Women, New York, July, 1995.

[1] Nechama Liebowitz, *Limmud Parshanei haTorah uDrakhim leHora'atam* (Jerusalem, 1978). Introduction, as quoted by Howard Deitcher in a lecture in honor of Nechama Leibowitz, October 1998, at Machon Schechter in Jerusalem.

all the means at one's disposal, including the halakhic and aggadic *midrashim*, the talmudic and biblical commentaries, as well as ancient and contemporary philosophers, scholars and biblical exegetes. A teacher must remain faithful to the text as it was intended to be delivered by the author (i.e., God or His prophets). In an essay entitled, "How to Read a Chapter of Tanakh," Nechama states:

> It is true that the reader is bound to the printed word. He does not, however, merely absorb it into his soul; he gives it expression from within his soul in order to bring the letters to life. "The relationship of words to a living work is like that of an architect to a constructed house. The reader is true in his reading to the blueprint, but it is he who builds the house of literary creativity from the material of his voice and soul" [Ludwig Strauss]. After these words it is even more understandable how difficult it is for one person to teach another to read, since the responsibility for rebuilding the book anew belongs to the builders themselves according to the instructions of the book and by means of the material of their voices and souls, in which they differ one from the other just as their appearances differ. If, in spite of this, we are still trying to teach reading, our justification is that the instructions given to the builder (that is the architect's blueprint with all its clauses, words and letters), they are the precise given objective facts which command respect. It is towards the understanding of these (letters, words and clauses) and to the acceptance of their authority, that we wish to lead the reader....[2]

A few years ago I was asked to give a *shiur* to a group of women in New York, on Tisha be'Av. Without hesitation, I turned to Nechama for advice. Her unique pedagogic style consisted of bringing the text to life by placing the person within the context of the story, the time period and the historical circumstances. The life and force of the Torah is much greater than we are, yet it can be made readily accessible if one has the appropriate tools and knows how to use them. Nechama exemplified a person whose worldview was characterized by the use of Torah as a lens

---

[2] The original Hebrew text is entitled *LeZekher A.L. Strauss* (Jerusalem, 1954) 90–104. An English version appears in *On Teaching Tanakh*, Moshe Sokolow trans. (Torah Education Network, 1986) 1–13.

for contemplating and understanding the world and she taught others how to interpret and utilize the Torah to this end.

Nechama referred me to the Book of Jeremiah, chapter 36. She explained that the chapter represents not only a tragic episode in the history of the Jewish people, but that it also contains within it a deeper, more symbolic message that connects directly to Tisha be'Av. It was only a matter of moments before Nechama was to show me by personal example how to apply literary analytical skills to a text that was written more than a thousand years ago, in order to extract guidelines for living in the present.

When Nechama taught Torah, she was always telling a story. She was the "narrator" par excellence, knowing how to create a dialogue between the text and the student. On that afternoon, Nechama drew a direct line between the events that transpire in Jeremiah chapter 36 and the symbolism of Tisha be'Av, according to its meaning and proper observance. Nechama brought me back to a time and place in Jewish history that a few moments before had only been a text to analyze. What follows is a description of the lecture that I gave, which was based on the inspiring experience that I had with Nechama that afternoon.

Background Information on Jeremiah, Chapter 36

The time frame is the fourth year of the reign of Yehoyakim,[3] the son of Yoshiyahu, and Jeremiah has received a prophecy commanding him to transcribe the words that God had relayed to him. There is the hope that *benei Yisrael* (Children of Israel), upon hearing the words read aloud, will repent from their evil ways (36:1–3). We know that Jeremiah did not have an easy time as a prophet and had met with a great deal of resistance from both *benei Yisrael* and the king (26). The text attests that only after some time had passed were the people convinced of Jeremiah's integrity (26:16). In the Talmud, R. Yohanan concludes that God held Yehoyakim

---

[3] Yehoyakim ruled Judea from 609 BCE until 598 BCE. During the first five years of his reign, the Egyptian empire ruled Judea. The Babylonians invaded the country in 604 BCE and ruled for the next three years. Judea rebelled against the Babylonians in 601 BCE and was finally defeated in 598 BCE, when Yehoyakim and the rest of the people were exiled from the country. Nebuchadnezzar, the King of Babylon, destroyed the Temple eleven years later, in 586 BCE (II Kings: 25:8).

accountable for the sins of his generation, and had it not been for the good deeds of *benei Yisrael*, the whole world would have been destroyed.[4]

We are told in verse 5 that Jeremiah is under house arrest (עצור), but the exact nature of his situation is unclear.[5] After hearing the prophecy of the future destruction, decimation of the Land of Israel and exile of the nation, the priests, prophets and people (who heard the prophecy) intend to kill Jeremiah (7:29; 8:10; 26:8; 29:26).[6] When the princes of the king are informed of the situation, they gather to determine the fate of Jeremiah. While they are conferring, another prophet, Uriah, is pursued to Egypt and returned to Judea where Yehoyakim kills him (26:22–23). Thanks to the intervention of Ahikam ben Shafan (26:24),[7] one of the king's advisers, Jeremiah is able to escape a similar fate.

Barukh ben Neriah, the Scroll and the Mission

In 36:2, Jeremiah calls Barukh, the son of Neriah and dictates to him "all the words of God," and commands him to "Take a scroll and write in it all the words which I have spoken to you about Israel and about Judah and about all the nations...." The commentaries suggest that the scroll Barukh

---

[4] *Sanhedrin* 103a. "R. Yohanan said: God wanted to return the world to its primordial state of null and void [*tohu vavohu*] because of Yehoyakim...but then He looked at [the deeds of] his generation and decided against it...." There is some dispute whether Yehoyakim was indeed tyrannical. Alternatively, he might have been acting in a manner justified by military law. See comments of C. Givaryahu, Y. Elitzur and Z. Beilin in response to Yochanan Aharoni in *Hoy Boneh Beitoh belo Tzedek, Iyunim beSefer Yirmiyahu*, vol. 2, Benzion Luria ed. (Jerusalem, 1952–54) 53–73.

[5] Jeremiah's "confinement" would explain why a significant period of time passed between the mandate he gave to read the scroll and its actual reading by Barukh the son of Neriah. But perhaps Jeremiah's statement "ואני עצור" would be more correctly interpreted as "I am prohibited" or forbidden to enter and prophesy in the Temple area (Jeremiah 26). The word עצור cannot mean arrested or detained; if he were incarcerated, why would the king be searching for him and Barukh later on in the chapter? Gershon Brynn, *Yirmiyah 36—Perek beHit'havut Sefer Nevui, Hagut beMikrah*, vol. 4, 46–54.

[6] Metzudat David explains that this is referring to the priests of Ba'al and the false prophets.

[7] A scribe appointed by Yoshiyahu (II Kings 22:12, 14; II Chronicles 34:20).

wrote is the book of Lamentations.[8] The Rabbis learn this from the cryptic conclusion of verse 32—"and there were added to them many other words."[9] After Yehoyakim burned the first scroll, Jeremiah has the "honor" of prophesying the rest of the contents of Lamentations—recorded in chapters two, three, four and five. The midrash cites verses from Lamentations (representative of the last four chapters) as corresponding texts to the words in Jeremiah 36:32. This indicates that when Jeremiah ordered Barukh to rewrite the scroll, he added these four chapters to the original text. In addition, the midrash explains that there are three different types of prophets: those who are concerned with the honor of God, those who are concerned with the honor of *benei Yisrael,* and those who are concerned with both. Jeremiah is the only prophet who is characterized as maintaining the honor of both God and *benei Yisrael.*

Nechama Reads a Story

These were some of the background sources that I included in the *shiur* I gave on Tisha be'Av. After conducting the brief historical, contextual and exegetical review, I then shifted my focus to the main point Nechama had explicated on the day I spent studying the chapter with her. To explain the *peshat* (literal meaning) of the chapter, Nechama had not turned to the classical biblical exegetes, nor to any of the *midrashim.* After searching a back bookcase for a solid five minutes, she pulled out a small, well-worn book. She told me to sit down and listen carefully because she had a "story" to tell me. As Nechama began reading from the book, the characters were brought to life and I felt as if I was witnessing the events first-hand. The chapter from which she was reading was a modern literary

---

[8] *Mo'ed Katan* 26a; Radak, Metzudat David and Abravanel on 36:2. There is a dispute amongst scholars as to what exactly was written in the scroll. In addition to the view cited above, some scholars are of the opinion that the scroll contained the first six chapters of Jeremiah, while others think that it might have been the whole Book of Jeremiah. See Aharoni 50–52. The Abravanel stipulates that it did not contain the prophecies as they were told to Jeremiah. Rather, the scroll consisted of lamentations for the forthcoming punishments that would befall the Jews, in addition to affirmations of vengeance that God will wreak upon the enemy. Henceforth, according to Abravanel, the scroll became known as the Scroll of Lamentations.

[9] *מכילתא* בא, פתיחתא דמס׳ פסחא ב; מובא *בילקוט שמעוני*, ירמיהו ס׳ שכה.

rendering of Jeremiah 36, entitled: *"Va'ani kotev al hasefer bidyo, o hapahad mipnei hanisgav,"* by D. Kimhi.[10] Nechama's choice of reference was guided by her continual insistence that one must read and understand the text as if it were happening at that very moment. Furthermore, in an article on how to teach a chapter of Tanakh, she comments that, "Ludwig Strauss taught us, according to the formulation of Nathan Rottenstreich, that true reading is: the completion of the work—as though it were taken from the potential to the actual. Reading a poem is: a reproduction which the reader accomplishes by means of his voice and soul."[11] Nechama was able to transport me back to a distant time and place—sixth century B.C.E., Palestine—not by simply using a literary device, but by infusing the text with the spirit of her voice and soul.

Analysis of Jeremiah, Chapter 36

We have already read in the chapter that it is the fourth year of the reign of Yehoyakim and Jeremiah had commanded Barukh not only to record his words in a scroll, but also to go out to the people and read it aloud:

Verses 6–8

...You go and *read in the scroll*, which you have written from my mouth the words of God...on the fast day.... And Barukh the son of Neriah *did* according to all that Jeremiah the prophet *commanded him, reading in the book the words of God* in God's house.

Verses 9–10

And it came to pass in the fifth year of Yehoyakim...in the ninth month, that they proclaimed a fast before God to all the people in Jerusalem.... *Then Barukh read in the book the words of Jeremiah* in the house of God in the chamber of Gemaryahu, the son of Shafan....

---

[10] D. Kimhi, *Beshvilei haTanakh* (Tel Aviv: Dvir, 1952) 66–73. The translations in the following pages are my own.

[11] *On Teaching Tanakh*, 1–2.

In the ninth month (*Kislev*) of the following year a fast day is pro-claimed,[12] and Barukh sets out to do what Jeremiah had requested of him (6). The wording of the text emphasizes that Barukh follows Jeremiah's orders exactly as prescribed (Abravanel). Radak suggests that the fast day had been proclaimed as a response to the troubles that had befallen *benei Yisrael*. Maimonides explains that it is a positive commandment to cry out and blow trumpets when troubles befall the community. This is considered an act of repentance and acknowledgment that the difficulties they are experiencing are the direct result of the deeds of the people themselves. The first "trouble" listed as a justifiable basis for the declaration of a public fast day is one that is brought about by an enemy of the Jewish people.[13] The logical inference is that the people are lamenting their fate, due either to the Egyptian conquest or the hardships inflicted upon them by their own king—probably a combination of both factors. Abravanel points out that Jeremiah specifically commands Barukh to wait for a fast day to read the scroll when people from all over the country gather in and around the Temple to hear the trumpet blasts and participate in communal prayers.

Moreover, it is no coincidence that the text mentions specifically in whose chamber Barukh reads the scroll. We are reminded that Gemaryahu was the brother of Ahikam, the man who had saved the life of Jeremiah (26:24). Barukh is acutely aware of the dangers involved in spreading the word of God and it is precisely because Jeremiah is prohibited by the king from entering the Temple area that it is Barukh who must speak to the

---

[12] During this period of time, Babylon was involved in its conquest of the western countries. According to the *Chronicles of Chaldaean Kings*, the "ninth month"—*Kislev*, is when Nebuchadnezzar conquered Ashkelon: "He marched to the city Ashkelon and captured it in the month of *Kislev*..." (D. Wiseman ed., in British Museum, 69, line 18). The Judean kingdom was probably quite frightened at the prospect of its own impending doom and declared a fast day to pray for salvation.

[13] Maimonides, *Mishneh Torah Hilkhot Ta'aniyot* 1:1–2; 2:1. Maimonides bases his ruling on the verse in Numbers 10: 9: "And if you go to war in your land against the enemy that oppresses you, then you shall blow an alarm with the trumpets, and you shall be remembered before the Lord your God, and you shall be saved from your enemies."

people (36:5). He has carefully chosen a safe zone, the chamber of an adviser he feels is trustworthy.[14]

Nechama read to me from Kimhi's book, carefully setting the stage for the unfolding of the events contained in verses 11–19:

> It is a cold winter day in the month of *Kislev* when Barukh sets out to do his master's bidding. He reads the scroll aloud with the voice and pathos of a loyal disciple. Because Jeremiah has been prohibited from conducting public speeches, the nation has endured many months without any word from God. Therefore, they now flock to the Temple to hear His message although they know the speech will contain heavy words of rebuke and retribution. Amongst the throng of people there also walks a certain Mikhayahu ben Gemaryahu (the grandson of Shafan) and others like him, sent by the military police (who are at that very moment sitting in the palace on Mount Zion) to spy amongst the people and sense the feelings of the populace towards the government. Specifically, they are looking for sentiments concerning the current war. And although official consent for the fast day had probably been given, the spies, of course, are not participating in it. Mikhayahu reports to his supervisors the news that Jeremiah's scroll is presently being read aloud to the people. Already inured to the terrible prophecies of doom and destruction, they send for the reader and his scroll purely out of a cynical sense of duty. They had spent the whole day reviewing, signing and affixing the official stamp to tax depositions, job transfers of Egyptian officers, law amendments and other such official documents and requests. Elishama, the scribe, is weary from transcribing protocol and from writing and reading the Egyptian memos, while the other advisers have grown increasingly bored as the day progresses.
>
> Suddenly the door opens and in walks the messenger with the disheveled Barukh, grasping to his chest the sheets of the scroll that he hadn't even had time to bind together. They command him to "sit down and read!" and gather around to hear what he has to tell them. Dilayahu stretches himself out on a pillow. Sitting across from him is the scribe with the quill in his hand, waiting to begin recording the raving prophecies of the demented prophet. And the rest of the king's

---

[14] Franz Werfel provides a moving depiction of how and why Barukh chose this specific adviser, *Yirmiyahu Ish Anatot Roman Histori* (Tel Aviv, 1947) 2, 290–95.

advisers are wondering what they are doing listening to Barukh expound on illustrations from the biblical text.

But as Barukh reads, one by one their sarcastic expressions start to change and as the oration continues and the disciple's tone picks up an emotional element, the mood in the room slowly shifts. It's almost as if Barukh himself is the prophet. The powerful reading begins to make a profound impact on his audience. They hang their heads in shame, shudder in horror over the shocking news and approach each other for solace. In a single moment they are shaken from their daily, mundane routine and thrown into a new incomprehensible reality, to be categorized simply as "פחדו איש אל רעהו"—"[turning] one to the other in fear." (Jeremiah 36:16)

Who or what had so frightened them? And why? "פחדו" here connotes surprise and fear, the trembling that accompanies a terrible storm replete with thunder and lightning. Each man is terrified and it is in this context that the gut instinct takes hold to produce the simple question: "Tell us, if you will, how did you write down all of these words from his mouth?" (36:7). Their query is actually one of wonderment—how were you *able* to record these words?! Why are you not trembling in fear from these words that have fallen upon our ears as sledgehammers fall upon a wall of stone, resonating with a far-reaching voice that throws into sharp relief the sound of reality— the truth need be told and when it is spoken, it must be heard— "איך כתבת?!"—"how did you write this?!" (Jeremiah 36:17)

And then Barukh, from the corner where he sits, his glance directed downwards, lost in his own thoughts, answers in child-like innocence—"He spoke these words from his mouth and I inscribed them in the scroll with ink" (36:18). But the advisers are no longer listening. They are gripped with fear. The psychological impact that issues forth from the dark place in their hearts produces a perplexing situation. The advisers who are sitting in the king's chambers are reduced to mere men, powerless in the face of the meek scribe sitting across from them. They whisper into Barukh's ear, "Go [quickly] and hide, you and Jeremiah and tell no man where you are!" (Jeremiah 36:19)[15]

At this point, Nechama closed the book and continued to expound on the rest of the chapter, using the same literary approach that Kimhi had employed. King Yehoyakim is dutifully informed of the contents of the

---

[15] *Beshvilei haTanakh*, 66–70.

scroll,[16] and he, in turn, demands to see it for himself. The biblical text plays its audience masterfully. We are once again told that it is the month of *Kislev*.[17] But now we are sitting in the king's winter house with a fire blazing in the hearth and it seems that no one is prepared for what occurs almost immediately. As Yehudi reads from the scroll, the king grabs the scribe's razor, rips out the pages and throws them into the fire until the entire scroll is consumed by the flames:

> And it came to pass that when Yehudi had read three or four leaves, he would cut it with a penknife and cast it into the fire that was in the hearth, until all the roll was consumed in the fire that was in the hearth. (Jeremiah 36: 23)

The Talmud (*Mo'ed Katan* 26a) explains that the scroll in the king's hands is the Book of Lamentations. Yehudi reads the first four verses without interruption since the king feels that these words have no relevance to him. However, upon hearing the beginning of the fifth verse: "...her adversaries have become the chief," the king has Yehudi pause to give himself time to absorb the words and then asks him to continue. But the message only gets worse, "...her enemies prosper; for God has afflicted her for the multitude of her transgressions..." ״אויביה שלו כי ה׳ הוגה על רב פשעיה״ (Lamentations 1:5). Immediately, the king tears out all references to God and throws them into the fire.[18]

---

[16] Gershon Brynn comments that, "It is important to note that the King's advisors reported the incident not because they objected to the content of Barukh's message, but rather because they felt it was important enough to be brought to the king's attention." Brynn, *Hagut beMikrah*, 48.

[17] According to *Megillat Ta'anit*, an Aramaic work written during the time of the Second Temple period, the exact date was 7 *Kislev*. Hananiah ben Hizkiyahu ben Gurion veSiyato, *Megillat Ta'anit*, Yehudah Leib Kratstein ed. (Vilna, 1925).

[18] *Mo'ed Katan* 26a. This story appears in various forms in many of the classic commentaries, for example: R. Menahem ben Helbo, Metzudat David, Rashi, Abravanel. The issue discussed by the commentators is the meaning of the word ״דלתות״. R. Yosef Kara explains that each section of the scroll was composed of three or four columns and was connected by stitches to the next section. As Yehudi read three or four columns; i.e., as he completed a section, Yehoyakim would tear the stitches with a scribe's razor and burn that section in the fire. He continued to do so until the entire roll was burned. Radak and Targum Yonatan define the word according to the literal interpretation—"doors," and in this context it is referring to

The Talmud then makes an interesting observation. The following verses state that neither the king nor his servants are frightened, nor do they tear their clothes. The advisers who had been present at the first reading attempt to prevent the king from burning the scroll, but to no avail. The Rabbis comment that the explicit remark that they did not rip their clothes teaches that it *should* have occurred. Furthermore, they derive a halakhic principle from this omission—additional liability is extended to the sinful error:

> אמר רב הונא אמר רב אין קורעים אלא על ס״ת ששרפה מלך ישראל
> בזרוע כגון יהויקים, וחייב לקרוע על הגויל בפני עצמו ועל הכתב בפני
> עצמו, מה טעם ״אחרי שרוף את המגילה״ זה הגויל, ״ואת הדברים״ זה
> הכתב.

> When one sees a Torah scroll being torn by the hand of a king of Israel, as in the case of Yehoyakim, one is required to tear one's clothing twice, once for the scroll and once for the letters.

This decision is based on the explication of the ostensibly superfluous words in verse 27, " and the words"—״ואת הדברים״. When the law was codified in the *Shulhan Arukh* in the sixteenth century, the halakhic principle of *keriyah* (ripping) was given a more generalized form:

> הרואה ס״ת שנשרף או תפילין או אפי׳ מגילה אחת מהנביאים או
> מהכתובים קורע שתי קריעות ודוקא ששורפין אותו בזרוע וכמעשה
> שהיה. (שו״ע, יו״ד, סימן שם)

> When one sees a Torah scroll being burned, or *tefillin*, or even a single scroll from the Prophets or the Writings, one must rip one's clothing twice and specifically when it is burned by hand [when the person who is burning the scroll has the deliberate intention of destroying it], like the instance that occurred.[19]

Here, no mention is made of a king of Israel and the instance of the scroll being burned is a separate issue. According to the *Shulhan Arukh*, the law

---

"pages." Just like doors open and close, so do pages. *The Book of Jeremiah*, Rabbi A.J. Rosenberg ed. (NY: Judaica Press, 1985) vol. 2, 294–95.

[19] The *Siftei Kohen*, a commentary on the *Shulhan Arukh*, comments that the instance which occurred (״כמעשה שהיה״) refers to Yehoyakim's burning the scroll.

of *keriyah* is applicable when one sees a biblical scroll being burned by hand.

The chapter closes with Yehoyakim ordering the capture of Barukh and Jeremiah. However, the order is never carried out. God hides them away. Jeremiah is commanded to take another scroll and rewrite the one burned by Yehoyakim. Emphasis is placed on the fact that Jeremiah carries out God's orders exactly as prescribed:

> Then Jeremiah took another scroll and gave it to Barukh the scribe, the son of Neriyah, who wrote in it from the mouth of Jeremiah all the words which Yehoyakim, king of Judah, had burned in the fire; and there were added to them besides many similar words.
> (Jeremiah 36:32)[20]

In retribution for burning the scroll, Yehoyakim's descendants will not merit to inherit the throne,[21] and he himself will meet with a horrible death.[22]

Nechama finished reading from Kimhi's book and asked me if I had a little more time to spend with her because she had another story to tell me. (Ironically, Nechama always thanked me profusely for the time that I spent with her, although without a doubt, it was I who was receiving far more from her than she from me. She always made me feel as if I were doing her a favor by simply sitting and engaging in a conversation, even though it was I who had asked for her time.) I replied in the affirmative and was treated to the following anecdote.

---

[20] In addition to the explanation given by the *Mekhilta*, Brynn comments that, "the explanation of the matter is that the second scroll was more comprehensive than the first. Although this fact seems to merely be a technical point, it serves a literary role as well. Not only can the word of God not be muted, it rises and grows stronger" Brynn, 49.

[21] Radak and Abravanel (36:30) explain that Yehoyakin ruled for only three months and was not considered to be "sitting on the throne."

[22] II Chronicles 36:6—"Against him came up Nebuchadnezzar, king of Bavel and bound him in fetters to carry him to Bavel." Jeremiah 22:19—"He shall be buried with the burial of an ass, drawn and cast forth beyond the gates of Jerusalem."

The Palestine Post

Prior to the establishment of the State of Israel, when the British were ruling the country, the Jews were permitted three hours of radio time a day. One half-hour was reserved for the reading of a chapter from Tanakh, accompanied by a brief explanation. Every week a different person would be asked to do the reading and eventually Nechama's turn came around. (This is how Nechama presented the scenario to me.) She was requested to read a few chapters from Jeremiah and proceeded accordingly. In the middle of the same week, there was a tragic occurrence—the offices and press of the *Palestine Post* were blown up.

At this point in the story, Nechama lowered her voice and told me that everyone knew the act had been committed by the British themselves, but of course the British denied it and their guilt was never proven. The editors of the Post, however, were determined to go to press and managed to organize enough resources to publish a special edition. What follows is an abridged version of column one on the front page of that edition:

> *The truth is louder than TNT and burns brighter than the flames of ar-son. It will win in the end. Last night's bomb smashed machinery.* **It is surprising what some men will do to destroy truth.** *The tyrant...the fool...***have tried to suppress the truth since history began; and tried vainly.** *They are still at their monstrous folly.*
>
> **What was done last night is an incident among many in the bru-tal history of this land.** *It was nothing new to see flames and hear the groans of hurt men. It was nothing new to see little children and old women and stumbling men silhouetted against fire as they hurried si-lently away from their homes. That is the modern history of Palestine. It is the recent history of Palestine.... It will be said in London that it is the consequence of the judgment of the earth's United Nations.* **To say just that accusingly, is to be in part responsible for the evil that is done.**
>
> *The bomb in Hassolel Street for a moment closed the mouths of the messengers of the world; and shut off, as a telephone is shut off, the news from a score of capitals. It did but throw into still sharper relief and sound with still farther-reaching voice, the truth of this land and the sureness of its triumph.* **And that truth will be told.** *The men who*

did last night's deed probably overlooked that. There is nothing they can do about it now or at any time. It has escaped them. It makes their triumph short-lived and hollow.[23]

I later went home and located the article. When I showed Nechama a copy of it, she quickly glanced at it, acknowledged that she had remembered the event accurately and then began to reminisce about the other news items recorded on the same page.

After telling me about the article, Nechama sat back, folded her hands on her lap, and with a smile tugging at the corners of her mouth, asked me if I could guess which chapter the radio station had asked her to read on the very same day. Yes, it was Jeremiah, Chapter 36. Nechama then proceeded to use the article as a modern-day commentary in order to interpret the end of the chapter. The words Jeremiah had told Barukh to commit to writing had been the words of God. These words represent the truth in its most overt form. Yehoyakim, in his perverse ignorance, had thought that he could expunge this Truth. Like the British, he suggested that he could "close the mouths of the messengers of the world." Yet in effect, "there was nothing he could do about it now, nor at any time. It had escaped him. It made his triumph short-lived and hollow." The truth of the Torah burns brighter and stronger than the flames of any hearth. Unquestionably, "it will win in the end."

The Ten Martyrs

All this talk of the truth never dying and the words of God that can never be extinguished reminded me of a tragic episode in Jewish history, remembered as the "Ten Martyrs."[24] The account of the Ten Martyrs appears in two slightly different versions in the midrashic literature:

> One of the martyrs, R. Hananiah ben Teradiyon, was best known for never having spoken against his fellow man. When the Roman ruler

---

[23] *Front Page Israel: The Palestine Post* (Jerusalem: Jerusalem Post, 1994, Fifth Edition) Monday, February 2, 1948. Emphasis mine.

[24] Otherwise known as the עשרה הרוגי מלכות. These were ten Sages from the rabbinic era who were tortured and murdered over a sixty-year period. The earliest account appears in Tractate *Avodah Zarah* 17b–18b.

decreed that it was forbidden to learn Torah, R. Hananiah went out to
the Roman marketplace, gathered people around him and began to
sermonize. He was seized, brought to the ruler and sentenced. A Torah
scroll was wrapped around his body, wet sponges placed on his chest
in order to prolong his agony and delay his death, and he was set
aflame. His students who were standing nearby, asked him what he
saw. He replied, "I see scrolls burning and letters flying [up to
Heaven]," and only then began to cry. They asked him why he was
crying and he answered, "If I alone were burning it would not be difficult, but now the Torah scroll is burning along with me."[25]

Once again, we find that the fire consumes the physical material of
the scroll, but the essence of its spirituality remains everlasting. The
letters return to the source from which they emanated. A form of this
midrash is found in the prayer liturgy and is read twice a year, once in
the *Mussaf* service of *Yom Kippur* and once in the *kinnot* (lamentations)
of Tisha be'Av.[26]

I believe it is no coincidence that we read of the tragic deaths of eminent Torah scholars during two of the most emotional periods in the
Jewish life cycle. The *kinnot* are read to commemorate and memorialize
the destruction not only of the Second Temple, but also of men and
women who were embodiments of the Torah. Yet in the midst of this
destruction there is hope. Maimonides teaches that when the Messiah will
come, the three major fast days, including Tisha be'Av, will be annulled
and replaced with days of festivity and celebration.[27] The *Mussaf* prayer is
one of the most emotional parts of the Day of Atonement. At its conclusion, *kaddish* is usually recited in a joyous tone. Many people heave a
sigh of relief, happy to know that the hardest part is over, and they begin
to ready themselves for the end of the day.

---

[25] "*Ma'asei Asarah Harugei Malkhut*," *Nusha'ot aleph ubet, Beit Hamidrash, Heder
vav, tzad* 19.

[26] The *kinnah* is entitled "*Arzei haLevanon*" and may have been written by R. Meir
ben Yechiel, c. 1140 CE. *Authorized Kinot for the Ninth of Av*, Abraham Rosenfeld
ed., 125.

[27] *Rosh Hashanah* 18b; *Tosefta Ta'anit* 3; Maimonides, *Mishneh Torah, Hilkhot
Ta'aniyot* 5:19.

The story of the Ten Martyrs punctuates the prayer and highlights its seriousness. On this awesome day, we cannot forget for a moment what it truly means to dedicate oneself to God and His Torah. The text of this *piyyut* concerning the ten martyrs serves to remind us that even amidst terrible persecution there is always hope. Our present-day existence attests to this fact. Even when we think that all is lost, we can rest assured in the knowledge that the truth of the Torah is indestructible.[28]

When I had asked Nechama to suggest a topic for me to teach on Tisha be'Av, she had interpreted my question to mean: what lessons can be learned from the *Hurban*, destruction of the Temple, and how can they be best conveyed to the students? Her first association was with everlastingness. She turned to the book, *Beshvilei haTanakh* as a source that conveyed this message in as clear a manner as possible. She referred to the article in the *Palestine Post* for the very same reason. These resources served the express purpose of bringing the text to life. She taught me how to find inspiration in a story that for most people would have spoken only of evil and corruption, and she succeeded in engaging my undivided attention by taking the present back to the past, and by making history as relevant as present-day reality.

In her *shiurim*, I would observe how Nechama allowed arguments to continue for just so long, knowing exactly when to interrupt and return to the original point that she had made. She always encouraged "give and take" in her lessons. Her approach, in the most simple of terms, consisted of getting a student to think, and at this she was a Master. I would let my mind wander to the other students. We would sit in her salon (a single room that served as her living room, dining room and study), twenty people clustered around a huge desk, absorbing every word she uttered. We ranged in age from twenty-five to sixty-five, and each of us waited with baited breath to hear her reaction to our answers. For Nechama and for us, the classroom was a living entity—the essence of reality.

---

[28] Throughout the ages the malicious destruction of the scrolls of the Torah has produced different genres that reflect both the anguish felt by the Jewish people and their perpetual faith in the survival of the Law. On Tisha be'Av, we read a *kinnah* entitled, "*Sha'ali Serufah be'Esh*," written by R. Meir ben Barukh of Rothenberg (1215–1293). It poignantly describes the public burning of the Scrolls of the Law in Paris, c. 1244 (*Authorized Kinot*, 161).

Nechama's Passing

Nechama's death, for me, was the equivalent of a *hurban*. Yet having studied the biblical text with her, I was able to acquire a perspective that allowed me the possibility of coming to terms with this loss. The way she lived her life imparted the lessons that she had been teaching for over seventy years. One time I asked Nechama to verify a story that had been circulating about her days as a student at the University of Berlin. Her initial response was a look of surprise and a question: "People talk about me? Don't they have anything better to do with their time?" She had no sense of how great she was in the eyes of others. It has been remarked that she was part of a generation of *talmidei hakhamim* who viewed themselves as mere *melamdim*–simple teachers.[29] She was shocked and refused to believe that her *Studies on...* was the classic bat-mitzvah gift, or that most "modern Orthodox" households owned a set of her books. This news made no impact on her and she forgot it almost as soon as I had told her. She had no interest in hearing about her popularity. Her sole concern was to teach Torah and to be a living manifestation of its values.

Many times, we would pass by the Central Bus Station on our weekly Friday morning walks. Inevitably, we would be stopped by someone who had recognized Nechama and wanted to say hello. Nechama would engage the person in conversation, inquiring as to the welfare of his or her family, where she or he was currently teaching and so forth. There were instances when the person had studied with Nechama more than sixty years ago, and the topic of conversation would shift to the "good old days." Often, after the former student had walked away, Nechama would turn to me and tell me that she had not recognized him or her, even after the five-minute discussion. I was struck by how sensitively Nechama had conducted the conversation, never letting on. Nechama had thousands of students and all of them remember her quite clearly. But as every teacher knows, it is not a simple task to remember all of one's students' names

---

[29] Jeffrey Saks, "*Melamdim* and *Mehankhim*–Who are We?: Implications for Professionalizing Orthodox Jewish Education," unpublished essay.

even after seeing them repeatedly, let alone after a separation of thirty years or more.

One morning, as we were walking, I told Nechama that my wallet had been stolen the previous night. She asked me repeatedly if I needed money and told me she would be more than happy to give me some. After our regular stop at the bank, she led me to a Lotto teller and had me buy her a scratch card. Although we lost the first two times, the third time we won back the initial "investment." Nechama insisted on splitting the winnings with me despite the fact that she had paid for all of the cards. I realized that this was the way Nechama had found to enable *her* to help me out. From that day on, we continued to play Lotto every Friday, until the last year when the walk to the stand became too fatiguing for her. That year the spark also began to wane from Nechama's eyes and her spirit began to falter. Our walks became shorter and shorter, until finally we would only be able to walk once up and down the block. I felt as if I was watching the light of a dimming flame.

R. Yosef Dov Soloveitchik *z"l*, in a talk comparing the Jew to a *sefer Torah*, mentions that one is obligated to stand when a Torah scroll is brought forth.[30] The source is the commandment, "You shall rise up before an elder and honor the old man" (Leviticus 19:32), which obligates one to respect a *talmid hakham*. The Talmud draws a further analogy and explains that "when one finds oneself in the presence of a person at the time that his *neshamah* leaves him [when he dies], one must tear one's garment. To what is this compared? To a Torah scroll that is burnt" (*Shabbat* 105b). Rav Soloveitchik elaborates: "when a Jew dies, the Torah departs with his *neshamah* and one is required to tear his garment for the burning of a Torah." Rashi comments that this law is derived from the scroll that was burned by Yehoyakim.

It was a Shabbat afternoon and we had just finished cleaning up from lunch. I had some students staying in my apartment who decided to nap for a few hours. Since it was a pleasant spring day, I chose to take a walk and visit Nechama, who had been in the hospital for almost a month. I had

---

[30] Beit Yosef Shaul, *"Iyunim uVi'urim beTorat Moran Haga'on,"* Rabbi Yosef Dov Soloveitchik *z"l, al Inyanei ST"M*, Elchanan Asher haCohen Adler ed. (New York, 1994) 68–69.

been visiting her almost every day and had witnessed the distressing progression of her illness. Most of the time, I would sit at the side of her bed hoping she would awaken for just a few moments so that I could share some words with her. Many times I would hear her mumbling to herself, barely conscious. Even in her weakened state, I could make out words that always had something to do with Torah. Sometimes she would be reciting verses; other times she would be clarifying a point that had possibly been raised by a previous visitor, or maybe a student from long ago. Whenever I would try to engage her in conversation, the topic I introduced always had something to do with Tanakh and in this vein she responded. On that same afternoon, I expected to walk in and find her resting, possibly with one or two students sitting nearby.

As I approached the doorway to the Intensive Care Unit, I realized something was wrong. The person lying in Nechama's bed was bare-headed. For all the years I had known Nechama, not once had I seen her without a hat. There have been many jokes made concerning the three hats and four dresses Nechama owned. The question always asked was whether the color of the day was blue or brown. As noted earlier, material possessions were of minimal concern to Nechama, to say the least. The one exception was a framed needlepoint hanging on the wall, containing the words: (תהילים קיט : צז) ”מה אהבתי תורתך כל היום היא שיחתי“—"How I love your Torah! All the day it is my meditation" (Psalms 119:97).

Her small three-room apartment contained one bed, one desk, a television, and a few benches and chairs for the classes she held in her home. The rest of the apartment was filled, wall to wall, with books and her *gilyonot,* and most of the time her bed was also covered with various reading material. One time, as I was helping her adjust her clothes before leaving the apartment, she went to the closet to look for a belt. I pointed out to her that there were no loops on her dress and hence there was no need for it. She picked up her head and gave me a look that made me wish I had never gotten out of bed that morning: "In *my* home no one ever left the house without a belt." A woman of unbending principles.

And so, when I saw the uncovered head in the hospital bed, I braced myself for news that her situation had worsened and she had been transferred to a different ward. When I entered the Unit and asked the nurse where I could find Nechama, the response was clipped, "Who are you?" Instinctively, I answered that I was someone who was very close to Nechama. I can only assume that I was misunderstood, as the Hebrew word for "close," *karov*, is the same as that for "relative." I was then informed that Nechama had passed away early that morning, and I was curtly dismissed. I walked out of the hospital in a daze, not sure how to absorb the news. With my stomach churning, I began to make my way back to my apartment and then remembered I had a house full of guests. Knowing that the last thing I wanted to do at that moment was to inform others of what had happened, I started circling the neighborhood. Curiously, the story of Beruriah and R. Meir kept running through my mind.[31] The Talmud relates that both of their sons died on a Shabbat, but Beruriah withheld the news from her husband until Shabbat was over so that his *oneg Shabbat* would not be disturbed. I was determined to follow her example.

I happened to meet one of Nechama's great nephews and asked him when the funeral would take place. He told me they were still unsure and that the family would be consulting a Rav after Shabbat. Traditionally, the Jerusalem custom is to bury a person as soon after his or her death as possible, even in the middle of the night. The issue in this case was whether or not to delay until Sunday so that Nechama's students who lived in outlying areas of Israel would be able to attend. I eventually made my way back to the apartment where, thankfully, everyone was still asleep. An hour later my brother-in-law dropped by to visit, with my one-year-old nephew. It was a struggle not to say anything, as I had decided to follow Beruriah's example. I was able to make it through

---

[31] "A woman of valor, where can she be found?" (Proverbs 31:10)—The Rabbis say: "A story was told about R. Meir. He was sitting and teaching in the study hall on Shabbat afternoon when his two sons died. What did their mother do? She put both of them on the bed and covered them with a sheet. When Shabbat was over, R. Meir returned to his home from the study hall.... She said to him: 'Rabbi, I have one question to ask you.' He said to her: 'Tell me your question.' She said to him, 'Rabbi, earlier today, one man came to me and left an object for safekeeping and now he is coming to reclaim it. Shall we return it to him or not?' He said to her: 'Whoever is responsible for the safekeeping of the object must return it to its owner....' She grasped him with her hand and brought him up to that room...." *Midrash Mishlei* 31:10 (Buber ed., 108).

se'udah shlishit, but the moment Shabbat was over I went into my room to call a friend and began to deal more openly with my pain. I emerged and informed everyone of what had happened. They quickly helped me clean up and then, at my request, left me alone. I had an important phone call to make to my Rav and needed time to carefully think through the questions I would be asking him.

The news that Nechama had died was a devastating blow. I had lost my teacher and friend. But Nechama was not only *my* teacher. In my eyes she had grown to the level of a *talmidat hakhamim*, a revered teacher of Torah who imparts her lessons to the masses. One should tear *keriyah* as a sign of intense mourning. Although my grief was overwhelming, I was not an immediate relative and therefore not necessarily obligated in this commandment. Nechama, however, did not have any children and her husband had died many years before. It didn't seem right that there would be no one performing the *keriyah* ritual. Would I be permitted to do so? Before I could make the call, the phone rang and I was informed that a ruling had been issued permitting the delay of the funeral until the next day. It had been decided that in the case of a *talmid hakham*, students are to be considered the same as relatives, and it is permitted to delay a funeral to allow time for the arrival of the children of the deceased who might have a great distance to travel.[32] As to the question of tearing *keriyah*, it would be my decision to make.

At this point, I was left to my own devices and instinctively reverted to a well-rehearsed habit that I had developed to help me resolve difficult questions: I turned to Nechama. But for the first time in more than ten years my question was met with a bleak silence. What *would* she have said? Would Nechama have viewed herself as a *talmidat hakhamim*? Or would she have considered this title to be too pretentious and undeserved?

I return to an earlier comment. Nechama's loss for me was like a *hurban*. I did not only lose a *sefer Torah*; I lost a whole Temple. However, given the overriding principle she had taught me concerning the main lesson of Tisha be'Av—to find the kernel of hope amidst the decimation, I felt the imperative to find a similar way to understand her loss.

---

[32] *Bava Kama* 82b; *Shulhan Arukh*, YD 357:1; TZ 1; *Shakh, Nekudat haKesef,* YD 357:1; *Mishnah Berurah* 526:2, *Bi'ur Halakhah* (end); *Gesher haHaim*, vol. 1, ch. 7.

Nechama's life provided me with a pattern after which I could model my own. The textual and pedagogical skills Nechama imparted to me and to all her students are her legacy. Nechama's ultimate success is in creating the next link in the chain of transmission that connects us back to Sinai, adding her voice to the collective experience of the Oral Tradition and enabling us to participate as well. Through these voices we, in turn, give vitality to the context—and to each word and letter of the text itself. The skills that Nechama taught give us the voice to transmit this to the next generation of students. In all her actions and teachings Nechama was the embodiment of a Torah scroll. Her essence was eternal truth which nothing can diminish or divert—"She [Torah] is a tree of life to those who lay hold of her and happy are those who hold her fast"— ‏״עץ חיים היא למחזיקים בה ותומכיה מאושר״‎ (Proverbs 3:18).

On the Sixth Anniversary of Your Parting
From This World:
A Letter to My Teacher Chana Balanson

Sarah Malka Eisen

בס״ד

9th of *Tevet*, 5759

Dear Chana,

Your sixth *yarzheit* is already here. Six years later, *Chana bas Leah* still slips from my tongue when I say the blessing of *Refaenu*, for the healing of the sick. I admit it: I am still in denial. And the never-ending conversation with you goes on and on in my head.

How one-sided is it? How much do you hear? I am looking for answers to questions in sublime, silent places. Places that cannot speak what they know. I will never get the answers, at least not in this world. Nor to other innumerable questions I am constantly asking you. Yet that has never stopped me; the conversation continues.

I have been thinking, though, that if I could direct the conversation outwards, people who never had the opportunity to meet you could in effect, encounter you. It could be beneficial to me as well. Perhaps it would lower the volume in my own brain.

Rest assured. No biographies. I will not write *about* you. How you detested most biographies with their idealized descriptions of saintliness and their obvious omissions of human weakness, failings and struggle.

I remember the image of the EKG that you used so often. You pointed out that the EKG graphically illustrates the movement of the heart—the life force of a person. It charts the heartbeat with a line that goes up and down, and up and down. If a long, horizontal line comes out on the screen, it indicates death—the absence of life. Struggle, symbolized by the up and down, is the sign of vitality. It is something that should be embraced and harnessed. Yet so many people spend their lives negating that reality, and yearn and strive for the smooth straight line. The peace of death.

So how *do* I pay tribute to you without offending you? How do I let people encounter you without painting you as a mummified model of greatness? How do I expose the real, live, struggling human being you were?

Not by describing you, nor by praising you. Not by teaching, nor by preaching. But perhaps by sharing. After all, that is the way you taught us all the years I knew you. You *shared* your enthusiasm, your encyclopedic knowledge, your penetrating insights and integrated experience with us. We—the students—became part of your larger learning-life adventure. How refreshing it was. That respectful distance ordinarily felt in a *Rav-talmid* (teacher-student) relationship simply did not exist. After all, this was no ordinary *Rav-talmid* relationship; it was a *Rav-talmid* relationship with an authentic female twist.

You were not afraid to share your vulnerability with us. Indeed, your stripping yourself down to the wire is what most commanded our respect. You did not need to hide anything. On the contrary, you thought it was important to be real, to be human, to be vulnerable. At the very same time, you dazzled us with your vast storehouses of knowledge, your ingenious creativity, and your uncanny ability to bring them to bear on life itself. Must there really be a contradiction? Must our great strengths be cordoned off from our weaknesses?

Indeed, the greatest symbol and demonstration of strength is the ability to admit weakness and muster all of our God-given gifts to grapple with it. No one demonstrated that peculiarly human symbiosis better than you. You exemplified the human paradox of infinite and finite coexisting within the same being—the mobilization of limitation towards a higher end. You demonstrated the role of vulnerability as catalyst for spiritual growth. The elevation of the conglomerate of body and soul specifically through the struggle with human limitation. Most of all, you demonstrated the natural, healthy interaction between the two poles.

From your sharing to mine.... May I share something of your ways, your ideas, your attitudes? Perhaps it would be best if I spoke about the impact of your teaching on me and on my teaching—the living chain, the dynamic transmission, *Torah sheBa'al peh* (the Oral Torah)...

After my first few classes with you, we met in the library of Michlalah Jerusalem College for Women. Having been so impressed with your classes and coming from an academic home, I asked the natural question. Do you write? You answered in the negative. Quite surprised, I asked you why. After all, it did seem like such a shame not to commit a bit of that brilliance to paper. "I love to teach. I have no interest in writing," you answered.

Torah sheBa'al peh—the Oral Torah. That is what you did best. I don't remember whether you actually used the term in speaking of yourself. Yet, I cannot think of a more appropriate phrase to describe your teaching. The Oral Torah, dynamic transmission, sharing the human experience, constant application and re-application, associative thinking...this was taking the black and white of the printed word and animating it with the color of life.

Chana, in my own life until now, I have engaged exclusively in *Torah sheBa'al peh*. I have not written a thing. Nor have I paid much attention to that fact; it only struck me now. I suddenly realize: this is the first time I am committing thoughts to paper instead of projecting them orally into a classroom. And in the end, what am I writing about? *Torah sheBa'al peh*.

Essentially, what I am doing is some form of transcription. Transcribing my live experience as your student. Including the aspect of the experience that is not contained in the redaction or reiteration of teachings, but in the effects and applications of that teaching on the student.

I remember a class in your midrash course at MaTaN (Machon Torani leNashim) that involved a midrash using animal metaphors. A student came up to you at the end of her class to show you her "notes." She presented you with a striking pencil drawing of the animal imagery. She was a talented artist. The ultimate translation of the inspiration and the message of the midrash into a medium that was hers. How thrilled you were with it. You were so happy she had written the notes in her own language. At the same time, you were grateful to her for enriching your own vision of the midrash with a fresh perspective.

You so enjoyed seeing your students filter your teachings through their own talents, personalities, circumstances and souls. You encouraged independence and a healthy dose of *hutzpah*. So I will now take the initiative and try to share a little bit of you using the media most familiar to me and to you: *Torah. Torah sheBikhtav* and its essential partner, *Torah sheBa'al peh*. I would like to travel through the looking glass of which you were so fond.

Through the Looking Glass

A cold and gray November day, 1992. A group of us from MaTaN pack into a gray Mitsubishi van headed for Telz Stone. We enter the inner sanctum of your house. Your bedroom. Shelves have been put up on the walls around your bed to accommodate your precious books. Surrounded by your sefarim, *you lie on your bed. I feel sick looking at you. Your face is bloated. Your eyes bloodshot and red. Your body ravaged by cancer. (Your little daughter told me at the Shiva that there were days she could not go into your bedroom. I understand her. She could not bear to look at you. Nor could I.)*

Yet despite the wreckage that was your body, you allowed us to come and learn from you. You separated soul from body and connected your soul to that living chain on your wall. Whatever vitality was left in you was eked out from the world up on your wall.

I hear you speaking about your birthday. (You had just turned 41.) I hear
you talking about the letters of your name. I hear you talking about your
namesake—the biblical Chana, the one who taught us how to pray.

To be honest, Chana, although I recall the subjects that were discussed, I
don't remember what you said. It was at once so inspiring and so disturbing that I could not really absorb the information, much less retain it. I
could only absorb the experience.

So allow me to return to the textual sources myself and get a glimpse of
Chana, the biblical heroine. Naturally, it will reflect on Chana, my contemporary heroine. (An authentically human one, I might add and all the
more impressive for your lack of angelic pretenses.)[1]

I confess that I have never been a great fan of courses on *Women in the
Bible*. For the most part, they seem slightly artificial, somewhat stilted. I
have always preferred an organic, holistic approach to Torah that is not
gender specific. For me, it is more awesome to see reality borne out on
every level of creation and every level of human behavior, rather than
limiting it to the lens of female experience.

So instead of a full-scale study of the biblical personality called Chana, I
would like to focus on one universal aspect. An aspect that is seen through
the words of the talmudic Sage, R. Elazar. His words are familiar to you,
Chana; how preposterous of *me* to explain them to *you*! In your life, how
you echoed those words. You spoke to God in exactly the same way.

The first chapter of I Samuel opens with a scene of the two warring wives
of Elkanah: Penina and Chana. Penina has many children. Chana, on the
other hand, is barren. Still, her husband loves her more.

---

[1] There is one book in particular, a collection of essays by R. Adin Steinsaltz, called
The Strife of the Spirit, that articulates your world view so succinctly. This issue of
angelic saintliness versus human greatness is discussed in the essay entitled, "Words,
Angels and Men." However, the title essay, "The Strife of the Spirit," you would
have loved most. The message of the legitimacy and positive nature of human
struggle was central to your teaching. I find the debunking of the peace-of-mind
myth to be so critical to emotional and spiritual health, that I have made "The Strife
of the Spirit" required reading in all my courses. Adin Steinsaltz, "The Strife of the
Spirit" (NJ: Jason Aronson, 1988).

Chana, not content with the good graces of her husband, goes to the Temple to supplicate God for a child. Her unusual form of prayer irritates the *Kohen Gadol* (high priest)—Eli. Undeterred by his perception of her, she continues in a fervent and forceful request from God that He grant her a child.

I Samuel, 1:10 reads:

והיא מרת נפש ותתפלל על ה׳ ובכה תבכה.

And she was bitter and prayed onto God and she cried.

The Hebrew word על usually translates as "on," as opposed to אל which translates as "to." The obvious syntactic problem raised about this verse is: why was the word על chosen instead of the word אל? אל would certainly have been more appropriate in the context. After all, didn't Chana pray **to** God? Besides, how *does* one pray **on** or **over** God?

R. Elazar in *Berakhot* 31b implies that the word על may literally mean "on," but as in all exegetical solutions, it adds additional information. Here, the word על describes the *way* in which she prayed. She prayed "on," as if to say, "over" God. But what does praying "over" God involve?

In his commentary on I Samuel 1:10, Rashi describes her prayer thus:

חנה הטיחה דברים כלפי מעלה.

Chana flung her words at God.

He explains that the verb *hetiah* is the same verb used for shooting an arrow. Chana directed her cutting words towards God. In other words, she exchanged powerful words with Him. She spoke *over* God.

The Maharsha (R. Shmuel Eliezer ben Yehudah Halevi Edels) in his commentary on this passage illustrates this manner of addressing God. He refers to examples from the rabbinic commentary on our chapter in Samuel, appearing in *Berakhot* 31b:

And she vowed saying, O Lord of Hosts [*Tzeva'ot*] (I Samuel 1:11).
Said Chana before the Holy One, blessed be He: "Sovereign of the
Universe, of all the myriad hosts that You created in Your world, is it
so hard in Your eyes to give me one son?" A parable: to what may this
be compared? To a king who made a feast for his servants and a poor
man came and stood by the door and said to them, "Give me a bite,"
and no one took any notice of him, so he forced his way into the presence of the king and said to him, "Your Majesty, out of all the feast
which you made, is it so hard in Your eyes to give me one bite?"

If you will indeed look [*im ra'oh tireh*] (I Samuel 1:11). R. Eleazar
said: Chana said before The Holy One, blessed be He: "Master of the
Universe, if you will look [*ra'oh*]—Good! And if not—[*tireh*]—you
will see [what I will do!] I will go and hide from my husband, Elkana.
[I will spend time alone with a man other than my husband. Thereby
setting up the legal conditions that] I will be forced to drink the waters
of the *Sotah*.[2] Yet, since I will clearly be innocent of the sin of adultery, I will thus have the ability to bear a child."

Now Chana spoke in her heart... (I Samuel 1:13). R. Eleazar said in
the name of R. Jose ben Zimra: she spoke of matters of the heart. She
said before Him: "Sovereign of the Universe, of all the things you
have created in a woman, none are without a purpose. Eyes to see,
ears to hear, a nose to smell, a mouth to speak, hands to do work, legs
for walking and breasts for nursing. Why have you put these breasts
on my heart? Not to nurse with them?! Give me a son so that I may
nurse him!"

These three examples clearly demonstrate the forthrightness with which
Chana spoke to God. The obvious question is: how did she allow herself
to speak to God in such a brusque manner? Yet strangely enough, for all
this seeming lack of deference towards God, we do not find a hint of
rebuke or punishment for Chana. On the contrary, God answers her
prayers. Was her harshness towards God justified? To take it even further,
is there a chance it was even laudable?

---

[2] Numbers 5:11–31. A woman who is suspected of committing adultery is given the
waters of the *Sotah* to drink to verify whether she indeed sinned. If she drinks it and
remains unaffected, she is compensated for the humiliation and trouble, with special
rewards. According to the opinion of R. Ishmael (*Berakhot* 31b), a woman who was
barren will bear children.

Perhaps the simplest answer is in the verse itself. The verse prefaces her manner of praying by saying that she was bitter "ותתפלל על ה' ובכה תבכה". In other words, she spoke harshly to God out of bitter pain. Her misery had led her to such a state that she could not help but speak harshly. Rashi explains that a person is not held responsible for his way of relating to God when he is in a state of intense suffering.[3] Had she been in a healthy emotional state, she would have been punished for her words. God "understood," however, how deeply distressed she was and accepted her anger as a natural outflow of that bitter, emotional state. It would be out of place to interpret her words in light of any philosophical or theological position—in fact, in light of any position, other than an emotional one.[4]

This idea of God excusing Chana for her harshness towards Him due to her suffering has broad implications. For one, it seems that there are differing ways of relating to God under different circumstances. What is considered legitimate in one circumstance is illegitimate in another. In other words, we do have some flexibility in the way that we approach God, depending on our situation.

Furthermore, God's way of relating to human beings serves as the ultimate model for human beings relating to one another. God did not judge Chana harshly despite the fact that she challenged Him. We can infer that one must exercise great caution in judging others who are in a state of intense suffering, even when they themselves are speaking harshly. This is especially true when that suffering is derived from a situation of exceptional circumstances. Infertility for a woman—the inability to produce new life—contains an element of inner death. Her behavior while in this

---

[3] Rashi, *Berakhot* 31b.

[4] God Himself states this position to the friends of Job. While Job's friends criticize his bitter complaint against God for the suffering inflicted upon him, God defends him. "Job has spoken without knowledge and his words are without wisdom" (Job 34:35). In other words, Job's harsh words for God did not come from an intellectual position, from a stance based on knowledge or wisdom; rather, pure emotion guided him. In *Bava Batra* 16b, the Gemara continues, "This teaches that a man is not held responsible for what he says when in distress." This same reasoning is applied in the instance of Chana's complaint as well.

state, however inappropriate, was accepted magnanimously by God. Surely she was not punished for it. Inappropriate behavior exercised by a person who is suffering must be viewed with gentleness and understanding.

Rashi's interpretation, though, is still perplexing. He seems to see her form of prayer as illegitimate, but excusable. That does not seem to fit in with the larger rabbinic portrayal of Chana, in which she is seen as our greatest model and teacher in the art and science of prayer. Her prayer forms the basis of the halakhic guidelines on prayer.[5] If that is the case, does it make sense to say that the paragon of Jewish prayer nonetheless fell short in one aspect? Or conversely, could this controversial aspect be interpreted as exemplary? Are there any grounds to say that her anger and demands of God were not only excusable, but legitimate and praiseworthy?

The later commentaries add a fascinating aspect to this issue. R. Hayyim of Volozhin interprets Chana's reproach in a completely different and ultimately positive light.[6] The simple interpretation of "*Chana hetiha devarim klapei ma'alah*" is that she "threw her words" at God. R. Hayyim's more profound interpretation is that she connected her sorrow to that of Heaven. In other words, she attributed her pain to God. She identified her own misery with Divine misery. While her pain was devastating her personally, she was aware at the same time, of another dimension of it. Her personal pain had a similar, if not worse effect on the

---

[5] *Berakhot* 31a: "Rav Himnuna said: how many great *halakhot* are learned from the story of Chana!".... This particular Gemara page is replete with the most basic laws of prayer derived from Chana. To cite a few examples: "And Chana spoke with her heart, only her lips were moving" (I Samuel 1:13). From here we learn that we must whisper and move our lips, rather than say the prayers out loud. We also learn that conviction of the heart, direction and understanding are essential elements of prayer. "And Eli thought she was drunk" (ibid.). From here we learn that it is forbidden to pray while in a drunken state.

[6] *Nefesh haHayyim* 2:12.

Divine Presence. When she appealed to God, she appealed to Him on His own account, as it were.[7]

There is a deep link between the pain of human beings and the pain of Heaven. Our Sages say that when we are in pain, the Divine Presence suffers with us. This phenomenon bears itself out even with regard to physical pain.[8] How much more so in the case of psychological and spiritual pain. Indeed, the anguish of a parent forced to watch his or her child suffer is more torturous than the pain experienced by the child.

Perhaps we could say that when Chana appealed to God, her question was not only, "Why are *You* doing this to me?" She was also asking, "God, why are You doing this to Yourself? Why do you allow Yourself to remain in agony? What benefit do *You* have from my misery and lack of female fulfillment? What do *You* gain by leaving me with emptiness instead of life, with this spiritual void, when I could bring the future leader of the generation into the world? *You*, the Almighty, all-powerful One, *You* have the choice to change my fate.[9] Why then must *You* continue to inflict this upon Yourself?"

---

[7] R. Hayyim devotes much attention to this issue in *Nefesh haHayyim* 2:11. The anthropomorphic overtones and implications of this concept pose great philosophical difficulties which he attempts to address in the above chapter.

[8] *Sanhedrin* 46a. R. Meir said: "When a person suffers for his sins, what does the *Shekhinah* say? 'I am burdened by my head. I am burdened by my arm.' If the Omnipresent is pained for the spilled blood of the wicked, how much more so for the blood of the righteous!" See *Nefesh haHayyim* 2:11 on this statement.

[9] *Tziyun leNefesh Haya* (*TzLaH*; R. Yechezkel Segal Landau, 1713–1793) on our Gemara expands on the notion of God changing her fate. He interprets Chana's grievance against God as a rational/polemical position. Her basis in confronting God was not emotional, he contends, but ideological. She maintained that if God did not give her a child, people would be led to believe that God was lacking ultimately in the power to change her fate. To understand his notion better, I will try to clarify the mechanics of fate he suggests.

The mechanics of fate are generally dependent on two factors: *mazal*—astrology and *zekhut*—merit. With regards to having children, the governing factor is *mazal*. Initially, whether one is worthy or not is not the deciding issue. One has a child if it is deemed so in the stars. However, the factor of worthiness or merit can occasionally override the power of the stars. A woman who was not allotted a child from the point of view of astrology, can override that with her own merit. (Conversely, if the governing factor were indeed merit and not astrology, there would be pitifully few children in the world!) God set it up in such a manner that the exercising of free will

With profound spiritual insight, Chana understood that crucial link between her pain and God's pain. She understood the purpose and effects of her suffering.

Interestingly enough, traditional sources discuss the connection between human pain and Godly pain with specific regard to the issue of infertility. The phenomenon of barrenness in our foremothers is indeed striking. Why were so many of them barren? The Rabbis answer, "The Holy One Blessed Be He desires the prayers of the righteous" (*Yevamot* 64a). A curious answer. Does God afflict the righteous in order to receive their prayers?! Surely not! The answer goes far deeper than meets the eye. God places the righteous under the type of circumstances that precipitate confrontation with God. What are those circumstances and what type of confrontation is He seeking? The circumstances are the types of suffering that only God can alleviate. This suffering compels the righteous to reach out to God for help. The vulnerability and dependence on God that results from such suffering enables the person to form an intimate, interdependent relationship with God. This relationship cannot be achieved in any other way. Certainly not in a situation where that person felt his or her own strength and independence. In the end, it is the utter dependence on God and consequent trust in Him which creates the conditions in which prayers can be answered.

Returning to the connection between Godly pain and human pain, Chana realized that this was her opportunity to connect on a deep level to God. Through this connection, she could then go on to effect a change in the world. She therefore gave herself the liberty of reproaching God, because her concern was essentially for Him. That does not mean she obliterated herself, her pain, her own needs. It does mean, however, that she saw the intimate connection between her soul and the Divine Presence. Her

---

in our behavior is the ultimate deciding factor in our fate. In other words, the essential point is that God allows us to earn our fate even in the case of having children, which is an issue that is usually astrologically predetermined.

According to this idea, Chana was confronting God with His own reputation, so to speak. The *TzLaH* continues: "God," she challenged, "if you do not fulfill my request by allowing my merit to overcome astrology, people will say that ultimately the stars are more powerful than you!"

suffering was God's suffering and her needs were ultimately God's "needs." She saw herself as a mere extension and reflection of the state of the Divine Presence.

There is no better proof of her innocence and sincerity than the fact that her prayers were answered. When the righteous suffer, the Divine Presence suffers with them. When they pray that their suffering be alleviated, their prayers are focused on cosmic rather than selfish interests. They recognize that the purpose of their pain extends beyond their personal concerns, particular causes and circumstances. R. Tsvi Hirsch of Novarno points out that precisely because they pray for the *right* motives—for divine rather than egotistical ones—they merit that their prayers be answered.[10]

Through the Looking Glass, Backwards

On that note, I shift back to you, the contemporary Chana.[11] It is not my place to focus on your relationship with God. Nor is it my place to focus on the way you prayed. All I *can* say is that your closeness to God and your dependence on Him was felt strongly by your students.

You had endless plans of books you wanted to read, subjects you wanted to research, courses you wanted to teach, music you wanted to listen to, countries you wanted to visit—a myriad of experiences you wanted to live fully. You could not get enough of life. The world was there to be devoured and there was not enough time in the day to do it. Often, in your

---

[10] R. Tsvi Hirsch of Novarno in his commentary *Tzemah Hashem leTzvi*, "*Vayetze*," (published 1848).

[11] It is with great difficulty that I must limit the discussion of *Chana hetiha devarim klapei ma'alah*. The issue of arguing with God is a deep and fascinating topic. Throughout our history and literature, Jews have argued with God, even to the extent, under certain circumstances, of taking God to rabbinical court (*beit din*)!

At this point, I would like to acknowledge the help of my relative, R. Chaim Pardes *z"l*, with this essay in particular and with all of my studies in general. R. Pardes was a world-class *talmid hakham* and a source of inspiration throughout the years. He always made himself available to answer my questions and solve my problems, despite his many other pressing responsibilities. May his memory be a blessing to us all.

classes, we touched on a subject that was fascinating, yet completely divergent from the subject matter at hand. You mentioned a plan to teach a course or treat the topic in a comprehensive manner. While you were undergoing treatment, you prefaced those plans with "אם ה' יתן לי כוח" "If God will give me strength." Those words struck a deep chord in me. There was nothing mechanical about the way you said them. It wasn't the phrase *be'ezrat Hashem* (with the help of God) that so many of us throw around loosely. On the contrary, your words demonstrated an acute consciousness of God's role in your life. You made a point of verbalizing clearly, both to yourself and to others, where the source of your strength lay.

Your love and awe of God, the simplicity of your faith and trust in Him— all existed harmoniously with the sophistication of your intellectual dimension. This could be discussed at length. However, I prefer to stay where I belong: away from your relationship with God and within the realm of your relationship to other human beings.

You were the ultimate anti-snob. When I talked to one of my neighbors about you, she told me an anecdote that I must share:

My neighbor took a course you taught on Rashi's methodology, a requirement in the first year of Michlalah Jerusalem College for Women. There were a few such courses given by different teachers. She happened to be in yours. She had married in the middle of the year, moved out of town, and soon afterwards became pregnant. She began to experience the difficult symptoms that many women experience in their first trimester. Although she was not visibly showing at the time, you, being no stranger to the process, figured it out. She began coming late and had a hard time keeping up with the level and the pace of the class. You noticed how she was struggling and approached her. You did not wait for her to overcome her embarrassment and her sense of failure to come to you. Gently you said, "I see how hard it is for you to keep up these days. Would it be easier for you to take this same course, but perhaps on a less demanding level, given by another teacher?" She, extremely relieved, nodded her head and immediately took you up on your offer.

You did not expect her to override or fight against her body. Nor did you expect her to stifle the changes and challenges entailed in adjusting to married life. What a striking contrast to the unhealthy attitudes unfortunately imposed upon women in so many workplaces and institutions. You knew that her tardiness and weak performance were not out of a lack of respect or a lack of desire. By preempting the next move and making a practical and reasonable suggestion, you allowed her both to save face and preserve her self-respect by following through on her responsibilities in spite of her difficult circumstances.

On that note, although you were a formidable intellect, your interest in academia was decidedly utilitarian. On the one hand, you were a crusader for serious education for women, uncompromising in your high standards. You saw the intellect as a tool that had been under-emphasized and often made unavailable for women. You were determined to cultivate and provide access to it. Yet for you, although the intellect was the single most important tool of religious experience, it remained but a tool. Intellectual accomplishment was always kept in perspective. Marriage, pregnancy and child rearing were also fundamental tools of religious experience. They were gifts from God to teach us how to serve Him. Surely, they were not given to us to be negated artificially in favor of the pursuit of academic achievement. All tools must function in harmony with one another—each in its place and time. Use of these tools was a holistic, female art that you mastered.

Another important lesson I draw from this anecdote is that you did not expect your students to be on your level of "mind-over-matter" bordering on self-obliteration. You understood that there are God-given differences between human beings. You never allowed your extraordinary gifts to obstruct your authentic sense of humility. You loved people regardless of their talents or accomplishments. Everyone's difficulties were equally legitimate in your eyes. All of these factors together (and more) made you into the ultimate anti-snob.

Sometimes I would meet you at the bus stop or on the bus. Once we talked about the nature of bus travel. I told you that riding the bus may have been the most productive part of my day. I spoke with you about what I was reading, learning or writing on the bus. By contrast, when I asked you what you did on your bus rides, you replied, "I think."

How much thought that remark engendered in me. There I was, in my early twenties, at the height of absorption/accomplishment madness. You, on the other hand, were busy turning things over and over, in that never-stop-for-a-minute brain of yours. You allowed your knowledge to seep deeply into you: you synthesized it and then applied it to every level of your being. You mastered the art of integration—an exceedingly rare talent. How much more subtle and internal a process than the largely external pursuit of absorption and accomplishment, so common in the Jewish intellectual world. Let me confess to you, Chana—I never did look at bus rides in quite the same way after that.

I could not resist that tangent. You too, were associative, not by default but on principle. Yours was a highly organized, critical and analytical mind. In the classes dedicated to teaching a specific skill, you stuck to it. But when it came to the classes that were content-oriented, provided you had the students mature enough to deal with it, your kaleidoscopic vision took us to many places that we would never have ordinarily seen or touched.

I must note, as well, that you were always developing. People who met you encountered many parts of you as well as a variety of intellectual trends at different stages in your life. You were ever-evolving. I noticed a shift towards the end of your life from a certain criti-cal-analytic-intellectual bent to a more associative-integrative-holistic way of thinking. Perhaps this was a natural result of your difficult life experience, which did not allow you the luxury of living in your head. It demanded that you squeeze every ounce of meaning out of your intellect into your experience.

In any case, I would like to return to your mind-over-matter attitude and your approach toward your students.

The year was 1989/1990. You were undergoing intensive radiation and chemotherapy. You traveled from your home in Telz-Stone to Hadassah Hospital in Ein Karem for treatment in the mornings. From there, you would come straight to Michlalah and belt out four hours of classes. I stood in awe of you.

At the same time, I was disturbed by the attitude of my fellow classmates, young girls in their first year of college. Most of them saw what was for you a soul-passion, as an obligation to be dispensed through a minimal investment of time and energy. I watched in disbelief as they haggled with you about tests, the amount of material on the exams, etc. Try as I may, I could not persuade them to change their attitude. What did they know about life and death, cancer and chemotherapy, about the soul, about passion, about the heroic struggle to fight the inevitable, about subjugating one's whole being to the forces of will and mind? I would look at your hairless, lined face, shocked by what was going on around me.

It was Lag Be'Omer. Classes were scheduled as usual. Three people (out of forty) showed up for class that day. You, me and another married woman who had made aliyah from Russia in the 1970's. Not one student, despite the fact that they had no excuses, had showed up. "Too busy from roasting marshmallows last night. It was obviously very exhausting," I joked sarcastically. But I didn't think it was funny at all. Reserved as you were, I could sense your pain, humiliation, the feeling of rejection. That upset me all the more.

Chana, I know you would want me to talk about your teaching career in all its facets, including the uncomfortable underside. It is through your attempts to deal with these aspects, perhaps, that we learn the most. What happens when things are not as ideal as they should be?

On another occasion you talked to me about this issue, about how difficult it was to teach those students. You said it was much more gratifying to teach mature women of your own standing, who could relate to real life. Women who were motivated and drank up every word with a real thirst. Women who were educated and applied their education to whatever they were learning. Women who thought deeply and who struggled to integrate what they were learning with their daily lives.

The gratification factor was important to you. You were far too honest to deny that reality. Of course, the positive response you received from your students propelled you. The critical element, however, that distinguishes you from so many others was that it was never your primary motivation. It would be presumptuous of me to attempt an objective or definitive answer to that question. But this is the way it appeared to me: you were determined to raise the level of God consciousness among your students. You wished to do so by raising the level of education, thus raising the level of sophistication in which Jews relate to God through Torah and *mitzvot*. You provided access to a deeper and more sophisticated, all-inclusive understanding of Judaism than the one they had ever encountered.

You proceeded to explain that the future lies with young people. The impact of your teaching on youth could instigate greater changes in them and thus in the world at large, than in older people. "We cannot give up on youth," you insisted. "If there's just one student in each class of forty that I have succeeded in reaching, it's worth all the frustration and pain." You were willing to forego the discomfort, rejection and humiliation to live out your ideals.

There's so much more I could say. But the children are calling and the business of "real life" beckons. I hope you won't be embarrassed or offended if I praised you. The purpose of this piece is certainly not to shower empty praise. Mostly, I wanted to share my experience, my perceptions, and all I gained with people who never had a chance to meet you.

However, there is one more reason I wrote this. It is to thank you.

While you were alive, I sensed that you knew you were having an impact on me. There was much about our backgrounds and personalities that were too uncannily similar for us to have been thrown together haphazardly in a teacher-student relationship. Nevertheless, I never had the opportunity to tell you myself how deeply you affected me. I am sure you sensed it to some degree from my enthusiasm, eagerness and the seriousness with which I studied from you. I am so sorry I never said it directly to you in words.

Chana, you were and will forever remain my *Mashpi'ah* (mentor) in the real sense of the word. One who has left me a changed person. I do not know how you perceive this letter in your present state. May you benefit from it in whatever way souls do in that strange, supernal reality you now inhabit. May you be blessed and compensated with endless *nahat ruah*, fulfillment and repose. All the *nahat ru'ah* that was missing in your tumultuous, all-too-brief stay in this world.

I love you, miss you and wish you were here....

And most of all,

I thank you.

Sarah Malka

"With Every Good-Bye You Learn": Reflections on Leave-Takings and the Passing of the Lubavitcher Rebbe

Susan Handelman

E-mail message, received April 25, 1998:

Dear Susie,

Your erstwhile office mate lives (by the skin of his teeth), and so he assumes doth you. These must be particularly exciting times in Israel with the 50th anniversary of its founding—I've been reading about it in **The New Yorker** *and elsewhere.... I would love to see Jerusalem, and envy you being there, clearly thriving in such an intense intellectual and political atmosphere. I'd give you news on the department these days, but I'm a particularly barren source since I'm hardly ever there (average once/month) since I went on sick leave after a bunch of hospitalizations and another surgery in November. We've run out of chemotherapies, so now I'm in home hospice care (their nurse comes in 2–3 times/week to change dressings, adjust my morphine pump, etc.), and also attended by an LPN, a large woman named Josephine who hails from—ironically enough, since I served in the Peace Corps there—Ghana. She feeds me lunch, bathes me, and is around to help me take things easy, which I didn't find all that necessary at first, but which has been more required lately as my energy wears down gradually.*

The tumor grows incrementally on my lower left side, whose front looks like a '56 Cadillac bumper breast (you may have to be into car culture to catch that reference), and clearly is sapping strength from me— had a transfusion last week in preparation for a trip to Williamsburg, and it helped me through the weekend there, but it's taken me 4 days to recover.

So that may well be my last trip, which saddens me. One of the things I miss most is the opportunity to travel and see places I've never seen, like Jerusalem (op cit), the Grand Canyon, Yosemite, Provence, Maine. But I've really been pretty privileged in that regard (I've taught or lectured on 5 continents, and lived for years in Africa and Europe), so I'm not complaining, just yearning.

All told, the past four months have been a pretty weird time, "laying low" back at the house, considering how my life has been spent, balancing off the professional things undone and challenges avoided, against... I'm not sure what, exactly. I could break into a chorus of "I did it my way," but that seems a bit too grand, and not entirely accurate. Anyway, I've achieved some spiritual growth, and probably nudged a few students in some good directions, and encouraged a lot of the average ones to love literature enthusiastically and see it as a way of framing life (a bit passé in these post-Deconstruction days). I persuade myself I've done more good than harm.

And I know you have, Susie, and wanted to let you know while there was still world enough and time.... For these and all the other things you've generously shared with me, I thank you, friend, and pray that God blesses you as He has blessed others by making you part of their journeys.

I'd like to see you "next year in Jerusalem," but reckon that's not in the cards. In the meantime, my Susan joins me in sending,

Love, Jamie

I received this e-mail message from a colleague with whom I have shared an office for many years at the university where I teach. I was in the midst of a fellowship in Jerusalem, studying Torah texts on "leave-taking" as part of a curriculum I was trying to write on how to teach classical Jewish sources to adults without background. I wanted to organize my syllabus around topics that would relate to their existential situations, to what presses on their hearts and minds in their daily lives.[1]

---

[1] As the famous theologian Paul Tillich once wrote in his essay, "A Theology of Education," that in speaking of things such as God and redemption: "...religious education mediates a material which cannot be received by the mind of those who have not asked the questions to which these words give answers. These words are like stones, thrown at them, from which sooner or later they must turn away.

But I didn't realize that the topic and the materials I was studying would themselves come to life in ways I had not expected. Yet who among the living is immune to loss, to so many kinds of leave-takings, whether it be the large painful ones, or the smaller partings we all endure in all the many transitional moments in our lives, even from week to week. So often throughout life, we are separated from, or have to let go of, beloved family members, teachers, friends, homes, jobs, relationships, or just certain cherished ideas. We move on, trying to take with us as we go all they gave to us.

The case of my friend Jamie put in such clear focus the sharp reflections that come to a person as he or she accepts the waning of life, considers what is important and what to leave behind, and how to say farewell. What could I write back to him, a sensitive, religious non-Jew who had come to see his illness as part of a "spiritual journey"? The following is an excerpt from the message I did manage to send back a few days later, with some reflections on life in Israel and its national losses and recoveries:

April 27, 1998

Dear Jamie:

You are right that this is a special time in Israel—though the country is always in some sort of crisis or another. This week, everywhere I look I see the blue and white Israeli flags hanging for the upcoming 50th birthday—from cars, buildings, balconies. Although I would say the general mood here is subdued due to all the problems...but life here is collectively manic-depressive. Either way up or way down.

You describe your process of thinking about and reviewing your life these past four months and what seems to have really counted—the effect on your students, your spiritual growth.... I was indeed so grateful for your words to me, about how you think I have helped my students and how somehow I have helped you in your journey. Because I often wonder

---

Therefore, every religious educator must try to find the existentially important questions which are alive in the minds and hearts of the pupils. It must make the pupil aware of the questions which he already has."

what remains of all those years of mine at the University. And what could at all make it worthwhile to be back there instead of here.

From my perspective here in Jerusalem—a 3,000 year old city, the focus of so much pain and yearning where you do indeed have "intimations of immortality"—I, too, think from afar about what that life in academia is finally all about, and it seems to me it is not ultimately about the "career" part—the publications, the latest theories—all of which become obsolete fairly quickly. But the enduring things are those human relations we were able to construct almost in spite of the University— those moments of touching each other's souls somehow, even obliquely.

Someone gave me a copy of an interview with Grace Paley in which she talked about teaching writing and said, "To me, teaching is a gift because it puts you in loving contact with young people."

How many moments of loving contact do I remember in my years of teaching—with students and colleagues? In the end, that is what it is about, I think. They redeem everything. I can remember some very specifically; I missed opportunities for others, but I want to try to remember that as my ultimate goal. The course material, the literature, the theories, all the rest of it are just a means.

And I have to tell you, too, Jamie, I know you, too, created many of those moments with those around you...I always sensed that in your approach to your students, in the many kindnesses you did for them, in the ways you related to everyone in the Department.

And in the family you had built...and built with such difficulty. I saw in you a man with a special gift of love—especially how you brought into your life the several children you adopted from abroad. In Judaism, the building of a family and home is the ultimate success, and part of eternity—in this, you are a real model. I think others feel this about you too— when Janet last wrote me about you in February, she said she had seen you in the office, and that though you were quite thin, you had, as she put it, an "aura" about you. Perhaps this whittling down also further revealed the core of your essential self—that man of luminous soul and love.

My spiritual teachers say that there aren't any coincidences in life— and I don't think it was coincidental that we came to share an office, you and I.

*So do we all live by the skin of our teeth—I think that phrase comes from the Book of Job. I still don't know how Job found comfort after all his tribulations, and I still don't understand God's answer to Job and I don't understand a lot of what God does, but being here in Jerusalem, one is fortified in faith despite all the difficulties, terror, conflict, bloodshed and sense of fragility. There was an op ed piece in the **New York Times** yesterday on the occasion of the 50th anniversary of Israel that said, Israel "is more than a country; it is an idea that inspires millions of Jews from around the world."*

It said that from the gas chambers and ruins of Europe and from dozens of countries around the world, "an indefatigable people created a new country sustained by an ancient faith." I thought I sensed in the tone of your message that you, too, despite all the pain, have been sustained by faith and made your way to a certain peace with yourself and your God. In this, too, I admire you so greatly.

I always loved the teaching of one of the great hasidic masters, R. Nahman of Bratslav, who lived about 150 years ago and endured much. He had a famous saying, that he wrote a famous melody to—"All the world is a very narrow bridge, a very narrow bridge, and the main thing is...not to be afraid...not to be afraid at all." Thanks for being a warm companion to me on that bridge.

I somehow still feel I have not been able to express to you all that is in my heart for you—but I trust you will understand and know....

II.

When I wrote this message back, I did not use any of the specific texts I had been studying from Torah. I didn't feel that was what was called for at the moment. But five months before, in November 1997, the day after one of my study sessions on the remarkable *midrashim* about the passing of Moshe, I received an e-mail message from the husband of one of my former graduate students, Mary Alice Delia, informing me she had passed away. Mary Alice was an award-winning Maryland High School teacher, who had been battling leukemia for four years. As her mentor and close friend, I was asked to write something for the memorial service her fellow teachers and former students were holding a month later in Washington,

D.C. which would be read aloud in my absence. The *midrashim* I was studying were now not just part of a curriculum I was writing, but gave me a language to eulogize my friend, and gave me comfort. Here is an excerpt of what was read at the service:

Dear Mary Alice,

You always wrote me such wonderful letters. Letters were so much the basis of our friendship, and then became part of the creative pedagogy we worked out together. So I know you would so enjoy my writing this memorial for you in the form of a letter. But even more than that: for me, our correspondence, our relationship, can never end.

Can it be already fourteen years since we first met—when you came back to graduate school at the University of Maryland in 1985 and took seminars on literary theory with me? I was your professor, but soon I became your student, for I learned so much from you about teaching.

We continued to write to each other long after you finished your Ph.D. The last e-mail I wrote you was this past September, a long description of my life on my fellowship here in Israel. I also described my reactions to the suicide bombings here in Jerusalem:

"One sees all the soldiers in the streets—the ages of our students at the University of Maryland—so full of vigor and camaraderie...so full of the joy of life despite dragging rifles on their backs. As a friend of mine here said after the bombings, the fact is that our lives always hang by a thread, but here in Israel that is so much more revealed. So life here is also lived ever so much more intensely."

You wrote me back, in the very last e-mail I received from you this past October and described your experiences trying to teach again:

"I developed migraines and had to cut my fall teaching to one course....

I'm not teaching next semester and am thinking seriously of not doing it any more at all. It's just too scary, wondering if I'll be able to finish the course or attend all the classes, or get sick IN class. And I think, Why? Why put myself through all that? The answer unfortunately is too obvious—because teaching keeps me connected, encourages me to grow

*mentally, gives me problems to solve, makes possible new relation-
ships...."*

*That was you, Mary Alice, the consummate teacher, always worrying
about and rethinking her classes, always beloved by her students, always
passing on a word of support and encouragement to your friends. And
how ironic that the letter I am writing now is for your memorial service.*

*It is also ironic that the day before your passing, I was talking about
you at length to my colleague here in Jerusalem. That day, that last day of
your life in this world, he and I were also examining texts from Jewish
tradition about various forms of leave-taking, and about teachers and
students. We were looking at the ways the greatest teacher in the Bible,
Moshe, responds to God's telling him that the time has come for him to
leave the world, and that he will not be able to go into the Promised Land.
At the very end of the Book of Deuteronomy, Moshe has to accept this
decree and make arrangements to pass his teachings and authority on to
his student and successor, Joshua.*

*In rabbinic tradition, there is a genre of literature called **midrash**
which fills in the gaps in the narrative and elaborates on the enigmas of
the biblical text. I want to end this letter with a story from that tradition
about the passing of Moshe, a story that we discussed on that day that
was also your last day.*

*In many of these rabbinic texts, Moshe does not easily accept God's
announcement that his end is near. In one of them, [Tanhuma, vaEt'hanan
5] Moshe asks God for the chance not to die. But God replies:*

> This is what I have decided and it is a universal law: each genera-
> tion has its interpreters, its economic guides, its political leaders. Until
> now, you have had your share of service before Me: now, your time is
> over and it is your disciple Joshua's turn to serve Me. Moshe an-
> swered: "Lord of the world, if I am dying because of Joshua, I shall go
> and be his disciple." And God replied: "Do as you desire!"
>
> Moshe rose early and went to the Joshua's door, where Joshua was
> sitting interpreting the Divine Word. Moshe stood before him but
> Joshua did not notice him. Meanwhile, the children of Israel came to
> Moshe's door as usual to study and learn with him. They asked,
> "Where is Moshe our Teacher?" and were told he had gone to
> Joshua's door. When they arrived, they saw Joshua sitting and Moshe

standing. Perplexed, they asked Joshua what was happening, for the teacher is usually the one who sits while the students stand.

No sooner did Joshua look up and see Moshe than he tore his garments, wept and cried, "Teacher, Teacher! Father! Father! Teacher!" The children of Israel begged Moshe to teach them the Divine Word, but he demurred: "I do not have permission." They pleaded: "Do not leave us." A voice from Heaven then said: "Learn from Joshua. Agree to sit down and learn from Joshua." Joshua sat in the head position and Moshe sat at his right. Joshua interpreted the law before Moshe.

The moment Joshua began to speak, saying, "Blessed be He who chooses among the righteous," the methodological and pedagogical rules of wisdom were taken from Moshe and given to Joshua. And Moshe no longer understood what Joshua was explaining. After the lesson, the children of Israel asked Moshe to give them what would be the concluding words of the Bible, but he replied: "I do not know what to tell you." And Moshe stumbled and fell. Then Moshe said to God: "Until now I asked for my life, but now my soul is given over to you."

III.

It must have been so painful for Mary Alice to have to stop teaching, to leave her students, to have to withdraw, not to go all the way to the Promised Land. She would have been so happy to see this letter published, and to know how writing about her gave me a new way to read this midrash, and a way of understanding what teaching is about—that Moshe was willing to abandon his role as teacher and become his student's student. But that perhaps is the way of any great teacher, both the way a teacher begins to learn how to be a teacher, and the way a teacher ends her career as a teacher.[2]

---

[2] The program printed for Mary Alice's memorial service included a poem she used to give her own students as they concluded her class; it was her way of saying good-bye each semester to them:

> After a while you learn the subtle difference
> Between holding a hand and chaining a soul...
> And you learn that you really can endure...
> That you really are strong
> And you really do have worth.
> And you learn and learn...
> With every goodbye you learn. (Anonymous)

This requires, to use a kabbalistic metaphor, a necessary *tzimtzum*, self-contraction, on the part of the teacher, which is itself also kind of "letting go." And indeed my own model of teaching is also influenced by hasidic interpretations of that concept as a paradigm of the teacher/student relation. Teachers and students need to know, too, how to enable and how to let go of each other as well. The teacher/student relation has its own life-cycle: becoming a student, acquiring a teacher, becoming part of a *hevrah*, a community of learning, becoming a teacher, the passing of one's teacher, transmission of one's life wisdom at the end of a career.

The tension between withholding and giving, holding on and letting go, is itself a highly spiritual act. The idea of "self-contraction," of a concealing or withdrawal of the Divine Light as the essential first step in God's creation of the universe, is central to the Jewish mystical tradition. *Tzimtzum* is God's "letting go," so to speak, the withdrawal of the infinite Divine Light in order to leave an "empty space," a space which can allow for finite beings, who otherwise would have no place and would be overwhelmed and nullified by the Divine Light. (In a sense one could also say that "self-contraction" is really the secret of human relations and of ethics: I let go and make space for the other person.)

In an intriguing text, the sixth Lubavitcher Rebbe, Rabbi Yosef Yitz-hak Schneersohn (1880–1950), explains the divine self-contraction by analogizing it to the teacher/student relation. Significantly, this passage comes from the very last essay he wrote before he himself passed away, *Bati Legani* 5710 ([1950], ch. 15). Perhaps one could also connect this essay to his own impending sense of departure. It begins with a discussion of the ways the *Shekhinah*, the immanent aspect of God's presence, comes into and departs from the world. Perhaps there is a sub-text here about how to understand all the disconnections and withdrawals in our lives, and how to retain bonds with what seems to have been irretrievably broken:

> Through the process of *tzimtzum*, the infinite light was concealed, and the first and basic perception became personal identity and independent existence; God's infinite light was not perceived openly. Yet after the *tzimtzum*, God is still one with creation, as the verse declares, "I fill the heavens and the earth." Now the *tzimtzum* only applies to us, for in relation to God, the *tzimtzum* does not conceal at all: He radiates

Godly light after the *tzimtzum* just as before the *tzimtzum*, as we say in prayer, "You were before the world was created; You are after the world was created." Both states are totally equal since the *tzimtzum*, for Him, does not conceal.

We can understand this through the analogy of a teacher communicating a concept to a student. The teacher desires that his "plantings" [i.e., his students] should be like him. He cannot, however, transfer his ideas directly. To enable the student to apprehend and absorb the influence of his teacher, the teacher must first entirely remove the light of his own intellect, and conceive an intellectual light that is on the receiver's level. Thus he will make a number of *tzimtzumim* and concealments in order for his thoughts to be apprehended by the receiver.

The same principle applies in the spiritual realms: the limiting aspects of the *tzimtzum* only effect ourselves, but in relation to God Himself, the *tzimtzum* does not conceal at all. In truth, though, even in relation to ourselves, the intent of the initial *tzimtzum* and all the subsequent ones is for the purpose of revelation. Just as in the example of the teacher and the student—the main purpose of the *tzimtzum* is to enable the influence to be accepted by the receiver. So from a deeper perspective, the *tzimtzum* does not conceal at all.

The late Lubavitcher Rebbe (and son-in-law of R. Yosef Yitzhak), R. Menachem Mendel Schneerson, used this notion of *tzimtzum* and "concealment" of the teacher from the student and the pain it involves, as a way of explaining some of the darknesses of Jewish history, the destruction of the Temple, exile—and also saw in it a mode of finding comfort amidst loss.[3] In the most holy precincts of the Temple in Jerusalem, the images of the two *keruvim* (a term often transliterated as "cherubs") were

---

[3] In 1950, in the days and months just after his father-in-law, the previous Lubavitcher Rebbe, passed away, Rabbi Schneerson gave many moving talks about the meaning of what had occurred. He cited the statement of the *Zohar* that "when the *tzaddik* departs, he is to be found in all worlds more than his lifetime" (1.71b). In hasidic philosophy, the life of a *tzaddik* is not viewed as a physical life, but a spiritual life consisting of faith, awe and love. And after his passing, his soul is no longer bound by the limitations of a physical body, but is connected to the world in new and different ways. R. Schneerson also explained why he did not use the conventional expression, *zekher tzaddik livrakha* ("of blessed memory"), about his father-in-law after the latter's passing: the activation of memory is relevant to distant matters about which there is a danger of forgetting; but in relation to his father-in-law, the previous Rebbe, who was still close and still connected, there could be no forgetting at all, and therefore there was no need to invoke memory.

found. These were not the chubby angels of Baroque paintings, but sphinx-like winged figures with human faces. The Talmud relates that at times of Divine favor, and when the Jews were performing the Divine will, the faces of the *keruvim* were positioned towards each other, locked in a loving embrace. When the Jews did not act according to the Divine will, and it was a time of Divine disfavor, the *keruvim* were positioned the opposite way. When the Temple was destroyed and the alien conquerors came into the Temple, they saw the *keruvim* positioned face to face; they dragged them into the street to mock and desecrate this strange "idol" of the Jews.[4]

The Rebbe asks, however: how could it be that at a time of greatest Divine disfavor, the destruction of the Temple, the beginning of the exile, the faces of the *keruvim* could be looking *towards* each other? He answers with the analogy of the teacher/student relation: when a teacher is transmitting knowledge to his or her student, the teacher's attention is fully engaged with the student. But if, in the middle of this process, the flash of a new idea suddenly comes to the teacher's mind, the teacher must suddenly stop, withdraw from the student, and turn his or her attention to grasping and developing this new insight—or else it will disappear and be irretrievably lost. And because of the teacher's deep inner love for the student, the intention in withdrawing and attempting to comprehend this new idea is later to be able to transmit it to the student. The deeper and more precious the new idea, the more the teacher has to withdraw attention from the student. The student, however, feels the disconnection and loss of the teacher as a kind of "exile" and "destruction." But that is only on the "external" level; on the inner level, the disconnection and withdrawal is for a higher revelation.

---

[4] "R. Katina said: When Israel would come on Pilgrimage, they [the Temple functionaries] would unveil the curtain [in the Temple] and show the Israelite Pilgrims the *keruvim* embracing one another. And they would say to them: 'Look! God's love for you is like the love of man and woman....' Reish Lakish said: When the gentiles entered the Temple, they saw the *keruvim* embracing one another. They took them out to the market place and proclaimed: 'These Israelites, whose blessing is a blessing and whose curse is a curse—that they should be occupying themselves with such matters!' Then they cast them down [destroyed the *keruvim*], as it is said, 'all that honored her cast her down, for they have seen her nakedness' (Lamentations 1:8)" (*Yoma* 54a–b).

Thus too, R. Schneerson goes on to say, although externally there was indeed a terrible destruction of the Temple and exile of the Jews, the "inner" meaning of it is for a higher revelation, specifically the revelation of the future redemption, a revelation of a new light so great that it temporarily requires a time of darkness and disconnection. And that is why, he continues, when the gentile conquerors came into the Holy of Holies, they saw the faces of the *keruvim* positioned **towards** each other—indicating a time of divine favor for the Jews. For the entire purpose and inner meaning of exile is to bring about the highest revelation, and the Holy of Holies is the place that expressed the deepest, innermost aspect of the spiritual. So precisely there it *was* a time of divine favor. The Jews, just like the "student" in the parable, therefore have to remember and know, he concludes, that the concealment and removal of the Teacher is only on the "external" level, while on the deeper inner level the highest revelation is being found. And so they need to continue their strong connection with and yearning for the Teacher amidst the darkness.[5]

IV.

I can't help wanting to apply some of these words to the painful loss of the Rebbe himself in 1994. His passing occurred at the end of the Shabbat on which the biblical portion *Hukkat* (Numbers 19–22) was read, a portion all about the passing of our great leaders. It includes the famous incident of Moshe's striking the rock, and the decree that he and Aharon will not enter the Promised Land; it also describes the death of Miriam and the death of Aharon. A remarkable midrash on the verses which deal with the death of Aharon reflects in another way on the idea of concealment and on the pain of loss:

The specific biblical passage, Numbers 20:22–29, reads as follows:

---

[5] R. Menahem Mendel Schneerson, *Likkutei Sihot*, vol. II, *parashat Devarim* (Brooklyn: Kehot Publication Society, 1975) 359–63.

And they journeyed from Kadesh.

And the children of Israel, the whole congregation, came to Mount Hor.

And the Lord spoke to Moshe and Aharon in Mount Hor, by the border of the land of Edom, saying:

"Aharon shall be gathered to his people.

For he shall not enter the land which I have given to the children of Israel—

because you rebelled against my word at the waters of Meriva.

Take Aharon and Elazar his son

and bring them up to Mount Hor and strip Aharon of his garments, and put them on Elazar his son.

And Aharon shall be gathered to his people and die there."

And Moshe did as the Lord commanded—and they went up to Mount Hor

in the sight of all the congregation.

And Moshe stripped Aharon of his garments and put them on Elazar his son.

And Aharon died there at the top of the mount.

And Moshe and Elazar descended from the mount.

And all the congregation saw that Aharon had died.

And they wept for Aharon thirty days, all the House of Israel.

What, one wonders, might Moshe and Aharon be thinking and feeling at this point? A trained reader of the Bible would also pick up right away the problem of repetition of the announcement of Aharon's death from first being to *both* Aharon and Moshe, and then just to Moshe. In what sense is Moshe supposed to "take" Aharon? How is he to tell him such news; how, indeed, is a brother to "take" another brother to his death? And why is Moshe being given the role of mediator of God to Aharon here? How should anyone, in fact, tell another such news?

The midrash from *Yalkut Shimoni* (*Hukkat* 20) on this verse has a striking interpretation of the verse, "Take Aharon and Elazar his son and bring them up to Mount Hor" (Numbers 20:25):

> The Holy One blessed be He said to Moshe: "Do me a kindness and tell Aharon of the death of which I am embarrassed to tell him."
>
> R. Huna said in the name of R. Tanhum bar Hiya:

What did Moshe do? He rose very early in the morning and went to Aharon's dwelling, and began to call out "Aharon, my brother!" Aharon came down to him.

Aharon said to him: "What did you see to make you rise so early and come here today?"

Moshe replied: "I was pondering a matter [*davar*] in the Torah last night and it was very difficult for me. So I rose early and came to you."

Aharon said: "And what is this word of Torah?"

Moshe said: "I don't know what the text is, but I do know that it was in the Book of Genesis. Come, let's read it."

They took the Book of Genesis and read through it, section by section, and about each one Aharon said: "How wonderfully and how beautifully God created!"

And when they reached the story of the creation of Adam, Moshe said: "What will I say about Adam who brought death to the world?"

Said Aharon: "Moshe, my brother, don't speak that way about this matter. Mustn't we accept the decree of God...how Adam and Eve were created, how they merited marriage and joy in the Garden of Eden, how they ate from the Tree, and then as it is said to him, 'For dust you are and to dust you shall return?' After all that praise, to such an end did they come."

Said Moshe to him: "And I, who ruled over the ministering angels, and you who stopped death [the plague in Numbers 17:13], isn't our end going to be like this?! How many more years do we have to live? Twenty?"

Said Aharon: "They are very few."

Moshe subtracted and subtracted, until he mentioned to him the day of his [Aharon's] death.

Immediately, Aharon felt it in his bones and he faltered.

Said Aharon: "Perhaps this word [*davar*] is intended for me?"

Said Moshe: "Yes."

Immediately, the children of Israel saw that his stature had shrunk, as it is said: "And all the congregation saw."

Said Aharon: "My heart is void within me and the terrors of death have fallen upon me" [Psalms 55:5].

Said Moshe: "Do you accept death?"

Said Aharon: "Yes."

Said Moshe: "Let us ascend Mount Hor."

* * *

This is an extraordinarily moving interpretation. I also think of this midrash as a paradigm of teaching. Moshe seems to be consciously enacting that pedagogical strategy, the kabbalistic metaphor I referred to earlier. The teacher always has to undergo a *tzimtzum*, a contraction and concealment of his or her knowledge, in order to be able to pass it over and have it received by the student. It seems that all the great teachers knew that one cannot really teach anything directly, which is why they so often resorted to parables and stories. I see the literary and pedagogical nature of biblical and midrashic narratives doing precisely that. Or as Adam Philips once said about child development and about psychoanalysis itself: "The child's freedom, the child's self-fashioning project, depends on her being able to treat orders and instructions as though they were also hints and suggestions: an education through hinting about hinting that hints, points, invites, but does not compel."

And indeed, the very deepest things we can only say indirectly. Especially at moments of leave-taking, even when we often attempt to pour out and reveal all that is in our hearts, we can't ever fully capture all we want to say. And so often, we take the opposite course, simply evading trying to say it at all, or doing so in a very hasty, improvised way. But why, I still wonder, is God "embarrassed" to tell Aharon of his impending death? Why should it be difficult even for Him?

My colleagues and friends suggested some possible answers. Rav Kook, the famous first Chief Rabbi of Palestine, once said that death is a *herpah*—"a disgrace, shame"—for human beings. That is, we really should not have to die at all, despite Adam's sin. And God, so to speak, is sensitive to this. It "embarrasses" Him, especially in regard to Moshe and Aharon, such great souls. What, indeed, had they done that could possibly justify this? The prophet Elijah, for example, merits an entirely different kind of departure: he does not die but ascends alive to heaven on a chariot of fire (II Kings 11). So how can God say this to Aharon—especially after Aharon was the one who in the previous story, during the rebellion of Korah, stopped the massive lethal plague that had broken out among the Israelites and "stood between the living and the dead"? (Numbers 17:13)

Another suggestion: sometimes one has to tell difficult things to people one loves. One has to give criticism or convey hard truths and this is embarrassing. God loved Aharon and did not want to have to tell him he would die; it was an embarrassing knowledge.[6]

The classic medieval Jewish commentator, Rashi, in his comment on the words "take Aharon," cites a midrash and interprets the directive to Moshe as follows: "With words of comfort: 'how fortunate you are that you will see your crown given to your son, unlike me who has not merited that.'" For Moshe was succeeded not by his son, but by his student and follower, Joshua, and went to his death alone.

The midrash (*Yalkut Shimoni, Hukkat* 20) continues to describe the scene of a very gentle, loving passing, one which Moshe himself yearns for as he witnesses it. Aharon takes off the special garments of the High Priesthood and they are put on his son Elazar. Then:

> Moshe said to Aharon: "Enter the cave." And he entered.
> "Ascend the couch." And he ascended.
> "Extend your arms." And he extended them.
> "Close your mouth." And he closed it.
> "Shut your eyes." And he shut them.
> At that moment, Moshe said, "Fortunate is the one who dies such a death."
> Thus it is written [Deuteronomy 32:50], "like Aharon your brother died"—the death that you desired.

Another midrash expands the dialogue:

> Said Moshe to him: "Aharon my brother, what do you see? Miriam died and you and I both took care of her. Now you are dying and you see Elazar and me taking care of you. And myself—when I die, who will take care of me?"
> Answered the Holy One blessed be He: "I will take care of you," as it is written [Deuteronomy 34:6]. "And he buried him there." Immediately, the *Shekhinah* descended and kissed him.

The last line comes from the moving and painful description of Moshe's own passing at the end of the Book of Deuteronomy (34:5–6):

[6] I thank my colleague R. Zion Weissman of the Mandel School for Educational Leadership in Jerusalem, and my friend Sara Aisenfeld Beyer, for these insights.

And Moshe died there, the servant of God, in the land of Moav—according to the word of God.

And he buried him there in the valley, in the land of Moav, over against Beit Peor,

And no one knows his grave unto this day.

The midrash above seeks to explain the ambiguous pronoun "he" in the phrase "he buried him there." Who in fact, buried Moshe? For after Moshe finishes speaking his final words to the people in Deuteronomy 32:44–52, God tells him to ascend Mount Nevo in the land of Moav facing Jericho, and view the Promised Land he will not be able to enter: "And die on the mountain which you ascend, and be gathered to your people, like Aharon your brother died and was gathered to his people in Mount Hor." But unlike Aharon, no one was to accompany Moshe. He went alone. God took care of his lonely passing.

And from that summit, he sees a glimpse of his dream from afar (Deuteronomy 34:1–5). According to the midrash, God showed him the entire Promised Land, in its times of peace and in its times of destruction, and all that would happen in the future history of the Jews until the Last Day and resurrection of the dead. Perhaps that was God's way of comforting and assuring Moshe that all would continue without him, that ultimately all he gave his life for would be realized.

Aharon saw his son succeed him, but Moshe's life moved far beyond the personal. His true children were the entire people of Israel, whom he led and with whom he suffered for so many years in the desert.[7] To see the Promised Land and a vision of his children entering, settling and building it until the Last Day, was perhaps a way of indeed seeing his "son" succeed him.

---

[7] Another extraordinary midrash from *Tanhuma, vaEt'hanan* 5 relates: "It was announced to Moshe: 'The time has arrived for you to leave the world.' Moshe said: 'Wait until I have blessed Israel, for they had no joy from me all my life because of all the warnings and rebukes with which I chastised them.' He began to bless every tribe separately. When he saw that the time was short, he included them all in one blessing. He said to them all, to Israel: 'Much have I pained you over the Torah and the *mitzvot* and now forgive me.' They said to him: 'Our Teacher and Master! You are forgiven.' And then Israel also stood before him and said to him: 'Moshe our Teacher! Much have we angered you and increased your troubles. Forgive us!' He said to them: 'You are forgiven!'"

I can't help but again think of the passing of the Rebbe as I read these texts. Of the way in which he died in a hospital room, surrounded not by family, nor with the consolation of seeing a child able to take up his mantle. Of a man who was also never able to set foot in the Land of Israel, but also of a leader who saw it all so clearly from afar, gave his life over entirely to the people, suffered with them, and who also strained to see that final End, that time of the Messiah which would bring an end to all the tribulations of Exile.

How hard it is to accept the passing of such a man. On the words "and they went up to Mount Hor in the sight of all the congregation" (Numbers 20:27), the midrash interprets that all the people saw Moshe, Aharon and Elazar ascend the mountain, but "if they had known that he was ascending to die, they would not have permitted him to go, but would have prayed for mercy for him. They thought, however, that perhaps God was calling those three." Afterwards, when "all the congregation saw that Aharon had died" (Numbers 20:29), another midrash (*Tanhuma, Hukkat* 17) relates:

> When Moshe and Elazar descended from the mount, all the congregation gathered together and asked, "Where is Aharon?"
> Moshe said: "Dead."
> They said: "How could the angel of death strike a man who stood up to the angel of death and stopped him?" As it is written: "And he stood [Aharon] between the dead and the living and stopped the plague" [Numbers 17:13]. "If you bring him, good—but if not, we will stone you!"
> At that moment, Moshe stood in prayer and said, "Master of the Universe! Help clear me of this suspicion!"
> God opened the burial cave and showed them, as it is said, "And all the congregation saw that Aharon had died."

It is now several years since R. Schneerson has passed on. His grave, however, is well-known and visited by many. His *hasidim* continue his life's work all over the world. His teachings continue to radiate from the hundreds of books of his Torah scholarship, and the many volumes of letters he left behind. The personal comfort, advice and inspiration he gave to tens of thousands is inscribed in their hearts. And he gave us all, too, a glimpse of his great vision of redemption.

V.

In a recent lecture, in a discussion of the midrash on the way Moshe so indirectly "took" Aharon and conveyed to him the day of his death, Avivah Gottlieb Zornberg, the well-known Jerusalem teacher and author on the Bible, explored the possibility that Moshe was not just manipulating Aharon: perhaps Moshe indeed forgot or repressed the terrible knowledge God had given him. He knows, however, that he has to tell Aharon something, and that the truth will emerge as he speaks and they read together, trying to apply the text to their own lives. They will find the "lost" word of Torah in the process. On a broader level, she continued, one doesn't "possess one's own truth"; rather one has to bear witness to it through one's reading, through an alert reading. One reaches it obliquely, one begets it—as Moshe joins Aharon to beget the truth together with him—to bring out the hidden dimension of the text through use of one's own life situation. Interpretation and finding truth are not, then, merely saying what one already knows. Instead, they are a dark, oblique process. In the obscurities and dark spaces, one finds an unpredictable truth. And that indeed is the way of Torah.[8]

Dark spaces and unpredictable truths. We all continue to search the Torah, to try to beget our truth and our consolation. The key line for me in that midrash is Aharon's question, *Shema bishvili hu haDavar*: "Perhaps this word is meant for me?" Aharon first learns it as theoretical knowledge, a nice lecture, a theme in Genesis about everyone having to die. But he doesn't realize, *bishvili hu haDavar*. The word of Torah is indeed for us on our deepest level in all our pain as well as all our joy, in our life and in our death. For all those who face and have faced leave-takings, I hope, too, there has been a word here for you.

---

[8] Paraphrase of an unpublished lecture given by Avivah Gottlieb Zornberg in Jerusalem, February 16, 1998.

* * *

As is evident in this essay, I had a special relationship with the Luba-
vitcher Rebbe, R. Menahem Mendel Schneerson (1902–1994). I would not
be the Jewish woman I am today were it not for him. He was my
"teacher" in many ways. The Talmud relates (Sanhedrin 58a) that when
R. Eliezer became critically ill and close to death, he took his two arms,
folded them across his heart and said to his disciples: "Woe are you. My
two arms are like two scrolls of the Torah that are rolled and closed up.
Much Torah I learned and much Torah I taught: much Torah I learned
and I did not absorb from my teachers even as much as a dog could lick
from the sea. Much Torah I taught, and what my students absorbed from
me was but as the drop of ink the quill takes from the ink well."All I
managed to learn from the Lubavitcher Rebbe's teachings and life are but
like those few small drops compared to the vastness of the ocean. It is not
possible for me to convey even them in their fullness, let alone who and
what he was.

As a woman engaged in intellectual and academic work, I also re-
ceived the greatest encouragement from the Rebbe—blessings to continue
my Ph.D. in English, advice about possible dissertation topics, advice
about how to negotiate politics within the university. The Rebbe also
edited and corrected some manuscripts I wrote in English dealing with
talks he had given on various topics. I always sensed he wanted me to
employ to the full my intellectual capacities, and all the secular knowl-
edge I had attained from my Ivy League education...to elevate this all in
the service of God and Torah. He was indeed a vigorous supporter of
Jewish women, spoke often of their greatness, held special gatherings
specifically for women alone. He initiated several campaigns to encour-
age Jewish women to perform the special mitzvot pertaining to them, and
advocated depth and breadth in their Torah study. I once wrote an article
based on one of his talks, comparing the truths found in secular fields to
those of Torah. I wrote of the ways in which secular forms of knowledge
are limited; yet these very limitations can give one a sense of satisfaction,
a feeling that she or he has mastered a field. The Torah, however, is
unlimited and infinite and I wrote, "Thus one can never contain Torah,

master it." In editing this manuscript, the Rebbe amended the sentence to read: "Thus one can never contain all the content of even one **Dvar** *(sentence of) Torah, master it."*

The Rebbe gave me, among so many other things, this sense of humility and awe before the greatness of Torah. This essay is one of the ways in which I take leave of him—and continue, nevertheless, always to be his student. I dedicate it to his memory.[9]

---

[9] An earlier version of this essay was published in *Wellsprings* 47 (Summer 2000): 25–33. I also deal with some of these ideas in "'We Cleverly Avoided Talking About God': Personal and Pedagogical Reflections on Academia and Spirituality," *Courtyard: A Journal of Research and Thought in Jewish Education*, Jewish Theological Seminary 1.1 (1999): 101–20; and "A Man Apart: The Legacy of The Lubavitcher Rebbe," *Crosscurrents: Religion and Intellectual Life* (Summer 1995): 234–40. On R. Schneerson's position on Torah study for women, see my essay "Women and the Study of Torah in the Thought of the Lubavitcher Rebbe" in *Jewish Legal Writings By Women*, Micah D. Halpern and Chana Safrai eds. (Jerusalem: Urim Publications, 1998) 142–77.

Readings of Biblical Texts

The Souls That They Made:
Physical Infertility and Spiritual Fecundity

Tamara Goshen-Gottstein

There are moments in life when searing pain drives us to desperation. Overcome by a sorrow that feels too great to bear, our entire life hangs by a single thread. Nothing we tell ourselves to keep things in perspective seems to help: we know that only one thing alone will salvage our life. This experience can haunt the infertile, the unmarried and the chronically ill, but it is not limited to special situations; we are all fair game. Each one of us may at times come to see our life through a lens of desperation; one unbearable problem can cloud our appreciation for life itself with its myriad of daily blessings. Yet, can that pain also empower? The lives and teachings of our barren matriarchs offer a unique window into the quest for fulfillment.

The agonized cries and fervent prayers of barren women resound throughout the Bible. Most of these stories have gratifying outcomes: God receives the desired prayers of the righteous and the couple is eventually blessed with a child. These are "special children," often significant figures in the destiny of the people of Israel.[1] Such stories and the commentaries on them can offer comfort and direction to couples who are temporarily infertile. These stories also, surprisingly, have much to offer women and men who may never bear children. Moreover, they address profound existential issues, revealing the richness of prayer and opening the possibility of moving beyond desperation to build purposeful lives. Despite the fact that Sarah precedes Rachel chronologically in the Bible, this essay is

---

[1] Sarah/Isaac the patriarch (Genesis 11:30, 16:1–3, 17:15–22, 18:9–16); Rebecca/Jacob the patriarch (Genesis 25:21); Rachel/Joseph (Genesis 30:1); Hannah/Samuel the prophet and judge, the first to anoint a king over Israel (I Samuel 1:1, 2:11).

constructed as an existential journey. It begins with Rachel's piercing cry for life and then looks at models of growth and fulfillment which both she and Sarah exemplify. It concludes with the hasidic Rebbe, the Be'er Mayyim Hayyim's expansive vision of "fecundity."

Approaching Religious Texts

In my teaching and learning, I have been encouraged by a comment made by R. Shlomo Twersky *z"l* (of blessed memory) of Denver, who said that there are two main ways to learn. One approach is linear, more typically "masculine," in which each idea leads to another and occasionally to a breakthrough, where the larger context is grasped. There is another, more "feminine" kind of learning, where one absorbs an idea like a seed and nourishes it until it blossoms, becoming an emanation that shines through one always. This mode he likened to the famous Shabbat lights of Sarah and Rebecca that never go out.[2]

My approach to learning and teaching Torah has never been exclusively intellectual. It is important to me to understand the historical context, a text's relationship to other strands of Jewish thought and to come as close as I can to understanding what the author was trying to communicate. This is the first stage. Afterwards I need to internalize the thought and let it challenge my preconceptions, hear it echo and practice what I learn from it, fall and reach again, pray, grow deeper in its practice, until eventually it becomes part of the fabric of my life. Contemplating the biblical characters makes them come alive and casts our pressing life issues in a new light.

And so, before beginning, I would like to say to the reader: do not be limited by my current perspective of the texts. Every year, open your life anew; notice details in the text that may never have caught your heart before. Ponder the life issues they pose. The modern world is inundated with quantitative knowledge. We need *Torat imekha*, "Torah of the Mothers," Torah that grows, emanates and nourishes. I'd like to share the

---

[2] Notes from a class R. Shlomo Twersky gave to women at a Shabbaton in Big Bear, California, Summer 1981.

following texts with this intention at heart. I pray that they open an expanded sense of fertility and fulfillment for us all.

Jealousy

> When Rachel saw she bore Jacob no children, Rachel became envious of her sister and said to Jacob, "Give me children or else I die." Jacob's anger flared up against Rachel and he said, "Can I take the place of God, who has denied you the fruit of your womb?"
> (Genesis 30:1–2)

It is possible to endure a difficult situation for years, then something suddenly will tip the scales, making it become unbearable. After living through years of infertility, Rachel "saw," and she became jealous. What did she see?

The biblical narrative points quite clearly to the cause of Rachel's envy. Rachel "saw" that she had no children, while Leah had just given birth to her fourth son. We can understand Rachel's desperation. Her prolonged infertility was sufficient cause for crisis. Why then does the biblical text emphasize her envy? Should we simply ascribe it to human nature? That we want something even more when someone close has it? The biblical text emphasizes Rachel's jealousy, yet a well known midrashic tradition sidesteps her envy, weaving together the threads of Rachel's life to portray her as a young woman who is able to transcend her nature.[3] As the people of Israel, many generations later, are sent into exile, Rachel's ability to overcome envy is precisely what gives her the power to intercede with God.

We recall that Rachel is buried "on the road to Efrat," not next to Jacob in the tomb of the patriarchs and matriarchs, as one would expect.[4] Jacob foresaw the future and buried her "on the way" to enable her to intercede for her children as they are forced into exile.[5] The midrash creatively renders Rachel's extraordinary behavior on her wedding night to exemplify the principle that our actions can have a profound effect on God:

---

[3] Proem to *Lamentations Rabbah* 24.

[4] Genesis 9:19.

[5] *Genesis Rabbah* 82.10.

At that moment, the matriarch Rachel broke forth into speech before the Holy One, blessed be He and said, "Sovereign of the Universe, it is revealed before You that Your servant Jacob loved me exceedingly and toiled for my father on my behalf seven years. When those seven years were completed and the time arrived for my marriage with my husband, my father planned to substitute my sister for me, to wed my husband. It was very hard for me, because the plot was known to me and I disclosed it to my husband; and I gave him a sign whereby he could distinguish between me and my sister, so that my father should not be able to make the substitution. After that I relented, suppressed my desire and had pity upon my sister that she should not be exposed to shame.

In the evening, they substituted my sister for me with my husband and I delivered over to my sister all the signs that I had arranged with my husband so that he should think that she was Rachel. More than that, I went beneath the bed upon which he lay with my sister; and when he spoke to her she remained silent and I made all the replies in order that he should not recognize my sister's voice. I did her a kindness, was not jealous of her and did not expose her to shame. If I, a creature of flesh and blood, formed of dust and ashes, was not envious of my rival and did not expose her to shame and contempt, why should You, a merciful King who lives eternally, be jealous of idols which aren't even real and exile my children and let them be slain by the sword and let their enemies do with them as they wish?"

The mercy of the Holy One, blessed be He, was stirred and He said, "For your sake, Rachel, I will restore Israel to their place." So it is written, "Thus says the Lord, 'A voice is heard in Ramah, lamentation and bitter weeping. Rachel is weeping for her children; she refuses to be comforted for her children, because they are not.' Thus says the Lord, 'Refrain your voice from weeping and your eyes from tears; for your work shall be rewarded...and there is hope for your future,' says the Lord, 'and your children shall return to their own border.'" (Jeremiah 31:14–16)[6]

---

[6] Proem to *Lamentations Rabbah* 24. This translation is based on the *Midrash Rabbah*, appearing in the Soncino CD-ROM.

Rachel emerges here as the paradigm of altruism. If Rachel, who is only "flesh and blood," can bear the unbearable, then why can't God "bear" something far less wrenching, especially when He views it from the perspective of eternity?

Rachel's merit came from her profound ability to do what is nearly unthinkable in human terms. She gave up her beloved after yearning for him for seven long years; she sacrificed her fulfillment to prevent her sister's shame. What changed noble Rachel into an anguished woman? How could Rachel, of all people, be jealous? Does her relationship with Jacob offer us any clues?

Strained Relationships

Other biblical couples, including Jacob's grandparents and parents, also faced infertility, but responded in less divisive ways. On Sarah's initiative, Abraham fathered a child with Hagar. Isaac and Rebecca's response was to pray together for a child.[7] Elkana tries to comfort his wife Hannah in her pain, asking, "Hannah, why do you weep? Why do you not eat? Why is your heart grieved? Am I not better to you than ten sons?" (I Samuel 1:8).

Elkana, so solicitous and concerned for Hannah, reaffirms his love, yet his attempt to comfort only reinforces the fact that her desperation is hers alone. Elkana has another wife, Peninah, who has given him abundant children. Hannah suddenly realizes that "Elkana is resigned to her childlessness."[8] She must face her pain alone, so she goes to the temple of the Lord in Shilo to pour her heart out before God.

---

[7] "[And Isaac entreated the Lord] for his wife (*lenokhah ishto*): this teaches that Isaac prostrated himself in one spot and she in another [opposite him] and he prayed to God, 'Sovereign of the universe! May all the children thou has granted me come from this righteous woman.' She too prayed likewise." *Genesis Rabbah* 43.5 citing Genesis 25:21.

[8] Bryna Jocheved Levy, "Sense and Sensibilities: Women and Talmud Torah," *Jewish Action* (Winter 1998): 19, who quotes Uriel Simon, "*Sippur Holadat Shmuel: haMivneh, haSug, vehaMashma'ut.*" *Studies in Bible and Exegesis*, vol. II (1986). Translated to English by Lenn J. Schramm, *Reading Prophetic Narratives* (Bloomington: Indiana University Press, 1997) 14.

In contrast to these biblical narratives, Rachel stands out. She does not turn to prayer as the others have. She *demands* of her husband Jacob, "Give me children or else I die" (Genesis 30:1). Is her cry calculated, or threatening?[9] Is she attacking Jacob, implying that he is withholding something from the process—that he could do more to ensure their fertility? Did she really reach a breaking point, feeling that without children her life was not worth living?

At the beginning of Rachel's marriage, the biblical text informs us that "He [Jacob] loved Rachel even more than Leah" (Genesis 29:30). Most of us carry this frozen image of the couple throughout their lifetime. Rachel's story, however, is far from static. Through analyzing the biblical narrative below, a more nuanced picture emerges. We begin to see the intimacy that can accompany childbearing as well as the strain that can develop between husbands and wives facing prolonged infertility.

> He consorted also with Rachel and loved Rachel more than Leah. God saw that Leah was unloved, so he opened her womb, but Rachel remained barren. Leah conceived and bore a son and she called his name Reuben,[10] as she had declared, "Because God has *seen* my humiliation, now my husband will love me." She conceived again and bore a son and declared, "Because God has *heard* that I am unloved, He has given me this one also," and she called his name Shimon.[11] Again she conceived and bore a son and declared, "This time my husband will become *attached*[12] to me for I have borne him three sons," therefore he[13] called his name Levi. She conceived again and bore a son and

---

[9] In a private conversation, Tikva Frymer-Kensky, Jerusalem, spring 1999, raised the possibility that it was a calculated move on Rachel's part. Rachel wanted to build herself up through Bilhah but was afraid that since Jacob already had children with Leah, her request would be rejected. In this way, the request came as the welcome solution to her anguish.

[10] From the word *ro'eh*, to see.

[11] From the word *shome'a*, to hear.

[12] From the word *laveh*, to accompany or attach to.

[13] James Kugel, in a personal conversation in June 1999, said that in biblical Hebrew if the feminine form of the verb "to name or call" (*vatikra*) is used, one can conclusively say that a woman named the child. When the masculine form is used (*kara*) it may also be an impersonal form, like *man* in German or *on* in French, meaning roughly, "one called," without specifying gender. Hirsch picks up on the difference in how the verb is conjugated and builds his thesis around the possibility that Jacob

declared, "This time let me gratefully *praise* God," therefore she called his name Yehudah;[14] then she stopped giving birth. (Genesis 29:30–35) [Italics added for emphasis]

R. Samson Raphael Hirsch shows that the names they gave their children chronicle the evolution of Leah's relationship to Jacob.[15]

> The successive names show how, with the blessing of each fresh child for which Jacob has to thank Leah, his attitude to her becomes increasingly more loving. At first, "God saw my affliction," so that up to then Jacob's preference for Rachel was *visible*. With the birth of Reuben, that disappeared, but by Leah's *ear* it could still be detected. Just in the tone of his voice to Rachel, Leah could feel that she still did not possess the full measure of her husband's love, so she called her second son Shimon.
>
> With the birth of her third son, however, she felt the difference had quite disappeared, yea she felt she could now express with full confidence, that now the purest, truest loving relationship between husband and wife was established…. It is accordingly highly significant that at Levi, it is not she, but he who expresses this in giving the baby its name. Had she done so, it might only have been supposition, or even wishful thinking on her part, but, coming from his mouth, it was the sweetest acknowledgment *al ken kara shmo Levi*. So that, when the fourth son was born, Judah, she no longer had primarily to welcome it as a means of progress in her husband's love towards her, which she now fully possessed, but could simply enjoy her baby purely for its own sake. She accordingly pronounced the words of a happy mother, "This time I can thank God, just for His gift itself," and called the child Judah (*Yehudah*).

The relationship between Leah and Jacob evolved as they built a family together. The birth of their fourth son may have represented a peak moment in their relationship, or at the very least in Leah's inner experience, which catapulted her to a new level of gratitude and well being.

---

named the child. In this case his argument is convincing, for one seeks clues in the context to understand who the subject is.

[14] From the word *lehodot*, to praise.

[15] R. Samson Raphael Hirsch, Genesis 29:32–35 (NY: Judaica Press, 1971) 473–74.

As long as they were both suffering, Rachel because of infertility and Leah because of her status as the *snuah* ("hated" or "rejected" one), they at least had their anguish in common. Did Leah's fulfillment trigger Rachel's pain? Rachel's self perception could have been that her beauty was being eroded by her grief. Did she feel excluded from the warm circle of family intimacy connecting Leah, Jacob and their sons? Did Rachel feel that she had lost forever her special beloved status with Jacob and that she was suddenly bitterly alone, both in her marriage and in her yearning for children?

(In modern times, we don't have an emotional experience comparable to that faced by two women, much less two sisters, sharing one husband, but many of us do live as part of an extended family in which large family events can be painful triggers. Though some find family celebrations welcome distractions and uplifting events, for others [infertile couples and single men and women, who want to have families] these events can carry a tyranny all their own. Mourners do not come to places of celebration for the first year of mourning, yet individuals anguishing and mourning the life they feel is eluding them not only attend these events but must grapple with their accentuated loneliness, amidst the joyous celebration that seems so far from their own reality.)

Rachel reaches a breaking point. Time has taken its toll. The young Rachel may have been strong, idealistic and sure enough in her love to sacrifice. It is not difficult to understand the evolution of Rachel's jealousy. As the years drag on, her faith waivers and despair sets in. In the face of despair, one's greatest strengths and ideals can falter.

Holy Envy

In contrast to these "emotional" explanations of Rachel's jealousy, Rashi, quoting the midrash, raises the possibility that a certain kind of envy may actually be beneficial. Envy of another's achievements in learning and good deeds can spur one to increase one's own acts of holiness. Rashi states, "She was jealous of her sister's good deeds, saying, 'If Leah were not more righteous than I, she would not have been privileged to bear children.'"[16]

Rachel's reasoning, as expressed in the midrash, stands at odds with the biblical text's clear statement regarding why Leah had children, or at least her firstborn: "And when the Eternal saw that Leah was hated He opened her womb."[17] Perhaps the reasons for our hardship are less important than how we allow them to challenge our lives. Rashi's suggestion of constructive envy raises the possibility that Rachel opened to her inner landscape, taking on the challenge of increasing her worthiness. Rachel's choice to embrace growth allowed for positive movement.

The Spiritual Challenge

The infertile often feel that there is a *gzar din* (evil decree) looming over them. Viewing hardships such as infertility as a challenge to increase our merit is a time-honored practice of the Jewish people. Throughout the centuries, Jews have sought to mediate this sort of judgment through *teshuvah* (repentance and return to a meritorious way of life), *tefillah* (prayer) and *tzedakah* (giving charity and assuring justice for the downtrodden). This is expressed in its most familiar form in the *Mussaf* prayer of Rosh Hashanah and Yom Kippur, "But repentance, prayer and charity annul the evil of the decree."[18]

To pray in Hebrew is *lehitpalel*, a reflexive verb meaning literally, "to judge oneself." R. Nahman of Bratslav encouraged his students to engage regularly in reflective prayer saying, "Through the fact that a person judges and evaluates himself, he mitigates and eliminates the judgment

---

[16] Rashi, Genesis 30:1.

[17] Genesis 29:31.

[18] This prayer formulation is a distillation of a teaching in *Rosh Hashanah* 16b. "R. Isaac further said, 'Four things annul the decree of a person, namely, charity, supplication, change of name and change of conduct.... Some say that change of place [also avails]." The Talmud adds the change of name. A letter of God's name was added to Sarah's name. The Talmud quotes this as a prooftext, "As it is written, 'As for Sarai thy wife, thou shall not call her name Sarai, but Sarah shall her name be,' and it continues, "And I will bless her and moreover I will give thee a son of her."

above. For where there is judgment below, there is no judgment above."[19]
What kind of self-judgment is this? It is not an exercise in giving the
harsh inner critic free reign, but rather, coming to the point where one
places oneself in God's presence and critiques one's life with discernment
and compassion. Rachel named the son that Bilha her maidservant bore
her—Dan (judge)—to honor the justice of God's ways. Although we
often view suffering as an unwelcome intrusion, the decisions we take and
the way we endure our suffering can have a profound potential for opening our wombs, both on a physical and metaphorical level. *Rehem* (womb)
has the same root in Hebrew as *rahamim* (compassion).[20]

Through compassionate reflective prayer and the deep instinct to become a better person, we are catapulted into another aspect of our fecundity: increasing holiness in the world. According to the kabbalistic notion
of *tikkun*, "fixing," we all come into the world to participate in a process
of repair, on both a personal and global level. Through the religious acts
of Israel: Torah, *mitzvot*, prayer and acts of lovingkindness we help
restore the harmony which heals the present unredeemed and broken state
of the world. If this is so, then using our most dearly sought-after dreams
as a motivating factor can certainly be fruitful. Even if we are not rewarded in the way we desire, our lives and the lives of those around us
can flourish with dignity and purpose. From this perspective, even unexpected harshness can generate constructive action.

Can I Take God's Place? The Spiritual Challenge

> Jacob's anger flared up against Rachel and he said, "Can I take the
> place of God, who has denied you the fruit of your womb?" (Genesis
> 30:1–2)

Commentators throughout the ages have grappled with Jacob's harsh
response. If Rachel was suffering so much, did she deserve such an

---

[19] R. Nahman of Bratslav, *Likkutei Moharan*, 169:2.

[20] There is a talmudic tradition that credits Abraham's compassionate prayer to heal
Abimelech and his entire household as the turning point that opened Sarah's womb.
Bava Kamma 92a.

answer? Nechama Leibowitz[21] addresses Jacob's criticism of Rachel in her penetrating commentary on the Book of Genesis. In her chapter entitled "Can I take God's Place?" she analyzes both Rachel's "appeal in her misery to her husband Jacob" and his "unfeeling reply."

"Didn't Jacob understand that a person cannot be blamed for what he says out of intense suffering?"[22] Leibowitz quotes the Ramban who takes Jacob to task.

> Our commentators explained that Rachel asked to pray for her or else she would die (Rashi). In that case why was Jacob so angry?.... Do not the righteous pray on behalf of others? [he goes on to explain:] "She spoke wrongly out of her envy and thought that Jacob out of his love for her would fast and put on sackcloth and intercede for her until she was granted children so that she should not die on account of her suffering.
> Jacob was angry because the prayer of the righteous is not in their power that it must automatically and invariably be granted.... This was why he told her that he was not in the place of God to be able to make fruitful the barren."

Leibowitz elaborates that Jacob's anger reflected his concern "with the misleading approach to prayer," evident in Rachel's words—"her incomprehension of the real relationship between man and God. Herein surely lay the difference between superstition, idolatrous media of intercession and the pure undefiled prayer of man to his Maker!"[23] Prayer is not a magical practice to bend God's will to suit one's own desires. "The offerer of sincere prayer to the Deity, however, knows that his prayer cannot force his Maker to do anything, but that the Lord will do what

---

[21] Unique among women of this century, Nechama Leibowitz was an eminent biblical scholar and teacher. Her analysis of Rachel's bitter cry to her husband reads with poignant vitality when one realizes that though she raised up many students, she never gave birth to biological children.

[22] Nechama Leibowitz, *Studies in the Book of Genesis: In the Context of Ancient and Modern Bible Commentary*, Aryeh Newman trans. (Jerusalem: World Zionist Organization, 1972) 332–33.

[23] Ibid.

seemeth good to him and that we must thank Him for misfortune just as we do for good fortune."[24]

Rachel, however, persisted, "in her desire that the righteous man should pray for her and cause Him to do her will."[25] Further refinement of Rachel's relationship to God is still required before she can conceive their child. "Now when the righteous woman saw that she could not rely on Jacob's intercession, she betook to praying herself to the Answerer of Prayer and this is borne out by the text, 'And God hearkened to her.'"[26] The biblical text indicates that when she finally did pray directly, it was her prayer that was effective.

Leibowitz also presents the attempt made by R. Isaac Arama (Akeidat Yitzhak) to justify Jacob's strong reaction. He reads Jacob's words as recalling Rachel to her larger purpose:

> The two names, "woman" (*isha*) and "Eve" (*Hava*) indicate two purposes. The first teaches that woman was taken from man, stressing that like him, she may understand and advance in the intellectual and moral field just as did the matriarchs and many righteous women and prophetesses and as the literal meaning of Proverbs 31 about "the woman of worth" (*eshet hayil*) indicates. The second alludes to the power of childbearing and rearing children, as is indicated by the name Eve—the mother of all living. A woman deprived of the power of childbearing will be deprived of the secondary purpose and will be left with the ability to do evil or good like the man who is barren. Of both the barren man and woman Isaiah (66:5) states, "I have given them in My house and in My walls a name that is better than sons and daughters," since the offspring of the righteous is certainly good deeds (see Rashi on Genesis 6:9). Jacob was therefore angry with Rachel when she said, "Give me children or I am dead," in order to reprimand her and make her understand this all-important principle that she was not dead as far as their joint purpose in life because she was childless, just the same as it would be in his case, if he would have been child-less.[27]

---

[24] Ibid.

[25] Leibowitz paraphrasing the Ramban.

[26] Ramban 5.22; Genesis 30:22.

[27] Akeidat Yitzhak, Commentary on Genesis quoted by Nechama Leibowitz, *Studies in Genesis*, 334.

Here we have a reprimand of great interest. Rachel was missing an essential understanding of the mutual purpose in life that she shared with Jacob, regardless of their inability to have children. Can this intellectual understanding defend against emotions that surge so powerfully? It often takes stronger medicine, but this kind of understanding can help one to regain perspective.

Viewed in this way, Rachel is being jolted back to herself. She must come to a whole new level of faith. At first, she desperately wanted her salvation to come through the agency of her husband's relationship to God, but his clear rebuke catalyzes her to forge her own intimate connection to her Creator. As pained and desperate as she is at this moment, she cannot force Jacob or God. When we stop trying to manipulate through emotional anguish and instead place ourselves honestly in God's presence, prayer from the depths of our suffering can indeed move us to another level. R. Nahman calls this form of prayer *hitbodedut*, secluded prayer, in which one comes to God in complete truthfulness: "Be totally honest and open your heart before God, whether to beg for forgiveness for what happened in the past or to appeal to God to help you in the future by releasing you from the traps you are caught in and by drawing you closer to Him."[28]

In solitude one can pour out the bitterness of heart, the dreams and prayers for the future. One can thus imagine Rachel, left to her own resources, finding a deeper root. Underneath desperation lie many emotions. In intimate prayer, when one listens and feels as much as one speaks, one inevitably comes to new understanding and inspiration.

Rachel came to terms with her infertility. She faced her desperation and embraced her moment, to allow life to come to her, even if it was not in the form of her own biological child. Through this willingness, her life began to flourish. She ceased to manipulate Jacob to pray for her and opened prayer, with all its pain, as an act of intimacy with her Maker.

---

[28] R. Nathan of Bratslav, *Advice* (*Likkutei Etzot*), translated to English by Avraham Greenbaum (The Breslov Research Institute, 1983) 84. See also R. Nahman of Bratslav, *Likkutei Moharan* 2:25 for instructions on the daily practice of *hitbodedut*.

There are two more aspects of her struggle that I want to address before leaving Rachel for Sarah's tent.

Yearning

Yearning is not an obsession that one has to transcend to come to "fulfillment." According to R. Nahman of Bratslav, real spiritual work takes place in the heart of one who desires deeply.

> All the barriers and obstacles that confront a person have only one purpose: to heighten his yearning for the holy deed which he needs to accomplish. It is part of human nature that the greater the barriers standing in the way of a particular goal, the more one desires to achieve it. When a Jew needs to do something whose purpose is to strengthen his very core, especially when it is something upon which his whole being as a Jew depends...he is given desire from above.... The desire is created through the barrier which is sent to him and the barrier itself causes the yearning to grow.... The entire purpose of the barrier is only to increase your desire. When you achieve the necessary desire and yearning for the holy act you need to accomplish, you will surely succeed in transforming the idea which is in your mind into an actual reality. The barrier itself can bring you to succeed by strengthening your desire to do so.[29]
>
> It may take a lot of effort for a person to break the barriers confronting him when he starts to grow close to God.... But all one's effort produces a vessel.... The greater the struggle one has at one's outset, the greater the vessel one forms.[30]

The power of this yearning and effort produces a vessel. There seems to be a genuine fruitfulness intrinsic in the struggle. When we contemplate the lives of Rachel and Leah, we see two women yearning. Leah's childbearing is a prayer of yearning for intimacy with Jacob. In the process of

---

[29] R. Nathan of Bratslav, *Likkutei Etzot, Meniyot* 119a (a thematic distillation of teachings from *Likkutei Moharan.*) Translation in English by Avraham Greenbaum, *Advice*, The Breslov Research Institute, Jerusalem, 1983, 163.

[30] Ibid., 165:5. The word **vessel** in the original R. Nahman version (*Likkutei Moharan* 66:4) comes from the Hebrew word *nekudot*, which literally means **dots** or **vowels**. It is impossible to speak without vowels. You cannot even name the letters. The vowels allow for the potential to be actualized. In R. Nathan's version, the word "*kli*" or vessel is used.

her deep desire for closeness, she is truly productive, giving birth to more than her share of the tribes of Israel. She lives close to the raw nerve of her pain. She doesn't run away from it—she even documents the stages of her process in the names of her children. She bears children and she also merits increasing closeness. Rachel's yearning is a powerful paradigm of tears that will not cease—tears that cry out to God through the many long years of exile of the Jewish people. This vision of Rachel crying for her children, as well as for the "Children of Israel" in exile, is a poignant image the Bible employs to express the unceasing prayer for the redemption of the people of Israel.

The Talmud teaches that the *Shekhinah* does not dwell where there is sadness.[31] I would venture to say that the sadness being described by this passage is despair—a complete erosion of faith. Rachel, however, presents a different model. A faith large enough to carry the pain and yearning. The forefathers were distinguished in the midrash by their willingness to die for God. Rachel's greatness was in her courage to *live* for Him.[32]

It takes astounding fortitude to sustain one's willingness to live and believe in the face of unbearable suffering. I find deep comfort in the fact that the Bible lets us see Rachel's fallibility. Rachel, who had to give up her beloved on her wedding night, years later confronts an even more difficult moment. She faces the death of her dream, yet goes on. Yearning, praying and staying present to the pain are very different from sinking into a pit of desperation.[33]

A friend shared this teaching with me as she sat *Shiva* for her four-year-old son who had died of cancer. "The pain is searing," she said, "but the love and extraordinary outpouring of support are as well. Now I understand what Reb Shlomo Carlebach meant when he said, 'You have to keep your heart open in hell.'" Without keeping one's "heart open in

---

[31] *Pesahim* 117a.

[32] This idea is expressed beautifully in the song "Rachel" by "Ashira," audio cassette (Castle of Water, 1983).

[33] In contrast to Rachel, Hagar models this collapse, when she and her son Ishmael run out of water in the desert. She cannot bear Ishmael's cries and casts him beneath the trees saying, "'Let me not see the death of the child.' And she sat at a distance, lifted her voice and wept. God heard the cry of the youth…" (Genesis 21:15–17), not the cries of Hagar!

hell," the fall into desperation can render us incapable of receiving or building anything. When we are desperate, there is nothing to lose, so the striving can be angry and demanding. It is easy to fall into the trap of implying that our suffering is someone else's fault. As a victim and a "blamer," we lose the power to change. We do not take Rachel's moment of desperation as her life's message, but as a legitimate momentary expression of her hardship. We remember her eternally as *Rachel imenu*—"our mother" Rachel, a mother who never stops loving and yearning.

Concrete Action

Rachel not only spiritualizes her suffering. She acts to engender a child, even if it is not biologically hers. A profound process is required to bring a woman to this point of readiness; one that Michael Gold describes as the death of a dream. "It is important to recognize that infertility involves a loss that is similar to the loss of a loved one. There are grief and mourning, anger and guilt, all the emotions that we associate with death. It is the death of a dream, a dream we hold from childhood."[34]

The following midrash introduces a pro-active Rachel, bringing dramatic life to the biblical passage following Jacob's rebuke:

> Am I in God's stead, who has withheld from you the fruit of the womb? (Genesis 30:2). He said, "From you He withheld it, but not from me." She said to him, "Did then your father act so to your mother? Did he not gird up his loins for her?" "He had no children," he retorted, "whereas I have children." "And did not your grandfather [Abraham] have children," she pursued, "yet he too girded up his loins for Sarah?" "Can you then do what my grandmother did?" he asked her. "And what did she do?" "She brought her rival into her home," he replied. "If that is the obstacle," she returned, "behold my maid Bilhah; go in to her...and I also may be built up through her" (Genesis 30:3). As she [Sarah] was built up through her rival, so was she

---

[34] Michael Gold, *And Hannah Wept: Infertility, Adoption and the Jewish Couple* (NY, 1950/1988) 56. Likening infertility to death, R. Gold cites *Nedarim* 64b: "R. Joshua ben Levi taught: a man without children is considered like a dead man, as it is written, 'Give me children and if not I shall die.' And it is taught, four are considered like they are dead, a poor man, a leper, a blind man and a man without children."

[Rachel] built up through her rival. Rachel said, "God has judged me (Genesis 30:6). He has judged and condemned me." But Rachel was barren (Genesis 29:31). Then "He has judged me and pronounced in my favor and has given me a son. Therefore she called his name Dan..." (Genesis 30:6).[35]

Rachel reaches a crisis, triggered by envy. What is her way out? She brings yet another rival into the picture. Often our solutions feel almost worse than the original problem, yet they truly are the next step necessary to open the gates.

Rachel ceases to be fixated on having her child be her biological progeny. She gives Jacob her handmaid Bilhah. Her willingness to change enabled Dan to enter her life and perhaps led to her eventual conception.

In biblical times, an infertile woman could build herself up through her maidservant. All the matriarchs except for Rebecca "offered" their handmaidens to their respective husbands as concubines, so that they could adopt their husbands' offspring as their own children. According to Rashi, each of the matriarchs expected to bear her own children as a divine reward for introducing a rival into her family life. R. Levi ben Gershon (1288–1344), Rabbenu Nissim (1310–1375) and R. Ovadia Sforno (1470–1550) appear to suggest psychosomatic mechanisms: a change of "temperament" (*lahafokh mizgah*), a change in her "system" (*yeshaneh ma'arekhet gevirtah*), or a stirring up of her "nature" (*yit'orer hatevah*), respectively. However, almost all the other classical commentators hold that the matriarchs merely expected to become adoptive mothers of the children of their husbands and their handmaidens.[36] "According to folk wisdom, adoption may promote conception in infertile women."[37] Although the link between adoption and conception may never be confirmed definitively by science, stories abound to comfort and inspire women to choose adoption.[38]

---

[35] *Genesis Rabbah* 71.7.

[36] S.H. Blondheim and D.E. Blondheim, "Matriarchal Infertility and Adoption as a Prelude to Conception" *Koroth* 9.1–2 (1985): 91.

[37] Ibid., 90.

[38] E.J. Lamb, et al. "Does Adoption Affect Subsequent Fertility?" *American Journal of Obstetrics and Gynaecology* 134.2 (May 15, 1979): 138–44. W.C. Weir, et al.

Often adoption, or the willingness to build one's family in a way that does not come from one's own genetic material, offers deep fulfillment in and of itself. The Talmud, citing the story of Michal, who raised her deceased sister's children states: "Anyone who raises an orphan in their home, Scripture considers it as if she or he gave birth to him."[39]

Adoption is looked on with great favor by the Jewish tradition, although "Jewish law does not recognize it as a legal institution. Adoption in civil law means a total severing of a child's relationship to his or her biological parents and the establishment of an equivalent relationship with adoptive parents."[40] Gold, in his supportive presentation of adoption for infertile Jewish couples, explains the esteemed value of adoption in our tradition and the centrality of the knowledge of the child's biological identity for many aspects of Jewish law.[41] Adoption, however is not the first option a modern Rachel and Jacob turn to when they have difficulty conceiving. Approximately eighty percent of infertile couples seek the medical route first.[42] The compassionate concern for the legitimate

---

"Adoption and Subsequent Conceptions," *Fertility and Sterility* 17.2 (March–April, 1966): 283–8. Both these articles find no statistical correlation. A third source evaluates the existing literature, citing questionable research parameters and basically agrees that there appears to be no correlation, but does not close the subject definitively. F.M. Mai, "Conception after Adoption: An Open Question," *Psychosomatic Med.* 33.6 (November–December, 1971): 509–14.

One true story illustrating this phenomenon took place about six years ago. A couple finally adopted. At the circumcision of the adopted baby, R. Shlomo Carlebach *z"l*, suddenly turned to the couple and admonished them to add an extra name to the baby's name. "Add the name *Yosef*," beamed Reb Shlomo, "*sheyosif lakhem od ben*—that God should add you another son." Sure enough, that month, the adopting mother conceived her first biological son, who was born ten months after the adoption took place. This is one of several stories I have heard in which the woman nursed her adopted baby. I have been unable to locate studies on the effects breast-feeding adopted babies has on subsequent conceptions, but the issue warrants further research.

[39] *Sanhedrin* 19b.

[40] Gold, *And Hannah Wept*, 157.

[41] Ibid. These issues include knowing whether the child is a Gentile or a Jew, Cohen, Levi or Israel, issues of *mamzerut*, preventing marriage to biological siblings, inheritance, etc.

[42] Frank van Balen, et al. "Choices and Motivations in Infertile Couples," *Patient Education and Counceling* 31.1 (1997): 19–27.

suffering of the infertile motivates modern halakhic authorities to bridge difficult issues, making some of these scientific solutions available to aspiring parents.[43]

Sarah and Abraham

Entering the tent of Sarah, we meet a completely different paradigm of infertility. Abraham and Sarah are a couple, in deep spiritual partnership, bringing masses of people to the knowledge and praise of their Creator and sustainer. Unlike Rachel, Sarah does not seem tormented by her childlessness nor is she feeling anguish over a lack of closeness in her relationship with her husband.

---

[43] Most halakhic authorities find solutions to make couples' own genetic conception possible. The fiery debates surface when the issue of donor reproduction is raised. At the conference on "Judaism, Ethics and Health Care" held at the Western Galilee Hospital, Naharia in October 24–27, 1999, R. Moshe Tendler recalled the very real mental suffering that the infertile face, but qualified the halakhic response limiting its relevance to primary and secondary infertility. He emphatically stated that there was no justification for a woman with several healthy children to engage in potentially dangerous medical interventions to have children. Multiple ethical issues surface regarding the new technologies; discussion of them exceeds the scope of this article. The following list will provide a starting point for those seeking sources in English. J.D. Bleich, *Bioethical Dilemmas: A Jewish Perspective* (NJ: Ktav, 1998) for articles on artificial procreation, sperm banking, surrogate motherhood, pregnancy reduction, etc. Elliot Dorff, "Artificial Insemination, Egg Donation and Adoption," *Conservative Judaism* XLIX.1 (Fall 1966). For resources in Hebrew, see: Dr. Abraham Steinberg, *Encyclopedia of Jewish Medical Ethics* (Jerusalem, 1998) on paternity, artificial insemination, in-vitro fertilization, fertility and sterility, etc., R. Steinberg gives a clear breakdown of the main opinions on each topic with extensive footnotes to the responsa literature. Dvora Ross, "Artificial Insemination in Single Women" [Hebrew], *Jewish Legal Writings by Women*, Micah D. Halpern and Chana Safrai eds. (Jerusalem: Urim Publications, 1998).

In looking at the literature, one is struck by the fact that technology is causing a revolution in the definition of family. Sperm and eggs are commodities one can buy; genetic material can be viewed and manipulated: "favorable traits" can be selected and parents do not need to be part of conventional family units to conceive. There is no legislation in Israel or in most other countries to require parents to disclose to their children their biological origins. There are also no central worldwide registries. Consequently, when these children come to marriage there is no way to determine absolutely that they will not marry half siblings. This brave new world of blurred genealogy is a far cry from the biblical ideal of certain lineage. The extensive changes that reproductive technology pose to individual identity as well as to the whole fabric of society need to be addressed with care.

We are introduced to Sarah as, "Sarai is *akara* (barren) she has no child" (Genesis 11:30).[44] Normally, biblical language is economic in its use of words. Of course Sarah has no child. Infertility is, by definition, not having a child.[45] The seeming redundancy generates a wide range of interpretation.[46] The next mention of Sarah is as they set out on a journey of faith to the place that God will show Abraham. As they set out, Abraham takes "the souls that they made" (Genesis 12:5). If they were infertile, then who were these souls? In the words of the midrash:

> R. Elazar observed in the name of R. Jose ben Zimra: If all the nations assembled to create one insect they could not endow it with life, yet you say "and the souls that they made"! It refers, however, to the proselytes [whom they had made]. Then it should say, "that they *converted,*" not "that they *made.*" That is to teach you that he who brings a gentile near [to God] is as though he created him. Then it should say, "That *he* made." Why "that *they* made"? Said Rabbi Hunia: Abraham converted the men and Sarah the women.[47]

How does the Talmud describe Abraham's gift for bringing people to God?

> "He planted an *eshel* in Be'er Sheva" (Genesis 21:33). He planted an orchard with all species of delicious fruits. According to one Sage, he built an inn and he caused every passerby to call God's name. How? After they ate and drank, they would want to bless Abraham. He would say to them, "Did you eat the food that belongs to me? What you ate is God's. Thank, praise and bless Him who spoke and the world came into being."[48]

---

[44] The word *akara* (barren or infertile) with its connotations of "root" or "uproot" also suggests "*ikar,*" the "mainstay" of her family. *Genesis Rabbah* 71.2.

[45] The medical definition is any couple that does not spontaneously conceive within a year of unprotected intercourse.

[46] The *Ba'alei Tosafot* understand this as signifying that she did not even have the necessary anatomical makeup, *makom yetzirat havlad,* translated sometimes as "womb." It is also interpreted as meaning that she does not have children now, but in the future she will, as the linguistic formation *ein la* indicates in other biblical contexts.

[47] *Genesis Rabbah* 39.14.

[48] *Sotah* 10b.

Through inspiring gratitude, these progenitors of monotheism brought people to such knowledge and love of God that they were willing to trust both God and Abraham to lead them to an unknown destination.

Sarah may not have given birth, but the midrash portrays her as an immensely generative woman. Their open tent, receiving, teaching, nourishing guests does not seem to give her much time to experience the distress of her barrenness. Abraham, however, is troubled. Despite God's repeated promises to Abraham to give this land to "his seed" (Genesis 12:7, 13:14), Abraham says to God, "What will you give me? I go childless. You didn't give me seed and my servant will inherit me" (Genesis 15:2–3). Even after a new covenant is made between Abraham and God and two more promises of progeny are given, Sarah still does not conceive (Genesis 16:1). Sarah decides to give her concubine to Abraham saying, "Since God has stopped me from giving birth, come into my concubine and perhaps I will be built up through her" (Genesis 16:2). No dramatic show of emotion precedes this moment. If anything, on the simple level of the text, we hear a matter-of-fact acceptance of her situation. We also hear two themes here that recur with Rachel. First, the recognition that their barrenness was God's will. (In Rachel's case, "God judged me.") Second, a similar phrase is used as each offers her handmaiden. "Perhaps I will be built up through her."[49]

What inspires Sarah to offer Hagar to Abraham? Can we glean any understanding of her feelings from this response to her barrenness? On the face of the biblical narrative, she offers a solution to Abraham's increasing discomfort that is in accordance with the custom of her time.[50] Her problems seem to begin only after Hagar conceives. Hagar's fulfillment triggers discord in the home in a way that foreshadows Rachel's pain. In Sarah's case, the text clearly shows Hagar taunting Sarah. Ishmael also

---

[49] Sarah in Genesis 16:2. Rachel in Genesis 30:3, "That I too may be built up through her." Sarah states this before giving her handmaid. After the birth of Dan, Rachel says, "God judged me" (*dananni*).

[50] "Indeed we find in the Hammurabi Code, that preceded the patriarch Abraham, that a barren woman had the right to give her husband a hand-maiden to beget children for her." Nechama Leibowitz, *Studies in the Book of Genesis* (Jerusalem: World Zionist Organization, 1972) 154.

"mocks" (*metzahek*), interpreted by Rashi as "worships idols."[51] Sarah deals with the situation by taking decisive action to put Hagar in her place and later banishes her and Ishmael altogether. As disturbing as this story is, she is not universally condemned for her harshness. The Ramban and Radak criticize Sarah, but other commentators see her as a visionary who ensures the pure monotheism necessary in building a holy nation.[52] The Bible clearly states God's evaluation of her actions: God tells Abraham to listen to her. She is fulfilling the will of God.[53]

God sends three angels to comfort Abraham on the third day after his circumcision. When Sarah overhears one of the angels telling Abraham that her time has finally come to bear a child, she greets the news with laughter. Is it a defensive, sarcastic sort of laughter to protect her from dashed hopes if the messengers are not right? Is it bemusement because of their advanced ages? Does her laughter give us any clue about how she has felt and lived the emotional challenge of infertility? How can we explain Sarah's acceptance of her infertility and her sense of humor and fulfillment? Sarah had both her life's work and an extraordinary partnership. Were they sufficient to offset her lack?

The Open Tent

The open tent of Sarah and Abraham offers a paradigm for coping with infertility that does not requires a long wait for adoption, nor grueling months and years of fertility and hormone treatments. Abraham and Sarah enjoyed an exemplary partnership and profound spiritual union. Sarah was not emotionally "alone" in her desire for children. This exceptional partnership may have given them the strength to open their tent. However, even marriages on a less exalted level, and singles as well, can provide a home base for young people at critical moments in their lives, where they can gain life skills, find direction and be nourished in a stable context.

---

[51] Rashi on Genesis 21:9.

[52] In *Tosefta Sotah* 5:7 and *Zohar* 1.118b, Ishmael's idolatrous practices are cited; Sarah is concerned that Isaac will learn from him. Abraham and Sarah disagree about banishing him and God sides with Sarah.

[53] Genesis 21:12.

Emulating the paradigm of the open tent is delicate. Not all of us are suited to a lifestyle like Sarah's, though most of us could find more modest ways to open our lives. Can these additional and potentially problematic relationships ever ease the yearning for our own biological children? On one level, there truly is no substitute. Most couples seek altruistic options only after medical interventions fail. Yet my own life has been immeasurably enriched by "the open tent," bringing me both spiritual parents and the daughter that I never had.[54] Those of us who can't bring people into our homes can go out to them. A variety of ways abound in the world to make a meaningful, sometimes life-saving difference in children's lives.[55]

I am compelled to focus on the open tent because of real needs that beg to be met. As family structures weaken, many children are in need. There is a haunting chasm. On one side is a growing number of children in distress: children neglected through poverty, orphaned by war and AIDS, abandoned because of handicaps, or simply unwanted—urgently needing love and care. On the other side of this chasm are a multitude of infertile couples and singles desperate to have children. Why is this chasm so vast and deep? How much is ordained by God and how much of this chasm is due to our desperate fixation on biological progeny? Would the chasm be bridged by profound shifts in our attitude?

R. Moses Cordovero, the great Kabbalist, in his work *Tomer Devorah* (The Palm Tree of Deborah), writes that the image of God in which

---

[54] One Friday night, my husband brought two young women home from the *Kotel* (Wailing Wall) who wanted to experience a Shabbat meal in a Jewish home. One of them became an integral part of our family, lived with us for the time she studied in Israel and has remained part of our family, though she is now back in her home country finishing her M.A. Her birth parents love her deeply, yet they divorced when she was very young and she never had a chance to develop in certain ways. I was amazed by how open she was to us. Like a camel in an oasis, she drank in a condensed second childhood, in a family context that had both mother and father under the same roof. She flourished both in our home and in the richness of her birth home in Mexico. She straddled two worlds and honored them both. She developed strong study skills and later was accepted to one of the top universities in her country. My precious Sabina has her *Mamacita* (an affectionate way to say mother in Spanish) but I am her *imah* and she is my spiritual daughter.

[55] Such as foster care, Head Start, tutoring, volunteer work in orphanages and special needs schools and helping children at battered wife centers, etc.

humankind is created is certainly not a physical likeness. It refers instead to the attributes of God. He delineates the spiritual work in which every person can engage to cultivate his Godly image. In describing the patience and humility of God, R. Cordovero says:

> For there is no patience and no humility like that of God.... No flaw, sin, judgment nor any other quality can prevent Him from constantly providing and flowing goodness. So too, should man behave; no reason in the world should prevent him from doing good and no sin or misdeed of an unworthy person should prevent him from doing good to all who need it at all times, at every moment. Just as God provides [for all], from the horned buffalo to the lice eggs, despising no creature (for if He were to despise any creature because of its insignificance, it could not exist for even one moment), showing mercy to them all, man too should be good to all creatures, despising none. Even the smallest of small creatures should be very important in his eyes and he should be concerned about it. He should be good to all who need his goodness.[56]

To most of us, this is a tall order: to live our lives open and aware, caring for all in need who cross our path, creature or human, allowing no judgment to limit our flow of support. Although most of us are unable to open all four sides of our tent, many of us could open one flap.

Making Souls

Many of us think of fertility as an exclusively physical phenomenon. I want to preface my analysis in these concluding sections by describing a very special couple, R. Ephraim Rottenberg and his wife Chana, of Los Angeles, whom I met in my late teens. They exemplified a wholly different form of fertility. The Rebbetzin's first husband died soon after the *brit* of their first son, of an illness he contracted while imprisoned by the Nazis. Chana and her son miraculously survived years in a work camp in Mogelov, Transnistria. R. Rottenberg's first wife was not so fortunate. The Rabbi was often haunted by her memory and the image of his seven-and nine-year-old sons' brutal murder at the hands of the Nazis.

---

[56] R. Moses Cardovero, *Tomer Devorah*, beginning of part 2 (Jerusalem: Tomer Press) 1988.

After the war, the Rottenbergs met and built a second home together. The Rabbi adopted and raised the Rebbetzin's son as his own. They never mentioned their history to me until the Rabbi's final years. They weren't blessed with biological children together, but their house bustled with young people, their "spiritual children," for whom they found mates, married off, helped through major life decisions and encouraged through doctoral dissertations. They hosted many celebrations in their home, defying the grief-torn years that preceded their alliance.[57]

In the last years of his life, I would learn with the Rabbi. Invariably, as we took leave of each other, standing by the front door, he would suddenly light up and say to me, "You are really my daughter." Entering the dignity of their home, where the hasidic courts of Eastern Europe before the war still flourished, one would never know how deeply they had suffered. From their courageous example, I learned that it is possible to build a life of celebration out of the ashes.

In this exceptional home, I chanced upon a hasidic teaching that put their lives in context. My own relationship to the Rottenbergs made this teaching especially meaningful to me. This text was an abstract[58] of a beautiful hasidic commentary by R. Hayyim ben Solomon Tyrer of Czernowitz, known by the name of his Torah commentary, the *Be'er Mayyim Hayyim*.[59]

---

[57] Rolinda Shonwald, in *Recollections of a Rabbi's Daughter: The Memoirs of Rebbetzin Chana Twersky Rottenberg* (San Diego: Rottenberg Publishing, 2000) describes their life together.

[58] R. Shalom B. Kowalski and R. Yitzchak HaCohen Faigenbaum. *Humash Peninay haHasidut: Sefer Bereshit* is an anthology of commentaries culled from the entire range of hasidic literature, arranged, adapted and presented in succinct style. (Jerusalem: *Ahva: Agudat Peninay haHasidut*, 1977) 86.

[59] Hayyim ben Solomon Tyrer of Czernowitz (c. 1760–1816) was a Rabbi and hasidic leader born near Buchach, Galicia. He was a disciple of Yechiel Michael of Zloczow (one of the disciples of the Ba'al Shem Tov). He served as the Rabbi of several different communities, among them, Mogilev, Kishinev, Czernowitz and the district of Botosani. He was deeply knowledgeable in rabbinic literature and mysticism. He was a gifted preacher and an avid proponent of the hasidic movement. Under his great influence, *Hasidut* was not met with opposition in Bokovina or in Bessarabia. R. Hayyim of Chernowitz was exceptional in his love for Shabbat and the Land of Israel. He was also a gifted writer. His first book, entitled *Siduro Shel Shabbat* was the only one to be published in his lifetime. His commentary on the Pentateuch, *Be'er Mayyim Hayyim*, is praised as one of the most important hasidic

In the following commentary, he deepens the midrashic concept of the "souls that they made," defining for us a new dimension of fecundity— that of "making souls." R. Hayyim begins his work by focusing on the verse, "And Sarah was barren; she had no child" (Genesis 11:30). To explain the apparent redundancy in the verse, he refers to a talmudic dispute regarding whether both men and women are commanded to procreate, or men only: (*Yevamot* 65b)

> And God blessed them and said unto them, "Be fruitful and multiply and fill the earth and subdue it." (Genesis 1:28)

The Mishnah states, "The man is commanded to be fruitful and multiply and not the woman." R. Yohanan ben Baruka disagrees, claiming both of them are commanded, because the Torah says, "And God blessed *them* and God said unto *them*, 'Be fruitful and multiply and fill the earth.'"

R. Yohanan ben Baruka has a case—the fact that the text is in the plural seems to indicate clearly that both the man and the woman are commanded to "be fruitful and multiply and fill the earth." On what basis do the Mishnah and the majority of later halakhic (legal) authorities form their opinions that only the man is commanded to be fruitful and multiply? There are three major approaches.

The first is that the commandment to be fruitful and multiply is *not* based on the utterance of *pru urvu* to Adam and Eve.[60] A second approach describes a range of differences in men's and women's natures and social realities.[61] The third is a general principle articulated by R. Meir Simcha

---

works written. *Sha'ar haTefilah* and *Eretz haHayyim* were written after he immigrated to Tzfat, Israel.

[60] One line of argument is that this utterance to Adam and Eve was a blessing and not a commandment. Most commentators say that the actual commandment was given to the sons of Noah after the flood (Genesis 9:1, 7) or to Jacob (Genesis 35:11). Cf. Rashi on *Ketubot* 5a and on Genesis 9:7, Tosafot on *Yevamot* 65b, Nahmanides on Genesis 9:7 and Marasha on *Sanhedrin* 59b. The Be'er Mayyim Hayyim formulates a variation of the argument in *Yevamot* 65b, attributing the commandment to the second part of the utterance to Adam and Eve, "Fill the earth and conquer it."

[61] In biblical society, one could solve the problem of a woman's infertility by the husband taking a second wife, without breaking up pre-existing family units. A woman did not have this option. Another argument focuses on the fourth word in the passage: "'and conquer' (or subdue) is applied to one whose business it is to subdue rather than to be subdued." *Yevamot* 65b, reiterated by the Be'er Mayyim Hayyim.

haKohen of Dvinsk, that "the Torah does not impose upon Israel burdens too difficult for a person to bear.... Women, whose lives are jeopardized by conception and birth, were not enjoined."[62]

The first explanation, based on *Yevamot* 65b, forms the structural basis for the Be'er Mayyim Hayyim's stance that "be fruitful and multiply" and "fill the earth and conquer it" are two different directives. "However, the commandment for physical progeny in its simple meaning, to give birth to children for the sake of the continuation of the human race, is brought later in the verse '*and fill the earth and subdue it.*'"[63] Since the Torah is never redundant, the two phrases must mean two different things.

The Be'er Mayyim Hayyim agrees with the majority legal opinion, yet he still asks the obvious question: What is it that both man and woman are commanded to do if "be fruitful and multiply" does not refer to physical procreation?

In classic hasidic fashion, R. Hayyim starts by citing a dispute and then proceeds to offer a metaphorical interpretation of it, which leads to an integration of the conflicting opinions in a "mystical message." The presence of layers of text—biblical, talmudic, mystical and hasidic—is not evident in a straight translation, so after quoting his teaching, I will "unfurl" its message, giving conceptual background which will make these layers more accessible:

> One has to explain the meaning of, "God said unto *them*, 'Be fruitful and multiply.'" Indeed, there are two kinds of birth, one in the material world, i.e., physical sons and daughters, to increase their offspring like the dust of the earth, because God created the world to be inhabited. The second [type of birth] is giving birth to souls in the upper world through *mitzvoth* and good deeds, from which come the souls of

---

A third explanation is, "The command need not be addressed to woman because her instinct for childbirth is already strong enough; Eve was so called because she was the mother of all living." R. Jakobovitz (Julius Pruess, Biblisch-Talmudische Medizin) 479. See David M. Feldman, *Marital Relations, Birth Control and Abortion in Jewish Law* (NY: Schocken, 1978) 53–56.

[62] *Meshekh Hokhmah* on Genesis 9:7, quoted by David S. Shapiro in *Jewish Bio Ethics,* F. Roser and J.D. Bleich eds. (NY: Sanhedrin Press, 1979) 65.

[63] *Be'er Mayyim Hayyim, parashat Noah,* on *Vetehi Sarai akarah,* 99.

converts and *ba'aleh teshuvah*[64] as we know from the words of our Master the Ari, may his memory be a blessing. When a man and a woman couple with one intention, for the sake of God's name, with fear and love, with intention that finds favor before "the One who spoke and the world came to be," and the woman does not become pregnant from this union, then these souls are born. This is how Abraham converted the men and Sarah the women, as the Sages say (*Genesis Rabbah* 39), "because they gave birth to these souls and it was said about them '...and the souls that they made in Haran.'" They *mamash* (actually) made, because the souls were from them. In this, the woman is equal to the man; she also has to see to it that her righteous actions cause the creation of new souls, because those good deeds are the primary "progeny" of the righteous.[65] So when God says to both of them, "Be fruitful and multiply," it means this kind of birth. In this [form of procreation] both of them are equally commanded in this [spiritual fecundity] to increase souls in the upper world.[66]

Remarkably, here the Be'er Mayyim Hayyim uses a teaching from the *Zohar*[67] to concretize the midrash's metaphorical understanding of "the souls that they made." He goes beyond the text we explored earlier from *Genesis Rabbah* that defined these souls as converts.

Questions abound regarding these souls. Who are they? Where do they live? Did the holiness of the union of Sarah and Abraham resonate so deeply in the world that the souls of many people around them were suddenly awakened to God? Or were these totally new souls, never before

---

[64] Literally "masters of return," which refers to Jews distanced from traditional observance who "come back" to a life of Torah and *mitzvot*.

[65] *Genesis Rabbah* 30: "The real progeny of righteous people are their good deeds."

[66] *Be'er Mayyim Hayyim*, ibid. The translation is mine. I would like to thank R. Meir Sendor, R. Alon Goshen-Gottstein and R. Menachem Kallus for helping me gain a deeper understanding of the piece and with adapting the translation.

[67] *Zohar* 168a. Rav Metifta said, "It was written, 'Sarai was barren; she had no child' (Genesis 12:5). Since they say that Sarai is barren, therefore we know that she does not have a child. Why is it written that she has no child? "So," said Rav Metifta, "she did not give birth to a child, but she did give birth to souls. Through the attachment and desire of these two righteous people, they were giving birth to the souls of the converts the whole time that they were in Haran, in the same way that the righteous do in Gan Eden. As it is written, 'and the souls that they made in Haran;' they actually made souls."

created? What does it mean to literally "make souls"?[68] The Talmud says that there are three partners in the creation of a human being: the mother and father contribute the physical components of the body and God contributes the soul.[69] Is the Be'er Mayyim Hayyim claiming that Abraham and Sarah, two humans, did the work of God?

A complex mystical worldview underlies the making of souls. Marriage, in Kabbalah, is considered "one of the most sacred mysteries." Every true marriage is a symbolic realization of the union of God and the *Shekhinah*.[70] The attention to the importance of holiness in marital relations is not limited to the *Zohar*; it permeates classical Jewish legal literature as well.[71] Physical procreation is not the exclusive purpose of conjugal life. Great care is taken to define the equally important *mitzvah* of *onah* (the wife's conjugal rights).[72] These laws encourage a union of heart and soul as well as of body and ensure that this union does not

---

[68] The "making of souls" is an extensive topic in kabbalistic thought. In R. Hayyim Vital's record of teachings by his master, R. Isaac Luria, he describes a range of practices that enable the making of souls. These practices require *kavannah* (full intentionality) for the sanctification and unification of the name of God through prayer. See *Sha'ar haPesukim* (Jerusalem, 1912) 10c, *Etz Hayyim*, gate 39 ch. 11, and *Ta'amei haMitzvot, parashat Behar*.

For creating unifications through the way one eats, see *Sha'ar haMitzvot, parashat Ekev* 38a–45b. Regarding conscious dreaming and the practice of conjugal relations on Shabbat Eve, see *Olat Tamid* (Jerusalem, 1997) 116b–117a. This particular practice appears only in an older edition of *Olat Tamid* (Jerusalem, 1907, 53a) and in no other recensions. Here, R. Hayyim Vital states that **new** souls descend only on Shabbat Eve. The source of the Lurianic teachings is the *Zohar*. See particularly *Zohar* 2, 166b and *Zohar* 3, 167b–168a, where it is said that the making of souls is the work of the righteous in the Garden of Eden. My thanks to R. Menachem Kallus for access to these sources.

[69] *Niddah* 31.

[70] Gershom G. Scholem, *Major Trends in Jewish Mysticism* (NY: Schocken, 1946) 235.

[71] Classic sources for the laws of *onah* (providing for the timely and intimate needs of one's wife) include: *Ketubbot* 5, Rambam, *Sefer haMitzvot*, prohibitive *mitzvah* #262, *Mishneh Torah, Hilkhot Ishut* 12:2, the Tur and the *Shulhan Arukh* in *Oreh Hayyim* 240 and *Even haEzer* 25 and 76. In English, see Avraham Peretz Friedman, *Marital Intimacy: A Traditional Jewish Approach* (NJ: Jason Aronson, 1996).

[72] The *mitzvah* of *onah* is based on the biblical verse, "He shall not diminish her conjugal rights" (Exodus 21:10).

degenerate into the mere satisfaction of physical needs. Perhaps righteous couples can create souls precisely because they live by the Torah's goal for marital intimacy: to be a finely tuned meeting of two souls within two bodies, which increases the couple's profound bond through the deep respect and love they build as they unite physically.

Making Vessels for the Souls

The way to conceive righteous children is discussed in a variety of sources. Desire is not seen as an impediment to holiness; our tradition lauds its intentional enhancement. "Only by increasing the desire [of one spouse for another] during intimacy [does one ensure that] one's children will be righteous."[73] A well-known medieval source describes in intimate detail the role of the parents' imagination and consciousness at the moment of conception and how this affects the holiness of the soul that is drawn down.

> A man needs to cleanse his thoughts and purify them while having sexual relations and not to think of anything sinful or lustful, but only to think of holy and pure things. He must turn his thoughts away from any wrong and improper thought and he should contemplate the pure and saintly righteous [people], because these thoughts will take hold of the seed and give it their form during intercourse. He should also appease his wife's mind and bring her joy and prepare her and draw her to matters that gladden the heart, so she will consent to the pure and refined thoughts. They should be united in the *mitzvah*, because then their thought will be united, the Divine Presence will dwell between them and they will give birth to a child in accordance with the pure form that they envision.[74]

In other words, the couple draws down a soul that unites with the physical embryo. The purity and loftiness of the soul will depend on the level of pure *kavannah* (intention) that they have. This teaching refers to the

---

[73] R. Yehudah haHasid, *Sefer Hasidim*, 362 (early thirteenth century).

[74] *Iggeret haKodesh* originally attributed to R. Moshe Ben Nahman (the Ramban), although later scholars generally agree that it is not his linguistic style. *Kitvei haRamban*, 331–37, collected from manuscripts by R. Hayyim Chavel (Jerusalem: Mossad HaRav Kook, 1964). The translation is mine.

sexual act that leads to physical conception, demonstrating the effect of our spiritual consciousness on the formation of the new soul.

The Be'er Mayyim Hayyim addresses a related issue. What happens if this level of holy union is attained, but the couple does not conceive a physical child? I understand him to be saying that when a couple unites at this level of holiness, real spiritual fruit results, hence the capacity to literally "make souls," whether or not they make bodies. Clearly, not all acts of intercourse result in physical conception. A woman may be pregnant or nursing, infertile or post-menopausal. The couple may nevertheless have come together in an extraordinary way that drew a holy soul into the world. What happens to this soul if it can not unite with their seed? The Be'er Mayyim Hayyim is implying that no soul is lost. Once this soul is made, it enters either a righteous convert or a seeking Jew and becomes that new soul within him. That person then becomes awakened to living for God on a whole new level.[75]

The Be'er Mayyim Hayyim's mystical synthesis allows him to solve eloquently the dispute cited at the beginning of his text. The commandment to be fruitful was clearly said to both Adam and Eve and is understood as a commandment to all of humanity. The talmudic discourse in *Yevamot* does not definitely resolve the issue, but most later halakhic works make it clear that "the man is commanded to procreate and not the woman." The Be'er Mayyim Hayyim resolves this by impressing upon us the dimension of procreation in which both are equally commanded: that of making souls.

It is moving to contemplate the power of loving relationships. The creation of love in the world does not just dissipate, but has reverberating effects in the world. Based on the integrity with which the couple lives their life—their *mitzvot*, prayer, learning, charitable acts together and purity of intention in their moments of intimacy—they come to a spiritual reciprocity. This continues to have an impact in the world and comes to rest in those who need and have merited to be helped from above.[76]

---

[75] This profound subject is beyond the scope of my discussion here. It is developed by R. Moses Cordovero in *Pardes Rimonim, Sha'ar haNeshamah*, section 3.

[76] Ibid.

The Be'er Mayyim Hayyim's approach suggests a sacred bond that is fruitful whether or not the couple conceive, a union that fulfills a wider vista of fecundity. Perhaps through his teaching, the dehumanization of sexual union that often accompanies fertility treatment can be lessened and marital relations imbued with holiness and full partnership. The Be'er Mayim Hayyim reminds us all—whether married or single, or with or without biological children—that through our righteous thoughts, prayers and actions we can increase Godliness in this world. This is the ultimate intent of the commandment to be fruitful: "To increase the image and the likeness of God in the world."[77]

---

[77] *Be'er Mayyim Hayyim, ibid.,* 99.

The Daughters of Tzlafchad: Towards a Methodology of Attitude Around Women's Issues

Sarah Idit (Susan) Schneider

We are blessed with a Torah of timeless truths, which means that every individual can find his or her own very personal story told somewhere in its sequence of words and verses. And since there is a one-to-one correspondence between root-souls and letters of the Torah (there being 600,000 of each) it follows, says R. Zadok haKohen, that each person is especially connected to the passage containing the letter that is the root of his or her particular soul.[1] And since the stories of the Torah spiral through history, each *generation* is also reliving some particular step in the Israelite's forty-two stage journey from Egypt to the Holy Land.

A growing number of Orthodox women are struggling to reconcile two aspirations which are not easily joined. One is the longing for marriage and children, the other a passion for study and more active participation in communal life. Successful role models are sparse, and for many communities the impulse itself is questionable. Is it a holy urge, or one prompted by secular values unsupported by spiritual truths?

The question is real for any woman who seeks to live by spiritual law and who trusts the Torah as her guide. One method of resolution is to identify the scriptural passage that holds the archetype of this dilemma and examine its teachings for relevant advice. The obvious place to start is with the daughters of Tzlafchad who present an unusual expression of femininity that draws unanimous positive regard. The encounter between these women and Moshe evokes God's unqualified praise.

---

[1] *Dover Tzeddek*, 100; *Tzidkat haTzaddik*, s. 114 and many other places.

A petition was presented by the daughters of Tzlafchad...and they stood before Moshe, Eleazar the priest, the princes and the entire community at the door of the Tent of Meeting with the following petition, "Our father died in the desert...without leaving any sons. Why should our father's name be disadvantaged in his family merely because he had no son? Give to us a portion of land along with our father's brothers." Moshe brought their case before God.

God spoke to Moshe saying, "The daughters of Tzlafchad have a just claim. Give them a hereditary portion of land alongside their father's brothers. Let their father's hereditary property thus pass over to them. Speak to the Israelites and tell them that if a man dies and has no sons, his hereditary property shall pass over to his daughter...."
(Numbers 27:1–9)[2]

There are many teachings in this passage, relevant both to women seeking halakhic support for the changes they are experiencing and to the Rabbis who are ruling on their questions. The passage suggests a methodology of attitude that if consciously adopted by both parties, will keep peace below and draw grace from on high. This article explores the subject from both perspectives.

Guidelines for Petitioners

I.

When the daughters of Tzlafchad heard that the land was being divided to the tribes but not to the women, they convened to discuss the matter. They said, "God's mercy and compassion is not like the compassion of mankind. Mankind favors men over women. God is not that way, His compassion is on men and women alike....
(*Yalkut Shimoni, Pinhas* 27; *Sifri* 27.1)

They identified the underlying spiritual principle being violated. Deep inside something did not feel right and they named it. Now they were working for truth and a higher good. This gave them the strength to persist despite inner and outer resistance.

---

[2] Translation by Aryeh Kaplan, *The Living Torah* (NY: Moznaim, 1981).

II.

> The daughters of Tzlafchad were wise women for they presented their
> petition at the right time.
> (*Bava Batra* 119b; *Deuteronomy Rabbah* 21.11)

They did not raise theoretical issues. Rather, they waited until the moment
of practical decision to speak their piece. We learn from them that the
criteria of truth are twofold: its content must be accurate and it must be
spoken at the "right time." When both conditions are met, the heavens and
earth will open to receive it.[3]

Each moment comes with its own lights and possibilities of transformation. The whole inner structure of metaphysical reality shifts and alters
through the cycles of time: spheres align and channels of possibility open
and close, appear and disappear.

The daughters of Tzlafchad understood the secret of timing. It is a
deeply intuitive wisdom. From their example, we derive an essential
principle of social action: one must wait till the moment when an injustice
or wrong attitude actually impacts upon the physical plane and blocks the
path of truth for someone who is ready, now, to travel that path.

The reasons for this "law" are threefold:

A. It might be that the "offending principle" will dissipate on its own from
other factors, alleviating a needless waste of time and energy dedicated to a
project that would run perfectly well unaided (while in the meantime no
actual harm is done).

B. It might be that the individual, who at an earlier point felt oppressed by
her anticipation of encountering the offending concept, will as her life
unfolds, arrive exactly where she needs to go, naturally and organically,
via a different path. Not because she accepted limited options or avoided
confrontation, but because the issue became irrelevant to the actuality of
her life.

---

[3] *Ken Dovrot* (an organization of Orthodox women teachers), *Foundation Principles*;
an unpublished manuscript.

C. The actual moment of contact marks the point in the structure of time when channels align to facilitate change in that particular matter.

III.

> The daughters of Tzlafchad were learned women. They presented their petition in a logical and halakhically sophisticated manner. (*Bava Batra* 119b; *Deuteronomy Rabbah* 21.11)

After identifying the larger spiritual frame, they supported their petition with halakhic principles and precedents. They built an argument that was true to the letter *and* spirit of authentic discourse.

They were not like ordinary plaintiffs who simply present a question in an orderly fashion. Their petition followed a razor sharp line of reasoning that incorporated all the laws and relevant principles and even formulated the proper decision. This is why Scripture says, "And Moshe brought their *judgment* before God," their *judgment*, not their question, for their petition included the legal argument *and* its ruling. (*Anaf Yosef; Ein Ya'akov; Bava Batra* 119b)

IV.

> They trusted in the Merciful One, the Master of the world...and came before Moshe...and the entire congregation at the entrance to the *Mishkan.* (*Targum Yonaton*, Numbers 27:1)

The word the Targum uses for *trust* is from the same root as the word, "to cleanse," רחץ. They gave the matter up to God and cleansed themselves of attachment to anything less than truth. Although they hoped for a favorable outcome, they *didn't* want it if it was not God's highest will for them and for all concerned.

This is the most critical step in the whole process. The purity of one's will for truth[4] determines the success of all subsequent stages. The more one renounces personal agenda and forgoes demands for specific outcomes, the higher are the lights of divine assistance one pulls down to support the cause.

---

[4] Truth is here defined as the most spiritually productive outcome under the circumstances, regardless of its outward appearance.

To become clean (רחץ) is to surrender *all* control, "entrusting (ירחיצו) the entire matter to the Merciful One, the Master of the world." Contamination at this stage will manifest as opposition at latter points in the process. While these obstacles may or may not be surmountable, they will definitely irritate.

In fact this practice of surrendering attachment to a particular outcome, or to anything less than the truth, must accompany the entire project. It marks the difference between one who does God's work and one who does political work, though their actions may be the same. At periodic points in the day, one should affirm his or her commitment through prayer, "God, not my will but yours be done. If my labors serve you, please prosper their path and if they don't, please block them and let me know as gently as possible how to adjust my course."

V.

Although reluctant to appear in public, Tzlafchad's daughters overcame their natural modesty because their question was fundamental. (*Tiferet Tzion*, Numbers 27:2)

The daughters of Tzlafchad were holding an actual piece of the written Torah, and their mission was to get it accepted into the text. There is no holier privilege than to reveal a Torah law that will influence the behavior of Jews till the end of time. The explication of beautiful insights is always a blessed task, but to originate one of the 613 *mitzvot* is the highest honor accorded a soul.

Though the written Torah is fixed and final, the Oral Torah is alive and evolving. Each generation has new technologies and cultural phenomena with halakhic implications that have not been explored. The process of formulating questions and generating halakhic discourse is the life source of the Jewish people. Spirit touches matter as the Torah enclothes itself in the bodies of Jews who live by the contemporary applications of Sinaitic law.

Every Jew of every generation is also carrying a piece of the Torah[5] and each of them, too, must discover how to insert it into the evolving body of law and teachings called the Oral Tradition. The daughters of Tzlafchad are role models for this labor.

VI.

> **Daughters**: Give us a portion of the land along with our father's brothers.
>
> **Moshe**: It is impossible for a daughter to inherit.
>
> **Daughters**: Why?
>
> **Moshe**: You are women.
>
> **Daughters**: Then let our mother enter into *yibbum*[6] and conceive an inheritor that way.
>
> **Moshe**: Impossible. Since once there are children, *yibbum* is not possible.
>
> **Daughters**: You are contradicting yourself, Moshe. Either we are not seed and the obligation of *yibbum* applies to our mother, or we are seed and can inherit the land ourselves.
>
> At that moment they convinced Moshe. When he heard the justice of their complaint he immediately presented their case before God.
> (*Yalkut Shimoni* 27)

The daughters of Tzlafchad did not back down when encountering resistance. Moshe said "no" repeatedly before he conceded to the logic of their position.

The system does not shift easily; that is its strength. It selects changes that have a momentum of belief and purity of intention that can propel them through layers of resistance. In this way, the changes themselves are also purified in the process and only those that are clean and strong get

---

[5] According to R. Zadok haKohen, every Jew has some piece of the Oral Torah that only becomes revealed through his or her life (*Likutei Ma'amarim*, 80–81; *Yisrael Kedoshim* 152). Sometimes this is an actual law, but more often a particular application of a law that only comes up in the singular circumstances of one's life. Some unique facet of truth and divine beauty is pressed forth through the configuration of forces and events that comprises that life.

[6] *Yibbum* describes the situation of a woman whose husband has died without fathering any children. In that case, the brother of the deceased marries the widow and their first child is considered the spiritual child of the dead brother, rather than the child of the living father.

through. Similarly, a convert is refused three times. Only candidates who are driven by the non-negotiable truth of their soul will find the motivation to overcome the obstacles and claim their place among the Jewish people.

Every new concept or halakhic innovation is a "convert" of sorts. A new spark is seeking entry into the community of Israel. It, too, will be refused at least three times, but if its proponents are strong and of clean heart, it *will* find its way in, for no spark is ever permanently exiled. Every truth will find its way back to Torah.

VII.

> "The daughters of Tzlafchad speak rightly...." Rashi explains that God was teaching through this statement that, "'[As the daughters of Tzlafchad spoke] so the section is written before Me on high.' This informs us that their eye saw what the eye of Moshe did not see."
> (Numbers 27:7; *Targum Yonaton* 27:7; *Yalkut Shimoni, Pinhas* 27; *Sifri Numbers* 27.7)

Moshe is the greatest prophet who ever lived and yet the daughters of Tzlafchad saw something he did not see.[7] Each soul comes into the world with some specialty. Whatever its level in the hierarchy of enlightened (or unenlightened) beings, there is some piece of truth that only it knows and only it can bring into the world.

A creative tension develops between the people and its leaders. On the one hand, we defer to the wisdom of our elders, yet on the other we *may* know something that they do not because it is *our* piece of the Torah. In that case we have no choice but to engage in respectful dialogue, following the model of the daughters of Tzlafchad, honoring the system, honoring our truth and finding a way to transform personal wisdom into Oral Torah. There is no other option.

---

[7] There are differing opinions about whether Moshe, in fact, knew the judgment but chose to consult God directly on the matter for other reasons (*Deuteronomy Rabbah* 21.14; *Targum Yonaton* 27:5; *Torah Temimah* 27:5). Regardless of whether Moshe knew the judgment already, God wanted the ruling to come down in the daughters' merit and so the matter was suspended until they initiated its discussion.

VIII.

> The daughters of Tzlafchad were righteous women (צדקניות). They
> did not marry until they were forty years old. They waited for suitors
> that were worthy of them. (*Bava Batra* 119b; *Deuteronomy Rabbah*
> 21.11; *Yalkut Shimoni, Pinhas* 27)

Every choice has consequences and when the costs outweigh the gains, an
option becomes less feasible. Sometimes, however, though the stakes are
high there is no choice, for integrity requires *that* path.

God designs each soul with specific talents, for He wants certain revelations to come through it. He then implants a drive for self-actualization
which compels it, from the inside, to fulfill its mission.

The daughters of Tzlafchad developed themselves in certain ways that
would narrow their options of appropriate marriage partners. Their
exceptional intellect and strength of integrity put them in a category that
was not easily matched. And yet, our Sages call them righteous *because*
they were willing to pay this price for authenticity, *because* they refused to
compromise the precious gifts that God had given them.

Guidelines for Rabbis

The story of the daughters of Tzlafchad also has lessons for the Rabbis
who are the gatekeepers responsible for selecting which changes come in
and which are shut out, which are Torah and which are not. Some of these
teachings are discussed in *midrashim* and commentaries, while others are
surmised by the absence of negative comment.

I.

Conspicuously absent is *any* criticism from Moshe himself, as well as from
later commentaries, regarding the gender appropriateness of their action.
No one even hints that they stepped out of line when they came before the
entire congregation, publicly presenting their petition before Moshe and
the elders.

II.

Also conspicuously absent is any sign that the Rabbis felt personally threatened by their assertiveness or intellectual prowess.

III.

The contrast is poignant. While the men were calling for mutiny, abandoning Israel and preparing to turn back to Egypt (Numbers 14:4),[8] the daughters of Tzlafchad kept their sights forward and asked for their own piece of the land. Moshe inquired after their strength of faith and they said,

> When the people are abandoning Your Torah (i.e., the men turning back to Egypt) that is the time to intensify one's commitment to service of God. (Psalms 119:126)[9]

The midrash then cites an example that supports the principle from Psalms 119:126 cited by the daughters of Tzlafchad. The story concerns a young Jewish woman captive who became the maidservant of a Syrian general.[10] Her knowledge of all the detailed laws of leprosy enabled her to engineer a great public sanctification of God, His people and His Torah. The midrash wonders how this woman became so educated in such an esoteric matter of law, especially at a time when even the men had abandoned learning. The midrash answers that she learned in her father's house:

> When the people are abandoning the Torah [one makes use of every resource at one's disposal, even presumably the women] to strengthen

---

[8] After Aharon's death the men despaired and cried, "*Give us* a [leader] and we will go back to Egypt..." (Numbers 14:4). It was in response to this crisis that the daughters of Tzlafchad said, "*Give us* a portion in the land...." The midrash contrasts the two requests, both stated in the imperative. The men are betraying faith with these words; the women are asserting it.

[9] This is a well-known halakhic principle called, "emergency measure." Its prooftext is Psalms 119:126 which reads literally, "It is a time to do for God, they are voiding Your Torah." The verse is sometimes also translated as, "It is a time to do for God by suspending [a *mitzvah* of] the Torah" (as an emergency measure to assure the survival of the people as a whole).

[10] II Kings 5.

the remnant that holds strong to the service of God. (Psalms 119:126, but inverted; *Sifri Zutra* 27.1; *Yalkut Shimoni, Pinhas* 27)[11]

Since we are now in a time of national crisis with Jews assimilating at a frighteningly rapid rate, the faith and intellectual strength of women is a resource we cannot squander. There are women in this generation who are deeply rooted in love and fear of God, and who possess a strength of mind and love of Torah that can be of great service to the Jewish people. This midrash implies that in such circumstances, "It is a time to act for God" and empower women wherever *halakhah* permits. If a law is clear and closed, so be it. But if the law has room to expand, then the midrash argues for empowering women to serve their people with *all* of their God given gifts.

IV.

The daughters of Tzlafchad began their petition to Moshe with the following words, "Our father died in the wilderness…he died in his sin…." (Numbers 27:3)

The *midrashim* bring several opinions about which of the sins recounted in the Israelites' forty-year sojourn through the desert was the one that caused Tzlafchad's demise. The *Zohar* presents an opinion based on the equivalency of two words, מדבר (desert) and מדבר (to speak). It then substitutes the latter for the former and rereads the verse above not as, "Our father died in the desert," but rather, "Our father died as a result of his speech (בדיבור)…. He didn't guard his mouth and spoke improperly against Moshe…."[12] Consequently Tzlafchad's daughters were afraid that Moshe might hold a grudge against them and not rule objectively because of his bias… Moshe understood their concern…and brought their case before God…instead of deciding on his own" (*Zohar* 3.205b, based on Hebrew translation, *Matok miDvash* by R. Daniel Parish).

---

[11] This is Psalms 119:126 inverted.

[12] Numbers 21:2–6: "And they journeyed from Mount Hor by way of the Sea of Reeds…and the soul of the people was much discouraged because of the way. And the people spoke against God *and against Moshe*…. And the Lord sent venomous serpents among the people."

Moshe was a perfectly transparent channel of prophetic transmission. All other prophets and Sages have some degree of ego density that distorts their perceptions of reality, even if only slightly. For Moshe alone is this not so. The *Zohar* goes on to explain:

> The daughters of Tzlafchad did not realize that because "Moshe was the humblest man on all the earth,"[13] unlike the rest of mankind, he would not hold a grudge and his conflict with Tzlafchad would not have affected his legal judgment. (Ibid.)

The *Zohar*, however, does not reproach the daughters of Tzlafchad for doubting Moshe on this matter, rather the opposite. It goes on to present their behavior as a model for all generations to emulate when a plaintiff fears that a judge lacks impartiality. Moshe, too, understood their concern and accommodated it. The *Zohar* praises him specifically for this behavior.

Our generation finds itself in a complicated knot. The predicament of women seeking more active participation in study and community life raises halakhic questions about the permissibility of their proposed innovations. And just as Moshe balked at the prospect of introducing a change into the system that seemed to have no clear precedent, how much more so is this true, and rightly so, for Rabbis today who have no direct prophetic connection. The difficulty runs deeper still, for the repercussions of women's strivings are not simply halakhic. They also affect (even if only slightly) the traditional role divisions of men and women in the Orthodox Jewish community. For example, the systematic study of Talmud until very recently was a field of expertise and role only available to men.

The problem is that since these questions carry such deeply personal implications, both for the community as a whole and each individual within it, all parties are at least theoretically biased. For the plaintiff, this bias is self-understood. He or she approaches the courts requesting a favorable judgment. There is no standard of objectivity required of the plaintiff.

For judges, this matter is more complicated. The general rule is that anyone with personal interests in a case should absent himself from its ruling panel. And so Moshe did exactly that when the daughters of

---

[13] Numbers 12:3.

Tzlafchad approached with their appeal.

For the particular questions discussed here, however, there is no one who will not be personally affected by their rulings. And, unlike Moshe, we cannot simply turn to God and request a heavenly verdict direct from the Source. There is no option but to admit the problem and minimize it wherever possible.

The Talmud provides a possible solution. It presents a method of halakhic analysis that enables its practitioners to relinquish their preconceptions by entering a place of *truly* "not knowing" what the correct verdict should be. And then, from that place of *not-knowing*, they formulate their ruling:

> Moshe said to God, "Master of the Universe, tell me the *halakhah* about...?" God answered, "The *halakhah* is whatever the majority decides. If the majority acquits, so it is; if the majority convicts, so it is." *This is in order that all of the Torah's possible interpretations of the question be elucidated*, i.e., forty-nine that prove the object's purity, forty-nine that prove its impurity.... As it says, "The words of God are pure. Silver refined in a furnace upon the ground, purified *sevens of* times [i.e., 7x7=49]."[14] (JT *Sanhedrin* 21a–b)

Since we have no Sanhedrin or formal court of Sages, each Rabbi must do this work on his own. The Talmud describes a halakhic master as one who can formulate forty-nine perfectly logical *and compelling* reasons to permit and forty-nine to forbid.[15] Significantly, it does not present this as an intellectual exercise, but rather as a heart-centered one:

> Seek to acquire an understanding heart that hears the words that prove unclean and the words that prove clean, those that prohibit and those that permit, those that disqualify and those that declare fit.
> (*Hagigah* 3b)

Maharsha adds: "And then, *with your discerning heart*, find the ruling that is best suited to serve as practical *halakhah*."

---

[14] Psalms 12:7.

[15] "...R. Akiva had a distinguished disciple who knew how to interpret the Torah in forty-nine aspects of uncleanness and forty-nine aspects of cleanness, not one reason being the same as another.... Whence did he learn all these? He was learned in the Scriptures, expert in the Mishnah, distinguished in Talmud and brilliant in aggadah" (*Sofrim* 16.7).

A person who fulfills the spirit of this advice, even if not to its letter (i.e., not necessarily forty-nine on each side) must reach a point where he or she truly doesn't know which path holds God's truth. It is there, in the place of *not-knowing*, that bias melts and purification occurs. Until that point, even with a long list of pros and cons, one is still "deciding on one's own," which is *not* what Moshe did. By touching the place of *not-knowing* there is at least the possibility of "bringing the matter before God" on whatever level we are capable in this generation. And then, from the place of true *not-knowing*, one selects the most spiritually productive solution for *these* circumstances and *these* times. And so the Talmud closes its discussion of this subject with the verse, "The words of God are...purified by [the practice of deciding *halakhah* through the methodology of generating] sevens [of options on each side], מזוקק שבעתים":

> When are the words of Torah heard as they were intended? When the one who speaks them formulates his ruling after having integrated the opinions of both sides. (Maharsha on *Hagiga* 3a)

Not only is the content of their decision conveyed, but even more, the purity of their intention and humility of their process will speak to the hearts of all who hear them (נשמע כתקנן).

V.

> The Torah is teaching us the power of the *tzaddik*. The daughters of Tzlafchad presented their petition to Moshe...and Moshe prayed to God to concede to their request and to permit them a portion in the land. God agreed to Moshe's prayer as the midrash says,[16] "Moshe commanded and God obeyed him." (*Me'or veShemesh, Masai*)

Moshe so empathized with their dilemma and respected their love of the land that he actually prayed for a favorable verdict. The midrash implies that it was Moshe's prayer itself that actually drew down the positive decision.

If women felt that Rabbis had this kind of empathy with their yearning for more formal study or fuller participation in community life, any

---

[16] *Exodus Rabbah* 21.2.

decision (even a bitter one) would still also be sweet. When, instead, they are admonished for their urge to express themselves in ways that are deeply rooted in Torah but not in keeping with the traditional female role, an adversary relationship develops. At that point every option brings loss.

Moshe prayed to be able to give them a favorable verdict. As much as he wanted truth, he wanted to share something with them that was an objectively good thing and for which he himself longed (i.e., the land) but which was not, under normal circumstances, available to women.

The Torah is teaching a powerful lesson to the Rabbis of today. If they are to imitate Moshe (which they must strive to do) then they must find a place of deep and authentic compassion for the women who approach them with halakhic petitions. Their empathy should be so compelling that it moves them to prayer:

> Let it be Your will Hashem my God...that Your *halakhah* permit
> a favorable judgment, a judgment that will enable the fullest ex-
> pression of service for all involved.

Only after touching this place of genuine empathy with the petitioner should the Rabbi begin his halakhic research.

The incident of the daughters of Tzlafchad occurs on the steppes of Moav, the last stop on the Israelites' forty-two stage journey from Egypt to the Holy Land. Thus its reenactment in the 6,000-year scale of history will be one of the last developments before the messianic age. The exact time correlations are not clear, though we are fast approaching the end of days which, apparently, must begin before the year 6,000 (244 years from now).[17] This means that if we are not yet collectively at the "steppes of Moav" we are very close, and the glow of its dawning light is certainly present. It is therefore no surprise that a growing number of women in this generation identify with the daughters of Tzlafchad and find their own stories, dilemmas and yearnings mirrored in their tale.[18]

---

[17] *Sanhedrin* 97b. See *Leshem, Drush Eitz haDa'at, siman* 13, for a lengthy and complex discussion concerning the Talmud's translation of "6 days" into 6 millenniums.

[18] This would also explain why many Rabbis today have a natural empathy for these questions.

The story of the daughters of Tzlafchad presents a methodology of attitude that if practiced in good faith by all parties, will draw the unfolding of God's highest will into the halakhic discourse generated by our times.

The Voice in the Shofar: A Defense of Deborah

Yael Unterman

I. The Meaning Behind the Shofar

The blowing of the shofar on Rosh Hashanah is one of the most powerful experiences in the rituals of the Jewish yearly cycle. To me, there seems to be something very raw about standing together in silence, allowing blast after blast of this strange, primitive hornblowing to wash over us.

Although we are used to functioning in "hearing mode" in synagogue, listening as we do every week to the prayer service or the reading of the Torah, this is the only time we are commanded to listen very carefully to sound that is non-verbal. Because it is wordless, this sound succeeds in bypassing the higher centers of our brain, striking at a point of deep emotion within us.[1] On a primary level, it also allows or even forces each individual to think, feel and interpret the sound without outside guidance, as he or she sees fit.[2]

Nevertheless, the Sages did not simply leave it up to the individual to fill this void; rather, they suggested a rich spectrum of symbolic meanings and associations for the shofar blowing. Some of them incorporate seminal events or concepts in the life of the Jewish nation and others call

* I would like to thank the women of AMIT for providing the initial impetus for this article, originally given as a *shiur*, and whose comments proved valuable in its development.

[1] R. Nahman of Bratslav, in *Likkutei Moharan* 3, comments that he who hears a tune from an evil person, will find it difficult afterwards to serve God. This was explained to me once as referring to the ability of music without words to bypass our rational minds and enter straight into the heart.

[2] It is perhaps not coincidental that the siren has been chosen as the shofar's secular counterpart for purposes of remembrance, as it achieves these same two effects.

directly to the individual Jew.[3] Two of these associations relate to *akeidat Yitzhak*, the binding of Isaac by his father Abraham.[4] One is the ram's horn itself, reminding us of the ram that was sacrificed in place of Isaac.[5] In the second, the shofar reminds us of Sarah's wailing upon being informed of the events of the *akeidah*.[6]

Another woman exists, however, whose wails teach us about the shofar blasts. This woman, unexpectedly, is none other than the mother of one of our worst enemies and this incongruous connection is to be found in tractate *Rosh Hashanah* 33b:

> It is written,[7] *"It shall be a day of blasting (teru'ah) unto you"* and we translate,[8] a day of *"yebava"*; and it is written of the mother of Sisera, "Through the window she looked forth (*nishkafa*) and she lamented (*vateyabev*)." One authority thought that this means drawing a long sigh and another that it means uttering short piercing cries.

The discussion in the Gemara of the lengths of the various shofar blasts unexpectedly turns to Sisera's mother (henceforth referred to in this article as *em Sisera*) and her vocal expression of grief at her son's delay— found in the Song of Deborah (Judges 5).

The verse of the Song that introduces us to *em Sisera* (Judges 5:28) contains two verbs. The first verb, *nishkafa*, is translated by all as "to look forth." Many commentators understand the second verb, *vaTeyabev*, as also meaning "to look." Followed as it is later in the verse by "through the lattice," it would thus serve to create the parallel imagery in the verse of

---

[3] For examples, see Eliyahu Kitov, *The Book of Our Heritage* (Feldheim: Jerusalem, 1962) 31–32.

[4] Genesis 22.

[5] *Rosh Hashanah* 16a.

[6] In *Pirke deRabbi Eliezer* 32, Satan tells her the story of the *akeidah* and she, believing that Isaac is actually dead, wails and dies. In *Tanhuma Vayera* 23 and *Leviticus Rabbah* 20.2, Isaac (or, in the latter version, Satan disguised as Isaac) is the one telling her of the events. Although it is obvious that he is alive, here too she wails (which corresponds to the shofar) and dies (see discussion below of the meaning of her death in this case).

[7] Numbers 29:1.

[8] This is referring to the Aramaic translation of the Bible by Onkelos in the 2nd century C.E.

looking through the window and also through the lattice. However, the Sages in the above Gemara prefer to connect *vaTeyabev* to Onkelos's *yebava*, the word with which he translates the blast of the shofar in Numbers 29:1, and thus to understand it as referring to a crying, ululating and lamenting sound.[9]

The central role *em Sisera* plays here means that anyone who is familiar with this *sugya* (topical section) will hear *em Sisera* sighing in the *shvarim* (shofar note), and groaning in the *yebavot* of the Rosh Hashanah shofar. Why is she given the spotlight here? Why does this central talmudic discussion not revolve around the figure of Sarah, who also groaned in the manner of the shofar blasts?

Clearly the word *yebava* is the linguistic reason for the connection here, linking as it does one biblical verse and the Aramaic translation of another to associate *em Sisera* with the shofar. It could also be claimed that *em Sisera*'s grief delineates the *form*, in a purely technical fashion, while for inner spiritual *content* and *meaning* we turn to our ancestress. The *midrashim* on Sarah exemplify this process: since no verse connects Sarah to the shofar directly, they transfer the "woman wailing like shofar blasts" motif (learned from *em Sisera*) to Sarah, whose significance for the Jewish people is much greater. Indeed, many later commentators do shift the emphasis over to our ancestress.[10] There is even a source that

---

[9] In the Aramaic of the Talmud, the root "*yabev*" takes on a group of related meanings, all of them denoting sound: sounding the alarm, lamentation and a trembling note (see entry in M. Jastrow, *Dictionary of the Talmud*, NY: Pardes, 1950). The traditional commentaries on Judges 5:28 all mention this meaning, and Robert Alter in *The Art of Biblical Poetry* (NY: Basic Books, 1985) 43 follows suit with "whined." Rashi and Radak also note the translation of "to look."

[10] Abudraham (quoted in Menahem Kasher, *Torah Shelemah*, Genesis 23:2, note 17) goes even further than the midrash. He says that Onkelos's *yom yebava* translation of the shofar blasts connect us to Sarah's wails (*yebavot*). Thus he completely bypasses this word's appearance in the Bible and its more obvious connection to *em Sisera*! By the same token, Kasher himself (ibid.) deems it proper, considering the weight of these *midrashim*, to amend a tradition that we blow 100 sounds to commemorate the 100 cries of *em Sisera*, so that it reads as a commemoration of Sarah's 100 cries. *Kitov* (35) retains the tradition of the *em Sisera* link for the 100 sounds, but in this version we learn that these sounds actually nullify the brutal cries of *em Sisera*, thus endowing the latter with a negative impact that is not explicit in the Gemara itself. The only positive words the traditional commentators have to say for *em Sisera* are

credits Sarah's death cries, in the form of the shofar, with the ability to atone for her children; what meaning could be greater than this on Rosh Hashanah?[11]

Thus, surely the Rabbis of the Talmud, with their flexibility and associative method of discussion, could also have found a way to bring Sarah into this evocative description of the emotional aspect of the shofar blasts. Why does no one reduce *em Sisera*'s monopoly of this discussion? Sarah's absence from this context requires some explanation, as it seems almost deliberate.[12]

This puzzle of the presence of *em Sisera* in the symbolism of the shofar and the simultaneous absence of Sarah may become clearer if we look at who *em Sisera* is, and at the nature of Deborah's attitude towards her as depicted by the author of the Song of Deborah.

II. Deborah's Strength and *em Sisera*'s Weakness

Firstly, let us look at the context in which *em Sisera* is mentioned. In Judges, chapter 5, Deborah sings her victory Song after defeating Sisera, the general of Jabin, king of Hatzor. This victory was aided by Yael, wife of Hever the Kenite, who enticed Sisera into her tent and killed him with a tentpeg. The Song ends as follows:

> (24) Blessed above women is Yael, the wife of Hever the Kenite, blessed is she more than women in the tent. (25) He asked for water, but she gave him milk; she brought forth cream in a lordly dish. (26) She put her hand to the tent peg and her

---

that one of her cries was an authentic cry of pain and therefore one blast of the shofar is actually in commemoration of her.

[11] A midrash aggadah, quoted in Kasher, ibid.

[12] As we have mentioned, at least four *midrashim* make the connection between Sarah's groaning and the shofar blasts; yet such a connection does not appear in the Gemara (neither in *Rosh Hashanah 33b*—the obvious place—nor anywhere else). This is in despite the fact that *Leviticus Rabbah* is an early midrash, dating from the amoraic period, approximately the time of the talmudic discussion. The Gemara mentions only that God visited Sarah on Rosh Hashanah. Thus, notwithstanding all later interpretations and even amendments, I would like to concentrate on this primary source. I feel that the Gemara's mention of *em Sisera* rather than Sarah is a purposeful one that cries out *"Darsheni!"* (search for my meaning!).

right hand to the workmen's hammer; and she hammered Sisera,
she smote through his head; she crushed and pierced his temple.
(27) At her feet he bent, he fell; where he bowed, there he fell
down, bereft of life.

(28) Through the window she looked and moaned, Sisera's
mother, through the lattice: "Why is his chariot so long in coming? Why are the hoofbeats of his steeds so tardy?" (29) Her
wise ladies answered her, she even returned answer to herself:
(30) "Have they not found booty? Have they not divided the
prey; to each man a damsel or two; to Sisera a booty of diverse
colors, a plunder of many colored needlework, dyed double
worked garments for the necks of the spoilers."

(31) So let all thy enemies perish, O Lord: but let them that love
Him be as the sun when it comes out in its might.

And the land was quiet for forty years. (Judges 5:24–31)[13]

This is all we are told about *em Sisera* in the Bible itself. For more
information, we must have recourse to the midrash. Midrash is a wonderful phenomenon. Characters and events in the Bible that are given barely
a mention, or remain in the gray one-dimensional region of background
plot, suddenly take on a vibrant life of their own through the eyes of the
midrash. It dares to flesh out and sometimes even reverse the basic thrust
of the biblical text.

One rather flat character, however, who is not granted any midrashic
dimension, is Sisera. He makes a brief appearance in Judges 4 and 5,
portrayed as the ruthless enemy, and the rabbinical authors of the midrash
content themselves with glorifying and magnifying his defeat. More
fascinating, however, is a biblical and midrashic portrayal of a group of
females who encircle Sisera in a whirl of powerful emotions. These
figures do not actually interact with one another *per se*; their interconnec-
tion takes place via his life and subsequent murder.

In feminist criticism, mention is often made of the presence or absence
of "women's voices" in the text. Like most other literature of past epochs,
the Talmud and *midrashim* were authored by men and have therefore been

---

[13] Koren translation.

criticized for not giving women the voice they deserve. The following midrash, based on the verses quoted above, is an example of a source that does give center stage to women—to the women surrounding Sisera, each of whom raises her voice in a different way:

> "Why is his chariot so long in coming?"—this was said by Sisera's mother. "Her wise ladies answered her": "His wife said, 'Have they not found booty? Have they not divided the prey...?'" The words of Sisera's mother were revealed to Deborah by the Divine Spirit and thus she said to her, "Do not expect Sisera your son—from now on, 'thus let all Thy enemies perish, O Lord.'" (*Yalkut Shimoni*, *Beha'alotekha*, 734)

In this scene, this veritable babble of female voices surrounds the silent figure of Sisera. A main actress, Yael, seems to have already exited at this point. Deborah, the rejoicing victor, has the upper hand over his concerned mother and reassuring wife; she sees everything and consequently gets the last word.

Who, further, is Deborah?[14] The image of Deborah in the text is a positive one, of course, in many respects: she was a judge, a prophetess and successfully led the people of Israel in battle against the Canaanites. The phrase used to describe her—"*eshet lapidot*" (Judges 4:4)—may be translated "a fiery woman,"[15] and she is certainly one of the strongest and most independent female figures in the Bible.

A painting by Rembrandt depicts Yael, Deborah and Sisera: the shadowy figure of Sisera lurks in the background; Yael is portrayed as a vital, feminine young woman, tentpeg in hand. In direct contrast, the Deborah figure is wizened, bent and old. In my view, this depiction indicates a superficial understanding of the essence of Deborah for it portrays her as being a hardhearted, gloating witch, speaking her line in the midrash in a

---

[14] After doing much of the following research, I discovered that several of the following points are also raised by Gabriel Cohn in his article dealing with feminist elements in the Song of Deborah, "*Hebetim Feministi'im beShirat Devora*" in *Al haPerek* 13 (1997): 8–13.

[15] See Metzudat David on Judges 4:4—"*lapidot*—a woman of valor, dexterous" which also fits in with a kind of fiery intensity. Other interpretations will be discussed below.

cackle of flinty glee and without a drop of sensitivity. She is, I believe, far more multifaceted than this.

It is obvious that Deborah is a strong personality. The Rabbis of the Talmud criticize her for being haughty and cite this trait as the reason why she, along with the prophetess Hulda, deserved to bear such ugly names (meaning a hornet and a weasel respectively).[16] Indeed, strength is Deborah's *persona*, the face she shows to the world. In the Song, Deborah says, "The inhabitants of the villages ceased, they ceased in Israel, until I Deborah arose, I arose a mother in Israel" (Judges 5:7).

Elisha Shefi and Shmaryahu Talmon[17] comment that the phrase which Deborah uses to describe herself, "*em beYisrael*," parallels "*em Sisera*" while nevertheless emphasizing the difference between the two women. This contrast is supported by Radak's[18] interpretation of this phrase as "a mother *to* Israel," (rather than its literal meaning "a mother in Israel")—i.e., concerned only for the nation of Israel. In that case, Deborah is presented as the strong, proud, collective-minded foil to *em Sisera*, a foolish, weak old lady, concerned solely for her son's safety. The Bible in general portrays many mothers as putting their sons' welfare above their own. They act through and for their sons, and to an extent play a secondary role to them, as can be seen from the relationships of Hagar and Ishmael, or Rebecca and Jacob.[19] Deborah, by virtue of being the "mother" to a whole nation, in contrast, is a leader; she stands in the background only insofar as any leader stands in the shadow of the nation whose good is his or her main concern.

Besides her small-minded worry over her son's safety, *em Sisera* had an even more selfish reason to be anxious: her very status depended on her son. The image of *em Sisera* staring through her window reminds us

---

[16] *Megillah* 14b.

[17] In *Olam haTanakh* (Tel Aviv: Dodson Iti, 1994) 53.

[18] RaDaK is the Hebrew acronym for Rabbi David Kimchi (approx. 1160–1235), Provençal exegete and grammarian.

[19] These and other examples are cited by Esther Fuchs in "The Literary Characterization of Mothers and Sexual Politics in the Hebrew Bible," *Semeia* 46 (1989): 162–3. She comments that mothers are far less likely to come forth for their daughters' sake, e.g., Leah's inaction in the case of Dinah.

of two royal women who looked out through theirs—Queens Michal and Jezebel.[20] This association hints to *em Sisera*'s standing as the mother of the famous general, a standing which was dependent on his remaining alive, just as widowed queens' standing depended on their sons being kings.[21]

Although *em Sisera* does not yet know that her son is dead, Deborah does. "The mother of Sisera," who is designated solely by her relationship to her son, will soon lose the meaning of her entire existence. Two of the women in the Song, Yael and *em Sisera*, both have men in the center of their lives. It seems to me that Deborah, on the other hand, is portrayed as seeing herself free from that kind of dependence on another human being; she does not merely wait yearningly for someone's chariot to come. Barak is not mentioned; the Song is Deborah's alone,[22] and she proclaims that she is "singing to God."[23] She is presumably in the ranks of those she mentions at the end of her Song who love God,[24] and God, unlike mortal human beings, cannot suddenly be killed by the enemy thus shattering a dependent female's world.

Even a certain subtle play of light and darkness in the narrative highlights this contrast between the two women. *Em Sisera* looks through the lattice—it is probably dark inside as she peers out into the sun. Ivories of Phoenician window scenes[25] depict the goddess Ashtoret peering half inside, half outside of the window, and *em Sisera* is at least partly

---

[20] For sources see below. There are many other window images in the Bible, but these two most closely parallel *em Sisera*'s situation as a woman of importance looking out through the window to view events in the outside world. A more detailed discussion of the window motif will follow.

[21] The position of the queen mother in the Bible is expanded upon by Patricia J. Berlyn in "The Great Ladies," *Jewish Bible Quarterly*, 24.1 (1996): 26–35. She mentions that Michal, due to her subsequent childlessness, lost the original standing granted to her as Saul's daughter and David's senior wife (27).

[22] See Judges 5 verses 7 and 12, where she speaks resoundingly of herself.

[23] Judges 5:3.

[24] Judges 5:31.

[25] See description in *Olam haTanakh* 61 and Nechama Aschkenasy, *Woman at the Window* (Michigan: Wayne State University Press, 1998) 1–2. The window motif was a common one in Near Eastern art, architecture and literary texts, and is generally connected in ancient art to fertility cults and temple prostitution.

involved with the darkness of the room and the darkness of her fears. By contrast, those *"who love the Lord"*—as mentioned, including Deborah—*"are as the sun when it comes out in its might."*[26] At the very least, *em Sisera* is clearly incarcerated in her tower, while Deborah is free to come and go as she pleases.[27]

So far, I have focused on the aspects of Deborah in the narrative that point to strength and scorn for the enemy and his mother. Yet sometimes when we attack someone, we reveal our own Achilles' heel. Perhaps in the place where Deborah's strength lies, there lies her weakness too. I would now like to explore the idea that an underlying theme in the Song of Deborah is a certain duality in Deborah's perception of other women and of herself as a woman. Deborah's image of Sisera's mother, and her relationship with her son, seem to highlight this duality and reveal to us an existential incompleteness within this bold prophetess.

III. The Private Deborah—Tenderness and Vulnerability

Deborah's Self-Image

The author of the Song has Deborah describe herself as *"em beYisrael."* Although the literal translation of this phrase is "a mother in Israel," she had no descendants as far as we know; as mentioned above, Radak prefers to read "a mother to Israel." Thus, an entire nation, Israel, in effect functions as her surrogate children. Another motive her language reveals is that by calling herself *em beYisrael*, she denies Sisera's mother the

---

[26] Judges 5:31. Interestingly, Rabbi S.R. Hirsch, in his essay on Jewish symbolism, *"Jewish Symbolism–Collected Writings"* vol. III (NY: Feldheim, 1984)—originally published in German as *"Grundlinien einer juedischen Symbolik"* as vol. 3 of his essays, *Gesammelte Schriften* (1902–12) makes the following comment (89). Unlike other religions, "which stem from man's feelings of dependence" and therefore "direct man towards the night," Judaism summons humans into the full, bright light of day and shows them that they are master over their world. According to R. Hirsch, this is why many of the commandments are to be fulfilled only during the day.

[27] See Aschkenasy 2–3; 26. She argues that the image in the ivory gives an impression of a woman confined, who longs to be able to see beyond her fixed horizons. See however Don Seeman's critique of Aschkenasy's whole premise and his reevaluation of the meaning of the figure at the window, soon to be published in *Prooftexts*. (I thank the author for sharing this information with me before publication.)

option of being the only mother in the Song, as that would highlight Deborah's barrenness. And since mothers *do* live through their sons' acts, she praises Israel in her Song, mentioning the individual tribes and chastising the tribes who did not heed the call. She speaks to the tribes personally, as if they were people: her sons.[28]

Previously, I suggested that *"eshet lapidot"* might be translated as "a fiery woman." Clearly the most simple reading of *"eshet lapidot"* is as "the wife of Lapidot." The Gemara, though, interprets the phrase in a different way: she made wicks for the Temple—she was "a woman of wicks," so to speak.[29] *"Eshet lapidot"* is the only indication in the text that Deborah is married. Thus by its interpretation, the Gemara leaves us with no explicit knowledge of Deborah's being married, while simultaneously depicting a woman active in her own right in the service of God. This is quite a shift of emphasis.

It is true that the talmudic Rabbis are not aiming at a literal meaning, but are rather informing us about her lifestyle;[30] however, even if Deborah were married, it does not appear to have been a successful affair. Ralbag[31] mentions that she was actually separated from her husband, whom he holds to be Barak.[32] Even if they were not actually separated, we may guess that married to Barak, her family life left something to be desired. She spent much time in her position as the leader, which might well take her away from her husband (as we see in Judges 4:6, where she has to send for Barak when she wishes to speak to him). And he comes across as

---

[28] See Gabriel Cohn's comments on this subject (9–10).

[29] *Megillah* 14a. Rashi follows this interpretation.

[30] See Radak, loc. cit. who explicitly separates between the literal meaning (*Lapidot* refers to a person, possibly Barak) and this midrashic information.

[31] RaLBaG is the Hebrew acronym for Rabbi Levi ben Gershom, also known as Gersonides (1288–1344), Provençal exegete, philosopher and astronomer.

[32] As does Radak, Ralbag suggests that the reason she had to send for him to come to her from afar (Judges 4:6) was due to her separation from him "because of her prophecy." This reminds us of Moshe, who separated from his wife Zipporah because of his prophecy. According to the commentators, Moshe was criticized for this by Aharon and Miriam and although God defends him, it seems that prophets of a lesser stature might not be justified in doing so (e.g., see discussion by Abravanel, the fifteenth century Portuguese statesman, philosopher and exegete, on Numbers 12:1–17).

a rather weak and passive character, at least in Deborah's eyes (Judges 4:8–9). All this makes for an unusual biblical woman, whose family life, if it exists at all, is very much on the periphery. In light of this background, her choice of the words "*em beYisrael*" to describe herself takes on an extra significance and reveals much about Deborah's self-image.

Deborah and Yael

When Deborah mentions Yael in her Song, she exclaims, "*Tevorakh minashim Yael...minashim ba'ohel tevorakh*" (5:24): Yael is to blessed more than women in the tent. "Women in the tent" seems to serve here as the ancient equivalent of the housewife, and Deborah seems to be praising Yael in her identification with her as being a stronger, more daring figure than the colorless housewife. Yet even as she blesses her "more than women in the tent," we may get the impression that Deborah cannot help but admit that Yael is "*eshet Hever Hakeni*"—the wife of Hever the Kenite. She has family and therefore is clearly *also* a woman in the tent. In fact, that is exactly where the bloody scene took place; Yael emerged briefly out of her female territory[33] in order to lure him back inside, where she executed her deed. She is not like Deborah, who sits out in the open under a palm tree, where she judges the people.[34]

Perhaps the narrator is suggesting a Deborah who would like to utilize Yael to rationalize her own lack of family, and to point to the advantages of a strong woman who does not sit in the tent all day. Nonetheless, the wording of her Song hints that she is honest enough with herself to admit that the two modes of existence, the active and influential, and the private and domesticated are not mutually exclusive: Yael would appear to have both.[35]

---

[33] Judges 4:18—"*and Yael went out towards Sisera.*"

[34] Judges 4:5.

[35] Even the Hebrew *mem* in "*minashim*" expresses this ambiguity. Does Deborah see Yael as having broken out of the housewife situation, or as excelling within that given state? "*Minashim*" may indicate that Yael is "blessed *more* than women in the tent" (she is not of that category), or "*out of all women in the tent*, Yael is the most blessed" (she is of that category). It is interesting that we are forced to try and guess Deborah's intention by the context. Aschkenasy holds that the latter is the meaning. She writes (26–31) that Deborah is indicating to women who, unlike her, are

However, it is Deborah's dialectical relationship with the figure of Sisera's mother which I find particularly interesting. I want to argue here that the latter's very presence in the Song, even if used in irony, highlights Deborah's feminine perspective most strikingly.

The Jewish philosopher, Martin Buber, speaks of a model of encounters, of dialogue. One type of interaction is the "I-Thou" encounter, in which each partner embraces the very essence of the other, in an authentic relationship of subject to subject, of mutuality without subordination or fusion. The second type is "I-it," in which the other is viewed as an object and there is no real seeing or understanding of the other.[36]

In her Song, Deborah portrays Sisera's mother as being heartlessly enthusiastic about the captives the conquering hero was to bring home. The "damsel or two to every man" are none other than the female Israelite prisoners who are to be despoiled. They are the only female figures in this scene who are not granted a voice; and it is no wonder, for that is precisely how Deborah wishes to portray *em Sisera*'s image of them. The Hebrew word used here for damsel is *"raham,"* a word which cannot help but remind us of the Hebrew word for womb—*"rehem."*[37] As depicted by Deborah, these women are not human in this scene; they are objects and wombs, in the eyes of the Canaanite women.

Deborah is commenting sharply on the "I-it" relationship that the Canaanite women evince towards the Israelite women.[38] We can be sure that Deborah, who describes herself as *em beYisrael* (Judges 5:7), a mother to all Israel, i.e., someone who is concerned for them, was sensitive to the implied depersonalization and denigration of her "daughters." The words

---

homebound, how much power they retain even as ordinary housewives. She views Yael, the "woman at the door," as the extension of the confining "woman at the window."

[36] M. Buber, *I and Thou* (Edinburgh: Scribner, 1958), originally published as *Ich und Du* in 1937.

[37] See Driver, *International Critical Commentary* (Edinburgh: T.&T. Clark, 1989) 170; Alter, 43.

[38] Aschkenasy discusses the coarseness of the imagery employed here. In addition, she comments that no other woman better epitomizes the adulation of the world of men, and the loss of sensitivity to the predicament of women, than the mother of the Canaanite chief (24).

she places into the mouths of Sisera's relatives with such barbed irony must surely have had an underlying ring of pain for her.[39]

Deborah's Song counterbalances their hard-heartedness with sensitivity to *em Sisera*, a female intuition of her pain, a certain "I-Thou"ness. She captures *em Sisera*'s concern and pain so well that we know she is looking into this woman's heart.

We can see this sensitivity clearly when comparing her Song with *shirat haYam*, the victorious Song that Moshe and the Children of Israel sang at the Sea after the Egyptians were drowned.[40] At the Song at the Sea, women sang too:

> And Miriam the prophetess, sister of Aharon took a timbrel in her hand; and all the women went out after her with timbrels and with dances. (Exodus 15:20)

Miriam goes out, after the main Song by Moshe, surrounded by women. Deborah, in contrast, *is* the main singer. Furthermore, although we are told that Barak sings with her (Judges 5:1), the Song itself refers solely to her, and often is spoken in the first person at that, with Barak remaining very much in the background. Deborah is pictured as fierce, proud and *alone*. She is not the counterpart to Miriam; rather, she draws her inspiration from Moshe. She sings her Song as a prophetess, as the great Moshe did and is the leading voice for the entire nation.

Yet despite the similarity, the comparison of the two Songs serves to highlight the imprint of a woman's perceptions in Deborah's poem.[41] Moshe's themes in his Song were God's might, the drowning of the

---

[39] See Cohn (13) who points to this passage as one of the clearly feminine parts of the Song.

[40] Sisera and Pharaoh, the vanquished enemies, actually have much in common in addition to having a song sung about their defeat. They often appear in the sources alongside another archenemy, Sanheriv, who does not, however "merit" a song. Radak (on Judges 4:7) comments that Sisera's astrologers foresaw his defeat, but God "drew his heart" so that he would nevertheless go out to war. This inevitably reminds us of God's hardening of Pharaoh's heart so that against his true will, he would not let the Israelites go. Additionally, both armies were drowned. Interestingly, another common motif is that the leaders both escaped—there is a midrash that posits that Pharaoh remained alive (*Mekhilta, Beshalah* 6).

[41] See Cohn *passim*.

enemy, fearful reactions by other nations, and Israel's salvation.[42] There is no mention of Pharaoh's grieving family. Of course, bearing in mind that Moshe was raised by Pharaoh's daughter, it would have been the height of insensitivity for him to use her as a motif. In any event, I would argue that in examining the content of *shirat haYam* we find that it is a very general Song, about national entities and their power vis-à-vis each other. The only emotions explicit in it are fear, awe and pride, and in this it differs from the Song of Deborah. Certainly we can suppose that after the intense effort it took to leave Egypt, Moshe's priority is to emphasize the fact that God's name has been glorified and His people saved. It should not surprise us if Moshe's experiences with the cruelty of the Egyptians and the stubbornness of Pharaoh may have obliterated any "I-Thou" relation he might potentially have had with them. Only God Himself, who preserves some connection to all humans, no matter how evil, is affected by their death. The midrash depicts Him rebuking the angels for their insensitivity when they want to sing the *Hallel* praise by the sea—"*My creatures are drowning in the sea and you are singing?*"[43]

Deborah's Song has a female aspect in that it is more personal in its relationship to the enemy. As far as we know, other biblical sections relating to the death of enemies are authored by men; and consistent with the line of thinking mentioned above, do not reveal much personal or emotional material. One source which does actually mention the enemy's mother is I Samuel 15:33. There the prophet Samuel kills Agag the king of the Amalekites saying, "as your sword has made women childless, so shall your mother become childless among women."

Nonetheless, it seems clear that the resemblance is superficial. There is no insight here into a mother's feelings; rather, it is an abrupt, down-to-earth statement of the justice being done, with a slight literary flourish in the parallelism.

An empathetic portrayal of the enemy is thus unique to the Song of Deborah. *Em Sisera* could have been omitted altogether; the focus could have been the downcast fear of the Canaanites when they heard of the

---

[42] Alter (50) terms it a "song of God working in History" as opposed to the "terse story of Yael."

[43] *Megillah* 10b.

catastrophe, or a portrayal of a wealth of other images. In my view, the deliberate mention of the enemy's family transforms Deborah from Rembrandt's witch into a deeply empathetic person.[44]

Yet this is obviously not the whole picture. In our day, there is a trend towards understanding and relating the "narrative of the other." It would be disloyal to the text, though, to claim that the narrator's insertion of the enemy's family in Deborah's Song is intended to grant them a voice as equals. We have already seen that there are elements of great scorn in Deborah's account of *em Sisera*. In fact, it could even be suggested that all this empathy and female sensitivity is used as an ironic weapon *against* the enemy's mother; Deborah's political self is utilizing the insights of her inner self to achieve an apogée of satire.

The transition from the previous scene is sharp,[45] with Sisera lying on the floor in a pool of blood—the active, bloody scene shifts into a passive, pensive mode. Deborah knows what really happened and therefore moves just as sharply into "*So let all thy enemies perish, O Lord*" (verse 31), leaving *em Sisera* dangling, in the climax of her self-delusion, without allowing her to finish her scene, so to speak. This is the Deborah expressed in the midrash, who knows via her prophecy (the "divine spirit") what is occurring and is extremely pleased to have routed the enemy. She does not have a heart of stone; on the contrary, the combination of her prophecy and her female empathy enable her to describe the scene vividly, while at the same time abruptly breaking it off with her victorious comment.

---

[44] I would like to point out here that everything we have said so far about Deborah would be more accurately assigned to characterize the author of the Song who puts the words in Deborah's mouth. Cohn and others suggest the author was a woman. If it was not Deborah herself, then my comments about female empathy in the Song are more attributable to the fact that the author was a woman than that the character in question (Deborah) was a woman. The same Song written by a man may have looked completely different. However, what is important here is that the author writes her female characters in a specifically female way, and the insights we gain on the author's view of Deborah.

[45] Alter (46) describes it as an instance of "false overlap," whereby we momentarily suppose the subject of "*Through the window she looked*" to be Yael, the subject of the previous verse.

As we noted, the Bible contains two other scenes of women looking through windows. The first features Michal, daughter of King Saul and wife of King David, who looks out and sees her husband dancing and making a fool of himself (from her perspective) in front of the Ark of the Lord (II Samuel, 6:16). The second involves Jezebel, Ahab's widow. In II Kings 9:30, this wicked queen proudly makes herself up for the last time and looks out of the window to greet Jehu, the slayer of her son Jehoram, with contempt; he then orders that she should be pushed out of the window to a horrible death. Both scenes involve royal women, strong emotions, a man and death (in the case of Jezebel), or subsequent childlessness (in the case of Michal).[46] In our story, the reader also acutely senses the crushing blow about to fall on the mother of Sisera, who looks out of her window unaware that her son is at this very moment lying lifeless in Yael's tent. The reader, being "in the know," is invited to appreciate the irony along with Deborah. If this is the case, though not wizened and hard-hearted as Rembrandt would have it, Deborah actually emerges all the more unkind. Is this, then, the final word on Deborah the prophetess?

Haim Gouri, a contemporary Israeli poet, wrote a poem called "*Immo*"[47] which fleshes out the scene in a way that is sympathetic to *em Sisera*. The original scene ends suddenly, leaving *em Sisera* and her ladies in the painful throes of their suspense, whereas Gouri follows them as they descend into silence, the sun sets and the twilight comes—a slow

---

[46] II Samuel 6:23. Through examining the wider context of window scenes, including that of Abimelech (Genesis 26:8); Proverbs 7:6–27; Rahab (Joshua 2:15) and others, Aschkenasy (*passim*) concludes that these scenes revolve around sexuality, vulnerability and a desire to participate in the world of men, with the central female figure thus betraying her own sex. Robert H. O'Connell, "Proverbs VII 16–17–a Case of Fatal Deception in a 'Woman at the Window' Type Scene" in *Vetus Testamentum*, 41 (1991): 235–39, adds deception to the list. It is interesting that in the cases of Michal and Jezebel, hatred, contempt and helplessness are involved. Sisera's mother was certainly feeling helpless. She was contemptuous too—but unlike the other two, her contempt seems to be reserved not for the man in the scene, but rather for the Israelite captives.

[47] The Hebrew and English versions (translated from the Hebrew by Dan Pagis) can be found in William Urbrock, "Sisera's Mother in Judges 5 and Haim Gouri's *Immo*" in *Hebrew Annual Review* 11 (1987): 423–34.

darkness.[48] He compassionately describes *em Sisera* as "a woman whose hair is a streak of silver." His poem follows her as she hears the news and stays with her right to the bitter end:

> Forty years—the land was calm. Forty years
> Horses did not gallop and dead horsemen did not stare with glassy
> eyes
> But she died a short time after her son's death.

This last sentence reminds us again of the midrashic account of Sarah dying very soon after hearing of her son's death—a mother's heart bursts.[49]

Gouri's poem suggests that Deborah was cruel in not finishing the scene, in leaving *em Sisera* forever suspended in her torturous anticipation and uncertainty, even as the words *"So let all thy enemies perish"* announce to the rest of the world the true outcome. His poetic completion of the scene is thus an implicit criticism of Deborah for what she omitted to do—for leaving the scene and not confronting the reality of another woman's life being ruined.

Yet perhaps Gouri is mistaken in his interpretation. Perhaps the reason the narrator of the Song does not have Deborah take the scene one step further, and describe what happened when the mother found out about her son's death is not due to her cruelty or even apathy. On the contrary, perhaps she is *so sensitive* that she finds herself unable to verbally articulate and delineate something so awful.

Consider the reaction of another parent, King David, to the death of his beloved son Absalom:

> ...and he wept and as he walked he cried, "My son, Absalom, my son, my son—would that I could die in place of you, Absalom, my son, my son." (II Samuel 19:1)

David's pain at this juncture was very deep, yet we might suppose that *em Sisera* has even more to lose. Unlike David, who retains his stature and

---

[48] Perhaps a contrast to the blazing sunrise of those who love God in Deborah's poem.

[49] *Pirke deRabbi Eliezer* 32.

self even after Absalom's passing, *em Sisera loses* the veritable center of her world with the death of her son; in fact, in the next moment of this scene, she essentially ceases to exist.

Perhaps we can then conclude that Deborah has ambivalent feelings about this other mother whom she herself has introduced into her Song—a woman so self-absorbed and so much the enemy, yet so maternal in her pain and so absorbed in her son. This duality means that Deborah is able to mock her up to a certain limit, but no further. She prefers to indicate subtly the power, grief, and potential for death and bereavement by use of the window-scene motif.[50] She then does *em Sisera* the kindness of leaving her at a point where she can still retain that small ray of hope, still reassure herself that all will end well and her victorious son will be restored to her waiting arms. Deborah steals away and a curtain falls over the tragic scene, allowing the newly bereaved their privacy.

IV. Deborah–The Key to the Puzzle of the Shofar

The outcome of the *em Sisera* scene, then, receives different treatment in different hands:

(1) Haim Gouri, as we have seen, gently draws the scene to its tragic close.
(2) We find that the Rabbis of the Talmud also give *em Sisera* a continuation of sorts, contending[51] that Sisera's descendants (including, according to one tradition, R. Akiva) learned Torah in Jerusalem.[52]
(3) My suggestion is that the Song's deliberate curtailing of the scene allows Sisera's mother a different conclusion to her story, achieved through the sound of the shofar on Rosh Hashanah.

To understand this connection, let us return to our initial question: why does Sisera's mother take a central role in the weave of emotional

---

[50] Aschkenasy (26) explains that Deborah's use of the window scene is actually her *justification* of how *em Sisera* came to be so cruel and dehumanized—it was due to her being imprisoned all her life.

[51] *Sanhedrin* 96b.

[52] See Steinsaltz edition of the Talmud, loc. cit.; R. Zadok haKohen of Lublin, *Resisei Layla* 46.

associations surrounding the shofar blowing on Rosh Hashanah, equal to or maybe even superseding Sarah in some way?

The answer lies in the difference between the existential situation of Sarah and *em Sisera*. As mentioned before, several *midrashim* connect Sarah's cries to the shofar blasts, but they do not explicate the cause of her crying and subsequent death, leaving us the task of deciphering their meaning. One midrash indicates she thought Isaac was dead.[53] According to this interpretation, her cries are of *grief for what has occurred*.[54] Other *midrashim*[55] have Isaac himself (or Satan in his guise) reporting the events; yet there, too, she wails and, even more perplexing, dies. In these latter *midrashim*, Sarah would seem to definitely know that her son is alive. If so, her sighs and groans must be an expression of *shock* rather than grief. This shock does not derive from her recognition of a calamity averted at the last moment, but from an acute perception that her world will never be the same.[56]

---

[53] *Pirke deRabbi Eliezer* 32. Satan informs her of the binding of Isaac without telling her that he was still alive. Assuming the worst, she cries three times, wails three times (corresponding to different sounds of the shofar) and dies.

[54] Thus Avivah Gottlieb Zornberg, in *Genesis: The Beginning of Desire* (NY: Doubleday, 1995) 124–25 posits that the atonement achieved by the shofar has a redemptive effect against her despair and anguish, dying as she does without hope of release.

[55] *Leviticus Rabbah* 20.2; *Tanhuma Vayera* 23.

[56] The question of what affects Sarah so deeply in this situation is raised in Yehuda Gellman's article, "And Sarah Died," *Tradition* 32.1 (1997): 57–67. Gellman considers why we should wish to remember this episode on Rosh Hashanah. If, as this midrash tells us, Sarah knew the *akeidah* was at God's bidding and that Isaac had come through it safely, her wailing and death seem to be an overreaction, an exhibition of weakness in her. His suggested explanation is that Abraham and Sarah represent two different spiritual modes of existence, those of *hesed* and *din* respectively. He posits that her shock is not at the outcome, but rather at *Abraham* and his deed. Abraham's aspect of *hesed*, his desire and ability to be so self-sacrificial, was the opposite spiritual orientation from her own mode, that of the concrete, immanent and non-sacrificial type. The deeper meaning of her wail comprises a plea to God not to demand of her children such "Abrahamic" self-sacrifice on the Day of Judgment, but rather to spare them from it. This form of sacrifice was so painful to her that she died from shock at its instigation. Zornberg (125) suggests a slightly different answer: that the emotion Sarah felt was a deep disappointment, consequent to Satan's success in destroying her vision of her husband and of her life's mission. This reaction was again irrespective of the "happy" ending. Indeed, in the *Midrash*

Thus in these *midrashim*, Sarah reacts to events that have already occurred. There is no uncertainty in her being; she looks only to the **past**
and it is this past that kills her. Its constant shadow strips the future of any
promise, and past and future merge as an irrevocable horror.[57] The opposite is true of Sisera's mother at the point where Deborah leaves her. True,
she feels worry, even grief; but there is also hope, and she looks to the
future for her salvation. As we watch her, we know that her son is already
dead; and on one level, *em Sisera* knows this too and her sighs and groans
are, like Sarah's, that of a mother who has actually lost her son.[58] Yet on
another level, she is still at a point in time where she may reassure herself,
imagining her son is still alive and is victoriously bringing home the
booty. On this level, our past is her present and our present, with its
knowledge of her tragedy, does not comprise her future for she lives in
hope of a different end.

It seems to me that *em Sisera*'s condition of dialectical emotions and
time-frames is a model for us as we hear the shofar on Rosh Hashanah: it
evokes grief and loss, but also hope.[59] The groan of the shofar arouses
deep feelings of alienation and lack of sense of self: on the Day of

---

Tanhuma, she does not even wait to see if all ends well, indicating that her shock lies
at the core of the story and not in its ultimate conclusion.

[57] In the *Leviticus Rabbah* version, she exclaims: "Were it not for the angel, you
would already have been slaughtered?!" This suggests that it is her imagination that
kills her, as she transports herself into the nightmare of "what might have been," as
Zornberg describes (see below).

[58] In my view, on this initial level, Sarah and *em Sisera* are partners in imbuing the
shofar with their anguish—even the tradition that maintains that *em Sisera* uttered
100 brutal sounds admits that one sound was nevertheless truly of a mother's pain
(Kitov, 35). Haim Gouri's ending of the scene makes the *em Sisera* story parallel to
the first midrash about Sarah, and the message is a simple and immediate one of
maternal bereavement. It is only when we stop the scene in the middle, or when we
see Sarah dying *despite* Isaac being alive, that we can engage in a complex dialogue
of comparison and contrast between the two.

[59] Interestingly, certain elements in the story of Hannah (I Samuel 1–2) resemble
those mentioned here. Her rival, Peninah, taunts her barrenness (I Samuel 1:6). But
when Hannah subsequently gives birth to Samuel, she sings a song of joy in which
she "raises her horn" (ibid., 2:1) as she *gains* a child. Thus perhaps the blowing of
our "horn" captures *em Sisera* at a moment while she is still functioning as a mother,
in a song that recounts and reflects upon motherhood and its nature, preventing her
from moving forward into the next moment, one of barrenness and loss.

Judgment we are stripped of our standing and of the delusions we hold dear the rest of the year, which comprise the core of our life. We grieve the loss of innocence and purity we brought upon ourselves by sinning. The sigh of the shofar echoes a sigh rising from the depths of our being, as our world seems to crumble around us.

Yet all is not lost because *teshuvah*, repentance, is by nature a restructuring of time. Human identity, as Rabbi J.B. Soloveitchik points out, is located in the anticipation of the future and is thus the key to the process of *teshuvah*.[60] We can be encouraged by the Jewish idea that our sins are not ensconced in an unredeemable past; they are not a *fait accompli*. We can live in a time zone in which we never actually transgressed. The past becomes our present and the present may be repaired, bringing a different more positive outcome for the future, in imitation of *em Sisera* and the women of her court.

In conclusion, the Gemara in tractate *Rosh Hashanah* emphasizes that it is actually *em Sisera*, rather than our mother Sarah, who teaches us about the interplay of time, *teshuvah*, and anguish that is simultaneously hope. Avivah Zornberg[61] proposes that what kills Sarah in the scenario where the real Isaac stands before her is the sudden existential realization of "what might have been"—the truth of the "hair's breadth that separates death from life." Sarah enters in her imagination into a world of existential "vertigo," where Isaac is "already-slaughtered" and nothingness reigns. Her pure analytical thought fails to provide her with the flexibility needed to overcome this trauma, to "negate negation" and emerge into affirmation; the only release is death.[62]

Based upon Zornberg's assertions, I would like to develop the idea that the *teshuvah* process provides the antidote to Sarah's existential malaise. Sarah has been propelled into a mode where a harsh and severe truth reigns, where the individual, being accountable for all his sins, is

---

[60] See Pinchas Peli, *On Repentance: The Thought and Discourses of Rabbi J.B. Soloveitchik* (NJ: Jason Aronson, 1996) 250.

[61] Ibid., 126–36

[62] Ibid., 133; 135–36.

condemned to die from the moment of birth.[63] There she remains stuck, with an immutable past forever casting its evil blight on life. The sound of the shofar, as Zornberg says, is a call for transcendence.[64] It evokes an irrational world of non-linear time, of surmounting the unyielding accountability in order to attain an even higher truth—an affirmative one, one of *hesed* (lovingkindness). Thus it seems to me that the shofar is not primarily an echo of Sarah's wails, as she has not apprehended the meaning of *teshuvah*. Rather, it is a lesson from *em Sisera*, who at this moment and forevermore, does not lose faith in her future, although the "reality" appears to dictate that it is actually her past. The non-rational situation, positioning her at ninety degrees to others' mundane reality, is precisely the formula for repentance and only she, not Sarah, can teach us about the infinity of hope.[65]

Let us not omit Deborah's part in the above process. Ultimately, the portrait of *em Sisera* and her thoughts and emotions, is Deborah's creation in her Song; thus despite the fact that she is not mentioned in the Gemara, Deborah's role here and her connection to the shofar must not be ignored. Everything we have discussed points to the talmudic Sages' implicit recognition of the ambivalent feelings the enemy's mother arouse in Deborah, and the latter's ability to transcend her natural disdain, reaching a point of a deeply empathetic perception of the other woman. The Sages themselves are able to recognize the element of goodness and truth in *em Sisera* that merits her appearing in the center of our associations and awareness on Rosh Hashanah, in the power of the shofar and its

---

[63] This mode of *din*, judgment, may be the one in which Jonah also functions; he too cannot countenance the idea of repentance, it contradicts all of his principles. See for example Uriel Simon, *Yonah im Mavoh uFerush* (Tel-Aviv and Jerusalem: *Am Oved* and Magnes, 1982) 7–9.

[64] Loc. cit., 133.

[65] In her situation, *em Sisera* must have had to invest great energy in her belief in her son's imminent return—in fact, the more apprehension she was suffering, the more optimism she needed to reassure herself. We can assume that she invested the emotional energy from her anxiety into her hope, channeling it into a positive function. This bears some similarity to the talmudic idea that upon repentance, one's sins are not erased but rather become merits; the energy invested into the sin is uplifted and purified until it transforms into a positive element (*Yoma* 86b). See discussion in Peli, 248–65.

symbolism. Her ever-hopeful voice has become an integral part of our *teshuvah* process. By calling to us from the depths of our shofar, the erstwhile enemy has become our adviser in religious emotion, and she is thus allowed to complete her story with a good ending, coming to life every year in a cry of hope that conquers anguish. And if *em Sisera* may still change her story, then surely *we* may hope to do so too; and thus be granted life, hope, and a clean slate with which to start the new year.

* * *

The unravelling of this talmudic puzzle has revealed to me the Talmud's teaching of sensitivity towards even our worst enemy; not for the sake of a superficial humanism but through a perception of what we have to learn from each of God's creatures. I believe it is not a coincidence that we find this sensitivity in a scene involving two women, and I sense that the Sages, too, were indicating their appreciation of this fact by placing one of these women at the heart of their discussion.

Certain scholars today examine external, sociological levels of the Talmud and find it lacking in sensitivity towards women. Committed as I am to the Talmud as a pivotal religious text that shapes my life, the philosophical and spiritual wisdom I attain through immersion in it and through appreciation of its subtleties, enable me to reconcile myself with any seeming discordance or outmodedness. I find myself able to link it directly to my concerns as a Jew, as a woman, and as a human being concerned with the questions of our time.

While some might view this process of study as "imposing one's own interpretations on the text," I believe that this mode is in fact the key to the ever-renewing Torah, which reveals itself in each generation as we gain fresh awareness via our unique experiences. For me, the divine spark contained in modern thought, including feminist critique, is precisely this new level of perception it bestows; and to this I owe many of the insights

I have gained here, which I hope may further my service of God and that of the readers of this volume.[66]

---

[66] For a different understanding of the connection between Sisera's mother and the shofar, see Mordechai Gafni's soon to be published book, *Dance of Tears*. He posits her tears as one of several models of crying on Rosh Hashanah. In this particular model, we cry due to our removal of our societal masks, as she of necessity did when her son—the locus of her whole identity, as evinced in her very name—dies and she is left to confront her own independent self. (I thank the author for sharing this unpublished material with me.)

Between Lines and Behind Masks:
Reading and Understanding *Megillat* Esther

Ilana Goldstein Saks

Every year on Purim, we read *Megillat* Esther to publicly recall the events that brought about the establishment of the holiday and to remind us of their significance. Ask any child to recount those events and he or she will explain with ease how Mordechai and Esther defeated the wicked Haman, enemy of the Jews. Salvation from what appeared to be certain annihilation is reason enough for a yearly celebration; indeed we know of many other holidays that were established for similar reasons.[1] The Rabbis tell us, however, that Purim is not like other holidays, which will one day be abolished.

Purim, we are taught, is eternal—וימי הפורים אינם בטלים לעולם.[2] Why is Purim distinguished in this way? Clearly Purim is not just another story of salvation. What is the holiday's significance?

If the answer to that question lies in the *Megillah* we read every year, then the means to finding that answer lies in understanding how to read the *Megillah*, approach the text, and determine the central issues and themes. This very question is at the heart of a discussion recounted in the *Mishnah Megillah* 2:3, in which the Rabbis debate whether one must read the entire *Megillah* to fulfill one's obligation on Purim.

According to one opinion, one must read from when Mordechai is introduced (2:5); another claims that the obligatory reading begins with the introduction of Haman (3:1). The real question under discussion is: which parts of the *Megillah* can be skipped without compromising its message?

---

* As always, thanks to my husband, Jeffrey, for all his help.

[1] A long list of such holidays is the content of *Megillat Ta'anit*.

[2] *Midrash Mishlei* 9. For related text see *Megillah* 10b.

The verdict in the Gemara, following the opinion of R. Meir, is that the *Megillah* must be read in its entirety. The Rabbis concluded, then, that in order to fully appreciate the significance of the story of the *Megillah* and not just glean isolated albeit important lessons, it must be read in full.

In the following close reading of the text of *Megillat* Esther, we will see that indeed it is the *entire* story of the *Megillah*, not just those portions which seem to be the most important, that conveys the significance of the Purim story. Skipping sections of the *Megillah* eliminates much of the depth, complexity and meaning it has to offer.

The Introduction

Two of the opinions cited above in the Mishnah suggest that part or all of the two introductory chapters of the *Megillah* need not be read on Purim. Chapters one and two, which precede the main narrative of the *Megillah*, in which Haman plots to kill the Jews and is eventually defeated by them, provide the reader with important background information necessary for appreciating the main story. For example, before describing how Esther, a secret Jew, became Queen, the introduction tells the reader about the banishment of the previous Queen, Vashti.[3] Similarly, in order to help the reader fully appreciate the account of Ahashverosh remembering that Mordechai had once saved his life,[4] the *Megillah* familiarizes the reader with that event in the introduction.[5] Providing this background information at the beginning of the story heightens the tension and suspense during the development of the plot.

Despite this important role, one can understand why those opinions in the Mishnah question the indispensability of these chapters. While they might add stylistically to the *Megillah*, these chapters do not seem to add anything intrinsic to the understanding of the main story. On the other hand, if this is the case, one has to wonder why two entire chapters—out of a total of just over nine—are dedicated to preparing the reader for the main plot of the story.

---

[3] Esther 1:9–19.

[4] 6:1–3.

[5] 2:21–23.

I believe the purpose of the introduction of *Megillat* Esther is not just to bring the reader up-to-date with the lives of the characters, nor is it meant simply to liven up the style of the narrative. Its purpose, rather, is to present readers with a means of understanding the time and place they are about to enter. Chapters one and two, we will see, are in essence a condensed version of the events recounted later. In these two chapters, the author first presents a "problem" that has permeated Shushan, and then offers a solution. This sheds light on the later events in the *Megillah* and illuminates their meaning. The "introduction," then, is the key to unlocking the meaning of the rest of the *Megillah*.

The Problem: Something Rotten in the State of Shushan

The *Megillah* opens with a description of the lavish, one-hundred and eighty-day feast of King Ahashverosh. The King's chief objective in throwing this party, as the *Megillah* explicitly states, is to show off "the vast riches of his kingdom and the splendid glory of his majesty."[6] A rich king, after all, is a powerful king. On the seventh day, however, when the King is full of wine and confidence, he calls upon Queen Vashti so that he can show her off as well and she refuses to come.[7] In one fell swoop, she shatters the image Ahashverosh had been attempting to create. One can almost hear the snickers emerging from under the twirled moustaches: "He can't even command his own *wife*, how much more so the *kingdom*!"

In an attempt at damage-control Ahashverosh speaks to his advisors. One of them, Memukhan, suggests the following:

לא על המלך לבדו עותה ושתי המלכה כי על *כל* השרים ועל *כל* העמים אשר בכל מדינות המלך אחשורוש. כי יצא דבר המלכה על *כל* הנשים להבזות בעליהן בעיניהן באמרם המלך אחשורוש אמר להביא את ושתי המלכה לפניו ולא באה. והיום הזה תאמרנה שרות פרס ומדי אשר שמעו את דבר המלכה לכל שרי המלך וכדי בזיון וקצף. אם על המלך טוב יצא דבר מלכות מלפניו ויכתב בדתי פרס ומדי ולא יעבור אשר לא תבוא ושתי לפני המלך אחשורוש *ומלכותה יתן המלך לרעותה הטובה ממנה. ונשמע פתגם המלך אשר יעשה בכל מלכותו כי רבה היא וכל הנשים יתנו יקר לבעליהן* למגדול ועד קטן.

---

[6] 1:4.

[7] 1:10–12.

Queen Vashti has committed an offense not only against Your Majesty but also against *all* the officials and against *all* the peoples in *all* the provinces of King Ahashverosh. For the Queen's behavior will make *all* wives despise their husbands, as they reflect that King Ahashverosh himself ordered Queen Vashti to be brought before him but she would not come. This very day the ladies of Persia and Media, who have heard of the Queen's behavior, will cite it to all Your Majesty's officials and there will be no end of scorn and provocation! If it please Your Majesty, let a royal edict be issued by you and let it be written into the laws of Persia and Media, so that it cannot be abrogated, that Vashti shall never enter the presence of King Ahashverosh. And let Your Majesty bestow her royal state upon another who is better than she. *Then will the judgment executed by Your Majesty resound throughout your realm, vast though it is*; and *all wives will treat their husbands with respect*, high and low alike. (1:16–20)

This plan is executed by the issuing of two new laws:

וישלח ספרים אל כל מדינות המלך אל מדינה ומדינה ככתבה ואל עם ועם
כלשונו להיות כל איש שרר בביתו ומדבר כלשון עמו.

Dispatches were sent to all the provinces of the King, to every province in its own language, *that every man should wield authority in his own house and speak the language of his own people.* (1:22)

The significance of Memukhan's words can be grasped only when one notices their similarity to the words of another, better-known member of the King's court. When, in chapter three, Mordechai refuses to bow down to him, Haman comes before the King with the following counsel:

ישנו עם אחד מפזר ומפרד בין העמים בכל מדינות מלכותך ודתיהם שנות
מכל עם ואת דתי המלך אינם עשים ולמלך אין שוה להניחם: אם על
המלך טוב יכתב לאבדם...

There is a certain people, scattered and dispersed among the other peoples in all the provinces in your realm, whose laws are different from those of any other people and who do not obey the *King's* laws; and it is not in *Your Majesty's* interest to tolerate them. If it please Your Majesty, let an edict be drawn for their destruction.... (3:8–9)

A careful analysis of the recommendations of Haman and Memukhan reveals striking parallels between them. Both Haman and Memukhan are reacting to the "transgression" of an individual—Vashti's refusal to come before the King and Mordechai's refusal to bow down. In response to the behavior of those individuals, both advisors generalize about entire populations. Memukhan assumes that just as Vashti disobeyed her husband so, too, will all women disobey their husbands. Similarly, Haman claims that if the Jew Mordechai acts defiantly, then so too, will all Jews act in the same way. As a result of this stereotyping, entire populations are punished for the actions of individuals.

Memukhan and Haman are similar not only in *what* they tell the King but in *how* they tell it to the King. Both men play upon the insecurities of Ahashverosh—his need to make his power known and to be in control—to get what they themselves want.[8] Ironically, both men themselves are obsessed with control and respect. Haman is preoccupied with Mordechai's lack of respect and his own inability to control the rebellious Jew. Memukhan's concern is that husbands should command the full respect of their wives and have full control over them.

Haman's real motive in coming before the King is to eliminate the man who doesn't pay him (Haman) proper respect. Killing *all* of the Jews, who do not obey the *King*'s laws and are not worthy of the *King*'s tolerance, is simply an "acceptable" means to the desired end. He cannot reveal to the King that he wants a specific Jew killed simply because that person won't show him respect. He can, however, tell the King that there is a dangerous threat to the *King*'s authority lurking about. Haman is ready to exterminate all the Jews—if that's what it takes—to get rid of Mordechai.

Though Memukhan's manipulativeness is a bit subtler, it is clear nonetheless. His plan to subdue all of the women of the kingdom, as he explains to the King, is an effective way to have the King's executed judgment resound throughout his vast realm.[9] Ahashverosh's power will be exerted not only in the palace but also throughout his entire kingdom.

---

[8] Amos Hakham suggests that Memukhan uses his position as advisor to the King to attain certain things for himself. *Da'at Mikra, Esther* (Jerusalem: Mossad HaRav Kook, 1990) 11.

[9] 1:20.

While this advice is certainly in the best interest of the King, there seems to be more to Memukhan's counsel than that. A careful reading of his words to the King reveals what the real crux of the matter was for Memukhan.

He was, it seems, far more concerned with the *ramifications* of Vashti's behavior among the wives of "all of the officials" (including, presumably, his own wife)[10] than he was about the Queen's insurrection itself. This is clear from the way he keeps returning, with much intensity, to the harm Vashti had caused throughout the kingdom, while barely dealing with the specific affront to the King at all. Even as Memukhan is explaining the purpose of the new laws concerning the women—that such laws will be a display of power for the King—he concludes with the point that "all wives will treat their husbands with respect, high and low alike."[11] His *main* concern it seems, then, is to keep womankind in line. If he has to use Vashti to achieve his aim by taking advantage of her lack of judgment—so be it.

Once one recognizes these parallels, the statement in *Megillah* 12b, which identifies Memukhan with Haman, takes on new meaning. The Gemara is not necessarily suggesting that they were literally the same person, but that for all intents and purposes they were one and the same. Haman and Memukhan represent the same evil; they are both, as the Gemara puts it, מוכן לפורענות, ready to destroy others.[12]

The Paradigm of Evil: Amalek

This evil which Haman and Memukhan both represent does not originate in them. Memukhan and Haman's behavior is patterned after that of

---

[10] See the comment of the *Tosafot* on *Megillah* 12b, *s.v. memukhan.*

[11] It is possible that Memukhan's speech to the King, with its emphasis on the problem of the women in the kingdom, is a presentation of what would be said to the general population to justify the new laws. The fact, however, that Memukhan emphasizes the issue of the women even when explaining the strategy of his plan to the King, when his words are clearly meant for the ears of the King alone (verse 20), seems to go against that interpretation.

[12] See Rashi's comment there: understanding פורענות as "punishment" rather than "destruction," he explains that Haman is called Memukhan because he is "ready" (*mukhan*), i.e., destined, for his *own* punishment.

Amalek, the infamous nation from which Haman is descended. Yet
Haman is not an Agagite by way of genetics only.[13] He and Memukhan,
by association, deserve that distinction because their behavior is distinctly
Amalekite. In order to appreciate this, it is necessary to analyze the
Torah's view of the nation of Amalek and why that nation is deemed so
evil.

In Deuteronomy 25:17–19 the Torah commands:

זכור את אשר עשה לך עמלק בדרך בצאתכם ממצרים, אשר קרך בדרך
ויזנב בך כל הנחשלים אחריך —ואתה עיף ויגע ולא ירא א-להים.

Remember what Amalek did to you on the way at your going-out from
Egypt, *how he encountered you on the way and attacked your tail—all
the beaten-down-ones at your rear—while you [were] tired and weary
and [thus] he was not God-fearing.*

The nation of Amalek is infamous not only for attacking Israel (which
many nations did), but for attacking those who were straggling behind the
nation, which as a whole was tired and weary. This act, says the Torah,
indicates that the Amalekites were not God-fearing (ירא א-להים).

This association between fear of God and proper treatment of the weak
is found in other places where the concept of the fear of God appears. In
Leviticus 19, among a long list of laws, two are specifically linked with
the idea of fear of God. Verse 14 states:

לא תחלל חרש ולפני עור לא תתן מכשל ויראת מא-להיך אני ה'.

You shall not insult the deaf, or place a stumbling block before the
blind. *You shall fear your God*: I am the Lord.

In verse 32 God commands:

מפני שיבה תקום והדרת פני זקן ויראת מא-להיך אני ה'.

You shall rise before the aged and show deference to the old; *you
should fear your God*: I am the Lord.

---

[13] Haman is descended from Agag (3:1)—the King of Amalek (see I Samuel 15:8).
Amos Hakham suggests that perhaps "*Agagi*" was a description ascribed to Haman
by the Jews because of his wickedness and was not an identification of his actual
genealogy (*Da'at Mikra, Esther* 22).

Why are these laws specifically associated with fear of God? *Kiddushin* 32b illuminates this issue in a discussion about the *mitzvah* of standing up for an old person:

יכול יעצים עיניו כמי שלא ראהו. ת״ל: תקום ויראת. דבר המסור ללב:
נאמר בו ויראת מא-להיך.

> He can close his eyes as one who does not see him. Scripture teaches: "stand up and you should fear." It is said of a thing that is within the heart: "and you should fear God."

Sitting on the bus, tired after a long day, one may be tempted to stare out the window or feign sleep in order to avoid standing up for the old man or woman who just boarded. Therefore the Torah says: "And you shall fear God." The Gemara goes on to explain that in cases involving what is hidden in a person's heart—one's true intentions and motives—there is a risk that one might try to avoid acting in the proper way; thus the Torah provides the extra reminder "and you should fear God." The relevance of this definition of "fear of God" to the laws protecting the deaf and the blind, who will never know what you have done, is clear. The concept of the fear of God protects those who are weak, vulnerable, and unable to shield themselves against those who might seek to take advantage of them.

The nation of Amalek, the Torah implies, epitomized the lack of יראת א-להים. They attacked when Israel was tired and weary. In addition, they attacked from behind. By doing so, they acted in a deceitful manner, intentionally victimizing those who were particularly vulnerable.[14] For this crucial lack of יראת א-להים—with all its implications—they must be destroyed.[15]

---

[14] In his commentary on the end of Deuteronomy 25, R. Shmuel David Luzzatto explains that the common denominator between the commandment to destroy Amalek and the laws preceding it is the attempt to eliminate deviousness.

[15] The idea of annihilating an entire nation—even an evil one—has often disturbed me. A partial solution might be found in what seems to be the central issue regarding this commandment.

We are told in Deuteronomy 25:19: תמחה את זכר עמלק מתחת השמים לא תשכח—we must blot out the *memory* of Amalek, i.e., that which they leave behind, their legacy. The emphasis then seems to be not on the annihilation of the people themselves, but rather what they stand for. If so, the commandment to both remember

Haman and Memukhan both represent this same type of evil. They both obtain what they want in a devious manner at the cost of a vulnerable population. If Haman were the *sole* representative of this Amalekite trait, then the message of the *Megillah* would be that defeating Amalek is equal to defeating the enemy of the Jews. By first introducing the Amalekite evil in the person of Memukhan, the *Megillah* takes the battle against Amalek out of the specific context of the plot against the Jews and broadens it to include any scenario in which an ungodly evil sets out to destroy an innocent defenseless population. This makes *Megillat* Esther not only the story of the victory over an enemy of the Jews, but of the victory over "Amalek" in the broadest sense. It is particularly appropriate that Esther, who was both a woman and a Jew, and therefore a victim of both Memukhan and Haman, was the individual ultimately responsible for the eradication of the evil that Memukhan and Haman represent.

The Solution: Bigtan and Teresh Revisited

The introduction to the *Megillah* not only prepares the reader for the evil of Haman, but also hints at Haman's downfall with the story of Bigtan and Teresh:

ויבקשו לשלח יד במלך אחשורש. *ויודע הדבר למרדכי ויגד לאסתר המלכה ותאמר אסתר למלך בשם מרדכי.* ויבקש הדבר וימצא ויתלו שניהם על עץ. ויכתב בספר דברי הימים לפני המלך.

> At that time, when Mordechai was sitting in the palace gate, Bigtan and Teresh, two of the King's eunuchs who guarded the threshold, became angry and plotted to do away with King Ahashverosh. *Mordechai learned of it and told it to Queen Esther and Esther reported it to the King in Mordechai's name.* The matter was investigated and found to be so, and the two were hung on the gallows. This was recorded in the book of annals at the instance of the King. (2:21–23)

(זכור) and to blot them out (תמחה את זכר), which seems contradictory, suddenly makes sense: we are told to remember *what they did* (זכור את אשר עשה לך עמלק) in order to ensure that everything they stand for (their "זכר") is removed from the world. See the commentary of the Netziv, *haEmek Davar*, on Exodus 17:14, who expresses a similar idea.

The mechanism by which Bigtan and Teresh are caught is identical to that which ultimately sends Haman to the gallows. Here we are told that Mordechai, while sitting at the palace gate, hears that Bigtan and Teresh are plotting against the King. He tells Esther, who is now living in the palace. Esther then tells Ahashverosh, who immediately has the traitors executed. Later, the bad news about Haman's plan follows the same trail. Mordechai hears—most likely at the palace gate—what has happened to the Jews. Mordechai comes before the palace gate and makes a scene in order to attract the attention of Esther who is inside the palace,[16] apparently unaware of what has happened. Mordechai then convinces Esther that she must speak to the King in order to prevent the destruction of the Jews.[17]

The fact that this process of communication is key to the upcoming story of the *Megillah* is emphasized by the two verses that immediately precede the Bigtan and Teresh story:

ובהקבץ בתולות שנית *ומרדכי ישב בשער המלך*. אין אסתר מגדת מולדתה ואת עמה כאשר צוה עליה מרדכי, *ואת מאמר מרדכי אסתר עשה כאשר היתה באמנה אתו*.

> When the virgins were assembled a second time, *Mordechai sat in the palace gate*. But Esther still did not reveal her kindred or her people, as Mordechai had instructed her; *for Esther obeyed Mordechai's bidding, as she had when she was under his tutelage*. (2:19–20)

The Bigtan and Teresh story is not only placed here, after the above verses, to provide the reader with information that will be necessary later on. It also serves to illustrate, as these verses describe, the relationship between Esther (who is now inside the palace) and Mordechai (who sits at the palace gate).[18]

---

[16] 4:2–4.

[17] 4:9–17.

[18] 4:1. The parallel between the Bigtan and Teresh story and the later events, and the claim that the Bigtan story describes the "mechanism" by which the Jews will be saved, are strengthened by a linguistic parallel. In the Bigtan and Teresh story, it says: ויודע הדבר למרדכי (it became known to Mordechai, 2:22). Concerning the plot against the Jews, it says: ומרדכי ידע את כל אשר נעשה (Mordechai knew all that had happened, 4:1). Amos Hakham comments that perhaps the two are linked. Just as Mordechai learned about the plot against the King because of his strategic location at

The way in which the story of Bigtan and Teresh is a harbinger of the story of Haman, however, goes beyond the technicalities described above. That story is not merely another example of the process of communication which was used to save the Jews. As we will see, the story of Bigtan and Teresh itself was a determining factor in Esther's plan to defeat Haman.

Esther: The "Better" Queen

In order to appreciate exactly how Esther saved her people, we must first better understand her character and situation. It is clear what Ahashverosh was seeking when he ordered all the beautiful maidens of his kingdom to be brought before him. Vashti had dared to defy him and in the process he was humiliated. His next wife would have to be, to use Memukhan's terminology, "better than she"—טובה ממנה.[19] "Better," of course, meant compliant, docile and well-behaved.[20] Esther, as she is described in chapter two, seems to fit the bill perfectly; she is undemanding,[21] rather passive[22] and, of course, pretty.[23] It is clear from her conversation with

---

the palace gate, he learned of the plot against the Jews in the same way (*Da'at Mikra*, *Esther*, 29.4). See *Megillah* 13b, which describes how Mordechai's position at the palace gate enabled him to overhear important conversations.

[19] 1:19.

[20] The irony, of course, is that Esther is "better" than Vashti, but not in the way Memukhan and Ahashverosh think. As many have noted, Memukhan's statement (1:19), "And let Your Majesty bestow her royal state upon another who is better than she"—ומלכותה יתן המלך לרעותה הטובה ממנה—echoes Samuel's words to Saul informing him that the kingdom was being ripped away from him: קרע ה' את ממלכות ישראל מעליך היום ונתנה לרעך הטוב ממך (I Samuel 15:28). The kingdom was taken away from Saul because he failed to destroy Amalek, and was given to someone more qualified for that job. So, too, Vashti was unable to fight this particular evil while Esther, as we will see, was "better" than she in that respect.

[21] 2:13–15.

[22] 2:8. The verb ותלקח—and she was taken—is passive. The Rabbis read this verse in the positive sense: that she did not go willingly to the King, but rather she was taken by force (*Aggadat Esther* 2:8). Whether her failure to act assertively was a result of the rules imposed upon her, or was an inherent part of her nature, it is a fact nonetheless. Interestingly, in *Sanhedrin* 74b, the question is raised why Esther was not obligated to die rather than publicly transgress the laws of forbidden relationships by marrying Ahashverosh and having marital relations with him. One opinion asserts that Esther was קרקע עולם—like the dust of the earth—when she was with Ahashverosh. Since she was not actively doing anything, she did not have to die. One

Mordechai that Esther quickly fell into the patterns and expectations of the palace. She is afraid and unwilling to go against the palace protocol and would not dare to approach the King without an invitation to do so.[24]

Only after Mordechai chastises her regarding her passive behavior does she realize that she must act.[25] She who knows the palace better than Mordechai, who only sits at its gate, realizes that she cannot, as Mordechai suggests,[26] simply march into the chamber of the King, proclaim that she is a Jew and demand what she wants. Acting too boldly did not serve her predecessor well. Ironically, rather, she is aware as Haman and Memukhan have proven—that only with cunning, not directness, can one get what one wants from Ahashverosh. Using Haman's (and Memukhan's) own tactics, she prepares to convince the King to kill Haman: not because it is in the best interest of the Jews, but because it is in the

---

could interpret the metaphor of קרקע עולם as saying that Esther exhibited passive resistance to the actions of Ahashverosh. It seems, however, that beyond passivity, the "earth" metaphor is meant to evoke the common comparison of a woman to the earth. Both have seed planted in them and give forth fruit (see e.g., Genesis 3:16–19). However while ordinarily, women and men are active partners, the earth by comparison, takes a rather passive stance. Through this metaphor, the Rabbis assert that Esther acted like the earth, i.e., passively. Although the Rabbis here are dealing with a halakhic issue, it seems that this explanation of her behavior is grounded in a close reading of the text.

[23] 2:7. In short, the ideal woman in Persia was one who would look pretty and not cause too much trouble. Vashti was the former (1:11), but not the latter (1:12). Gavriel Cohn points out that the degree to which women in Persia were treated like bodies rather than people is emphasized in the description of the year-long mandatory perfume bath the women had to have before they were brought to the King. The phrase used to describe this, כי כן ימלאו ימי מרוקיהן (2:12) is strikingly similar to the description of the mummification of Jacob in Egypt, כי כן ימלאו ימי החנטים (Genesis 50:3). This phrase appears nowhere else in the Bible. (*Da'at Mikra*, *Esther*, introduction, 9.)

[24] 4:10–11.

[25] 4:13–14. It might seem strange that Rabbis praise Esther for the very thing for which Mordechai chastises her (see note 22). This is not really difficult. Mordechai rebukes her for her general passive behavior in the political realm, while the Rabbis note her passive nature and use it as a way of dealing with the halakhic problem of her relationship with Ahashverosh.

[26] 4:8.

best interest of the *King*.[27] Accordingly, she hides her true intentions from Ahashverosh—puts on a mask, to use Purim terminology—and in that way ensures she will achieve her goal:[28]

ויהי ביום השלישי, ותלבש אסתר מלכות ותעמד בחצר בית המלך הפנימית נכח בית המלך והמלך יושב על כסא מלכותו בבית המלכות נכח פתח הבית. ויהי כראות המלך את אסתר המלכה עמדת בחצר נשאה חן בעיניו. ויושט המלך לאסתר את שרביט הזהב אשר בידו ותקרב אסתר ותגע בראש השרביט. ויאמר לה המלך מה לך אסתר המלכה ומה בקשתך עד חצי המלכות וינתן לך. ותאמר אסתר אם על המלך טוב יבוא המלך והמן היום אל המשתה אשר עשיתי לו.

On the third day, Esther put on royal apparel and stood in the inner court of the King's palace, facing the King's palace, while the King was sitting on his royal throne in the throne room facing the entrance of the palace. As soon as the King saw Queen Esther standing in the court, she won his favor. The King extended to Esther the golden scepter which he had in his hand, and Esther approached and touched the tip of the scepter. "What troubles you Queen Esther?" the King asked her. "And what is your request? Even to half the kingdom, it shall be granted to you." "If it please Your Majesty," Esther replied, "let Your Majesty and Haman come today to the feast that I have prepared for him."[29]

---

[27] Esther later says to Ahashverosh (7:4) that if the Jews were *merely* sold as slaves she would not have bothered him. This indicates that Esther was aware that Ahashverosh did not really care one way or the other about the Jews.

[28] One might question Esther's virtue, if she was willing to utilize those tactics employed by Haman. An important difference is that while Haman would destroy anyone who might stand in the way of his ambition—even innocent bystanders—the only one who receives punishment as a result of Esther's plot against Haman is Haman himself. Even in the subsequent battle, in which a disturbingly large number of people were killed (9:6, 15–16), the *Megillah* emphasizes that the Jews only killed in self-defense (8:11; 9:1–2, 16) and they did not even take from the spoils of war (9:10, 15–16). The only reference to indiscriminate systematic killing—which included women and children (8:11), which is uncomfortably similar to what Haman wanted to do to the Jews, is found in the context of the letter which was sent out to the kingdom, proclaiming what the Jews were *allowed* to do. In this light, however, the commandment to kill all of Amalek, men, women *and* children (see: I Samuel 15:3), is troubling. See note 15.

[29] 5:1–8.

Esther comes before the King—a most daring act in the court of Ahashverosh—and when asked by the King what it is that she desires, she replies that she would like to prepare a feast for him.[30] Her message appears to be that nothing would make her happier than to serve the King; her devotion alone empowered her to defy the law and risk coming to see him without an appointment. By doing this, Esther immediately succeeds in neutralizing any possible disapproval of, or speculation about, her daring behavior. Ahashverosh may rest assured that she is indeed the same woman he so carefully selected. In this way, Esther ironically utilizes her subservient status as a woman—Memukhan's legacy—in her fight against Haman.

Déja Vu

At the very moment that Esther ostensibly demonstrates her great devotion to her husband, she simultaneously begins to work subtly at making him feel, at least on a subconscious level, very insecure. This idea, proposed in different forms by many commentators throughout the ages, already appears in a number of sources in the Talmud and the midrash. In one formulation, Esther wanted to make Ahashverosh jealous of Haman, i.e., to make him think that she and Haman were having an affair:

יבא המלך והמן אל המשתה. תנו רבנן : מה ראתה אסתר שזימנה את המן?.... רבי יהושע בן קרחה אומר : אסביר לו פנים כדי שיהרג הוא והיא. אמר רבן גמליאל : עדיין צריכין אנו למודעי דתניא, רבי אליעזר המודעי אומר : קנאתו במלך, קנאתו בשרים.

> *Let the King and Haman come to the banquet* (5:4). Our Rabbis taught: What was Esther's reason for inviting Haman?.... R. Joshua ben Korha said: [She said] I will look favorably upon him so that both he and I may be killed.... R. Eliezer of Modi'im says: She made the King jealous of him and she made the princes jealous of him.[31]

---

[30] Only later, at the first feast, when she invites Ahashverosh and Haman to a second feast, does she say (that at the second feast) she will do His Majesty's bidding (i.e., will tell him her request) (5:8). However, in their initial conversation, she gives no indication that she has another request.

[31] *Megillah* 15b. See also: *Midrash Panim Aherim* (Buber), versions 2 and 5, which illustrates what Esther did at the feast to arouse the jealousy of Ahashverosh.

It is easy to understand the rationale of this midrash. Ahashverosh, as we have seen, is quite concerned with control and consequently is very suspicious of anyone whom he perceives as undermining that control. His suspicion and insecurity were particularly strong with regard to his wives, a case in point being the story of Vashti's disobedience. He undoubtedly is very pleased that Esther is preparing a feast for him, but at the same time is probably also wondering, "But what is *he* doing here?"

Another selection of *midrashim* posits that as a result of Esther's feast, Ahashverosh began to suspect that Haman (or Esther and Haman!) was plotting against him.[32] One source of this midrash is the continuation of the passage quoted above:

רבא אמר : שנת המלך אחשורוש ממש נפלה ליה מילתא בדעתיה, אמר : מאי דקמן דזמינתיה אסתר להמן? דלמא עצה קא שקלי עילויה דההוא גברא למקטליה. הדר אמר : אי הכי לא הוה גברא דרחים לי, דהוה מודע לי? הדר אמר : דלמא איכא איניש דעבד בי טיבותא ולא פרעתיה, משום הכי מימנעי אינשי ולא מגלו לי. מיד ויאמר להביא את ספר הזכרנות דברי הימים.

> *On that night the sleep of the King was disturbed....* Raba said: literally the sleep of King Ahashverosh.[33] A thought occurred to him: What is the meaning of Esther inviting Haman? Perhaps they are conspiring against me to kill me? He thought again: If so, is there no man who is my friend and who would inform me? Then he thought again: Perhaps there is some man who did me a favor and I have not rewarded him; and therefore men refrain from informing me. Immediately, he commanded to bring the book of records of the chronicles.[34]

---

[32] The idea that Esther might have wanted Ahashverosh to suspect them both is found also in *Megillah* 15b, which suggests that she hoped that on the suspicion of an affair between Esther and Haman, Ahashverosh might kill them both. Esther's martyrdom in these scenarios may be based on her expression of willingness to risk her own life to save her people in 4:16.

[33] This comment follows another opinion which states that the "King" refers to God.

[34] *Megillah* 15b.

A variation of this midrash is found in *Esther Rabbah*:

ונדדה שנת המלך אחשורוש שראה בחלומו את המן שנטל סייף להרגו
ונבהל והקיץ משנתו ואמר לסופריו הביאו ספר הזכרונות לקרות ולראות
מה שעבר עליו ופתחו הספרים ומצאו את הדבר שהגיד מרדכי על בגתנא
ותרש וכיון שאמרו למלך הנה המן עומד בחצר אמר המלך אמת הדבר
שראיתי בחלומי לא בא זה בשעה זו אלא להרגני.

> *On that night the sleep of the King was disturbed...*King
> Ahashverosh's sleep was disturbed because he saw in his dream
> Haman seizing a sword to kill him, and he awoke in terror from his
> sleep and told his scribes to bring the book of chronicles to read and
> see what events had occurred. And they opened the book and found
> how Mordechai had informed against Bigtan and Teresh. And when
> they told the King, "Behold Haman is standing in the court" (6:5), the
> King said, "What I saw in my dream is true; he has only come at this
> time of day to kill me."[35]

Both of these *midrashim* try to establish why Ahashverosh could not
sleep the night of Esther's first feast. The text in *Megillah* explicitly
connects the feast to the sleeplessness, claiming that Ahashverosh was
kept awake first by wondering why Esther had invited Haman to the feast,
and then by trying to ascertain if there was someone he might have
wronged in the past. The book of chronicles is brought to help him
remember who that might have been. When he recalls the Bigtan and
Teresh story, he realizes Mordechai went unrewarded for saving his life.

The midrash in *Esther Rabbah* proposes that Ahashverosh was awakened because he dreamed that Haman wanted to kill him. Here, too, the
book of chronicles is brought to the King and he recalls the Bigtan and
Teresh event. Immediately afterwards, he is told that Haman has come to
the court and concludes that Haman has come to kill him.

The logic of the sequence of events in this midrash is less obvious than
in the previous one, yet the wording of the midrash implies that those
events are connected by cause and effect. Why does the dream prompt
Ahashverosh to have the book of chronicles read? Why does he want to
know "what events had occurred"? What is the significance of the Bigtan

---

[35] *Esther Rabbah* 10.1.

and Teresh story? Why does the King then conclude that Haman has really come to kill him?

To answer these questions, another one not dealt with explicitly in this midrash must be posed as well: why does Ahashverosh dream that Haman wants to kill him? As in the version in *Megillah*, it seems that Esther's feast prompts the King's nightmare. Let's reconstruct what might have been festering in Ahashverosh's mind: Why can't he sleep? Something is nagging at him; he feels as if he has forgotten something, but he can't grasp it. He finally falls asleep and in his dreams, the midrash suggests, all of his subconscious fears rise to the surface. He abruptly awakes and immediately calls for the book of memories in order to decipher what has been disturbing his subconscious all day—"what events had occurred" that would trouble him so and, as the midrash puts it, cause him to dream of Haman killing him. They read and read and read—finally the King finds what he is looking for—the Bigtan and Teresh story. Before Haman knocks at the door, the King has become convinced that Haman is coming to get him.

Why would Ahashverosh's subconscious mind link Bigtan and Teresh to Haman? The connection becomes clear when one recalls the recent events around the palace and, as we noted earlier, their resemblance to previous events. Mordechai, the text emphasizes, is situated and even causing quite a commotion at the palace gate.[36] This is exactly where he was during the Bigtan and Teresh insurrection.[37] For two days now, Esther has been very anxious to speak with Ahashverosh. The last time she had important news for the King was when she informed him that Bigtan and Teresh wanted to kill him. Lastly, Haman has certainly been moving up the ranks recently,[38] and even seems to have won the admiration of the Queen. The latter may not seem to be tantamount to an assassination attempt, but in the eyes of the insecure King, it was close enough.

After reading in his chronicles about the Bigtan and Teresh incident, the final link is made between Haman and the previous

---

[36] 4:1–5.

[37] 2:21. See note 18.

[38] 3:1.

would-be-assassins. Haman, by killing all of the Jews, was eliminating Mordechai, the Jew who once saved his life.[39] This connection is intimated at the end of the midrash in *Esther Rabbah*, in the remark that when Haman appeared at the King's court, Ahashverosh immediately concluded he had come to kill him. The verse in the *Megillah* itself, which mentions Haman's real reason for coming, says:

והמן בא לחצר בית המלך החיצונה לאמר למלך לתלות את מרדכי על העץ אשר הכין לו. ויאמרו נערי המלך אליו הנה המן עמד בחצר. ויאמר המלך יבוא.

> For Haman had just entered the outer court of the royal palace, to speak to the King about having Mordechai hung on the gallows had prepared for him. (6:4–5)

While Haman may not have been coming to murder Ahashverosh, he did intend to kill the very person whom, the King just learned, had saved his life. Knowing that someone wanted to kill the man who had protected him in the past made the King feel threatened or, as the midrash puts it, as if Haman were standing over him with a sword.[40] If so, the Bigtan and

---

[39] Mordechai is consistently referred to as "the Jew" throughout the *Megillah*. This seems to be a way of distinguishing him from the others in the court and therefore indicates that he was something akin to the "court Jew." That he was some sort of official in the King's court is also indicated by his continuous presence at the palace gate (see especially 3:2 where Mordechai's behavior is compared to that of the other ministers). On this topic, see M. Lehmann, "A Reconstruction of the Purim Story" in *Tradition* 12.3 (1972): 95–98.

[40] In effect, Ahashverosh never does learn why Haman had come to see him (see 6:6–10). The midrash, though, seems to pick up on the irony of the juxtaposition of Haman coming to ask the King to kill Mordechai, and the reading of the story in which Mordechai saved the King's life. The irony is heightened by the fact that Ahashverosh might have connected Haman's plot against the Jews with Mordechai, the Jew. This claim, that Ahashverosh was wary of Haman and perhaps even made the connection between Haman's plot against the Jews and a personal vendetta against Mordechai, is strengthened by the two questions the King asked during his sleepless night. Immediately after hearing that Mordechai had saved his life, he asked what has been done (נעשה) for Mordechai, to which the servants reply that nothing has been done (נעשה) for him. This evokes the only other time in the *Megillah* that that word is used: "And Mordechai knew what had been done (נעשה)" (i.e., the plot against the Jews, 4:1). Not only has nothing been done to reward the savior of the King, but quite the opposite: *somebody* wants him killed. The second question the King asked is to Haman himself, immediately after Haman enters the King's chamber: מה לעשות באיש אשר המלך חפץ ביקרו—What should be done for a man whom the

Teresh story in the beginning of the *Megillah* indeed does more than just present the mechanism which leads to Haman's downfall. That incident provided a precedent which allowed Esther to manipulate the current events of the palace to evoke feelings of suspicion against Haman.[41] She recreates the atmosphere of that event for the King so that he feels as if it is happening all over again. The account of that episode at the beginning of the *Megillah* not only *foreshadows* what is to transpire later on, it sets the later story in the proper context in which it can be understood.

The rest of the story leading to Haman's demise plays itself out exactly (or even better) than Esther had planned. Upon hearing that Haman wants to annihilate Esther's nation, Ahashverosh reacts with immediate anger. It

---

King desires to honor? Upon hearing Haman's answer the King immediately sends him to bestow such honor upon Mordechai. The fact that Ahashverosh would appoint Haman, his highest officer, to lead Mordechai on a horse might indicate that he is trying to put Haman in his place. It also seems likely, as many commentators have suggested, that Ahashverosh asked Haman how he thought a person should be honored by the King in order to find out Haman's own ambitions. The fact that Ahashverosh has Haman honor Mordechai might also suggest he had figured out Haman's plan to kill Mordechai.

[41] Perhaps the subconscious activity of the King can also shed light on Haman's exaggerated enmity toward Mordechai. Haman, too, is very much aware of what has been going on in the court. Perhaps Haman is even more aware than the King, since he, being power-hungry, has reason to stay in control of the situation. He knows that Mordechai's presence at the palace gate, of which he is all too aware, is dangerous since Mordechai is liable to acquire all sorts of information there. He might even be aware of the commotion Mordechai made there as of late. Quite possibly, Haman remembers, even without the help of the King's diary, that in the past Mordechai has informed the King of certain goings-on in the palace. Therefore, when Haman says:

וכל זה איננו שוה לי בכל עת אשר אני ראה את מרדכי היהודי *יושב בשער המלך* ..

Yet all this means nothing to me every time I see that Jew Mordechai *sitting at the palace gate*. (5:13)

perhaps what he *really* means is: as long as I see Mordechai *sitting at the gate of the King*, all this is worth nothing, because as long as he is there I am not safe. For that reason, Haman is so ruffled by Mordechai's presence at the gate and feels it neces- sary to get rid of Mordechai *as soon as possible*. If he waits until the thirteenth of *Adar* (which is at least nine months away, see 3:12–13; 8:9) it may be too late. Only when his wife, Zeresh, suggests that he kill Mordechai right away, is Haman able to go happily to the feast (5:14). What Haman does not know and what Mordechai, Esther and the reader do know, is that he is *already* too late. Mordechai's contact in the palace, the last person Haman would suspect, has already been informed. Even if he would kill Mordechai that moment, he has already lost the game.

is the exact cause of his anger, however, rather than the reaction itself, that is particularly significant. Esther says to Ahashverosh:

תנתן לי נפשי בשאלתי ועמי בבקשתי. כי נמכרנו אני ועמי להשמיד להרוג ולאבד. ואילו לעבדים ולשפחות נמכרנו החרשתי כי אין הצר שוה בנזק המלך.

> Let my life be granted me as my wish and my people as my request. For we have been sold, my people and I, to be destroyed, massacred and exterminated. Had we only been sold as bondmen and bondwomen, I would have kept silent; for the adversary is not worthy of the King's trouble. (7:3–4)

Significantly, Esther does not mention her nation by name, minimizing her Jewish identity, thereby allowing a different issue, the King's authority, to take center stage.[42] The King is angered not because he cares about the Jews, but because someone had dared threaten his queen without his knowledge, thus undermining his authority. What upsets the King is that his authority was undermined. Haman will be executed because he is an enemy of the King—not because he is an enemy of the Jews.

In the next scene, Ahashverosh storms off to the garden. Meanwhile:

והמן עמד לבקש על נפשו מאסתר המלכה כי ראה כי כלתה אליו הרעה מאת המלך. והמלך שב מגנת הביתן אל בית משתה היין והמן נופל על המטה אשר אסתר עליה.

> Haman remained to plead with Queen Esther for his life; for he saw that the King had resolved to destroy him. When the King returned from the palace garden to the banquet room, Haman was lying prostrate on the couch on which Esther reclined.

---

[42] Also see note 27 above. The fact that Ahashverosh asks subsequently מי הוא זה ואי זה הוא אשר מלאו לבו לעשות כן—who is it that wants to do this—indicates that he did not make the connection between Esther's words and Haman's plot against the Jews. This might be due to the fact that neither Haman nor Esther refers to the Jewish people by name (3:8; 7:3–4). Nevertheless, one might surmise that Ahashverosh knew that Haman had plotted against the Jews, since the letters calling for their destruction were sent throughout his kingdom *and* the decree was announced in Shushan.

Upon seeing this, the King roars: "הגם לכבוש את המלכה עמי בבית" —
"Does he mean to conquer[43] the Queen while I am in the house?" The
significance of Ahashverosh's statement comes into focus when one
realizes that once again, control over one's wife is used as a metaphor for
authority in one's home.[44] In addition, in the case of Ahashverosh this
metaphor has even greater significance than for the average husband. His
wife is the Queen, his home is the palace and by extension, the entire
kingdom. Ahashverosh is not simply accusing Haman of conquering his
wife; he is accusing him of conquering his kingdom.[45] Once again it is
clear that Haman is executed because he is perceived as a threat to
Ahashverosh's authority.

Esther's success in eliminating the danger to her people was due to her
intimate understanding of the psyche of Ahashverosh and the environment
of the palace. Intensely familiar with her husband's concerns and weaknesses, she was also painfully aware of the consequences of stepping out
of line. Using her acute understanding of these factors, she turned all
disadvantages to her favor. Knowing what was expected of her as a
woman and a wife, she was able to conceal her true actions from the King.
Understanding what lay beneath the surface of her husband's anxieties
allowed her to lead him to his—and the Jews'—enemy without him
realizing she was doing the leading.

The Final Reversal

Although the greatest threat to the Jews is eliminated with Haman's
execution, all of the nations in the kingdom remain prepared to kill the
Jews on the thirteenth of *Adar*. Haman's evil endured beyond his own

---

[43] Rashi suggests he was accusing Haman of trying to rape Esther. (See also Amos
Hakham, *Da'at Mikra, Esther* 46.) Ahashverosh's words may also be interpreted as
an accusation that Haman was trying to seduce Esther. This would be in keeping with
the hypothesis mentioned above that Esther hoped that Ahashverosh would suspect
Esther and Haman of having an affair.

[44] See Ibn Ezra on 7:8, "הגם לכבוש".

[45] It is interesting that except for one possible exception (see Genesis 1:28 and Rashi
"וכבשה") the verb "conquer" is always used in the Bible in the context of conquering
land. See note 22.

death.[46] To avert this, Esther and Mordechai send a new letter to all the nations of Ahashverosh's kingdom. This letter proclaims the Jews' rights:

להקהל ולעמד על נפשם להשמיד להרג ולאבד את כל חיל עם ומדינה
הצרים אותם טף ונשים ושללם לבוז.

> The King has permitted the Jews of every city to assemble and fight for their lives; if any people or province attacks them, they may destroy, massacre, and exterminate its armed force together with women and children, and plunder their possessions. (8:11)

This letter empowers the Jews to fight back against those who attack them—the people of the nations in which they live. No longer must they passively accept their fate at the hands of their neighbors; they may now actively assert themselves and fight for their rights. Like all the other letters dispatched during the story,[47] these, too, were sent to every province in its own language and script—מדינה ומדינה ככתבה ועם ועם כלשנו. Unlike those other letters, however, this letter was also sent to the *Jews* in their own language—ואל היהודים ככתבם וכלשונם (8:9). What a symbolically perfect reversal of Haman's decree which was modeled, after all, on the decree proclaiming "every man should wield authority in his own home and speak the language of his own people—"להיות כל איש שרר בביתו ומדבר כלשון עמו (1:22). The Jews had been subject to the authority of the nations in which they lived, just as the women were subject to the authority of their husbands. Never before had a letter been addressed to them in their own language.[48] As a direct result of the actions of Esther and Mordechai, the situation of the Jewish people was completely reversed. The evil of Shushan had been blotted out.

---

[46] This is similar to the "memory" (זכר) of Amalek which must be destroyed. See note 15.

[47] 1:22; 3:12.

[48] The fact that every nation, except for the Jews, received a letter in its language underscores the fact that the Jews did not have a country of their own, but rather were "scattered and dispersed among the other peoples" of Ahashverosh's kingdom. That, of course, is what enabled Haman to rise against them in the first place.

Conclusion: Do Not Forget

The introduction to *Megillat* Esther can be divided into two parts. The first includes Vashti's banishment from the palace and the choosing of Esther to take her place. The second part is the story of Mordechai saving Ahashverosh from Bigtan and Teresh. These sections foreshadow the events that later occur in the main narrative of the *Megillah*. Memukhan's advice is parallel to that of Haman. The way in which Ahashverosh was informed by Mordechai, via Esther, that his life was in danger is analogous to the mechanism used later to eliminate the dangerous Haman. The stories at the beginning of the *Megillah* lay down templates which are utilized in the later parts of the story. Through the association of the later events with the earlier templates, the common elements of the parallel events are highlighted. This brings into focus the significant issues which the *Megillah* addresses.

In addition to foreshadowing later events, the earlier stories also introduce psychological structures which will serve as a format for later action. These structures allow both for the rise of Haman and for his subsequent downfall. Only within a certain type of atmosphere would Memukhan and Haman succeed in oppressing their victims. Ironically, however, Esther uses that which is seemingly most to her disadvantage, her societal position, to keep her plans a secret until the right moment. Similarly, only because of same insecurities of Ahashverosh, of which Haman and Memukhan took advantage, is she able to turn the King against Haman.

It is clear why the opinion of R. Meir, that one must read the entire *Megillah* on Purim, prevailed. Just as the events of the Purim story are traditionally understood as being a miracle in disguise, so too, the narrative of the *Megillah*, particularly the first two chapters, contains much more than a cursory reading reveals. Starting with chapter three would not really be jumping ahead to the heart of the matter as one might think. Quite the opposite. Omitting the first two chapters eliminates much of the enduring significance that the *Megillah* has to offer.

The story of the *Megillah* tells of the defeat of Haman. Significantly, it also touches on the fight against Haman's "partner," Memukhan. Esther, as the protagonist of the story, personifies the empowerment of both the Jews and the women of the Persian empire. The message of the *Megillah*, however, is so much greater than the sum of these two parts. The purpose of twinning the Jews' situation to that of the women was to expand the battle against Haman and Memukhan to include all evil oppressors, rather than focus on any one specific enemy of one particular population. The battle is against the evil of "Amalek," not against the enemies of the Jews and of the women specifically.

I read the *Megillah* with a deep appreciation of, and identification with, the struggles of both the Jews and the women whose tales it tells. I believe, however, that my understanding of the message of the *Megillah* is greatly influenced by the fact that my personal experience is completely different from theirs. My right to live as a Jew is unquestioned. In the family in which I was brought up and in the schools in which I was educated, I was as a female given equal opportunities. Particularly, I was not only allowed, but encouraged to proclaim out loud—unlike Esther— my "nation and my birthright," which included the right to proudly sit in the *Beit Midrash* to study, examine, interpret and teach Torah. Ironically, that perspective allows me to gaze beyond the particulars of these battles and see the broader picture, and to realize that the message of the *Megillah* is much more far-reaching than is generally assumed. Reading the text in this way, for me, is completely natural.

When the Rabbis discussed whether or not to include the *Megillah* in the biblical canon, their underlying *assumption* was that the *Megillah* was the story of a battle against Amalek. Their initial concern was whether the Bible could contain yet *another* reference to the ongoing battle against Amalek in addition to those already included.[49] Their conclusion: the *Megillah* has a message that could and must be told. Purim and the *Megillah* will remain even after all other holidays are deemed superfluous, because its message endures forever. If the centrality of the Jews in the *Megillah* has a purpose, it is to teach us that we—a nation which has all too often been the victim of evil—must listen every year to the *Megillah*, in order to *remember* what evil is capable of and to ensure it is *erased* from the world.

---

[49] See *Megillah* 7a.

Serah bat Asher:
Songstress, Poet, and Woman of Wisdom

Rachel Adelman

Serah bat Asher, though hardly known, is a critical player in our nation's history—both as one who stirs the embers of our collective memory and as one who survives, unextinguished, as a source of continuity. In rabbinic tradition, she sang to Jacob the message that his son, Joseph, was still alive; she was the one who told Moshe where Joseph's bones were buried in Egypt and she was the wise woman of Abel, who argued with King David's general, Joab, to save the city. Songstress, poet and woman of wisdom, her lifetime spans over ten generations. Some even grant her immortality. She appears by name only three times in the Torah, yet from these fragments, the Rabbis have created a character of tremendous vitality. She emerges out of the rabbinic literature at critical junctions in Jewish history—a facilitator in the transition of the people from a small family to a great nation.

In this article, I'd like to outline the difficulties found in the original biblical contexts where she is named, and suggest why the Rabbis make an "immortal" figure of her. Her legacy has largely been overlooked and has only recently been brought to the fore by scholars such as Avivah Zornberg,[1] Leah Bronner[2] and Marc Bregman,[3] a result of the search for positive female role models in Jewish sources. This essay is a thorough

---

[1] Avivah Gottlieb Zornberg, *Genesis*: *The Beginning of Desire* (Philadelphia: Jewish Publications Society, 1995).

[2] Leilah Leah Bronner, *From Eve to Esther: Rabbinic Reconstructions of Biblical Women* (Kentucky: Knox Press, 1994).

[3] Marc Bregman, "Serah bat Asher: Biblical Origins, Ancient Aggadah and Contemporary Folklore" (The Albert T. Bilgray Lecture, University of Arizona, 1996, pamphlet).

study of her role throughout her extraordinary life span. My sources include aggadic literature, classic commentators, such as Radak and Rashi, as well as modern literary and biblical critics. I've also included the insights of Thomas Mann, who eloquently wove many *midrashim* into his epic *Joseph and His Brothers*, lending the stories a poetic and a modern sensibility. As a result of this work, I hope she will, once again, become a household name. It is said she never died, but entered Paradise alive,[4] but I believe her status of immortality rests with us, not in the heavens, through our retelling her stories.

In the Torah, Serah is mentioned by name three times in the genealogies—in the census taken at the end of Genesis, at the beginning and at the end of the Jewish people's sojourn in the desert. Though nothing more than her name is mentioned, the Oral Tradition compensates for the paucity of information, giving her a critical role at four crucial points of transition in the history of the Jewish people:

1) As a child, she was the bearer of tidings to Jacob, telling him, in a song, that his son Joseph was still alive.

2) She survived into the fourth generation of the Egyptian exile and won Moshe credibility before the elders of Israel.

3) She also knew where Joseph's bones lay and was the one to whom Moshe turned at the critical hour, enabling the Jews to flee Egypt with the patriarch's remains.

4) According to late midrashic sources,[5] she even survived to the last years of King David's reign and was the woman who advised the inhabitants of Abel of Beth-maacah to surrender the traitor, Sheba, thereby

---

[4] "Nine entered Paradise alive; they are Benjamin ben Jacob, Caleb ben David, Serah bat Asher, Batya bat Puah, Eliezer Abraham's servant and the servant of the Kushite King, the Messiah Eliyahu and Ya'abotz the grandson of Judah Hanassi; and some even say Joshua ben Levi." (From *Otzar haMidrashim*, Eizenstein—original sources can be found in *Yashar Vayigash* 110a; *Pesikhta deRav Kahana* 10.86a–87a; *Derekh Eretz Zuta* 1 [end]). In another version (translated from *Torah Shelemah*, by Menachem Kasher, on Genesis 45:26, footnote on 88), "There are those who say that some humans entered Paradise alive.... Serah bat Asher, because she told Jacob that Joseph was still alive and Jacob said to her 'The mouth that told me the news that Joseph is alive, that mouth will never taste death'" (based on the *Targum Pseudo-Yonatan* on Genesis 46:17).

[5] See Radak on II Samuel 20:16.

saving her city from siege. Using the play between poetry and memory, she represents a unique source of continuity in the Oral Tradition.

If we restrict ourselves to the genealogies in the Torah, her life spans from the last generation of Genesis to the surviving generation of the desert. She was but a child when the seventy souls went down from the Land of Canaan to Egypt and was still alive in the fortieth year of their meandering.[6] The meaning of her name, in fact, reflects her endurance. The verb form of the root, *sameh/resh/het*, means to go free, be unrestrained, *overrun, exceed*.[7] The first context in which the term is found (Exodus 26:12) refers to the remnant of the curtain that overhangs the back of the Tabernacle, said to be *saru'ah*, a neutral term. In contemporary Hebrew, *saru'ah* has negative connotations, of being left over, in a state of decay, moldy, aged beyond appeal. Serah bat Asher, however, is a survivor, a "remnant," overhanging in the positive sense—the quintessential woman of wisdom who belongs rightfully to "the immortals." She earns this status, though, not through birth; her wisdom was gained not by emerging from Zeus' temple like the goddess Athena, but through the words she speaks and the deeds she performs.

Naming and Numbering

In the first context, at the end of Genesis, when all seventy souls who go down from Canaan to Egypt are named and counted, the only two women mentioned are Serah, Jacob's granddaughter and Dina, Jacob's daughter. Yet the text says:

> Thus Jacob and all his offspring with him came to Egypt: he brought with him to Egypt his sons and grandsons, his *daughters* (*banot*) and his *granddaughters* (*banot banav*), all his offspring.[8] (Genesis 46:6–7)

---

[6] She is named again at the end of Numbers (26:46) and according to Rashi, "because she was alive she is counted here" (*Sotah* 13a).

[7] See Brown, Driver and Briggs, *Hebrew and English Lexicon of the Old Testament*, entry 5628.

[8] The new translation of the Jewish Publication Society (Philadelphia: Jewish Publication Society, 1985). I will use this translation unless otherwise indicated.

Rashi, commenting on the plural form *"banot banav,"* suggests it refers to Serah bat Asher, who is named in this context and Yocheved (bat Levi), who is not.[9] Accordingly, Yocheved, the mother of Moshe and Serah bat Asher are Jacob's only "known" granddaughters, out of all fifty-five grandchildren. One wonders whether this was indeed the case or whether, in fact, he had other granddaughters who were neither mentioned nor counted because of their gender (as was the case for the sons' wives, who were not counted, cf. Genesis 46:26). Nahum Sarna, in his commentary on Genesis, makes this suggestion as to why Serah is mentioned by name:

> It is inconceivable that Jacob's twelve sons, who themselves had fifty-three sons in all, should have had only one daughter. In light of the general tendency to omit women from the genealogies, there must be some extraordinary reason for mentioning her in this particular one, although no hint of it is given in the text.[10]

Midrashic sources make up for the paucity of information about Yocheved and Serah. Both stand out as exceptional women in the generation going down to Egypt and are therefore worth noting. Both have been accounted as *the* potentially mysterious "seventieth" soul, who makes up the discrepancy between those sixty-six who went down from Canaan and the seventy, including Joseph and his two sons, who were already in Egypt (see Exodus 1:5).[11] Yocheved, however, is not mentioned in this context because according to midrashic sources, she had not yet been born. The expression used for her birth is strange, in itself, *"nolda bein hahomot,"* born between the walls—meaning on the border between Egypt and Canaan. Yocheved comes into being **in a no-man's land, a hinterland** of neither here nor there. She is liminal. Like Serah bat Asher, she is "overhanging" as the curtains of the Tabernacle, running over,

---

[9] Ramban takes issue with this reading and suggests that *"banot banav"* is meant to be singular, just as his daughters, *"banot,"* refers only to Jacob's one daughter, Dina.

[10] Nahum Sarna, *Torah Commentary on Genesis* (Philadelphia: Jewish Publication Society, 1989) 315 on Genesis 46:17.

[11] See Ginzberg, *Legends of the Jews* (Philadelphia: Jewish Publication Society, 1938) vol. v, 359, note 321 (sources cited there include *Genesis Rabbah* 94.1; *Pirkei deRabbi Eliezer* 10; *Targum Pseudo-Yonatan* Genesis 46:27; *Bava Batra* 123a).

extending between two lands, two nations, two periods in the history of her people. Both women span four generations in their lifetime, from the tail end of Jacob's life to Moshe's rise to leadership. They both play a peculiar role in bridging the transition from Genesis, "the book of family," to Exodus, "the book of the nation"—a period in which the Jews are transformed from a straggling tribe of twelve families to a people 600,000-strong. Both women come to embody a source of power and authority which is pre-Sinaitic, prior to the giving of the Law. Yocheved, as Moshe's mother (and according to midrash, identified as one of the midwives, Shifra), is instrumental in the birth of the nation; Serah bat Asher is the one who grants Moshe his credibility.[12]

Strangely enough, neither woman has the full-status of being named *and* numbered in the original context.[13] Serah bat Asher, paradoxically, is named and not counted. The verse reads:

> Asher's *sons*—Imnah and Ishvah and Ishvi and Beriah and *their sister Serah*…. These are the *sons* of Zilpah, whom Laban had given to his daughter Leah. These she bore to Jacob—sixteen persons. (Genesis 46:17–18)

Serah is conspicuously left out of the count of sixteen. Furthermore, her relation is as "*sister*," not daughter (see also I Chronicles 7:30 where she is also referred to as "Serah their sister"). Though in rabbinic tradition she is called "Serah *bat* Asher," an analysis of her lineage links her to another father altogether, Asher being her adopted father, having married her mother with a daughter from a previous marriage. Asher's sons are Serah's half brothers (sharing a mother, not a father).[14] Accordingly, she

---

[12] See my comments below on the midrash in *Pirkei deRabbi Eliezer* 48.

[13] Both women are posited as the seventieth figure.

[14] Ginzberg, in reconstructing her genealogy, has this to say: "Asher's first wife was Adon, the daughter of Ephlal, a grandson of Ishmael. She died childless and he married a second wife, Hadorah, a daughter of Abimael, the grandson of Shem. She had been married before, her first husband having been Malchiel, also a grandson of Shem and the issue of this first marriage was a daughter, Serah by name. When Asher brought his wife to Canaan, the three-year-old orphan, Serah came with them. She was raised in the house of Jacob and she walked in the way of pious children and God gave her beauty, wisdom and sagacity" (*Legends of the Jews*, vol. v, 39). See also Radak, I Chronicles 4:3.

inherits a portion in the Land of Israel along with the tribe of Benjamin. Fatherless, possibly without husband, she is the disowned, the disengaged one, who becomes a woman in her own right—singled out by name, yet not numbered in the counting at the end of Genesis. The Rabbis fill in the gaps where her naming seems anomalous.

Because she is named, she is granted importance as one who may be the "seventieth" soul who came into Egypt (Genesis 46:27). The discussion as to who this mysterious figure is—whether it be Serah bat Asher, or Yocheved, or Jacob himself—raises questions as to the significance of the number.[15] It foreshadows the seventy elders (those who "see God" after the Revelation at Har Sinai, Exodus 24:9) and those who are chosen to help Moshe bear the burden of judging the people (Exodus 18:24–25). In Numbers 11:23–25, they even act as prophets, when "the Divine Presence rested upon them." The seventy elders are, in turn, a prototype for the Sanhedrin. The number seems to mark the founding of a new order—a nation ruled by the judgment of law. Yet at this juncture, as the Israelites move into their first exile, they are not yet governed by law. Their loyalty is to the family—the patriarchs and heredity. The key is continuity and memory. This juncture involves the gestation of a people, prior to Revelation, prior to the giving of Torah at Sinai. The fact that the "seventieth" chair may be filled by a woman at this point in history is unique and not incidental, for a woman contains the secret of continuity within her very physiology, in the potential to "body forth" the future. For Serah, her "biological potential" may never have been fulfilled. We do not hear of her children. Her future resides in the role she plays in ensuring her people's redemption.

Serah–"Telling the News"

Our first encounter with Serah bat Asher in the *midrashim* takes place in one of the most moving moments in the story of Joseph—when his brothers face the prospect of telling their father that their brother, thought

---

[15] Some *midrashim* even suggest the *Shekhinah* is counted as the seventieth figure because "God counts Himself among the pious" (Psalms 106:31). See Ginzberg, *Legends of the Jews* (vol. v, 357, note 321).

to be dead, is still alive. The biblical passage on which the *midrashim* are
based reads thus:

> And they told him, "Joseph is still alive; yes, he is ruler of the whole
> land of Egypt." And his heart went numb (*va'yifag libo*) for he did not
> believe them. And they told him all the words of Joseph, which he had
> said to them: and when he saw the wagons which Joseph had sent to
> transport him, the spirit of their father Jacob revived (*va'tehi ruah*
> *Ya'akov avihem*). (Genesis 45:26–27)

Two questions arise from the text—what is meant by the expression
va'yifag libo, his heart went numb? Is it close to a stroke, a sudden rush of
blood, or does the heart skip a beat, or even stop? And how does Jacob's
spirit revive? The *midrashim* explore the nature of the brothers' anxiety in
telling their father. They fear both for themselves and for him. Perhaps the
secret of their treachery against the favored son would become known,
their guilt exposed and they would then be disowned. Perhaps Jacob
would withdraw in disbelief, or worse, expire with shock. So they plot to
have one of "the innocents" sing him the news, condensing the story to
poetry, accompanied by the harp:

> [The brothers said:] If we tell him right away, "Joseph is alive!" per-
> haps he will have a stroke [lit., his soul will fly away]. What did they
> do? They said to Serah, daughter of Asher, "Tell our father Jacob that
> Joseph is alive and he is in Egypt." What did she do? She waited till
> he was standing in prayer and then said in a tone of wonder, "Joseph is
> in Egypt/ There have been born on his knees/ Menasseh and
> Ephraim"/ [three rhyming lines: *Yosef beMizrayim/ Yuldu lo al*
> *birkayim/ Menasheh ve'Ephrayim*]. His heart failed, while he was
> standing in prayer. When he finished his prayer, he saw the wagons:
> immediately the spirit of Jacob came back to life.[16]

Jacob could only receive the news, without endangering his life,
through poetry and music. The truth of his son's survival had to reach him
through his senses before touching his rational mind; and it is by virtue of
Serah's poetry and her music that the father survives the knowledge.

---

[16] *Midrash HaGadol* 45:26, translated by Avivah Gottlieb Zornberg in *Genesis: The*
Beginning of Desire (Philadelphia: Jewish Publication Society, 1995) 281.

In another version of the midrash, "Serah Bat Asher entered Paradise alive because she told Jacob that Joseph was still alive and Jacob told her—'The mouth that told me the news that Joseph is alive, that same mouth will never taste death.'"[17] She gains immortality by giving "life" back to her grandfather; she grants him access, once again, to God's presence in his life, *ru'ah hakodesh*. Radak understands the revival of Jacob in response to the news, *vatehi ru'ah* (Genesis 45; 28), as a return of the *Shekhinah* to his life:

> *And his spirit was revived*, for he had been as dead as it is written, "*va'yifag libo*" [and his heart *had been* numb, that is, until then]. Our Rabbis, of blessed memory, say that the spirit of prophecy had left him from the day Joseph disappeared, for the spirit of prophecy rests only upon those who are happy (*ain ru'ah nevuah shorah ele mitokh simhah*). Because he was happy on account of the news of his son, the spirit of prophecy returned to him....[18]

In fact, God does reveal Himself to Jacob immediately following this scene—"And God called to Israel, in a vision by night: 'Jacob! Jacob!' He answered, 'Here I am (*hineni*)!'" (Genesis 46:2)

Radak suggests that the "numb heart" may be traced back to the original refusal, on the part of Jacob, to mourn Joseph's death. After the brothers brought their father Joseph's bloody cloak, Jacob cast a desperate judgment, "'A savage beast devoured him! Joseph was torn by a beast (*tarof toraf Yosef*)!'—All his sons and daughters sought to comfort him but he refused to be comforted, saying, 'No, I will go down mourning to my son in Sheol.' Thus his father bewailed him" (Genesis 37:34–35). The image of descent is infernal, a burial alive in Sheol, in which Jacob must struggle with his conscience—both in having sent Joseph in the first place to Shehem, to find out how his brothers were faring and in pronouncing his death sentence. By speaking the words, "Joseph was torn by a beast," he creates an irreversible reality, confirming his son's death. Yet he refuses to be comforted. Either he is committed to an inconsolable

---

[17] Translated from *Torah Shelemah* on Genesis 45:26, footnote 88.

[18] Rashi similarly basis his interpretation on the Targum Onkelos, "*usharat ru'ah kudsha al Ya'akov avuhon.*"

despair, or he lives in a state of suspended animation, doubting the certainty of his own interpretation. Rashi comments on Jacob's refusal to be comforted as a denial of his son's death, his unwillingness to accept the decree that the deceased must be forgotten.[19] Perhaps the father has an inkling that this decree, a kind of death certificate, cannot be stamped—an intuition that the evidence is not what it appears to be. In mourning, Jacob would be accepting that pronouncement of death, the signing of the certificate, thereby committing himself to the irrevocable process of loss of memory. His refusal to mourn, then, is an act of defiance against the commitment to forget his son and move on.

Dylan Thomas, in his poem "A Refusal to Mourn the Death, by Fire, of a Child in London," writes of this phenomenon as a deafness to truth:

> Shall I let pray the shadow of a sound…to mourn
> The majesty and burning of the child's death.
> I shall not murder
> The mankind of her going with a grave truth
> Nor blaspheme down the stations of the breath
> With any further
> Elegy of innocence and youth.[20]

The poem is an anti-elegy, a denial of the child's tragic death. Paradoxically, committing it to poetry is an admission of the irreversible "grave truth," the truth that she may exist now only as memory. Likewise, Jacob's "refusal to mourn," while admitting the possibility of Joseph's death, is a means of preserving him unburied, outside the grave, outside truth. Zornberg reads the ambiguity—both the denial of death and the state of perpetual mourning—within the very language. The term "to comfort," *nahem*, suggests a willingness to turn to other thoughts (*mahshavah aheret*) in the broadest sense, to change one's mind. Thus, in the story of Noah, the root, *n.h.m.* can denote both comfort and "regret" (Genesis 6:6), a "change in cognitive gestalt."[21] She writes:

---

[19] Rashi on Genesis 37:35.

[20] Dylan Thomas, "The Refusal to Mourn the Death, by Fire, of a Child in London" in *The Modern Poets* (NY: McGraw-Hill, 1963).

[21] Zornberg, 414, note 34.

Jacob, on some subconscious level, *knows* that Joseph is alive; while consciously, he thinks him dead. That is why he cannot accept comfort for him. The point is obviously paradoxical: normally, one might imagine that a mourner who refused to be comforted is over-involved in the despair of death. The midrash shifts the reader's perspective: the willingness to be comforted becomes a mode of despair at the finality of death—it is a "decree" that allows the dead to recede from the heart of the living, a kind of treachery to the loyalty of memory. Conversely, the refusal to be comforted is a refusal to yield up the dead, to turn one's mind to other thoughts.[22]

So Serah bat Asher is the oracular messenger of truth. Like Orpheus, she plays the role of a poet who *resurrects* the dead—asserts the truth of Joseph *never having died*. She allows Jacob to imagine another possibility, the alternative narrative to "Joseph was torn by a beast," thereby enabling *Jacob* to live. For it is not Joseph, but Jacob who bore a kind of death—the exile of the divine word.

Thomas Mann, in his epic version of *Joseph and His Brothers*[23] enhances the midrashic version of this story and suggests Serah "of the song-lips" was the necessary messenger because poetry "is always the gentlest, whether sweet or bitter or bitter-sweet in one." The shift to an alternative view for Jacob, the real comfort or *nehamah*, required a radically different mode of transmission: an aesthetic one, touching the visceral, before the rational consciousness, where one's senses are struck by the beauty of the words before their meaning is scrutinized. It is the mode of Keats' Grecian Urn—"Beauty is truth, truth beauty." And yet Jacob does not initially give in to its influence. Thomas Mann argues against the aesthetic, remaining all too skeptical along with Jacob:

> "But listen now, my gifted one" [as he addresses Serah after hearing her song], "while I say I have heard with pleasure the music and the poetry, but yet not without some misgiving the sense. For poesy, dear little one, poesy is always an alluring, seductive, dangerous thing. Sense and senses lie close together and song rhymes all too easily with

---

[22] Ibid., 300.

[23] Thomas Mann, *Joseph and His Brothers*, translated from German by H.T. Lowe-Porter (London: Sphere, 1968).

wrong...the rhymes are well enough but not the reason and so it hath neither rhyme nor reason."[24]

Finally, though, she does get under his skin, as it were, past his sense and convinces him that indeed Joseph is alive, alive and "already quite fat with the years and the fleshpots of Egypt."[25] Jacob, whose spirit is revived, to whom the *Shekhinah* returns, tells her she will be rewarded with the gift of entering Heaven alive. Like Elijah who rose up to Heaven in a chariot of fire, also having granted *life-after-death* to the widow of Zarephath's son,[26] Serah bat Asher never tastes death. She enters Gan Eden alive.

Serah and the Code Words of Redemption

The "power of poesy," of language as a transformative force, carries Serah through the generations. In our next encounter with her, she plays the role of adjudicator—the elders of Israel turn to her in determining whether Moshe is the true redeemer of the Israelites. While she holds a seat as the people's "oracle," Moshe must earn his.

In the revelation at the burning bush, Moshe quavers at the prospect of being the leader of the Exodus from Egypt, "Who am I, that I should go to Pharaoh and free the Israelites from Egypt?" (Exodus 3:11). In this scene, he objects to the delegation at least four times—hinging on his belief that the nation will not trust him ("What if they do not believe me and do not listen to me..." Exodus 4:1) or that he would fail to move them, not being an eloquent man ("...I have never been a man of words...I am slow of speech and slow of tongue" Exodus 4:10). He is continually anxious about his own ability to use language fluently and refers to himself on several occasions as *aral sefata'im* (Exodus 6:12 and 30), literally "of uncircumcised lips."[27] In contrast, Serah has a fluency with language which allows

---

[24] Thomas Mann, *Joseph the Provider* (London: Sphere Books, 1968) vol. 6, 363–64.

[25] Ibid., 364.

[26] I Kings 17:17–24.

[27] R. Sa'adia Ga'on suggests he had a speech defect; Moshe stuttered. Rashi rather opaquely comments that his lips were sealed, *atum.* In his supercommentary on Rashi, *Gevurot Hashem*, the Maharal of Prague suggests Moshe's speech impediment is indicative of the purity and intensity of his words. He was *nivdal*, set apart, so close to God was he, that he needed the mediation of his brother, Aharon, as his

the incredible to be credible, the unbelievable, believed. This contrast is played out in the midrash, *Pirkei deRabbi Eliezer* 48, in which Serah recognizes the code words that Moshe uses, "*pakod pakadeti*" (Exodus 3:16 and echoed in 4:31)—meaning God has surely noticed/remembered His promise to you as a nation. She gives the stamp of approval that he, indeed, is the redeemer. Before I analyze the contents of the midrash, I would like to examine some original contexts in which the term *pakod pakadeti* appears.

In the revelation at the burning bush, God answers Moshe's first query about why he in particular was chosen to be the emissary ("Who am I?" Exodus 3:11)—with the sign of the bush, which burnt without being consumed, as symbolic of his role: "I will be with you; and this [the burning bush] shall be a token (*ot*) to you, that I have sent you" (Exodus 3:12). To Moshe's latter query of what he is to respond when asked, "What is [God's] name?" God provides a theological credential, a metaphysical *asmakhta*, to grant him the authority he needs as a leader. The answer can be broken down into three components which overlap—the actual name *Ehyeh-Asher-Ehyeh*,[28] loyalty to the patriarchs and the promise to fulfill the covenant by bringing the people out of Egypt into their own land:

> *Ehyeh-Asher-Ehyeh...Eheyeh* has sent me to you.... Go and assemble the elders of Israel and say to them: "the Lord, the God of your fathers, the God of Abraham, Isaac and Jacob, has appeared to me and said, 'I have taken note of you (*pakod pakadeti*[29] *etkhem*) and of what is being done to you in Egypt.'" (Exodus 3:15–6)

---

spokesman. Ibn Ezra offers yet another interesting interpretation: Moshe is imputed with an accent, perhaps even to the point of unintelligibility, because of his many years abroad. His Egyptian upbringing and his sojourn in Midian would be reflected in his speech, perhaps arousing distrust among his people.

[28] A full explication of the meaning of this name is beyond the bounds of our discussion.

[29] The doubling of the verb, *pakod pakadeti*, is an intensification of the verb (absolute infinitive in tautological form), *pakod* being the direct object of the verb *pakadeti*, literally "I will have remembered the remembering." The use of this form suggests that it will surely happen, being part of an irrevocable promise. Once the people hear this phrase, they will know that God "has surely noticed them"—with the purpose of fulfilling His words. See *Gesenius Hebrew Grammar*, E. Kautzch ed. (Oxford University Press, 1910) 342, par. 112n.

Yet Moshe is still uneasy and God grants him three miraculous signs (*otot*) with which to convince the elders of Israel of his authority—his rod becomes a snake, his hand turns leprous and the Nile water changes into blood. The verbal message is not trusted as sufficient, Moshe not being privy to its power. Having grown up in Pharaoh's court and then fleeing to Midian, he has been cut off from the Oral Tradition, which travels from father to child. The impact of "*pakod pakadeti*" is lost to him. The letters, "*otiot*," give way to the power of signs, *otot*, in Moshe's mind. Yet it is the former which become transformative in Moshe's career as prophet.

When Moshe *does* appear before the elders with Aharon as his spokesman, he performs the three miraculous signs (*otot*) that God had given him. Note that the term *pakad*, is repeated:

> And Aharon repeated all the words that the LORD had spoken to Moshe and he performed the signs in the sight of the people. And the people were convinced. When they heard that the Lord had taken note of, *pakad*, the Israelites and that He had seen their plight, they bowed low in homage. (Exodus 4:30–31)

What exactly did they hear? And what is meant by the term *pakad*? The syntax in English impedes us from exploring the full ambiguity of the Hebrew phrase. Ibn Ezra suggests that they were convinced because they had heard. He rearranges the verse; hearing (*va'yishme'u*) comes before being convinced (*va'ya'amen*), understanding before acceptance ("because," *ki*, is attached to the clause *pakad Hashem*).

This interpretation seems to draw on two possible meanings for the root *pakad*—*peh/kuf/dalet*—either as "counting" or as "taking note/remembering." That is, literally the four hundred years[30] of affliction, of being a stranger in a land not their own, had come to an end—God had counted the years out on His abacus and the beads had reached the end of

---

[30] According to "the covenant between the pieces," God said to Abraham, "Know well that your offspring shall be strangers in a land not theirs and they shall be enslaved and oppressed four hundred years" (Genesis 15:13). Rashi and Ibn Ezra argue that the exile itself lasted only 230 years (some *midrashim* suggest only 220—see *Pirkei deRabbi Eliezer* 48), but the years from the birth of Isaac to the Exodus add up to 400 (Rashi on Genesis 15:13 and Ibn Ezra on Exodus 40:12).

the line. And now came the time for focusing on their deliverance—"taking note/remembering" the Israelite people.

To understand the unique usage of the term *pakad*, as recognized by Serah, we must examine its varied connotations. The verb itself, based on the root *peh/kuf/dalet*, has many interrelated meanings; the paradigmatic use being when Sarah conceives Isaac: "And the Lord [*yud/kay/vav/kay*] took note of Sarah (*pakad et Sara*) as He had promised and the Lord did for Sarah as He had spoken" (Genesis 21:1). What happens, literally, is the conception of a child, but in "the mind of the Omniscient" it is the fulfillment of a promise. Here the word *pakad* is commonly translated as "remembered," yet remembering implies forgetting and one would not impute such an omission to God here.

Another translation suggests "visit," which in older English translations of the Bible means a revelation of the Divine Presence. This "visitation," though, leaves a permanent mark on her skin. I think of it metaphorically, as the focus of dispersed light into a beam, the focal point being Sarah. In contrast, the expression used when Rachel conceives is: "And God remembered Rachel" "*va'yizkor Elokim et Rahel*" (Genesis 30:22). Here, God as *Elokim* "calls her to mind" without there having ever been a promise. She was physically "forgotten" and then recalled *to her body*; having been barren for so long, but the "recall" has no transformative power for the nation. It is a judgment reversed on her personally; hence the name of God there is *Elokim*. Sarah's "remembrance" is of a different dimension altogether. Here the Tetragrammaton is used—which connotes a particular relationship with the Israelites, beginning with the promise to Abraham that through his seed the nation would be built (Genesis 15:4).[31] The verb *pakad* suggests a transition larger than the

---

[31] R. Yoel Bin Nun has suggested that the difference between the name, *yud/kay/vav/kay* (the Tetragrammaton) and *Elokim* is like the difference between a first name and a last name. The former connotes the unique presence of God for the individual, as in the fulfillment of a promise, which has classically been understood as the characteristic of *hesed* (lovingkindness), whereas the latter connotes God in His transcendent, perhaps universal, impersonal form, associated with the characteristic of judgment. The Tetragrammaton in Hebrew is actually the third person present form of the verb "to be"—yet "being" in Hebrew takes an active, dynamic form as God's *personal* presence for the individual as *yud/kay/vav/kay*. (Yoel Bin Nun,

person "visited." It thrusts the nation forward by implanting the particularization of the covenant into the child Sarah bears, while at the same time "remembering" the promise to Abraham. The term, then, is like a barbed arrow, drawn by the archer of the past and directed towards the target of the future, the redemption of the people.

In Exodus, the term *pakad* is consistent with its use in speaking of the conception of a child. Just as the child draws on its parents' genetic make-up as the blueprint for its *becoming*, so too, the nation, in its beginning stages, draws on its link to the forefathers. And just as the child must grow into his or her potential, so too the nation must move into its future as a free people. God uses the term as a means of convincing the nation of Moshe's authority:

> Go and assemble the elders of Israel and say to them: "the Lord, the God of your fathers, the God of Abraham, Isaac and Jacob, has appeared to me and said, 'I have taken note of you (*pakod pakadeti etkhem*) and of what is being done to you in Egypt.'" (Exodus 3:15–16)

The covenant is recalled through the forefathers and the transformative power of "taking note" is implied. The midrash draws on this double meaning present within the word *pakad*, inclusive of a past link and future fulfillment of a promise:

> Rabbi Eliezer said: Five letters are doubled in the Torah and all of them contain the secret of redemption... *kaf-kaf... mem-mem... nun-nun... peh-peh...*and *tzadi-tzadi...*[32] through which our forefathers were redeemed from Egypt, as it says, [*pakod pakadeti etkhem*] "I have taken note of you" (Exodus 3:16).... These letters (*peh-peh*) were delivered solely to our father Abraham. Our father Abraham delivered them to Isaac and Isaac [delivered them] to Jacob and Jacob delivered the mystery of the Redemption to Joseph, as it is said, "But God will surely take notice of you (*pakod yifkod etkhem*)" (Genesis 50:24). Joseph his son delivered the secret of the Redemption to his

---

"Being as Dynamic and as State in the Bible: The Literal Meaning of the Name of God" [Hebrew] *Meggadim* 5 (1988): 7–23.

[32] In this midrash, all the "redemptive" letters, including "*peh*," differ in form when at the end of a word (*kaf, mem, nun, peh, and tzadi*), suggesting the *telos*, the ultimate end they are meant to signify.

brethren. Asher, the son of Jacob, delivered the mystery of the Redemption to Serah his daughter. When Moshe and Aharon came to the elders of Israel and performed the signs in their sight, the elders of Israel went to Serah, the daughter of Asher and they said to her: "A certain man has come and he has performed signs in our sight, thus and thus." She said to them: "There is no reality in the signs." They said to her: "He said, '*Pakod yifkod*—God has surely taken notice of you'" (Exodus 4:31). She said to them: "He is the man who will redeem Israel in the future from Egypt, for thus did I hear from my father, '*peh-peh*,' '*pakod pakadeti*'—'I have surely taken note of you'" (Exodus 3:16). Forthwith the people believed in their God and in Moshe, as it is said, "And the people believed when they heard that the Lord had taken note of the children of Israel." (Exodus 3:31)[33]

In this drama, Moshe gathers the Elders of Israel and performs signs and wonders (*otot*) before their eyes. While impressive, these visual tokens are not accepted as an ultimate source of authority. They turn to Serah, who "spans the generations,"[34] the last survivor of the generation that came down to Egypt from Canaan and therefore the sole link to the forefathers. It is a time of disjunction in history. "A new king arose in Egypt who did not know Joseph" (Exodus 1:8)—when memory is askew, a great leader in Egypt, "Joseph the provider," is forgotten. Serah, then, is an anomaly—a relic, "hanging over" as her name implies. In the midrash, she is loyal to her past role as one who stirs memories; she reasserts links at a time of rupture. The old woman outrightly disregards the power of the *otot*, saying, "there is no reality in the signs"—and confirms Moshe as the redeemer only when she hears him repeat the code words he received directly from God (Exodus 3:16). She heard these same words in Joseph's parting statement to his brothers:

> I am about to die. God will surely take notice of you (*pakod yifkod etkhem*) and bring you up from this land to the land that He promised on oath to Abraham, to Isaac and to Jacob. So Joseph made the sons of

---

[33] *Pirkei deRabbi Eliezer* 48; the translation is my own.

[34] This is Marc Bregman's term and I think it is appropriate since it includes both the *meaning* of her name and her significance in history. See "Serah Bat Asher: Biblical Origins, Ancient Aggadah and Contemporary Folklore" (The Albert T. Bilgray Lecture, University of Arizona, 1996, pamphlet).

Israel swear, saying, "When God has taken notice of you, you shall carry up my bones from here" (Genesis 50:24–25).

The words, originally given over as a promise to Abraham, were transmitted to Joseph's brothers through *an oath*—coupling the promise to bring his bones out of Egypt with the time for redemption (when the "*pakod yifkod*" would be fulfilled). The words were internalized by Serah, as a code and were metaphorically engraved on Joseph's bones. The continuity with the past generation must come through the re-assertion of that oath made to Joseph, echoed by Moshe in reiterating God's promise to the people (Exodus 3:16).

In our midrash, Moshe gains credibility only through language, through the words "*pakod pakadeti etkhem*." The power of the letters (*otiot*), *peh-peh*, displaces the power of the signs (*otot*). Serah bat Asher becomes the adjudicator by being the sole repository for these code letters, *peh-peh*, which have traveled by Oral Tradition, *me-peh el-peh*, from mouth to mouth. The letters are placed into an intensive verb form, *pakod yifkod*, which itself is barbed in time, pointing towards a redemptive act and calling on a past covenant with the forefathers. In the drama between Moshe and Serah, she embodies the source of authority Moshe lacks. Displaced as an infant, brought up in Pharaoh's court, having fled to Midian, he has no apparent relation with the Israelites, neither in upbringing nor heritage. Yet it is this very "outsider" status which makes him a prime candidate as God's prophet and the people's redeemer. He must, however, earn the elders' recognition; the direct revelation from God, word for word, must match the weight of Serah's Oral Tradition, her "*peh el peh*" inheritance. She stands in contrast to Moshe precisely in her continuity with the past, her rootedness in the Oral Tradition. As a poet who stirs memory and longing, she operates in the mode of *Torah sheBe'al peh* even before there is a formal Oral Tradition. Moshe, on the other hand, is a man of revelation, *Torah sheBikhtav*, who stands face to face, *panim el panim* with God. He is the *mehokek*, the inscriber, carving into solid rock the words of God, while she, as songstress and poet now old, still relies on the power of spoken language, the mode of *peh-el-peh*. For her, words alone affirm God's promise of remembering His nation and reasserting continuity in a time of disjuncture and loss of memory.

Serah and the Bones of Joseph

According to the midrashic scenario, Serah bat Asher also plays a critical role at the final hour, when the Israelites are preparing to leave Egypt. She alone knows where Joseph's bones are buried. When the time for the Exodus finally arrives, the people are busy with preparations to leave while Moshe searches the collective memory for the whereabouts of Joseph's remains. The people are eager to proceed with future ventures; their leader, on the other hand, insists on literally dredging up the past, finding those bones upon which the promise of redemption hinges. One midrashic version reads, "And Moshe took the bones of Joseph with him" (Exodus 13:19). This proclaims the wisdom and the piety of Moshe. For all Israel were busy with the booty while Moshe busied himself with the duty of looking after the bones of Joseph. "Of him, Scripture says: 'One who is wise in heart takes on duties' (Proverbs 10:8)."[35] This is a juncture—a moment in which the future hinges on a link to the past and Serah, as an advisor to Moshe, guarantees that link. The original biblical passage reads thus:

> Now the Israelites went up armed out of the land of Egypt. And Moshe took with him the bones of Joseph, who had exacted an oath of the children of Israel saying, "God will be sure to take notice of you (*pakod yifkod etkhem*): then shall you carry up my bones from here with you." They set out from Sukkot and encamped at Etham, at the edge of the wilderness. (Exodus 13:18–19)

I mentioned earlier that Joseph's oath exacted from his brothers linked the time of redemption to the act of carrying his bones out of Egypt (Genesis 50:26). That is, when the time comes, Joseph has every intention of travelling with them. He would not be left behind—neither as remains nor as a fading memory. Marc Bregman notes that "Joseph had made the oath concerning his bones incumbent not upon any one single Israelite leader, but upon all the children of Israel." He suggests that the break in the continuity of generations, implied at the beginning of the book of Exodus

---

[35] *Mekhilta deRabbi Yishmael, Beshalah* (*petihta*), Horowitz ed., 78.

1:6–8, could only be reasserted by one who "spans the generations."[36] Serah is, once again, the only one who can link Joseph with Moshe through her unfailing memory. I would like to propose, however, that finding his bones and bringing them on the sojourn in the desert does not *follow* the timing of the redemptive moment. Rather, the timing is *contingent on* the fulfillment of the oath. As suggested in *Pirkei deRabbi Eliezer*, only through Serah's recognition of the words, *pakod yifkod*, embodied in the oath, can the promise be fulfilled. Likewise, unless the bones of Joseph are found, the moment of redemption is lost. Moshe seems to understand the urgency of this task, but, not having a link to that generation, how could he know where Joseph's remains were buried? The *Midrash Tanhuma* suggests an answer:

> How did Moshe know where Joseph was buried? They say that Serah bat Asher had survived from that very generation and she told Moshe where Joseph was buried. Egypt tried to stand in the way [*amdu*, i.e., they knew that without the coffin the Israelites wouldn't be able to leave]. They made an iron casket and sunk it in the Nile. Moshe came along and stood by the Nile. He took a small stone and engraved upon it, "Rise Ox," (*alei shor*)[37] and then cried out saying, "Joseph, Joseph, the time has come for the Holy One blessed be He to redeem his children. His Presence (*haShekhinah*) is waiting for you.[38] Israel and the Clouds of Glory are waiting for you. If you reveal yourself, well and good! And if not, herein we should be free of your oath." Immediately, up floated Joseph's casket. And you need not be surprised at this, for it says, "As one of them [a disciple of the prophet Elisha] was felling a trunk, the iron ax head fell into the water. And he cried aloud, 'Alas, master, it was a borrowed one!' 'Where did it fall?' asked the man of God [Elisha]. He showed him the spot; and he cut off a stick and threw it in and he made the ax head float" (II Kings 6:5–6). Now, if Elisha, the disciple of Elijah, could cause iron to float, how much more so (*kal vehomer*) could Moshe do so, the master of Elijah![39]

---

[36] Bregman, ibid., 5.

[37] Ox, *shor*, refers to Joseph. See Jacob's blessings (Genesis 49:6).

[38] The term in Hebrew is "*me'akevet lakh*," or "*me'akvim lakh*"—which could be read either as "holds back" because of you, or in a non-literal translation "waits for" you.

[39] *Tanhuma, Beshalah* 2, Buber ed., my translation.

Here the elements themselves, iron and water, are at war in holding back the redemption of Israel. The Egyptians have been resistant all along to the Israelites' redemption; and somehow, at the last moment, they realize that the final restraint lies with Joseph's remains, which they sink to the bottom of the Nile. Ironically, the "not knowing Joseph," the relegation of the hero to the realm of the forgotten, imputed in the first chapter of Exodus, is now reversed and the Egyptians use his remains to impede events. The future can only be realized with the fulfillment of the oath when "God will indeed take notice" of the Israelites and they carry up Joseph's bones from there (Genesis 50:25). The sunken casket is a means of freezing history, mummifying it within iron in Egyptian memory, impermeable to air, impermeable to God's remembering.

Moshe racks the nation's collective memory for Joseph's whereabouts. Serah again, as the sole source of continuity, tells the prophet that the patriarch's remains are to be found at the bottom of the Nile. Now Moshe must use two tactics—the one, symbolic, engraving words on a stone in order to force the casket to float to the surface and the other, an apparent verbal threat. This midrash seems to contrast the two modes, as in *Pirkei deRabbi Eliezer*, when Moshe appears before the elders of Israel. The first mode is miraculous, operating through signs and wonders; the latter is verbal. The prophet posits the written word against the oral. Here the *mehokek*, the engraver, carves the words "Arise Ox" onto stone.[40] The appellation for Joseph, "ox" (*shor*), is the one with which Moshe blesses the whole tribe (Deuteronomy 33:17) as if recalling Joseph to his role as one of the twelve who must assume his position among the nation. Stone, on which these words are engraved like the tablets of Torah themselves, is pitted against the weight of the iron. Yet sinker, alone, cannot counter sinker. Only after Moshe speaks is the cued response elicited. In raising Joseph's casket from the river Nile, both the spoken and the written word

---

[40] In another version of the midrash (cited as the *Mekhilta*, in *Torah Shelemah* on Exodus 13:19, note 272), it is God's name, the Tetragrammaton, that he engraves on the stone. This recalls the use of God's name in the ritual of the bitter waters with the woman accused of adultery (Numbers 5: 23). In the *Sotah* ritual, God is prepared to have His name erased for the sake of reconciliation between husband and wife (*Hullin* 141a). In our case, God's name is used to call Joseph to rise to the surface, as an act of "reconciliation" between Himself and the nation.

are necessary for Joseph's recall. As in our previous aggadah, the written Torah is coupled with the authority of the Oral Torah at a critical juncture in the redemption of the people. Again, the key hinges on Serah's knowledge.

Serah as the Wise Woman of Abel

Our next encounter with Serah, chronologically, is found in the story of the anonymous wise woman of Abel of Beth-maacah (II Samuel 20). The reasons she is considered to be this mysterious figure over six hundred years after her original appearance in the Bible are intriguing.[41] One might be the phenomenon of "the conservation of biblical personalities," in which stories of obscure and unnamed people are identified in midrash with well-known biblical figures for the sake of continuity within and between texts. Or it could be that her quality, as the one who bridges generations, is just what is needed to resolve the conflict between king and countrymen. The biblical context can be summarized thus: Joab, the king's chief henchman, has been sent to rout out the traitor, Sheba son of Bichri, a Benjaminite.[42] Sheba threatens to split the nation as he rallies the men of Israel against the tribe of Judah, in his declaration of non-allegiance to David, the king. When Sheba finds refuge in a walled city, Abel of Beth-maacah,[43] Joab and his troop attack, ostensibly to extract the traitor, but potentially to pillage, burn and kill the inhabitants as well. While they are battering the wall, a wise woman (identified by the Rabbis in the midrashic tradition as Serah) shouts over the ramparts.

---

[41] Calculations suggest she was 686 years old at this point (*Midrash Derekh Eretz Zuta*).

[42] It is significant that he is from the tribe of Benjamin, for since the incident of the concubine of Gibeah (Judges 19), the nation is continually threatened by disunity often arising within the tribe of Benjamin. While appointing Saul (also a Benjaminite) as king may have been an attempt at correcting that disunity, it fails. And David (from the tribe of Judah) is meant to be his better-suited successor. Insurrection from among the tribe of Benjamin, however, is par for the course in King David's attempt to unite the nation.

[43] The city itself may have been in Benjaminite territory, hence the citizens of the town may have been torn between loyalty to king and tribe.

Herein ensues a very interesting dialogue between the military leader, Joab, and the aged woman, in which she manages to save the residents of her town—both from death and from transgression—surrendering the head of the traitor, Sheba to his pursuers. The whole dialogue takes place over a wall, in itself a defense, on a symbolic level a barrier between outside and inside, yet the woman turns this barrier into a bridge between the people and the king. Just as Serah links the generation between Joseph and Moshe through her memory, here too she mediates between the king's henchman and her people through her clever rhetoric.

I would like to analyze the dialogue as it is presented in the midrash. The original source is primarily concerned with the question of who fills the honored seventieth seat of those who left Canaan for Egypt. Serah seems to merit being counted retroactively as "the seventieth" because of her longevity and her unique role as woman of wisdom, arbiter of the law. In her own words:

אני השלמתי מנינן של ישראל אני השלמתי נאמן לנאמן.

> I completed the number of seventy children of Israel who accompanied Jacob to Egypt. I linked one faithful leader of Israel, Joseph, with the next faithful leader of Israel, Moshe.[44]

The midrash plays with two meanings to the word: 1) השלים–*to fill in*, as an act of completing or rounding-out the number "seventy," and 2) *to link* or bridge, as Serah does in spanning the generation from Joseph to Moshe. According to a simple reading of this passage, she merits completing the seventy Israelites, being counted among them, by virtue of filling in the years between Joseph and Moshe. Yet a third meaning to the Hebrew term comes to the fore in the stories of Serah bat Asher—*to reconcile*, to make peace between people, derived form the words *shalom* (שלום) or *shalem* (שלם). It is this meaning that becomes significant when Serah comes to save her town from siege. Following is my translation of the retelling of the story in *Genesis Rabbah*. For the sake of comprehensibility, I have

---

[44] *Pesikhta deRav Kahana, Beshalah*, Mandelbaum ed. (189). Joseph is *ne'eman*, faithful or trusted, because he was "keeper of the keys" in Potiphar's house (Genesis 39:4) and Moshe is called *ne'eman* because God speaks to him directly, "He [the prophet] is trusted throughout My household" (Numbers 12:7).

taken the liberty of including, in brackets, the narrative sections the midrash has left out.

[All the troops with Joab were engaged in battering the wall] when a wise woman shouted from the city, "Listen! Listen! Tell Joab to come over here so I can talk to him." He approached her and the woman asked, "Are you Joab?" Meaning, "You are a father (*av*) of Israel, yet you do nothing but shorten the life of man. You don't behave according to the meaning of your name. Neither you nor David are learned (*benei Torah*)." [...She continued, "In earlier times they would have spoken saying, 'Let them ask Abel to surrender,'] and so they would have ended the matter" by which she meant, "Have the words of Torah ended here?! Is it not written, "When you approach a town to attack it, you shall offer it peaceful terms (*ve'karata eleiha shalom*)" (Deuteronomy 20:10). And he [Joab] asked her, "Who are you?" She answered, "I am one of those who seek the welfare of the faithful in Israel (*anokhi* **shlumei** *emunei Yisrael*)—I am the one who completed the number of Israel (**hishlamti** *minyan shel Yisrael*); I am the one who linked the 'faithful' to the 'faithful' (**hishlamti** *ne'eman lene'eman*), Joseph to Moshe.... But you seek to bring death upon a city...and upon me for I am a mother in Israel." And Joab replied, "Halila! Halila! Far be it, far be it for me [to destroy or to ruin]!" Halila is said twice—once for David and once for Joab; far be it for the Kingdom of David. "Not at all! But a certain man from the hill country of Ephraim, named Sheba son of Bichri, has rebelled against King David. [Just hand him alone over to us and I will withdraw from the city.]"[45]...The woman assured Joab, "His head shall be thrown over the wall to you." How did she know this? She said, "He who is insolent toward the royal house of David will be decapitated by divine decree." Immediately, the woman came to all the people with her clever plan. "Do you not know David's reputation?" she urged them. "Which kingdom has successfully resisted him?" "What does he demand?" they asked her. "A thousand men," she replied, "and is it not better [to sacrifice] a thousand men than have your city be destroyed?" "Let every one give according to his means," they

---

[45] Herein ensues a rather technical discussion over the redundancy in the verse, "*against* the king, *against* David." One opinion suggests "Whoever rebels against the king rebels against a scholar.... How much more [heinous is his offence] when he rebels against a king and a scholar!" The other opinion suggests that "Whoever is insolent toward a king it is as though he were insolent toward the *Shekhinah*."

proposed. "Perhaps he would be willing to compromise," she suggested. She then pretended to go and appease him and returned with the number reduced from a thousand to five hundred, then to one hundred, to ten and finally to one, who was a lodger [stranger] there and who was he? Sheba the son of Bichri. And they cut off the head of Sheba the son of Bichri [and threw it down to Joab. He then sounded the horn; all the men dispersed to their homes and Joab returned to the king in Jerusalem].[46]

This is an elaborate retelling of the biblical story, highlighting the conflict between loyalty to one's king and betrayal of a stranger seeking refuge within one's walls. The wise woman of Abel is faced with a dilemma—does she convince the people to adopt a cruel attitude of taking inventory of "strangers" within the city, or does she "win them over" by showing it would be better to sacrifice the one to save the many? The ensuing halakhic discussion in the midrash is fascinating.[47] Can one sacrifice an individual to save a city? The answer suggests that if the individual remains anonymous, he cannot be sacrificed and the people of the town must die a collective death. "But if they singled out a particular person, as in the case of Sheba the son of Bichri, they should surrender him and all should not be killed." Serah understands, however, that Sheba may be residing as a stranger, unknown among her citizens, so she feigns a "plea bargain"—give up a thousand and perhaps Joab can be persuaded to take only five hundred. She seemingly bargains him down from a thousand, to five hundred, to one hundred, then to ten and finally to one, who *happens to be* the traitor, Sheba. How is this method effective? It echoes the dialogue between God and Abraham over whether to save Sodom from destruction.

Abraham confronts God (Genesis 18:22): "Will You destroy the innocent along with the guilty? What if there should be fifty innocent within the city; will You then wipe out the place and not forgive it for the sake of the innocent fifty who are in it?" The same expression, *"Halila,"* punctuates his rhetoric, "Far be it from You to do such a thing, to bring death

---

[46] *Genesis Rabbah* 94.9.

[47] See also *Tosefta Terumot* 7.20; *Genesis Rabbah* 94.9; *Midrash Shemuel* 32.140 and *Midrash Ecclesiastes* 9.18.

upon the innocent as well as the guilty, so that innocent and guilty fare alike. Far be it from You! Shall not the Judge of all the earth deal justly!" (Genesis 18:25).

While, on a personal level, Abraham may be vested in saving his nephew, Lot, who is succored within the walls of this city, the plea bargain with God assumes a much grander moral scale. "Save the individual at least!" Collective punishment is surely not true justice. Serah, on the other hand, "plea bargains" to release an individual, *as a sacrifice*, in order for her people not to suffer collective punishment. True, there isn't a strict parallel between Lot and Sheba. One is an innocent stranger in Sodom, a city renowned for its cruelty, where the men would "have their will" with visitors to the town; while the other is a traitor to the king, a threat to national unity, Abel of Beth-maacah merely being his city of refuge. But because the story is told in the shadow of the Judges, when the tribe of Benjamin was pitted against the rest of the Israelites, I think this midrashic Serah is wary of replicating the sins of Sodom, or the incident involving the concubine of Gibeah in sacrificing the stranger.[48] She must negotiate a fine moral line between loyalty to king and loyalty to individual, tracing a line of light through the shadows of her people's history.

However she is cautious in her tone, clever with her measures. On the one hand, she challenges Joab about his learning, citing a passage from Deuteronomy—don't you know that "When you approach a town to attack it, you shall offer it peaceful terms" (*vekarata eleiha shalom*) (Deuteronomy 20:10), before bombarding it. And he is forced to back down from battering the walls. On the other hand, she doesn't want her people to be corrupted by cruel measures, by sacrificing a stranger, even if he is a traitor to the king. He must remain anonymous till the end. She understands her role as the one who seeks reconciliation (*hishlamti ne'eman lene'eman*), spans generations and thereby merits completing the number seventy (*hishlamti minyan shel Yisrael*). In this role of judge, of a wise woman accusing the king and his henchmen of ignorance, she stands as a "Sanhedrin"—a body of seventy, a complete judiciary of her own, as it were. She knows the law well, but knows the frailty of human nature, the potential for cruelty, even better. Her capacity for reconciliation in the

---

[48] Judges 19.

broadest sense of the word—singing the "truth" to Jacob, forging bridges between Joseph and Moshe, loyal to her king and the sensibilities of her citizens—earns her the "seventieth" seat. Ultimately, she affirms life over death and thereby earns the right never to taste death. Upon her demise, she enters Paradise alive, not on a fiery chariot but with a legacy we are left to cherish.

Strange Words Between Strangers: Jacob's Encounter With Pharaoh

Erica Brown

Jacob is the last of the triumvirate of patriarchs mentioned in our liturgy. To receive our praise and consider our petitions, we call upon the "God of Abraham, Isaac and Jacob." It is Jacob who established through his children the tribes of Israel. It is Jacob who brought his household to Egypt where they become a nation. It is Jacob whose name becomes associated with the house of Israel, as reflected in the words of the psalmist: "For the Lord has chosen Jacob for Himself; Israel, as his treasured possession" (Psalms 135:4). Jacob's life was both rich and complex. Jacob's complexity is reflected in one of the most prominent *leitmotifs* in his narratives, repeated acts of blessing and suffering.

Jacob was a man of many blessings, both those that he received and those that he gave. As a young man, Jacob achieved notoriety by stealing a blessing. As an old man, he left the world by giving his sons blessings. As a young man, Jacob fought an angel to grant him a blessing; as an old man, he offered blessings to his children and grandchildren. The blessing can function as both prayer and prediction, conferral of divine favor or material legacy. The act of receiving blessings and awarding them seems to frame much of Jacob's existence. One such act of blessing, perhaps the most curious of all, is the set of blessings that Jacob bestowed upon Pharaoh.

There is a brief encounter near the end of Genesis in which two men who figured prominently in the life of Joseph came together. Joseph presented his father before Pharaoh, and Jacob and the powerful Egyptian leader shared a private moment of conversation. We anticipate that the two would discuss the one matter they have in common: Joseph. After all, both leaders assigned Joseph a position of importance within a hierarchy, be it family or polity. Both presented Joseph with physical symbols of their respective confidence in his future: the striped coat and the signet ring. Both leaders passed on, through these symbols, their hopes that Joseph would achieve success. Joseph's name, however, is never mentioned in this dialogue:

> Joseph then brought his father and presented him to Pharaoh. And Jacob greeted [lit., blessed] Pharaoh. Pharaoh asked Jacob, "How many are the years of your life?" And Jacob answered Pharaoh, "The years of my sojourn [on earth] are one hundred and thirty. Few and hard have been the years of my life, nor do they come up to the life spans of my fathers during their sojourns." Then Jacob bade Pharaoh farewell [lit., blessed] and left Pharaoh's presence.[1]

There are not many extensive dialogues in our sacred Scriptures. Adam and Eve hid and God called to them in one word; Adam replied with few words. Cain spoke to Abel, then rose up against him in the field. The midrash explores the words that prompted this first murder;[2] the biblical text, however, offers no such speech. God called Abraham to the dramatic task of offering his son in a few words and in one word, Abraham responded. Jacob summoned Joseph to the fateful task of inquiring about the welfare of his brothers and Joseph responded with one word. We wonder why the details of conversation, so often lauded as a critical aspect of good literature, are absent in our sacred literature. This economy of words presents us with a biblical convention often misunderstood. In the words of one modern Bible scholar: "Given the reticence...direct speech assumes even greater importance. Within the scenic mode typical of much biblical narrative, it is dialogue that adds dramatic presence to the story and encourages confrontation between the characters."[3] Precisely because of the minimalism of the dialogue, can we feel the full

---

[1] Genesis 47:7–10. All translations of biblical text are from *JPS Hebrew-English Tanakh* (Philadelphia: Jewish Publication Society, 1999) second edition.

[2] See *Genesis Rabbah* 22.7 for the argument that took place between the brothers. Essentially, the varying opinions highlight the roots of human contention: money, love and religion.

[3] George W. Savran, *Telling and Retelling: Quotation in Biblical Literature* (Bloomington: Indiana University Press, 1988) 12.

weight of the drama. The silence itself speaks. With this in mind, we approach what is perhaps the strangest of biblical conversations: Genesis 47:7–10.

Setting the Scene

The context of this conversation must first be established. Joseph has brought his family to Egypt following several tests of character and a striking revelation of identity to his brothers. Joseph's family has been settled in the land of Goshen and offered the best of the land and its produce. Juxtaposed with Joseph's generosity are the increasing hardships of Egypt and its dependents:

> So Joseph settled his father and his brothers, giving them holdings in the choicest part of the land of Egypt, in the region of Ramses, as Pharaoh had commanded. Joseph sustained his father and his brothers and all his father's household with bread, down to the little ones. Now there was no bread in the world, for the famine was very severe; both the land of Egypt and the land of Canaan languished because of the famine. (Genesis 47:11–13)

Joseph provided well for his family, but the rest of the country was impoverished. Joseph had to sell the stored provisions. He purchased land and enhanced Pharaoh's fortunes while addressing the needs of the common man. The children of Israel became wealthy and great in number. Jacob's years ebbed; he made Joseph swear to bury him in Canaan. He then called his children to his deathbed for his blessings, and just as in his conversation with Pharaoh, his predictions and reflections were dark and ominous. Jacob died. Joseph died. The book of Genesis comes to an abrupt close. The gifts of Joseph to his people were rescinded when new leadership took over Egypt. Where in these events, does our conversation belong? Does it shed light on the above events or is it a disconnected fragment, as mysterious in its placement as the jagged texture of the conversation itself? The medieval French exegete, R. David Kimche, confesses his own bafflement at the passage: "I cannot find a reason why this story is recounted."[4]

---

[4] Genesis 47:7.

The Dialogue's Content

It is not strange that Jacob and Pharaoh meet. According to Nahmanides,[5] it was Pharaoh who requested the meeting. He was so impressed by the capabilities of Joseph that he wanted to meet his father. An alternative reading would have Jacob requesting a chance to meet royalty. In the text itself, however, it is Joseph who brought his father in and stood him before Pharaoh. This physical support may suggest old age and frailty, which would confirm Jacob's own reflections about his age. But Jacob had just made the journey from Canaan to Egypt with his whole household; one senses that such a traveler, as he identified himself here, would not require the physical assistance of his son. Perhaps the son, whose absence had weighed his father down, must now try to uplift him to greet a fellow leader as an equal.

Jacob and Pharaoh were strangers, yet the patriarch revealed to the Egyptian king what he had not confided to any member of his family or tribe. He offered the man who had control over his livelihood an intimate and almost tragic summation of his life. Curiously, at the same moment, Jacob blessed Pharaoh upon his entrance and exit. There is a dissonance between Jacob's presumptuousness in blessing the monarch, and his humility in confessing his unworthiness to the same individual. A contemporary scholar offers this insight: "The reason for the separate audience, after that of his brothers, is probably that Joseph felt it would not be dignified for the aged patriarch to appear in the role of supplicant."[6] Sensitive as Joseph may have been to the difference in status between these two powerful men, it still seems that Jacob humiliated himself with his autobiography of misfortune.

Pharaoh's Question

Pharaoh's conversational initiative is also troubling. His first words convey confusion or astonishment at Jacob's age. One would expect,

---

[5] Ibid., 47:9.

[6] Nahum Sarna, *The JPS Torah Commentary: Genesis* (Philadelphia: Jewish Publication Society, 1989) 320.

rather than this personal prying, a dialogue of national or spiritual import. Several medieval exegetes read Pharaoh's question as a statement of respect. R. Ovadiah Seforno stages this as a question of wonderment.[7] Pharaoh was struck by the old age of the patriarch and blurted out the question. Such old age was not common in Egypt.[8] Hidden in Pharaoh's question is an inquiry about the secret of Jacob's longevity. To reach such ripe years is surely a divine reward. Pharaoh's question would then read: what merit did the patriarch have to age so gracefully? It is through this interpretation that one might understand Jacob's response to read, "This is not as much of a reward as that which my fathers received, whose years were many more than my own."

R. Hezekiah ben Manoah,[9] the thirteenth-century French exegete, offers a different strategy: "You look very old and at the end of your days." Jacob is not surprised by this question and responds that in truth, he is not very old but that the exigencies of life have aged him beyond his years.[10]

---

[7] Genesis 47:8.

[8] Sarna suggests that the ideal life expectancy in Egypt was 110 years and that when Pharaoh saw a man who exceeded these years, he asked Jacob this question (JPS Commentary) 320.

[9] Genesis 47:8.

[10] In *The Poetics of Biblical Narrative: Ideological Literature and the Drama of Reading* (Bloomington: University of Indiana Press, 1987), Meir Sternberg writes that the myth of the elderly patriarch who ages with contentment is true of Abraham—"Abraham was advanced in years and the Lord had blessed Abraham in everything," (Genesis 24:1)—but is not the description offered of Isaac. "Isaac was old and his eyes were dim so that he could not see" (Genesis 27:1). Sternberg writes, "Here old age goes neither with admirable character nor with happiness and success but with failing powers all around, notably spiritual as well as physical decay" (349–50). One wonders if Jacob created a more positive view of the aging of his predecessors than was actually the case. Sternberg offers the aging of Abraham and Isaac as two different possibilities for patriarchal geriatrics. Where would Jacob fit in? He certainly seems to resonate more with the Isaac model than with the Abraham model on one level. The text even records a similar state of physical demise: "Israel's eyes were dim with age; he could not see." But Jacob seems to take more control of his progeny in his dying years than Isaac, whose blindness led him to be deceived and give the birthright to the younger son. Jacob, in contrast, very much controls the blessings he gives his children and even, perhaps especially, those he gives his grandsons, Ephraim and Menashe. If, as Sternberg writes, "old age does carry favorable implications for character, except when overridden by failing vision" (351), then Jacob follows both models. He ages poorly but retains a keen sense of vision. All three patriarchs thus offer different models of aging, with Jacob's perhaps

Don Isaac Abrabanel asks the obvious: Jacob has not yet died. How does he know that he will not achieve the years of his fathers?[11] He was already 130 years old. Abraham died at 180, Isaac at 175. Jacob may yet have another fifty years and if not, as the father of the twelve tribes, he certainly must have accomplished his life's work. In progeny alone, Jacob went unrivaled by his predecessors. If Genesis, on some level, is a battleground where humans struggle with God and each other over fertility and legacy,[12] Jacob of all the patriarchs, could call himself triumphant.

Abrabanel posits that Jacob measured his life not in years but in travels.[13] He did not simply offer a number but repeated, "the years of my sojourning." From that perspective, Jacob claimed that he had not achieved what his fathers had. Rashi adds here: "All of my life I have lived in the country of others." His travels were so extensive and beyond his control that he defined his very existence by what he was unable to achieve: a life of harmony in his homeland.

The Blessings

Regarding the blessings, two strands of interpretation are pursued by the classic exegetes. Jacob's blessing of Pharaoh was either an act of humility or strength. Both Rashi and Radak are of the opinion that blessing, in this case, was a simple formality expected by royalty, the biblical equivalent of a bow. In the words of Rashi,[14] "This is a gesture of courtesy, done by all who appear before royalty." To verify this reading, Radak adds an

---

being the most complex.

[11] Genesis 47:9.

[12] Naomi Steinberg in *Kinship and Marriage in Genesis: A Household Economics Perspective* (Minneapolis: Fortress Press, 1993) writes cogently of the need to understand the dilemmas of fertility and legacy to comprehend the structure of the book of Genesis. Lapses in the recording of genealogy occur whenever there is a doubt about fertility or heirship. If one concurs with this theory, then of all the patriarchs, it is Jacob who is most "successful," having multiple wives and thirteen children. Although his most beloved wife, Rachel, struggles with barrenness, Jacob is not limited to her progeny, and thus narrative lapses occur with less frequency in narratives concerning him than earlier in Genesis.

[13] Genesis, ibid.

[14] Genesis 47:7.

example from another biblical context in which the root *brkh* (ברך) is also used as a simple greeting: "If you meet any man, greet [literally "bless"] him not."[15] In II Samuel 16:16 and in I Kings 1:31, the term is used as a "salute" and a wish for the long life of a monarch.[16] Nahmanides faithfully records Rashi's view but disagrees.[17] "The servant does not inquire about the welfare of the master." He suggests that it was literally a blessing, like those given by the pious and the elderly for the enhancement of the king's welfare and good fortune. Implicit in his reading is that Jacob is still the subordinate of the two. Even giving a blessing did not position him above the status of a servant.

R. Ovadiah Seforno will not admit of servile status, saying that Jacob blessed him, "and did not bow to him, neither when he arrived nor when he departed."[18] R. Naftali Tzvi Berlin adds that he did not bow to Pharaoh to indicate that, "They were considered guests of Joseph and not servants of Pharaoh."[19] R. Samson Raphael Hirsch contends that the two were equals; Jacob quickly initiated the encounter with his blessing to demonstrate that although the two may not be of equal stature at that particular point in time, both were leaders of nations. Jacob would not settle for subordination but asserted his equality through the dispensation of a blessing. "Jacob does not wait for the king to address him first. He feels himself on equal footing with a greeting of blessing."[20]

None of these exegetes, however, connect the blessing to the content of Jacob's speech itself. They treat the blessing as a detached fragment of conversation, the contents of which have not been revealed, but which

---

[15] II Kings 4:29.

[16] Nahum Sarna in the JPS commentary draws attention to these verses and suggests that "The content of the greeting is not given, but widespread custom in the ancient Near Eastern world dictated wishing the king long life...." He considers this as the basis for the rabbinic custom of reciting a blessing upon seeing a non-Israelite king (320).

[17] Genesis 47:7, cf. *Shabbat* 89a.

[18] Genesis 47:7.

[19] *HaEmek Davar*, Genesis 47:7.

[20] Genesis 47:6 (London: translated and published by Isaac Levy, 1963), second edition.

frame Jacob's reflections. The midrash does attempt to connect, however loosely, the content of the blessings with Jacob's conversation. In one midrash, Jacob blesses Pharaoh with a life longer than his own, which would be in consonance with what he actually says to Pharaoh, that his own life is shorter in years than he had hoped.[21] In another midrash, Jacob blesses Pharaoh with the wish that he should not experience the predicted famine.[22] While this is not directly spoken about in their conversation, it is clear that the meeting between these two figures would not have occurred had there been no famine in the Land of Israel. It is as if Jacob blessed Pharaoh that he be spared the humiliation of famine from one who has known hunger well.

If we understand the blessings as somehow conforming to the rest of the conversation, rather than as detached formalities, it may enhance our understanding of the dialogue or the relationship of Jacob, Joseph and Pharaoh. In a text so economical and sparse in the details of ordinary living, the inclusion of a bow or formal salutation would seem out of place or trivial. In addition, these two acts of speech do not seem to form one unit. Blessing is generally viewed as an act of spiritual outreach to another. The content of Jacob's conversation with Pharaoh, however, is centered on him. Is Jacob reaching out to Pharaoh with his blessing, or is he using Pharaoh as a sounding board for his own reflections on life's disappointments?

In order to understand the function of the blessings here, one must see the centrality of blessing to Jacob's identity. The word "blessing" in Genesis 27, in its noun and verb form, appears no less than twenty-three times, as the struggle to acquire the blessing of the birthright entrenched Jacob and Esau in a life-threatening battle that will take chapters to resolve. Thus his father first blessed him. He acquired this blessing, destined for his elder brother, through deception. "Cursed be all who curse you and blessed be all who bless you" (Genesis 27:29). Jacob then battled in earnest for his next blessing. In Genesis 32, he fought the angel but did not leave until he earned his blessing:

---

[21] Genesis, *Midrash HaGadol* 47.7.

[22] *Sifrei, Ekev* 38.

> And Jacob was left alone and there wrestled a man with him until the breaking of the day. And when he saw that he prevailed against him not, he touched the hollow of his thigh; and the hollow of his thigh was strained as he wrestled with him. And he said, "Let me go, for the day breaks." And he said, "I will not let you go, except if you bless me." And he said to him: "What is your name?" And he said: "Jacob." And he said: "Your name will not be called Jacob anymore but Israel since you have striven with God and with men and you have prevailed.

This is the most direct and powerful expression of Jacob's life of struggling and blessing—it is this very confluence of seemingly disparate acts, struggling and blessing, which earned and defined his name.[23] Wherever Jacob went he struggled, but at the same time he was blessed and he blessed others. He left Laban's house a wealthy man. He went to Egypt where his children prospered. Jacob's promotion of Joseph was penultimately a blessing for Pharaoh. This capacity to be a blessing and to transmit blessing was a divine gift, as is stated in Genesis 28:14, "And in you and in your seed, shall all the families of the earth be blessed."

At the same time, there are few figures in Tanakh who suffer more than Jacob. Even in his brief conversation with Pharaoh, Jacob referred to incidents of evil and malcontent but provided no details. He described his life not in years but in movement, and resigned himself to the tragedy of his history.

The biographical details of Jacob's life read like a catalogue of misfortunes. When he was finally able to make his escape and set out for home after two decades in the service of his scoundrel uncle, he found his erstwhile employer in hot and hostile pursuit of him. No sooner had this trouble passed than he felt his life to be in mortal danger from his brother Esau. Arriving at last at the threshold of Canaan, Jacob experienced the mysterious encounter that left him with a dislocated hip. His worst troubles awaited him in the land of Canaan. His only daughter Dinah was violated,

---

[23] Aviva Gottlieb Zornberg, *Genesis: The Beginning of Desire* (Philadelphia: Jewish Publication Society, 1995) 235 asks who prevailed in this wrestling match? "Evenly matched, Jacob wants to prevail, to absorb into himself the power of his partner. He wants to become Israel, by mastering the angel. The wrestling match is an occasion for clarification, for discovery of the parameters of personal power."

his beloved Rachel died in childbirth, and the first son she had borne him was kidnapped and sold into slavery, an event that itself initiated a further series of misfortunes. All the foregoing makes quite clear Scripture's condemnation of Jacob's moral lapse in his treatment of his brother and father. In fact, an explicit denunciation could hardly have been more effective or more scathing than this unhappy biography.[24]

It is not surprising, therefore, that a contemporary scholar of the Bible sees the stones present in many of the Jacob narratives as emblematic of Jacob's hardships:

> ...stones are a motif that accompanies Jacob in his arduous career: he puts a stone under his head as a pillow at Beth-El; after the epiphany there he sets up a commemorative marker of stones; and when he returns from Mesopotamia, he concludes a mutual nonaggression pact with his father-in-law by setting up on the border between them a testimonial heap of stones. These are not really symbols, but there is something incipiently metaphorical about them: Jacob is a man who sleeps on stones, speaks in stones, wrestles with stones, contending with the hard unyielding nature of things....[25]

Jacob was a wrestler. He wrestled with Esau. He wrestled with an angel. He wrestled with his father-in-law and on some level, with his sons. He wrestled with deception: from the birthright to the striped coat returned on false pretenses, under the wedding canopy, in Rachel's theft of Laban's idols, and in the deception of Simon and Levi. Dishonesty punctured his weary existence. His mother told him to deceive, he deceived, his children deceived. Knowing this of Jacob, it becomes especially difficult, to the point of irony, to understand the verse: "Esau was a cunning hunter, a man of the field; and Jacob was a plain man, dwelling in tents." The verse suggests Jacob's contentedness and the stability of a life indoors, but such was not Jacob's life. His life was filled with movement, far removed from the stability, innocence and pastoral simplicity depicted

---

[24] Nahum Sarna, *Understanding Genesis: The Heritage of Biblical Israel* (NY: Schocken, 1972) 184.

[25] Robert Alter, *The Art of Biblical Narrative* (NY: Basic Books, 1981) 55–58. Alter's description of the contrast in well scenes (which he terms a biblical type-scene) between Jacob's meeting of Rachel, and Isaac's betrothal to Rebecca sheds much light on the "unyielding" nature of obstacles in Jacob's life.

in the verse.

With the last blessing of our narrative, the dialogue between Jacob and Pharaoh ends as curiously as it began. If Joseph was in the room, he was silent. Jacob did not explain himself further. Pharaoh did not respond to Jacob's confession of inadequacy. He offered no healing words, no empathy, sympathy, or compassion. Pharaoh failed to recognize that with the loss of Joseph, Jacob's life crumbled and through the gain of the very same individual, Pharaoh succeeded. While Jacob struggled to put bread on his table during the famine, and under the shadow of grief caused by the loss of his beloved wife and their first child, his son was growing in power by augmenting the very thing that his father lacked: physical sustenance. The gift to one became a loss to the other; this is most acutely conveyed when the two leaders meet. Jacob communicated his dissatisfaction with life. Pharaoh did not need to display his success. It was evident. Mentioning it would only rub salt in Jacob's wound, and possibly for that reason, Pharaoh chose not to respond to Jacob. Silence was the more noble response. Jacob simply offered another blessing and left. Given Jacob's disappointment, we wonder if the blessings of such a heartbroken man were desirable.

Jacob's Response to Tragedy

One midrash records that Jacob was actually punished with a life shortened by thirty-three years, corresponding to the thirty-three words of complaint he uttered to Pharaoh.[26] On a more profound level, however, the biblical text reflects resignation rather than complaint as Jacob's response to tragedy. R. Samson Raphael Hirsch, in his comments on this passage, speaks of Jacob's resignation:

> In his reply, Jacob differentiates between living and existing. You ask after the days of my *life*. I have not *lived* much. I have sojourned on earth during one hundred and thirty years. The days of the years that I can really call my *life* were in reality only few and they were bad, were just the bitterest and those most full of worry. I had the mission of doing the duties of unhappiness in unhappiness. The contents of my

---

[26] See the *Torah Shelemah* 23 on Genesis 47:9.

life can in no way be compared to the contents of the lives of my fathers. They lived more; every day of existence here below was living,
and they had to carry out the mission of their lives under cheerful conditions. This was no complaint against the shortness of his life, but
modesty in looking back at the moral worth of the life he had lived.[27]

R. Hirsch alerts us to the statement Jacob makes about the quality of
his life and his readiness to relinquish it. Several biblical verses inform us
that Jacob's resignation was actually longstanding, beginning with the
moment that Joseph's striped coat was returned in blood. In an etching by
Rembrandt, Jacob is presented with the coat as one of the brothers points
off in the distance suggesting where he found it. Jacob's hands are raised
in horror, away from the bloody garment and his eyes reflect the terror of
the loss.[28]

From this moment on, Jacob mentioned his own death or its en-
croachment no less than six times.[29] He told his sons on more than one
occasion: "You shall bring down my grey hairs with sorrow to Sheol." He
was elated at the thought of reuniting with Joseph, and claimed that his
only need was to see him, "And then I will die." Once reunited with him,
this was affirmed: "Now let me die since I have seen your face while you
are still alive." One might argue that death was not a singular event for
Jacob but an ongoing response to the "unyielding" nature of his life:
resignation. Death is the ultimate resignation. Constant mention of death
is a statement of living resignation. Jacob could not wrestle anymore. He
was too tired. When he told Pharaoh that his years were numbered, he
may not have been referring to death itself, but to what death represents.
Death in this sense is a slow, painful relinquishment of the energy required to live each day wrestling with one's surroundings. Jacob's constant reference to death may be an acknowledgment that every hardship is
in some way mimicking death; "...death is not a confrontation. It is simply

---

[27] Genesis 47:9.

[28] "Joseph's Coat is Shown to Jacob," Rembrandt, 1633 (Amsterdam, Rijksprentenk-
abinet). Another pen and ink drawing with the same title, done more than twenty
years later (1655), has Jacob in a similar pose with his hands held heavenward and
his head bent back in grief.

[29] See Genesis 42:28, 44:28, 44:31, 46:31, 45:28, 46:30.

an event in the sequence of nature's ongoing rhythms...death is the
surcease that comes when an exhausting battle has been lost."[30] There is
not one moment of death for Jacob, but many. Death is not a singular
confrontation but the final act of ongoing resignation.

Emily Dickinson captures this essence of resignation to death while
life presses on. She demonstrates that there can be some sense of mortal
surrender to death even though life continues:

> I felt a funeral in my brain,
> And mourners, to and fro,
> Kept treading, till it seemed
> That sense was breaking through.
> And when all were seated,
> A service like a drum
> Kept beating, beating, till I thought
> My mind was going numb...
> As all the heavens were a bell,
> And being but an ear,
> And I and silence some strange race,
> Wrecked, solitary here.[31]

Dickinson captures the loneliness of this resignation and its weight. It
pounds heavily and its escalation numbs the mind. One can imagine the
"funeral in Jacob's brain" as he descended in defeat to Egypt, holding the
blood stained striped coat of his most beloved son.

A Fitting End

Jacob's words to Pharaoh signaled a need to resolve the many abrupt and
open-ended obstacles he faced. He sought closure for two conflicts before
he died: he requested burial in Canaan and a final reconciliation for his
sons—an end to the fraternal discord sown throughout Genesis. These
conflicts were resolved, however, only after Jacob's death. In Genesis
47:29–30, Jacob beseeched Joseph to bury him in the land of his fathers:

---

[30] Sherwin B. Nuland, *How We Die: Reflections on Life's Final Chapter* (NY:
Knopf, 1994) 10.

[31] *The Collected Poems of Emily Dickinson*, Martha Dickenson Bianchi ed. (NY:
Barnes and Noble Books, 1993) 238, poem 112.

"Deal kindly and truly with me; bury me not, I pray you, in Egypt but I will lie with my fathers and you shall carry me out of Egypt and bury me in their burying place." Although it would have sufficed to request burial in Canaan, Jacob mentioned it twice, emphasizing that he should not be buried in Egypt, but must be removed from that foreign place. This man of movement would move yet again, but this time to his final resting place. His sojournings would end by joining the very ancestors of whom he deemed himself unworthy in his conversation with Pharaoh. This place of burial might have given Jacob the settlement in his death that he had sought in his life.

His second and final request in Genesis 50:17 is mentioned only post-humously, but resolves yet another aspect of Jacob's malcontent. Joseph received a message from his father through his brothers after Jacob's death:

> So shall you say to Joseph, "Forgive I urge you, the offense and guilt of your brothers who treated you so harshly. Therefore, please forgive the offense of the servants of the God of your father." And Joseph was in tears as they spoke to him.

The brothers could have fabricated this request. They may very well have feared that Joseph would exact his revenge once Jacob died. However, in his poignant speech in Genesis 45:5, Joseph assures the brothers that they are not in danger of his revenge: "Now, be not distressed or reproach yourselves because you sold me hither; it was to save life that God sent me ahead of you." If one believes the brothers, then the constant wrestling of Jacob's life ended with a sense of finality and reconciliation. We do not expect happy endings, or that the "plain man who dwells in tents" would suddenly look back with contentment on life's hardships. It is enough to arrive at small solutions. His bones were carried back. The brothers committed themselves to living together peaceably.

The Dialogue's Broader Context

Returning to Jacob and Pharaoh's conversation, one fundamental question remains: why does Jacob have this conversation with Pharaoh of all people? To reach an answer, we must put the conversation into a broader context. In this biblical chapter, the nation of Israel begins its long and arduous history of dislocation, settling in Goshen. From Abraham onward, individual leaders did leave Israel. Genesis 47, however, presents the first national account of movement to the Diaspora. Although it begins with success, it spirals into oppression, like so many subsequent records of Jewish national dislocation. It is a movement by choice that becomes a forced exile. This theme is repeated in many places throughout the Hebrew Bible. David Daube, in *The Exodus Pattern in the Bible*, traces linguistic and thematic parallels between texts from the Bible with the story of Exodus:

> The kind of salvation portrayed in the exodus was not, by its nature, an isolated occurrence, giving rise to nebulous hopes for similar good luck in the future: it had its root in and set the seal on, a permanent institution—hence it was something on which absolute reliance might be placed.... By being fashioned on the exodus, later deliverance became manifestations of this eternal, certainty-giving relationship between God and his people. It will emerge as we go on that, conceivably, even events prior to the exodus were made to approximate the latter....

One example Daube offers is Jacob's encounter with Laban. Like the Egyptians, Laban initially welcomes Jacob as a guest but then treats him as a servant. As a result of his increasing wealth, Laban becomes harsher. Jacob flees, taking with him great substance as a self-delivered reward for hard labor, only to be pursued by an angry Laban.

I believe that the isolated incident between Laban and Jacob represents a pattern which will expand and eventually include all the children of Israel with the move (in our chapter) to Egypt. The brief conversation between Jacob and Pharaoh presents a sub-text and a signal to look between the lines.[32] Genesis 47 is, in essence, the beginning of all national exiles.[33] Even though Jacob and his sons go willingly to Egypt, the

---

[32] David Daube, *The Exodus Pattern in the Bible* (London: Faber & Faber, 1965) 14.

[33] To be sure, the theme or punishment of exile is present from the beginning of Genesis. Adam and Eve are banished from the Garden. Cain's punishment is to be a wanderer. Noah leaves his land in a torrent of water. Only verses after Abraham gets to Canaan does he leave for Egypt for sustenance. Exile becomes an almost anticipated consequent of malfeasant behavior. Here, though, is the first record of national exile.

relationship between the foreign power and the temporary visitors soon changes and becomes one of oppression. A note of explanation must accompany this most significant move out of Israel, this first national movement to the Diaspora. This note occurs in the form of a conversation between the one in power and the one in pain, between the person of privilege and permanence, and the person oppressed and in constant movement. Jacob describes a life that is bitter and short, one of wanderings and discontent. Yet it is the figure of power, Pharaoh, who wonders about the secret of his subordinate's longevity. If Jacob indeed revealed the secret of survival to Pharaoh, it is hard to detect it amidst Jacob's negativity. All we find is the weariness of self-imposed exile and its heavy price; there is no other record.

Aside from the words of conversation, however, we do have an additional act of speech in these few lines: the blessings. Perhaps the acts of blessing that frame the dialogue are not incidental to the text, a disconnected formality, as some medieval exegetes posited. Rather, they may be a key to unlocking the meaning of the encounter within a broader reading of exile and redemption. When Jacob entered, he blessed and when he left, he blessed. In effect, the blessings themselves were the secret to Jacob's longevity. Jacob was blessed and Jacob blessed. This dimension of his life endured despite his wanderings and hardships. Jacob's empire was not built with material wealth. He sometimes had to leave the Land of Israel for physical sustenance. However, he had the spiritual dimension, encapsulated in the act of blessing here, to outlast stronger, foreign powers. If Jacob bears the name Israel and thus in some way mirrors the identity of the nation that took his name, then at issue is not only a conversation between two men but an ongoing dialogue between nations. The sub-text is Jewish history. We stray from our homeland—whether by choice or by force—and we are successful in foreign lands. That success, however, sours and our fortunes change. We become frustrated in exile but we survive. Our survival itself becomes an enigma, perhaps explainable only through a divine gift. We have been blessed and we bless others.

Jacob's conversation with Pharaoh reflects the tragedy of exile, even that which is self-imposed. The geographical distance between himself and the land of his fathers represents yet another tragedy for Jacob—his frustrating proximity to achievement without obtaining it. This theme is present in several dimensions of the Jacob narratives. In love, he struggled to marry Rachel only to find Leah beside him. Rachel then died just before returning to his homeland; her death on the roadside is itself symbolic of the proximity to home without reaching it. Jacob's remains lie eternally beside those of the woman he confessed he did not love. As a father, he was unable to love his children equally and without judgment. He pined for Joseph. As a leader, he confessed the shame of not living up to his ancestors. Exile, too, is this state; it is a numbing awareness that there is a goal, an achievement, a homeland and that one remains on the margins. Exile presents itself as constant, unrequited longing:

> There are two kinds of exiles. There is national exile which begins with *Hurban*, with the destruction of the sovereignty of the people and their dispersion into alien lands. However, prior to national exile and more fundamental and universal, is cosmic exile. National exile is a phenomenon in the history of nations; cosmic exile bespeaks the spiritual quality of the universal human condition at any one time in history.[34]

Extending this classification to our narrative, we can see that it effectively communicates these two exiles: the beginning of exile for the nation, and the personal exile of the patriarch. Exile is limitation; it is longing. However, "If there is tragic limitation in life there is also possibility. What we call maturity is the ability to see the two in some kind of balance into which we can fit creatively...character is the restrictive shaping of possibility."[35] Although his life was marked by intensive suffering, Jacob retained his capacity for blessing until the last moment. Despite the tragedy of limitation he endured, Jacob was able, perhaps more realistically as a consequence of misfortune, to determine a course for his children through the act of blessing them. Blessings are redemptive in the Jacob narratives. The book of Genesis ends with the blessings he offered his sons and grandsons. Through those blessings, he both foresaw and shaped the

---

[34] Eliezer Berkovits, *Crisis and Faith* (NY: Sanhedrin, 1976) 154.

[35] Ernest Becker, *The Denial of Death* (NY: Free Press, 1973) 266. Becker here quotes from Rieff, "The Impossible Culture: Oscar Wilde and the Charisma of the Artist," *Encounter* (September 1970): 40.

character of national destiny. Between the blessings, however, is the hardship of exile, to be resolved only with Jacob's burial in his homeland and ultimately with the nation's return to its homeland.

The conversation of blessing and suffering started thousands of years ago in the first chapter describing national exile. The conversation continues. There is weariness and there is longing, but there is also the capacity for receiving spiritual gifts and bestowing them in the act of being blessed and blessing others. Such was it for Jacob in exile and such has it been for the nation that bears the name Israel.

From the Earth's Hollow Space to the Stars: Two Patriarchs and Their Non-Israelite Mentors

Judy Klitsner

In exalted terms, God instructs Avraham[1] to become great:

> Go forth from your native land and from your father's house to the
> land that I will show you.
> And I will make of you a great nation and I will bless you;
> I will make your name great and you shall be a blessing.
> I will bless those who bless you and curse him that curses you;
> And all the families of the earth shall bless themselves in you.
> (Genesis 12:1–3)

Yet seven short verses later, the patriarch embarks on a vexing downward spiral that seems to mock the sublime messages of God's initial charge. A famine afflicts the Promised Land and Avraham is forced into exile in Egypt. Out of mortal fear of the godless population, Avraham lies, claiming that his wife, Sarah, is his sister. She is abducted anyway and in a morally dubious conclusion, husband and wife are sent away with great riches. Avraham's material wealth leads to the next crisis—incompatibility with his next of kin and probable heir, Lot.

The spiral is briefly interrupted by a moment of upward focus, in which God tells Avraham to "lift your eyes and look" in all four directions, symbolizing his descendants' acquisition of the Promised Land. Yet Avraham's gaze is quickly redirected downward in the following abstruse account of a series of wars between two sets of allies, one comprised of five kings, the other of four. Lot, who has chosen to live among the wicked people of Sodom, is taken captive. Avraham is then

---

[1] Note that in Genesis, Avram undergoes a name change and becomes Avraham. For the sake of convenience, we will refer to him as Avraham throughout.

faced with choosing between two unsavory options: he can either rescue his next of kin by aligning himself with Sodom, a nation known for its moral depravity (Genesis 13:13), or retain the moral high ground by remaining militarily neutral, while forfeiting his "brother" (14:14). Avraham chooses the former and wins the war for Sodom and her allies. At this point, arguably the moral nadir of Avraham's experiences, the king of Sodom makes his entrance, presumably to propose a victor's division of spoils. The text relates the following:

> When he returned from defeating Chedorlaomer and the kings with him, the king of Sodom came out to meet him in the Valley of Shaveh, which is the valley of the king. (Genesis 14:17)

Surprisingly, this king does nothing but "go out to meet" Avraham; at this point the text assigns him neither action nor speech. Instead, quite suddenly, the king's entrance is upstaged by that of another king, of whom the reader has no prior knowledge—Malkizedek, King of Shalem:

> And Malkizedek, King of Shalem brought out bread and wine; he was
> a priest of God Most High.
> He blessed him saying, "Blessed be Avraham of God Most High,
> Creator of heaven and earth.
> And blessed be God Most High,
> Who has delivered your foes into your hand."
> And he gave him a tenth of everything. (Genesis 14:18–20)

It is only after this cryptic appearance and utterance that the king of Sodom returns and the reader finally discovers what prompted his appearance in the first place. The king now makes his offer to divide the spoils of war with Avraham:

> Then the King of Sodom said to Avraham, "Give me the persons and take the possessions for yourself."

> But Avraham said to the King of Sodom, "I swear to the Lord, God Most High, Creator of heaven and earth: I will not take so much as a thread or a sandal strap of what is yours; you shall not say, 'It is I who made Avraham rich.' For me, nothing but what my servants have used up; for the share of men who went with me—Aner, Eshkol and Mamre—let them take their share." (Genesis 14:21–24)

This textual sequence presents the reader with many difficulties:

- Why is the Bible's presentation of the king of Sodom interrupted? One would have expected the king to "go out to meet" Avraham, immediately say his piece and only then would the next king enter.
- Who is Malkizedek? What is his connection with Avraham's war? Why does he offer food and blessings?
- What is the meaning of his dual title "priest" and "king"? What is the symbolism inherent in the names ascribed to Malkizedek (literally "king of justice"), who comes from Shalem (literally "complete")?
- What is the function of this non-Aronite, non-Jewish priest? Are there other biblical examples of priests fulfilling a similar role?
- More generally, after relating the lofty messages to Avraham to go forth and become a great nation, why does the text then burden the reader with greatly detailed vicissitudes of a decidedly ungodly existence? This question is intensified by the account of the wars, which aside from failing to provide inspiration, seems to have marginal relevance to the Abrahamic narrative.

Malkizedek as Moral Contrast to the King of Sodom

Or haHayyim (Haim ibn Attar, eighteenth century) suggests that the Malkizedek narrative interrupts that of the King of Sodom to highlight and contrast the characters of the two kings.[2]

The King of Sodom, who should have felt himself greatly indebted to Avraham for helping him win the war, greeted him with empty hands. Yet Malkizedek, who owed Avraham nothing, brought bread and wine.

Support for this notion can be found by contrasting the names of these kings: one is "king of justice" (the translation of מלכי-צדק) and the other

---

[2] The Hebrew letter "*vav*" here means not "and," but "but." It is combined with the relatively unusual subject-verb form: hence we find "ומלכי-צדק מלך שלם הוציא" instead of the more usual biblical style employing the verb with the vav conversive, followed by a verb-subject sequence, in which the verse could have said "ויוצא מלכי-צדק". For an example of this style, see Proverbs 10:1: "בן חכם ישמח אב ובן כסיל תוגת אמו"—"a wise son makes a glad father *but* a foolish son is the grief of his mother." Example taken from Rivka Raviv, "*Munokhon leLimud haMikra*," *Kedumim* (*Ulpanat Lahav*) 90.

reigns "in evil" (the translation of his name, ברע). In addition, the latter is king of the nation that becomes the biblical symbol of the absence of justice:

> Hear the words of the Lord,
> You chieftains of Sodom;
> Give ear to our God's instruction,
> You folk of Gomorrah!
> What need have I of all your sacrifices?
> Says the Lord…
> Learn to do good,
> Devote yourselves to justice;
> Aid the wronged.
> Uphold the rights of the orphan;
> Defend the cause of the widow. (Isaiah 1:10, 11, 17)

While Malkizedek offers bread and wine, Sodom is known for its refusal to offer sustenance to the needy:

> Only this was the sin of your sister Sodom: arrogance! She and her daughters had plenty of bread and untroubled tranquility; yet she did not support the poor and the needy. (Ezekiel 16:49)

This latter passage attributes Sodom's penury to an underlying arrogance, a trait that provides further contrast with the essence of Malkizedek, King of Shalem. Malkizedek's message was one of humility, attributing all military and material success to God, *El elyon* (Most High), who is at all times in control of human enterprise.

Malkizedek as Provider of Moral Reinforcement to Avraham Prior to His Encounter with the King of Sodom

Or haHayyim's interpretation notwithstanding, it is Avraham and not these two kings who demands the reader's attention. While we may have some interest in contrasting the characters of two marginal figures, the narrative has thus far focused on our main protagonist, Avraham. We must therefore ask: how does this interlude and the characters within it affect the development of Avraham?

Faced with the onerous choice of abandoning his nephew, Lot, or forging an unholy alliance with the king of Sodom, Avraham finds himself in a state of moral confusion and spiritual exhaustion. This state is the cumulative result of the above-mentioned string of events interrupting Avraham's fulfillment of his divine task.

Against this background, the King of Sodom "goes out to meet" Avraham, treaty in hand, expecting Avraham's signature. If Avraham agrees to this union, his moral crisis will be perpetuated, becoming further estranged from the original divine ideals and mission introduced in chapter 12.

But suddenly the text provides a cinematic "freeze frame" of the King of Sodom and from left stage a new character appears—Malkizedek. His words and actions dramatically alter the focus of events:

- Instead of addressing the mundane protocols of a sullying experience, Malkizedek enjoins Avraham to direct his thoughts heavenward—to God Most High (*El elyon*), an expression that appears three times in these few short verses.

- Malkizedek blesses Avraham and his God, echoing the blessings given to Avraham at the beginning of his journey. In fact, the root ברך (bless) appears three times in these verses, hearkening back to Genesis chapter 12 in which this root appears five times in verses 2–3. Malkizedek refers to God as the one who protects Avraham by delivering his enemies to him (מגן צריך בידך). Though unstated, it is broadly implied that these enemies are not only the military nemeses Avraham has just defeated, but the much more dangerous *ally* as well—the enemy of justice, who is ready to co-opt Avraham for his own dubious purposes.

- Malkizedek exhibits great generosity, giving Avraham bread, wine and perhaps the tithe.[3] By giving, he provides a model of spiritual and fraternal uprightness. In addition, Malkizedek's very name suggests righteousness, thus introducing this theme into the narrative.

In sum, by arriving at this critical juncture, Malkizedek seeks to remind Avraham of his purpose and his calling: he is to look upward to God and deal righteously with his fellow human beings.

---

[3] Resolving the textual ambiguity of who gives the tithe to whom—Avraham to Malkizedek or vice versa—is beyond the scope of this article.

The messages have been broadcast, but has the patriarch received them? Is he capable, given his troubled mindset, of altering his viewpoint in favor of the perspective now offered by Malkizedek? This question is difficult for the average reader to answer, as the biblical text does not offer free viewing into the internal feelings of its characters. On the whole, actions rather than sentiments are emphasized. Yet the astute reader will note the Bible's sophisticated intertextuality; that is, literary links between one section and another, which often supply the reader with added insight into the psyche of its characters. In a fine example of intertextuality, Avraham is seen as internalizing Malkizedek's messages when he echoes the language that the priest has used.

Immediately following Malkizedek's enigmatic appearance, the King of Sodom is released from suspension. Malkizedek returns to his mysterious origins and the King of Sodom speaks. He begins with the expected words: "תן לי הנפש והרכוש קח לך" which means literally, "Give me the soul(s) and take the booty for yourself." The plain sense of this statement is the proffering of an exchange in which the king of Sodom gets his hostages and Avraham becomes rich. But a more literal, though less evident, reading can provide deeper understanding: the king of Sodom demands *Avraham's* soul, which is the price exacted for the riches to follow. The king's meaning is thus: "Keep the booty and your soul will be mine."

Against the background of Malkizedek's inspiring words, Avraham recalls the promises, the covenant and God's protection. He has no need of an earthly, corrupt pact with the devil; his future lies in following a much loftier course. Thus Avraham finds the strength to rebuff the king's offer, thereby relinquishing material gain. His behavior here is especially noteworthy, as it contrasts with his acceptance of riches from Pharaoh, king of Egypt. In that instance, Pharaoh rewarded Avraham, following the abduction of his wife, Sarah, whom out of fear of the local inhabitants, Avraham had claimed was his sister (Genesis 12:16). In Egypt and now with the king of Sodom, Avraham could claim that by receiving compensation, he technically did no wrong. Yet here, bolstered by Malkizedek, Avraham distances himself from receiving any ethically questionable rewards. In his response, Avraham echoes more than the sentiments of

Malkizedek—he goes on to invoke the very *language* used by the king-priest:

Avraham – אברהם	Malkizedek – מלכי-צדק
הרימתי ידי אל ה׳ **א-ל עליון קונה שמים וארץ**	והוא כהן **לא-ל עליון**...ברוך אברם **לא-ל עליון קונה שמים וארץ** וברוך א-ל עליון
I have raised my hand to **God Most High Creator of heaven and earth** (Genesis 14:22)	He was a priest to **God** Most High...Blessed is Avraham to **God Most High Creator of heaven and earth**. And blessed is **God Most High** (Genesis 14:18–20)
הרימתי **ידי**	אשר מגן צריך **בידך**
I have raised my **hand** (Genesis 14:22)	Who has delivered your Enemies into your **hand** (Genesis 14:20)
ולא תאמר אני **העשרתי** את אברם	ויתן לו **מעשר** מכל
so you shall not say, "It is I who made Avraham rich" (*he'esharti*) (Genesis 14:23)	And he gave him a tenth (*ma'aser*) of everything (Genesis 14:20)

- Avraham reiterates Malkizedek's reference to God as א-ל עליון and קונה שמים וארץ, "God Most High," who presides over all of creation. Avraham adds a dimension of his own to Malkizedek's words by referring to God as He was manifested in their early encounters, with God's particular, ineffable name. Perhaps Avraham was reminded of this initial divine encounter by Malkizedek's repeated use of the word *barekh* (bless), a key word, or *leitwort*—a central, recurring "leading" word that guides the leader through God's first charge to Avraham in chapter 12.
- Malkizedek praised God for delivering Avraham's enemies into his **hands** (*asher migen tzarekha beyadekha*). Avraham now exhibits how those hands have been morally strengthened when he raises his **hand** to God Most High (*harimoti yadi el Hashem el elyon*) to reject the dubious offer of the king of Sodom. Avraham's hand, as introduced by

Malkizedek, becomes the symbol of the moral strength gained by having God at his side.

- In his response to the King of Sodom, Avraham makes yet another reference to his encounter with Malkizedek when he says that he does not want to enable the king of Sodom to say, ‏"אני העשרתי את אברם"‎—"I made Avraham rich." The verb ‏העשרתי‎ draws the reader back to the tithe (‏מעשר‎) offered, either by Avraham to Malkizedek, or vice versa. Bolstered by the tithe, Avraham feels no temptation to accept the riches of the King of Sodom.

By drawing on Malkizedek's language of rejuvenation and moral reinforcement, the text presents an Avraham who has internalized and has consequently been fortified by the messages he received.

The Malkizedek Interlude as Laying the Groundwork for the Covenant Between the Pieces

Immediately following Malkizedek's appearance and Avraham's refusal to accept the post-war terms offered by the king of Sodom, comes a chapter apparently detached from that which precedes it. Chapter 14 is occupied with the prosaic, chapter 15, with the celestial. Chapter 14 is concerned with war, human alliances and moral compromise, while chapter 15 focuses on God forging a sublime, unshakable covenant with humankind.

Were it not for the opening words of chapter 15, we may have read this chapter as signaling the arrival of a new Avraham, whose coming undertakings owe very little to earlier, sorrier events. But the text instructs us otherwise. Chapter 15 begins, "After these things, the word of the Lord was to Avraham." Rashi, following the midrash, views this opening as the literary equivalent of an arrow pointing back toward the preceding chapter. Such linkage helps to explain God's enigmatic charge to Avraham in verse 2:

> Fear not, Avraham, I am a shield to you; your reward shall be very great.

What unexpressed fear does God seek to allay? It seems that Avraham's fear must somehow be related to his wars with the kings in chapter 14.

For Rashi, the connection between chapters 14 and 15 ends with verse two. Chapter 15 then moves ahead, away from the earthly struggles of the past to speak of a loftier future.

Yet if we again take note of the Bible's intertextuality, we will find that there are in fact numerous literary links throughout these two chapters, suggesting a much more extensive relationship, with the Malkizedek interlude at the epicenter. In an impressive show of literary word play, the Bible draws broadly on the language of chapter 14, which presents Avraham's sullying war experiences and Malkizedek's uplifting messages. Chapter 15 uses the same terminology to reinforce the messages that Malkizedek introduced, and to reverse the messages Avraham culled from war and his encounter with the king of Sodom.

Chapter 15 – פרק טו	Chapter 14 – פרק יד
אנכי **מגן** לך I am a shield (***magen***) to you (Genesis 15:1)	אשר **מגן** צריך בידיך , who delivers (***miggen***) your enemies into your hands (Genesis 14:20)
ובן משק ביתי הוא **דמשק** אליעזר the one in charge of my household is **Damascus** Eliezer (Genesis 15:2)	וירדפם עד חובה אשר משמאל **לדמשק** He chased them to Hobah **Damascus** which is north of.... (Genesis 14:15)
ויוצא אותו החוצה ויאמר הבט השמימה אני ה' אשר **הוצאתיך** מאור כשדים He **brought him** outside and said... "I am the Lord who **brought you out** from Ur of the Chaldeans" (Genesis 15:5, 7)	ומלכי-צדק מלך שלם **הוציא** לחם ויין Malkizedek king of Shalem **brought out** bread and wine (Genesis 14:18)
ויתן איש בתרו **לקראת** רעהו He placed each half opposite (***likrat***) the other (Genesis 15:10)	ויצא מלך סדום **לקראתו** The king of Sodom went out to meet him (***likrato***) (Genesis 14:17)

והאמן בה' ויחשבה לו **צדקה**	ומלכי-**צדק** מלך שלם
Because he believed in God, He considered it to him as righteousness (*tzedakah*) (Genesis 15:6)	Malki*zedek* king of Shalem (Genesis 14:18)
מה **תתן** לי, **ויתן** איש בתרו	**תן** לי הנפש
What will you **give** me He put (**gave**) each half (Genesis 15:2, 10)	**Give** me the souls (Genesis 14:21)
קחה לי עגלה משלשת	והרכש **קח** לך
Take for Me a three-year-old (Genesis 15:9)	**Take** the possessions for yourself (Genesis 14:21)
וגם את הגוי אשר יעבדו **דן** אנכי	וירדף עד **דן**
I will execute judgment (*dan*) on the nation they shall serve (Genesis 15:14)	He chased them until *Dan* (Genesis 14:14)
ואחרי כן יצאו **ברכש** גדול	**והרכש** קח לך
Afterward they shall go free with great **possessions** (Genesis 15:14)	And take the **possessions** for yourself (Genesis 14:21)
ואת **הרפאים**	ויכו את **רפאים**
and the *Rephaim* (Genesis 15:20)	And they smote the *Rephaim* (Genesis 14:5)
והנה **אימה** חשכה	ואת **האימים**
a dark dread (*eima*) (Genesis 15:12)	And the *Eimim* (Genesis 14:5)
וגם את **הגוי**	ותדעל מלך **גוים**
and also the **nation** (that enslaved them will I judge) (Genesis 15:14)	And Tid'al king of *Goyim* (**nations**) (Genesis 14:1)
כי לא **שלם** עון האמרי	ומלכי-צדק מלך **שלם**
for the iniquity of the Amorites is not yet complete (*shalem*) (Genesis 15:16)	Malkizedek king of Shalem (*Shalem*) (Genesis 14:18)
כי לא שלם עון **האמרי**	והוא שכן באלני ממרא **האמרי**
for the iniquity of the **Amorites** yet complete (Genesis 15:16)	he dwelled at the oaks of Mamre the **Amorite** (Genesis 14:13)

ביום ההוא כרת ה' את אברם **ברית**	אחי אשכל ואחי ענר והם בעלי
	ברית אברם
On that day God made a covenant (**brit**) with Avraham (Genesis 15:18)	kinsmen of Eshkol and Aner, these being allies (ba'alei **brit**) of Avraham (Genesis 14:13)

To begin to understand the above comparisons, let us return to the opening words of chapter 15. Rashi comments there:

> Fear not, Avraham,
> I am a shield to you;
> Your reward shall be very great. (Genesis 15:1)

God's words seem to be offered in response to Avraham's fear, yet no such fear has been mentioned in the text. Rashi, in an adaptation of R. Levi's opinion in *Genesis Rabbah* 44.5, comments:

> [I will be a shield to you] from punishment, that you shall not be punished for all those souls you killed and as to your concern about receiving your reward—your reward is very great.

According to this reading, Avraham is concerned about the corrupting effect the war has had on him. Killing, even in self-defense, is a morally debilitating experience and Avraham feels defenseless in the face of ethical challenges to his behavior. God's response to his unspoken fear is unwavering: you have nothing to fear, for I am your shield against such claims. You did what you had to do, but that behavior does not define you. Your definition and your rewards are yet to come. Strikingly, like Avraham in his encounter with the king of Sodom, God recalls the words of Malkizedek: Malkizedek had blessed God who protects Avraham by handing over his enemies to him (מגן צריך בידיך) and God now invokes these same words to assure Avraham of the veracity of this sentiment. God's message is: I will protect you (אנוכי מגן לך) from both your moral and mortal enemies.[4]

---

[4] מגן in the *pi'el* verb form (intensive active conjugation) means "to deliver," while the noun form means to act as a shield. God here extends Malkizedek's thought: not only do I hand over your enemies, allowing you to win wars, I also provide complete protection by acting as a shield against all other kinds of adversity as well. The appearance of the root מגן in these two chapters represents two of a total three times

Avraham's concern is not completely allayed, as he proceeds to express apprehension about his future. In rejecting the advances of the King of Sodom, it has become conclusively clear to Avraham that Lot, with his Sodomite association, will never be his heir. Yet the question remained: in the absence of any other foreseeable prospect, who would be? Avraham expresses this fear with great hesitation: will his household servant, Damascus-Eliezer, inherit all that is his? This name, too, refers us back to chapter 14, in which Avraham pursued them (the armies of the five kings) as far as Hobah, which is north of Damascus (אשר משמאל לדמשק). In chapter 15, Avraham continues to wonder if he would be succeeded by the types of battles and counter-battles that encumbered him in chapter 14. When God promised (13:16–17) that Avraham's seed would be as numerous as the dust of the earth, and that those multitudes of descendents would inherit the land, what did that mean? Would every inch of gain be at great cost to Avraham's moral and physical well being? Here, in chapter 15, Avraham wonders aloud if "Damascus," the gritty experiences of pursuit and ultimately hard-won victory will be his real legacy. Here again, God reassures Avraham in Malkizedek's style: your legacy will be true to your exalted beginnings.

The next literary connection between these two chapters lies in the repeated use of the root יצא, to go out:

ויוצא אותו החוצה ויאמר הבט נא השמימה וספר הכוכבים אם תוכל לספר אותם.
ויאמר לו כה יהיה זרעך.

> He took him outside and said, "Look toward heaven and count the stars, if you are able to count them."
> And He added: "So shall your offspring be." (15:5)

ויאמר לו אני ה' אשר הוצאתיך מאור כשדים.

> He said to him, "I am the Lord who brought you out of Ur of the Chaldeans...." (15:7)

---

this root appears (in both verb and noun forms) in all five books of the Torah. This makes its doubling here especially noteworthy.

The verb יצא appears twice in these verses in the causative (*hiph'il*) form, meaning "He brought him out." This choice of verb and form reminds us of Malkizedek, who "brought out bread and wine" (הוציא לחם ויין).[5] By bringing an offering and reviving Avraham's troubled spirits, Malkizedek sustains him morally and physically, preparing him to be "brought out" by God in chapter 15. There, God brings Avraham outside of his earthly, worried mindset, redirecting his thoughts to the celestial sphere. Perhaps this is the intent of the midrash as cited by Rashi: "He brought him out from the hollow space of the world and elevated him above the stars" (*Genesis Rabbah* 44.10; Rashi on Genesis 15:5). God's message now is that the earlier, hollow experiences that confront Avraham should be left behind, as God has a more sublime destiny prepared for him. This message is taken further in verse 7, when the same form of the verb יצא is used. Here, God extends the scope of the "bringing out" of Avraham: after freeing him from the burdens of the ordinary, he projects an exalted legacy of a Promised Land.

As Avraham draws closer to God, we see that certain doubts persist in the mind of the patriarch: he asks for assurances that he will inherit and God offers him affirmation in the form of rich symbolism. God tells Avraham to take (קחה לי) a three-year old heifer, along with other animals, cut them in half and walk between the pieces, thus conducting an ancient rite of covenant-making, or *brit*. Here, too, the language of the text sends us back to chapter 14, but this time for contrast: Avraham's "taking" of the covenantal animals is to replace the kind of taking offered by the King of Sodom when he ordered Avraham to "take the possessions" (קח את הרכש). Instead of taking for his own material gain, or to consolidate an unholy alliance, Avraham now takes at God's bidding those things that will further the divine-human alliance and lead to a state of "*brit*."

In place of the King of Sodom who went out to "meet" Avraham (ויצא מלך סדום לקראתו), here we have the pieces of the animals "meeting" each other (איש בתרו לקראת רעהו). Again the text emphasizes the

---

[5] The same root is used for the King of Sodom, but in the simple (*kal*) form, since he came out alone, bringing nothing that could be of any benefit to Avraham.

constructive process of forging a *brit* with God, which was a notable departure from past meetings and alliances.

There are numerous other literary associations between chapters 14 and 15 which highlight Avraham's transition from prosaic warrior to partner in God's covenant. The symbols of brutal human warfare, *Rephaim*, *Eimim* and *Goyim* of chapter 14 (verses 1 and 5) are transformed into symbols of God's covenantal protection in chapter 15 (verses 12; 14; 20).

Additional allusions from chapter 15 back to chapter 14 can be found in some of the central elements of the *brit*. Following the promised enslavement and affliction, God vows to judge the enslaving nation and see to it that Avraham's descendants will emerge from their ordeal with great wealth. Again, intertextuality provides the key to understanding: God promises to **judge** the nation that has enslaved His people (Genesis 15:14—וגם את הגוי אשר יעבדו **דן** אנכי). Afterwards, the Israelites will leave with great property (ibid.—יצאו **ברכש** גדול). Here, in contrast to Avraham's experiences in chapter 14, God pledges to stand beside him in his adversity. Instead of leaving Avraham alone to chase his enemies until **Dan** (Genesis 14:14—דן), God promises to chase the enemies of Israel until "*dan*"—that is until a final, just **judgment** is meted out for their crimes (ibid., 15:14). After that, God will see to it that Avraham's descendants receive great possessions (ibid.—**רכוש**), with no need to rely on the provision of property by such morally skewed allies as the King of Sodom (Genesis 14:21—**והרכוש** קח לך). And this is all because Avraham no longer needs to rely solely on his own earthly abilities to forge military alliances and treaties (Genesis 14:13—בעלי **ברית** אברם), but instead will have a treaty with God, who now promises to look after Avraham and his descendants on a covenantal level (Genesis 15:18—ביום ההוא כרת ה׳ את אברם **ברית**).

Following a series of moral and physical challenges, Avraham is now concretely reminded of God's initial inspiring charge: he was to go forth and create a nation, now fortified by the messages of the *brit*. At the core of the *brit* lay the notion that military strategizing and alliance-building were to defer to a nobler system of merit and promise. No matter how strong an army Avraham would assemble, the land was not to be his

during his lifetime, for the "sin of the Amorite was not yet complete"—
"*ki lo **shalem** avon ha'Emori*" (Genesis 15:16). And when their sins
became so numerous as to disqualify them from continued inhabitance of
the Holy Land, no martial strategy could keep the Amorites there since
God had judged otherwise. It was Malkizedek, King of *Shalem* (שלם—
lit., "complete") who delivered this message: completion is defined as
justice, and justice is at the core of God's complete world.

This notion is reinforced by the definition of this king's name
("Malkizedek" translates as "king of justice"). It is this concept of justice
in chapter 14 that presents the most valuable message to be received by
the patriarch in chapter 15. In the latter chapter, the text momentarily
breaks with the normative narrative style to extol the virtues of Avraham:

והאמין בה' ויחשביה לו **צדקה**.

> And he believed in God and *he* considered *it* to *him* as righteousness
> (*tzedakah*). (15:6)

This is one of the most perplexingly ambiguous statements of the Bible,
giving rise to much exegetical debate.[6]

If we define *tzedakah* in its biblically normative way, the verse reads:
And Avraham believed in God, and God considered Avraham's belief to
be to Him (in God's eyes, as it were) righteousness (צדקה). Thus
Avraham's unwavering belief is equated with the notions of justice and
righteousness at the core of his faith. This reading would again send us
back to Malkizedek, whose very name evokes a sense of moral rectitude
and justice. Following his encounter with Malkizedek, Avraham's belief
system is reinforced with these ideals. We are to find out three chapters
hence that the election of Avraham by God was for the very purpose of
upholding "*tzedakah*."

---

[6] To whom and what do all these pronouns refer? **Who** considered **what** to be
righteousness and to whom? What is the meaning of *tzedakah* in this verse? What is
its connection to Avraham's belief in God? Rashi suggests that **God** considered
Avraham's belief to be as a **merit** for **Avraham**, placing the emphasis on Avraham's
faithfulness and suggesting that he would find his reward for it. But this solution is
problematic, in that *tzedakah* in the Bible most often means not merit, but righteousness.

In chapter 18, verse 19, God says:

> For I have singled him out (literally "known him") that he may in-
> struct his children and his posterity
> to keep the way of the Lord by doing *tzedakah,* what is just and right
> (ושמרו דרך ה׳ לעשות **צדקה** ומשפט).

This is the divine teleology offered by Malkizedek which is reinforced several chapters later directly by God.

Based on the messages introduced by Malkizedek, Avraham is now enjoined to do justice, look heavenward and through these merits, God will uphold His promises to him. By echoing Malkizedek's terminology, God has signaled to Avraham that he will emerge from the morass, not just to the safety of *terra firma*, but he is to be thrust heavenward, directly toward the lofty future awaiting him.

Avraham as Archetype of the Jewish Nation

Malkizedek has paved the way for more than Avraham's personal emergence: empowered by their encounter, Avraham will become a microcosm of the nascent Israelite people. Chapter 15 presents a potent case of dramatic foreshadowing, as God's covenant with Avraham provides a basis for the national events in the book of Exodus, chapter 19. In line with the rabbinic dictum "מעשה אבות סימן לבנים"—"the deeds of the fathers prefigure the deeds of the sons," Avraham's theophany is a symbolic microcosm of the great national revelation to come:

שמות פרק יט **Exodus Chapter 19**	בראשית פרק טו **Genesis Chapter 15**
וגם בך **יאמינו** לעולם [the people] will **trust** you forever (Exodus 19:9)	**והאמן** בה׳ ויחשבה לו צדקה Because he put his **trust** in the Lord (Genesis 15:6)
והר סיני **עשן** כלו Mount Sinai was all in **smoke** (Exodus 19:18)	והנה תנור **עשן** There appeared a **smoking** oven (Genesis 15:17)

מפני אשר ירד עליו ה' **באש** For the Lord had come down upon it in **fire** (Exodus 19:18)	ולפיד **אש** And a flaming torch of **fire** (Genesis 15:17)
וענן כבד על ההר and a **dense cloud** upon the mountain (Exodus 19:16)	אימה **חשכה** גדלה **ועלטה** היה a **great dark** dread descended (Genesis 15:12)
ויחרד כל העם אשר במחנה and all the people in the camp **trembled** (Exodus 19:16)	והנה **אימה** חשכה גדולה a great dark **dread** descended (Genesis 15:12)
ויוצא משה את העם Moshe **brought** the people **out** (Exodus 19:17)	**ויוצא** אותו החוצה He **brought** him **outside** (Genesis 15:5)
לקראת הא-להים **Towards** God (Exodus 19:17)	איש בתרו **לקראת** רעהו Each half **towards** the other (Genesis 15:10)
אנכי ה' א-להיך אשר הוצאתיך **I am the Lord your God who brought you out** of the land of Egypt (Exodus 20:2)	אני ה' אשר **הוצאתיך** מאור כשדים **I am the Lord who brought you out** of Ur of the Chaldeans (Genesis 15:7)

The physical environment created by God, in His covenant with Avraham, presages the atmosphere prior to the Israelites' receiving of the Torah. Both sections contain a statement of belief; there is smoke, fire, great darkness, fear and trembling; the partner to the treaty is "brought out," and God is introduced as the deity who "took [the people] out" from one place to another.

The above comparison highlights Avraham's prefiguring of the Israelites' theophany at Sinai. It was the king/priest, Malkizedek, who enabled Avraham to receive this personal, symbolic revelation.

In sum, the appearance of the mysterious king of Shalem has accomplished the following:

- It helped Avraham confront and find the appropriate response to the moral challenge presented by the King of Sodom.

- It provided Avraham with a language enabling him to comprehend God's messages in the Covenant Between the Pieces (*Brit bein haBetarim*).

- It helped to establish Avraham as archetype of the future Israelite people.

Another Priestly Enabler: Yitro, Priest of Midian

Where else in the Bible do we find a pivotal priestly figure such as Malkizedek who attaches himself to a patriarchal figure, helping to create clarity out of confusion and moral exhaustion? Let us examine the role of Yitro, Priest of Midian, and his relationship to Moshe.

The second chapter of Exodus begins with the actions of an unnamed man, or "*ish*":

> And a man from the house of Levi went and married a Levite woman.

The term "*ish*" serves as a *leitwort*, a central, recurring term that provides the key to understanding the passage before us. This word recurs a further eight times in this one chapter, with constantly varying referents. The passage ends with Moshe sitting with an "*ish*," in this case his father-in-law to be, Yitro, thus providing a ring composition to the entire section. Moshe's father makes only one appearance in the chapter's introduction and then plays no further recorded role in Moshe's life. His mother, on the other hand, by twists of fortune and cunning, manages to raise her own son under the aegis of the princess of Egypt. Moshe had the opportunity to learn a great deal from the selfless, courageous and devoted women in his life.[7] Yet the text speaks of no male role model for

---

[7] Cassuto suggests an ironic literary foiling of Pharaoh's murderous plot: Pharaoh orders the murder of male babies, but allows the girls to live, "*vekhol habat tekhayun*" (וכל הבת תחיון), as the latter presumably pose no threat to the Egyptian nation. Following the use of the term "*bat*" in Pharaoh's decree in Exodus chapter 1, the word recurs a further seven times in chapter 2, referring to a series of heroic women, all of whom poignantly disprove Pharaoh's theory about the challenge presented by women. It is their moral might, not their physical prowess, which in the end defeats the Egyptian ruler. Yocheved, Pharaoh's daughter, and Zipporah are specifically referred to as "*bat*," while other heroic women are introduced without this epithet: the midwives and Moshe's sister, Miriam.

Moshe. Perhaps as a result of this absence, Moshe goes out in search of an "*ish*," which might be viewed as the Hebrew equivalent of the Yiddish term "*mensch*." In order to grow successfully into a man himself, Moshe looks at his world for direction. His first efforts meet with dismal failure: he sees an Egyptian *ish* striking a Hebrew *ish*—and understands that his world is populated with promulgators of violence and injustice. Compounding this outrage is the fact that he looked around and "saw that there was no man" (2:12—וירא כי אין **איש**) which means, in the words of haEmek Davar (R. Naftali Zvi Yehuda Berlin, nineteenth century):

> He searched for ideas as to how to complain about the Egyptian who had gratuitously stricken the Hebrew, "but he saw that there was no man" before whom to report this inequity, as all around him were traitors and haters of the Israelites.

If Moshe had harbored illusions that the situation was better amongst his brethren, these were dispelled on his next outing where he saw two Hebrew men (אנשים) fighting. When Moshe tried to stop them from emulating their oppressors, the "wicked" party showered him with ironic rhetoric: "Who made you a **man** ("*ish*") who is chief and ruler over us?" (Exodus 2:14—מי שמך ל**איש** שר ושופט). Moshe is taunted for his efforts to act as an "*ish*," and now, realizing the total absence of "men" among the Egyptians and Hebrews, he flees.

While he has found no other "*ish*" with whom to associate, Moshe himself continues to act as a man. His first deed in the land of Midian is to save seven strangers, the daughters of Yitro, the Priest of Midian. When they report his noble deeds to their father, they refer to him as an "Egyptian man" (**איש** מצרי). Yitro concurs with their assessment and deems Moshe worthy of his company, his bread and ultimately his daughter. The denouement is that "Moshe consented to stay with the **man**" (Exodus 2:21—ויואל משה לשבת את ה**איש**), thus conferring reciprocal recognition of the humanity, maturity and decency of the other man.

This relationship presents us with an intriguing parallel to the story of Malkizedek and Avraham examined above:

יתרו כהן מדין Yitro Priest of Midian	מלכי-צדק, כהן לא-ל עליון Malkizedek Priest to God Most High
קראן לו ויאכל **לחם** Call him to eat **bread** (Exodus 2:20)	ומלכי-צדק מלך שלם הוציא **לחם** ויין Malkizedek King of Shalem brought **bread** (Genesis 14:18)
ולכהן מדין שבע בנות the **priest** of Midian had seven daughters (Exodus 2:16)	והוא **כהן** לא-ל עליון He was **priest** to God Most High (Genesis 14:18)
ויתן את צפרה בתו למשה he **gave** Zipporah his daughter to Moshe (Exodus 2:21)	**ויתן** לו מעשר מכל he **gave** him a tenth of everything (Genesis 14:20)
וירא כי אין **איש** he saw that there was no **man** (Exodus 2:12)	**ואנשי סדום** רעים וחטאים לה׳ מאד the **men** of Sodom were very wicked sinners against the Lord (Genesis 13:13)
וירא כי אין **איש** he saw that there was no **man** (Exodus 2:12)	**ואנשי סדום** רעים וחטאים לה׳ מאד the **men** of Sodom were very wicked sinners against the Lord (Genesis 13:13)
ויך את המצרי he **smote** the Egyptian (Exodus 2:12)	ויחלק עליהם לילה...**ויכם** at night he deployed against them… and **smote** them (Genesis 14:15)
ויצא משה **לקראת** חתנו Moshe **went out to meet** his father-in-law (Exodus 18:7)	**ויצא** מלך סדום **לקראתו** the king of Sodom **went out to meet** him (Genesis 14:17)
ברוך ה׳ אשר הציל אתכם **מיד** מצרים ומיד פרעה **Blessed** is the Lord who	**ברוך** א-ל עליון אשר מגן צריך **בידיך** **Blessed** be God Most High who

delivered you from the Egyptians and from the **hand** of Pharaoh (Exodus 18:10)	delivered your enemies into your **hands** (Genesis 14:20)

ושפטו את העם בכל עת	ויבאו אל עין **משפט** ומלכי-**צדק** מלך שלם ושמרו דרך ה׳ לעשות צדקה ומשפט
and they **judged** the people at all times (Exodus 18:26)	They came to *Ein Mishpat* (spring of **justice**) (Genesis 14:7) And Malk**izedek** (king of **righteousness**) (Genesis 14:18) They [Avraham's posterity] will keep the way of the Lord by doing **justice** and **righteousness** (Genesis 18:19)

Moshe, like Avraham before him, is at a critical moral juncture in his life. Yet, unlike Avraham, Moshe has no promises to rely on and so he embarks on a self-propelled quest to find his place among like-minded people. The result of his efforts is that his own humanity is called into question ("who made you a man who is chief and ruler over us?" Exodus 2:14). Like Avraham, he finds himself in a moral quandary; it seems that in a world without "men," any alliance he would choose to make would compromise his ethical standards. Avraham was nearly compelled to accept the fraternity of the King of Sodom whose "men" were evil before God (Genesis 13:13). Moshe's search led him to such frustration and agitation that he found himself taking the life of one to preserve the life of another. Here, as with Avraham before him, the onerous act of slaying is forced upon Moshe.[8]

At this juncture, the priest enters to provide moral reinforcement. While Malkizedek reminded Avraham to look to God for support, Yitro introduces Moshe to morality among men, thus giving him an ethical

---

[8] See Genesis 14:15 and Exodus 2:12.

community with which to confer. Both priests provide material succor as well, as both feed bread to their weary guests. Significantly, this passage ends with Moshe naming his son Gershom, "because I was a stranger in a foreign land" (Exodus 2:22). Here Moshe recognizes and publicly acknowledges his estrangement from the type of humanity he witnessed in the land of Egypt. This statement bespeaks a sense of solace that Moshe finds in his association with the priest, or kohen of Midian.

There are further compelling parallels between these two *cohanim* and the enabling role they play in relation to God's chosen leaders. Yitro reappears in chapter 18 of Exodus, and in a resounding echo of the blessing offered by the kohen, Malkizedek, he proclaims:

> Blessed be the Lord… who delivered you from the Egyptians and from Pharaoh, and who delivered the people from under the hand of the Egyptians. Now I know that the Lord is greater than all gods.… (Exodus 18:10)

As in the Malkizedek interlude, this proclamation follows a war with a morally debased nation (in this case, Amalek) and precedes a theophany. This priest, like the priest before him, helps the patriarch make the transition from moral ambiguity to moral and theological certainty.

Yet another common element in these two passages warrants scrutiny. Based on the translation of Malkizedek's name and place of origin, he is the "king of justice," living in the "land of completion." Avraham's battle took place in "the spring of justice"—(Genesis 14:7– עין משפט). Malkizedek's words, actions and essence helped catapult Avraham toward his goal as transmitter of righteousness and judgment (Genesis 18:19). It is only when this realization becomes internalized that Avraham is ready for his encounter with the Divine.

Similarly, Yitro has a great deal to teach Moshe about justice, belatedly offering him his answer to the taunts of the Hebrew in Egypt: "who made you [Moshe] a **man** who is an **officer** and **judge** over others?" (מי שמך **לאיש שר ושופט**). Through Yitro's guidance, these very distinctions are now conferred upon Moshe. By judging correctly, that is by knowing when to delegate authority to "officers" (שרים) and "men" (אנשים), Moshe becomes a judge worthy of the title. Ultimately, as a result of Yitro's moral reinforcement, Moshe ironically reverses the denial of these titles by the wayward Hebrew and truly becomes an *ish*, a *sar* (officer) and a *shofet* (judge).

Uncharacteristically, the Bible allows Yitro to be quite loquacious on the subject of justice, and only after the correct method of judgment is established are preparations made for the receiving of the Torah. Given the context in which we have placed the character of Yitro, the emphasis afforded this interlude becomes clear. As with Malkizedek and Avraham, the role of the priest is to prepare the patriarch for his theophany—to fortify God's chosen leader so that he can successfully commune with God, and fully embark on God's mission to promulgate justice to the rest of humanity.

Kings and Priests on a National Level

We have spoken thus far of the priest Malkizedek preparing Avraham for his personal revelation, which prefigured the great theophany at Sinai. Yitro, Priest of Midian, propelled the Israelite leadership a step further by instructing Moshe in the ways of justice, thus preparing him to receive the divine word. The next step was for the people collectively to receive God's word as *priests* and accept as their mandate the dissemination of the word to the world at large. We see this in Exodus chapter 19, verses 5–6:

> Now, then, if you will obey Me faithfully and keep My covenant, you shall be my
> treasured possession among all the peoples. Indeed, all the earth is Mine, but you
> shall be to Me a kingdom of priests (ממלכת כהנים) and a holy nation....

Ibn Ezra (Abraham ibn Ezra, eleventh century) takes note of the conditional nature of this verse—*if* you obey, *then* you shall merit the accolade "a treasured possession among all the peoples." For Ibn Ezra, this term carries with it a benefit along with an obligation:

> **A kingdom of priests.** In my opinion, every kohen in the Bible is a kind of servant and the support for this is "וכהנו לי" (Exodus 28:41, where the root כהן is in verb form meaning "to service"). And so it is

with the Priest of Midian [Yitro] (Exodus 18:1); he was a servant of God as was Malkizedek. And so "the children of David were *co-hanim*" (II Samuel 8:18). We know that the sons of the King had greatness, but the text informs us that they were servants of God. And "a kingdom of priests" means "My kingdom will be seen through you, when you act as My servants."

Broadening the common definition of kohen from being a member of a small elite caste, Ibn Ezra defines the term as a person from any one of the tribes of Israel who has been chosen to provide service to God. Perhaps aware of the connections we are drawing, Ibn Ezra cites as prime examples the two priests we have studied, Malkizedek and Yitro.[9] In his opinion, a kohen is chosen in order to bring God's message to others: this is precisely the mission performed by Malkizedek and Yitro, and the same mission is given the Israelites at the foot of Mount Sinai. Ibn Ezra views the election of Israel as a sign not of racial superiority, but primarily as an obligation—to teach humanity about God and justice.

Just as the two priests, Malkizedek priest to God Most High and Yitro Priest of Midian, instructed the patriarchs in the ways of divine justice, so too at the foot of Mount Sinai, the Jewish people were enjoined to follow this model and become a ממלכת כהנים, a "kingdom of priests." This is an expression with clear echoes of the "king/priest," Malkizedek (מלכי-צדק מלך שלם והוא כהן). By the Israelites' assuming this role, the model of enabler/priest was to be extended and magnified to a nation of priests who were to bring the notion of divine justice to all of humanity.

The universal messages here are powerful: two non-Jewish priests tend to the spiritual needs of two Israelite patriarchs. Malkizedek and Yitro point to God's role as the source of all blessing, and as the sustainer of the prophets and their people. By leading the patriarchs to this recognition, the priests brought them to an understanding and appreciation of justice as a manifestation of God's will. At Sinai, in poignant reciprocity, God enjoins the descendants of these patriarchs to enlighten all of humanity with this same recognition.

---

[9] Similarly, as Ibn Ezra points out, the sons of David, from the royal, not priestly tribe of Judah, are referred to as *kohanim.*

The following comparison highlights the themes common to the non-Israelite priests and to the Israelite nation in its priestly role:

עם ישראל כממלכת כהנים **Israel as a Kingdom of Priests**	הכהנים מלכי-צדק ויתרו **The Priests Malkizedek and Yitro**
ואתם תהיו לי **ממלכת כהנים** וגוי קדוש You will be for me a **kingdom of priests** (Exodus 19:6)	**ומלכי**-צדק מלך שלם ...**והוא כהן** לא-ל עליון Malkizedek **king** of Shalem was a **priest** (Genesis 14:18)
כי לי כל הארץ **For all the earth** is Mine (Exodus 19:5)	ברוך אברם לא-ל עליון **קונה** **שמים וארץ** Blessed is Avraham to God creator of **heaven and earth** (Genesis 14:19)
ונברכו בך כל משפחות האדמה All the nations of the world will be **Blessed** through you (Genesis 12:3)	**ברוך** א-ל עליון **ברוך** ה' אשר הציל **Blessed** is God Most High (Genesis 14:20) **Blessed** is God who has delivered you (Exodus 18:10)

At Mount Sinai, the Israelites are awarded a new dual title: "kingdom" and "priests." In their new capacity, they are selected from among the nations for a particular relationship with their creator, while at the same time they are singled out to bear a weighty responsibility. Because God says, "all the world is Mine," He charges His newly elected priests to care for the rest of creation by promoting notions of justice and right-eousness.

Ultimately, God's blessing is not the sole domain of the Israelites. The kindness of the early priests is not forgotten: the blessing they bestowed will come back to them, through the agency of their priestly Israelite heirs. Surely Avraham is blessed, as is his seed, but they are enjoined not to be satisfied with their own blessings. The national promise will not be fulfilled until "all of the nations of the world will be blessed through you"

(Genesis 12:3). It is not enough to be blessed; the charge to the Israelites was "והיה ברכה" (Genesis 12:2), to "be a blessing" as well.

Conclusions

In treating the questions posed at the outset, we have suggested the following:

- an understanding of the contrast intended by the Bible's unusual interposing of the Malkizedek narrative into the narrative of the King of Sodom.
- a key to understanding the enigmatic character of Malkizedek and a paradigm for the function of non-Aronite priests later in the Bible.
- an intricate literary relationship between Genesis chapter 14 (the wars and their aftermath) and chapter 15 (God's covenant with Avraham).
- a comparison between the Malkizedek-Avraham relationship and that of Moshe-Yitro.
- a connection between these early stories, and the delicate relationship between the particularism of the chosen nation, and the universalism of a kingdom of priests enjoined to serve all nations.

Yet in all of these narratives—that of Avraham, of Moshe and of the Israelite nation—we are struck by the persistent and disturbing dialectic between a transcendent, majestic mission and a circuitous, sometimes turbid route to its fulfillment. At times, the view of heaven is obscured, at times, entirely forgotten. What is one to make of a narrative that leaps heavenward, and plunges to the depths of coarse reality and then back again, all within the space of several short verses? What is the relevance of this model to the reader of the Bible who looks to it for inspiration?

Inspiration may be provided in many forms and one is as a recognizable, relevant model for human existence. The infallible patriarch or matriarch is no relevant archetype for his or her struggling posterity. Rather, fateful fluctuations and the mundane transposing itself into the divine, unite the reader with his or her forebears. Once this paradigm has been established, the probing reader asks: what applicable messages may I cull from the tribulations presented by the biblical chronicle?

One such message is that the idealist must also be a realist. There must be an understanding that the success of any mission depends on one's ability to navigate between exalted vision and earthly necessity, the latter carrying with it a powerful downward gravitational pull. This may account for the seemingly inordinate biblical emphasis on the minutiae of the prosaic struggles of the matriarchs and patriarchs. These details are an essential part of the message: vision without struggle is not part of the human experience. We are privy to Avraham's daily strife, because therein lies the model for human existence. This is a basic element of the rabbinic dictum "מעשה אבות סימן לבנים" ("the deeds of the fathers prefigure the deeds of the sons"): not only will Avraham's descendants emulate his encounters with the Divine, they will also inevitably face his moral challenges and experience his earthly vicissitudes. There is solace and validation to be found in the biblical models; though sainthood eludes them, they have struggled well to succeed.

The model we have studied presents the patriarchs in situations of impasse: at times they are unable to sufficiently combat the flow of the ordinary, and instead encounter a blurring of the larger perspective of their life's mission. At this point, a fresh figure presents itself: the priestly enabler who, in part by virtue of his being an outsider, retains perspective and reminds the patriarch of his original mandate. This role was filled by Malkizedek for Avraham, by Yitro for Moshe and is presented as a charge to the Jewish people toward the rest of humanity. Ultimately the Israelites, the perennial outsiders, are exhorted even when threatened by the quagmire of daily strife, to help keep the eyes of humanity firmly fixed on the beckoning firmament above. When the hollow spaces of the earth threaten to expand and devour, Avraham's descendants are taken out "and elevated above the stars."[10]

---

[10] *Genesis Rabbah* 44.10 cited by Rashi, Genesis 15:5.

Readings of Rabbinic Texts

"Na'aseh Adam": Should We Make Adam?
A Midrashic Reading of Genesis 1:26

Simi Peters

...the story of Creation is a deep secret, not to be understood from the [biblical] verses. And it cannot be thoroughly known except by means of the tradition going back to Moshe, our teacher, as received from the mouth of God, and those who know [this secret] are obligated to conceal it.... (Nachmanides' Commentary on the Torah, Genesis 1:1)

In this essay, I will attempt to present a nuanced reading of a narrative expansion—a "story" (aggadic) midrash. My goal is to demonstrate that midrashic sources, when read carefully, yield a far deeper understanding than is gained by simply skating over the surface of the text. Naturally, a reading of this type does not presume to be exhaustive. It is axiomatic that a midrash can be understood at many levels, some far simpler than the one offered here and some, such as the commentaries of the Maharal, the Alshich and the great masters of the Hasidic and *Mussar* movements, far more profound. The approach offered here is not necessarily incompatible with approaches taken elsewhere. The ultimate goal of this essay is to provide the reader with food for thought as well as analytical tools in his or her next encounter with a midrash.

I. The Interpretive Problem: The Midrashic Starting Point

Readers of Genesis 1 quickly notice that the language of the text follows a certain pattern in describing the seven days of Creation.[1] First, God commands that something come into being. Next, God contemplates what

---

[1] I highly recommend that the reader review the first chapter of Genesis for a framework within which to understand what follows.

He has created and sees that it is good. Finally, the day of the Creation is numbered. This pattern is followed almost invariably[2] throughout the chapter, although the descriptions differ in detail according to what has been created on a given day.

In only one case does this pattern vary. In all the verses of Genesis 1, which describe God ordering the creation of something, the language is unambiguously one of commandment, with the following exception. Genesis 1:26 reads as follows, "And the Lord said, 'Let Us make *Adam* [humankind] in Our image, after Our likeness....'" This verse might also be translated as, "We will make *Adam* in Our image...." The midrash cited below actually reads it as a question best translated, perhaps, as, "Shall/Should We make humankind in Our image?"

Elsewhere in Genesis, the word *Adam* (אדם) is used to refer to the first man, and Eve—or *Havva* (חוה)—is used to refer to the first woman. In this particular passage, the classical Jewish commentators interpret the word *Adam* to mean "humankind," both male and female. The midrashic reading of the passage clearly understands this verse as referring to humanity and its discussion deals with human nature, rather than masculine nature. My translation of the term reflects this understanding.

In any event, the language of the verse, at the very least, is somewhat surprising. To whom can God be speaking and for what purpose? Even if we wish to assume that God, for some reason, is employing the royal "we" in this utterance, it is unclear why He should do so here and not elsewhere in the text. This use of language is particularly odd from the perspective of Jewish tradition because as Rashi points out, this use of the plural "gives heretics room to rebel."[3] What, then, are we to make of this odd shift in the pattern of language we see throughout Genesis 1?

Genesis Rabbah, an early midrashic commentary on the book of Genesis, uses the interpretive problem posed by Genesis 1:26 to explore the possibility that humankind *might* not have been created, or even that it *should* not have been created. The midrash asks whom God consulted

---

[2] With the exception of the second day of Creation (verses 6–8), in which the act of creation is not completed. In the description of this day's Creation, the text does not have God contemplating that which He has created.

[3] See Rashi on Genesis 1:26.

when He said, "Let Us make *Adam...*" and, in the answers which it proposes, suggests that the real issue is whether the creation of human beings is theologically justified. In the course of their exploration of this question, the Rabbis offer a complex range of understandings of human nature, clothed in language and imagery of rare literary beauty. The full discussion in *Genesis Rabbah* 8.3–5 follows:

> And the Lord said, "Let Us make *Adam*."

Section One

(1)   With whom did He consult?

(2)   R. Yehoshua says in the name of R. Levi: He consulted the work of heaven and earth [Creation].

(3)   This may be compared to a king who had two advisors,[4]

(4)   and would not do anything without their knowledge.

(5)   R. Shemuel bar Nahman said: He consulted what had been made each day.

(6)   This may be compared to a king who had an associate regent,[5]

(7)   and would not do anything without his knowledge.

(8)   R. Ami said: He consulted His heart.

(9)   This may be compared to a king who built a palace by means of an artisan.[6]

(10)   He saw it and it was not pleasing to him.

(11)   With whom should he be discontented—not the artisan?!

(12)   This is [what it means when it says] (Genesis 6:6) "And it grieved His heart."

(13)   R. Yosi said: This may be compared to a king who did business through an agent and lost [his investment].

(14)   With whom should he be discontented—not the agent?!

(15)   This is [what it means when it says] (Genesis 6:6) "And it grieved His heart."

---

[4] This term may also be translated as "senator" or "councilor."

[5] This term may also be translated as "associate" or "assessor."

[6] This term may also be translated as "architect" or "stonecutter."

Section Two

(16)　R. Berekhia said: At the hour that the Holy One Blessed be He came to create *Adam harishon* [the first human],

(17)　He saw righteous people and wicked people coming from him.

(18)　He said, "If I create him, wicked people will come from him;

(19)　[but] if I don't create him, how will righteous people come from him?"

(20)　What did the Holy One Blessed be He do?

(21)　He separated the path of the wicked from before His face,

(22)　and partnered to Himself the quality of mercy,

(23)　and created him.

(24)　That is what it says [in] (Psalms 1:6), "For God knows the path of the righteous, and the path of the wicked will perish."

(25)　He destroyed it[7] from before His face, and partnered to Himself the quality of mercy and created him.

(26)　R. Hanina did not say thus.

(27)　Rather, [he said that] at the hour that the Holy One Blessed He came to create *Adam harishon*,

(28)　He consulted the ministering angels and said to them,

(29)　"Should We make humankind in Our image, after Our likeness?"

(30)　They said to Him,

(31)　"This human, what is his nature [characteristics]?"

(32)　He said to them,

(33)　"Righteous people come from him."

(34)　That is what it says [in] (Psalms 1:6), "For God knows the path of the righteous"—

(35)　for God made known the path of the righteous to the ministering angels;

(36)　"and the path of the wicked will perish"—

---

[7] We should note here that the first chapter of Psalms from which the prooftext on lines 24 and 34 is taken is a paean of praise to the virtues of the righteous, which mentions the wicked only in the last line. The word '*toved*' (translated in line 24 as "will perish") is a conjugation of the root א.ב.ד. which, depending upon the construction in which it is conjugated, can have the meaning of "lose," "destroy," "perish," "ruin," "forfeit" or "commit suicide." The variant readings of Psalms 1:6 play upon the different possible meanings of the root א.ב.ד.

(37)   He caused [knowledge of the path of the wicked] to be lost to them.[8]

(38)   He revealed to them that the righteous arise from him [*Adam*],

(39)   and He did not reveal to them that the wicked arise from him;

(40)   for had He revealed to them that the wicked arise from him,

(41)   the quality of judgment would not have permitted [humankind] to be created.

Section Three

(42)   R. Simon said: At the hour that the Holy One Blessed be He came to create *Adam harishon*,

(43)   the ministering angels formed parties and factions.

(44)   Some of them said, "Let him be created,"

(45)   and some of them said, "Let him not be created."

(46)   That is what is says [in] (Psalms 85:11), "Lovingkindness and truth met; justice and peace kissed."[9]

(47)   Lovingkindness says: "Let him be created, because he does acts of lovingkindness";

(48)   and Truth says: "Let him not be created, because he is all lies."

(49)   Justice says: "Let him be created, because he does acts of justice."

(50)   Peace says: "Let him not be created because he is all discord."

(51)   What did the Holy One Blessed be He do?

(52)   He took Truth and cast her to the ground.

(53)   That is what it says [in] (Daniel 8:12), "and truth was cast to the ground."[10]

---

[8] See footnote 7.

[9] It is significant that Psalms 85 is a song in praise of God's desire for repentance, given that the issue in R. Simon's story is whether, in light of *Adam*'s negative propensities, he should be created. The prooftext in line 46 is given an ironic twist by its placement in the context of this narrative. Although the plain sense of the verse is as translated in line 46, the words *nifgashu* ("met") and *nashaku* ("kissed") can be twisted to mean "encountered" (with a negative connotation), and "met in armed combat," respectively. Once again, this is possible because R. Simon can play with the variant meanings of the roots .ש.ג.פ and .ק.ש.נ. (It should be noted, however, that the meaning "met in armed combat," assigned to the word *nashaku*, is a fabricated meaning for the word which does not actually exist in Hebrew.)

[10] The verse in Daniel has been translated in the passive voice to avoid the confusion that would occur if it were translated literally, as "and it cast truth to the ground."

(54)   The ministering angels said before the Holy One Blessed be He,

(55)   "Master of the universe, why are You abusing Your seal?"[11]

(56)   "Let Truth rise up from the ground."

(57)   That is what it says [in] (Psalms 85:12), "Truth will grow up from the earth."

(58)   The Rabbis say in the name of R. Hanina the son of Idi and R. Pinhas and R. Hilkiya in the name of R. Simon said, "very" [me'od]—this is "Adam."[12]

(59)   This is what it says [in] (Genesis 1:31), "And the Lord saw all that He had made and behold it was *very* good"—

(60)   And behold, humankind is good.

(61)   R. Huna, the Rabbi of Tzippori said,

(62)   While the ministering angels were arguing with each other and engaged with each other, the Holy One Blessed be He created him.

(63)   He said, "What are you arguing about? *Adam* has already been made!"[13]

II. Some Methodological Problems

The careful reader has no doubt noticed that the first section of this midrashic text—the parables of R. Ami and R. Yosi—raises a number of serious theological difficulties. For one thing, if we assume that God has total foreknowledge of everything that will ever come to pass, how is it that His heart is grieved over something that He should certainly have been able to anticipate, and indeed forestall, by simply not creating humanity?

Furthermore, it is difficult to understand what can possibly be meant by "God's heart." One of the tenets of Judaism found in the Bible is that

---

[11] See Rashi on these words: "The seal of the Holy One Blessed be He is truth" (*Shabbat* 55a).

[12] The rabbinic pun we see here makes use of the fact that a Torah scroll is written without vowels. The word "very," without vowels, is spelled מאד and "Adam," without vowels is spelled אדם. The letters are the same in both words, though the order is different. Thus, the Rabbis are able to play with the meanings of the words and relate them.

[13] R. Huna's play on words here also makes use of the fact that a Torah scroll is written without vowels. See footnote 12. The word *na'aseh* in Genesis 1:26 which we have translated as "Let Us make..." changes in meaning with a slight vowel shift (*na'asah*) to "he (it) is made."

God is an absolute unity, not divisible in any way, just as He is non-corporeal in any way.

Questions of this sort arise in the second and third sections of the midrash as well. "The quality of judgment" and "the quality of mercy" were not perceived by the Rabbis as entities external to God, but as His attributes. What then can it mean to say that "the quality of judgment would not have permitted [humanity] to be created" (line 41) had God revealed the truth about human nature?

By the same token, if angels have no free will—and it is clear that the Rabbis defined the angels in this way—how can they quarrel over the creation of humanity? For that matter, why does God bother to consult them, if He simply intends to ignore their arguments?

This list of questions is by no means exhaustive, but is indicative of the kinds of interpretative difficulties that arise in *midrashim* of this type. How are we to reconcile the definition of God that is axiomatic in Judaism with the sort of anthropomorphism that is given such free play here?

One approach, which goes far beyond the scope of this article and my realm of knowledge, is to interpret the midrash within a kabbalistic framework, such as the Maharal or the great hasidic masters. Within the various kabbalistic frameworks, different symbolic values are assigned to the roles in *midrashim* of this type, and the questions we have raised are interpreted as part of a coherent world-view which accounts for them.

The approach I will take here is not incompatible with the one outlined above, but functions at a different interpretive level. My analysis assumes that *midrashim* of this type, like those in which inanimate objects are anthropomorphized, are designed to discuss difficult theological or philosophical questions in language accessible to readers of all types. The thought processes attributed to God, His act of "consulting" the angels, and the objections they raise to *Adam*'s creation are simply rhetorical devices; they are metaphors, uses of figurative language which represent the range of rabbinic opinions concerning the theological value of creating humankind.

III. Methodological Tools: Structure and Comparison

In analyzing a midrash, it is usually helpful to examine its structure, on the assumption that the way in which the midrash is constructed is designed to draw our attention to certain ideas.

The first section (lines 1–15) opens with the question that sets the stage for the discussion that follows: whom did God consult in His decision to create humankind (line 1)? This is followed by four possible answers to the question, presented in parable form (lines 2–15). On our first reading, we immediately see the similarity between the parables of R. Yehoshua (lines 2–4) and R. Shemuel bar Nahman (lines 5–7) on the one hand, and the similarity between the parables of R. Ami (lines 8–12) and R. Yosi (lines 13–15) on the other. Thus, the structure of section one is an introductory question followed by two sets of parables.

At this point we might ask, given the similarity of the parables within each set, why the editors of *Genesis Rabbah* included all four of them. Furthermore, if we examine the parables, we will note that they are hardly more than sketches. In fact, it is not at all clear on a first reading what the parables actually add to our understanding of the four rabbinic opinions. For example, in answer to the question of whom God consulted, R. Yehoshua says that He consulted Creation. That answer seems to stand perfectly well on its own. What does the parable of the king and the senators add? To answer these questions, we need to examine each opinion individually and see how, if at all, it differs from the others.

In saying that God consulted "the work of heaven and earth" (line 2), R. Yehoshua is implying that the creation of humanity is legitimate only if it is harmonious with the rest of Creation. Given the nature of free will, humankind has the power to alter, and even damage, God's perfect world. R. Yehoshua's parable seems to place Creation at center stage and humanity in the wings; if *Adam* harms or damages Creation, humans ought not be created.

That humanity has to conform to Creation, and not vice versa, is made clear by the parable portion of R. Yehoshua's statement. In the parable (lines 3–4), God is compared to a king, while heaven and earth are compared to two advisors without whose knowledge the king will not act. The parable implies that heaven and earth have veto power here; the king's consultation with his advisors is not merely a matter of protocol since, as we are told in line 4, he "would not do anything without their knowledge." If the creation of *Adam* does not harmonize with "the work of heaven and earth," on R. Yehoshua's reading, it will not be allowed to take place.

How does R. Shemuel bar Nahman differ from R. Yehoshua? In R. Shemuel bar Nahman's reading, it is not sufficient for God to consult Creation as a whole in order to determine whether the creation of *Adam* is legitimate. He contends that each element in nature has to be consulted individually—"[God] consulted what had been made each day" (line 5). R. Shemuel bar Nahman's parable points out that each element of Creation is an "associate regent" to the king (lines 6–7), and that the creation of *Adam* must be harmonious not only with the *overall* scheme of Creation, but with each *detail* of it.

Common to both R. Yehoshua's and R. Shemuel bar Nahman's readings are two ideas. The first is that God *considered* the creation of *Adam* before actually implementing it. This implies that the creation of *Adam* was by no means a certainty; perhaps the world might well have been complete without humans. Both R. Yehoshua and R. Shemuel bar Nahman appear to contemplate with equanimity a world without humankind on the assumption that, at the very least, its creation is by no means an unequivocal good. (This view, like much of what follows in this midrash, challenges the anthropocentrism which governs much of our thinking.) The second shared idea is the notion that in debating whether or not to create humanity, God "consulted" something outside Himself. In contrast, the second set of opinions views this process of decision-making as purely internal to God.

Both R. Ami and R. Yosi deal with the problem raised by the words "Let Us make *Adam*..." by stating that God "consulted His heart." On this reading, God, figuratively speaking, is thinking out loud. The decision-making process described here involves only God; no one is granted veto-power. In fact, each of these parables picks up the story *after* the decision to gamble on the creation of *Adam* is already made.

In R. Ami's parable, God is likened to a king and *Adam* to a palace that the king has commissioned from an artisan. The artisan of the parable is God's heart. When the king sees that the palace is not pleasing to him, he is discontented with the artisan, just as God's heart, by analogy, is later filled with grief over humanity's wickedness. R. Ami seems to be saying that humankind is a plan flawed in the execution—the completed palace does not come up to the king's expectations.

R. Yosi also sees God as consulting His heart, but his parable presents yet a more pessimistic assessment of the success of God's endeavor in creating humanity. In R. Yosi's parable, God is a king who has made a business investment ([the creation of *Adam*) through an agent (His heart). Unlike the king of the previous parable, who at least is left with *something*, however much it displeases him, R. Yosi's king has lost everything. The venture is a total loss and, by analogy, that is how the creation of humankind is portrayed in R. Yosi's parable.

IV. Stories as Dialectic

The second section of our midrash (lines 16–41) presents us with two stories that further explore the question of the justification of *Adam*'s creation. The paragraph is easily divided between R. Berekhia's account and R. Hanina's. Although these two accounts seem similar, the editors of *Genesis Rabbah* make it clear that the resemblance is only superficial by pointing out that whereas R. Berekhia said such and such, "R. Hanina did *not* say thus" (line 26).

R. Berekhia's story (lines 16–25) outlines two stages in the process of the creation of humankind. The first stage (lines 16–19) describes God's contemplation of His dilemma. To create *Adam* means, by definition, that there will be both righteous and wicked people; to refrain from creating *Adam* is to prevent the existence of the righteous as well as the wicked. The problem is summed up in lines 18 and 19: "If I create him, wicked people will come from him; [but] if I don't create him, how will righteous people come from him?"

The second part of R. Berekhia's story gives us the second stage of humanity's creation and opens with the words, "What did the Holy One Blessed be He *do*?" (line 20). Instead of simply telling us that God created humanity, R. Berekhia describes a rather tortured procedure that involves first, God's removal of the path of the wicked from before His face and second, the partnering of Himself with the quality of mercy in order to create *Adam*. For R. Berekhia, then, God's decision to create *Adam* is no simple matter. The fact of the existence of the wicked is so terrible that in order to create humanity, God must, so to speak, conceal it from Himself. Even then, having removed "the path of the wicked from before His face," God cannot create human beings without joining to Himself the quality of mercy.

R. Berekhia's story echoes elements of R. Ami and R. Yosi's parables. In R. Berekhia's story, as in both parables, God consults only Himself. R. Berekhia, like R. Ami and R. Yosi, is deeply pessimistic about the outcome of humankind's creation; and in both the story and the parables, it is the human potential for wickedness that raises the question of whether the creation of *Adam* is justifiable.

R. Hanina's reading of *Adam*'s creation (lines 26–41) is less pessimistic. In his account, God consults the ministering angels, apparently after having decided independently to create humankind. When the angels ask about the nature of *Adam*, in order to make a decision about whether or not he should be created, God tells the angels only about the righteous, "for had He revealed to them that the wicked arise up from him, the quality of judgment would not have permitted [humankind] to be created" (lines 40–41).

How does R. Hanina's reading differ from R. Berekhia's? First, in R. Hanina's view, God is not ambivalent. He wishes to create *Adam* **despite** being fully cognizant of the human potential for evil. Second, in R. Hanina's version, there appears to be no need to add the weight of the quality of mercy to tip the scales in *Adam*'s favor. God only conceals the complete picture of human nature so that the quality of judgment will not prevent the creation of humankind—not because He Himself cannot, as it were, bear to contemplate it.

I would suggest that R. Berekhia's portrait of God's thought processes is analogous to that of a person who wishes to take a course of action against his better judgment, and chooses not to look squarely at the real facts of the situation in order to permit himself to do so. In contrast, the proper analogy for R. Hanina's portrayal of God's actions is a person who is confident in the course of action he or she wishes to take, despite being aware of its pitfalls. Nonetheless, such a person still might wish to avoid the objections of others to his plans and, therefore, would take steps to conceal the true situation from them.

R. Hanina's story takes us back to the first set of parables in section one. Like R. Yehoshua and R. Shemuel bar Nahman, R. Hanina reads "Let Us make *Adam*..." as God speaking with someone outside Himself, and like them, R. Hanina is fully aware that the creation of humankind poses a theological problem. R. Hanina differs from the authors of the first set of parables, however, in seeing God's "consultation" of the angels as more a matter of protocol than application. R. Hanina recognizes that from the perspective of the quality of judgment, the creation of *Adam*— that creature with his unlimited potential for evil—is impossible. However, while R. Yehoshua and R. Shemuel bar Nahman's parables give veto power to Creation, R. Hanina constructs his story so that the quality of judgment is circumvented by an act of God's will.

The third section of our midrash opens with yet another account of the creation of *Adam*, that of R. Simon (lines 42–57). R. Simon's story differs from everything that precedes it. First, unlike the accounts in sections one and two, R. Simon's description does not state that God consulted the angels, or even His own heart. In fact, in R. Simon's story there does not seem to be any decision-making process, even from God's internal perspective, as there is in both the parables of section one and the stories of section two.

The second difference between R. Simon's description and that of the opinions which precede it is in the focus of the story. The parables in section one, for example, don't explicitly describe human nature, even as they indicate by indirection that the creation of humanity is problematic. The parables focus primarily on God. In the first set, the issue is God's interaction with forces outside Himself and their potential impact on the creation of humankind. In the second set, the issue is the nature of God's reaction to His failure with *Adam*.

The stories in section two introduce an element not present in the parables. Here, the crux of the matter is human nature, which is described as potentially righteous or wicked. Although the stories differ in their conclusions about whether *Adam* should have been created, they portray the possibilities of human behavior in the same way: humankind can be either good or bad.

By contrast, R. Simon's view of human nature is more nuanced. In his story, human nature is not reducible to the black and white of righteous people and wicked people. Instead, it is represented as a complex of qualities: *Adam* is incapable of attaining truth and peace, but *is* capable of acts of righteousness and lovingkindness. The implication is that even righteous people cannot, from a heavenly perspective, attain absolute truth and peace, while even wicked people may sometimes perform acts of righteousness and lovingkindness.

The opposition which R. Simon sets up is, significantly, between absolute qualities (truth and peace) and relative qualities (justice and lovingkindness). By definition, truth and peace cannot be partial or relative; a partial truth, strictly speaking, is a lie and an incomplete peace, at best, is an uneasy one. R. Simon makes this clear with the extreme language he gives voice to in the utterances of Truth and Peace: "Let him not be created because he is *all* lies" (line 48), and "Let him not be created because he is *all* discord" (line 50).

While the creation of *Adam* means the disruption of those absolute qualities, if humankind is not created, the human qualities of justice and lovingkindness cannot come into being. Justice is not possible, after all, from the perspective of the angels, since there is no injustice to be corrected in heaven. Similarly, acts of lovingkindness are not possible where there is no free will. The qualities of truth and peace, on the one hand and justice and lovingkindness, on the other, cannot exist on the same plane. Yet from R. Simon's perspective, a world without the potential for justice and lovingkindness is incomplete. And since justice and lovingkindness are not possible without *Adam*—the only being in Creation with free will—the creation of *Adam* is justified.

R. Simon's story does not, however, simply set up the oppositions we have noted, and end with God's creation of *Adam* against the backdrop of the angels' bickering. Instead the story *begins* with "the hour that the Holy One Blessed be He came to create *Adam harishon*" (line 42), which implies that He is engaged in the act of creation even as the angels argue, and *ends* with God casting Truth to the ground, to the horror of the ministering angels who ask, "Master of the universe, why are You abusing Your seal?" (lines 51–55). We should note that the speaker of the line that follows this question is unclear. Is it the ministering angels who say, "Let Truth rise up from the ground?" (line 56) as part of their protestations against the abuse of God's identifying characteristic? Or is it God Himself, answering the objections of the angels to this desecration of the truth? We might also ask why R. Simon structures his story so that it ends in this way.

To answer these questions, we should examine the prooftext with which the story concludes. Lines 56–57 read: "'Let Truth rise up from the ground.' That is what it says [in] (Psalms 85:12), 'Truth will grow up from the earth.'" If we read line 56 as God's answer to the angels, we can see that in this story, R. Simon is not only asserting that *Adam* is valuable because of his potential for qualities which angels cannot manifest, but he is also addressing the vexed question of what to do with the human potential for evil and its effect upon the supreme value of Truth. Unlike the parables and the previous stories that simply note the problematic nature of humankind, R. Simon offers a solution, namely the verse in Psalms. If Truth has been dethroned by the ascension of *Adam*, it will have to be restored by growing up from the earth. Truth will no longer be a static, absolute, divine quality, but an evolving, organic component of the created world—something for which human beings will have to strive. The ending of R. Simon's story is highly significant because it is ultimately so optimistic about humankind. If people are flawed, on R. Simon's reading, they are nonetheless also capable of at least striving for—if not totally attaining—divine qualities.

V. The Final Word

R. Simon's story is followed by two more rabbinic comments. The first, which actually quotes R. Simon (lines 58–60) uses a pun to re-read Genesis 1:31. The verse says that God, in contemplating all He has made, sees that "it was very good." Since the Hebrew letters for "very" are identical to the letters for "*Adam*," differing only in their order in the different words (see footnote 12), the Rabbis read the verse to mean that in contemplating all that He has made, God sees that "*Adam* is good." In making the equivalence between the goodness of Creation and the goodness of humanity's existence, the Rabbis make explicit what is implied in the previous narrative, namely that the creation of *Adam* is unequivocally a "*very good*" thing and needs no apology. In fact, on this reading, the creation of humankind is equal in weight to "*all that He had made*" and, quite possibly, the existential purpose of Creation.

The second rabbinic comment, that of R. Huna (lines 61–63), brilliantly reverses everything that precedes it. Instead of reading Genesis 1:26 as "Let Us make *Adam*..." or even "Should We make *Adam*...")?, R. Huna reads these words as a peremptory, even dictatorial statement: "*Adam* has already been made" (see footnote 13). According to R. Huna, God is not consulting anyone; He is proclaiming that the competing positions of the angels are totally irrelevant to His desire to create *Adam*. On this reading, the only thing that matters is God's will—His desire, for whatever reason, to create humanity. In two pithy sentences, R. Huna has dismissed all the philosophical speculation that precedes his own expansion of the narrative. We do not know why God has chosen to create human beings, implies R. Huna, and ultimately it is not for us to say what value the creation of *Adam* has, or in what ways human beings are problematic. It is enough that God has created us—"*Adam* has already been made!" (line 63).

Each rabbinic opinion cited in *Genesis Rabbah* 8.3–5 is a philosophical and literary gem in its own right. It is important to note, though, that the text before us in fact is a compositional work, a carefully constructed argument which adds up to more than the sum of its various parts, however impressive those parts may be when read in isolation. The editors of *Genesis Rabbah* not only selected each of these rabbinic positions; they also arranged them in an order that shows the relationships and disjunctions between them. For example, the juxtaposition of the four parables at the beginning of the midrash enables us to note the superficial similarities between them, and more significantly, the different ways they present God's relationship to the problem of the creation of humankind. Is the creation of *Adam* a problem because of its effect upon the world, or is it because *Adam* will inevitably disappoint God?

Significantly, the editors of *Genesis Rabbah* order the rabbinic opinions from the most pessimistic view of humankind to the most optimistic. *Almost* the last word is given to R. Simon, whose bottom line is that "*Adam* is good" (line 60). This would seem to indicate that the editors of *Genesis Rabbah* give greater weight to those who see the creation of humanity as, ultimately, a positive thing. But even that is not the final word on the creation of *Adam*. The last opinion cited, of R. Huna's, is a humbling reminder that all our philosophical speculations, in fact, are only speculations. God does as He wills, and whatever our opinion of His actions, in the final analysis we must recognize that God is God and His will is beyond our understanding, or even our approval.

Three *Meshalim* of the King and His Daughter in Rabbinic Thought

Batya Hefter

The Role of Midrash

דורשי הגדות אומרים ״רצונך להכיר את מי שאמר והיה העולם״ למוד
הגדה שמתוך כך אתה מכיר את מי שאמר והיה העולם ומדבק בדרכיו.
(ספרי דברים, פיסקא מט, ד״ה ׳ולדבקה בו׳)

> If you wish to know "Him who spoke and created the world" learn ag-
> gadah, since through doing this you will come to know Him and ad-
> here to His ways. (*Sifre Devarim* 49)

While many may relate to aggadic and midrashic literature as merely
enjoyable anecdotes, the Sages in this *Sifre* insist that intensive study of
aggadah is key to "knowing Him" for those who are seriously motivated.
For the most part, *Hazal* (an acronym in Hebrew, *hakhameinu zikhronam
livrakha*, meaning "our Sages of blessed memory") did not express their
beliefs and opinions systematically—rather, they are imbedded and
concealed in the varying forms of aggadic literature. These ideas are often
expressed through a genre of midrashic literature known as the *mashal*.

A *mashal* (pl., *meshalim*) is a parable, a short fictional story whose
purpose is to illustrate or illuminate some concept in need of explanation,
which is called the *nimshal*. A good example is the following *mashal*
which stresses the overall importance of *meshalim* to Torah study:

ורבנן אמרין אל יהי המשל הזה קל בעיניך שעל ידי המשל הזה אדם יכול
לעמוד בדברי תורה משל למלך שאבד זהב מביתו או מרגלית טובה לא על
ידי פתילה באיסר הוא מוצא אותה? כך המשל הזה לא יהיה קל בעיניך
שעל ידי המשל אדם עומד על דברי תורה. (שיר השרים רבה א:ח)

Our Rabbis say: Let not the parable be lightly esteemed in your eyes, since by means of the parable a person can master the words of the Torah. If a king loses gold from his house or a precious pearl, does he not find it by means of a wick worth a farthing [literally "assarius," a small Roman coin]? So, too, the parable should not be lightly esteemed in your eyes, since by means of the parable a person arrives at the true meaning of the words of the Torah....
(*Song of Songs Rabbah* 1.8)

How does the *mashal* help us arrive at the true meaning of the words of the Torah? The *mashal* itself is compared to an inexpensive wick, with which the king's lost precious items can be found. In the *nimshal*, the Torah is the precious object lost somewhere in the dark. One who is in search of the Torah cannot find it without the light. The inner meaning of the Torah eludes him and remains hidden. The *mashal*, then, is the vehicle which can access and unravel the inner meaning of the Torah. The *mashal*, therefore, must be seen as valuable in and of itself, regarded as the light revealing the significance of the Torah, without which one would remain forever groping in the dark. We therefore learn not to be misled by the simple appearance of the *mashal*, for it is a means of acquiring Torah.

The King-Daughter Parable

This essay focuses on how *Hazal* viewed God as the "father" of the "beloved daughter" in three different contexts. Since the Rabbis constructed *meshalim* for the purpose of illuminating the *nimshal*, there is a natural tendency, when reading the *mashal*, immediately to try and apply its meaning, without first paying careful attention to the choice of characters and other details. While the *nimshal* is the reason why the *mashal* was created, the *mashal* has a life of its own and can provide us with a glimpse into the inner thoughts of *Hazal*—in our case, how they viewed the dynamics in family relationships.

We need to ask who and what were the personalities and images that *Hazal* portrayed in their *meshalim*? Through these *meshalim*, what did they want to teach us about our relationship to God? Why did they select certain characters and not others? These choices are not arbitrary. In particular, the idea that *Hazal* want to express by employing the image of the king-daughter relationship is different from that implied by the portrayal of the king-son relationship.

There are no lack of *meshalim* in which the king is angry at his son, or even his "*matrona*" or aristocratic wife, but never do we find the king angry with his daughter. The specific choice of king and daughter, as opposed to king and son, or king and workers, is thus highly significant. Each relationship carries with it different expectations and emotional interactions.[1]

The main characters in the narrative of the three *meshalim* discussed here are the *melekh* (king) and the *bat-melekh* (king's daughter). We will explore the dynamics of their relationship in the *mashal* and then see how *Hazal* apply this dynamic to the relationship between God and the Jewish People, openly and unabashedly exploring the complex and often conflicting aspects of the father-daughter bond. Each *mashal* focuses on one type of relationship. When these *meshalim* are viewed together, a fuller picture of the complexity of human relationship emerges, which further reflects the intricate and even contradictory nature of the divine-human bond. R. Chaim Brovender once suggested that our understanding of the parent-child bond reflects our own perception of the divine-human relationship. In that light, it is particularly interesting to see how *Hazal* drew on their insights into personal family relationships to understand and transmit the divine-human encounter.

Reaching Maturity (and the *Ohel Mo'ed*)

The first of these three *meshalim* describes the father-daughter relationship in terms of the daughter's maturation process, from childhood to adulthood and the father's role in that process:

"'אפריון עשה לו.'" ר' עזריה בשם ר' יהודה בר' סימון פתר קרייה במשכן, אפריון זה משכן, אמר ר' יהודה ברבי אלעאי למלך שהיתה לו בת קטנה, עד שלא הגדילה ובאת לידי סימנים היה רואה אותה בשוק ומדבר עמה בפרהסיא במבוי ובחצר, כיון שהגדילה ובאת לידי סימנין אמר המלך אין

---

[1] A methodology of analyzing parables, including the significance of the choice of protagonists, can be found in Yona Fraenkel's Hebrew book, *The Way of Aggadah and Midrash* (*Yad haTalmud*, 1991), section on *mashal*.

שבחה של בתי שאהא מדבר עמה בפרהסיא, אלא עשו לה פפליון
וכשאהיה צריך לדבר עמה אדבר עמה מתוך הפפליון.
כך כתיב (הושע י"א:א) "כי נער ישראל ואהבהו." במצרים ראו אותו
בפרהסיא. בים ראו אותו בפרהסיא.... בסיני ראו אותו פנים בפנים כיון
שעמדו ישראל על הר סיני וקבלו את התורה ואמרו (שמות כ"ד) "כל אשר
דבר ה' נעשה ונשמע," נעשה לו אומה שלימה, אמר הקב"ה אין שבחן של
בני שאהיה מדבר עמם בפרהסיא אלא יעשו לי משכן, וכשאני צריך לדבר
עמהם אהיה מדבר עמהם מתוך המשכן ההי"ד (במדבר ז:ט"ו) בבא משה
אל אהל מועד לדבר אתו. (שיר השירים רבה פרשה ג ד"ה אפריון עשה)

> "King Solomon made himself a palanquin" (Songs of Songs 3:9). R.
> Azariah in the name of R. Judah ben Simon interpreted the verse as
> applying to the Tabernacle. "A palanquin" refers to the Tabernacle.
> Said R. Judah ben R. Ila'i: It is as if a king had a young daughter and
> before she grew up and reached maturity, he used to see her in the
> street and speak to her in public, in an alleyway or in a courtyard, but
> after she grew up and reached maturity, he said: "It is not becoming
> for my daughter that I should converse with her in public. Make her
> therefore a pavilion and when I need to converse with her, I will do so
> within the pavilion."
>
> So it is written, "When Israel was a child, then I loved him" (Ho-
> sea 11:1). In Egypt, the Israelites saw God in the open.... At the Red
> Sea they saw Him in the open.... At Sinai they saw Him face to
> face.... But after Israel stood before Mount Sinai and received the To-
> rah and said, "All that the Lord has spoken will we do and obey"
> (Exodus 24:7) and they had become a whole nation, the Holy One
> Blessed be He, said: "It is not becoming for My people that I should
> speak with them in the open. Let them therefore make for Me a Tab-
> ernacle and whenever I need to speak with them, I shall speak with
> them from the midst of the Tabernacle." And so it says, "But when
> Moshe went in before the Lord that He might speak with Him..."
> (Numbers 7:89; *Song of Songs Rabbah* 3.9)

The narrative in the *mashal* illustrates two stages in the relationship
between the king and his daughter: in the first stage she is a young girl
and in the second she has reached maturity. When the daughter is young,
the king "speaks" to her wherever he sees her "in the street, in the alleyway, in the courtyard"—in other words, in all public places. The Rabbis'
usage of "speech" is not limited to verbal communication, as is demonstrated by its reference in the tractate of the Mishnah *Ketubot* 1:8, "They

saw her **speaking** with someone in the marketplace...." In that context, "speaking" is a euphemism for sexual relations.[2]

In our *mashal*, the usage of "speech" in all the public places indicates a type of playful, innocent intimacy in the relationship. Through his continuous speech, the daughter experiences the father's love and constant presence. This special focus on "public" not only stresses the king's affection for his daughter, but more specifically his omnipresence—the father is emotionally and physically present at all times. This significant point is not fully realized until we compare the *mashal* and the *nimshal*. The close, intimate relationship between father and daughter is necessary while she is young. For the child, the parent is the universe. The child's own inner sense of stability is reflected by the stable presence of the parent—in this case, the father, whose unconditional love and presence is essential to the child's well-being and feeling of wholeness. The *mashal* also points out that while the king-father relates to his young daughter in this manner, he does so, all the while, with the conscious awareness that she has not yet reached maturity ("before she grew up and reached maturity, he used to see her in the street and speak to her in public..."). This mode of relationship is necessary and beneficial to her while she is still young, but as the king sees her reaching maturity, he says: "It is not becoming for my daughter that I should converse with her in public. Make her therefore a pavilion and when I need to converse with her, I will do so within the pavilion."

The king, as he adapts to and encourages his daughter's maturity, no longer speaks to her in public. The meaning of "not speaking to her in public" is that the maturing daughter can no longer benefit from the constant and even overbearing presence of her father. Although most children, as they grow older, want their parents to be in the vicinity, to observe their activities, they no longer want to be the recipients of outward displays of their affection. Here, the king, a very noble father, who is concerned on her behalf, separates himself from his daughter. Her maturity is contingent on separation from her father, allowing her to

---

[2] כתובות א:ח: ראוה **מדברת** עם אחד בשוק אמרו לה מה טיבו של זה איש פלוני וכהן הוא רבן גמליאל ורבי אליעזר אומרים נאמנת ורבי יהושע אומר לא מפיה אנו חיין אלא הרי זו בחזקת בעולה לנתין ולממזר עד שתביא ראיה לדבריה.

develop her own sense of independence and existence in the world. Paradoxically, while this very need for independence necessarily leads to distance, ultimately it will result in a more refined and appropriate intimacy.

While the father's separation from his daughter may seem realistic, building a pavilion to talk with her defies a believable plotline. But as we know, a *mashal* is an analogy, offering some points of comparison but not all. In this case, the plot of the *mashal* describes the mundane (profane) reality of the interpersonal relationship which is then applied to shed light on the human/divine reality. Since the human reality can never adequately reflect the divine reality, there will always be a point where the precise application and intended meaning of the details of the *mashal* to the *nimshal* will fall short. While the idea of a father building a pavilion is unconvincing in the *mashal*, it does draw our attention to the king's ultimate concern—to best facilitate his daughter's maturity by respecting and encouraging her privacy. This concern of the king for his daughter and his choice of pavilion take on new meaning when applied to the *nimshal*.

Hazal apply the image of a king speaking to His beloved daughter at every location ("in the street, in the alleyway, in the courtyard") to the image of God who, through his love of Israel ("When Israel was a child then I loved Him") revealed Himself to them in public via miraculous events (splitting the Red Sea, Mount Sinai). As previously mentioned, the king-father's love, expressed by his omnipresence, becomes abundantly clear in the *nimshal*. While God's love is a factor, it is not the only reason for His constant presence. The meaning of the revelation of God, through miracles, is to ensure that God's presence is undeniably *clear* to His young, immature people. Here, the imagery of the *mashal* contributes toward a fuller understanding of the *nimshal*. Like the father who made his presence known and served as the foundation for his daughter's stability, so too, God revealed Himself in His overwhelming and continuous presence to ensure that the people would know with certainty who their father is. At this stage of development, the people are passive, as belief in miracles requires no effort on behalf of the believer and God, the miracle-maker is active.

In other words, the nation of Israel is, at first, in need of God's constant presence. When the people show signs of independence, represented by their willing acceptance of the Torah, God distances Himself, only to reemerge in a new context. In the *nimshal*, the *Mishkan* (Tabernacle) becomes the place where God and the people will meet, in the private, hidden domain.

We can also see the stages of Israel's history as the maturation process of Israel's relationship to God through the three prooftexts (verses brought to support and enhance the conclusions drawn in the *nimshal*), cited in the *nimshal*.

First Prooftext: Childhood-Miracles

> When Israel was a child, then I loved him. (Hosea 11:1)

This verse expresses the unabashed love of a father for his child. Here, the love of God for Israel is expressed through public miracles ("At the Red Sea they saw Him in the open.... At Sinai they saw Him face to face..."). The idea that the miracles represent God's love and omnipresence as opposed to His power is reinforced by the image of the father in the *mashal*, whose *speech* and not his power or awesome presence is an expression of love for his daughter. This close attention to the details in the plot of the *mashal* enhances our understanding of the *nimshal*.

Second Prooftext: Entering Adulthood-Sinai

> All that the Lord has spoken will we do and obey. (Exodus 24:7)

The turning point at Mount Sinai occurs when the people are transformed from being in a youthful and passive mode, to a more mature and active one. Here the midrash rereads the famous words "we will do," which Israel say to express their obedience and acceptance of the Torah. The midrashic reading of the word "נעשה" *na'aseh*, "we will do," is reread "*na'asah*," meaning "they have become" a complete nation. In other words, it is their active and mature (free-willed) act of accepting the Torah that enables them to reach for perfection. In this model, God, like the father-king, desires that the people mature by becoming wholly active in their relationship with Him. (This reading supplements the more well-known midrash cited by Rashi on Exodus 19:17, that at Sinai the people received the Torah under duress as God held the mountain over their heads like a basin, גיגית.) We can learn that the *nimshal* informs the *mashal*. As in the *nimshal*, God is interested that the nation become active, so too in the *mashal*, the father's withdrawal is designed to encourage the daughter's active search and self-definition. This new awareness paves the way for the next stage in their relationship.

Third Prooftext: Adulthood-*Mishkan*

> Let them therefore make for Me a Tabernacle and whenever I need to speak with them, I shall speak with them from the midst of the Tabernacle and so it says, "But when *Moshe* went in before the Lord that he might speak with him." (Numbers 7:89) (*Song of Songs Rabbah* 3.9)

We now move to the final stage of development—the mature adult whose relationship with God is in the private domain—reflected by the *Mishkan* (specifically, the *ohel mo'ed*, the special location within the *Mishkan* which served as the meeting place between God and humanity).

The *nimshal* expresses the idea of God shifting from "speaking in public"—revealing Himself through miracles—to "speaking in private"—the new and preferred relationship—as a result of the nation's increased maturity.

It is particularly interesting to note how miracles are viewed in this midrash. Miracles are generally seen as a reflection of a greater revelation, a revelation where God's will is clear, where His Presence is known and absolute. Due to their low spiritual state, subsequent generations are not normally the recipients of miracles. According to this midrash, however, the exact opposite is true! The dimension of the relationship with God based on miracles is only necessary until sufficient maturity has developed, allowing for a new, fully refined relationship. In the *mashal*, where the daughter shows signs of maturity, the father withdraws because it is time to cultivate within her an inner sense of self which is necessary for the next stage of their relationship. The idea that belief based on miracles is inadequate or "immature" is also expressed by the Rambam

(Maimonides) *Mishneh Torah*, section "The Foundations of the Torah" (chapter 8).

The Rambam clearly states that belief in the prophet Moshe, which resulted from witnessing revealed miracles, is flawed belief— (יש בלבו דופי) albeit necessary for those of insufficient intellectual maturity. Viewed in this light, miracle-based belief is simply inferior and has no place in either national or individual religious development. Ideally, according to the Rambam, one should aim to reach beyond such simplistic understanding. The midrash, however, views a relationship with God which is based upon miracles as the first stage in religious development. Later stages do not replace the first, but are built upon it. The first stage can not be omitted anymore than can early childhood in the development of an individual.

Here, the effect that the revealed miracles of the Exodus had upon the young Nation of Israel is likened by *Hazal* to the effect that the father's omnipresence has on his young daughter. The miracles enabled the people of Israel to internalize God's presence so that when He later seemed absent or hidden, they would know to seek Him out and find a new, mature and reciprocal mode of discourse in the privacy of the *Ohel Mo'ed*.

Prooftext

In the above midrash we defined the mature relationship as one that is reciprocal. The prooftext supports a reading of the *Ohel Mo'ed* as a "place of meeting," where "meeting" implies reciprocity between God and humankind.

Commentaries on nearly identical phrases in Exodus inform our reading on this verse in Numbers. The verse in Numbers 7:89, "And when Moshe was going into the tent of meeting *to speak with him*" contains the same grammatical ambiguity as the following verses discussed by Nechama Leibowitz *z"l* (of blessed memory), in her commentary on the book of Exodus. In her commentary, she notes that there are three verses about Moshe meeting with God, in which it is not at all clear who is addressing whom:

"Moshe knew not that the skin of his face shone *on his speaking with him*" (Exodus 34:29).

"Whenever Moshe came before the Lord *to speak with him*" (Exodus 34:34).

"Moshe removed the veil...until he came *to speak with him*" (Exodus 34:35).

"Is the reading: Moshe came before the Lord so that he (Moshe) should speak with Him, or so that He (God) should speak with him (Moshe)? Verse 35 is even more mystifying: 'until he came to speak with him.' Who came? Who spoke?"[3]

These "syntactic peculiarities" are explained by Rabbenu Bahya (Exodus 34:35) as the Torah's deliberate ambiguity for the purposes of enhancing "Moshe's spiritual stature." It is written:

> "...*untill* he came to speak with Him." The text should have read: "*untill* he came to speak with the Lord." The proper noun "Moshe" is repeated several times in the same discourse without pronominaliza- tion. Why then is the name of God pronominalized where to avoid ambiguity, the proper noun should have been used? Perhaps the ambi- guity was deliberate to enhance Moshe's spiritual stature by legiti- mizing the alternative reading—"*untill* God came to speak with Moshe." The text implied that just as Moshe came to speak with God, so God came to speak with Moshe. The same idea (of reciprocity or symmetry in relationship with the divine) is implicit in the text: "As one man speaks to another" (31;11); one speaks and the other replies without an intermediary.

This is not to imply that human beings are ever God's equal. That is why Moshe, who in these verses engages in a reciprocal relationship with God, is described elsewhere in the Torah as the most humble person of all, one who would be completely aware of his inferior position vis-à-vis God.

It is probably not coincidental that the midrash chose this verse with its connotations of reciprocity for the prooftext in the *nimshal*. The use of this prooftext suggests that the mature relationship is not only one in which a person seeks for God in His absence, but also one in which when there *is* an encounter, it is a reciprocal one.

---

[3] *Studies in Shemot*, "Ki Tissa," (World Zionist Organization, 1981) 629–31.

A Conditional Marriage (and the *Kiton*)

Whereas the first midrash deals with the stages of childhood, entering adulthood and adulthood itself, the following midrash deals with separation from and "replacement" of the father figure in the daughter's life when she marries. This source carries the greatest emotional charge and also shows rabbinic artistry in dealing with weighty psychological and social issues:

ויקחו לי תרומה, משל למלך שהיה לו בת יחידה בא אחד מן המלכים
ונטלה ביקש לילך לו לארצו וליטול לאשתו אמר לו בתי שנתתי לך
יחידית היא, לפרוש ממנה איני יכול, לומר לך אל תטלה איני יכול לפי
שהיא אשתך אלא זו טובה עשה לי שכל מקום שאתה הולך קיטון אחד
עשה לי שאדור אצלכם שאיני יכול להניח את בתי.
כך אמר הקדוש ברוך הוא לישראל נתתי לכם את התורה לפרוש הימנה
איני יכול לומר לכם אל תטלוה איני יכול אלא בכל מקום שאתם הולכים
בית אחד עשו לי שאדור בתוכו שנאמר (שמות כב:ח) ועשו לי מקדש.
(שמות רבה לג:א)

> God, however, said to Israel: "I have sold you My Torah, but with it, as it were, I also have been sold," as it says, *"that they take me* [rather than 'for me'] *for an offering"* (Exodus 25:2). It can be compared to a king whose only daughter married another king. When he wished to return to his country and take his wife with him, he [the father] said to him: "My daughter, whose hand I have given you, is my only child. I cannot part from her, neither can I say to you, 'Do not take her,' for she is now your wife. This favor, however, I would request of you: wherever you go to live, have a chamber ready for me that I may dwell with you, for I cannot leave my daughter."
> Thus God said to Israel: "I have given you a Torah from which I cannot part and I also cannot tell you not to take it; but this I would request: wherever you go, make for Me a house wherein I may live, as it says (Exodus 22:8), 'And let them make Me a sanctuary, that I may dwell among them.'" (*Exodus Rabbah* 33.1)

Our *mashal* opens in typical narrative fashion, with one king marrying another king's daughter. The new son-in-law wishes to make his home with his new wife in his own land. This natural desire on the part of the son-in-law evokes in the king feelings of great love and affection for his only daughter. While not denying his daughter's nuptial relationship, the father-king expresses his inability to separate from his beloved only child. The entrance of the son-in-law into the family requires a shift of the initial king-daughter relationship, introducing tension and an aspect of competition. Perhaps the king's love seems somewhat excessive, but it is based on the fact, emphasized by the *mashal*, that she is his only daughter. The king, desiring to remain close to his beloved daughter within the new context of her marriage, then tenders a request which is also a solution, that a *kiton* or chamber be provided for him so that he can be close to his daughter. The king's love places him in an unusually vulnerable position, as he is now dependent upon the good-will of the son-in-law to fulfill his request.

The content of our *mashal* can be best appreciated when seen within the context of "*peshuto shel mikra*"—that is, the straightforward reading of the verse in the Torah, ״ויקחו לי תרומה״, "that they take for me an offering."

A careful reading of the verses of the Torah in their context discloses the motive for the interpretation which gave rise to this *mashal*. The frame of the *mashal* are the verses of Exodus 25:2–7, "Bring *me* an offering" ending with:

> They will make for *me* a Tabernacle. Speak to the children of Israel that they bring me an offering: of every man whose heart prompts him to give, you shall take my offering...[followed by the details of what to take]. And let them make me a sanctuary that I may dwell among them. (Exodus 25:7)

In these verses we see two images of God. On the one hand—the model of God appears as distant ruler from above. He commands the nation to build Him a sanctuary according to meticulous requirements, thereby fulfilling the divine will for a *Mikdash*. On the other hand, the ultimate purpose of the *Mikdash* is to allow for God's indwelling. The language of "*shokhen*," meaning "dwell," does not have a commanding tone and connotes a different kind of relationship. The straightforward reading of the verses strives to maintain the commanding voice within the immanent image.

This midrash exploits the ambiguity in the verse (specifically the meaning of the word "*li*" (meaning "to me") and uses it to depart from the commanding image of God altogether. "Speak to the children of Israel that they bring *me* an offering. And let them make *me* a sanctuary that I may dwell among them." There are two ways that the word "*li*" or "me" can be understood: 1) as a command, "take an offering 'for me,'" meaning (according to Rashi) to honor me, or 2) in the bolder midrashic reading, "take Me—myself!" Our midrash is most likely based on an earlier rabbinic source where the bold reading was stated emphatically:

אמרתי לכם (שמות כ״ה:ב) ״ויקחו לי תרומה״ בשביל שאדור ביניכם.
(שמות כ״ה:ח) ״ועשו לי מקדש״ כביכול אמר הקב״ה קחו אותי ואדור
ביניכם. ״ויקחו תרומה״ אינו אומר אלא ״ויקחו לי״ **אותי אתם לוקחים**.
(ויקרא רבה פרשה ל:יג)

> I said to them (Exodus 25:2) "And you shall take for me an offering so that I may dwell with you [plural] and you shall make me a *Mikdash*." It is as if to say that The Holy One Blessed be He said "take Me and I will dwell among you." It is not written "take an offering" but rather, "*Take me—it is Me that you are taking*." (*Leviticus Rabbah* 30.13)

In *Leviticus Rabbah*, the midrash mines the word ״לי״. Here, the midrash interprets it to mean that God is in need of the people and their desire to create a place for Him to dwell among them. Make the Tabernacle for Me! Take Me that I may dwell among you.

In our *mashal*, the king's great love for his daughter is expressed through his desire to continue to live with her and his new son-in-law. According to the *nimshal*, God gives His Torah conditionally. The nation of Israel must acknowledge the relationship between father and daughter. In this midrash, God did not reveal His Torah and remain a distant law-giver. God is portrayed as being intimately bonded with the Torah and is present in the physical world together with the Torah and the Nation of Israel. When the Jewish people received the Torah, they received, as it were, God Himself with the Torah and when they learn Torah they are, in a sense, engaging with God Himself. The *kiton* in this midrash represents the people of Israel's constant awareness of God's presence that they need to have when they learn Torah. Without that awareness, there is Torah without God. The midrash is telling us that this would be an orphaned Torah, without roots, devoid of the vitality which gave birth to it.[4]

This concept of God as bonded with the Torah requires a major paradigm shift: from an understanding of God as Creator and lawgiver to a God who is in need. For it is undeniable that at the heart of this *mashal* and *nimshal* lies God's vulnerability. The king is dependent upon the good-will of the son-in-law to include him. One may ask: why can't the king simply command the young couple to include him by virtue of his being the supreme monarch?

The answer lies in the details of the *mashal*. Once the son-in-law has married the king's daughter, the relationships change. The king and the son-in-law are not just formal acquaintances governed by protocol; they have entered into a familial relationship. The familiarity of the relationship necessarily erodes the feeling of awe one holds toward the king, since awe is founded upon "otherness." He cannot command the son-in-law to provide a place for him. Once God has given the Torah to Israel, the relationship shifts from the transcendent, regal relationship to a familial one. Because the people of Israel have the Torah, they should perceive God as part of their family.

On the other hand, this midrash also implies that God's relationship with the people of Israel is not direct. The medium through which Israel will "engage" with God, as it were, is through His Torah. This encounter is contingent on Israel's providing a place for God in their learning. It is up to the people to allow God to enter into their lives, becoming a tangible part of their reality. An indirect relationship with God, through the Torah, relates to the ambiguity in the verses mentioned above. On the one hand, the Torah is an intermediary which creates a sense of distance between the

---

[4] The midrash raises the possibility of the nation with Torah, but without God! Although we are indeed limited in our ability to understand the meaning of the relationship between God and the Torah, we do understand from this midrash that from God's point of view, as it were, the new relationship of the Nation and the Torah without Him is inconceivable!

The idea of "The Holy One and the Torah are One," קודשא בריך הוא ואורייתא חד הוא is rooted in rabbinic literature. Later, it is further developed and becomes a foundation in mystical literature such as the *Zohar*. An in-depth discussion of this topic is beyond the scope of this essay. See also the first section of *Nefesh haHayyim* by R. Hayyim of Volozhin.

people of Israel and God. This distance is reminiscent of the model of God in the Torah as an All-Powerful King, Creator and Commander. On the other hand, the immanent image of God is of a father, a close member of the family.

The *kiton*, or *Mishkan*, made by the people will be the meeting place for God, Torah and the people. The *Mishkan* is not the meeting place between God and the people of Israel alone (which is the apparent reading of the verses). Nor is it a venue for the son-in-law and his wife alone, or for Israel and the Torah; rather the *Mishkan* is to serve for all three—God, Israel and the Torah. According to the midrashic reading of the verse, "And you shall take ME into the Tabernacle and I will dwell among them," the word "them" referring to both the Torah and the people of Israel.

Hazal, in meditating upon their own relationship to the Torah, imagine God's ambivalence in giving away His Torah. They contemplate that image to deepen their understanding of how they must treat Her (the Torah) as the beloved offspring of God and as one who reflects His essence. The deeper the son-in-law appreciates the love the father has for his daughter, the easier it is for the father-in-law to accept and eventually delight in the new relationship. This brings us to our final *mashal*, in which the king separates from his daughter with apparent ease.

An Unconditional Marriage

The Rabbis draw a comparison with a king who gave his daughter away in marriage to someone from another country.

ורבנן אמרי למלך שמשיא בתו חוץ למדינה, אמרו לו בני המדינה: אדוננו המלך שבח הוא ובדין הוא שתהא בתך אצלך במדינה. אמר להם: וכי מה איכפת לכם? אמרו לו: שמא למחר אתה הולך אליה ודר אצלה ועמה בשביל אהבתה. אמר להם: בתי אשיא חוץ למדינה, אבל אני דר עמכם במדינה.

כך בשעה שאמר הקב"ה ליתן תורה לישראל אמרו לו מלאכי השרת להקדוש ב"ה: רבש"ע אשר תנה הודך על השמים, אישורך הוא, הודך הוא, שבח הוא שתהיה תורה בשמים. אמר להם: וכי מה איכפת לכם? אמרו לו: שמא למחר אתה משרה שכינתך בתחתונים. אמר להם הקב"ה תורתי אני נותן בתחתונים, אבל אני דר בעליונים, אני נותן את בתי

בכתובתה במדינה אחרת שתתכבד עם בעלה ביפיה ובחמדתה שהיא בת
מלך ויכבדוה, אבל אני דר עמכם בעליונים, ומי פירש זה חבקוק שנא׳
(חבקוק ג:ג) ״כסה שמים הודו ותהלתו מלאה הארץ.״
(שיר השירים רבה, פרשה ח, ד״ה בדבר אחר)

> The people of his country said to him: "Your majesty, it accords with
> your honor and it is only right that your daughter should be in the
> same country with you."
> He said to them: "What does it matter to you?"
> They replied: "Perhaps later you will visit her and stay with her on ac-
> count of your love for her."
> He then replied: "I will give my daughter in marriage out of the coun-
> try, but I will reside with you in this town."
> So when the Holy One, blessed be He, announced His intention of
> giving the Torah to Israel, the ministering angels said to the Holy One,
> blessed be He, "Sovereign of the Universe, You are He whose majesty
> is over the heaven; it is Your happiness, Your glory and Your praise
> that the Torah should be in heaven."
> He said to them: "What does it matter to you?"
> They said: "Perhaps tomorrow You will cause the Divine Presence to
> abide in the lower world."
> Then the Holy One, blessed be He, replied to them: "I will give My
> Torah to the dwellers on earth but I will abide with the celestial be-
> ings. I will give away My daughter with her marriage portion to an-
> other country in order that she may pride herself with her husband in
> her beauty and charm and be honored as befits a king's daughter. But I
> will abide with you in the upper world."
> As it says, "His glory covers the heavens and the earth is full of His
> praise" (Habakkuk 3:3). (*Song of Songs Rabbah* 8.2)

This third *mashal* offers a model of the father-daughter relationship
which is in direct contrast to the previous midrash. Previously, we read of
the king's inability to separate from his daughter, while in this *mashal*, the
king accepts the separation with no apparent ambivalence or conflict. The
difficulty in this plotline is the ease with which the king separates from
his daughter. She is married to the king of another country and they may
never see each other again. The separation does in fact cause anxiety,
which is experienced by the king's subjects. The subjects fear the king
will desert them out of love for his daughter. Here again is the awareness
of the great love the king has for his daughter, but is this time expressed

by the king's subjects and not the king himself. Its expression by the people clarifies that the king's love for his daughter is publicly acknowledged—an objective fact—which is much more apparent than in the previous *mashal*. From the former *mashal*, we could understand the king's love as private, whereas in this *mashal* the king's love of his daughter is common knowledge. The depiction of the angels' reluctance in relinquishing the Torah, in allowing it to be brought to earth is a familiar theme in rabbinic literature. The angels, like the king's subjects, pretend to be concerned on behalf of the king, but are, in truth, worried about losing the Divine Presence.

In the *nimshal*, God addresses the anxiety of the angels: "I will give My Torah to the inhabitants of the earth but I will abide with the celestial beings. I will give away My daughter with her marriage portion to another country so she may be honored with her husband in her beauty and charm, as befits a king's daughter. But I will abide with you in the upper world." These words unmask the gap between the king's and the angels' understanding of the ultimate destiny of the Torah.

From the moment the king's daughter was born, he knew that the day would come when she would marry. He prepared for that day by providing her with a generous dowry in the hope of finding a suitable match. For the father, her marriage does not mark a moment of separation, but rather of closure. By enabling her to reach maturity she fulfills her destiny. This element is absent from the *mashal*, because it is precisely this point that the king's subjects do not understand. The Torah was not created to remain in its pristine form in heaven, but rather to be given to humanity. The argument whether to keep the Torah in the heavens is reminiscent of the angels' plea to God in other *midrashim* not to create Adam (humanity) or the world. In this midrash, although God gave His Torah to Israel, He remains transcendent. God the father must separate from his daughter, the Torah. She will be honored by her husband for all of her qualities, especially in light of her being the king's daughter, but God Himself will ultimately remain in heaven. The people of Israel are, as it were, married to God's Torah. Through their love of and commitment to the Torah, they express their love of God.

Overview

The common thread woven through our three *meshalim* is acknowledgment of the developing and changing nature of the father-daughter relationship. This dynamic sometimes generates anxiety over separation and engenders feelings of ambivalence. In our *meshalim*, we find three different reactions of the father. In the first ("Reaching Maturity"), the father acknowledges his daughter's emerging maturity and adapts accordingly. He allows for a new mode of interaction which takes into account the new reality of his daughter's maturation. In the second ("A Conditional Marriage"), the father experiences anxiety and seeks to avoid total separation while at the same time adjusting to the new reality. In the third ("An Unconditional Marriage"), the father separates from his daughter with relative ease, the anxiety about the change being expressed by those around him.

Hazal do not deny or repress such authentic human emotions. On the contrary, these emotions are affirmed and drawn upon to capture the complex and paradoxical nature of the divine-human relationship. Just as the human interpersonal relationship is multifaceted, how much more so is the divine-human encounter.

The close-but-separate nature of the father-daughter relationship in the *mashal* becomes the blueprint for the divine-human relationship in the *nimshal*. Issues of intimacy, maturity and separation become, in the *nimshal*, issues of immanence, revelation and transcendence. In the first *nimshal*, the ideal model of revelation, the meeting between humanity and God, changes from that which is public and overwhelming, to that which is private, personal and concealed. There is a shift from God's imposing omnipresence and man's passivity to a more subtle presence requiring human effort to search Him out. The second *nimshal* primarily describes God's immanence in the world with His Torah and the nation of Israel, although the immanence is countered by the fact that the Torah acts as an intermediary between Israel and God. The third *nimshal* portrays God as being more remote than in the previous two *meshalim*. The ease of God's separation from His people is a result of the nation's commitment to the Torah.

In all these *midrashim*, conflicting emotions regarding interpersonal relationships are accepted as part of the fabric of human experience. However, when these images are applied to the *nimshal*, a complex and even contradictory picture of God emerges, in which a God who dwells with the people of Israel and with the Torah coexists with a God who is remote and concealed from human experience.

By employing *meshalim* such as these, *Hazal* help us maintain the feeling of God's presence and closeness; they do not allow God to become a philosophical abstraction irrelevant to our religious life. God's distance is balanced by the metaphoric familial imagery, a reminder of His caring and affection.

In our *meshalim* (as in aggadic literature of a theological nature in general), we find a transition from the prophetic relationship, to one which is based on the Oral Law: in other words, from a revealed God to the hidden God, from the God who makes His will and presence known, to the God whose will and presence must be sought out. In these *meshalim*, particularly in the first, we see that *Hazal* relate to this new relationship as the ideal mature one between Israel and God. They have found a way to continue to relate to God, in the absence of prophecy through the medium of His beloved Torah, specifically the development of the Oral Law. From seeking God in the Torah, or in the hidden domain of the *Mishkan*, the Rabbis find His subtle yet continuous loving presence.[5]

---

[5] The notion that the ideal religious reality is based not on manifest revelation, but on relating to God in His obscurity seems to be among the dominant themes in the hasidic writings of R. Zadok haKohen of Lublin. He describes the hidden nature of the revelation of the Oral Law: "Even though this is a type of concealment, it led to greater revelation...for according to the strength of the concealment is the strength of the revelation." See Ya'akov Elman, "R. Zadok HaKohen: On the History of Halakha," *Tradition: A Journal of Orthodox Thought* (Fall 1985) 17.

Reading Midrash Today:
A Study of "Rabbi Hanina ben Dosa and His Stone" in *Song of Songs Rabbah* 1.4

Rella Kushelevsky

The story of R. Hanina ben Dosa (*Song of Songs Rabbah* 1.4) tells of a *tanna* who lived during the end of the Second Temple period. A pietist (hasid) and man of deeds, he maintained high moral standards, was assiduous in his observance of the commandments, and learned in miracles. When he died, "men of deeds ceased and piety came to an end."[1] Stories about him are scattered throughout tannaitic and amoraic sources,[2] and the one that concerns us here appears in *Song of Songs Rabbah* as a homily interpreting the verse in Proverbs (22:9): "See a man skilled [lit., "swift"] in his work...he shall attend upon kings":

> It is related that once, seeing the men of his town taking burnt-offerings and peace-offerings up to Jerusalem, he [R. Hanina ben Dosa, renowned for his poverty] exclaimed, "All of them take peace-offerings up to Jerusalem and I have nothing to take! What am I

---

* Dedicated to my mother Jepta Geffen, *z"l* (of blessed memory), with love.

[1] *Mishnah Sotah* 9:15; JT *Sotah* 9.16. The term *tanna* refers to the sages from the period of Hillel to the compilation of the Mishnah, i.e., the first and the second centuries. The word *tanna* (from the Aramaic *teni*, "to hand down orally," "study," "teach") generally designates a teacher either mentioned in the Mishnah or of mishnaic times. (See Daniel Sperber, "*Tanna*," *Encyclopaedia Judaica* 15, cols. 798–803). On the figure of the hasid, or righteous person, see S. Safrai, "*Hasidim ve'Anshe Ma'aseh*," *Zion* 3 (1985): 133–54; also cf. Hasid in *Encyclopaedia ha'Ivrit*, 3, cols. 750–52.

[2] Most notably a group of four stories in *Ta'anit* 24b–25a. Other sources dealing with R. Hanina ben Dosa include: *Tosefta* on *Berakhot* 3.20 and on *Sotah* 15.2; *beraitot* in *Berakhot* 33a and 34b and *Yevamot* 121b; JT *Berakhot* 5.1; *Yoma* 53b. On the figure of R. Hanina ben Dosa, cf. E. Heiman, *Toledot Tannaim ve'Amoraim* (London, 1910) 481–84; Zvi Kaplan, "Hanina ben Dosa," *Encyclopaedia Judaica*, 7, cols. 1265–66.

to do?" Forthwith he went out to the desert land near his town [*midbara shel iro*], to the ruins of his town [*behurva shel iro*],[3] and found a stone there, which he went and chiselled and polished and painted, and then he said: "I vow to take this up to Jerusalem." He wanted to engage some carriers and said to them: "Will you take this stone up to Jerusalem for me?" They said: "Pay us a hundred gold coins and we will take your stone up to Jerusalem for you." He replied: "And whence am I to get a hundred gold coins or even fifty to give you?" He could not raise the money just then and they went away. Straightway the Holy One, blessed be He, placed in his way five angels in the form of men. They said to him: "Master, give us five *sela* and we will take your stone up to Jerusalem, only you must lend a hand." He lent a hand and immediately they found themselves standing in Jerusalem. He wanted to pay them but they had disappeared. The incident was reported in the Chamber of Hewn Stone and they said to him: "It would appear, sir, that ministering angels brought your stone up to Jerusalem." Forthwith he gave the Sages the sum which he had agreed to pay the angels.[4] [translated by Rachel Rowen, based on the Soncino Press translation by Maurice Simon.]

---

[3] In ms Vatican 76 and other manuscripts it reads: "*Rehova shel Iro*," meaning: a wide and open space out of town. Both readings refer to an open and desolated area out of town. "*Midbara shel Iro*" also means a desolated area out of town. I am using the printed edition reference because it is the most well known. Other, less important differences between the printed and the manuscript versions will not be discussed in this article.

[4] *Song of Songs Rabbah* was redacted at the sixth C.E., thus belonging to the early phase of the midrashic collections. A similar legend appears in *Ecclesiastes Rabbah* 1.1, with the following differences: 1) *Ecclesiastes Rabbah* says R. Hanina ben Dosa saw the people of his town bringing "vows and donations," whereas *Song of Songs Rabbah* says "burnt-offerings and peace-offerings." The actual reference is to a pilgrimage festival where people bring burnt offerings for the pilgrimage and peace-offerings in celebration. The latter are comprised of vows and donations. 2) *Ecclesiastes Rabbah* only says "to the desert land near his town," without the words, "to the ruins of his town." 3) According to *Ecclesiastes Rabbah*, he "hewed, chiselled and shined" the stone, whereas in *Song of Songs Rabbah*, he "chiselled, polished and painted" it. 4) The sum demanded by the workers in *Ecclesiastes Rabbah* is "five *sela*" as opposed to "a hundred gold coins" in *Song of Songs Rabbah*. In mss, different sums of money are mentioned. 5) *Ecclesiastes Rabbah* omits the concluding passage found in *Song of Songs Rabbah*, in which R. Hanina ben Dosa paid the Sages the wages he had promised to the angels. The former version relates his concern about paying the wages because of the sudden disappearance of the workers and mentions the Sages' deduction that they were angels; with this the story concludes.

How are we to understand this story? On the one hand, the moral and happy-ending of R. Hanina ben Dosa's predicament evokes empathy as good will overcomes seemingly insurmountable obstacles. On the other hand, however, many of the story's details arouse skepticism. For example, giving a stone as a donation is surprising, considering that Jerusalem is a city surrounded by hills that abound in stones. To bring a stone to Jerusalem is somewhat like carrying coals to Newcastle. Moreover, what purpose was there in donating a single stone, however chiselled, polished and painted it may have been, when the Temple was standing?[5] Finally, there is a disparity between the account of the miraculous way R. Hanina ben Dosa, the stone and the angels were all transported to Jerusalem, and the following account of R. Hanina ben Dosa's insistence on paying for the transportation of the stone. If he realized that angels had carried the stone to Jerusalem, why did he insist on paying them their wages? Or if he believed that laborers transported the stone to Jerusalem, how did he understand the stone's sudden appearance in Jerusalem?

As modern readers of midrash and aggadah today, these specific questions relating to R. Hanina ben Dosa allude to more general issues confronting us. For how are we to understand stories that depart from a rationalistic view of reality and focus on miraculous events? How are we to follow short and tightly-formed stories that relay only essential events, leaving large gaps in the plot? This is all the more complicated when the language is replete with symbolism that is not self-evident. Moreover, the stories are set in a non-narrative context, either as part of a talmudic discussion or scriptural exegesis in compilations of midrash. We must interpret them then within a broader context.

---

[5] This sort of interpretive approach can be found in Admiel Kosman's article, "All Will Bless the *Etrog*, But I Will Bless the Horse" (*Ha'aretz*, Literary supplement, March 20, 1998). Underlying Kosman's interpretation is apparently the view of the hasid as a simple man, whose deeds overweigh his learning, in contrast to the scholar of *halakhah*. (This notion is suggested by Shmuel Safrai, "*Hasidim ve'Anshei Ma'aseh*," 144–54.)

Destruction versus Construction

The story conveys the experience of life at the historic crossroads between destruction and rebuilding. R. Hanina ben Dosa left his city to go to the desert land; from there he returned with a hewn stone to the city, to Jerusalem.[6] The desert land sets the limits of the city, and from its desolation the city is built. Its stone serves as a hewn stone to be used for building. Bringing the stone to the Temple could be interpreted as an act of re-building the Temple in the context of its tangibly imminent destruction. Awareness of the upcoming destruction nurtures forces of re-construction and from its own ruins, the Temple is rebuilt. R. Hanina ben Dosa was a disciple and contemporary of Rabban Yohanan ben Zakkai and lived in the late Second Temple period. The Temple was still standing, but the threat of its destruction could be felt in the air.[7]

Descriptions of time in the story also suggest an awareness that the destruction was imminent. The emphatic repetition of the word "immediately" conveys a sense of urgency and trepidation, seeking to thwart the chronological march of time. A similar atmosphere is conveyed by the accelerated rhythm in the description of R. Hanina ben Dosa's actions concerning the stone: "he went and chiselled and polished and painted." Here we have a series of verbs joined by the conjunction "and." Near the end of the story an inner, synchronistic view of time takes over the chronological view, and the dimension of space is erased as well: R. Hanina ben Dosa instantly finds himself in Jerusalem.

The dialectical tension between destruction and construction is deeply imprinted in Jewish sources, in descriptions of the cornerstone of the city of Jerusalem or the Temple. The psalmist, singing the song of pilgrims to Jerusalem, notes in thanksgiving: "The stone that the builders rejected has become the chief cornerstone" (Psalms 118:22). An unclaimed, unwanted stone, became fundamentally important. In *Pesahim* 119a, the cornerstone metaphorically stands for David, the youngest son of Jesse and the

---

[6] According to JT *Berakhot* 4.1, R. Hanina ben Dosa lived in "Arab," a city in the lower Galilee, not far from Sepphoris.

[7] The Second Temple was destroyed in 70 C.E.

shepherd of his sheep, who became King of Israel.[8] The potential of becoming King and Messiah is found precisely among those who tend to be held in low regard. The stone as a metaphorical expression of the dialectic of destruction-construction also connects with the giving of the Torah. According to *Exodus Rabbah* 1.6, the Torah was given on stone tablets precisely because "anyone who does not place his life like this stone, does not merit the Torah." The desert is viewed with the same sort of dialectic in the Talmud and midrash as a metaphor of depletion as well as repletion. The Torah was given in a desolate, dangerous wasteland; yet there, the men and women who took part in the exodus from Egypt were forged into a people.[9]

The Stone "Transporting Itself"

The story of R. Hanina ben Dosa features a similar sort of doubleness, contrasting two divergent vantage points. In this instance, they oppose one another. According to the view of the Sages as represented by the narrator, the stone and R. Hanina ben Dosa were transported to Jerusalem by angels. According to R. Hanina ben Dosa, however, they were transported by people who offered their assistance; thus he was troubled by the matter of paying them their wages. The depiction of R. Hanina ben Dosa lending a hand, and the angels handling the stone, creates an interesting configuration. It is not clear who transported whom: R. Hanina ben Dosa needed the angels to transport the stone, yet they could not transport it without R. Hanina lending a hand. The result is an iconic depiction of the angels and

---

[8] Cf. Rashi. In *Midrash Tannaim* on Deuteronomy 1:17, in a similar homily, David is characterized, not only as King of Israel but also as the Messiah.

[9] The following examples describe the positive aspects of the desert, dialectical to its obvious dangerous aspects. *Nedarim* 55a: "When a person makes himself like the desert, open to all, the Torah is given him as a gift." *Leviticus Rabbah* 13.2: "The Holy One, blessed be He, evaluated all the generations but did not find one worthy of receiving the Torah, save for the generation of the wilderness." *Song of Songs Rabbah* 2.2: "The wilderness said, 'I, the wilderness, am beloved, for all the good things of the world are hidden in me.'" *Tanhuma* on Exodus 14: "The choicest part comes from the wilderness, the Torah comes from the wilderness, the manna and quail come from the wilderness, the Tabernacle comes from the wilderness, the *Shekhinah* comes from the wilderness, the priesthood and kingship come from the wilderness...."

figures all moving together through the air. A stone so large that several laborers were required in order to move it from its place and bring it to Jerusalem suddenly seems to *transport itself.*

Surprisingly, the massive stone flies through space, denying the natural consequences of its dimensions. Its paradoxical nature in the story is expressed in its ability to defy the factors of weight and size, to dislodge itself from its place and transport itself to some other location. This alteration of the laws of nature is made possible by the touch of a hand, expressing the intention that the stone in essence be part of the foundation of the Temple. This resolve is also reflected in the description of R. Hanina ben Dosa's actions in the beginning of the story. By chiselling and painting the stone and by vowing to bring it to Jerusalem,[10] an insignificant stone (simply "a stone") becomes unique. According to R. Hanina ben Dosa's perception of reality as revealed in the story, the laws of nature are determined by a sense of resolve that is attuned to God's will. Reality is open to varying definitions, depending on inner criteria. This is a dynamic view of reality, one that does not distinguish between nature and miracle, but defines them in dialectical relationship to one other. Miracles are natural phenomena, just as nature is miraculous. Thus reality may be more a function of one's way of contemplating things than an expression of an objective situation.

Miracles versus Nature

The Sages suggested this dialectic between miracles and nature when they said that "Ten things were created in the twilight on the eve of the Sabbath" (*Avot* 5:6). The Mishnah lists things with which miracles were wrought, such as the mouth of the earth that engulfed Korah and his followers, the mouth of the well that moved along with the Israelites and supplied them with water in the wilderness, the mouth of Balaam's she-ass that spoke, and the staff with which the omens were produced in Egypt. Implicit here is the notion that miracles are part of Creation, definable in temporal and spacial terms.

---

[10] On the formulation of vows, cf. *Mishnah Kinnim* 1:1.

Yet miracles are also set apart from nature as phenomena unto themselves, created in a niche of timelessness within time, during the interregnum of twilight on the eve of the Sabbath, when the act of Creation was being concluded. The same notion is expressed in *Genesis Rabbah* 5.5: "The Holy One, blessed be He, set a condition with the sea [at the time of Creation], that it split before the Israelites [during their exodus from Egypt]." The midrash continues with a list of miracles, such as the sun being halted in Gibeon to answer Joshua's needs and Daniel being delivered from the lion's den, all of them stipulated in advance during Creation and realized under unique circumstances. The dialectic of nature-miracle is also reflected in *Mishnah Avot* 5:5, where the Temple is described as a place where a series of miracles regularly took place. In the Temple, "no woman ever miscarried from the odor of the sacrifices; the meat of the sacrifices never turned putrid; and no fly was ever seen in the slaughterhouse." The Mishnah continues to list a total of ten such miracles that happened in the Temple, all of them having a regularity similar to that found in nature. The dialectic lies in the fact that this regularity itself is what determined that certain phenomena in the Temple were miracles and not incidental occurrences.[11]

Such a point of view, which does not distinguish between nature and miracle, is employed in the story of R. Hanina ben Dosa to express constant and keen awareness of the Divine Presence in the midst of everyday life. It is also found in other stories about him, such as his saying that "whoever told the oil to ignite, let him also tell the vinegar to ignite" (*Ta'anit* 25a). This sense of being reflects an especially close spiritual bond with God, and defines the figure of R. Hanina ben Dosa as a hasid. In other words, his characterization in the sources as being an expert in miracles is more an expression of a mode of existence than it is a testimony to magical capabilities. The Sages in the story represent a static perception of reality, contrasting the regularity of the laws of nature with

---

[11] The view that nature is a hidden miracle that depends on Divine Will and not on necessary causality also appears in medieval exegesis. Cf. Nahmanides' commentary on the Torah, Exodus 9.12; ibid., 13:16; and Leviticus 26:11. For further development of this position from a modern approach, cf. R. E. Dessler, *Mikhtav me'Eliyahu*, I (Jerusalem, 1987) 177–86.

the one-time appearance of the miracle. That the stone was transported to Jerusalem by angels does not abrogate its physical characteristics, but puts them in abeyance for the purpose of Divine intervention. This interpretation explains the mixture of a legendary code (the point of view of the Sages) and a realistic code (the point of view of R. Hanina ben Dosa). The definition of reality as perceived by R. Hanina ben Dosa is plastic and changeable.[12]

The Story in its Homiletic Context

The homily that follows the story of R. Hanina ben Dosa in *Song of Songs Rabbah* also depicts a stone that transports itself to the Temple. According to this story, Solomon did not build the Temple, rather the Temple built itself. Solomon did not transport the stones to the site of the Temple, rather the stones transported themselves and set themselves down row upon row. Thus the Temple stands, irrespective of human involvement. In

---

[12] By realistic code I infer that R. Hanina ben Dosa does not distinguish between miracles and nature—both are part of human existence. On the Sages' perception of miracles and their relationship to reality, cf. E.E. Urbach, *The Sages: Their Concepts and Beliefs*, Israel Abrahams trans. (Cambridge: Harvard University Press, 1975) 104–23. Urbach relates in particular to the story of the wild ass (for example *Berakhot* 33a) and the story of Nehunya, the digger of wells (for example *Bava Kama* 50a) in connection with R. Hanina ben Dosa's perception of miracles, namely that miracles are a means of sanctifying the Lord (ibid., 109–10). In an article on the figure of R. Hanina ben Dosa in two other stories, Rachel Nissim sheds light on his traits as a hasid as reflected in the way he worshipped the Lord—out of fear of Heaven, negating any personal interest and expecting no reward. This is another aspect of awareness of the Divine Presence, in addition to its manifestations in the way miracles are viewed in the present discussion. Cf. Rachel Nissim, "*Dmut heHasid: Imut bein R. Hanina ben Dosa levein R. Pinhas ben Yair le'Or Amadot Hazal beVa'ayat haGmul*," *Alei Si'ah* 12–14 (1982): 136–54.

Y. Frankel discusses R. Hanina ben Dosa's perception of reality as reflected in the story of the daughter of Nehunya, the digger of wells. Underlying it are belief in retribution, in reward and punishment and in the power of a good deed to change reality. Miracles are the natural result of the spiritual state of utter purity in which the hasid, such as R. Hanina ben Dosa, exists. Cf. Y. Frankel, *Iyyunim be'Olamo haRuhani shel Sippur ha'Agaddah* (Tel Aviv: haKibbutz haMe'uhad, 1981) 18–22; "The Individual Facing His Maker" 23–40; "Man and Miracle." On miracles as a general cultural phenomenon, cf. J.A. MacCulloch, "Miracles," *Encyclopaedia of Religion and Ethics*, vol. 8 (NY, 1915) 676–90; Mircea Eliade, "Miracles," *The Encyclopaedia of Religion*, vol. 9 (NY and London, 1987) 541–52; Eliezer Schwied, "Miracle," *Encyclopaedia Judaica*, vol. 12, cols. 73–79.

terms of time, this lends expression to the notion that the Temple is eternal, independent of the temporal nature of any builder. The homily is an interpretation of I Kings 6:7: "'When the House was built, only finished stones cut at the quarry were used.' It was built of itself, as it is said, 'only finished stones cut at the quarry were used.' It does not say *banu*, 'they built it,' rather *nivne*, 'it was built,' to indicate that the stones transported themselves and set themselves down row upon row."

A third interpretation, a few lines later, concerns the same phenomenon, although without any connection to the Temple. When Belshazzar threw Daniel into the lion's den, "a stone flew from the Land of Israel and landed on the mouth of the den" to protect him from those who sought to harm him. The distance between the Land of Israel and Babylon became as naught. Thus three successive homilies in *Song of Songs Rabbah* all describe the same phenomenon—that of inanimate entities made autonomous in a miraculous manner.[13]

The Symbolism of the Stone

The miraculous occurrence of weighty objects being radically altered in nature appears in other sources as well. There, as here, this motive symbolizes the stone as center of the world and corner stone of the Temple. The Foundation Stone from which the world was created lay in the Holy of Holies.[14] When Jacob wished to spend the night in Beth El on his way to Haran and sought a stone on which to lay his head, the stones began arguing among themselves, each wishing this righteous person to lay his head on it. Ultimately they were all joined into a single stone. Jacob erected this large stone as a monument to the Lord and vowed that it would be "God's abode" (Genesis 28:11–22), "and that is the gateway to

---

[13] This is an indication of deliberate redaction. Several studies concerning the redaction of midrashic anthologies include: Joseph Heinemann, *haDerashot beTzibbur beTekufat haTalmud* (Jerusalem: Bialik Institute, 1982) 24–28; Ophrah Meir, "*Retzifut ha'Arikhah keItzuv Hashkafat Olam*," *Mahashevet Hazal* (Haifa: Haifa University Press, 1990) 85–100; David Stern, "Midrash and the Language of Exegesis: A Study of *Vayikra Rabbah*" in *Midrash and Literature*, Geoffrey H. Hartman and Sanford Budick eds. (New Haven: Yale University Press, 1986) 105–24.

[14] *Yoma* 53a; *Leviticus Rabbah* 2.4, Margaliyot ed., 455; *Tanhuma Pekudei* 3.

heaven."[15] Twelve stones melded into a single monolith under Jacob's head, leading him to understand that he would be progenitor of the people.[16] The analogy is based on the notion of the stone as the foundation of the edifice. Thus Jacob is also called the "Stone of Israel."[17] Furthermore, when Jacob met Rachel by the well in Haran, he rolled away the stone sealing the well "like someone taking a lid off a saucer." Scriptures say this was a large stone requiring all the shepherds to gather together in order to roll it aside (Genesis 29:2–3).[18] In all these sources, physical stones have metaphysical significance. Stone, despite its prominent physical characteristics, contains a metaphysical essence.

The idea of a stone that transports itself is also paradoxically related to the notion of *tzimtzum haShekhinah*, or the Divine Presence contracting itself. This is a paradox difficult to understand. In the Temple, the Divine Presence, which has no material boundaries but fills the entire world, contracts itself to the confines of the Temple. This concept finds expression in the biblical account of Solomon's prayer at the Temple's dedication: "Even the heavens to their uttermost reaches cannot contain You, how much less this House that I have built!" (I Kings 8:27). The idea can also be described from the opposite direction: contraction of the Divine

---

[15] *Hullin* 91b.

[16] *Genesis Rabbah* 68.11.

[17] *Exodus Rabbah* 41.6.

[18] *Genesis Rabbah* 70.10. Additional related examples of inanimate entities endowed with spiritual attributes are: *Exodus Rabbah* 52.4, which mentions that the Tabernacle miraculously set itself up and *Genesis Rabbati* (Albeck ed.), an eleventh-century work from the school of R. Moses HaDarshan of Provence, which describes the heavenly Temple descending when the ordained hour arrives and building the Third Temple (136). According to *Sotah* 35a, when the Israelites crossed the Jordan on their way to the Land of Israel, as described in chapters 3–4 of the book of Joshua, the Ark of the Covenant carried those who were bearing it. The stone monument that Joshua erected at the Jordan was intended as testament to this miracle. It is said further that the Ark of the Covenant did not take up any space in the Temple (*Yoma* 21a). Just as the Ark of the Covenant transported those who bore it, so too the Tablets of the Covenant were carried by the letters of the Decalogue inscribed on them by the finger of God. It only appeared that Moshe was carrying the Tablets as he descended from the mountain. When the Israelites sinned, the letters disappeared and Moshe, feeling the weight of the Tablets, had to break them (*Exodus Rabbah* 46.1, 47.6). In all these various sources we find the phenomenon which is embodied in the metaphor of "the stone transporting itself."

Presence eliminates the dimension of space, much as the Temple transports itself. What makes this paradoxical contraction of the Divine Presence in the Temple possible? Husserl's concept of "intention" helps us understand this.[19] The category of the relations between a person and God makes it possible to conceive of the contraction of the Divine Presence. The Temple is where the individual contacts God.[20] The intimate contact between human beings and God in the Temple is reflected in our story by the involved actions of R. Hanina ben Dosa concerning the stone, "which he went and chiselled and polished and painted," and his contact, together with the angels, with the stone.

Conclusion: Midrash and Self-Understanding

In interpreting the text, the reader discovers a possible way, independent of time and space, of defining reality. Thus R. Hanina ben Dosa accepts

---

[19] The concept of the *intentionally* is a key concept in the phenomenological analysis of knowledge and experience. For Husserl (1859–1938), the intentional nature of consciousness means that it is always consciousness of something. Every intentional act of consciousness has its intentional object, that towards which consciousness is directed. This object need not be actual, but might exist only in the context of a mental act. See: Marie H. Loughlin, "Intention/intentionality" in *Encyclopaedia of Contemporary Literary Theory*, Irena R. Makaryk ed. (Toronto University Press, 1993) 564–66.

[20] On the function of the Temple as *axis mundi*, cf. Mircea Eliade, *The Sacred and the Profane* (NY: Harcourt, Brace & World, 1959) 36–42.

the ability of a stone to transport itself to Jerusalem as a viable reality. Similarly, the dialectic of destruction-construction takes the place of logical notions that perceive a contradiction between these two states of being. The existent is built precisely out of the non-existent. As it is on a national level, so it is on a personal level: in a state of depletion we can find resources whithin the soul, of which we were previously unaware.[21]

---

[21] For a possible psychological interpretation of the phenomenon of miracles, see C. G. Jung, "Synchronicity: An Acausal Connecting Principle," *The Structure and Dynamics of the Psyche*, R.F. Hull trans. (London: Routledge and Kegan Paul, 1969) 417–531.

Inui Nefesh (Self-Affliction) on Yom Kippur: A Literary and Conceptual Analysis of a Talmudic Discussion

Leah Rosenthal

For many contemporary Jews, one of the highlights of Jewish experience is the day of Yom Kippur. For most, this is a day of introspection, soul-searching and repentance, a day of spirituality and religious feeling unlike all others.

What is it about this day that creates such an intense experience? How is this moment in time imbued with such special meaning? How has Jewish tradition defined the components that make up this experience, and how have these definitions contributed in creating such a unique and intensely spiritual experience?

After studying the biblical material regarding the day of Yom Kippur, it soon becomes apparent that the central, personal commandment of the day is *inui nefesh*—self-affliction.[1] This command is presented by the Torah in connection with other themes of the day: *kaparah*–atonement and *taharah*–purity. Although the Torah repeats the commandment of *inui*

---

[1] I refer here only to the material that defines and regulates the day of Yom Kippur in general. In so doing, I am disregarding the larger portion of biblical material that relates primarily to the Temple rites of Yom Kippur. The distinction between the general laws of the day and the special Temple service of Yom Kippur is also apparent in the structure of the Mishnah. The first seven chapters of the tractate of *Yoma* describe the Temple services of Yom Kippur, and only the last chapter deals with laws of Yom Kippur that are applicable outside the Temple area as well. It is worthwhile therefore to note that Yom Kippur as we know it reflects only a very small proportion of Yom Kippur as it was defined by the Torah. A large proportion of the mishnaic discussion was also largely theoretical for the Rabbis of the Mishnah themselves—and only their discussions in the eighth chapter actually reflect their own first hand experiences of Yom Kippur. One of the discussions in that context will be the focus of this essay.

nefesh five times within the context of prescribing the day, it does not define precisely what the meaning of this affliction is. How is one actually expected to perform this command? What are the exact requirements of this obligation?

Furthermore, how is the concept of self-affliction connected to the concepts of atonement and purity? What is the conceptual structure underlying this formula? Does the experience of affliction and specifically *self*-affliction, achieve atonement and purity? Is this a confirmation of the basic intuition that suffering and pain cleanse one of sin and guilt—a familiar enough concept in human culture and religion?

In this article, I propose to look at the talmudic discussion of the biblical commandment of *inui nefesh*.[2] This discussion appears to be primarily technical, concerned for the most part with legal and formalistic definitions, somewhat disappointing to one searching for inner meaning and spiritual depth. It is my contention, however, that underlying these formalities and technical details lies a conceptual structure of great spiritual force. Although the Rabbis do not seem to give a systematic philosophic presentation of the laws of Yom Kippur, once these underlying structures are revealed, a clear image of this day and that which it represents does begin to take form in our minds.

The Mishnah begins its discussion of the *halakhot* of Yom Kippur[3] by defining the special prohibitions of the day:

יום הכפורים אסור באכילה ובשתיה וברחיצה ובסיכה ובנעילת הסנדל ובתשמיש המטה.

> On the Day of Atonement it is forbidden to eat, to drink, to wash, to anoint oneself, to put on shoes, or to have marital intercourse....[4]

Although the Mishnah does not explicitly identify these prohibitions as being the practical application of the imperative of self-affliction, it seems

---

[2] *Yoma* 74b.

[3] The laws pertaining to Yom Kippur in general—see note 1 regarding the structure of the tractate.

[4] *Mishnah Yoma* 8:1. Translations of the Mishnah and Talmud are adapted from the Soncino edition.

reasonable to view them as such. Not until further on in the chapter[5] does the Mishnah, while referring to these acts, use the term *inui*, thereby confirming our intuition that these are indeed the manifestations of the afflictions prescribed by the Torah for Yom Kippur.

Characteristically, the Mishnah does not share with us the methods used to arrive at these definitions of *inui nefesh*. How were the Rabbis of the Mishnah able to define the biblical term? Is there a basis for this interpretation or is it solely a result of Oral Tradition accompanying the written Torah?

These questions are high on the agenda of the Rabbis of the Talmud. It is their reconstruction of the process leading to the definition of *inui nefesh*, formulated in the above Mishnah, that concerns me here. Through this discussion, I would like to attain a deeper understanding of the rabbinic idea behind the law—the conceptual underpinnings of the halakhic definition—the abstract structure behind the definitive details.

The literary structure of this particular talmudic discussion is quite straightforward. The Talmud quotes three tannaitic sources, all of which present different discussions of the term *inui nefesh* used by the Torah. Following each *baraita* (tannaitic source), the Talmud adds a brief comment or discussion regarding the quoted source. Finally, the Talmud presents a seemingly tangential aggadic discussion of a theme that seems to be connected, by association alone, to the discussion of *inui nefesh*. Let us consider closely the various stages of this discussion.

1a. First *Baraita*–Passive Self-Affliction

תנו רבנן : תענו את נפשותיכם יכול ישב בחמה ובצנה כדי שיצטער **תלמוד לומר וכל מלאכה לא תעשו מה מלאכה שב ואל תעשה אף עינוי נפש שב ואל תעשה.**

> Our Rabbis taught: "...you shall afflict your souls." One might assume that one must sit in heat or cold in order to afflict oneself. Therefore the text reads: "And you shall do no manner of work"; just as the prohibition of labor means "sit and refrain from action," so does the enjoinment of affliction signify "sit and refrain from action."

---

[5] *Mishnah Yoma* 8:4.

This *baraita* seeks a definition of the commandment to afflict oneself. It suggests a possibility—that the application of this *mitzvah* involves actively pursuing situations of discomfort and suffering. The examples given by the *baraita* (sitting in the heat and cold) are relatively tame; with a bit of imagination, one could suggest even more creative and extreme examples of active self-affliction.

This possibility, though, is subsequently rejected by the *baraita* on the basis of the juxtaposition in the biblical text between this commandment and another commandment—that of the prohibition for doing work (*melakhah*) on Yom Kippur. This second commandment is more familiar to us given that it appears in other contexts as well—Shabbat and many other of the holidays prescribed by the Torah. It is now used to shed light on the unique, unfamiliar *mitzvah* which appears only in the context of Yom Kippur. As a result of this analogy, the *baraita* now concludes that the basic nature of *inui nefesh* must be defined as being similar to the basic nature of the prohibition against work. Namely, it must be a *negative* commandment, implying that this *mitzvah* is fulfilled by *refraining* from performing certain acts, as opposed to taking action to perform any given deed.

The original suggestion of the interpretation of the commandment is undeniably closer to the literal meaning of the biblical text. The wording of this commandment is clearly styled as a *positive* commandment—one which, in order to fulfill, requires taking action. Nevertheless, the *baraita* prefers a midrashic reading of this text—rejecting the "simple" or *peshat* meaning—and establishes the commandment of *inui nefesh* as a negative precept instead of as a positive one.

This preference, this shift of perception from active to passive, from positive to negative, is extremely significant in enhancing our understanding of the commandment of *inui nefesh* and its experience. To perform an act of active self-affliction is very different from enduring discomfort as a result of not taking action to prevent it. The psychological effect of this new type of *inui*—namely, passivity, silent endurance of discomfort brought upon us not directly by ourselves but by some other, presumably natural, process—differs greatly from the effect of engaging in an active procedure of self-affliction. A strong element of control is present in the act of bringing upon oneself pain and suffering, which might also engender an almost intoxicating sense of self-mortification.

The rejection of the active definition in favor of the passive causes us to focus on some serious differences between these two options. The active definition bears an inherent danger of limits: what are the qualitative and quantitative definitions of the self-affliction that one is required to perform in Yom Kippur? How should people avoid underdoing or, perhaps of greater concern, overdoing this *mitzvah*? This concern draws our attention to yet another difference between positive commandments and negative commandments. Within the context of positive commandments, the possibility always exists of doing more, of performing the *mitzvah* with greater zeal and more enthusiasm. An element of competitiveness sometimes exists within these contexts. Negative precepts, on the other hand, are defined in absolute terms: it is basically impossible to perform a negative precept "more" than anyone else, or with greater care than one had previously done. To refrain from an action is definitive; there is no room for grading or personalizing performance.[6]

Let us note, as well, that the performance of a positive commandment demands focus, whereas the observance of a negative command requires little attention. Certainly it takes less active energy to observe a negative prohibition than to perform a positive commandment. By turning the definition into a negative one, the focal point of the day is effectively steered away from the act of affliction occupying our minds and actions. The commandment of self-affliction is transformed into a required state of being that serves as the background for other activities that become more actively central to the day. Whereas the active definition of *inui* would have claimed central stage during the day of Yom Kippur, it takes on in its passive definition secondary status, in terms of the attention it demands as part of the day's experience.

---

[6] Although it would seem that there are options of observing stringencies and stretching categories of prohibitions, this is not the same as performing the *same* obligation more qualitatively.

1b. **Talmudic Discussion of First** *Baraita*

ואימא היכא דיתיב בשימשא וחיים ליה לא נימא ליה קום תוב בטולא
יתיב בטולא וקריר ליה לא נימא ליה קום תוב בשימשא דומיא דמלאכה
מה מלאכה לא חלקת בה אף עווי לא תחלוק בו.

> But say perhaps: If a person sits in the sun and is warm, one may not
> say to him: "rise and sit in the shade"; or, when he sits in the shade
> and is cool, one may not say to him: "rise and sit in the sun"?
> It is as with labor: Just as you have made no distinction with regard to
> labor, so in connection with the prescribed affliction is no distinction
> to be made.

Here the Talmud picks up on the words of the *baraita* and further investigates the definition of "*inui nefesh.*" The *baraita* has just established that the commandment of self-affliction is negative, passive. In other words, at this point all we know is that one must afflict oneself by refraining from taking action. The Talmud therefore now suggests that any action one would ordinarily take to relieve oneself of pain or discomfort would be forbidden on Yom Kippur. While it may be that one is not obligated to actively create situations of suffering, would it also be true to claim that if one happened to be in an uncomfortable situation on Yom Kippur, one would be prohibited from taking any action to alleviate the suffering? If one happened to be sitting in the sun and was becoming uncomfortable as a result of this—would it be forbidden to get up and move? This would be applying the *baraita*'s definition of self-affliction as a passive obligation to suffer.

The Talmud rejects this possibility by returning to the *baraita*'s definition of *inui nefesh* as being basically similar to the prohibition of work. This time, the Talmud stresses yet another characteristic of the prohibition of work and claims that it must apply to *inui nefesh* as well. The prohibition of work is uniform and common to all people. In other words, the prohibitions of labor are non-conditional and non-subjective. If something is forbidden through the category of "*melakhah,*" it is forbidden to everyone, in all situations. There is nothing that would be forbidden to one person and not to another.

The same must be true for self-affliction: it is not possible that there would be an action that would be forbidden to one person and permitted to another. Nor is it possible that one person would be exposed to a particular kind of affliction whereas another would not be obligated to endure that same experience. If the obligation of self-affliction is the prohibition to take *any* action to relieve discomfort, the result would be very different experiences of affliction among various individuals. There would be no common unifying experience of *inui nefesh* on Yom Kippur.

The Talmud now proceeds to reject this model: the experience of self-affliction must be the same for all involved. There must be a common underlying experience for everyone on this day. The actions that are forbidden for us to do on this day must be those which alleviate discomfort common to us all—discomfort that is non-conditional, non-subjective and non-contingent to a particular, individual situation at any given moment. The experience of suffering must stem from the basic conditions common to us all—the basic human condition.

At this point, let us consider again the Mishnah's definition of affliction as refraining from eating, drinking, washing, anointing, wearing shoes and engaging in sexual relations. We now become aware that these are actions we ordinarily perform that minimize our sensations of the natural physical processes that are a part of us, our bodily functions.

We wash and anoint ourselves to erase traces of the less dignified aspects of being physical beings, flesh and blood. We downplay the fact that our bodies create waste, that we are so much part of the biological, physical world.

We wear shoes to protect our feet from exposure to harmful and damaging elements from which we are not naturally protected.

We engage in acts of procreation—creating a sense of continuity, of reaching into the future, of everlasting eternity.

We eat and drink so as not to feel thirst and hunger, not to experience the weakness and dizziness that accompanies that state even in its early stages. We eat and drink so as to feel strong and vibrant. We eat and drink to stay alive.

The act of affliction of Yom Kippur is the stripping away of the routinely performed actions that create our illusion of strength, stability and dignity. The experience of affliction is the return to consciousness of the basic human condition and our vulnerability. It is the experience of our weakness, of the fact that when we refrain from taking action, our bodies weaken, diminish and eventually die. It is the realization that death is the result of non-interference, of not taking action to avoid it. Life is the constant effort to keep death away. Death is not an unnatural interruption of life—rather the opposite. Our bodies, left alone, will naturally drift towards death. Life is the result of interfering in that natural process and delaying it again and again.

2a. Second *Baraita*–Precedented Self-Affliction

תענו את נפשותיכם—יכול ישב בחמה ובצנה ויצטער תלמוד לומר וכל מלאכה לא תעשו מה מלאכה דבר שחייבין עליו במקום אחר אף עוני נפש דבר שחייבין עליו במקום אחר ואיזה זה זה פגול ונותר אביא פגול ונותר שהן בכרת ולא אביא את הטבל שאינו בכרת תלמוד לומר תענו ועניתם את נפשתיכם ריבה. אביא הטבל שהוא במיתה ולא אביא את הנבילה שאינה במיתה תלמוד לומר תענו ועניתם את נפשתיכם ריבה אביא את הנבילה שהיא בלאו ולא אביא את החולין שאינן בלאו תלמוד לומר תענו ועניתם את נפשתיכם ריבה. אביא החולין שאינן בקום אכול ולא אביא את התרומה שהוא בקום אכול תלמוד לומר תענו ועניתם את נפשתיכם ריבה אביא את התרומה שאינה בבל תותירו ולא אביא את הקדשים שהן בבל תותירו תלמוד לומר תענו ועניתם את נפשתיכם ריבה. ואם נפשך לומר הרי הוא אומר והאבדתי את הנפש ההיא עני שהוא אבידת נפש ואיזה זה זה אכילה ושתיה.

> "You shall afflict your souls." One might assume that one must sit in the heat or cold to afflict oneself. Therefore the Scripture said: "And you shall do no manner of work." Just as in connection with work the reference is to something for which one may become culpable, so also in another connection. So with affliction it is to something for which one might become culpable in another connection. And what is that? "An abhorred thing" or "that which remains." I shall then include only the abhorred thing or that which remains, because the penalty involved there is extirpation (*karet*), but not include "*tebel*"[7] since the penalty involved therein is not

---

[7] *Tebel*–produce from which the priestly dues and tithes have not been separated. The Torah prohibits the consumption of *tebel*. (This definition, as well as those in further

extirpation. Therefore the text reads: "you shall afflict" and "you shall afflict your souls," which is inclusive. I might then include *'tebel*," the punishment for which is death, but not include carrion, the penalty for which is not death. Therefore the text reads: "you shall afflict" and "you shall afflict your souls," which is inclusive.

I might then include the eating of carrion, which involves the transgression of a prohibition, but not profane food, the eating of which is not prohibited at all. Therefore the text reads: "you shall afflict" and "you shall afflict your souls," which is inclusive.

I might then include profane food, the eating of which is not commanded, but exclude "*terumah*,"[8] the eating of which is commanded. Therefore the text reads: "you shall afflict" and "you shall afflict your souls," which is inclusive.

I might then include "*terumah*" which is not subject to the law concerning remaining over, but exclude sacrifices, in connection with which the law concerning remaining over applies. Therefore the text reads: "you shall afflict" and "you shall afflict your souls," which is inclusive.

And if you should have any remark in objection thereto, I can reply: Behold Scripture said: "And I will destroy that soul," i.e., an affliction which causes a destruction of life and what is that but the denial of eating and drinking?

This second, rather long and somewhat complicated source addresses the same question that the previous source addressed: the definition of *inui nefesh*. This *baraita*, however, while employing the same analogy with *melakhah* as the previous *baraita*,[9] focuses on another element of similarity. Just as the prohibition of working on Yom Kippur is a familiar concept from other halakhic contexts (Shabbat, other holidays) so, too,

---

notes, is quoted from R. Adin Steinsaltz, *The Talmud–the Steinsaltz Edition: A Reference Guide* (NY: Random House, 1989).

[8] *Terumah*–A portion of the produce that must be set aside for the priests. *Terumah* is considered holy and may only be eaten by a priest and his household when they are in a state of ritual purity.

[9] The relationship between these two tannaitic sources is an interesting issue in and of itself. The first tannaitic source appears only in the Talmud Bavli, the second appears in the Yerushalmi and the Sifra. The striking similarity of style creates the impression that these are not two unrelated texts formulated independently of each other.

must the prohibition involved in the commandment of *inui* have a precedent elsewhere in *halakhah*.

To claim that the *inui* of Yom Kippur is a commandment with precedent, one that is familiar from other halakhic contexts, is an interesting claim indeed. Surely, one of the striking elements of this commandment is how unique and unusual it seems to be. It is a commandment that certainly does not seem to have a parallel elsewhere[10] in biblical law.

I would therefore venture to suggest that the author of this *baraita* is primarily motivated to formulate his conclusions in this particular way in order to shift our perception of the *mitzvah* of *inui nefesh*. He presents not only the definition of the command to afflict oneself, but also makes a claim about this seemingly extraordinary *mitzvah*: it is *not* unprecedented. The day of Yom Kippur is not one whose essential experience is separate from that of the rest of the year. Even this unique element of self-affliction has its roots deep within routine, normative *halakhah*.

The *baraita* presents the conclusion that the prohibition referred to by the term *inui nefesh* must be some kind of forbidden act of eating that, if done elsewhere, in a different context, would also make one liable for the penalty of *karet* (the same punishment prescribed for performing this act on Yom Kippur).[11] The *baraita* identifies this act as being the eating of *pigul* and *notar*.[12] After a series of midrashic maneuvers,[13] the *baraita* extends the prohibition to *all* types of eating—including the prohibited, the sacred and the profane.

Of course, a logical flaw does seem to exist in the above discussion. After establishing that the commandment of self-affliction must be a

---

[10] On the contrary, according to some rabbinic opinions, there are biblical injunctions against causing oneself injury or harm. See, for example, *Bava Kamma* 91b.

[11] *Karet*—a divine punishment for serious transgressions. The precise definition of the term is a matter of debate among the commentators.

[12] *Pigul*—a sacrificial offering disqualified by improper intention. Anyone willfully eating from such a sacrifice is liable to the penalty of *karet*.

Notar—Part of a sacrifice left over after the time permitted for it to be eaten. One who eats *notar* is also subject to *karet*.

[13] Various commentators debate the precise methodology used by the *baraita* to stretch the prohibition and include all categories of eating. See, for example, *Tosafot Yeshanim, Yoma* 74b, Raabad's commentary on the *Sifra, Aharei Mot* 7.

prohibition that has a precedent, this prohibition was identified as that of *eating*, *pigul* and *notar*. On what basis did the search for the unidentified precedented prohibition focus solely on prohibitions of eating?[14] Surely there are other types of prohibitions that are punishable by *karet* that could serve as the required precedent?

The Talmud is aware of this problem and in its comment following the *baraita*, explains that the second part of the *baraita* supplies us with the answer to this question. Based on a midrashic interpretation of the biblical verse,[15] the *baraita* concludes that the *inui* must not merely cause discomfort or pain, but diminish the actual life force within us (*aveidat nefesh*). What action, when we refrain from performing it, immediately affects our life, our strength?[16] Clearly this must be a reference to eating and drinking.

Presented here is a direct connection between the experience of *inui* and the concept of life and death. *Inui nefesh* is not merely the sensation of pain and discomfort. It touches on the very essence of ourselves as living beings. It affects our deepest selves. It taps our life energies; it targets the center of our existence as creatures of flesh and blood.

3a. Third *Baraita*–An Intertextual Approach

The third and last source that the Talmud quotes in this context is the shortest and the most straightforward of all the tannaitic sources cited:

---

[14] This is particularly noticeable in Rashi's commentary on the *baraita* where he inserts the requirement that it be a type of eating into his explanation of the *baraita*'s methodology.

[15] The verse describes the penalty for one who transgresses the prohibition of *melakhah* on Yom Kippur. As this particular phrasing is unusual, the Rabbis interpreted this choice of words as alluding to the nature of the transgression as well as a description of the penalty. Although this is stated with regard to *melakhah* and not *inui*, the Rabbis have already established the analogous relationship between the two categories.

[16] Obviously, there are other acts necessary for the preservation of life. However, none of these others are totally voluntary. The individual cannot stop these acts through will alone. The human body will take over and perform the necessary requirements of life. It is, indeed, only eating and drinking that are essential to life and are completely under the control of the conscious will of human beings.

דבי רבי ישמעאל תנא נאמר כאן עני ונאמר להלן עני,
מה להלן עני רעבון אף כאן עני רעבון.

> The School of R. Ishmael taught: here the term "affliction" is used and
> there the term "affliction" is used; just as there an affliction through
> hunger is meant, so here an affliction through hunger is meant.

Here, the School of R. Ishmael deduces the meaning of the vague command of *inui* by utilizing a classic method of midrash—the *gezeira shava*.
The *baraita* makes the reasonable claim that if the meaning of a phrase is
unclear in one context, it would be enlightening to search for that same
phrase in another context in which the meaning may be clearer.

Our attention is then drawn to another appearance of this phrase in the
Torah, in which the meaning, according to the *baraita*, is clear. On the
basis of this analogy, the *baraita* concludes that the meaning of *inui* is
hunger. The Torah commands us to afflict ourselves on Yom Kippur by
experiencing the sensation of hunger.

The exact reference regarding which the *baraita* draws the analogy is
not explicitly stated. To which biblical appearance of the term *inui* are we
referred?

Rashi suggests that the verse referred to is Deuteronomy 8:3:[17] "...He
suffered you to hunger..." (ויענך וירעבך). In this verse, the term *inui* indeed
appears in the context of hunger. As we will soon see, the context of this
particular verse plays an important role in the continuation of the talmudic
discussion.

This *baraita*, therefore, draws on the story of Israel's wanderings in the
desert to clarify the meaning of the term "affliction" as used by the Torah.
The term that the Torah uses to describe one aspect of desert life serves as
the basis for interpreting the central *mitzvah* of Yom Kippur.

The Talmud seems to suggest that the analogy drawn is not merely a
literal, lexicographical one. Rather, the comparison between the experience of *inui* in the desert and the command to experience *inui* on Yom
Kippur defines for us not only the practice of this *mitzvah*, but also the
inner nature of the experience itself. The analogy here is not only an

---

[17] There are other possibilities. See for example R. Hananel's commentary to *Yoma*
74b.

external, technical one, but rather one that offers us insight into the existential implications of experiencing *inui* particularly on the day of Yom Kippur. This suggestion is made, in effect, by the Talmud's comments following this *baraita*.

3b. Talmudic Discussion

The Talmud challenges the conclusion of the *baraita* by drawing our attention to the fact that there are other appearances of the phrase *inui* in the Torah. It is possible, therefore, to construct alternative *gezeirot shavot* producing different conclusions as to the meaning of *inui*. The Talmud refers us to the term *inui* as it appears in the context of Laban's parting words to Jacob as he prepares to leave Laban's home and return to the Land of Israel along with his wives, Laban's daughters:

ונילף מאם תענה את בנותי.

But let us infer from: "If thou shalt afflict my daughters."

The Talmud understands this term to mean that Laban is warning Jacob not to withhold sexual relations from his daughters.[18] The meaning of *inui*, therefore, would be abstinence from sexual relations and that would be the experience of *inui* that we are obligated to experience on Yom Kippur.[19]

The Talmud rejects this option and defends the choice of the *baraita* to compare the *inui* of Yom Kippur to the *inui* mentioned in the desert because:

דנין עינוי דרבים מעינוי דרבים ואין דנין עינוי דרבים מעינוי דיחיד.

One should infer concerning the affliction of a community from another affliction of a community, and not infer the affliction of a community from the affliction of an individual.

---

[18] See *Yoma* 77a–77b.

[19] Abstinence from sexual relations is, of course, one of the afflictions that the Mishnah mentions. The Talmud, though, is clearly stating that not all of the prohibitions mentioned in the Mishnah are *the inui nefesh* of the Torah. That is solely defined as refraining from eating and drinking. The halakhic status of the remaining prohibitions is discussed at great length by many halakhic authorities.

The Talmud claims that the analogy between the affliction of Yom Kippur and the affliction in the desert is a stronger one than that which exists between Yom Kippur and the Laban-Jacob story. This is due to the simple fact that the desert situation involved the entire community, the entire nation, whereas the Laban case is an individual's particular story. Yom Kippur, of course, involves the entire community of Israel. There is, therefore, stronger ground for comparison in the analogy drawn by the *baraita* than in the analogy suggested by the Talmud's challenge. The Talmud thereupon raises yet another challenge. We are directed to yet another appearance of the term *inui*, one that is also in the context of a "communal affliction"—the affliction of Egypt.

ונילף מעינוי דמצרים דכתיב וירא את ענינו ואמרינן זו פרישות דרך ארץ.

> But let us infer it from the affliction of Egypt, as it is said: "And the Lord saw our affliction" and in connection with which we said: "This is the enforced abstinence from marital intercourse."

The Torah uses the phrase *inui* to describe the suffering of Israel in Egypt; the Talmud adds that the particular affliction referred to here is abstinence from sexual relations. This analogy, if adopted, would once again suggest that the affliction of Yom Kippur is abstaining from sexual relations.

The Talmud responds by pointing out yet another element of similarity between the desert experience and that of Yom Kippur:

דנין עינוי בידי שמים מעינוי בידי שמים ואין דנין עינוי בידי שמים מעינוי
בידי אדם.

> One infers a divine affliction from another divine affliction, but one should not infer a divine affliction from an affliction brought on through human beings.

The source of both these cases of *inui* is God. The affliction of Egypt, however, was humanly designed. It is therefore disqualified from being a choice source of inspiration for understanding the divine commandment to afflict oneself on Yom Kippur.

The Talmud seems to be encouraging us to take note that the *gezeira shava* used by the *baraita* does not only compare on the basis of external-ities—the appearance of the same word in the two contexts. There are also

essential elements of similarity between the desert experience of affliction
and the experience one is expected to create on Yom Kippur.

On this basis, a clearer understanding of the experience of the desert
could give us more insight into the meaning of the *mitzvah* of *inui nefesh*
on Yom Kippur. The Talmud suggests that the desert experience serves as
the model for the experience of Yom Kippur, and that to a certain extent
the day of Yom Kippur serves to recreate and relive that experience.
Understanding more about the *inui* of the desert leads to a more profound
understanding of the *inui* of Yom Kippur.

Interestingly enough, that is precisely what the Talmud next proceeds
to do. In what seems to be a loose associative flow, the Talmud proceeds
with a wealth of aggadic material on life in the desert, primarily dealing
with the miracle of the manna. The introductory midrash to this section is
of special relevance to the topic of affliction:

המאכילך מן במדבר למען ענותך רבי אמי ורבי אסי חד אמר אינו דומה
מי שיש לו פת בסלו למי שאין לו פת בסלו.

> "Who fed thee in the wilderness with manna...that he might afflict
> thee."[20]
> R. Ami and R. Asi, one of whom said: "You cannot compare one who
> has bread in his basket with one who has none...."

Here, the Amoraim, R. Ami and R. Asi, debate the meaning of a verse
that, somewhat surprisingly, describes the experience of being fed by
manna as a type of affliction, and speculate as to the nature of that affliction. The first of the two opinions cited focuses on the manna as an
experience of complete dependency with no possibility of security, of
saving, of putting away for a rainy day. One needs to rise every morning
and lift one's eyes to heaven yet again to see if today, as well, God has
supplied one's needs. For the human psyche this is an affliction, a type of
suffering. The sense of vulnerability, instability, and insecurity is an
intensely disconcerting and troubling state of being. In the desert, being
fed with manna, this sense created an intense consciousness of dependence on God which eventually became the foundation for an intense
relationship with Him, a vividly present religious experience.

---

[20] Deuteronomy 8:16.

This, to a large extent, ties in with all that we've seen in this talmudic discussion of the definition of *inui nefesh*. It is not meant to be an experience that focuses on pain and suffering for its own sake. Rather, it focuses us on the pain and suffering that is the natural state of being, the human condition. It is the consciousness that at the root of our being, when stripped of our protective layers, stripped of the actions that we routinely perform to create the illusion of stability and strength, we confront our selves as fragile, vulnerable, dependent creatures. This consciousness lies at the foundation of the religious experience. It is the basis of our people's relationship with God, and is recreated for each individual on the day of Yom Kippur through the careful interpretation and fulfillment of the commandment of *inui nefesh.*

The talmudic discussion serves not only to define this commandment in practical terms. Indeed, had that been the primary goal of the Talmud, it would have been much more efficient to only bring the third *baraita*— which directly interprets *inui* as hunger, and reaches the final conclusion with little bother and effort.

The redactor or redactors of this talmudic *sugya* (topical section), though, seemed to have had more on their agenda than merely defining in precise terms the requirements of *inui nefesh*. For comparison's sake, it is interesting to note the parallel discussion in the Talmud Yerushalmi.[21] There, only the second and third *baraitot* appear, with no discussion following either. The halakhic conclusion as to the definition of *inui nefesh* is absolutely identical, but the difference in presentation leaves one with a very different perspective on the nature of the commandment. No attention is drawn to the transition from an active definition of affliction to a passive one, nor to the common, non-conditional nature of the affliction involved. Neither does the Yerushalmi suggest that the basis for comparison with the *inui* of the desert (as suggested by the *Tanna d'bei R. Ishmael* and quoted by the Yerushalmi as well) is more than just linguistic and external. It becomes clearer, in contrast, how the Bavli in its presentation of the discussion, subtly directed our attention to the basic elements of *inui nefesh* as understood and defined by *halakhah*, thereby providing a

---

[21] JT *Yoma* 8.1, 44d

conceptual context in which to understand this central and unique commandment on this central and unique day.

In conclusion, a methodological note. It is important, in my opinion, to approach the talmudic text with the expectation of finding more than legal and formal discussions within. A student in search of meaning and spirituality needs to develop the methods required to uncover the levels of discussion that will gratify those demands. Such levels do exist within the text and it is up to us to uncover and reveal them. Our Torah learning need not be confined solely to legalistic halakhic details, but should afford us insight into human nature, spirituality, and the inner depths of religious experience. Nothing less does credit to the traditional texts that have been, for generations, the focus and inspiration of Jewish wisdom and practice.

Exile and Redemption

"This is the Essence of Spiritual Exile":[1]
Galut haNeshamah in Traditional Jewish Sources and as a Contemporary Condition

Miriam Birnbaum

"And the Lord God expelled him from the Garden of Eden to till the ground from which he was taken." (Genesis 3:23)
Rabbi Judah said: "He was expelled from the garden of Eden in this world and he was expelled from the Garden of Eden in the world to come." (*Genesis Rabbah* 21.7)

I. Introduction

Exile as an Existential Paradigm

My identity is almost exclusively a Jewish one. As a Jew who tries to be halakhic, a Jewish woman, and as a student and teacher of Torah, I find my life to be deeply meaningful. I feel grateful to be living in historically unprecedented conditions which allow me to lead an intensely Jewish life unencumbered by poverty or persecution. And yet.... Though the material conditions of life in contemporary North America or Israel seem, for the most part, decidedly "unexilic," inner life is often quite turbulent. According to the tannaitic opinion quoted above, exile (*galut*) is as much a state of banishment from a spiritual realm as it is from a geographic space.

The scope of the idea of *galut* is further broadened in midrashic, kabbalistic and hasidic literature to include not only a historical and national phenomenon, but also a spiritual and personal condition—a soul dynamic. As a contemporary observant Jew, the existential condition in which I and many of my peers find ourselves could certainly be described as exilic.

---

[1] R. Shneur Zalman of Liadi, *Torah Or, Va'era*, 55b.

We live in multiple realities while never fully identifying with any of them. We are a product of many different worlds, yet find ourselves not quite at home anywhere. Seeking fragments of truth in far-flung places, we find them disturbingly compounded with falsehood. Our relationships with God, with others, and even with ourselves are obstructed by a vague sense of numbness and isolation. Communication functions inadequately, breaks down, or fails us entirely, often leaving us mute and cold.

The restlessness associated with *galut* is particularly familiar to us as young, Jewish women. Like so many observant North American Jews, we find ourselves straddling religious and secular societies. As women, we also shuttle between our families and careers or studies, oscillating between the sometimes conflicting stereotypically male and female priorities of relationships and ambitions, between conventional roles and untraditional possibilities. The specific association between women and exile is conceptual as well as practical, ancient as much as modern. The biblical prophets, the Rabbis of the Talmud, the liturgical poets and the Kabbalists frequently use feminine imagery to represent the exile of the Jewish people and of the *Shekhinah*, the presence of God.[2] The metaphors which are ubiquitous throughout Jewish literature in describing exilic and pre-redemptive conditions are those of a lover's quarrel, pregnancy, and the travail of childbirth—"*Wail, O Zion and her cities, like a woman in the pangs of birth.*"[3]

The Problem of Voice

Any single phenomenon moves each of us in different ways; since exile is by definition an isolating condition, responses to it vary widely from person to person. I am able to discuss exile only as I experience it. I hope that in describing my condition, others may be better able to relate to aspects of their own experience in terms of exile.[4]

---

[2] The indwelling presence of God, referred to in the feminine gender in rabbinic literature, becomes a hypostasis of the feminine in kabbalistic thought.

[3] The refrain from the final *kinah* (dirge) of the Tisha be'Av service, "*Eli Tzion.*"

[4] While the focus of this essay is *galut*, the idea of exile cannot be fully understood without its conceptual parallel of *ge'ulah*. But that is the subject for another essay....

Finding an appropriate voice in which to express these thoughts has been difficult. Conventional academic discourse generally distances itself from its subject and tends to address ideas rather than experience. A detached, scholarly tone seemed unsuitable for this essay, though, because I make no pretense of objectivity, nor do I see reason to apologize for having a highly personal interest in the matter. A strictly personal composition also appeared to be inadequate. I believe that thoughts and experiences which deepen one's understanding of what it means to be a Jew, which have a kind of redemptive value, need to be conceptualized and expressed in normative Jewish terms—in the linguistic, cultural and religious idiom of Torah. So I turned to classical Jewish literature. I tried to define my own ideas and emotions in the mode of traditional Jewish texts and ways of seeing, not in order to validate my thoughts and feelings, but to make them part of what I see as authentically Jewish spiritual experience.

Sources

In the end, it seems that what I have written is neither an academic treatise on the subject of exile, nor a purely personal essay. Instead, it is a collection of excerpts from traditional Jewish sources (with explanatory passages added as necessary), loosely stitched into a narrative by a thread of associative personal response. I hope that the voice heard most distinctly in this essay is not mine, but those of the texts cited, the voices of their holy authors. The theme of *galut* is not developed in these works in a unified, systematic fashion—exile is characterized by fragmentation. The assortment of Jewish sources offered here refracts diverse understandings of a multi-faceted concept.

Many of the ideas and texts presented are from hasidic sources. Though hasidic thought is expressed in traditional Jewish language, it often deals with experiences which are strikingly familiar to us as Jews living in the modern world. In redefining in classical Jewish terms what appears to be a postmodern complaint afflicting secular persons, I remind myself that Jews have been wrestling with these "contemporary" issues for generations. An ancient religious Jewish existential condition links one's own distress with that of one's people. Between the lines of these old texts, perhaps we perceive ourselves. Looking in the mirror these works hold up to our lives, we catch a glimpse of our own image standing nearer to King David than to Kafka; we may find more of a perceptive common language with the Alter Rebbe of Lubavitch than with the perceptive literary theorist Jacques Derrida.

This essay is a meditation then, rather than a *mussar shmooze* (moralizing homily). It is more narrative than expository, more cathartic than instructive. In writing it, I seek not so much answers as a more nuanced understanding of questions. Questions as to the nature of the existentially exilic condition—both collective and individual, the specific spiritual toll *galut* takes on our souls, on our relationship to God and on our service of Him, and the particular opportunities for growth that are available to us as exiles.

II. Exile as Barrier

Mediated Relationship with God and Torah

In the very first verse of his book, the prophet of *galut*, Ezekiel, describes his situation as being "among the exiles, by the river Kevar." Ezekiel's vision of the Divine Chariot[5] is traditionally considered to be one of the most sacred and esoteric of prophecies. R. Shneur Zalman of Liadi (1745–1813), the father of Habad Hasidism points out, however, that Ezekiel's prophecy was not a "face to face" encounter with God as was the revelation the Jews received at Sinai and, in a less dramatic fashion, during the period of the Temple.[6] Rather, it was a vision of divinity mediated through angelic forms—"the face of a lion" and "the face of an ox" (Ezekiel 1:10). Like Ezekiel, our souls are in *galut* and they too cannot bear the intensity of direct contact with the Holy One. But exile is not a natural condition and an exiled Jewish soul, diminished though it may be, craves the immediacy of God and the unmediated revelation of His Truth.

Even deeply Jewish communities are not immune to the subtly pervasive effects of "Western" cultural patterns. Although Jewish

---

[5] Ezekiel 1–3.

[6] *Likkutei Torah, Ha'azinu*, 77c.

consciousness very much informs them, their primary frame of reference might in many ways be secular and technological, their notions of causality, scientific. Contemporary Jewish communities—even ones that are quite sheltered—create and function in what they hope is an authentically Jewish social and psychological setting. But their relationship to concepts as fundamental as God, Godliness and Torah may still be indirect. Though rejecting and shunning many aspects of the ubiquitous popular culture, their vision of God is nevertheless sometimes unconsciously perceived through pop culture's crass forms, and understood using the blunt instruments of its logic. For some, reference to "the King" conjures up a fleeting image of Elvis, before it brings to mind the *Melekh Malkhei haMelakhim* (The King of Kings). The language of the sacred—both literally and figuratively—has historically been our mother tongue. Now, that language sometimes has the strange rhythms of foreign speech and must be converted back into religious terms. Much is lost in translation.

In Exile from Oneself

"*Myself am Hell!*" cries one of the personae in John Milton's *Paradise Lost*, the sixteenth-century epic poem about humankind's fall from grace and banishment from Eden.[7] The most isolating exile is that which we experience within ourselves. R. Dov Ber Schneerson, the "Mitteler Rebbe" of Habad (1773–1827), explains that one's "Godly soul" (*nefesh elokit*), having been fragmented and dispersed among the desires and passions of the baser parts of oneself, is in exile to one's "animal soul" (*nefesh haBehamit*). Only by means of sincere repentance, writes the Rebbe, can all the scattered scraps of the *nefesh elokit*, of ourselves, be gathered together and melded again into a seamless whole soul which parallels the oneness of God, and is therefore able to ascend to the realm of Unity (*olam haYihud*).[8] "*If your dispersed ones be at the utmost ends of the heavens, from there will the Lord your God gather you.*"[9]

---

[7] *Paradise Lost*, book IV, 1.75.

[8] *Shaarei Teshuvah* II (Jerusalem: Makor, 1971) 62:3.

[9] Deuteronomy 30:4, quoted by R. Dov Ber Schneerson, loc. cit.

Exile inside oneself.... Within me, disparate—perhaps diasporate—parts of personality, worldview and experience swirl about, clashing against each other, never quite merging to form an integrated whole, a cohesive Torah personality. Conflicting values and moral priorities introduce themselves, and interrupt each other like noisy participants in a bizarre, never-ending courtroom drama. The internal cacophony is muted, however, even silenced by a muffler of numbness which deadens the ability to feel on an intense level and shake off the lethargy. *"Rouse yourself! Rouse yourself!... The glory of God is revealed to you...."*[10]

Exiled Speech

It is difficult enough to articulate thought and feeling even to ourselves; how much harder is it, then, to relate deeply to other people and to God. The failure of communication and the alienation, which is typical of a certain kind of contemporary Western experience, is a recurring theme in existential literature such as the novels of Kafka and Camus, and the writings of postmodern thinkers and critics like Derrida and Foucault. A similar concept already appears in the *Zohar*, albeit in a theological rather than a philosophical or literary context. Moshe complained to God that he would not be able to speak articulately to Pharaoh: "Behold I am of uncircumcised lips (*aral sefatayim*) and how shall Pharaoh hearken to me?" (Exodus 6:30). It is from these words that the *Zohar* derives its concept of "the exile of speech" (*galut haDibbur*).[11]

The *Zohar*'s cryptic statement is expanded upon by R. Yehuda Aryeh Leib Alter, the third Gerrer Rebbe known as the *Sefat Emet* (1847–1905), who points out that orifices of the body are blocked by coverings. A Jewish male undergoes a painful circumcision to remove the obstruction with which he is born. Later in life, a Jew must struggle to dislodge a

---

[10] Although these phrases are biblical, the particular formulation cited here is found in R. Shlomo haLevi Alkabetz's "*Lekha Dodi*" hymn, part of the *Kabbalat Shabbat* liturgy for Friday night.

[11] *Zohar* 2.25b.

virtual occlusion that plugs his mouth, says the Rebbe.[12] Closing the space between idea and expression, between emotion and utterance…. The tongue fumbles for speech, for words that will explain paradoxes, heal pain, express Torah-truth, and proclaim sincere praise to the Creator. Why is it so difficult to speak? The *Sefat Emet* suggests:

> Every place where there is openness and inwardness [i.e., an opening], there is covering (*orlah*) and concealment, so that "not everyone who wishes to utter the Name [of God] may come and [nonchalantly] do so."[13]

The implication is clearly that speech is not be taken for granted, that the power to utter words of holiness should not be used in a cavalier fashion. The "*orlah*" of the mouth must be cut away before pronouncing Torah.[14]

The Metaphor of the Fetus

The processes of national exile and redemption are frequently described in metaphorical terms in the written and Oral Torah as pregnancy, labor and birth. R. Shneur Zalman further extends the metaphor and likens the exilic condition to a fetal state.[15] The comparison he draws is based on the Talmud's description (in an entirely different context) of the unborn child:

---

[12] *Sefat Emet, Va'era*, 5654. The term *berit haLashon* is found in a different context in earlier kabbalistic works including the thirteenth-century *Sha'are Orah* by R. Joseph Gikatilla (ch. 2, *Sefirah* 9).

[13] This is the *Sefat Emet*'s original and free interpretation of the phrase from the Mishnah "*Lo kol harotzeh litol et Hashem yitol*" (*Mishnah Berakhot* 16b). The Mishnah presents R. Shimon ben Gamliel's opinion that a bridegroom may not recite the *Shema* prayer on his wedding night, since on that occasion he might lack the requisite mindfulness.

[14] The *Sefat Emet* points out, however, that there is a vicious circle here. The only process which can purge us of impurities and blockages of the mouth and spirit (that prevent us from articulating Torah)—is Torah study itself. Only the grace of God grants us the "oral purity" that is a prerequisite for achieving the *berit haLashon*, "(circumcision/covenant) of the tongue," thereby inducting us into the covenant of the Torah. The *Sefat Emet* argues that the removal of the Jewish people's "blockage of the mouth" was also one of the central spiritual effects of their suffering and exile in Egypt.

[15] *Torah Or, Va'era*, 55a–b.

> To what is the fetus in the innards of its mother likened? To a folded pamphlet...its two heels lie on the sides of its rump...its head is between its knees...its mouth is sealed and its navel is open...it is nourished from what its mother eats.... When it emerges into the atmosphere of the world, that which was sealed becomes opened and that which was open becomes sealed....[16]

The child, *in utero*, possesses all the limbs and organs he or she will need throughout life, but is not yet able to use them. Though the child has a mouth, he cannot eat with it; the sustenance received from the mother reaches the digestive system via the umbilical cord, altogether bypassing the upper parts of the body. No life-force animates the respiratory system and the child will not breathe with heart and lungs until he or she utters the first cry. The Alter Rebbe continues:

> So too are the Jewish people in the time of exile compared to [a fetus]..."they have mouths, but they cannot speak: eyes have they but they cannot see" (Psalms 115:5) the light of God...for God has withdrawn His presence and the revelation of His Godliness from the netherworld—"The Lord roars from the heavens" (Jeremiah 25:30) [i.e., not from the earth] *and it appears to human eyes as if the world is an entity unto itself.*[17]

"Nothing else exists aside from Him!"[18] God's active presence in the world—as well as the absence of anything that is *not* part of His presence—is a basic tenet of mystical Jewish theology. However, accepting an idea as an article of faith, or even understanding it as a conceptual reality is not the same as internalizing it as an overwhelming, self-evident, living truth. God dwells in the sacred spaces of the Heavens, atop lofty mountain peaks, and in the synagogue. Is He also encountered in the concrete apartment blocks of the faceless city, in the frigid halls of academia, or on the Greyhound bus at midnight?

---

[16] *Niddah* 30b.

[17] *Torah Or*, loc. cit. Note that the verse from Psalms (115:5) that the Alter Rebbe quotes to describe the unresponsiveness of the fetus refers to *idols* in its original biblical context (!).

[18] *"Ein od milvado,"* Deuteronomy 4:35. In hasidic writings, this phrase was given additional meanings beyond the Bible's declaration of monotheism. See *Tanya, Sha'ar haYihud vehaEmunah.*

The Alter Rebbe's words seem remarkably descriptive of our present condition:

> [We perform *mitzvot* not] "in order to know God, to love Him," and to serve Him with all [our] hearts, with a willing soul and with a heartfelt passion "like a fiery flaming torch and a great thirst"—but rather [we do *mitzvot*] as a matter of "you shall fear me" [i.e., motivated by fear], as a "commandment learned by rote."[19] That is to say, [our *mitzvot* are] fulfilled only on a physical level, coldly: **this is the essence of spiritual exile.**[20]

R. Shneur Zalman is certainly not implying that the many *mitzvot* performed by Jews are of no value. Indeed, in prescriptive *halakhah*, commandments carried out in a habitual manner are valid, and *mitzvot* performed with a cerebral acknowledgment of God are of great value as representations of a firm commitment to God's will.[21] But what, at least on a conscious level, do such *mitzvot* do for the soul?

> Even the influence of *mitzvot* and good deeds which [normally] are sustenance to the spirit, [in our case] do not give vitality [*hiyyut*] to the heart and brain, through breathing [*neshimah*].[22]

Rote service motivated by a visceral sense of fear and duty leaves the worshipper cold. Absent is the warm breath of passion for God.

The *Shekhinah* in Exile

We are not the only ones in exile. "The *Shekhinah* was exiled to Edom with them," says the Talmud.[23] When the Jewish nation is expelled from

---

[19] "*Mitzvot anashim milumada,*" Isaiah 29:13.

[20] "*Zehu ikar haGalut beruhaniyyut,*" *Torah Or,* loc. cit.

[21] "*Mitzvot einan tzerikhot kavannah.*" See *Rosh Hashanah* 22b, *Shulhan Arukh, Orah Hayyim,* 60:4.

[22] *Torah Or,* loc. cit. "*Neshimah*" is a play on words, meaning breathing, but also suggesting a soul-process.

[23] *Megillah* 29a. In rabbinic literature, Edom is usually a reference to the Roman empire and was later used as a code word for Christendom. The present exile, which began with the expulsion of the Jews from their homeland following the destruction of the second Temple in 70 C.E., is referred to as "the exile of Edom." In kabbalistic

its land and, through its own misdeeds or for some other reason, is sent into exile, the presence of God goes into exile too, as it were.[24] One of the functions of *galut haShekhinah* is pedagogic. The Talmud rules that a teacher whose disciple is exiled is obligated to accompany that student into *galut*.[25] If punishment is to serve a didactic purpose, the student must be provided with a means of understanding the moral instruction that accompanies the pain. Likewise, the *Shekhinah* remains with the Jewish people in exile in the form of their sacred scrolls and books, and those who study them. "Since the day that the Temple was destroyed, the Holy One has no [dwelling place] in His world except the domain of the *halakhah*."[26] Even in *galut*—especially in *galut*—Jews continue to study Torah, to internalize a worldview based on biblical and rabbinic perspectives, infusing their exilic lives with *Shekhinah*.

The self-imposed exile of the *Shekhinah*, in addition to being a source of instruction and protection, is also an act of empathy on the part of the Divine. Like a loving mother whose offspring have been sentenced to expulsion, the *Shekhinah* prefers to accompany them on their wanderings, rather than leave them to their own devices. How can she remain comfortably at home while her forlorn children wander the earth? "...*A voice is heard in Rama, lamentation and bitter weeping: Rachel weeping for her children; she refuses to be comforted, for her children—they are gone.*"[27]

Yet the profundity of the concept of *galut haShekhinah* cannot be expressed only in pedagogical or maternal metaphors. The *Shekhinah* is considered by the Kabbalists to be another name for the Jewish people, not as a social collective entity, but as a metaphysical one. *Knesset Yisrael* (The Congregation of Israel) *is* the *Shekhinah*, the indwelling presence of

---

theosophy, Edom signifies the attribute of strict judgment untempered by compassion. See *Zohar* 3.128a.

[24] See *Mekhilta* (Horovitz-Rabin ed.) 51–52.

[25] *Makkot* 10a.

[26] Lit., "the four cubits of *halakhah*," *Berakhot* 8a.

[27] Jeremiah 31:14. According to the Kabbalists, the matriarch Rachel symbolizes the *Shekhinah* which they hypostasized as the image of the feminine.

God in the universe.[28] The displacement of the Jew in physical, spiritual or existential *galut* is described as a reflection of disorder in the celestial spheres. The historical exile of the Jewish nation, and the private exile of an individual Jew, is seen as paralleling the exiling of an aspect of God Himself. The *Shekhinah*'s identification with the suffering of her children is empathetic, but it is also sympathetic: though she suffers for her children, her anguish is for herself as well, and for her sake as well as for theirs, she will redeem them. "*For My own sake, for My own sake, will I do it.*"[29] To the Psalmist, God gives the assurance, "I am with him in his distress" (91:16). This declaration is provided with a more far-reaching significance in the aggadah. It is explained there as signifying that exile is personal and painful for God.[30]

The particular emotion which perhaps most characterizes going into *galut* is regret—the chagrin of being faced with the discrepancy between what should have been and what in fact happened. Regret is a central motif of Jeremiah's account of the conquest of Jerusalem, in the Book of Lamentations:

> *Eikhah*—Alas! How does the city sit solitary, that was full of people! How is she become like a widow. She that was great among the nations and princess among the provinces, how is she become a vassal. (Lamentations 1:1)

The *kinot* (dirges) recited on the fast day of Tisha be'Av, commemorating the destruction of the Temples and the attendant exile from the Holy Land, also describe the wretchedness of the fallen Jewish people in sharp contrast to its former splendor:

---

[28] See *Sefer haBahir*, par. 45 in Scholem, par. 66 in R. Margoliot edition; *Zohar* 3.197a; *Sha'are Orah*, *Sha'ar* 1, beginning of *Sefirah* 10.

[29] Isaiah 48:11, quoted in R. Menahem Mendel Schneerson's *Likkutei Sihot (5748)* (Brooklyn: Kehot, 1982) vol. 18, *Vayeleh*, 199. Note that in the original biblical context, the speaker is not the *Shekhinah* (a post-biblical concept), but God. R. Schneerson's exegetical technique is based on the traditional assumption that the Bible is eternal and prefigures all later developments in Jewish thought. This permits him to understand this phrase as being spoken by the *Shekhinah*.

[30] See *Lamentations Rabbati, Petihta*, par. 25.

My house was established and the cloud of glory rested upon it
when I went forth from Egypt;
But God's fury rested upon me like a heavy cloud
when I went forth from Jerusalem.[31]

God Himself, states the Talmud, "regrets" having created *galut*.[32]

God regrets exile. Do we? As one of my more outspoken teachers once acidly questioned us—"Do you want? Or do you want to want? Or want to want to want...?"[33] A hasidic interpretation discusses the curse with which God punished the serpent in Eden (Genesis 2:14), "...and you shall eat dust all the days of your life," and asks why it is considered a punishment. Did not such a sentence in effect guarantee the serpent a never-ending supply of food? Certainly it did. However, never to be hungry, never to desire, not to feel a yearning for sustenance from the Lord is a severe curse indeed.

III. Exile as Bridge

Is that all? Is exile nothing less banal than a painfully protracted punishment? It would be difficult to accept that we alone bear full responsibility for national and personal *galut*, that exile is merely a penalty for collective transgressions and individual iniquities. Would not such a punishment have long ago exhausted its purpose? "Why have you forgotten us forever, forsaken us for so long?" (Lamentations 5:20). Surely exile achieves a more positive end. Can it be that we are growing in particular ways not in spite of, but *because*, of *galut*? Might exile, rather than being a gross deviation from God's original historical design, be part of the divine redemptive scheme? A midrashic comment on a famous verse from Ecclesiastes 3:1 seems to suggest this:

---

[31] *Kinah* 32 (Goldschmidt edition), based on *Midrash Eikhah Zuta* 19.

[32] *Sukkah* 52b. The description of God as experiencing regret is striking in its anthropomorphism. While rabbinic literature is firmly rooted in belief in an omniscient Deity whose every act is purposeful and good, this sort of audaciously anthropomorphic description of Divine processes is not uncommon in aggadic material.

[33] Heard from R. Mendel Blachman, Jerusalem, 1998.

> To everything there is a season, and a time to every purpose under the heaven—there was a time for Adam to enter the Garden of Eden, as it says "and He placed him in the Garden of Eden" (Genesis 2:8), and there was a time for him to leave it, as it says, "and He banished man from the Garden." (Genesis 3:23)[34]

This midrash introduces the possibility of a pre-determined exile: at least for a certain period, we are *supposed* to be in *galut*. Exile has a meaningful purpose. There are specific tasks for which we are responsible, tasks that can only be accomplished in an exilic state.

Birur & Tikkun: Purifying the Sparks and Preparing a Dwelling Place Below

Rabbinic sources, dating from as early as the second and third century, mention the notion that a certain kind of spiritual rectification can only be achieved through being in a situation that is physically, emotionally or religiously negative.[35] Within the Jewish mystical tradition, Lurianic Kabbalists developed the concept of "purifying" or "raising the sparks" (*birur/he'alat hanitzotzot*).[36] When God desired to create the world, they explained, His essence was too intensely holy and too ethereal to allow the existence of a universe separate from Him. To ensure that the creation would not be completely overwhelmed by His presence, He created "vessels" which would contain His spirit enough to allow the existence of a world. However, the pressure of the Godliness held within these vessels was too great for them to bear, and they shattered in an event of cosmic proportions known as *shevirat hakelim* (the Breaking of the Vessels).[37]

As a result of the Breaking of the Vessels, writes R. Hayyim Vital, two hundred and eighty-eight "sparks" (*nitzotzot*) of holiness were released and scattered—exiled, as it were—through every level of the cosmos. Some of these sparks became "trapped" in places of non-spirituality, and

---

[34] *Ecclesiastes Rabbah* 3.1.

[35] See *Berakhot* 5a, *Sifri, vaEt'hanan* 32 and *Nazir* 23b. Also see Birger A. Pearson, *Gnosticism, Judaism and Egyptian Christianity* (Minneapolis: Fortress Press, 1990).

[36] See R. Isaac Luria, *Sefer haGilgulim*, ch. 38.

[37] *Etz Hayyim*, ch. 9.

even of defilement, and must be restored to their sacred origins. How? Every time a Jew uses a non-sacred object or idea for holy purposes, the lost sparks lodged in it are raised, writes R. Hayyim, on the authority of his teacher, R. Isaac Luria.[38] They are reintegrated into the supernal realms, from which they were discharged when the vessels broke and a measure of redemption is brought to the world. By extricating the "sparks" from the realm of the demonic in which they are ensnared (*birur hanitzotzot*), the Jew contributes toward the restoration (*tikkun*) of a fallen world to its primordial and ultimate condition of cosmic perfection,[39] a world which will once again be holy enough for God to dwell in our midst.

Though the kabbalistic model of the "raising of the sparks" is highly abstract, certain aspects of our own situation seem to be reflected in it. Perhaps intellectual exile—feeling compelled to seek *emet* (truth) not only in Torah, but also in traditions and wisdoms far from one's own, searching for nuggets of pristine meaning in distant and possibly unclean places and finding them there—is an awesome opportunity, as well as a terrible burden. It is a bewildering and dangerous task delicately to pry profound truth from its near-identical twin of deep lie, and to try to restore it to the service of the sacred. Could it be that attempting to do so is not necessarily an act of cultural adulteration, evidence of religious estrangement, but is sometimes holy work? The *Zohar* compares the Jewish people in their exile to a bride standing in a reeking tanner's market. God is likened to her groom who not only goes among the stinking hides to fetch her, but from the power of his love for his bride, feels himself to be in a market of fragrant spices.[40] "The ultimate purpose of the creation of the universe is

---

[38] Loc. cit., I, ch. 18, 170.

[39] "The Holy One, blessed be He, exiled Israel among the nations only so converts would be added to their numbers" (*Pesahim* 87b). "Converts" is interpreted by the Kabbalists as referring to the sparks of holiness redeemed from the situation of impurity in which they are trapped. "Just as a convert was initially distant [from God] and afterward was brought closer, so the sparks were initially under the dominion of the shells (*kelippah*) and by means of purification (*birur*), were brought closer to holiness," summarizes R. Yosef Yizhak Schneersohn in *Sefer haMa'amarim 5702* (Brooklyn: Kehot, 1985) 69.

[40] *Zohar* 3.115b.

to make [even] the lowest of the low [worlds] into a dwelling place for the Blessed One."[41]

Looking for truth in muddy trenches, one's hands and soul may not always remain immaculate. Self-doubt intrudes obsessively: am I doing the right thing? Or is my rationale merely the sophistry of the *yetzer hara* (evil inclination), a lofty-sounding justification for spiritual infidelity? I beg the One "who separates between the sacred and the profane, between light and darkness"[42] to grant me the discernment to differentiate between purity and impurity, the humility to acknowledge when I am unfit to do so, and the opportunity to be cleansed when I fail in the process. "A pure heart create for me, O God and renew a steadfast spirit within me. Cast me not away from Thy presence; and take not Thy holy spirit from me." (Psalms 51:12–13).

"Estheresque"

Aggadic and mystical interpretations of the Book of Esther describe the predicament of the heroine who, by force of circumstance, became the consort of the degenerate King Ahashverosh. In a religiously inhospitable situation, Esther was able not only to preserve a pristine spirit, but even to draw holiness out of impurity.[43] God's name never appears in the Book of Esther. References in it to the unnamed monarch, however, are understood by midrashic tradition as veiled allusions to the Supreme King.[44]

The *Zohar* mentions that the *Shekhinah* in exile cannot reveal herself in a manifestation of holiness, but only cloaked in darkness[45] and sullied

---

[41] *Midrash Tanhuma, Naso* 15. See also, R. Menahem Mendel Schneerson's *Likkutei Sihot* 15 (Brooklyn: Kehot, 1982) 293.

[42] From the liturgy for the outgoing of Shabbat and Festivals (*Havdalah* ceremony). Also see JT *Berakhot* 5.2. "If there is no wisdom, how can there be differentiation?" [*Im ein de'ah, havdalah minayin?*].

[43] See *Sanhedrin* 74b, *Megillah* 15a and Rashi on *Megillah* 16a, s.v. *ad akhshav, ve'akhshav* and *avedeti mimkha*.

[44] *Midrash Rabbah* 3.10, "Every place in this book where it says 'to King Ahashverosh,' the text is speaking of King Ahashverosh. Every place where it says only 'to the King,' it refers to both the sacred and the profane [King]," i.e., on a certain level, it is a reference to God.

[45] See *Zohar* 1.20a.

garments[46]—the illusory semblance of an aspiritual, superficial reality. R. Zadok haKohen of Lublin (1823–1900) writes that Esther perceived the presence of the divine, even through the sackcloth by which the divine is covered in exile.[47] She recognized the King of Kings disguised in the robes of the dissolute gentile ruler, "peeking through the lattices" (Song of Songs 2:9). Through an act of will—the force of her belief in her people's capacity for holiness—Esther wrested power away from Ahashverosh and his kingdom of concealment, and onto herself as representative of the redemptive power inherent in every Jew.[48] Within the soul of every Jewish woman dismayed to find herself in spiritually hostile circumstances, is there not an element of Esther?

The Torah of Exile

Some see truth as absolute, understand good and evil to be polar opposites, and consider an upright life to be a function of moral fortitude. For others, the challenge of living according to the will of God is not only a matter of mustering strength to resist evil, but also of discerning what is good. The Talmud relates that the second Temple was destroyed because of baseless hatred, referring to it cryptically as "a sin which was not revealed."[49] Rashi explains this to mean that the Jews of the era were secretly full of hate and wickedness.[50] R. Shneur Zalman of Liadi, however, interprets the Talmud's words homiletically as being reflexive: "their sin was not revealed, *to themselves*, the perpetrators." Not only did the Jews of the Second Temple era believe they had done no wrong, writes the Rebbe; they were also under the impression that their sins (of baseless hatred) were justified, even righteous, deeds![51] And us? Can we

---

[46] *Zohar, Ra'aya meHemna* 3, 45b.

[47] *Mahshavot Haruz*, ch. 24, 91a–b.

[48] *Mahshavot Haruz*, ibid. R. Zadok adds that it was the failure of the Jewish people alone that prevented Esther from bringing eternal salvation to her people and redemption to the entire world.

[49] *Yoma* 9b.

[50] Rashi on *Yoma*, loc. cit., s.v. "*Aharonim lo nitgaleh avonam*."

[51] *Likkutei Torah, Matot* 85d.

always distinguish between our sins and our *mitzvot*, between good and evil, holiness and depravity, truth and falsehood?

Moral confusion and the corruption to which it leads brought about the destruction of the Temple. Paradoxically, however, its effects have also contributed to our survival in exile. Aspects of Oral Torah were born out of the cessation of prophecy, crises of authority, and the uncertainty resulting from exilic conditions. The Talmud is largely concerned with questions pertaining to halakhically ambiguous situations:[52] kosher or *treif*? Permitted or forbidden? Innocent or guilty? The talmudic corpus, perhaps the most innovative creation of the Jewish people, is indeed a quintessentially exilic production. The Torah of ambiguity has kept us thinking Jewishly for generations, because multiplicity of meaning is all-consuming in ways that clarity is not. Would we have God on our minds constantly if His presence, His ways, were always clear to us? Would we internalize a Torah whose black fire and white fire[53] were crisply distinct from each other, which did not burn within us a crackling, chaotic gray?

And then there is the hidden (*nistar*) aspect of the Torah—Kabbalah and its later, more popular but no less profound manifestation, Hasidism. Its dissemination is itself considered to be a sign of the advent of the messianic era[54]:

> Just as the Jews merited receiving the Torah because of the mortar and bricks (*livenim*) of the slavery in Egypt, so too will we merit the

---

[52] See also *Likkutei Torah*, *Matot* 85a and *Likkutei Torah* on *Shemini Atzeret* 91c.

It is important to note here that while the Rabbis of the mishnaic and talmudic periods disagreed on countless halakhic matters, they shared a basis of axiomatic truths concerning which there was no disagreement. Their situation is not analogous to our own in which dispute and uncertainty extend even to the fundamentals of Jewish belief and praxis.

[53] JT *Shekalim* 6.1.

[54] Hasidic works refer to the emergence of Hasidism as "*At'halta dege'ula*" (the beginning of the Redemption), a phrase from *Megillah* 17b, employed there in a different context. *Keter Shem Tov* (Brooklyn: Kehot, 1972) opens with the Ba'al Shem Tov's description of a vision he had in which he ascended to Heaven and asked the Messiah when he would finally arrive. The Messiah answered "At the time when your knowledge is disseminated and revealed in the world, and your wellsprings [of hasidic wisdom] will spread outward."

revelation of the internal dimension [i.e., the essence] of the Torah [*gilui pnimiyut haTorah*] by means of the fiery glow [*libbun*—a play on words] of halakhic argumentation, in the course of this exile.[55]

The physical and existential travail of exile has given rise to Torah of unparalleled intellectual intensity and emotional profundity.

Descent as an aspect of *Ascent*

Must we learn the hard way? Had we never been separated from God—during Creation, in Eden, after the Golden Calf, at the destruction of the Temples—could we not have developed the depth of insight of the exoteric and esoteric Torah without having had to go through the agonies of national and personal exile? On a certain level, perhaps yes. But there is a kind of insight, of truth, which is the product of suffering. There is a Torah of achievement and exultation and a Torah of adversity and anguish. Pain is not the price to pay for wisdom—it is itself often a source of revelation. Service of God under difficult physical or psychic conditions exercises another part of the soul altogether. It engages at both a micro-and macro-cosmic spiritual level, the *sefirah* of *Netzah* ("Endurance"), the divine attribute which is aroused when the soul is afflicted, when the yoke of God chafes on our necks. In such moments, God is present to us in His aspect of fear and dread, when our own sense of self is crushed almost into oblivion. R. Kalonymus Kalman Shapira, the Piaseczna Rebbe, and later a spiritual leader of the most tortured of congregations, the population of the Warsaw Ghetto, offered the following message:

> Such…must be the faith of the Jew: he must take courage and believe that God will save him, not only at a time when he sees a logical and natural way open for his salvation…. One must say "It is all true: 'The people that dwell in the land are fierce,'[56] it is correct that 'the cities are fortified,'[57] nevertheless I believe that God—who transcends all boundaries and limitations—will save us. 'We should go up and

---

[55] *Torah Or, parashat Shemot* 49a.

[56] Numbers 13:28.

[57] Ibid.

possess it'—*without rationale and without reason.*" Such a faith and trust in God hastens our salvation.[58]

During the period of the Temple, religious life may have been more exalted than our present-day attempts at divine service. But in the actual or metaphorical context of the Sanctuary, worship "made sense." Pagan or monotheist, everyone defined themselves based on the deity in which they believed. In the modern or postmodern world, by contrast, a life devoted to service of God (*avodat Hashem*) may appear both intellectually and socially to be hopelessly passé. Many of us are more secular than we like to believe. And yet we serve God anyway, in spite of ourselves, in spite of our surroundings, against everyone's "better judgment." Ours is an *avodah* transcending rationality and above emotion; for this reason, asserts R. Shneur Zalman, it is in many ways even dearer to God than the obeisance of our ancestors in the Temple.[59] Musing on the phrase, "To see Your power and Your glory as I have seen You in the sanctuary" (Psalms 63:3), the Ba'al Shem Tov exclaimed: "Would that I had been able to perceive You in the time of the Temple as I see you now [at a time of destruction and exile]!"[60]

Fiery Thirst

Although contemporary Western society is in many ways overwhelmingly secular, paradoxically—or perhaps even consequently—a sincere questing for spirituality is on the rise. "*Days are coming, says the Lord God, when I will send a famine in the land. Not a famine for bread, nor a thirst for water, but for hearing the words of the Lord*" (Amos 8:11). The most encouraging, and perhaps the most important effect of *galut* is the intensification of a yearning for the holy and the Godly. In Genesis, Judah passes a death sentence on his apparently adulterous daughter-in-law Tamar and declares, "Bring her out and let her be set on fire" (*hotzi'uah vatisaref*)

---

[58] *Eish Kodesh, Shlah, 5700* (1940) 55. Translated by Nehemia Polen in *The Holy Fire: The Teachings of Rabbi Kalonymus Kalman Shapira, the Rebbe of the Warsaw Ghetto* (NJ: Jason Aronson, 1994) 71–72.

[59] *Torah Or,* loc. cit.

[60] *Torot uFitgamei haBesht, Tehillim* 52, page 35 printed in *Keter Shem Tov.*

(Genesis 38:24). The *Zohar* freely interprets this biblical phrase as a description of the response of the Jewish people to exile: "'Bring her out and let her be set on fire!'—with blazing flames, in *galut*" (*bishalhuvei tihara bigalutah*).[61] The *Zohar*'s cryptic comment is elucidated by the Alter Rebbe of Lubavitch as follows: *hotzi'uah*—when the soul is "sent out," i.e., in a state of exile, *vatisaref*—it is consumed by fiery flames of love for the Holy One.[62] "My soul thirsts for You. My flesh longs for you in a dry, parched land with no water" (Psalms 63:2).

IV. Surrender, Silence and Hope

> *God did an act of kindness to the Jewish nation by dispersing them among the nations.* (*Pesahim* 87b)

After the intellectual, spiritual and emotional rationalizations, beyond apologetics, didactics, angst, soul-searching and *teshuvah* (repentance), there is silence. Ultimately, we have no idea why there is *galut*. We find it incomprehensible that an all-powerful, merciful God chose not to create some other means of redemption and growth, one that does not entail estrangement and acute suffering. Exile defies logic, defies our ability to control by means of understanding. It forces us into the ultimate acts of submission to divine will: suspension of reason, acceptance of the justice of God, and hope that one day we may gain more understanding. "Thus says the Lord: keep judgment and do justice: for my salvation is near to come and my righteousness *will be* revealed [i.e., in the future]" (Isaiah 56:1).

Is a stoic, silent sufferance of the anxiety and misery of exile the only appropriate response for the faithful? While it may be considered saintly to endure one's own pain with a Job-like affirmation of God's justice and mercy, it seems far less virtuous to accept quietly the distress of others. How can one witness the suffering of another and *not* cry out to God? "Silence is acquiescence!"[63] If one is indeed convinced that God is

---

[61] *Zohar* 3.72a.

[62] *Likkutei Torah, parashat Bamidbar* 2c.

[63] "*Shetika kehoda'ah*," *Bava Metzi'ah* 37b.

righteous, that *galut* serves a didactic purpose, that the Creator wishes human beings to participate in shaping their own history, then can one *not* respectfully but urgently appeal—even demand—that the world's collective and individual states of exile be transformed into redemption, that the Holy One no longer hide His face?

Honi, a *tzaddik* of tannaitic times, is known in the Talmud by the sobriquet, "Honi the circle maker" (*Honi haMe'agel*), because of an act he is said to have performed after finding that his earnest prayers did not bring an end to a severe drought. He drew a circle around himself and exclaimed:

> Master of the Universe...I swear by Your great name that I will not move from here until You have mercy upon Your children![64]

The righteous Honi was certainly in a better position to wrangle with God than we are. But we too have a responsibility to our people as he had to the Jews of his time. One can approach God with an unshakable belief in the wisdom of His ways, as well as with a firm protest against aspects of the exilic condition.[65] Objecting to the estrangement and affliction of exile is neither a refusal to accept God's will, nor an attempt to manipulate Him or remake Him in our own image. God acts in order to provoke a response from us: it *is* His will that we react, that we vigorously respond. Protest is part of our national character. The name of our forefather Jacob was changed to "Israel" because he "contended (*sarita*) with God and with men and...prevailed" (Genesis 32:29).

While fighting with one hand, one surrenders with the other, submitting to God, deferring to the inscrutability of His providence, to the promise of His ultimate goodness. "*A song of ascents: when God will bring back the captives of Zion, we will be as dreamers...*" (Psalms 126:1). The Alter Rebbe points out that it is only in *our* reality that ideas or events of an opposite character are logically incompatible. In a dream,

---

[64] JT *Ta'anit* 3:8; *Ta'anit* 23a.

[65] The patriarch Abraham "bargained" with God in such a manner regarding the destruction of Sodom: "And Abraham drew near [the Lord] and said, 'Will you destroy the righteous with the wicked?.... Far be it from You to do this, to slay the righteous with the wicked...far be it from You. Shall not the Judge of all earth do right?'" (Genesis 18:23–26).

in the higher and entirely altered state of consciousness a dream represents, observes the Rebbe, we find that contradictory concepts can peacefully coexist. In fact, we are commanded to dream—to dream of salvation. The Talmud recounts that when a person arrives before the Heavenly court, he is asked: *"tzipita liyshua?"* Did you look forward to redemption?[66] Indeed! We anticipate acquiring a true understanding—and identification with—the experience of kindness found in pain, growth in diminution, sanctification in desecration, elevation in the fall, redemption within exile.[7]

---

[66] *Shabbat* 31a.

[67] I benefited from the expertise and support of many teachers and friends who, directly and indirectly, helped me think about, research and write this essay. I am deeply grateful to my wonderful father and mother, Eleazar and Mrs. Rivka Birnbaum, *ad me'ah ve'esrim.* Thanks in particular to Danny and Sarah Malka Eisen, to R. Dovid Lawrence and R. Avrohom Birnbaum. I am indebted to R. Mendel Blachman *shlit"a* of Nishmat: The Jerusalem Center for Advanced Jewish Studies for Women, R. Moshe Weinberger of Congregation Aish Kodesh, Woodmere and especially to Elliot Wolfson of New York University, for familiarizing me with many of the ideas and sources discussed in this essay. A special thank you to the dedicated editors of this volume. *"From all my teachers I have gained understanding"* (Psalms 119:99).

The Book of Exodus: A Search for Identity

Caroline Peyser

I. Introduction

The early chapters of the book of Exodus mark the transition of the Hebrew people from a small tribe invited to settle in a foreign land, to an enslaved and alienated nation struggling to forge an independent national identity. The narrative opens with a list of individuals who arrive in Egypt from their homeland, Canaan:

> ואלה שמות בני ישראל הבאים מצרימה את יעקב איש וביתו באו. ראובן
> שמעון לוי ויהודה יששכר זבולון ובנימין דן נפתלי גד ואשר.
> (שמות א:א–ג)

> Now these are the names of the children of Israel who came to Egypt, with Ya'akov; every man came with his household. Re'uven, Shimon, Levi and Yehuda; Yissakhar, Zevulun and Binyamin; Dan, Naftali, Gad and Asher. (Exodus 1:1–3)

Through the process of enslavement and redemption, this group of individuals emerges as an independent nation, separated physically and spiritually from its host environment, Egypt.

Woven between the layers of the narrative of the nation's developing identity is the parallel story of one member's struggle to discover his personal identity. Moshe, the future leader of this nation, is born into a Hebrew family, but is soon separated from his birth mother and is subsequently adopted by the daughter of Pharaoh. He, like the nation as a whole, grows up in the shadow of two opposing cultures: the emergent Hebrew people and the surrounding Egyptian empire. Through a careful reading of the text, one hears repeated echoes of Moshe's oscillation between these two conflicting identities as he progresses toward a commitment to the Hebrew people and dons the mantle of its leadership. With an empathic understanding of Moshe's struggle, the reader can more readily identify with the corresponding national process.

Moshe's adoption serves as a pivotal event for his subsequent identity development. His separation from his biological family at the age of weaning, and his adoption by the house of Pharaoh, the arch-enemy of his people, would have had a profound effect on his emerging sense of self and his later life experiences. Yet the effects of adoption on Moshe's identity, a modern avenue of inquiry, have not been the focus of discussion in traditional literature.

In this essay, I would like to examine the stories of Moshe's birth and adoption, his youth and his later recruitment as God's messenger, from a perspective informed by current psychological theory and research regarding adoption and identity development. This theoretical framework offers an additional lens with which to view the text, allowing previously unnoticed nuances to surface. My intention is not to paint a psychological portrait based on mere theoretical conjecture, but rather one that is firmly rooted in the specific language and details the text provides. While no retrospective psychological study can presume to be conclusive or comprehensive, the fruits of such an approach can suggest ways in which critical events may contribute to shaping a character's development and subsequent roles and choices. In exploring the narrative of Moshe's development recounted in the opening chapters of Exodus, I will emphasize how an awareness of the profound and long-term effects of adoption on a child's emerging identity, and the unique circumstances of Moshe's adoption, allow for new interpretations of a familiar story.[1]

II. Identity Formation: Theory and Research

The terms identity and identity formation are central to this essay. I would like to define these psychological concepts, and explain the unique challenges facing the adopted child in order to lay the necessary groundwork for our study of the Exodus narrative.

---

[1] The text, of course, lends itself to multiple interpretations and I have chosen those that fit with the psychological picture that I develop. I have noted alternative interpretations, both traditional and modern, in the footnotes.

The term identity eludes simple definition:

> Identity is the result of multiple emotional, social and cultural influences which contribute to the building of an integrated self. Personal and social identity denote the kind of consciousness that we all carry within us about who we are…a secure identity is characteristic of deep feelings of security and belonging, and of being conscious of oneself as an individual uniquely different from others, yet at the same time part of one's environment and of the human community.[2]

Although we often speak of identity as a static entity, it continues to evolve and change throughout the life cycle. Eric Erikson, a leading theorist on identity formation writes, "While the end of adolescence is the stage of an overt identity crisis, identity formation neither begins nor ends with adolescence: it is a lifelong development largely unconscious to the individual and to his society."[3] Identity need not be unified even at a given stage of life but instead one may speak of an occupational identity, religious identity, social identity, national identity, and so forth.[4]

The identity struggles that pervade the book of Exodus are aptly alluded to in the Hebrew title of the book—*Shemot*, or "Names." A midrash on the opening verse expresses the intrinsic connection between names, *Shemot* and identity:

ואלה שמות בני ישראל, שלשה שמות יש באדם, אחד שקרא לו הקדוש ברוך הוא, אדם אחד שקראו לו אביו ואמו, ואחד שקורא הוא לעצמו וכוי.[5]

These are the names of the Children of Israel—Each person (*Adam*) has three names. One by which the Holy One, blessed be He,

---

[2] John Triseliotis, "Identity and Genealogy in Adopted People" in *Adoption: International Perspectives*, E.D. Hibbs ed. (Connecticut: International University Press, 1991) 36.

[3] Eric Erikson, *Identity and the Life Cycle* (NY: W.W. Norton, 1980) 122.

[4] David M. Brodzinsky, M.D. Shechter and R.M. Henig, *Being Adopted: The Lifelong Search for Self* (NY: Doubleday, 1992) 101.

[5] Machir Ben Aba Mari, *Yalkut haMakhiri: Minor Prophets*, A.W. Greenup ed. (London, 1913) on Exodus 1:1. Quoted in the name of *Midrash Tanhuma*.

called him Adam, one by which his parents called him, and one by which he calls himself.

The midrash highlights the factors that shape a person's identity and by which he or she is called or known. A person's genetic endowment, the early environment in which he or she was raised, and the choices he or she makes in light of biological and environmental influences, contribute to one's self-definition. A name also forms a thread of continuity that bridges one's historical past and future.

Like the midrash, psychological research points to three corresponding factors which contribute to the development of personal identity: the quality of a child's experiences within his natural or substitute family; knowledge and understanding about one's background and genealogy; and community perceptions and attitudes toward the child.[6]

Adopted children face a greater challenge as they try to piece together a coherent sense of self, due to their separation from their biological family and the lack of information regarding their origins:

> For adoptees and nonadoptees alike, an understanding of the self is one of the primary tasks of psychological development.... As many authorities in the adoption field have noted, adoptees have a particularly complex task in their search for self. When you live with your biological family, you have guideposts to help you along. You can see bits of your own future reflected in your parents, pieces of your own personality echoed in your brothers and sisters. There are fewer such clues for someone who is adopted. Adoptees often talk about certain "cutoffs" in their history—from their birth parent, their extended birth family, their awareness of their genetic inheritance and sometimes their ethnic and racial origins.[7]

In addition to the search for self, an adopted child experiences a pervasive sense of loss regardless of the age of adoption.[8] While this seems self-evident for children adopted at later ages with articulated memories of their biological family, it remains true for children adopted in infancy

---

[6] Triseliotis, 35–42.

[7] Brodzinsky, 13.

[8] Ibid., 10.

as well.[9] The adopted child experiences this loss differently at various developmental stages. Thus the personal meaning of adoption changes as the child moves through adolescence and later marries and becomes a parent himself or herself.

Numerous factors made Moshe's adoption particularly traumatic. Moshe's mother nursed him for several years[10] with the daily knowledge that she would be forced to relinquish custody to Pharaoh's daughter, the offspring of the oppressor of her people. The hostile relationship between the Hebrew slaves and the house of Pharaoh could have only produced a complex set of feelings toward the adoption, in both his mother and Pharaoh's daughter. In addition, his cross-racial adoption made integration into his adoptive family more trying as the status, cultural norms, and possibly even language of the palace differed so markedly from his earliest years.

Finally, the stage at which Moshe was separated from his mother marks a particularly vulnerable point in a toddler's developing sense of self and autonomy.[11] A child at this age already possesses a memory and can recall meaningful relationships from the past.[12] Separation at this age instills within the child a sense of loss and abandonment.

We turn now to examine the biblical narrative in light of the processes of identity development in general, and that of the adopted child in particular.

---

[9] Ibid., 12.

[10] According to rabbinic tradition, the age of weaning is at two years (see *Exodus Rabbah* 1.31). Benno Jacob, a modern German commentator, suggests that weaning occurs up until four years of age. See Benno Jacob, *The Second Book of the Bible: Exodus* (NJ: Ktav, 1992) 2:10.

[11] Vera I. Fahlberg, "A Developmental Approach to Separation/Loss" in *Adoption: International Perspectives,* E.D. Hibbs ed. (Connecticut: International University Press, 1991) 27–34.

[12] Brodzinsky, 55.

III. The Narrative

Family Allegiances

Exodus, chapter two, verses 1–22 span the period of Moshe's birth until his marriage and the birth of his first child. This section can be divided into two subsections. Verses 1–10 describe Moshe's early childhood. Verses 11–22 describe Moshe's adolescence and entry into adult life as a husband and father. Both sections contain parallel stories of a marriage and the birth of a child, and conclude with the naming of this child. While the first section describes Moshe's birth and childhood years, the second covers the period of his emergence from the house of Pharaoh, his exile, and his establishing a family of his own. The first section provides the biographical and psychological backdrop against which the events of second section unfold.

Verses 1–10

And there went a man from the house of Levi and took as a wife the daughter of Levi. And the woman conceived and bore a son: and when she saw that he was a goodly child, she hid him three months. And when she could no longer hide him, she took for him a box made of papyrus and daubed it with lime and with pitch and put the child in it; and she laid it in the rushes by the river's brink. And his sister stood afar off, to know what would be done to him. And the daughter of Pharaoh came down to wash herself at the river; and her maidens walked along the river's side; and when she saw the box among the rushes, she sent her maid to fetch it. And when she had opened it, she saw the child: and behold, a weeping boy. And she had compassion on him and said, "This is one of the Hebrews' children." Then said his sister to Pharaoh's daughter, "Shall I go and call to thee a nurse of the Hebrew women, that she may nurse the child for thee?" And Pharaoh's daughter said to her, "Go." And the maid went and called the child's mother. And Pharaoh's daughter said to her, "Take this child away and nurse it for me and I will give thee thy wages." And the woman took the child and nursed it. And the child grew and she brought him to Pharaoh's daughter and he became her son. And she called his name Moshe: and she said "Because I drew him out of the water."[13]

The paragraph describing Moshe's infancy is noteworthy for the absence of proper names until his naming by Pharaoh's daughter. The list of characters mentioned but not named includes his father, a man from the house of Levi, his mother also from the house of Levi, his sister and the daughter of Pharaoh. The absence of names stands in marked contrast to the many names listed in the opening chapter of the book of Exodus.

Modern scholars explain this as an intentional literary device to draw the reader's attention to the central character.[14] The lack of names here, however, may also be viewed as a reflection of the psychological perspective of the central character, Moshe. By age two, most toddlers do not yet speak in full sentences and rarely can memories from this early stage of life be recalled in adulthood. Nevertheless, the pivotal events of this period imprint themselves upon the emerging psyche and leave their mark upon the evolving personality.[15] Although traumatic memories from this early period remain unarticulated, studies suggest that they are internalized and can be expressed later in non-verbal ways.[16] The series of nameless relatives identified only by their relationship to Moshe may reflect the pre-verbal internal representations of the significant figures in Moshe's infancy. His separation from his mother at this critical age, and adoption by a family so unlike his own, must have left Moshe with a profound sense of loss of a family he once knew. Perhaps the coincidence of this traumatic separation with the age of speech development contributed to Moshe's speech impairment.[17]

---

[13] Translation from English text of Koren Bible, revised and edited by Harold Fisch (Jerusalem, 1992).

[14] See *Da'at Mikra: Sefer Shemot*, Meir Medan, Aharon Mirsky and Yehuda Kil eds. (Jerusalem: Mossad Harav Kook, 1991) 32.

[15] Theodore J. Gaensbauer, "Traumas in the Preverbal Period," *The Psychoanalytic Study of the Child* 50 (1995): 122–49.

[16] Gaensbauer, 124.

[17] Trauma has been associated with some cases of speech impairment although much of the evidence is anecdotal. See Charles Van Riper, *The Nature of Stuttering* (NJ: Prentice Hall, 1982). However, the coincidence of Moshe's adoption with the age of speech development makes this possibility more likely. "The primary task for the

כי כבד פה וכבד לשון אנכי. (שמות ד:י)

But I am slow of speech and of a slow tongue. (Exodus 4:10)[18]

This section, which lacks all proper names, closes with the naming of Moshe when he is brought to live in the palace. Pharaoh's daughter calls her adopted son Moshe, "for I have drawn him from the water." The usual birth and naming sequence that one finds in other places in the Bible— ותהר, ותלד ותקרא שמו "She conceived, she bore a child and she called him"—is interrupted here. Instead, the adoption story intervenes between the two events, a device that reflects the discontinuity in Moshe's sense of his personal history. The name or identity that should have been bestowed by his mother is overwritten by the name chosen by his adoptive mother. Although Pharaoh's daughter recognizes his Hebrew lineage, she selects a name that dates his history from the point at which he entered her life.[19]

---

toddler is mainly the switch from dependence to independence with increasing autonomy. Concomitant with the autonomy issues are those of identity. This is the time of life when the youngster becomes aware of himself as a person separate from his primary caretaker, and the time when true ego development begins.... This, too, is a time of very rapid language acquisition. These, then, will be the areas of development most affected by parent loss or separation at this stage" (Fahlberg, 29). In addition, it is possible that Moshe spoke Hebrew at home and was exposed to Egyptian for the first time in his adoptive home.

[18] Different interpretations have been suggested regarding the nature of Moshe's speech difficulty. These include: stuttering (midrash, Hirsch), slowness of speech (Rashi), a problem in articulating certain letters (R. Hannanel), difficulty speaking Egyptian specifically (Rashbam, Ibn Ezra) and a lack of eloquence (Cassuto).

[19] Who named Moshe and what the name means are questions debated among traditional and modern commentaries alike. Some suggest that Pharaoh's daughter named Moshe. Ibn Ezra writes that the name Moshe is a Hebrew translation of the Egyptian equivalent bestowed by Pharaoh's daughter. Chizkuni, in his first explanation, opines that she converted (based on *Sotah* 12b), learned Hebrew and subsequently gave her adopted son a Hebrew name. Hirsch maintains that she specifically chose a Hebrew name to recall his origins. Modern scholars, N. Sarna and U. Cassuto, trace the name to the Egyptian word for "born" or "son."

Others maintain that Yocheved, Moshe's birth mother, named him. Abravanel suggests that she named her son Moshe to recall the way in which Pharaoh's daughter drew him from the Nile. Chizkuni in his second explanation writes that Yocheved named Moshe while Pharaoh's daughter offered the meaning for the name. My explanation here follows the Ibn Ezra's interpretation of the verse.

While serving to link him to his adoptive mother, this name severs him from his biological family and his past.

Although the text does not provide details about Moshe's relationship with his birth mother during his years in the house of Pharaoh, or his knowledge regarding his adoptive status, one can easily imagine that Moshe experienced a nagging, yet growing sense of otherness.[20] As Moshe matured, he must have observed the differences between his physical appearance and that of the rest of his adoptive family. His circumcision served as a further proof of his distinctiveness. Together, these anomalies likely aroused his suspicions and curiosity about his past. In addition, the relationship between himself and his adoptive family was not a simple one. By adopting a Hebrew infant, Pharaoh's daughter defied her father's command to kill all Hebrew male infants and thereby subvert the Israelite nation. If Pharaoh indeed was made aware of Moshe's true lineage, he may have harbored underlying hostile feelings toward his adoptive grandson.[21] If he was not told, then a weighty secret regarding Moshe's past hung in the palace air. Finally, memory fragments of an earlier time and place may have intruded into Moshe's consciousness from time to time—a mother who nursed him, a sister who cradled him, a home, another name—leading to an unarticulated awareness of another past and another history. Moshe's sense of being different, and his uncertainty regarding his origins, may help explain his readiness to identify with the suffering of the non-native Hebrew minority whom he encountered upon emerging from the palace.

Verses 11–22

And it came to pass in those days, when Moshe was grown, that he went out to his brothers and looked on their burdens: and he noticed an Egyptian smiting a Hebrew, one of his brothers. And he looked this way and that and when he saw that there was no man, he slew the

---

[20] The text leaves the reader to speculate whether Moshe maintained contact with his Hebrew family while in the house of Pharaoh. I am assuming that he did not maintain contact with them as this seems unlikely, given Pharaoh's public policy regarding the Hebrews. However, the text remains inconclusive on this point.

[21] See the well-known midrash regarding the infant Moshe's test of loyalty in *Exodus Rabbah* 1.26.

Egyptian and hid him in the sand. And when he went out the second day, behold, two men of the Hebrews strove together: and he said to him that was in the wrong, "Why dost thou smite thy fellow?" And he said, "Who made thee a prince and a judge over us? Dost thou intend to kill me as though didst kill the Egyptian?" And Moshe feared and said "Surely this thing is known." Now when Pharaoh heard this thing he sought to slay Moshe. But Moshe fled from before Pharaoh and dwelt in the land of Midian: and he sat down by a well. Now the priest of Midian had seven daughters: and they came and drew water and filled the troughs to water their fathers flock. And the shepherds came and drove them away: but Moshe stood up and helped them and watered their flock. And when they came to Re'uel their father, he said, "How is it that you are come so soon today?" And they said, "An Egyptian man delivered us out of the hands of the shepherds and also drew water enough for us and watered the flock." And he said to his daughters, "And where is he? Why is it that you have left the man? Call him, that he may eat bread." And Moshe was content to dwell with the man: and he gave Moshe Zippora his daughter. And she bore him a son; and he called his name Gershom: for he said, "I have been a stranger in a strange land."

Moshe grows up, leaves the palace and "goes out to his brethren." One can easily imagine that Moshe searches out his family of origin, as many adolescents do upon learning of their adoptive status.[22] Gnawed by a pervasive sense that he does not belong and plagued by memories of another family, he seeks out his people and begins to identify with their lot. Yet, he cannot easily integrate his newly acquired identity with his Egyptian upbringing due to the antagonistic relationship between the two nations. Moshe must have undergone a great deal of psychological turmoil as he began to realize that his adoptive grandfather's edicts against the Hebrews were responsible for his separation from his biological mother.

His internal conflict finds expression metaphorically in his encounter with the Egyptian taskmaster who is beating a Hebrew, "from his brothers." ויפן כה וכה—"he turns this way and that." Moshe is tormented by the clash between his two loyalties. The term *Vayifen* can denote not only a

---

[22] E.B. Rosenberg, *The Adoption Life Cycle: The Children and their Families Through the Years* (NY: The Free Press, 1992) 114.

physical turning but also a psychological turning point.[23] Moshe decides to strike the Egyptian and hide his body in the sand, an act of betrayal against his adoptive family. With this action, he attempts to bury or silence the internal conflict, choosing to side with the oppressed rather than the oppressor.[24]

The following day, Moshe confronts two Hebrews fighting with one another. Moshe attempts to intervene, but they rebuff his aid. Through his act of killing the Egyptian, he has irreversibly separated himself from the house of Pharaoh; yet the Hebrews, too, reject his involvement in their affairs. Here, interestingly, the text does not refer to the Hebrews as his brethren. When they allude to his murder of the Egyptian, Moshe responds "Surely, the thing is known." On one level, Moshe refers to the murder itself; yet, on another level, he fears that Pharaoh has been made aware of his disloyalty. If not for Pharaoh's suspicions regarding Moshe's loyalty to him, it seems hard to explain why a prince of Egypt should be sentenced to death for killing an Egyptian subject. In addition, Moshe's fears may relate to his own sense of anxiety as he comes to recognize his alienation from both nations. Feeling rootless and estranged, Moshe runs away.

Moshe escapes to Midian. In his encounter with the daughters of Yitro, in contrast to the two previous stories of his intervention, his initiative and assistance here lead to an invitation to join a new home, family and people. It is here, in the midst of this newfound family, that Moshe sets down roots by marrying and begetting a son.

---

[23] See Avraham ibn Ezra's commentary to Exodus 32:15, "And Moshe turned and descended from the mountain."

> **And he turned**: Like a person deciding what should be done, and he discerned that he must go down quickly from the mountain, like *Vayifen Ko vaKho*.

ד"ה **ויפן**: כאדם מסתכל מה יעשה וראה כי חייב לרדת מהרה כדרך ויפן כה וכה.

[24] It is possible that Moshe's sense of compassion, even at the expense of defying Pharaoh, was learned from his adoptive mother. See Hirsch's comments on 2:10. He explains that Pharaoh's daughter sought to instill a sense of compassion in Moshe by reminding him through his name of her act of kindness toward him that she performed in defiance of her father's cruel edicts.

At a distance from his place of birth and adoptive family, Moshe can gain a perspective on his earlier years. As he becomes a father for the first time and looks into the face of his biological son, it is easy to imagine that his own earliest experiences of separation and adoption flood his consciousness. Adoption literature notes that:

> For adoptees the birth of a child has special meaning. They achieve
> the reality of having a blood relative in their lives, perhaps for the very
> first time…. Having, keeping and raising a child of one's own is likely
> to stir up old and new feelings about birth parents.[25]

Through his son Gershom's birth, Moshe relives his own infancy and adoption. It is only at this moment, through the naming of his own son, that he can articulate with clarity the effects of his abrupt separation from his biological mother. He recognizes that he never truly belonged in the house of Pharaoh; he was always a stranger there.[26]

ותלד בן ויקרא את שמו גרשם כי אמר כי גר הייתי בארץ נכריה.

(שמות ב:כ״ב)

> And she bore him a son and he called his name Gershom: for he said,
> "I have been a stranger in a strange land." (Exodus 2:22)

Most commentators explain this verse as referring to the period of Moshe's exile in Midian. Why, though, would he choose to express his stranger status precisely at the point when he has successfully settled down and started a family of his own? Furthermore, why does he use the past tense—"I *was* a stranger…"? Instead, it seems possible that Moshe refers here to his stranger status in his former homeland, Egypt. Although he once perceived himself as part of the royal family, having a family of his own underscores his sense that he never belonged there. While the first section of the chapter closes with a naming that links Moshe to his

---

[25] Rosenberg, 116.

[26] Compare the names of Moshe's two sons to Joseph's sons (Genesis 41:51–52). Moshe and Joseph both were estranged from their families and found refuge in the house of a Pharaoh. Yet their different experiences, a function of the circumstances and age at the time of separation, find expression in the names each chooses for their sons.

adoptive family and Egyptian identity, the second section ends with a naming that separates him from this identity.

Moshe at this point seems content to settle in Midian and forget about his past. In the next chapter, however, God confronts him with his history and lineage and sends him on a mission to redeem his people.

The Encounter with God

During his stay in Midian, far away from the home of his youth, Moshe realizes who he is *not*. Yet with little contact with his biological family and people, he has yet to learn conclusively who he *is* and to fully identify himself with the Hebrews. During the encounter at the burning bush, God provides Moshe with this biographical information. Throughout the conversation, echoes of Moshe's identity struggle can be discerned.

In Chapter 3:6, God reveals himself to Moshe stating:

ויאמר אנכי אלקי אביך, אלקי אברהם, אלקי יצחק, ואלקי יעקב....

He said "I am the God of your father, the God of Abraham, the God of Isaac and the God of Jacob...."

He commissions Moshe to redeem the Children of Israel from bondage. Moshe's initial response becomes clearer when viewed in the context of his evolving identity:

...מי אנכי כי אלך אל פרעה וכי אוציא את בני ישראל ממצרים.
(שמות ג:י"א)

...Who am I that I should go to Pharaoh and that I should bring the Children of Israel out of Egypt? (Exodus 3:11)

At first glance, this statement can be interpreted as an expression of Moshe's humility. Yet, it can also be read as the question of one who is uncertain of his own identity. "Who am I?" asks Moshe. What is my national identity? This verse contains two separate clauses—1) I should go to Pharaoh, and 2) I should lead the Children of Israel. These separate clauses express the two aspects of Moshe's identity. I am a Hebrew—how can I go to Pharaoh? And yet I was raised as an Egyptian separate from my Israelite brethren—how can I serve as their leader who will redeem them from Egypt?

Moshe's preoccupation with names and identity is further expressed in his second question: "I will come to them and say that the God of your forefathers has sent me to you and they will say 'What is His name'— what will I say to them?" Moshe asks to know God's identity. Interestingly, Moshe here refers to himself as separate from the people— "the God of *your* forefathers," rather than *our* forefathers. Perhaps God's answer can be seen as a response to Moshe, no less than to the Children of Israel: "I will be that I will be" (Exodus 3:14). Despite the fact that you have not known me during the first eighty years of your life, and you were not raised with a historical consciousness regarding your Hebrew ancestry, our relationship will develop from this point onward.

Moshe raises numerous objections in the course of his discussion with God. Nevertheless, the primacy and the particular formulation of his first two questions—namely, who am I and who are You—allow us to glimpse Moshe's internal struggle.

After Moshe's many challenges, God finally lays his qualms to rest by telling him that he will send Aharon, his brother, to stand by his side and speak for him. In answer to Moshe's claims that he is an outsider to the people, God responds that Aharon will speak on his behalf. Aharon, Moshe's biological brother, serves not only as his mouthpiece, but more importantly as a link between Moshe and the people from whom he was estranged as an infant. Through a connection to his birth family, Moshe forges a tie to his people. At the same time, Aharon also acts as a buffer between Moshe and his adoptive Egyptian family.[27]

A shift in Moshe's identity development occurs upon his return from his encounter with God. Moshe declares to Yitro, "I will go now and

---

[27] Aharon alone speaks to the people initially (see Exodus 4:30) and speaks together with Moshe to Pharaoh (see Exodus 5:1). When Moshe speaks to the people directly for the first time (Exodus 6:9), they do not heed him and he reacts by attempting to reject his mission. Again, God responds by sending Aharon to stand at Moshe's side (Exodus 6:12–13). This conversation is retold more elaborately in Exodus 6:29; 7:2. Between these two renditions, the text lists Moshe and Aharon's lineage. The interposition of Moshe's lineage between these two renditions expresses structurally Aharon's function as a link between Moshe and his historical family.

return to my brethren in Egypt and see if they are still alive." This is the first time that Moshe refers to the Children of Israel as brethren. Rather than stating, "I will return to Egypt to my brethren," the emphasis is placed instead upon his returning first and foremost to his estranged brethren who are enslaved in Egypt.

Yet Moshe must take a final step in securing his Hebrew identity. It is easy to imagine the inner turmoil that Moshe experienced facing his return to Egypt. Aside from the immediate threat to his life that caused him to run away (which God assured him no longer exists), he must now return to join a people who are brutally enslaved and confront the heir to his adoptive family. Perhaps Moshe only became ready for this encounter when God informed him of the death of the former Pharaoh.

Even if he himself decides to throw in his lot with the Israelites, Moshe remains hesitant to endanger his newly established family. At this point in the story, God reiterates his mission to Moshe:

ויאמר ה׳ אל משה בלכתך לשוב מצרימה ראה כל המופתים אשר שמתי בידך ועשיתם לפני פרעה ואני אחזק את לבו ולא ישלח את העם. ואמרת אל פרעה כה אמר ה׳ בני בכורי ישראל ואמר אליך שלח את בני ויעבדני ותמאן לשלחו הנה אנכי הרג את בנך בכורך. (שמות ד : כ״א–כ״ג)

> And the Lord said to Moshe, "When thou goest to return to Egypt, see
> that thou do before Pharaoh all those wonders which I have put in thy
> hand. But I will harden his heart, that he shall not let the people go.
> And thou shalt say to Pharaoh, 'Thus says the Lord, Israel is my son,
> my firstborn. And I say to thee, Let my son go, that he may serve me.
> And if thou refuse to let him go, behold I will slay thy son, thy first-
> born.'" (Exodus 4:21–23)

Significantly, this is the first reference in the Torah to the Children of Israel as God's "son." The father-son imagery used in this passage, both Israel as God's son held captive by Pharaoh, as well as Pharaoh and his own son, must have resonated deeply with Moshe, leading him to identify personally with his mission.

Circumcision at the Inn

On the return journey to Egypt, Moshe stops at an inn where a bizarre set of events transpire:

ויהי בדרך במלון ויפגשהו ה' ויבקש המיתו ותקח צפרה צר ותכרת
את ערלת בנה ותגע לרגליו ותאמר כי חתן דמים אתה לי וירף ממנו
אז אמרה חתן דמים למולות. (שמות ד : כד–כו)

And it came to pass on the way, in the place where they spent the
night that the Lord met him and sought to kill him. Then Zippora took
a sharp stone and cut off the foreskin of her son and cast it as his feet
and said, "Surely a bloody bridegroom art thou to me." So he let him
go. Then she said, "A bloody bridegroom thou art, because of the circumcision." (Exodus 4:24–26)

Traditional commentators, medieval and modern alike, struggle to make
sense of this story. Why didn't Moshe circumcise his son? Whom did God
come to kill and why?[28]

Circumcision represents for males the quintessential sign of allegiance
to the people of Israel. This act binds the child's religio-historical identity
with the destiny of the Jewish people. Although unstated in the text, it is
easy to imagine that Moshe's circumcision served as the key through
which he unlocked his own identity. It is not coincidental that this mark is
made on the male organ of reproduction, the part of the body most symbolic of the continuity of the generations. While Moshe may have been
ready to endanger his own life in returning to Egypt, he hesitated to mark
his children with an identifiable and irreversible sign of allegiance to the
Hebrew people, thereby placing his future generations at peril.

In this story, God requires Moshe to imprint on his son's flesh the mark
of their shared Israelite identity before allowing him to serve as the
redeemer of the Children of Israel. Only when he is ready and willing to
join his child's destiny with that of the Children of Israel has he made a
full commitment to this identity.

It is interesting to note that even though Moshe joined his destiny to
that of the Israelites, he never became a fully integrated member of the
people. Instead, he remained separate from the people he led—physically
apart from the central encampment and distanced from even his immediate

---

[28] Some commentators explain that God sought to kill Moshe for not circumcising his
son (Rashi, Chizkuni), or for taking his family along and thus slowing down his
travelling time (Rashbam). Others suggest that God intended to kill Moshe's infant
son (Eliezer according to Ralbag; or Gershom in the opinion of Shadal), since Moshe
failed to circumcise him.

family. Perhaps God served the function of family for Moshe. Thus when Moshe's siblings criticized his conduct regarding his separation from his wife, God chastised them, explaining, "Not so my servant Moshe, for he is the trusted one in all my house" (Numbers 12:7).

Parallels Between the Individual and the Nation

The centrality of the search for identity in Moshe's life serves as a microcosm of the experience and development of the people as a whole. Using the metaphor of human development to describe the process of national development, one can discern parallels between Moshe's experience and that of the people of Israel.

Moshe's Development	National Development
Infancy with his biological mother	Infancy as a nation in their homeland, Canaan
Separation from his biological mother at an early age and adoption into an Egyptian family	Separation from Canaan and settling in Egypt
Threat to Moshe's life because of a suspicion of dual loyalty	Enslavement and slaughter of male infants due to a claim that the Israelites are not loyal to the Egyptians
Removal from the adoptive home in an abrupt manner— exile to Midian	Removal from the adoptive home in an abrupt manner— Exodus from Egypt
Full recognition of his historical identity through the encounter with God at the burning bush	Recognition of identity through encounter with God at Sinai and the giving of the Torah
Forging a commitment to this identity through a covenant of blood—circumcision	Forging a commitment to this identity through a covenant of blood

Although the sons of Israel grew up in the land of Canaan, their "mother" land, they eventually relocated in their infancy as a people to the land of Egypt. Joseph, who had achieved princely status in Pharaoh's house, encouraged his family to join him in Egypt and settle in Goshen by the king's invitation. There, they slowly assimilated into the surrounding nation and developed a dual identity common to the Diaspora Jew—that of their birthplace and that of their host country. Yet their reception by this foreign country, even at the outset, remained ambivalent and they were placed in Goshen due to their shepherding, a profession abhorrent to the Egyptians. Time passed and as their numbers increased, Pharaoh accused them of disloyalty:

ויאמר אל עמו הנה עם בני ישראל רב ועצום ממנו. הבה נתחכמה לו פן ירבה והיה כי תקראנה מלחמה ונוסף גם הוא על שנאינו ונלחם בנו ועלה מן הארץ. (שמות א:ט–י)

> And he said to his people: "Behold, the people of the children of Israel are more and mightier than we. Come, let us deal wisely with them; lest they multiply and come to pass, that when any war should chance, they also join our enemies and fight against us and so go up out of the land." (Exodus 1:9–10)

Through this accusation, Pharaoh successfully convinced his people to enslave the Israelites and to kill their male infants. Just as Moshe experienced a painful realization of his strangeness in a house that he once mistakenly imagined as his true home, so too, the Children of Israel were jarringly awakened to their foreigner status in Egypt. Through their enslavement, the Israelites were forced to reexamine their identity as a people. The plagues served as a further means of separating the Children of Israel from their host environment.[29] Finally, with the redemption from Egypt, the Children of Israel achieved full physical separation from this adopted land. The gaps in their national identity were filled by their encounter with God at Mount Sinai. This identity was eventually sealed with a covenant following the revelation at Sinai:

---

[29] See specifically the fourth, fifth, seventh, ninth and tenth plagues where the text explicitly states that the plague did not affect the Israelites.

ויקח ספר הברית ויקרא באזני העם ויאמרו כל אשר דבר ה׳ נעשה
ונשמע ויקח משה את הדם ויזרק על העם ויאמר הנה דם הברית אשר
כרת הי עמכם על כל הדברים האלה. (שמות כ״ד:ז-ח)

> And he took the book of the covenant and read in the hearing of the
> people. And they said, "All that the Lord has said will we do and
> obey." And Moshe took the blood and sprinkled it on the people and
> said, "Behold the blood of the covenant which the Lord has made with
> you concerning these words." (Exodus 24:7–8)

Like Moshe, however, the people's identity struggle does not resolve itself
all at once but rather continues to evolve throughout their travels in the
desert. There, they frequently demand to return to Egypt and the remnants
of Egyptian culture surface repeatedly. The generation that leaves Egypt
can never fully shed their Egyptian identity and experience. Instead, God
chooses to wait until this generation dies out before bringing the Children
of Israel to Canaan.

Conclusion

Alienation and identity play a central role in the Exodus narrative. Both on
the individual and national levels, the experience of being a stranger and
searching out one's past figure prominently in the process of psychological
development.

Moshe, the estranged son of his people, who grew up in the house of
the enemy and oppressor, did not share in the immediate history of his
people. In his privileged status as a prince in Pharaoh's house, a safe
distance from the mud pits of his enslaved brethren, he remained physically and culturally disconnected from their experience. Yet he too knew
on a personal level the meaning of being a stranger in a foreign land, and
the struggle to separate from the surrounding culture in an attempt to
establish an independent identity. The correspondence between his
personal odyssey and that of the Children of Israel provided him with
intimate knowledge of their psychological experience, making him
uniquely suited to serve as their leader.

Moshe: Portrait of the Leader as a Young Man

Bryna Jocheved Levy

A brief but dramatic passage in the Exodus narrative (Exodus 2:11–14) recounts Moshe's ethical coming of age. Rising above the environment of cruelty and suffering which was Egypt of the Pharaohs who knew not Joseph, Moshe emerged as a man among men. Raised in the palace of the oppressors, he displayed outstanding moral fortitude and sensitivity to the suffering of others. Up to that point in his life, he had been a passive beneficiary of a remarkable course of events, which spared his life and made him part of the Egyptian royal family. That fateful day, however, on which he went forth from the palace saw him transformed into an active agent in the redemption of his people. Through the episodes described in this passage, Moshe became prepared to lead.

These events are portrayed economically; every word and nuance is laden with meaning. The reader of the Bible must mine the text to discover the multifaceted valences embedded within. A close reading of the text, along with a study of the interpretations it has generated throughout the ages, will disclose the story of a son of enslaved Hebrews who rose to lead his people through his moral commitment and courage, and demonstrate how he made the leap from ethical concern to religious consciousness.

Providence or Bravery

Moshe's ascent to greatness is unlike that of other biblical characters. Among the leaders of biblical Israel, some were born great, others achieved greatness, while others still had greatness thrust upon them. Scripture endorses the notion that many of the leaders of the Jewish people were inexorably destined for their roles. Samuel and Jeremiah, for example, were even singled out *in utero* to serve as leaders of the people of Israel. They were not consulted, nor did they have to prove their spiritual or moral mettle. They were chosen and sanctified; their destinies and the destiny of the people became one.

Yet being sanctified at birth was not the only way to achieve greatness in ancient Israel. Abraham, for example, began his mission as the founding father of the Hebrew nation at age seventy-five, with the command of "*Lekh lekha*"—"Go forth from your native land...to the land that I will show you." The text does not inform us of any religious or moral distinction between the progenitor of the Jewish people and his contemporaries. In fact, the Book of Genesis leaves us wondering why Abraham merited selection. And so, the commentators, from even the earliest times, attempt to solve the mystery of Abraham's early life in the hope of explaining his unique and historic role. He is depicted as iconoclast, martyr and philosopher—each image attesting to his worthiness for future greatness.[1] Thus the Rabbis, who knew that Abraham would prove his spiritual valor in the course of his later career, assert the appropriateness of his having been chosen as the addressee of "*Lekh lekha.*" This was the command which brought Abraham onto the stage of Jewish history and bound him in eternal covenant with God.

In the case of Abraham, father of the nation, rabbinic literature alone provides the backdrop against which the reader may understand how he was qualified to assume the responsibilities inherent in his position and how he achieved lasting greatness.[2] By contrast, Moshe, perhaps the

---

*My sincerest thanks to Anne Gordon, who provided extensive editorial assistance and direction in the preparation of this article.

[1] The rabbinic portrait of the twenty-year old salesman in his father's idol shop, who actively demonstrated the futility of paganism (*Genesis Rabbah* 38.13; *Seder Eliyahu Rabbah* 5.27), surely presents a ready foreshadowing of the monotheistic trailblazer he was to become. Similarly, the classic story of Abraham's salvation from the fiery furnace (*Genesis Rabbah* 44.13, *Pesahim* 118a) suggests that the would-be martyr was indeed beloved of God. And as a philosopher who argues the logic of an Omnipotent Creator, Abraham is seen as one with the ability to convince others of his view. See L. Ginzberg, *Legends of the Jews* (Philadelphia: Jewish Publication Society, 1909), vol. v, 217–18, notes 49–51.

[2] Rabbi A.I. Kook suggests that Abraham's pagan origins actually prepared him for his role as the founding father of the Jewish people: the passion and spontaneity of paganism were to be harnessed for the service of the One God. See Jerome I.

leader most significant in molding the nation, is granted a nearly full biography in the Torah itself; we are allowed a glimpse of his greatness long before he stands at the burning bush and is given the parallel charge of "*Lekha ve'Eshlahakha*" (Exodus 3:10).

We encounter Moshe at the very beginning of his life: the second chapter of the Book of Exodus begins with the story of his birth. This text can be read as an account of the divine intervention on Moshe's behalf, marking him from the outset as one selected for a special role. Moshe, born during a reign of terror (the Egyptian despot decreed that every Hebrew male baby must be cast into the Nile), was hidden for three months in his mother's home. When she could no longer conceal the child, she prepared an ark for him and set it afloat on the Nile. None other than the Pharaoh's own daughter found the ark and was drawn to the child, whom she adopted and raised in the palace of Pharaoh.

Midrashic amplifications of this narrative, which emphasize the supernatural character of the events portrayed, drive home the idea that God's redemption of Israel already began with the birth of Moshe. For example, *Exodus Rabbah* 1.19 claims that Moshe's mother, Yocheved, conceived Moshe at the miraculous age of 130. This midrash further states that upon the baby's birth, the house in which he was born was filled with light (1:20). The miracles continued. The midrashic texts depict the supernatural events surrounding the salvation of the baby Moshe.

On the banks of the Nile, as Pharaoh's daughter and her handmaidens prepared to bathe, all those who raised obstacles to the rescue of the infant were instantaneously struck dead by the Archangel Gabriel (*Exodus Rabbah* 1.23). Moshe's cry was that of a mature boy, louder than that of a newborn, designed to capture the attention of Pharaoh's daughter. Leaving nothing to chance, the angel Gabriel struck the baby, orchestrating his crying, so as to draw the attention of the princess at precisely the right moment. The hand of Pharaoh's daughter magically lengthened, extending her reach, enabling her to rescue Moshe's basket herself. Moreover, in touching the basket, she was immediately cured of leprosy, from which

Gellman, *The Fear, the Trembling and the Fire* (Maryland: University Press of America, 1994) 99–120.

she suffered. When she opened the basket, she discovered not only the baby boy, but also the Divine Presence together with him (1:23).

Rabbinic literature is replete with *midrashim* which tell of the miracles, revelations and angelic visitations punctuating each critical juncture in the life of young Moshe. These *midrashim* show that Divine Providence accompanied Moshe at every step along his journey into adulthood, assuring his survival and safety. Interestingly, Rashi, in his biblical commentary includes these midrashic amplifications together with his *peshat* or plain reading of the narrative. By doing so, he stresses that the rabbinic understanding which emphasizes God's guiding hand, in fact, is the true *peshat* of the story; that the events of Moshe's salvation were not the products of chance. Rather, readers of these embellishments are left feeling certain that it is the Hand of God which selected Moshe for his role.

But another reading of this story is possible and perhaps even preferable. Scripture itself portrays the events, which result in the adoption of Moshe by Pharaoh's daughter as the function of natural human actions. There are no miracles to be found in the biblical text. The Torah, in fact, makes no mention of God until the concluding passage of chapter two.[3] Instead, it is the courage of the baby's mother and that of his sister, together with the compassion of the princess, which save his life.[4] It is no accident that precisely these qualities will in turn distinguish his own leadership style.

---

[3] See Nechama Leibowitz, *Studies in Shemot* (Jerusalem: World Zionist Organization, 1981) 17–19.

[4] We should note that the omission in this story of the names of Moshe's family members, whom we know quite well to be Yocheved and Miriam, serves a variety of functions. Maharal suggests that the anonymity in the biblical text serves to distinguish Moshe as having been not of ordinary birth (*Gevurot Hashem*, 15). More simply, on a basic literary level, the anonymity focuses attention on the protagonist, Moshe, insofar as the other figures are defined, as they relate to him. The concealed identities also lend an aura of secrecy to the narrative, as it recounts the dangerous birth and the hiding of the infant. Another reading allows the use of this text as a polemic. By withholding details of this nativity scene of the redeemer of Israel, the text discourages adoration of the members of Moshe's family. Alternatively, one may experience the universality of this anonymous portrayal, as it is transposed from a biographical episode of Moshe's family to a paradigm for every Jewish mother facing the horror of Yocheved's dilemma.

The courage of Yocheved is evident in verse three, where the Torah uses a surprisingly large number of verbs to convey the forceful and determined actions she takes to save her child:

ולא יכלה עוד הצפינו ותקח לו תבת גמא ותחמרה בחמר ובזפת ושם בה
את הילד ותשם בסוף על שפת היאר.

> When she could hide him no longer, she got a wicker basket for him
> and caulked it with bitumen and pitch; she put the child into it and
> placed it among the reeds by the bank of the Nile.[5]

Similarly, the extensive series of verbs which describe the actions of Pharaoh's daughter (in verses 5–6), leading to the salvation of the infant, attest to the active involvement of the Egyptian woman. Perhaps the parallel structure of the verbs is used to credit the adoptive mother; that is, she acted admirably, as the natural mother herself did.[6]

Growing Up in Pharaoh's Palace

And so, through the moral fortitude of Moshe's two mothers, the boy comes to be raised as an Egyptian in Pharaoh's court. Again, we may ask how to interpret this turn of events. This unusual upbringing of an Israelite boy (who by Egyptian law should not even be alive!) can be viewed as an ironic twist of fate—or the hand of Providence, if you will; for it is the prince of Egypt who will bring about the kingdom's doom.

Alternatively, we can understand events differently: being raised in the palace was essential in Moshe becoming the person capable of leading the Israelites out of Egypt. That is to say, Moshe's placement in the royal setting does far more than add dramatic detail; it prepares him for the choices he will later make and the stances he will have to take.

In this reading, through its account of Moshe's experience in Pharaoh's court, the Torah teaches us not only of God's providence, but also of the need for human participation in determining the destiny of the nation of Israel—participation through acts of courage, difficult moral choices and

---

[5] The translations of all the biblical verses are from *Tanakh: The Holy Scriptures* (Philadelphia: Jewish Publication Society, 1985).

[6] My thanks to Rivy Poupko Kletenik for this insight.

faith. That Moshe was a fitting leader for the people is evidenced by his conduct in the second chapter of the Book of Exodus. First, Moshe championed the cause of justice by defending a Hebrew slave victimized by his Egyptian overlord. Next, he attempted to settle a dispute which had erupted between two Hebrews. And lastly, he protected the shepherdesses and their flocks from the shepherds who competed for their water. Nechama Leibowitz points out that these three episodes form a series which illustrate Moshe's moral tenacity.[7] Leibowitz notes that in this triad, Moshe intervened in altercations between Jew and non-Jew, Jew and Jew, and non-Jew and non-Jew. He sought justice and he did so regardless of race, color or creed.[8]

Even a cursory reading of the text affords us this glimpse into the character of Moshe. Ahad ha'Am develops the idea further in his essay "*Moshe.*"[9] One might think that when Moshe struck the Egyptian, he was naive, responding impulsively to the oppression he beheld. The second act, however, and certainly the third, show true resolve. Even the negative reaction he encountered in the second incident did not deter him from zealous moral intervention. These events educated Moshe about the world in which his convictions found expression, and refined his character until he was indeed a paradigm of moral rectitude.

Abraham ibn Ezra in his commentary on Exodus 2:3 argues that from the very beginning, Moshe had the makings of a champion of the ethical. Simply by virtue of his noble upbringing, Moshe had access to the moral high-ground:

אולי סבב ה' זה שיגדל משה בבית המלכות להיות נפשו על מדרגה העליונה בדרך הלימוד והרגילות ולא תהיה שפלה ורגילה להיות בבית עבדים. הלא תראה שהרג המצרי בעבור שהוא עשה חמס והושיע בנות מדין מהרועים בעבור שהיו עושים חמס להשקות צאן מהמים שדלו.

---

[7] Ari Z. Zivotovsky describes the effect the four experiences (which occur before Moshe is commissioned at the burning bush) had on his ability to lead. The fourth experience is Moshe's career as shepherd. See his "The Leadership Qualities of Moses," *Judaism* 43 (1994): 258–69.

[8] Op. cit. Nechama Liebowitz.

[9] "*Moshe,*" *Kol Kitvei Ahad ha'Am* (Jerusalem: Dvir, 1947) 244.

ועוד דבר אחר כי אלו היה גדל בין אחיו ויכירוהו מנעוריו לא היו יראים
ממנו כי יחשבוהו כאחד מהם.

> Perhaps God caused Moshe to be reared in the royal house so that his
> soul would be trained to be on an exalted level through education and
> experience, and that it not be lowly and accustomed to be in a house of
> slaves. Indeed, he killed the Egyptian because of his violence, and
> saved the Midianite maidens from the shepherds who did them
> violence, watering their sheep with the water which they [the maidens]
> had drawn. Moreover, if he would have been raised among his
> brethren, so that they would know him from his youth, they would not
> have had reverence for him, considering him one of them.

Ibn Ezra points out that an ethical standard is not all Moshe developed
in the house of Pharaoh, nor was it all he needed to lead his people
effectively. By being raised among nobility, outside of the Hebrew slave
society, the young man earned a degree of respect from his brethren; he
achieved a certain mystique in their eyes and thereby avoided the contempt bred by familiarity.

Ibn Ezra's point, in fact, is reminiscent of a midrashic hypothesis,
found in *Exodus Rabbah* (5.2):

א"ר חמא: בן י"ב שנה נתלש משה רבינו מבית אביו, למה כן? שאילו גידל
בבית אביו ובא ואמר להן לישראל המעשים לא היו מאמינים בו שהיו
אומרים אביו מסרה לו לפי שיוסף מסרה ללוי ולוי לקהת וקהת לעמרם.
ולכך נתלש מבית אביו וכשהלך והגיד לישראל כל הדברים לפיכך האמינו
בו שנאמר ויאמן העם.

> R. Hamma said: Moshe was twelve when he was plucked from his
> father's house. Why so? For were he to have been raised in his fa-
> ther's home and then reported to the people [of God's deliverance],
> they would not have believed him. They would have asserted that he
> was merely quoting from the family tradition, since Joseph transmitted
> it to Levi, who in turn passed it on to Kehat, who in turn passed it to
> Amram, father of Moshe. Therefore he was uprooted from his home,
> so that when he spoke of his mission to the Children of Israel they be-
> lieved him.

Ibn Ezra and the passage in *Exodus Rabbah* both relate to Moshe's
royal upbringing as vital for the leadership role he was to assume. Ibn
Ezra describes the ethical advantage it yielded, as well as the chance for

Moshe to establish credibility in the eyes of the Hebrews. *Exodus Rabbah*, however, adopts a different approach. Israel, under the Egyptian taskmasters, had lost sight of the promise of redemption and only an outsider had a chance of restoring that vision. Perhaps the Israelites, cowed by oppression, had forgotten their inherent privileges as the descendants of Abraham. But Moshe, raised in Pharaoh's house, was uniquely fit to contemplate delivering his enslaved brethren from their servitude. It was the perspective of a free man which enabled him to deliver the slaves from their oppression.[10]

In contrast to Ibn Ezra, Philo of Alexandria, the first-century Jewish philosopher, claims in his biography of Moshe, that Moshe's ethical nature was unexpected. Unlike most ethical people, Moshe achieved his moral stature *despite* the fact that he was raised in the lap of luxury: "Now, most men, if they feel a breath of prosperity ever so small upon them, make much ado of puffing and blowing and boast themselves bigger than meaner men, and miscall them offscourings and nuisances and cumberers of the earth and other such names...."[11] Whether Moshe's morality was achieved despite his upbringing or because of it, the events which forged his character clearly strengthened him to become the model of ethical virtue for the Jewish people throughout his career.

Moshe Emerged

Let us now turn our attention to a closer analysis of the first two formative experiences in the life of young Moshe. The Bible relates:

ויהי בימים ההם ויגדל משה ויצא אל אחיו וירא בסבלתם וירא איש מצרי מכה איש עברי מאחיו. ויפן כה וכה וירא כי אין איש ויך את המצרי ויטמנהו בחול. ויצא ביום השני והנה שני אנשים עברים נצים ויאמר לרשע למה תכה רעך. ויאמר מי שמך לאיש שר ושפט עלינו הלהרגני אתה אמר כאשר הרגת את המצרי וייִרא משה ויאמר אכן נודע הדבר.

---

[10] Ibn Ezra also relates to the difference in mentality between a slave and a free person on a national level in his *Perush ha'Arokh* to Exodus 14:13.

[11] Philo provides an elaborate description of Moshe's upbringing, discussing Moshe's education at length, lauding his natural intellectual and philosophical abilities. See *De Vita Mosis*, F.H. Colson trans. (Harvard University Press, 1935) book I, vol. vi, lines 18–33.

> In those days, Moshe grew up. He went out to his brethren and saw
> their labors. He saw an Egyptian beating a Hebrew, one of his breth-
> ren. He looked around and saw no one, so he struck down the Egyp-
> tian and hid him in the sand. Another day, he went out and behold,
> two Hebrews were fighting, so he said to the offender: "Why do you
> strike your fellow?" He replied: "Who made you master, chief and
> judge over us? Do you plan to kill me, as you killed the Egyptian?"
> Moshe was afraid, thinking: so the deed is known! (Exodus 2:11–14)

The Bible presents these episodes as Moshe's coming of age: "And in those days, Moshe grew up." The mature Moshe displayed moral tenacity in the face of an immoral world.

This strength of character is revealed not only through Moshe's actions in each episode, but also in the transition between the two of them (verse 13): "*vayeitzei bayom hasheini....*" The Bible depicts the two incidents as happening *seriatim*. The most obvious translation of these words is, "He went out the next day."[12] However, "another day," meaning, "some time thereafter" (but not necessarily twenty-four hours later) is a possible reading of the phrase. This sense of the text is preserved in various translations, such as in the poetic, "Moshe sallied forth a second time,"[13] or the more prosaic, "in the second incident."[14]

Indeed, the Rabbis of the midrash favor the idea that some time elapsed between the two incidents. A *drashah* found in *Exodus Rabbah* 1.27 suggests as much: "שתי יציאות יצא אותו צדיק וכתבם הקב"ה זו אחר זו" "This righteous man went out on two occasions and the Holy One, Blessed Be He, recorded them one after another." This text implies that were it not for the juxtaposition, we would not think that these two events were immediately sequential. Thus, the purpose of recording them as having been temporally continuous is not for chronology, but to provide a vehicle to accentuate Moshe's unflinching moral resolve. By presenting

---

[12] This is the translation found in *Tanakh: A New Translation of The Holy Scriptures* (Philadephia: Jewish Publication Society, 1985); U. Cassuto, *Commentary on the Book of Exodus* (Jerusalem: Magnus, 1974); Brevard Childs, *The Book of Exodus* (Philadelphia: Magnus Press, 1974); and Benno Jacob, *The Second Book of the Bible* (NJ: Ktav, 1992).

[13] See Moshe Greenberg's *Understanding Exodus* (NY: Behrman, 1969).

[14] See Nahum Sarna's *Exploring Exodus* (NY: Schocken, 1986).

the events as consecutive, the narrative generates dramatic power, bringing Moshe's indignation and outrage into sharper focus. We are forced to
note that despite the turn of events of "day one," Moshe persists in his
sorties from the palace. His persistence shows that his behavior is not a
rash emotional response to a chance encounter, but is in direct compliance
with his convictions.

The Italian exegete, Yitzhak Shmuel Reggio (1784–1855), recognizes
the same ethical valor that the Rabbis perceive, but claims that two
consecutive days are described. On the very next day, Moshe went out:

ביום השני. כי כל כך היה אוהב את אחיו שלא יכול למנוע עצמו מלצאת
אליהם יום יום. אלא שלא האריך זאת ימים רבים כי הוכרח לברוח.

> As he loved his brethren so intensely that he could not prevent himself
> from going out to them day after day, though this did not last long, as
> he was compelled to flee.[15]

From Reggio's first comment we are to understand Moshe's powerful
affinity for his brethren which was a daily motivating force. Yet in
commenting on verse thirteen, he adds:

שני אנשים עברים. להגיד בשבחו של משה שלא הרג תמול את המצרי
בעבור היותו מצרי ולפי שנפשו קשורה בנפש אחיו אלא להציל את העשוק
מיד עושקו. והראיה כי ביום השני גער באיש אחד שעורר מדנים את רעהו
ואע״פ שהיו שניהם עברים והיה ראוי לחמול על המעול בהיותו מאחיו.

> *Two Hebrews.* [This is mentioned] in praise of Moshe, and to indicate
> that he did not kill the Egyptian the previous day because he was
> Egyptian and because his soul was intertwined with that of his breth-
> ren, but rather to save the oppressed from the oppressor. The proof is
> that on the second day, he castigated the man who threatened his fel-
> low, though they were both Hebrews, while he should have had com-
> passion upon the victim insofar as he was his brother.

The reader might have expected Moshe to save the Hebrew on the second day as well. After all, the same scenario presents itself: a Hebrew is
being beaten. Yet from Reggio's perspective, the words of the Bible
imply that he sought to correct the ills of society. There was a principle at

---

[15] Y.S. Reggio, *Commentary on the Pentateuch* [Heb.] (Vienna, 1821), Exodus 2:11.

stake—not only the life of a Hebrew. Moshe put himself out on a limb for the sake of justice.[16] A similar view is implicit in Ramban's commentary, written many centuries earlier. He describes Moshe's irrepressible sense of righteous indignation: "And he saw their sufferings and toils and could not tolerate it, and therefore he killed the Egyptian smiting the slave...." Thus Moshe possesses not only a philosophical and intellectual commitment to justice, but indeed an emotional, instinctive sense. Not even the gratitude and appreciation which he surely felt for his adoptive family could quell his indignation.[17] Furthermore, the nineteenth-century commentator, R. Meir Leibush Malbim, contends that it is precisely this innate willingness, or even need, to extend one's self for the sake of justice which is a prerequisite for "one who is worthy of leading the people."[18]

The narrative does more than illustrate Moshe's unwavering moral resolve; it presents us with the unfolding process of its development. R. Yitzhak Arama suggests that each incident in this section enhanced a different dimension of Moshe's character, and that each event constituted a rung on the moral-religious ladder which Moshe ascended, culminating in his achieving the status of leader.[19] On the first day out, Moshe was outraged at the plight of the victimized Hebrew and gave violent expression to his indignation. On the second day, he acted as a judge "applying the lash of justice to the assailant who had lifted his hand against his friend."[20] And the third episode, at the Midianite well, catalyzed Moshe's ability to come to the aid of the oppressed.

---

[16] The Rabbis introduced the phrase "Moshe put himself out on a limb" (נתן נפשו על) in a number of salient midrashic passages which describe the degree to which Moshe was outstanding in his dedication. For an in-depth analysis, see Avigdor Shinan, "*Bein Kiddush Hashem leMitat Beit Din: Amadot Shonot beSifrut haYehudit haKedumah Kelapei Sippur Mosheh vehaMitzri,*" *Sefer Kedushat haHayyim veHiruf haNefesh* (Jerusalem, 1993) 55–68.

[17] See Philo, *De Vita Mosis* I:33–40.

[18] See Malbim on Exodus 2:13.

[19] See also *Yefeh To'ar,* commentary to *Exodus Rabbah* 1.27, where R. Shmuel Ashkenazi suggests that the incidents demonstrate a progressive development in Moshe's moral and religious life.

[20] *Akeidat Yitzhak,* Introduction to the Book of Exodus, *Sha'ar* 34. Arama also makes reference to these ideas in his commentary, *Sha'ar* 34.

As Arama paints the picture, the ethical attributes these encounters illustrate also stood Moshe in good stead afterwards—in the national responsibilities he came to bear.[21] His moral outrage was utilized when the Egyptians were punished through the Plagues; his intolerance of injustice pushed him to deliver the slaves from their oppressors; and his compassion for the people brought him to teach God's Torah of righteousness to the Children of Israel. Furthermore, Moshe's ethical sensibilities are understood to be in perfect consonance with those of the Divine. God phrased His resolve to redeem the Israelites in terms which parallel Moshe's actions. And so, the prophet Moshe is seen as God's ideal agent on earth.[22]

These explanations of Moshe's behavior elevate the story from its dramatic, literary framework to the loftier moral-religious plane. The external tension reflects Moshe's internal development, until he is forced to flee Egypt, in both the literal and figurative senses.

Indeed, these encounters serve to introduce Moshe to the real world in which his moral convictions will find expression. They represent a series

---

[21] Maimonides presents these developments as the ethical prerequisites to prophecy. See *Guide of the Perplexed* II.45, cf. *Makor Hayyim*, R. Shmuel Zarzah ibn Seneh, Exodus 2:10 and Reggio op. cit. Exodus 2:13 and Genesis 15:1.

[22]

והיה ספור אלו העניינים הנכבדים אשר באו לידו להודיע לבעלי לב כי מצא האלקים איש כלבבו לעשות את המעשים האלה עצמם על ידי ההשגחה הא-להית אם לעשות משפטים במצרים הרודים בעמו ובנחלתו בפרך והמכים אותם בכל מכה ואם להושיע עם עני ואביון משופטי נפשו. ואם לתת להם תורה ומצות בה יתנהגו על היושר הא-לוהי בכל ענייניהם ומי כמוהו ראוי לכל המעשים האלה זולתו. והוא מה שא"ל השי"י ראה ראיתי את עני עמי אשר במצרים ואת צעקתם שמעתי מפני נגשיו כי ידעתי את מכאביו. ועתה לך ואשלחך אל פרעה והוצא את עמי וכו'.

The recounting of these significant events which occurred to him is intended to inform the wise that God found a man after His own heart, who could act in this fashion when Providence so required. This could be to punish the Egyptians who oppressed and struck down his nation, or to deliver the poor people from those who mete out punishments to them, or to give them the Torah and commandments through which they will behave according to divine rectitude in all their affairs. And who was more worthy in all of these matters than he. And it is this which God told him, "I have marked well the plight of my people in Egypt and have heeded their outcry because of their taskmasters; yes, I am mindful of their sufferings." "Come, therefore, I will send you to Pharaoh and you shall free My people, the Israelites, from Egypt."

of transitions which prepare him for the struggles he will face and transform him from being a moral individual into a leader. In the first incident, Moshe confronted the harsh reality of the Egyptian establishment and divorced himself from his illustrious upbringing. In the second, he discovered the dubious character of the Hebrews. He had assumed them to be innocent victims, but through this initial contact with them, he learned of their impudence and ingratitude, traits with which he was to become all too familiar through forty years of guiding them through the desert. From the outset, he was given a taste of what his leadership would demand, and so was forced to progress from theorist to pragmatist.

Again, the text provides a window of insight into the formative nature of these experiences in the life of Moshe. "It came to pass in those days, Moshe grew up." The events that catalyzed Moshe's ethical coming of age follow immediately upon the verse recounting that Moshe was brought to Pharaoh's daughter after being weaned. Obviously, considerable time had elapsed, for Moshe was no longer a little boy. Of course, the text does tell us outright that Moshe "grew up." Initially, we may understand this detail to mean that we should view him as an adult.[23] But "Moshe grew up" can also be understood to be the focus of that which follows. Thus, "In those days, Moshe grew up," can be interpreted not only as a preliminary factual detail for the scene (he is no longer a child), but more as a descriptive heading for the events to come—as the experiences presented here play a role in Moshe's spiritual development. Through these experiences, he ascends the moral-religious ladder of leadership.

---

[23] *Exodus Rabbah* 1.27 suggests that just as the previous verse indicates Moshe's chronological age, so too does this "*vaYigdal Moshe*":

ויגדל משה בן עשרים שנה היה משה באות השעה ויש אומרים בן ארבעים.

The implication, of course, is that he has reached adulthood, but whether he is twenty or forty, the Torah does not specify. Implicit in the different views of his age are different takes on his conduct: age twenty implies impetuous behavior; age forty, reasoned, planned action. See also *Avot* 5:21. For the wide range of possible ages, see Menachem Kasher, *Torah Shelemah* 72–74 [81] and Avigdor Shinan, *Exodus Rabbah* 1.27, note 84.

Active Intervention

What do we gain from being told, "It came to pass in those days"?[24] Perhaps this phrase reminds us of the world outside the palace. We recall that Moshe grew up in the context of Hebrew suffering and enslavement. Though he himself was sheltered in the palace from the terrible circumstances described in the first chapter of Exodus, his kinsmen groaned under oppression during his formative years. Their plight looms as a cloud of destiny over Moshe as he reaches manhood.

Consonant with this approach, *Midrash Lekah Tov* (Exodus 2:7) identifies Moshe's awareness of his environment in our verse:

ויהי בימים ההם ויגדל משה ויצא... שהרי משה רבינו אע״פ שהיה
בפלטין של פרעה, הלך לראות בסבלותן של ישראל, היינו דתנן הלל אומר
אל תפרוש מן הצבור, שלא יהיה אדם רואה צבור בצער ויאמר אלך
לביתי, ואוכל ואשתה, ושלום עלי נפשי, אלא יהא נושא בעול עם חבריו.

> In those days, Moshe grew and went out…. Although Moshe was in Pharaoh's court, he went to witness the sufferings of Israel. This is what Hillel taught: "Don't separate yourself from the community" (*Avot* 2:4). One should not see the community in pain and say to himself, "I'll go home, eat, drink and [enjoy] peace unto my soul." Rather, he should share the burden of others.

Other midrashic texts suggest that the same words focus attention upon Moshe's life in the palace. That is, it came to pass in those days when Moshe was in Pharaoh's palace that he grew up. Placing Moshe in a royal setting is crucial both to the narrative and to our sense of the young man: it grants Moshe the power and position to take the law into his own hands, and it highlights the risk of absolutely everything in his pursuit of justice.

The significance of Moshe's royal upbringing is noted by two *midrashim* which illuminate the circumstances that led to him meeting his brethren. They both depict his interaction with the slaves as the direct outgrowth of an official appointment—one of them interpreting the word "*vayigdal*" to mean "appointing," which is to say, growth in stature. The

---

[24] Alternatively, Yosef ibn Kaspi, in *Mishneh Kesef* (Krakow, 1900), suggests that "those days" refers to a broader previous time frame. Cf. Amos Hakham, in his *Da'at Mikra* commentary to Exodus 2:11, 23, note 14.

first *drashah* presents Moshe's clever planning which made his presence in the field possible:

אמר לו פרעה רוצה ולא רוצה בן בתי אתה, כל פרוקופי שאתה מבקש
אמור ואני נותן לך. אמר לו משה מבקש אני ממך להיעשות על ארגון
שלך. ומשה נתכוון לראות בשעבודן של ישראל לפיכך ויגדל משה.
(תנחומא ב׳ וארא 17, דף טז עמ׳ ב׳ הערה 151)

> Pharaoh said to [Moshe], "Whether I will it or not, you are my daughter's son. Name any distinction you desire and I shall award it to you." Moshe said to him, "I request of you to be in charge of your labors." But Moshe's intent was to look into the enslavement of Israel; therefore, [it says], "*vayigdal Moshe*."
> (*Tanhuma Va'era*, Buber ed. 17, p. 16b, n. 151)

Pharaoh was reluctantly obliged to assign his daughter's son a respectable appointment. Moshe used this sense of obligation to his advantage and negotiated for a position designed to aid his brethren. His intent is transparent to the reader, but presumably Pharaoh was left in the dark. The conclusion, "and Moshe grew," attests to Moshe's increased political stature. In the eyes of the reader, however, his political savvy has increased as well.[25]

The second *midrash* elaborates, depicting Moshe as actively seeking to alleviate the suffering of the Hebrews—made possible only because of Moshe's presence in the palace:

---

[25] The initial passage upon which this text is predicated served as the basis for Rashi's comment on verse 11. An additional midrashic text which assigns Moshe an official role in Pharaoh's court can be found in *Ecclesiastes Rabbah* 9.14:

וגם לא לחכמים לחם, זה משה אתמול עביד קומיס קלטור בפלטין של פרעה שנאמר
(שמות ב:יא) ויגדל משה ויצא אל אחיו. מהו ויגדל שהיתה גדולתו להכניס ולהוציא,
והיום קראן לו ויאכל לחם יוונים. (שמות ב:כ)

> "And the wise are not guaranteed bread." That is Moshe. Yesterday he was made *Comes Calator* (officer arranging royal receptions) in Pharaoh's palace, as it says, "And Moshe became great and went out to his brethren." What is the meaning of *vayigdal*? His greatness is that he was an attendant of magistrates and today, "Call him that he may eat bread" (Yitro says to his daughters to have pity upon this stranger). Cf. A.A. Halevi, *Parshiot be'Aggadah* (Tel Aviv: Haifa University, 1973) 173, note 1.

ד"א וירא בסבלותם ראה שאין להן מנוחה הלך ואמר לפרעה מי שיש לו
עבד אם אינו נח יום אחד בשבוע הוא מת. ואלו עבדיך אם אין אתה מניח
להם יום אחד בשבוע הם מתים. א"יל לך ועשה להן כמו שתאמר הלך
משה ותקן להם את יום השבת לנוח. (שמות רבה א.לב)

> "He looked upon their labors"—[Moshe] saw that they had no rest. He
> went and told Pharaoh, "If one who has a slave does not allow him to
> rest one day of the week, [the slave] will die. These are your slaves
> and if you do not allow them to rest one day of the week, they will
> die." [Pharaoh] said to him, "Go and do for them as you say." Moshe
> proceeded to establish the Sabbath day for them to rest.
> (*Exodus Rabbah* 1.32)

Here, too, Moshe is credited with strategic thinking. He presented his
case as an industrial psychologist would, suggesting that Pharaoh could
derive maximum effectiveness from his workers by giving them a day off.
Needless to say, Pharaoh approved of the idea. But Moshe is presented
here not as a shrewd Egyptian businessman, but as a religious personage.[26] Surely the Rabbis of the *midrashim* were pleased to reveal that
Moshe had an intuitive understanding of the need for Shabbat long before
he undertook his formal role as spiritual leader of the people of Israel.[27]

---

[26] Rabbinic emphasis on his inherent religiosity is found also in *midrashim* which
describe Moshe's knowledge of the ineffable name of God long before the encounter
at the burning bush (*Exodus Rabbah* 1.29, 30). In contrast, the biblical narrative itself
suggests that Moshe is not religiously knowledgeable. He asks God's name at the
burning bush, reacts intuitively by hiding his face, and does not know to remove his
shoes when standing on hallowed ground. The biblical text portrays a developmental
process in which Moshe matures ethically and then moves from the ethical to the
religious. In the midrashic perception, Moshe undergoes no such transition; he is a
religious personage from the outset, as is attested in his knowledge of the ineffable
Name and his institution of Shabbat, and so on. Midrashic assertion of religiosity is
also found in the portrait of Bitya, daughter of Pharaoh. The noble humanitarianism
she demonstrates by saving the infant Moshe is attributed by a midrash to her
religious convictions. She is depicted as having renounced paganism even prior to
finding the baby. See *Exodus Rabbah* 1.23.

[27] This interpretive move is not without linguistic basis. In Exodus 5:5 we find:
"ויאמר פרעה הן רבים עתה עם הארץ והשבתם אתם מסבלתם" (שמות ה:ה). And Pharaoh
continued, "The people of the land are already so numerous and you would have
them cease from their labors?" The juxtaposition of the words *sivlot* and *Shabbat* is
what allows the midrash to introduce Shabbat as the antidote to suffering, necessarily
provided by Moshe, the one who "saw their suffering." See also Kalman Spektor,
Iyyunim be'Aggadah (Tel Aviv: Shahaf, 1964) 79.

Both of these *midrashim* interpret the introductory phrase of the verse as setting the stage for Moshe. As a court appointee, he was able to wield royal clout. Of course, this approach places Moshe's killing of the Egyptian in an altogether different light. Only after he had exhausted all of the official channels and procedures with which he was quite familiar, did he take matters into his own hands. Moshe's act of killing, then, is presented less as impetuous and more as the immediate demonstration of a deep-seated concern which has been long before expressed.[28] This episode, however, is only the first of the triad which constitutes Moshe's ethical coming of age. His indignation at the treatment of his brethren was long-lived, but only by taking action was Moshe able to take his first steps in developing his ethical intuition. It is the deed itself which transforms.

Search For Identity

Moshe "goes out to his brethren." The biblical usage of "brethren" reveals Moshe's self-image: he is a Hebrew in his own eyes. Indeed, he sees "an Egyptian striking a Hebrew, one of his brethren." We would have assumed him to perceive the Egyptian as kin, yet the Bible informs us otherwise. Despite the long years in the palace, Moshe has not lost his fraternal association with the Israelite nation. But how was this connection preserved? Did Pharaoh's daughter, or someone else in the court reveal Moshe's origins to him? Did he maintain some connection with his family after he was brought to the palace? Did he retain some irrepressible memory of early childhood which even the grandeur of being an Egyptian prince could not erase? Scripture does not say. From the Bible itself, we are left to imagine that family ties with the House of Levi ended at the age of two or three, when he was weaned from his mother, Yocheved. Still, his earliest memories may have been from that time, and it is safe to assume that he retained some sense of familial identity.[29] After all, none

---

[28] Perhaps this approach supports the idea that he is forty at this time, his action being the result of mature consideration.

[29] See Devora Steinmetz, "A Portrait of Miriam in Rabbinic Midrash," *Prooftexts* 8 (1988): 41. Cf. *Exodus Rabbah* 3.1 which portrays God as communicating with Moshe, through his father's voice. Ordinarily, this midrash is understood to convey God's desire to not frighten Moshe, but implicit in it is the familiarity of the voice to Moshe.

other than God acknowledges Moshe's awareness of his family, in pro-
posing the assistance of Aharon, "your brother," to help deliver the Jewish
people (Exodus 4:14).[30]

Despite this divine testimony, Ramban implies that at this primary
venturing-out, Moshe did *not* recall his origins himself. Rather, he went
out in search of his brethren, "…because they told him that he was Jewish
and he desired to see them [the Israelites] since they were his brethren"
(Exodus 2:11). *Sefer haYashar* depicts "the boy [who] yearned for his
father and mother, '*vayitav el aviv ve'imo.*'"[31] This overpowering urge of
an adopted child to find his birth family provided the psychological
motivation which propelled Moshe to leave the sheltered environment of
the palace and seek out the Hebrews.[32]

We can, however, interpret the repetition of "brethren" differently,
recognizing that Moshe may well have considered himself to be a
full-fledged Egyptian. Ibn Ezra adopts this approach in his commentary
on this verse:

ויצא אל אחיו המצרים, כי בארמון המלך היה וטעם מאחיו, אחר הזכיר
עברי ממשפחתו, (בראשית יג:ח) "כמו אנשים אחים אנחנו."

> And he went out to his brethren—the Egyptians, as he was in the pal-
> ace of the king. The meaning of *mei'ehav*—his brethren [second ap-
> pearance] after mentioning *ivri*—connotes "brethren" [in the broad
> sense] [as in Genesis 13:8] "for we are brethren."[33]

---

[30] Philo also claims that Moshe was aware of his origins and his biological parents
(VII.31–37). *Jubilees* 47:9 maintains that Amram taught his son to write, indicating a
relationship extending beyond the age of weaning, and *Exodus Rabbah* 5.2 places
Moshe in his father's house until the age of twelve.

[31] Yosef Dan ed., *Sefer haYashar* (Jerusalem: Mossad Bialik, 1986) 292. Cf. *Divrei
haYamim shel Moshe Rabbenu*, in *Beit Hamidrash of Aaron Jellinik* (Jerusalem:
Bamberger et Warhman, 1998) 4.

[32] For an extensive discussion of Moshe as an adopted child, see Caroline Peyser's
essay in this volume.

[33] Ibn Ezra defines אחיו as brethren in the broader sense, pointing out that it was not
his blood brother, Aharon, whom Moshe approached. In a similar vein, in his short
commentary to Exodus 2:4, Ibn Ezra claims that אחותו, his sister, is not Miriam, but
a sister in a broader sense "יתכן היותה אחת ממשפחתו"—"it is likely that she was a
member of his [extended] family." In contrast, *Pirkei deRabbi Eliezer* 48 takes the
term quite literally:

That is: one day, Moshe went out among his Egyptian brethren to survey their public works. Logic dictates that he should identify with the Egyptians; after all, he was raised in the palace—and so, the first appearance of the word "brethren" refers to them. Then, when he sees one of his "kin" striking a Hebrew, his perception shifts. Now it is the Hebrew who is "of his brethren" ("*ish ivri mei'ehav*" indicates Hebrew brethren necessarily, removing the ambiguity found in the first incident). It would seem that the cruel act encourages Moshe to renounce his identification with the ruling ethnic majority, in order to champion the cause of the enslaved.[34] Would this transformation have occurred had Moshe not already been torn

---

ויצא משה במחנה וראה מצרי שהכה אחד מבני קהתי שהיה משבט לוי שנאי וירא
איש מצרי מכה איש עברי מאחיו.

[34] Ibn Ezra's supercommentaries were disturbed by the idea that Moshe once identified with the Egyptians. Yitzhak Shrem, in his supercommentary, *Be'er Yitzhak*, contends:

...ויש גירסא אחרת **העברים** במקום מלת המצרים.

Similarly, Samuel Zarah ibn Sneh, in his supercommentary, *Makor Hayyim*, explains:

המצרים כי בארמון המלך היה. ר"ל אחיו היהודים הדרים במצרים וקראם מצריים
לפי שהיו דרים במצרים.

It is clear that these comments influenced Yehudah Krinsky in his commentary *Mehokekei Yehudah* (Bnei Brak, 1971):

ויצא אל אחיו היהודים הדרים במצרים וקראם מצרים לפי שהיו דרים במצרים ויש
גורסים **העברים** והרדיי"א יפרש דעת החכם ז"ל שקורא למצרים אחיו וגו'.

To ascertain whether or not Ibn Ezra really intended to call the Egyptians Moshe's brothers, one must examine the manuscripts of his commentary. Preliminary findings disclose that the prevalent reading is indeed as cited above:

ויצא אל אחיו **המצרים** כי בארמון המלך היה וטעם מאחיו אחר הזכיר עברי
ממשפחתו כמו אנשים אחים.

This is the case in Oxford Bodlean 216, 223, Florence 11/3 and St. Petersburg IV 206. The point of view expressed in the supercommentaries may be reflected in the manuscript version of Moscow 1656 and Oxford Bodlean 214 where the word "המצרים" is missing, yielding the unclear reading of the comment: "ויהי אל אחיו כי בארמון המלך היה..." or Oxford Bodlean 238 which reads:

ויצא אל אחיו **המצרים** כי בארמון המלך היה וכוי ופי' אל תחמה איך יהיה ויצא
במצרים שהרי לא היו עבדים רק ברעמסס א"כ מי נתן למשה במצרים שיצא
מהארמון.

Although it is unclear that further investigation is necessary to sort out the relationship between manuscripts, these initial findings prefer the original intention of Ibn Ezra's comment that Moshe, did in fact, go out to his **Egyptian** brethren.

by doubts? Perhaps. But as a witness to violence, to the absolute corruption by absolute power, his moral sense was outraged. He was left with no choice but to shake off the bonds of upbringing and convention, and act boldly. As he killed the Egyptian assailant, Moshe killed the Egyptian within himself. From this point onward, it is the Hebrews who will be his brethren.

Ibn Ezra's comment, on which my reading is grounded, is characteristically terse and obscure, and he himself may not have read such a radical interpretation into the verse. Nevertheless, Ibn Ezra had solid analytic and grammatical reasons for recommending this unconventional approach. He interprets the rest of the verse so that it is consonant with this perspective: "וירא בסבלותם" *vayar besivlotam* is not to be understood as object genitive—the sufferings *endured* by the Hebrews—but must be read as subject genitive—the sufferings *imposed* by the Egyptians.

This phrase carries intense literary impact, for it highlights the complex dynamics of Moshe's personal identity, through which Moshe the Egyptian was transformed into Moshe the Hebrew. Simply translated, the phrase means, "he witnessed their labors." Yet in that case we should expect the verse to read, "*vayar et sivlotam.*" "*Vayar besivlotam*" is a bit puzzling—which may make more sense in light of other biblical instances of "*vayar be....*" In Genesis 29:32 and I Samuel 1:11, the phrase is used to imply sympathy. The text may therefore be emphasizing Moshe's love and compassion for his Hebrew brothers. Similarly, the midrash recognizes Moshe's deep compassion and empathy:

וירא בסבלותם מהו וירא שהיה רואה בסבלותם ובוכה, ואומר חבל לי
עליכם מי יתן מותי עליכם. שאין לך מלאכה קשה ממלאכת הטיט. והיה
נותן כתפיו ומסייע לכל אחד ואחד מהן. ר"א בנו של ריה"ג אומר ראה
ומשוי אשה על איש ומשוי אשה על איש. משוי זקן על בחור ומשוי בחור
על זקן. והיה מניח דרגון שלו והולך ומיישב להן סבלותיהם ועושה כאילו
מסייע לפרעה.

"He saw their labors"—What is meant by "he saw"? That he would see their labors and cry and say: "I feel for you; would that someone would allow me to die for you, for there is no more difficult labor than work with mortar." And he would lend his shoulder and aid each and every one of them. R. Eleazar ben R. Yossi the Galilean said: He saw the burden of the large on the small and the burden of the small on the large; the burden of the man on the woman and [that of] the woman on the man; the burden of the elderly on the young and [that of]…the young on the elderly—and he would put aside his staff and help them to rearrange their burdens, [though] making it appear that he was helping Pharaoh. (*Exodus Rabbah* 1.28)

Here, once again, the Rabbis of the midrash portray Moshe as demonstrating strategic care. Not surprisingly, we see Moshe spurred to action by the travesty of the distorted justice to which he was a witness. The midrash first presents Moshe as reacting to the severity of the oppression, to the hardship of the demanding physical labor (שאין לך מלאכה קשה ממלאכת הטיט). The second interpretation offered is that he acknowledged the inappropriateness of their labors. Moshe was not only witness to the men, women, old and young slaving beyond their capacities. He also perceived that slavery was far more than blood, sweat and tears. The ultimate harm is found not in the physical privations, but in the psychological ones. By stripping the slaves of their identities, the oppressors irreparably broke the slaves' morale. They abused the laborers psychologically and emotionally, and in so doing, committed a crime against human dignity. Thus do we encounter the humiliating and debilitating offense of role reversal—as well as the Rabbis' sensitivity to it.[35] Moreover, Moshe's understanding of the face of oppression shows him to possess not only a sense of justice but sincere compassion as well.[36]

Justified

How is it that the spiritual giant who comes to lead the Jewish people out of servitude embarks on his career with an act of murder? The Rabbis of the midrash found this behavior disturbingly discordant, and apply all of their interpretative powers to legitimate the deed and remove the onus of

---

[35] See Menachem Kasher, *Torah Shelemah* on Exodus 1:14, note 147 and also Zivotofsky, ibid., 263–64.

[36] The Rabbis of the midrash emphasize the rare combination of compassion and justice in Moshe's character on two other occasions. *Exodus Rabbah* 1.32 describes Moshe's coming to the aid of the daughters of Yitro, not simply out of pity, but out of concern for justice. Similarly, *Exodus Rabbah* 2.2–3 claims that Moshe's tending to Yitro's sheep is a prelude to Moshe's commissioning to lead the Jewish people— precisely because of the compassion and justice demanded of the shepherd.

imprudence and guilt from Moshe. Their task is a difficult one, but since the text itself does not flesh out the circumstances of the murder, the possibilities for explication are open. "And he saw an Egyptian smiting a Hebrew of his brothers," records the Bible. But where are the details? Who was the Egyptian? Who was the Hebrew? What was Moshe thinking as the events transpired? What caused him to resort to violence? What manner of weapon did he use? Almost predictably, the overriding consensus is that Moshe demonstrated courage and righteousness: the "dastardly deed" was, in fact, an act of saintly heroism.

The following passage from *Exodus Rabbah* 1.28 goes to great lengths to fill in all the details absent from the biblical text, in the effort to paint a morally palatable portrait of Moshe:

אמרו רז״ל נוגשים היו מן המצרים ושוטרים מישראל נוגש ממונה על עשרה שוטרים שוטר ממונה על עשרה מישראל והיו הנוגשים הולכים לבתי השוטרים בהשכמה להוציאן למלאכתן לקריאת הגבר. פעם אחת הלך נוגש מצרי אצל שוטר ישראל ונתן עיניו באשתו שהיתה יפת תואר בלי מום. עמד לשעת קריאת הגבר והוציאו מביתו וחזר המצרי ובא על אשתו והיתה סבורה שהוא בעלה ונתעברה ממנו. חזר בעלה ומצא המצרי יוצא מביתו שאל אותה שמא נגע בך אמרה לו הן וסבורה אני שאתה הוא. כיון שידע הנוגש שהרגיש בו החזירו לעבודת הפרך והיה מכה אותו ומבקש להרגו. והיה משה רואה אותו ומביט בו וראה ברוח הקודש מה שעשה בבית וראה מה שעתיד לעשות לו בשדה אמר ודאי זה חייב מיתה. כמו שכתוב (ויקרא כד) ומכה אדם יומת ולא עוד אלא דכתיב ויפן כה וכה וגו׳ ראה מה עשה לו בבית ומה עשה לו בשדה. שבא על אשתו של דתן על כך חייב הריגה שנא׳ מות יומת הנואף והנואפת והיינו דכתיב ויפן כה וכה וגוי ראה מה עשה לו בבית ומה עשה לו בשדה.

"And he saw an Egyptian"—what was it he saw?.... There were Egyptian overseers and Hebrew officers. One overseer was in charge of ten officers and one officer was in charge of ten Israelites. The overseers would go to the officers' homes at the crack of dawn to awaken them to work when the cock crowed. Once an Egyptian overseer went to the home of an Israelite officer and became enamored of his wife, who was perfectly beautiful. At the crack of dawn, he hurried the officer out of his house. The Egyptian then returned to the house and lay with the wife, who assumed he was her husband and conceived. Her husband returned and seeing the Egyptian leaving, asked, "Did he touch you?" to which she replied, "Yes, but I thought he was you." When the Egyptian realized the Hebrew was on to him, he sent him back to hard labor and beat him in an effort to kill him. Moshe witnessed this and saw, by means of divine inspiration, what the Egyptian had done in the home and what he was intending to do in the field. He said, "Assuredly, he deserves death, as it says, 'He who beats a man must die' (Leviticus 24:17). Moreover, he lay with the wife of Dathan. For that too, he deserves to die, as it says, 'Death to the adulterer and death to the adulteress.'" For that reason, [the text records] "He looked this way and that"—Moshe saw what had been done to him in the home and in the field.

We are asked to direct our attention to the evil character of the Egyptian in question. This is no commonplace beating such as any overseer might inflict. Rather, the Egyptian himself is plotting murder. Surely Moshe is not only justified, but obligated to save the Hebrew from this plight. Moreover, this is no standard aggravated assault and battery; the midrash introduces a sexual felony as well.[37] With such insult piled upon injury, Moshe could not help but take the law into his own hands. And if we harbored any doubts as to the legitimacy of his action, we are informed that divine inspiration provided Moshe with a glimpse into the future as well as to the past.[38] He was able to establish, with certainty, the Egyptian's criminal record. Moshe merely struck one who was deserving of death on many counts.[39]

---

[37] By adding the sexual crime, the midrash escalates the perpetrator's wrongdoing and glorifies Moshe's reaction. See also the midrashic embellishment to the story of the shepherdesses (*Exodus Rabbah* 1.32) and the sexual favors the Rabbis add to the demand Pharaoh makes of the midwives (ibid., 1.12). The women are thus presented as even more exalted in the eyes of the reader. This may be the first instance, at least according to this midrashic interpretation, of sexual harassment on the job, though a student of mine once suggested that Joseph in the house of Potiphar's wife may have that honor. Another student, Zahava Safran, explained that the rabbinic addition to the narrative conveys a complete picture of moral integrity. That is, the women withstood the test of each of the three cardinal sins: murder, idolatry and illicit sexual relations. The Bible itself records that they refused to shed the blood of the babies and they feared the Lord. Only sexual propriety is not acknowledged, and so the Rabbis filled in this detail thereby providing the third element in their standard of moral perfection.

[38] Other *midrashim* have Moshe consult the heavenly angels before striking the Egyptian (ibid., 1.29 and *Midrash Avkir* 33).

[39] For a general discussion of the different opinions offered in *Exodus Rabbah*, see Avigdor Shinan, "*Bein Kiddush Hashem leMitat Beit Din: Amadot Shonot beSifrut*

With justice on his side and concern for his brethren in his heart, Moshe therefore looked "both ways" to determine that the coast was clear. This careful surveying may signal caution, or mere nervousness. Or, with the rabbinic insight provided by *Exodus Rabbah*, we may understand that he assessed the guilt of the assailant from all vantage points. Next we are told that he "saw no man about." Given that Moshe had just cased the scene, this phrase is apparently extraneous, and therefore can be used to further vindicate the behavior of our hero. "No man about"? Then, surely, the man present, the Egyptian, does not count for a thing, an indication that he is doomed—as good as dead already. Alternatively: no other man was present to champion the cause of God and exact justice from the overseer. Or, perhaps no man was able to utter the ineffable Name to kill the Egyptian. Or even: no future righteous person was to be born of this Egyptian, who may have justified Moshe having mercy[40] in the fields. According to the midrash, having considered all these angles and having exhausted even the remote possibilities of acting otherwise, Moshe struck the fatal blow. *"Bemakom she'ein ish"*[41]—with no other man present, Moshe was compelled to fulfill the task demanded of him.

Both R. Naftali Tzvi Yehudah Berlin ("Netziv") and R. Yaakov Tzvi Meklenburg (*haKetav vehaKabbalah*) regard this phrase as highlighting the catalyst which compelled Moshe to shift from idealism to realism.[42] Netziv treats "no man present" as painful social commentary: "...there was no man to whom to report the travesty, for they were all a band of infidels and haters of Israel...."[43] Moshe had no recourse to a system of

---

haYehudit haKedumah Kelapei Sippur Moshe vehaMitzri," Sefer Kedushat haHayyim veHiruf haNefesh (Jerusalem, 1993) 60–62. See also A.A. Halevi, *Parshiot be'Aggadah*, 176, note 18. For a discussion of the midrashic treatment of this incident, see Reuven Kimelman, "Torah Against Terror: Does Jewish Law Sanction the Vengeance of Modern Day Zealots?" *BBIJM* 99.2 (1984): 16–22. (This article also appeared in Hebrew in *Gesher* 31, 1985, 76–81). For a recent discussion of the moral questions involved in this action see Avi Sagi, "He Slew the Egyptian and Hid Him in the Sand: Jewish Tradition and the Moral Element" *HUCA* 67 (1996): 55–76.

[40] All of these interpretations are from *Exodus Rabbah* 1.29.

[41] *Avot* 2:5.

[42] Cf. Nechama Leibowitz, *Studies in Shemot* (Jerusalem, 1970) 38.

[43] וירא כי אין איש להגיד לפניו את העול כי כולם עצרת בוגדים ושונאי ישראל ויך את המצרי, במקום שאין אנשים השתדל להיות איש (העמק דבר שמות ב:יא).

justice; the entire Egyptian establishment is dismissed as a politicized machine. This individual crime disclosed to Moshe a whole society which was morally bankrupt and rife with corruption.[44] And so, he is rudely awakened to the need to break with his Egyptian past. In killing the overseer, he renounces his affiliation with the kingdom and all that it symbolizes.

If Netziv sees "no man present" as reflecting a lack of Egyptian presence, Meklenburg finds no Israelite to fill the role. "Moshe thought that one of his Hebrew brethren standing nearby would rise up against the Egyptian and save his brother who was being beaten to death.... None were manly enough and none...cared enough about his brother's suffering to try to save him."[45] Mecklenburg, too, suggests a different kind of harsh surprise for Moshe: the apathy born of years of slavery. Moshe was shocked by the slave mentality (from which he himself had been spared, as a result of his privileged upbringing) that rendered the oppressed Hebrews incapable of helping each other. It was an important rite of initiation for him as well. It reflected his advantage as "outsider," and informed him of the Israelite need for reeducation. They must learn to love their neighbors, but first they must learn to love themselves. That task proved to be one of the most challenging of Moshe's illustrious career as lawgiver and rehabilitator of the people of Israel. Thus was Moshe introduced to his own new reality, one in which he could not trust the establishment in which he was raised, nor could he take refuge in his own idealism. Rather, he had to act autonomously.

And so: "He struck the Egyptian and buried him in the sand." Again, the midrashic interpreters maneuver in the silence of the text to discern Moshe's true intentions—by investigating the murder weapon.

---

[44] Netziv's struggles with the Russian authorities of his own day are well known. The cynicism for the establishment which he attributes to Moshe may, indeed, reflect his own experiences. See Jacob J. Schachter, "Haskalah, Secular Studies and the Close of the Yeshiva in Volozhin in 1892," *The Torah U'Madda Journal* 2 (NY: Yeshiva University, 1990): 76ff.

[45] ״חשב משה שאחד מהעברײם העומדים סביבו יתקומס על המצרי ויציל את אחיו המוכה מכת מות ראה שאין בניהם גבר שבגוברין ואין מהם שם על לב צרת אחיו להשתדל על הצלתו.״ (הכתב והקבלה שמות ב:יא)

במה הרגו ר' אביתר אמר הכהו באגרוף, וי"א מגריפה של טיט נטל
והוציא את מוחו רבנן אמרי הזכיר אליו את השם והרגו שנאמר הלהרגני
אתה אומר. (שמות רבה א:כט)[46]

One midrashic view says he struck the Egyptian simply, with his fist. Another suggests that he extracted his brain with a bricklayer's trowel. Yet another view proposes the ineffable Name was used as a murder weapon.[47] Of these depictions, the first smacks most (though not necessarily) of impetuous rage. The second attests to deliberate behavior (excising the Egyptian's brain)—though not premeditated. The bricklayer's trowel is the tool of the enslaved laborers and in the moment of rage, Moshe grabbed whatever was most accessible. The poetic justice of the trowel as the murder weapon is impressive. In his wrath at the enslavement of the Hebrews, Moshe uses the very tool of servitude to beat out the brains of the Egyptian taskmaster.

The third interpretation is the most difficult literarily, and is the most distant from the plain meaning of the biblical text. Its clear thrust is that Moshe's violence was not only carefully orchestrated, but also commended by the highest authority. Again, the rabbinic impulse is to ally the supernatural with Moshe along every step of his way.[48]

Whether or not Moshe was morally correct in killing the Egyptian, we at least expect that he would be traumatized by the result of his violent action. Scripture does not explicitly relate to the psychological aftermath of the incident—except, perhaps, by telling us that Moshe furtively buried

---

[46] One logical means by which to evaluate this act is to define "makeh." The verb in biblical parlance can mean to smite fatally or to smite non-fatally. In context, the same word teaches that the term does not inherently entail killing. The midrash, however, understands that the Egyptian's goal was to kill despite the fact that the Hebrew did not die.

[47] We must acknowledge that the first opinion in the midrash allows for the possibility that Moshe is not a murderer. That is, he may have struck the Egyptian with his fist, allowing for the possibility that the Egyptian's death was caused by his fall. We can therefore understand that Moshe had not intended to cause death. Cf. Saul Lieberman ed., *Deuteronomy Rabbah* (Jerusalem: Wahrman, 1974) 2.29, 59. Ibn Ezra opposes the midrashic view here and espouses the less personal rock or spear as the weapon of choice.

[48] Only one midrashic source holds Moshe accountable for murder. See A. Jellinek, *Beit haMidrash: Midrash Petirato shel Mosheh Rabbenu* (Jerusalem: Wahrmann Books, 1967) vol. 1, 118–19.

the body in the sand. By this action, Moshe hopes to bury the memory as well.

Compassion and Disappointment

On the second day Moshe sets out, like Joseph before him, in search of his brothers and like Joseph, he is shocked into a rude awakening. The only brethren he has left disappoint him painfully. They are the victims of the persecution he has just combated; nevertheless they assault him—verbally—and betray his confidences.

> ויצא ביום השני והנה שני אנשים עברים נצים ויאמר לרשע למה תכה
> רעך. ויאמר מי שמך לאיש שר ושופט עלינו הלהרגני אתה אמר כאשר
> הרגת את המצרי ויירא משה ויאמר אכן נודע הדבר.

> Another day he went out and behold, two Hebrews were fighting, so he said to the offender: "Why do you strike your fellow?" He replied: "Who made you master, chief and judge over us? Do you plan to kill me, as you killed the Egyptian?" Moshe was afraid, thinking: So the deed is known!

When Moshe encountered aggression among the Hebrews, he did not intervene physically. Rather, he rebuked the assailant: "Why do you strike your fellow?" Seemingly, this altercation was not as serious as the earlier beating; or perhaps Moshe contained himself precisely because those involved were his brethren. But if we are to understand that these events contributed to Moshe's increasing ethical sophistication, we may also infer that his restraint in this case was the result of a lesson learned of not striking out impulsively, even in the face of a situation which warrants it. Moshe's immediate goal was humanitarian—to break up the fight. Yet he was confronted with a vicious reprimand: "Who made you master, chief and judge over us? Do you plan to kill me, as you killed the Egyptian?"

R. Levi ben Gershom (Ralbag) asserts in his commentary on the Torah that this encounter teaches Moshe and the reader about the sorry state of his brethren after the many years of toil and travail:

> להודיע רוע מנהג ישראל בעת ההוא שהיו מריבים קצתם עם קצת ומכים
> קצתם קץ. והיו מואסים המוסר, עד כאשר הוכיחם משה על זה לא רצו

לקבל תוכחתו. אבל הרשיעו יותר ופרסמו הריגת המצרי באופן שנודע הדבר לפרעה והוכרח משה לברוח. וזהו כלו להורות כי מה שהיה להם מחוזק הגלות היה רוע מעשיהם סיבה לו. (שמות ב :יג)

> …to describe the poor behavior of Israel at that time. They squabbled with each other and attacked each other. They disdained discipline to the point that when Moshe rebuked them they were unwilling to accept his criticism. They did worse: they made known his killing of the Egyptian so that word reached Pharaoh and Moshe was forced to flee. All this to illustrate what the exile had done to them and it caused their evil ways. (Ralbag commentary on Exodus 2:13)

Indeed, the exhausting years of affliction had left the Israelites irritable, irascible and incorrigible. This brief encounter under the Egyptian sun opened Moshe's eyes to the harsh realities of leading a stiff-necked people.

The dramatic irony of this scene is palpable. The Hebrew who verbally assaulted Moshe, "Who made you ruler and judge over us?" had clearly forgotten his place. After all, Moshe was an Egyptian officer; he *did* rule over them! In fact, Moshe was destined to rule over them, not in Egyptian garb, but as leader of their entire people. This Hebrew resented Moshe's intrusion into his "private" affairs; yet it was Moshe who would later overturn reality as he knew it—a far more extensive intrusion. The slave hoped, by means of his knowledge of Moshe's act of murder, to undermine Moshe's status as an Egyptian overlord. Yet it was Moshe who would later achieve a greater status among the Hebrews' own people than any other before or since.

R. Bahya ben Asher sums up this idea beautifully:

ובשלש לשונות הללו שדברו כנגדו מצינו שלקח עטרה. הם אמרו לו מי שמך לאיש מצינו שנקרא איש שנאמר האיש משה ענו מאד, ונקרא שר שנא' באר חפרנוה שרים כרוה נדיבי עם, ונקרא שופט שנא' וישב משה לשפוט את העם.

> With these three expressions which they hurled against him he was crowned. They said: "Who appointed you a man…" and we found him [Moshe] called "a man" as it says: "And the man Moshe was very humble." He was called "an officer" as it says: "And the officers dug a well." And he was called "a judge" as it says: "And Moshe sat in judgment of the nation."

The foreshadowing of Moshe's struggles with the people he was chosen to lead is palpable as well—and the rabbinic renditions of this narrative are quite cognizant of those later struggles. Although the Torah is silent as to the identities of these fighting Hebrews, the Rabbis disclose the identities of these characters: Dathan and Abiram, key players in the rebellion of Korah, who actively sought to undermine the leadership of Moshe and his family.[49]

In their interpretation of the various acts of insurrection during the Israelite sojourn in the desert, the Rabbis of the midrash consistently identify any and all anonymous instigators as Dathan and Abiram.[50] The rabbinic inclination to "conserve personalities" is seemingly extended here, designating the "prototype of inveterate fomenters of trouble" as those who tormented Moshe even before he was commissioned as leader.[51] Moshe was singed now by that which would sear him later.

The first part of the Hebrew's retort left us wondering how he had the gall to address Moshe so insolently. The second part of his response leaves us with a different question: how did he know that Moshe had killed an Egyptian? Was this a blind accusation? After all, the Bible records that Moshe checked and found no one about. The extensive passage in *Exodus Rabbah* 1.28 which seeks to absolve Moshe of any wrong-doing, provides an answer: the Hebrew victim of the first day was none other than Dathan. He knew that Moshe had killed an Egyptian

---

[49] See *Exodus Rabbah* 1.29 and Numbers 16:1–3. Cf. Rachel Stern, "*Hu Dathan ve'Aviram*" (Elkana: *Talelei Orot*, 1990) 32–36.

[50] Cf. *Exodus Rabbah*, ibid.

[51] The phrase "prototype of the inveterate fomenters of trouble" coined by Nahum M. Sarna, "Dathan and Abiram" (*Encyclopedia Judaica*) vol. 5, 1312. The felicitous notion of "midrashic law of conservation of personalities" was formulated by Moshe Sokolow. This concept is found in *Midrash Avkir* 33, 12–13 (in *Likkutei Midrashim Shonim*) Solomon Buber ed. (Vilna, 1886):

אילולי אילו רשעים לא יצא הדבר לעולם ומי היו? דתן ואבירם. ולמה? **כל מה שאתה יכול לתלות ברשעים תלה.** הם שאמרו הדבר הזה, והם שהותירו מן המן, והם שאמרו נתנה ראש ונשובה מצרימה.

Cf. Amos Geulah (Jerusalem, 1998) 145, among other places. Cf. Yitzchak Heinman, *Darkhei ha'Aggadah* (Jerusalem, 1970) 29. This concept is stated in rabbinic terms in *Midrash Avkir*, ibid. (Jerusalem, Hebrew University).

because he himself had been the beneficiary of Moshe's violent act of righteousness. And so we see that his ingratitude knew no bounds—the kind of *hutzpah* which was later mirrored exponentially by the complaining Children of Israel in the desert. Poor Moshe—elected to a role for which he was uniquely qualified because of his unerring devotion to justice and his deep-rooted compassion for the needy, yet mistreated by just those individuals for whom he is to provide succor!

Moreover, the Hebrew's arrow struck its target, for Moshe was indeed shaken: "Moshe was frightened and said, 'Aha, the matter is known.'" Here, for the first time, Scripture explicitly comments on Moshe's emotional state. But why should Moshe, a royal grandson, fear repercussions for killing one Egyptian taskmaster during a reign of terror? It is possible that the slain Egyptian was far more important to the regime than the Bible makes known, or that Moshe's own position as adopted child was far more precarious than we are given to understand. Or perhaps Moshe's anxiety is rooted in his own emerging moral posture. The confidence to take action may not yet have matured into the strength to defend his ground when challenged. The midrash offers another alternative: this was not the first time Moshe had challenged Pharaoh and overstepped his bounds. Killing the taskmaster was the proverbial straw that broke the camel's back. Moshe knew that the time had come to fear for his life.[52]

Moshe's statement: "Aha, the matter is known," is seen by the midrash as a reference not to knowledge of his deed, but rather to knowledge of a deep truth about the enslavement of the Hebrews:

ר' יהודה בר רבי שלום בשם ר' חנינה הגדול ורבותינו בשם רבי אלכסנדרי אמרו: היה משה מהרהר בלו ואומר חטאו ישראל שנשתעבדו מכל האומות? כיון ששמע דבריו אמר לשון הרע יש ביניהן היאך יהיו ראויין לגאולה? לכן אמר אכן נודע הדבר עתה ידעתי באיזה דבר הם משתעבדים.

And he said, "Aha, the matter is known."—R. Yehudah the son of R. Shalom, in the name of R. Hanina the Great, and our Rabbis in the name of R. Alexandri said: Moshe wondered what sin Israel committed to warrant their enslavement more than any other nation. When he heard [the Hebrew's] words, he said: Tale-bearing is rife among them;

---

[52] *Deuteronomy Rabbah* 2.29 (S. Lieberman ed.) 59.

how, then, can they be worthy of salvation? Thus, "surely the matter is known"—now I know the reason for their bondage.[53]

The rabbinic authorities who endorse this interpretation support the notion that the problem of informers was of contemporary as well as exegetical relevance. Betrayal, slander and collaboration was rife among the Jews of the rabbinic period.[54] By inserting their own concerns into their commentary on Moshe, they educate their constituency, while providing a new perspective on Moshe's place in ancient Egypt. They assert that at that moment Moshe comprehended that which had eluded him: Why were the Hebrews enslaved? Why do Jews suffer? The resolution offered here resonates for every generation: because of the slander and malice which emerge from disunity. Moshe first encountered that kind of strife with these two Hebrews. But what Moshe experienced here on a personal level will never cease to challenge him on a national level. That is why he was gripped by fear: he had discovered an inherent flaw in the character of the Jewish people. The trait troubled him then on the smallest of scales, and would cause incessant grief to him and the people themselves in the years to come—for it is not easily overcome.[55]

Rabbinic tradition recognizes in Moshe a wiser man after this assault than he had been when he first emerged from the palace. In two days, he endured trial by the fire of experience which would prove crucial to his leadership of the Children of Israel. It prepared him for his standing before Pharaoh and for the task of freeing the Hebrews. He learned the ugliness of the Egyptian establishment and the imperfections of the people he would liberate. The awareness that his brethren were ethically wanting was painful. In the years to come, the absence of reverence, loyalty and

---

[53] *Exodus Rabbah* 1.30.

[54] Note that R. Alexandri of the midrash concerns himself with the problem of *lashon hara* elsewhere as well (*Avodah Zarah* 19b) and apparently, he had an audience for this message. For references to *delatorin* in the rabbinic period see Samuel Krauss, *Griechische und Lateinische Lehnwoerter im Talmud, Midrasch und Targum* (Berlin: S. Calvary, 1898/9) 203–4. Reuven Kimelman, "*Birkat haminim* and the Lack of Evidence for an Anti-Christian Jewish Prayer in Late Antiquity," *Jewish and Christian Self Definition* (Philadelphia: Fortress Press, 1980–1982) vol. 2, 226–403.

[55] See for example Exodus 15–17, Numbers 11.

gratitude among the people Israel would prove an ongoing source of disquietude for Moshe.[56]

Years later, Moshe the shepherd will be chosen to lead the flocks of Israel. He will be formally commissioned at the burning bush. But as the champion of the ethical, he had already been singled out by virtue of his own passion for justice. Later, Moshe will hesitate. He will give expression to his own self-doubt. But he will never question where his loyalties lie—he has killed the Egyptian. Nor will he deprecate his brethren, despite their shortcomings. Rather, he will lead them with compassion and justice. With dignity, he will rise to the challenges of leadership for which he has been prepared.

---

[56] For God, too. See *Exodus Rabbah* 1.42 for a moving description of God's awareness of His people's shortcomings and His resolve to redeem them nonetheless.

Rhetorical Questions:
The First Words of the Children of Israel

Jane Falk

The first weeks of the Children of Israel's post-slavery experience are checkered with dramatic "highs" and "lows" as the people encounter God's saving hand and fear its limitations. They are new to their role as the Chosen People, and their initial experiences as free men and women introduce them to the bliss of God's protection, as well as the despair engendered by their lack of confidence in the perpetuity of that protection. As they succumb to these challenges to faith, they gain a sense of what God expects of them, and even more, how to communicate with the divine.

Introduction

At the crossing of the Red Sea, the Children of Israel find that words are insufficient to convey the ecstasy they feel and they are moved to song, their joy captured in exquisite poetry.[1] But the former slaves lack confidence in the miracles that have been rendered on their behalf; as events unfold, they shift into a panic mode as they perceive danger to their well-being. Their anxiety, markedly different from their joy, is expressed in brief prose, a prose that marks the emergence of the collective voice of the Children of Israel as they leave slavery behind them. As we shall see,

* Dedicated to Ze'ev W. Falk, *z"l* (of blessed memory). I wish to thank the following people for their comments and support: Steven Bailey, Ilana Friedman, Robin Lakoff, R. Yosef Leibowitz, Stuart Margolis, Lawrence Zalcman, and Anne Gordon for her fine editing.

[1] Lecture given by Avivah Gottlieb Zornberg, January 4, 1998. Zornberg's comments sparked my investigation of the Israelites' questions, as well as much else in my approach to Torah.

that emerging voice resembles a series of moans and groans, yet it carries the people's initial relationship with God and therefore represents their first steps in becoming a free nation in their own right.[2]

Following the Exodus from Egypt, the people of Israel speak en masse in five different episodes—each time when they perceive a threat to their physical well-being. The prose that conveys their panic consists entirely of a series of questions. They question Moshe in the shadow of Pharaoh's approaching army; at Marah, of the bitter waters; twice at Zin—once when they are hungry and again when they are puzzled by the manna; and lastly, at Refidim, when they are thirsty. If we were to place these verses together, their thrust is formidable:

- Were there no graves in Egypt that you took us to die in the wilderness?
- What is this that you have done to us to take us out of Egypt?
- Did we not tell you in Egypt, "Let us be and we will serve Egypt"?[3]
- What shall we drink?[4]
- Who will grant that we should die [would that we had died] by the hand of God in Egypt as we sat by the pot of meat, when we ate bread to satiety?[5]
- What is this?[6]
- Why is this that you have brought us up from Egypt to kill me and my children and my livestock through thirst?[7]

---

[2] For the purposes of this article, I will not entertain the notion, put forth elsewhere, that different groups were responsible for different statements in the case of consecutive quotes (but see note 18 below).

[3] These three questions are from Exodus, *Beshalah* 14:11–12.

[4] At Marah—Exodus 15:24.

[5] Exodus 16:3. Here the Hebrew, *"mi yiten"* is an idiom for an unobtainable wish. See Bruce Waltke and Michael O'Connor, *An Introduction to Biblical Hebrew Syntax* (IN: Eisenbrauns, 1990).

[6] Upon first encounter with the manna, Exodus 15:16.

[7] Exodus 17:3.

Each of these questions has the feel of a complaint and the apparent absence of any request for help may surprise us. Let us remember, however, that the Israelites have only recently been freed from the shackles of servitude. Let us realize that as slaves, they had enjoyed little opportunity to make requests of their overseers. After all, even that which is formulated as a request ("please sir, may I...?") is fundamentally begging, by virtue of the utter dependency of the slave on his master.

Asking questions of a higher authority is not in the linguistic repertoire of a slave. And so, the greatest freedom of speech enjoyed by the Children of Israel while in Egypt was the ability to complain—if only to each other and despite the absence of hope for respite. Now, as they begin to learn to talk, to gain a voice as a people, it is the formulation of their complaining, their panicked prose, which deserves our attention, for it reveals that there is more to their words than might first appear. Before we can probe the full force of their words, however, we must first comprehend the mechanisms by which they function, for it is the role the words play, beyond their plain meaning, which opens a new mode of interpretation for us— and that is our current project.

The Tools of Analysis

In order to communicate properly, one requires an abundance of information: a sense of whom one is addressing; the location of the one being addressed; what that person knows about the speaker and about the matter at hand; the appropriate time to register one's comments and what one can expect in response.[8] Of course, the particular words used are not all that one has to convey meaning. A vast storehouse of information about language and the world at large enables one to import meaning to an utterance. The process of deriving the meaning conveyed by the grammar and context of someone's speech is technically called "conversational inference,"[9] and its tools, the myriad components of communication, are

---

[8] Charles J. Fillmore, *Santa Cruz Lectures on Deixis* (IN: Indiana University Linguistics Club, 1975).

[9] See John J. Gumperz, "The Linguistic and Cultural Relativity of Conversational Inference" in *Rethinking Linguistic Relativity*, John Gumperz and Paul Levinson (Cambridge: Cambridge University Press, 1996).

those considered by the academic field of Linguistic Pragmatics. The way the words are couched, their grammar, the contexts in which they occur, their interactional effect, and the subtle parallels between them all demand interpretation.

Indeed, the moans and groans in the questions of the Children of Israel reflect all the novelty, ambiguity, tentativeness and drama of their contexts. They are structurally complex, internally consistent, and interactionally sophisticated. The questions possess a uniform grammar and theme. That is, in Hebrew, they either begin with the prefix "*heh,*" which is a question marker,[10] or with a question word, such as "what," "who," "why" and so on. They are not, however, to be confused with ordinary questions, which demand an answer. Rather, they are rhetorical and therein lies the subject of our analysis.

Rhetorical Questions

In the field of Linguistics, the Rhetorical Question is a hybrid form.[11] Grammatically, it is a question. It looks like a question and it sounds like a question. But it does not have the feel of a question. That is, a question typically solicits information from the one to whom it is addressed. A question is rendered appropriately if the questioner lacks information, has reason to believe that the respondent has the information being solicited, and will share that information with the questioner who is seeking it. Such tacit understanding between questioner and respondent of how common discourse works is technically known as "the Cooperative Principle of Conversation."[12] A rhetorical question, by contrast, violates the Cooperative Principle by implying its own answers. It may suggest that its answer

---

[10] *Heh* often carries an exclamatory nuance as well. See Paul Jounon and T. Muraoka, *A Grammar of Biblical Hebrew* (Rome: Subsidia Biblica, 1991) vol. 14.1.

[11] The description of rhetorical questions here is based on Cornelia Ilie, *What Else Can I Tell You?* (University of Stockholm, 1994, Doctoral dissertation).

[12] H.P. Grice, "Logic and Conversation" in *Syntax and Semantics* 3, J.L. Morgan and P. Cole eds. (NY: Academic Press, 1975) 41–58.

is obvious, or it may be fundamentally impossible to answer. Hence, it is truly a statement, despite its question form.[13]

The fundamental difference between a real question and a rhetorical question is evident in the simple utterance, "Is it 5 o'clock?" If this phrase is uttered by a questioner who is not wearing a watch and a respondent who is (and no clock is visible), we assume that the questioner is asking the time and the respondent (presumably) will answer appropriately ("yes" or "no"). However, if the phrase is uttered by a boss in response to the employee's "I'll be leaving now," the same question takes on quite a different communicative force. A condition of real questions is not being met: the questioner is not ignorant of the information being solicited. The boss is well aware of the time. This utterance, therefore, does not solicit information or even acknowledgment, as a real question would.

In many rhetorical questions, the propositional content of the statement is asserted indirectly or is "backgrounded."[14] A rhetorical question does not lay information on the table for scrutiny. Rather, underlying assumptions are presented definitively, closed to debate. The onus of responding to the backgrounded information, therefore, is placed on the addressee. Of

---

[13] Thus, the question functions as some other Speech Act as discussed by J.R. Searle in his *Speech Acts* (Cambridge: Cambridge University Press, 1969). As far as I know, Speech Acts are first mentioned in J.L. Austin, *How to Do Things with Words* (MA: Harvard University Press, 1962) 148. Speech Act theory is based on the observation that every utterance we make does something—changes reality in some way. A genuine question, for example, solicits information or agreement. Some verbs perform their act just by virtue of being said. For example, "I promise you" constitutes a promise. As often as not, we have to infer which Speech Act is intended from context, for the same form and even the same words, can comprise different Speech Acts, depending on the speaker and the circumstances. Among such conveyed Speech Acts are requests ("Can you pass the salt?"), threats ("Do you want to take a long walk off a short pier?") and greetings ("How's it going?"). Here we see what appear to be questions, insofar as their grammar goes, functioning as requests, threats and greetings, none of which intends to solicit information or agreement. So too, the Speech Act of a rhetorical question is not dependent on the grammar of the form.

[14] The classic example of this occurs in courtroom scenarios when the prosecutor asks a question, such as "Why did you beat your wife?" The fact that the man beat his wife is backgrounded as a presupposition. One could, of course, respond to the backgrounded assertion, but to do so, one must go outside the parameters of the question as it is posed: "Wait a minute, I didn't beat my wife!" Thus, when a statement is presented as closed to discussion, it comes across more definitively— and may place the respondent on the defensive as well.

course, interpreting the statement of a rhetorical question correctly is not easy, especially given the misleading form. The rhetorical question taxes the interpretive abilities of those to whom it is posed, as they seek to determine its implicit message. Moreover, the effort exerted serves to ingrain that message all the more effectively.[15] In the ambiguity and capacity for misinterpretation, however, lie power and drama.

On the one hand, an assertion made by means of a rhetorical question is stated far more forcefully than it would be were it found in a simple declarative statement. By virtue of its form, the rhetorical question retains the implicit challenge of a question: "Answer me!" And because it is unanswerable as posed, the challenge is intensified: "Answer me despite the fact that I'm not giving you room to do so." In argument, therefore, a rhetorical question wields a forceful challenge and it is often the use of rhetorical questions which transforms a debate into a quarrel.

On the other hand, because the form is inherently ambiguous and intentionally indirect, the rhetorical question provides a mask of politeness to the confrontational, which facilitates a denial of the combat and leaves the questioner an escape. The implicit remark is presumably less offensive than a direct accusation would be.[16] The rhetorical question, therefore, diminishes the risk to both questioner and respondent of "losing face." At the same time, however, the rhetorical question locks both questioner and respondent into its claim, for while the respondent has no opportunity to articulate his or her own side of the matter, the questioner, in choosing a syntax which does not allow for argument, leaves no linguistic opening to recant his or her own statement. We therefore find that rhetorical questions indicate the mettle of both those who phrase them and those who respond to them. Insofar as they cloak the substance of the communication, when stripped away, they reveal the underlying positions and attitudes.

---

[15] Robin Lakoff, personal correspondence.

[16] Robin Lakoff, "The Logic of Politeness" in *Papers from the Ninth Regional Meeting of the Chicago Linguistic Society* (Chicago: University of Chicago Press, 1973) 292–305.

1. Five Biblical Rhetorical Questions

Now we may return to our biblical narrative, for the first utterances by the Children of Israel upon their departure from Egypt well illustrate the point: "Were there not enough graves in Egypt that you took us to die in the wilderness? What is this that you have done to take us out of Egypt? Didn't we tell you in Egypt, 'Let us be and we will serve Egypt?'…" (Exodus 14:11–12).[17] Certainly, these pronouncements appear to be questions. In Hebrew, the first and third begin with the question marker "*heh*" and the second begins with "*mah*" ("what"). But with equal certainty, we understand that the pronouncements are not intended to solicit the information they appear to demand. After all, we realize that the Israelites are not seriously wondering about the number of graves available in Egypt![18] Furthermore, while technically one may answer the first and third questions in the affirmative, these questions border on the absurd, as the Children of Israel paint slavery as rose-colored. For all intents and purposes, these so-called questions are unanswerable as posed. As such, they constitute complaints, accusatory in tone, directed at Moshe.

Alternatively, we may regard these utterances as equivalent to one simple question: "Why ever did you bring us here?!"[19] In this formulation, we realize all the more easily that the Israelites' words serve a function far more subtle than the sarcastic questions they appear to form, for it is a concern near panic which tacitly underlies the biblical phrasing. The verses themselves, therefore, are understood to be metaphorical, if only

---

[17] In this first and paradigmatic example, we find, in fact, a series of consecutive rhetorical questions. This series may be a "duet" (in this case, a "trio"), where different groups of the same mind play the role of one speaker, taking turns that continue the thread of the preceding turn, which are addressed to the same hearer. See Jane Falk, "The Conversational Duet" in *Proceedings of the Sixth Annual Meeting of the Berkeley Linguistics Society* (CA: Dept. of Linguistics, University of California, 1980).

[18] Moreover, the Israelites knew that Moshe knew that there were enough graves in Egypt and that he knew they knew he knew. Sarcasm is conveyed by the "of course" element.

[19] "Shotgun Questions." See Deborah Tannen, *That's Not What I Meant* (NY: William Morrow, 1986).

for a more looming question—an understanding supported by Moshe's response to them. For Moshe does not answer the Children of Israel literally ("Yes, of course there are graves in Egypt; that's not why I brought you out" or even "No, I didn't bring you here to die"). Rather, he infers the unspoken worry which underlies their words and responds accordingly: "Do not fear. Stand by and witness the deliverance which the Lord will work for you today..." (Exodus 14:13). His soothing reply indicates that he has understood the implications of their words and from his reaction, we too infer their fear, unspoken, but indicated nonetheless by their rhetorical questioning.

And so we begin to understand that each of the statements in the emerging collective voice of the Children of Israel carries a hidden meaning, hidden by its form as a rhetorical question. We therefore must unearth the message of each utterance by analyzing its content together with its form. Using the tools of Linguistic Pragmatics, we do so by: 1) determining that the utterance is a grammatical question; 2) giving the question's implicit answer; 3) identifying the function (Speech Act) which the question performs; and 4) describing the response to that Speech Act which takes the place of an answer to the surface question.

2. At Marah

The Israelites' second rhetorical question is uttered at Marah, upon their realization that the waters of Marah are bitter: "What shall we drink?" (Exodus 15:24). Again, in Hebrew, the sentence begins with the question word "*mah*" ("what?"). The implicit answer here is "nothing," for had there been an obviously present beverage (or had the waters been sweet to begin with), they would not have asked. The Speech Act is again a complaint, essentially whining, "There is nothing to drink!"—blaming Moshe for his role in bringing them to such an apparently dire situation. At this point, however, Moshe does not respond to the Israelites directly; he cries out to God for assistance. As we shall see, Moshe reveals his fine insight into their psyche with his refusal to defend himself, for engaging in a quibbling match of accusations would have given credence to their complaints. Instead, he allows the One responsible for the situation to take control. Again, we see that Moshe does not treat the utterance as seeking the answer to the question posed.[20]

3. At Zin

The Children of Israel continue in this vein at Zin, in their hunger: "Who will grant that we should have died [would that we had died] by the hand of God in Egypt as we sat by the pot of meat, when we ate bread to satiety? For you have taken us out to this wilderness to kill this entire congregation by famine" (Exodus 16:3). Here, the question word is "*mi*," (who?) and the implicit answer here is, "everybody and anybody"—that is, we were much better off in Egypt with food in our bellies, as anyone and everyone knows. This question does not mask a simple complaint, like that voiced at Marah. Instead, it carries with it an accusation, similar to the initial complaints raised out of fear of the pursuing Egyptians. Afraid of starvation, they hold Moshe responsible for their apparent predicament—for just as the rhetorical question masks the complaint, so too, the complaint masks the continued anxiety about the unpredictable sojourn in the wilderness. As at Marah, Moshe himself makes no direct response; after all, he is not directly responsible and the formerly placating "Do not fear" will not suffice in this case. It is God Himself who "hears their complaints" and instructs Moshe and Aharon as to the manna.

God's provision of manna at first seems incongruous: only an exceedingly permissive parent would give in to children who express themselves this way. How can God countenance their accusation? Granting the manna would seem to legitimate their complaint! But once we recall the nature of the rhetorical question and see the form for the disguise that it is, we understand that God's manna, the supernatural gift that appeared predictably and regularly, answered their need precisely. They fear the unknown, their fear manifest in the insecurity regarding their next meal.

---

[20] That God has Moshe turn the water sweet should capture our attention. He seems to give the people exactly what they ask for—a fine way to spoil the child, as it were. And so we can understand that God can give into them without fear of spoiling them because He knows better than any that their complaint is not for the sake of itself, but to mask their insecurity about the future. Just as a parent might do, God fulfils their request in the efforts of building their confidence in the future. We will return to the function of complaints later in this article.

God offers protection and comfort—and makes no criticism of their tone, recognizing their true circumstances.

4. The Children of Israel, however, panic again at this unexpected response, His strange gift: "What is this?"—in Hebrew, "*man hu*" (Exodus 16:15).[21] The commentaries differ as to whether "*man*" is a variation of "*mah*," in which case, the question asked is "What is this?" or whether "*man*" is a new noun, the traditional manna or food. Even if "*man*" refers to food, the statement can still be understood to be a question, as in "Is this food?" But only the context then indicates that it is a question and not its grammatical form. Nonetheless, the context seems to indicate that it is a question, rhetorical or not, because the verse continues: "for they did not know what it was." While this comment may serve to explain why they had asked the question, had their question been one of idle curiosity, this addition by the text would have been superfluous. Perhaps we can resolve the matter by considering the statement in the context of the other four statements made by the Children of Israel in the wilderness—in which case, we are left to suppose that this utterance, too, is a rhetorical question. The comment, "for they did not know what it was" is thus an explanation of why they were complaining (fear or dissatisfaction with the unfamiliar, perhaps).

The implicit message of this statement, assuming that the question is rhetorical, is "This is not food,"[22] and Moshe's response can be understood as a direct retort to it: Indeed, "This is the food that God has given you for eating" (Exodus 16:15). His contradiction of their assumption here, more direct than any of the previous responses, may be understood to indicate that his patience is wearing thin. Alternatively, his direct retort may be an astute means of dissolving their doubts.

---

[21] Note that this verse is not classically included as one of the "complaints."

[22] Alshich also understands the verse as a complaint, but he understands it to mean "It's not food"; "it's angel food!" "It's angel food" could also be the implied answer.

5. At Refidim

But the Children of Israel are a stiff-necked bunch and sharpen their complaint at Refidim, when they have exhausted their water supply and are thirsty: "Why is this that you have brought us up from Egypt to kill me and my children and my livestock through thirst?" (Exodus 17:3). As a literal question, this "why" statement cannot be answered. The Speech Act is one of accusation, now couched in complaint, as compared to the earlier complaints with an undertone of accusation. Moreover, immediately prior to this verse, the people demand: "Give us water that we may drink" (Exodus 17:2). First they seek water and then by means of the rhetorical question, they accuse Moshe of precipitating the circumstances which led to their thirst. Moshe does not respond to their accusation at all. He relinquishes the responsibility, as it were, and cries out to God, who has led their way thus far and who indeed tells him how to proceed.[23]

Moshe's Response

The special properties of the rhetorical questions heightens the drama of these interchanges in the wilderness. Moreover, they allow us insight into the nature of the relationship between the Children of Israel and Moshe— as they set out to test the strength of their leader. We might have thought that Moshe would fail to grasp the message underlying the rhetorical

---

[23] This sequence has spurred debate over the centuries. Why both utterances? Why does Moshe reject the first out of hand and God come to the rescue only in reaction to the second? Nechama Leibowitz addresses these issues in her *Studies in Shemot Part I* (Jerusalem: World Zionist Organization, 1976) 280–2 and cites the following: Ibn Ezra maintains that there were two groups, one addressing Moshe and one addressing God, and therefore two questions. Regardless, virtually all commentators agree that the tone of the first verse is belligerent. Or haHayyim suggests that Moshe actually had water and the people felt he owed it to them to hand it over. Others suggest that the Israelites themselves had water, but they wanted to store up more for themselves. And some commentators attribute the belligerent tone to the fact that the people's situation was the most dire they had encountered. Perhaps more importantly is the criticism that the Children of Israel here are not only rude, but also wrong-headed, for in their dire straits, they failed to pray (*Mekhilta*). Note that the first verse is not a rhetorical question (perhaps because the people were not yet desperately thirsty) and therefore would be read as *less* belligerent by the linguistic analysis developed in this essay.

questions, but he is never misled. This comprehension is all the more impressive, not only because of the inherent challenge in interpreting a rhetorical question correctly, but also because of the different cultural background he brings to the conversation. Raised among the Egyptians, it may well be that Moshe does not consider Hebrew to be his mother tongue. Nonetheless, he is attuned to his people Israel and responds to their complaints accurately and immediately. As their leader, he cannot ignore their indirect accusations; to do so would validate their fear. Yet he never allows himself to become defensively embroiled in argument. When he addresses them, he does so calmly, encouraging trust in the God who freed them—and only God (and we the later readers) knows of his mounting frustration with their anxiety.

Despair and Its Salvation

That anxiety, however, is genuine and again it is the rhetorical question form which reveals. The rhetorical questions allow us to eavesdrop, as it were, on the collective thinking process of the people Israel. For as much as we have understood their utterances to be challenges to Moshe, we may also understand that a verbal form which does not expect an answer may be seen as tantamount to thinking out loud.[24] We are privy to the internal murmur, the worrying of the people. Yet even as challenges, the distinctive characteristics of this form make it a revealing tool of the Children of Israel. By secreting the accusations which mask their fear within rhetorical questions, the Children of Israel prevent easy rebuttal of their claims. By making statements instead of asking real questions, they allow themselves no room for comfort in answers. It would seem that they believe that there is no remedy to be had—the epitome of despair. And so we uncover the people's perception of the severity of their plight. Again, the form of their utterances sheds light on the meaning of the words; the rhetorical questions reflect the tension as the Israelites embark on their travels in the wilderness, dependent on God.

But the rhetorical questions do more than reflect the tension; they also provide the catalyst which propels the Children of Israel to emerge as a

---

[24] Cf. Rashi on Exodus 15:24, "What shall we drink?"

people. The commentaries suggest that the scenarios which give rise to the rhetorical questions are purposive challenges to the nation by God, to teach them of His power.[25] When Moshe, God's chosen leader for the people, responds to the Israelites' accusations with equanimity, ignoring their contentiousness, he enables the people to begin to let go of their quarrel. They now begin to understand what it means to be cloaked in the mantle of God's chosen ones, for to each complaint God responds (often through Moshe), sustaining them with the protection of His omnipresence.

The rhetorical question, therefore, provides the newly freed Israelites with an initial vehicle through which to learn a new mode of conversation. In their ignorance of convention, uncertain as to the efficacy as well as the appropriateness of making a direct request for change, or even explanation, they choose a form of speech which enables them to ask without asking. The ambiguity of the rhetorical question leaves them the escape route of denying the challenge which underlies the question, but enables them to both vent their frustration and convey their request to one sufficiently astute to recognize the need beneath the form. Indeed, Moshe's responses are admirably attuned to the true purpose of the Israelites' words and in time, they will learn to make requests directly, in the manner of freedom.

Complaints

A rhetorical question may, of course, also function as a request. Indeed, our original example of the boss who chides his departing employee saying, "Is it 5 o'clock?" is making the not-so-subtle request that he stay at his post. But there are other functions (again, Speech Acts) which may be performed by a rhetorical question and in the passages we have seen above, they are primarily complaints. Ironically, complaints themselves may perform a variety of Speech Acts. For example, a complaint may be designed to elicit sympathy, to lay blame, to make an excuse, or even to make a request or plea. The context of the complaint is what identifies its function in the communication. Perhaps we could understand that these rhetorical questions *qua* complaints are really an indirect strategy for

---

[25] See Ramban on Deuteronomy 8:2.

soliciting assistance, but the text at large does not seem to support this view. After all, their only apparent request is to return to Egypt, an unrealistic one at best; rather, we understand that their comments express their distress with the current situation. Furthermore, when one makes a request, one generally assumes that it is in the power of the addressee to grant the request. Here we would have to assume that the Israelites understood the extent of God's compassion to legitimate the claim that their complaints are intended as veiled requests.

Let us remember, however, that the relationship between the Children of Israel and God, for all intents and purposes, is still in its infancy. As such, their sense of God's mercy may well have been under-developed. Or we may wonder whether they lacked faith in the role of God in their lives. They may not have grasped the nature of the Exodus, or they may have been, as suggested earlier, in the throes of despair. That is, the tension which underlies each of the rhetorical questions is the threat the people perceive to their physical well-being. Thus, they convey the fear, "We are going to die!" It would seem that the rhetorical questions are sparked by the situation of perceived dire physical threat and express despair.[26] In turn, the rhetorical questions themselves mark the presence of these emotions to those of us who are examining their travails in the wilderness from a distance.

In any case, whether the Children of Israel are doubting God, or merely lack a sense of His role in their destiny, they challenge Him (or His messenger Moshe) each time they are overwhelmed by intensity of their emotion. They do not yet understand that mercy is the bedrock of their relationship and they have not yet learned to communicate through prayer. Rather, they formulate questions which are not real questions, and the underlying messages of their comments are hidden from easy view. The rhetorical questions do not end with our fifth example above; the Israelites revert to this method of discourse intermittently throughout their

---

[26] Indeed, the rhetorical questions resonate with these propositions and feelings, regardless of whether they are articulated. That is, the rhetorical question form in the Israelites' dialogue is a "contextualization cue." See John J. Gumperz, "Contextualization Conventions" in *Discourse Strategies*, John J. Gumperz ed. (Cambridge: Cambridge University Press, 1982) 130–52.

travels.[27] Indeed, the repetition of the linguistic form sheds light on the mindset of the people for the duration of their travels, and so we gain a penetrating understanding of the Israelites' psycho-spiritual state in the context of their burgeoning relationship with God.

Leaving Complaint Mode

The rhetorical questions of the Children of Israel facilitate an observation of the human psyche's negative underpinnings—because they resort to this form particularly when they encounter danger. In the face of the threat, they flee to "complaint mode," trapped in their own emotions. Let us remember that the statement which takes its form as a rhetorical question is nonetheless a statement and therefore definite. It does not carry the escape hatch that a real question—which allows for withdrawing, hedging and rebuttal—would. But it is the knee-jerk response to their situation which precipitates the rhetorical questions. We are hard-pressed to accept that they do want to return to Egypt, or that they believe that Moshe brought them out of Egypt to let them die. We instead assume that their instinct to flee colors their memories of their time in Egypt, so they channel their fear into anger, which they levy at Moshe, to alleviate their need to blame. Despite the ever-present clouds of glory, emblematic of God's protection, the anxiety over the provision for their basic human

---

[27] The Israelites return to this complaint mode of rhetorical questions four times in the Book of Numbers, following the model established in *parashat Beshalah*, in grammar as well as theme: 1) Tired of their diet of manna, "Who will feed us meat?" (Numbers 11:4); 2) After hearing the report of the spies, "Would that we had died in the land of Egypt, or would that we had died in this wilderness. Why is God bringing us to the Land to die by the sword? Our wives and young children will be taken captive. Is it not better for us to return to Egypt?" (Numbers 14:2–3); 3) In Kadesh, when their water source had dried up, "Would that we had died as our brethren died before God. Why have you brought the congregation of God to this wilderness to die there, we and our animals? And why did you have us ascend from Egypt to bring us to this evil place?" (Numbers 20:3–5); 4) After detouring to avoid Edom, "Why did you bring us up from Egypt to die in this wilderness, for there is no food and no water and our soul is disgusted with this insubstantial food?" (Numbers 21:5). Some of these questions are responses to situations which are not life-threatening, but the language does hearken back to the real crises in *parashat Beshalah*. It would seem that either the Israelites now lapse into darkness (reflected in the rhetorical question mode) habitually, or that they are using the form the way a child whines—to get what he or she wants, having succeeded by using it in the past.

needs devolves to hopelessness. When the Children of Israel are confident in the Divine protection, however, they follow Moshe's lead without hesitation. As much as there is a pattern in the recurrence of the rhetorical questions, they are also an aberration.

And so we implicitly learn a lesson from the rhetorical questions of the Children of Israel. As they panicked when they perceived their well-being to be at stake, so too, we risk that kind of panic. As they are shown that indeed God guides their journey, so too, we pause to recall that He oversees ours. And the more we maintain that sensitivity, the less prone we are to fits of doubt. In place of tension or anxiety or worst, despair, we may hope to gain clarity of vision and hope—yielding the mode of mature, direct communication, the speech of the free, both as individuals and as the nation as a whole.

Conclusion

Paying attention to repetition of patterns in biblical text is a common method of Torah study. Generally speaking, the patterns we notice are formed by words recurring at intervals of the text, or by recurring parts of speech. Here, we note repetition in the grammatical discourse. And, as always, we learn from the repetition. We see that just as children do, the Children of Israel mature as a people by taking two steps forward and one step back. It is their regressions that are indexed by the grammatical repetition—by the preponderance of rhetorical questions. Of course, we do not need the rhetorical questions as a tool in order to recognize their regression, their experience with despair. Nonetheless, the frequency of this mood is much more apparent when we do notice the grammatical repetition, for it enables us to fully grasp its meaning and its trap.

Just as the Children of Israel are bombarded with challenges to their faith and trust in the future so, needless to say, are we all. Their rhetorical questions reveal the ease with which they fall prey to despair. But we have the advantage of knowing the end of the story: God never fails to come to their aid—even as He does not "answer" their questions, He responds to them, as they need. And the very repetition of the mood of despair which results in this mode of interaction teaches us to avoid it—not because we are any less prone to despair (far from it!), but because we see that ultimately it is unwarranted. We have the opportunity to gain from the growth pangs of the Children of Israel in the wilderness.

Exodus and the Feminine in the Teachings of Rabbi Yaakov of Izbica

Ora Wiskind Elper

> When the Great Mother (*imma ila'ah*) was revealed to you [Moshe], you responded, "I will approach and see that fearsome sight—why the bush is not consumed." For it is a wondrous act of mercy that the bush does not burn. (*Beit Ya'akov*, *parashat Shemot* 36)

My perception of "the feminine" as an aspect of hasidic teaching has emerged more as an unexpected discovery than as the result of conscious and systematic labor. In teaching, in learning, in reading, radically innovative interpretations by hasidic masters of canonical Jewish texts have leapt out at me and demanded attention. I would like to share some of them here, as I believe they have much to say about problems of our own time. As they confront the texts, the hasidic masters, at times, devote a great measure of attention to "original experience"—to fundamental aspects of humanness beyond gender, as well as to an awareness of "origins" such as conception, birthing and being born.[1] What interests me here are the aspects of the "feminine" that transcend physiological, biological, or culturally conditioned differences between men and women. An understanding of these aspects, I think, need not be reached dialectically, by identifying and defining an external Other, fundamentally alien to a self. That is, I do not expect to understand the feminine by defining "the masculine," nor attempt to oppose the psychic tendencies of women to those of men.

---

[1] In this manner, Emmanuel Levinas describes Maurice Blanchot's notion of the poet's transcendent vision. Cf. "On Maurice Blanchot" (originally published in 1976), in *Proper Names*, Michael Smith trans. (Stanford University Press, 1996) 130.

What I will call "feminine modes of being"—nurturing, protecting, selflessness, indwelling presence—are portrayed throughout the Bible, the Talmud and *midrashim*. While the actions connected to these modes are clearly not the exclusive domain of women, the imagery embodying them is very often linked to feminine elements. Hasidic thought in general, from its inception in the teachings of R. Israel Ba'al Shem Tov, shows a striking interest in such moving figures. Mother's milk, for instance, becomes a metaphor for the holy wisdom learned in childhood; the devoted rebbe is "midwife" to his students' nascent understanding; a Jew in prayer longs for God like a young wife for her husband. This reawakened sensitivity in hasidic teaching to experiences unique, in a literal sense, to women is surely linked to certain historical factors that deserve some mention, although I will not speculate on them here. Hasidism responded and contributed to the revival of spirituality, inwardness and emotion within the Jewish world in the late eighteenth and nineteenth centuries. That period also witnessed revolutionary changes in social, economic and political orders in both Eastern and Western Europe, among them the drive toward emancipation of women in the wake of the Enlightenment. A "modern consciousness" came to pervade Jewish intellectual life, and by the late nineteenth century it affected even the most insulated enclaves, from Russia and Galicia to Congress Poland. Although the subject is compelling, I will not address the actual role of women within the hasidic community as leaders or mystics, nor their intimate spiritual lives. Instead, I will concentrate on the metaphors used in hasidic texts to describe femininity (in an abstract, non-"embodied" sense). I hope that this will lead us to a deeper and more nuanced understanding of how these texts confront questions of great existential, religious and intellectual urgency. For example: how can spiritual freedom be preserved in times of oppression? Can we, in loyalty to the sources, think of God as "maternal"? What do concepts such as "mercy," "judgment," "punishment," or "desire" really mean?

The following pages will examine two passages from the teachings of R. Ya'akov Leiner of Izbica (1828–78), appearing in his commentary *Beit*

Ya'akov on the book of Exodus.[2] R. Ya'akov is the second prominent figure of the Izbica-Radzin dynasty, founded by his father, R. Mordechai Yoseph Leiner (1802–1854), who is commonly known as "the Izbicer" and author of *Mei haShiloah*. R. Ya'akov, like his father and his own son, R. Gershon Henoch of Radzin (the famed "*ba'al haTekhelet*"), presents his teachings in a rich texture of interwoven traditional sources, integrated through probing insights into the workings of the human psyche. Rather than imposing a conceptual structure of my own, I have chosen, in the following discussion, to follow R. Ya'akov's own associative train of thought, loosely based on selected verses from the weekly *parashah*, in presenting his teaching.

Forgetting in the House of Bondage

In the first of these passages (*parashat Shemot* 20–21), R. Ya'akov speaks of the insidious forces that gradually drew the Jewish people from their comfortable status as a privileged guest-population, settled in the Land of Goshen, into enslavement to an alien ruler. While the verse he selects to open his commentary—"And the Egyptians put the children of Israel to hard labor" "ויעבדו מצרים את בני ישראל בפרך" (Exodus 1:13) sounds rather unequivocal (particularly in the usual English translation), R. Ya'akov notes that the Rabbis are of two minds about its meaning. In the Talmud *Sotah* 11b we find R. Eleazar interprets the word *befarekh*, not as "hard labor," but the very opposite—as "soft-speak," *befe rakh*. R. Shmuel bar Nahmani, however, understands it more literally as "back-breaking work," *beferikha*. R. Ya'akov now makes a subtle psychological analysis of the conditions that insidiously rob people of their autonomy, gradually reducing them to total servility:

> At first, the Egyptians spoke kindly to them, concealing all evil intent, in order to accustom them gradually to being slaves. They were to forget they had ever been free; rather, the only enduring memory should be of themselves as subservient. The ultimate plan was to cause them

---

[2] *Sefer Beit Ya'akov al haTorah* (Lublin: 5664/1904; Jerusalem: 5758/1998). The commentary is presented according to the weekly *parashah*. The passages cited in my discussion all appears in the first *parashah* of the book of Exodus, in Hebrew— *Shemot*.

to forget how to pray, so that the very hope of being delivered from their exile would no longer live in their hearts. For the Egyptians knew that if the Jews would appeal to God for redemption, their prayers would be answered immediately. Thus, they provided favorable conditions to silence them from within. Egypt, for the Jews, was like a pleasure garden and they indulged themselves royally. So great was their desire and delight that the heart's repose was complete. "No slave was capable of escaping from Egypt, for it was more comfortable to live there as a slave than as a nobleman in some other country" (*Mekhilta, Yitro*). Thus the Torah speaks of the "house of bondage" (Exodus 20:2), for they felt enveloped and shielded from all evil; they were unaware of their own enslavement.

The ominous tone of this scenario turns on two ambiguous elements. The notion of comfort (*no'ah*) with its positive connotation of ease and non-confrontation is shaded by its negative, euphemistic sense of ultimate repose, i.e., death, being "laid to rest" (like the Aramaic *nah nafshei*). Comfort, then, turns into a sinister force as the Jewish people are slowly buried alive, as it were, smothered in the sensual embrace of material satisfaction, becoming willful prisoners in their House of Usher. At this stage, R. Ya'akov continues, the "soft-speak" initially adopted by the Egyptians is exchanged for outright aggression. When Pharaoh saw he had not fully succeeded:

> He forced them to cruel labor—*beferikha*—to break them and make them forget their lineage. They were to see themselves as born slaves with no faculty to pray, their sole desire being to find favor in the eyes of their masters. Thus were they shattered, growing so used to work that they were numb to their own pain and distress. Sometimes we see such a thing—when a person is so miserable that everyone pities him, yet he himself is oblivious to his own degradation.... This, then, is the worst sort of oppression—not to know or even sense one's enslavement and alienation.[3]

---

[3] The following testimony of a "slave" sucked into the Soviet gulag drives R. Ya'akov's words home: "I stood and dished out the food, methodically dipping my ladle into the caldron of soup and holding out a mess tin to each of the weird creatures that passed before me, muffled in rags and bits of sacking, with black, frostbitten cheeks and noses covered with running sores, with bleeding, toothless gums. Had they issued from primeval night, or from the sick fantasy of a Goya? I was paralyzed by horror, but I went on mixing and stirring the soup in the caldron so that what I

Thus, in a bold stroke, R. Ya'akov unites the seemingly contradictory meanings of the expression *befarekh*. Oppression begins with "soft words"; if the victim still resists, the iron club descends.

The biblical institution of the Jewish bondsman (*eved ivri*), with its concomitant moral dangers to the Jewish master, leads R. Ya'akov to add the following reflection:

> Indeed, the Torah warned, in the case of a Jewish bondsman, "Do not rule over him unduly (*befarekh*)" (Leviticus 25:46). That is, give him a place and a moment each day to remember that he is not a slave in essence or by birth; once he was free. This will preserve in him the passion to be redeemed; he will hope and pray for liberation.

And his conclusion: the most lethal attack against the Jewish people has always been directed against the soul—to obscure and extinguish the very memory that one can pray. R. Ya'akov now shifts to the crucial spiritual reflex of "desire" (*teshukah*)—that existential state of the soul Kierkegaard calls "infinite passion"—which alone ensures human freedom.

I Am Ready

How, R. Ya'akov asks, was the critical turning point reached? How did the Jewish people manage to awaken to their true identity as "children" of God (*bannim*), with the implicit and organic sense of origin the term entails, rather than as slaves held in a vacuum of isolation? It was God, he explains, who reminded them by revealing Himself in the guise of EHYEH. This divine name, which is uttered for the first time to Moshe in his vision of the burning bush (Exodus 3:14–15), is central in R. Ya'akov's unique vision of redemption. While many elements of his discussion do appear in midrashic, medieval and kabbalistic pre-texts, I

---

ladled out to them might be as thick and nourishing as possible.... Still they came. There was no end to the black procession. With their stiff fingers they took the bowl, stood it on the edge of the long, plank table and ate. They partook of the soup as though of a sacrament that held the secret of the preservation of life...." Eugenia Ginzburg, *Journey into the Whirlwind*, Paul Stevenson and Max Hayward trans. (Orlando: Harcourt Brace, 1967) 393.

believe they are transmuted in R. Ya'akov's thought, with important implications for our understanding of the feminine. At the outset, we must put aside the most common translations of the name EHYEH as "the Eternal," or as "I am what I am." The changeless duration of eternity, like the more immediate but equally static continuous present, fail to reflect the essence of this Name. Rather, in keeping with the most basic rules of Hebrew grammar, we note that the letter *aleph* with which EHYEH begins signifies the verbal future tense:

> In showing them His name as "EHYEH," that is, "I am ready to give birth" (*ana zamin le'oleda*),[4] He aroused them to hope for Him and pray to Him. Then they could be redeemed, as it says, "And they cried out to the Lord in their trouble (*betza'ar*) and He freed them from their distress..." (Psalms 107:13, 19) for God is merciful (*rahum*) and willing to save.

Here, in effect, R. Ya'akov suggests a radical shift in perspective, a new definition of genre and identification. As he notes in the lines that follow: "The holy R. Yitzchak Luria compares the experience of exile to the gestation process (*yetzirat havalad*)." When God announces, "I am ready to give birth," His words are directed, as it were, to an entity still unborn, to a presence that must become aware of the increasingly narrow confines in which it grows. The indwelling and still dormant fetus, then, represents in this context the nascent Jewish people, while the maternal body "pregnant with the future" is a metaphor of God "Him"self. Such an assertion, as radical as it may sound to modern ears, is nonetheless firmly grounded in the complex of images R. Ya'akov has inherited from biblical, rabbinic and mystical tradition.[5] The concepts of exile and redemption are also redefined, gaining metaphysical and meta-historical dimensions: "exile" bespeaks alienation; "redemption" is experienced as a joyful return, a

---

[4] R. Ya'akov employs the language of the *Zohar* 3.65a–b here to clarify the significance of this divine name.

[5] Consider, for example, the image in Isaiah 46:3: "Hearken to me, O House of Ya'akov and all the remnant of the House of Israel, who are borne by me from birth, carried from the womb." In the Blessing of Sanctification of the New Moon (*kiddush levanah*), the same language and imagery of pregnancy, fullness and birthing are adopted to speak of the messianic age as an ultimate re-birth.

reunion with some higher level of existence. In such a context, then, one may indeed say the unborn baby is estranged, or in exile from its still faceless mother (despite the extreme proximity) and that the Jewish people emerge forcefully from the innermost depths of oppression in a redemptive (re-)birth. A dynamic tension between the two extremes pervades the destiny of Israel, and the search for the meaning of that recurrent cycle of crisis, longing and deliverance underlies many of the images on which R. Ya'akov draws.

Perhaps most difficult to comprehend, however, is the curious state of mutual passivity he describes. The expectant mother feels "ready" to bear and yet she is vulnerable, wholly dependent on the initiative of the baby in her womb. R. Ya'akov invokes, on this point, a fragment of a talmudic statement in order to speak of the strange lull between the subjective sense of readiness for birth/redemption and its ultimate realization somehow beyond all will: "So if He is waiting and we await, what is the delay?" (*Sanhedrin* 97b).[6] To enable a fuller understanding of the final state of gestation—labor and birth—R. Ya'akov first turns his attention to the beginning of the process: the wholly concealed moment of conception.

> For everything contains something of the primordial Will (*haratzon harishon*) expressed in the words "Let there be light" (Genesis 1:3), which preceded the awakening of all created entities. As it is written: "Remember Your mercy (*rahamekhah*), O Lord, and Your compassion, for they are from time everlasting" (Psalms 25:6). It is from that germinal point that Creation begins.

The key word in this description is mercy (*rahamim*), etymologically linked to the image of the womb, or *rehem*. The original and primordial gesture of divine "mercy," he recalls, was in conceiving (of) our world, in enabling the existence of alterity, or otherness, within the infinite expansiveness called God. In Lurianic mysticism, this willful contraction

---

[6] In the Talmud, however, the order of the question he quotes is actually the reverse—"So if *we* are waiting and *He* awaits...." I have quoted the text as R. Ya'akov cites it. This surely unintentional alteration of the original statement may reflect the depth of R. Ya'akov's sensitivity to God's "predicament" as conceived in hasidic thought in general: divine will is predicated by and subject to human resolve to be redeemed. Cf. Teachings by R. Dov Baer, the Maggid of Mezericz, *Maggid devarav leYa'akov*, s. 24, 26, 85, 127.

(*tzimtzum*) is weighted with emotional and ethical significance: it is a supreme gesture of unselfish devotion, of renunciation and of patience. For in making room for a separate and autonomous self, an irrevocable subjectivity is also engendered. (Emmanuel Levinas describes this aspect of becoming a mother as the passivity of the "for-the-other in vulnerability,"[7] an occurrence in a past "prior to all memory and recall…an irrecuperable time."[8]) It is of this almost imperceptible point of origin (*nekudah*), R. Ya'akov teaches, that the name EHYEH speaks as well. The eventual "I am ready" of EHYEH begins to be possible at the moment of conception.

Shrieks and Echoes

This initial stage, however, is still exceedingly precarious. The diminutive embryo, so fragile, is compared to a seed planted in the earth: "After sowing, it seems as if each seed has decomposed, has been totally lost in the soil." This is R. Ya'akov's reading of the years following the death of "Yosef and all his brethren and all that generation" (Exodus 1:6). The Jewish nation multiplies and becomes scattered throughout the land of Egypt, yet they are slowly becoming dismembered as well, the Egyptian soil drawing them into grave moral and psychological putrefaction. At this most critical point of extreme decay, R. Ya'akov explains, Pharaoh unleashed his destructive forces in the attempt to snuff out their last spark of life. Recalling a chilling image from the *Zohar* (2.34b), R. Ya'akov describes Pharaoh as "a great and mighty dragon who sought to extinguish the sparks gathered from those worlds destroyed." Pharaoh's audacity (*hutzpah*), he explains, was in waging war against God Himself, in trying to negate His ultimate power as Creator and protector of His world.

The primordial events R. Ya'akov alludes to here are in fact drawn from a complex of traditional images. Among them are the biblical suggestion of chaos, or *tohu*, preceding the beginning of Creation; the

---

[7] *Otherwise than Being or Beyond Essence*, Alphonso Lingis trans. (The Hague: Martinus Nijhoff, 1981) 71.

[8] Ibid., 104–5.

midrashic probing of that primeval disorder—"God created worlds and destroyed them, created and destroyed, until He created ours" (*Genesis Rabbah* 9.2) and the interpretation of these events in Lurianic mysticism known as "the shattering of the vessels." R. Ya'akov integrates this complex of images in his own discussion, adding a psychological dimension: "Those worlds could not endure," he explains, "because they received the [divine] light in all its immensity, unmitigated by any sense of awe (*beli yirah*) and exploded." The annihilation, however, was not total. Fragmentary remnants of those lost worlds remained to echo the disaster. Drawing on yet another haunting image, R. Ya'akov portrays the shards as audible signs:

> This, our own world, came into being from those shrieks (*tza'akot*) and that dread (*yirot*) resounding from the worlds obliterated. In their wake, a trace of reverence (*yirah*) remained for the new world, a world in which restoration is possible (*olam hatikkun*)—that trace is the imperative to remember that all is in divine hands. Then the worlds will never again be destroyed.

The disembodied screams of beings unable to endure—it strikes us as a surrealistic and unsettling notion. I'd like to consider, for a moment, other instances in Jewish sources in which such voices are heard, in the hope of shedding light on R. Ya'akov's understanding of this primitive mode of expression.

The descending darkness of oppression described in the first chapters of Exodus brings the children of Israel to a nadir of despair. Chapter two closes with these words:

> And it came to pass in the course of those many days, that the king of Egypt died and the children of Israel sighed under their bondage and their cry (*tza'akatam*) rose to God. And God heard their groaning and He remembered His covenant with Avraham, with Yitzchak and with Ya'akov. And God looked upon the children of Israel and God knew.

This cry *de profundis* is, in effect, a turning point.[9] God responds by apprehending, by manifesting His presence—albeit yet passively—for the

---

[9] Note that here (Exodus 2:23–25), they sigh and cry in an existential vacuum, as it were (*veye'anu...veyitzaku*), and God "overhears" them. Only later in the narrative,

first time in the biblical narrative of the exile. In the revelation at the burning bush a few verses later, God speaks to Moshe directly of this "awakening":

> I have surely seen the affliction of my people in Egypt and have heard their screams (*tza'akatam*) evoked by their taskmasters and I know their sorrows.... (Exodus 3:7)

What was it about the cry of the children of Israel that finally succeeded in evoking divine attention? And why is the talmudic Sage, R. Yitzhak, in his turn, so convinced that "The most worthwhile appeal is to cry out to God (*yafeh tza'akah*), whether before or after the decree has been made"? (*Rosh Hashanah* 17a). Prayer may very well sound eloquent and convincing (particularly to the person praying). In crying out, by contrast, one "says nothing." Yet, as R. Yehudah claims (*Zohar* 2.20a), "For that very reason crying out has the greatest strength, for it emerges from the heart, as it is written, 'Their heart cried to the Lord' (Lamentations 2:18) and this is dearer to God than all prayer and groaning."

For R. Ya'akov, the crucial moment of awakening actually coincides with the revelation of the divine name EHYEH:

> When God told them "EHYEH," He reminded them who they really were and they *began* to scream to the Lord to save them. For when a person prays to God, He in His mercy will respond. God *began* to save them by revealing His name EHYEH to Moshe—at once they *began* to feel the bitterness of their exile, to *become* aware of their pain....

Note the emphasis in this passage on *beginning*. A process is set in motion at last; the impasse of long waiting starts to give way. This quickening, although apparently motivated more by anguish than by hope, nonetheless marks the commencement of a possibility yet unknown. The "courage to wish," as Franz Rosenzweig names it, finds voice "in the cry of an open question...to fulfill the wish, to answer the question, to still the cry—that is beyond its power. What is present is its own; into the future it only casts

---

after the revelation of the name EHYEH, are they able to turn to God with their sorrow. My thanks to R. Mark Kuzovsky for calling my attention to this distinction.

the wish, the question, the cry."[10] It is the revelation of a promise—EHYEH, "I will be with you" (Exodus 3:12)—that brings the Jewish people to a critical awareness of their straits. This awareness impels them to act, to begin wishing to be born. And in imagining such a new horizon, they initiate its ultimate realization.

The Great Mother

We recall the conviction, voiced by the talmudic sage R. Yitzhak above, that a wordless plea rising from the heart's depths can have the power to alter one's destiny. The language used by the Rabbis is telling on this point and close attention to it may clarify another aspect of the process we have been examining. A divine judgment, usually concerning the decision to punish or constrict the individual's actions, is customarily referred to, both in rabbinic and mystical parlance, as *din*. In more esoteric contexts, *din* is also often conceived in conjunction with *tzimtzum* or "contraction," a forceful retention of naturally expansive forces. Most people intuitively react to the idea of "judgment," or *din*, as an unpleasant, even undesirable experience—an unwelcome limitation placed on personal freedom and spontaneity. The instinctive response to such a threat, then, would be to plead for mercy, to attempt to have the decree revoked, the constriction eased. In turn, God's hoped-for response, in rabbinic terms, could then be "to rise from the seat of judgment and take the seat of compassion."[11] But despite the "unpleasantness" we associate with chastisement, rabbinic literature devotes much energy to considering its potentially desirable spiritual effects. Later, in mystical thought, the attributes of *din* and *rahamim*—of censure and mercy—acquire explicit gender differentiation. The feminine "left side" of judgment and severity is often portrayed in dialectical opposition to the masculine "right side" of grace. This stereotypical male-female polarity is frequently reiterated, and many

---

[10] *The Star of Redemption*, Book 2, "Revelation or the Ever-Renewed Birth of the Soul" (1930), William Hallo trans. (Notre Dame: University of Notre Dame Press, 1985) 185.

[11] Cf. *Leviticus Rabbah* 29.10, among other instances.

consider it a distinctive feature of theosophic Kabbalah as a whole.[12] We would do well, however, to notice other, less conventional and commonly overlooked mystical imagery, which may lead to radically different possibilities of interpretation. Indeed, only with an appreciation of alternate imagery can we hope to understand R. Ya'akov's (re-)reading of the Exodus story.

In subsequent reflections on the name EHYEH (*parashat Shemot* 45), R. Ya'akov associates that formulation with the *sefirah* of *Binah* and augments the association with these words from the *Zohar* (3.65a): "For she is called Mother, the feminine (*nukba*), strength (*gevurah*) and the source of strict judgment (*dina*)." He then adds, however:

> Yet in truth, we also find in the *Zohar* (3.99a): "That river, although [harsh] decrees (*dinin*) seem to emerge from her, they are not really decrees at all, but rather tremendous mercy." …Indeed, contracted in that name [EHYEH] is all of God's boundless light.

Remarkable in these comments is the denial of any objective dichotomy or separation between attributes. The impression of strict judgment, he implies, is merely that—an initial resemblance that conceals, yet eventually gives way to resolution in its opposite. At issue here is not a transmutation; the feminine element is not "annulled" or "effaced," nor does it become masculine in any sense. Rather, what R. Ya'akov describes are two stages, both of them "feminine" experiences in the extreme. The futurity implicit in the name EHYEH, as we have seen, symbolizes expectancy, pregnancy, the hidden reality of an impending birth. Restraint and constriction, both of them intrinsic aspects of *din*, are vitally necessary in such a state: the fetus must be held inside, hermetically sealed so to speak, until the time is ripe. At birth, a threshold is crossed, not only by the infant but by the birthing woman as well. As R. Meir puts it (*Behorot* 6b, *Niddah* 9a), "Blood changes into milk." The lifeblood that sustained the

---

[12] Consider, for example, Elliot Wolfson's discussion "Woman–The Feminine as Other in Theosophic Kabbalah: Some Philosophical Observations on the Divine Androgyne," *The Other in Jewish Thought and History: Constructions of Jewish Culture and Identity*, L. Silberstein and R. Cohen eds. (NY, 1994) 166–204. See also I. Tishby's and F. Lachower's extensive overview in *The Wisdom of the Zohar* (1949), David Goldstein trans. (Oxford: Oxford University Press, 1991) 269–308 and 371–82.

fetus becomes superfluous and flows away; another fluid, white rather than red but equally nourishing, comes in its stead to permeate the nursing mother's body. *Din* has given way to *rahamim*, to a face-to-face relationship of love, responsibility and compassion.

This second stage, though, is certainly no less feminine than the first, despite the "active" role the mother takes as the source of effulgence (*mashpi'ah*) rather than as a "passive" recipient of seed. Moreover, the "miracle that saves the world," as Hannah Arendt describes natality, can occur only after earlier, formative trials have been endured.[13] Clearly, then, the hierarchical relationship commonly attributed to the (inferior, disagreeable) concept of *din* and the (superior, gratifying) concept of *rahamim* must be reevaluated. Only within limitation and concealment can an inceptive occurrence take place. The power to hope germinates in that darkness; emerging, a promise is realized, bringing the consolation of a welcoming, open space.[14]

Body and Soul

The seed, the spark, the embryo—these minute vessels, containers of a future, are an exceedingly tenuous presence. We recall R. Ya'akov's portrayal of Pharaoh as "a great and mighty dragon who sought to extinguish the sparks gathered from those worlds destroyed." Pharaoh's ultimate failure is symbolized, in R. Ya'akov's eyes, in the counter-image

---

[13] *The Human Condition* (Chicago: University of Chicago Press, 1958, 1998) 247.

[14] Andre Neher, in his work relating the lives of prominent contemporary and near-contemporary Jews, *They Made Their Souls Anew* (1979), David Maisel trans. (Albany: S.U.N.Y., 1990) 133–35, speaks of spiritual rebirth in terms very similar to those used by R. Ya'akov. He describes the changing dynamics of the German-Jewish milieu from the period of the Weimar Republic to that of the Third Reich and through the Holocaust. "The slow but continuous erosion which detached, despite themselves, all these Jews from German society, Bloch perceived in the form of a Jewish biblical legend to which Benjamin Fondane, murdered at Auschwitz, gave its poetic expression and Ernst Bloch its philosophical pattern, the Exodus.... What was the Exodus if not the religious Utopia par excellence, the idea of going forth, of opening up, of passage and arrival?...[This Utopia] exists in the Promise...which led Bloch to another principle, even more central to his thought than the Exodus: the principle of *Hope*, the title of the key work of his entire spiritual edifice."

of an eternal, undying fire. He refers the reader parenthetically to his commentary on a later verse in the *parashah*, in which he offers a close reading of the inner dynamics of God's first appearance to Moshe at Horev. R. Ya'akov notes in passing that Moshe is compelled by the strange sight of the flaming bush and draws closer to understand why it is not consumed. Only then does God call to him "out of the midst of the bush," recount His awareness of the people's suffering and reveal the divine Name promising redemption (Exodus 3:1–16). R. Ya'akov's discussion there (*parashat Shemot* 36) will now aid us in understanding the complex vision guiding his thought:

> And Moshe said, "I must turn aside and see this great sight..." (Exodus 3:3). Moshe *rabbenu* was amazed by the union of the soul with the body, for by nature they are opposites. Why doesn't the soul, with its divine origin, overcome the body and draw it to God's will? And if the body is stronger than the soul, how can the soul survive within it?.... By showing Moshe that "the bush burned with fire but the bush was not consumed" (Exodus 3:2), God taught him that divine will alone determines whether or not destruction is possible.

While everything achieved by human efforts may be wasted by fire, R. Ya'akov explains, the nuclear core (*nekudah*) of all created entities is indestructible, for it, like fire itself, was generated by divine will. These reflections now lead R. Ya'akov to a striking reappraisal of the paradoxical duality of body and soul:

> As the midrash says (*Leviticus Rabbah, Shemini* 11.5): [Moshe asked], "What preciousness (*yekara*) is contained within [the bush]?" And God answered him, "My glory (*yekari*) is within it." In other words, God explained that the body has/contains tremendous value (*yekarut*). The midrash (*Shohar Tov* 62.3) recounts that the soul ascends, leaves the body, yet descends once again. In response to its desire to reunite with its [divine] root, God shows it that "the whole earth is filled with His glory" (Isaiah 6:3) and it goes back down.

The drama of the soul's ambivalence toward the body, its displacement between upper and lower realms in the restless, perhaps irreconcilable search for completeness—this, for R. Ya'akov, is the symbolic message contained in the vision of the burning bush. To appreciate the real originality of R. Ya'akov's thought here, however, we must become aware of the weighty and composite subtext on which his reflections are founded.[15]

The trials of the soul, for the Rabbis, begin not on earth but in the Garden of Eden. After being hewn from the Throne of Glory (known by mystics as "the mother of all souls," *em haneshamot*),[16] they flow onward to be gathered in a metaphysical storehouse called *guf*[17] where they await, doubtless with some trepidation, their inevitable descent into our world. The *Zohar* portrays with great pathos the soul's reluctance to fall from the heights of heavenly purity to the murky depths of corporeality.[18] Yet descend it must, for as R. Sa'adya Ga'on explains, the soul can serve its Creator, thereby meriting eternal life, only through the organs of the human body.[19] And so, submitting at last to divine decree, the soul descends to begin a life of contingency.

From Plato and Plotinus to Jewish thinkers such as R. Bahya ibn Paquda, R. Shlomo ibn Gabirol, R. Moshe de Leon and in the worldview of the *Zohar*, incarnation is incarceration—the soul languishes, imprisoned and alienated, in the shackles of the body.[20] Its sole yearning is to escape upward and return to its source and this accounts for its fugitive existence. While the body slumbers, it snatches moments of freedom until dawn

---

[15] The subject, of course, is vast. My treatment of it here is associative and impressionistic rather than analytical, and makes no claim to being comprehensive. Nor will I address distinctions between the "subdivisions" of the soul—intellect, *nefesh*, *ru'ah*, *neshamah*—so central to Hellenistic and medieval Jewish philosophical discourse, nor the five-part division perceived by the Kabbalists. Notably, R. Ya'akov uses many of these terms interchangeably, leading me to conclude that such distinctions (although he was surely aware of them) are not his concern.

[16] *Shabbat* 152a; *Hagigah* 12b; *Zohar* 1.125b (*Midrash haNe'elam*).

[17] *Yevamot* 62a, with Rashi's comments there. The cryptic term "*guf*," which translates in modern Hebrew as "body," does not share that connotation in the talmudic context.

[18] *Zohar* 2.96b.

[19] *Emunot veDe'ot* VI, 4. R. Moshe Cordovero, in *Pardes Rimmonim*, ch. 31, sec. 5 adopts this philosophical view and adds another, more mystical perspective.

[20] *Phaedo* 62b, 82e; *Enneads* IV, 8:1; *Hovot haLevavot* III.2, VI.5, VII.3, IX.3; *Hegyon haNefesh*, 11b, 16a; *Mekor Hayyim*, 1:2, 5:43; *Shekel haKodesh*, p. 5; *Zohar* 1.245b, 2.96b, 2.150a.

breaks; then it is compelled to return and dutifully restore life to the "shell" it inhabits in the world below.[21] The body itself, continually torn between good and evil,[22] a near-defenseless victim embattled with the powers of impurity,[23] is a mere "garment" (*levush*) to be cast off at death.[24]

Common to all these ideas is the tenacious and seemingly irreducible principle of *dualism*. The antithesis may be between matter and form, body and soul, darkness and light, left and right, or feminine and masculine. Yet all of these anthropomorphic symmetries serve to reinforce the implicit moral contrast upon which dualism is founded. Whether seen as an impediment or as an instrument, corporeality remains negative; obscurity must be bitterly endured until illumination finally comes; "husks" and shells are disposed of when the fruit grows ripe. One might argue that the best way to rectify the *de*valorization of all these stereotypically "female" entities is through reversal, to replace "inferiority" with superiority. Understandable as such a reaction may be, the alternative it offers is, in effect, equally reductive. To replace one dualistic system with its mirror image wins no one freedom. I believe another more viable response to the classic polarity does exist. Voiced in many forms by other hasidic masters as well, it is cogently expressed in R. Ya'akov's teachings. Let's listen, then, to his suggestion that the uncompromising notion of dualism outlined above must be expanded into a more complex vision of plurality. In it,

---

[21] *Ta'anit* 11a; *Zohar* 2.213b–214a, 3.67a.

[22] *Berakhot* 61a.

[23] *Shabbat* 105b; *Sefer Galya Raza*, 6b, 21a. The reaction to such a conviction of the body's vulnerability to evil forces is, most naturally, asceticism. By deliberately humiliating and negating bodily needs—that is, when the body is weakened—perhaps physical and spiritual liberty from those forces may be won. Needless to say, such a reaction has been a strong force in a range of religious and political movements throughout history.

[24] *Zohar* 1.59b–60a (*Tosefta*). This notion, to be sure, is counter-balanced by another concept of the human being as a microcosm (*Genesis Rabbah* 14.8), the body created from the four elements, from the dust of four corners of the world (*Zohar* 2.13a–b, 23b), or as a reflection of the divine *sefirot* (*Zohar* 1.20a, 186b). Just as each *sefirah* is the outer "garment" or manifestation of the essence concealed in the *sefirah* immediately above it, so the body serves as the shell, in which the invisible soul may be glimpsed (*Zohar* 1.103b).

polarities become nuances; tonalities of major and minor are exposed as inextricably interdependent.[25]

Embodiment and Becoming

We return now to the image of the disembodied cries reverberating from worlds destroyed and their role, according to R. Ya'akov, in the creation of our brave, new world (*olam hatikkun*). The following passage from the midrash *Pirkei deRabbi Eliezer* 34 seems to have served as a pretext for R. Ya'akov's own teaching:

> Six are the voices that echo to the ends of the earth, yet the voice cannot be heard. They are: when a fruit-bearing tree is chopped down—the voice echoes to the ends of the earth; when the snake sheds its skin—the voice echoes to the ends of the earth; when a woman is divorced from her husband—the voice echoes to the ends of the earth; when a woman has relations with her husband for the first time—the voice echoes to the ends of the earth; when an infant emerges from its mother's womb—the voice echoes to the ends of the earth; when the soul departs from the body—the voice echoes to the ends of the earth. And the soul does not depart until it sees the *Shekhinah*, as it is written, "For no one can see Me and live." (Exodus 33:20)

Note, first of all, that these "voices" emerge not from individuals (the tree, the woman, the infant, the snake) but from *moments* of crisis, charged with rending emotion. The tree made useless, the cast-off skin, the ruptured union, the passing of a living soul—all of these speak of a parting which somehow leaves its mark on the world itself as a lingering echo that never completely fades away. But what of the voice "when an infant emerges from its mother's womb"? The midrash speaks neither of the infant's first cries nor of the mother's travail. It seems to me that this disembodied

---

[25] In other creative modes, this notion of interdependence is self-understood. Consider, for instance, the interplay of light and shadow. First developed as an artistic technique in Renaissance painting and used by the Impressionists to a revolutionary extent, it is essential in evoking the sense of a real, living and dynamic subject. The aural dimensions in music that is polyphonic in texture similarly depend on the interplay between melodic lines—each heightens and enriches the other with no claims of superiority or inferiority.

voice is, in effect, the voice of the soul about to become embodied, with all the unspoken emotional burden that moment contains.[26] Compare, now, a very similar comment made by the sages of the *Zohar*:

> Come and see: three are the voices that never perish: the voice of a laboring woman (*hayya*)[27] on the birthstones—that voice travels through the air, echoing to the ends of the earth; the voice of a person when the soul departs from the body—that voice travels through the air, echoing to the ends of the earth; the voice of the snake shedding its skin—that voice travels through the air, echoing to the ends of the earth.

Here, in contrast to the midrash above, the source of the voice is named. Moreover, the sound emitted serves explicitly to "give voice" to some internal, mysterious experience. This parallel passage figures prominently in a number of other kabbalistic and hasidic teachings, particularly, as we will see, concerning the shofar on Rosh Hashanah. Missing, however, is the striking reflection in the last line of the midrash: "And the soul does not depart until it sees the *Shekhinah*, as it is written, 'For no one can see Me and live.'" The moment of death, then, would arrive in an ultimate, humanly unbearable revelation. As our discussion progresses, the implications of this intuition will become clear.

While R. Ya'akov does not refer openly to this midrash, nor to the similar passage from the *Zohar*, his son, R. Gershon Henoch of Radzin, interprets them both on a symbolic plane. The notion of the cry (*tza'akah*) is, in fact, a *leitmotif* in the teachings of three generations of the Izbica-Radzin dynasty. It appears in numerous contexts in the thought of R. Gershon Henoch; I believe his words in the following passage may help us integrate the two teachings of his father that we have been studying. In his work *Sod Yesharim, Hoshana Rabbah* 4, R. Gershon Henoch writes:

---

[26] There are divergent views expressed in the Talmud concerning when the soul enters the body: from the time of conception; gradually over the course of gestation; or at birth itself. In all these cases, however, birth remains the crucial turning point in the "active" interaction of body and soul. Cf. *Sanhedrin* 91b.

[27] Literally translated as an animal, but the word often appears both in rabbinic and kabbalistic contexts, in reference to a woman giving birth or a midwife.

This voice [heard] at birthing alludes to the cry when the [primordial, divine] light became clothed in the created world. Indeed, it is the [same] cry heard at every birth, for when the soul begins its descent from on high into the material body, it shouts out loud. How unpleasant (*aino no'ah*) to have to enter the obscurity of the body, that "tree of doubt" (*ilana desafeka*)—as it says (*Eruvin* 13b), "It would have been easier for a person never to have been created (*no'ah le'adam shelo nivra mishenivra*)!" But as my grandfather, may his holy memory be blessed,[28] explained, [the Sages] did not say, "It would have been *better* for a person not to have been created".... Because truly it *is* better that people were created [than not to have been]; as God wills that the soul inhabit the body, surely that is the best thing for the soul and He is certain it will succeed in its mission to this world. The fear, then, comes from people themselves—the terror is that being created will be very difficult; the pure soul is unwilling to descend...thus it cries bitterly: "Why have you raised me to such heights, only to cast me away?" (Psalms 102:11)

The pervasive reality of hiddenness, of doubt, discomfort and darkness that plagues our world, then, is what so troubles the unborn soul.[29] God's "certainty" stands in sharp contrast to the acutely human plight described. I think it is precisely this discrepancy in perception that R. Ya'akov addresses in his understanding of the revelation to Moshe at Horev. Moshe is astonished to witness a seemingly impossible "union": the flaming bush, the body unscathed by the burning soul. And God, through the divine name EHYEH, speaks to him of the mystery of all beginnings. That mystery hinges, once again, on the paradox of concealment and revealing so fundamental to R. Ya'akov's thought. We have considered it in the

---

[28] R. Mordechai Yoseph Leiner, whose teachings were collected posthumously by the author, R. Gershon Henoch, in two volumes of *Mei haShilo'ah*, published in 1860 (vol. 1) and 1922 (vol. 2).

[29] Note that the talmudic statement to which R. Gershon Henoch refers is actually the conclusion of a theoretical dispute between the schools of Shammai and Hillel. In mystical thought (cf. *Zohar* 3.245a), the worldview of *beit* Hillel is informed by the attribute of *hesed*, while the worldview of *beit* Shammai, in contrast, is informed by the attribute of *din*. In their evaluation of the "comfort level" of human existence, the Sages, on a collective level, eventually favor the conclusion voiced by the school of Shammai—"It would have been easier for people never to have been created." Yet, as R. Mordechai Yoseph teaches, the discomfort endemic to an experience of *din* may well be vitally formative, concealing within it an act of great love.

context of the Egyptian bondage and of the period of gestation preceding birth. But in truth, R. Ya'akov teaches, the same process recurs throughout the lifetime of every individual. Just as the children of Israel, reduced to servitude, were unaware of their own abjection, so too, every person is in some sense subject to his body's demands, while remaining blind to his own servility and alienation. Living this darkness, however, is an existential necessity, as R. Ya'akov proceeds to explain (*parashat Shemot* 36):

> For all creatures, the more distant they are, the more encumbered by coarse and heavy garments—the greater is the treasure (*yekarut*) they contain. It is only that their [innermost] light is concealed within garments so opaque that human eyes cannot perceive it; great effort is needed to arouse that light. And no individual alone can achieve [such an awakening]—God Himself must aid him. But God, in His kindness, wishes people to endure even in this world. For if He were to reveal the brilliant light concealed in the body, a person's life would end instantly, "For no one can see Me and live" (Exodus 33:20). Thus, God does not show one straight away how to reach a state of wholeness (*lehashlim haguf*). Rather, He leads the person with one detail and then another, enabling him to grow over time and in the end the labor will be complete. Then, at last, God will show him how to purify his bodily strength as well and he will realize that his very body is imbued with immense brightness. God guides him in that as EHYEH.

Coming to terms with one's physicality, then, is a long and arduous process fraught with uncertainty. The guiding force to that final discovery of the indwelling soul is named EHYEH, the divine feminine mode of Becoming, of potentiality and hiddenness. At Horev, Moshe comes to understand how "matter" may be redeemed from the stereotype of subordination to the spirit. Beyond its role as a shell, a garment, an instrument enabling perfection, the body has a vitally important mission in this world. In this passage, I believe that R. Ya'akov replaces the traditional notion of dualism with a vision that transcends the hierarchy of pure and impure, inside-outside, end and means. Recall the verse R. Ya'akov has God invoke in praise of embodiment: "For the whole earth is full of His glory" (Isaiah 1:6). In this sort of plenitude, container and contents reach a state of near total integration—just as soil may be saturated with water and the bush enflamed, so is the body infused with the omnipresent soul. Truly, the two are one.[30] The divine presence leading Moshe to this understanding, in R. Ya'akov's mind, is fundamentally maternal. Citing the *Zohar* (3.280a), he continues:

> When the Great Mother (*imma ila'ah*) was revealed to you [Moshe], you responded, "I will approach and see that fearsome sight—why the bush is not consumed." For it is a wondrous act of mercy (*rahamei*) that the bush does not burn.

The supernal or "Great Mother," as the *sefirah* of *Binah* is often named, has an intimate understanding of the child-life taking form within her. Most naturally, then, it is her insight, patience and gentle care that ultimately help her child reach the synthesis that R. Ya'akov envisions. In the final reflection with which this section (*parashat Shemot* 36) concludes, R. Ya'akov speaks of the change engendered in Moshe by the revelation at Horev:

> Moshe had been fearful that the Jewish people, heaven forbid, would remain in Egypt forever; God showed him that what He wills will never be destroyed, but will flourish with ever greater strength.

In the name of EHYEH, then, God reassures Moshe of the inevitability of birth and equally, of the boundless love secretly guiding the children of Israel in their passage to freedom.

Voices of Hope

Returning now to R. Ya'akov's earlier teaching (*parashat Shemot* 21), the link between those reverberating cries left from primordial worlds destroyed and the renewed cries of the enslaved nation becomes clear. We recall his explanation there, cited above: "Those worlds could not endure

---

[30] Vladimir Jankelevitch develops this concept of interpenetration, by which he effectively transforms the Platonic and neo-Platonic conviction of dualism, in his book *Le pur et l'impur* (Flammarion: Champs, 1960) 49–57. His insights there have enriched my reading of the *Beit Ya'akov* in many ways. Cf. also pages 115–31 on the notions of duality and plurality mentioned earlier, and pages 240–62 on the fluid subject-object relationship possible between body and soul.

because they wished to receive the [divine] light in all its immensity, unmitigated by any sense of awe, and they exploded." At the same time, though, "What God wills will never be destroyed, but will flourish with ever greater strength" (*parashat Shemot* 36, end). It is for this reason, then, that the sparks of those shattered vessels (or worlds) remained, endlessly echoing their desire for the creation of a new world in which they themselves might have the chance to live in fullness.[31] R. Ya'akov closes this teaching with a description of the nascent self-awareness that will enable such a re-creation and rebirth:

> One of the midwives was named Shifra and the second, Pu'ah [Exodus 1:15].... "**Shifra**," as the Talmud says (*Rosh Hashanah* 16a), "That I [God] may remember you with favor and how?—by the **shofar**." In other words, the cries and pleas uttered in the world below take the form of a shofar...because the Jewish people's sole desire is to receive God's blessing *in measure* (*rak betzimtzum*), within the confines of the shofar. Thus the Talmud states (*Berakhot* 34b), "To pray in an open valley is arrogance." That is, to ask God to shower one with boundless and unrestrained goodness is like praying in a valley with no clear borders—as if one rejects the guidelines and restrictions given by the Torah and the Sages. The shofar, on the other hand, teaches of the containing nature of a vessel (*tzimtzum keli kibbul*), as "awe before God—that is His treasury." (Isaiah 33:6)

In their courageous defiance of Pharaoh's will to extinguish every spark of Jewish life, R. Ya'akov teaches, the midwives named (or pseudo-named) early in the Exodus story are the true agents of spiritual as well as national rebirth. Focusing, like the talmudic Rabbis, on the first midwife, R. Ya'akov too reads Shifra's name as an allusion to the highly charged image of the shofar. On the yearly Day of Judgment, wordless cries emerge from its narrow confines; in Jewish tradition, these cries alone have the power to evoke God's mercy. What R. Ya'akov stresses here, though, is the dimension of interiority the shofar itself represents. It was the virile self-conceit of those primeval worlds, he contends, that led to their ruin. Similarly, the wish to live unencumbered, like the egoistic

---

[31] R. Ya'akov adopts the mystical term of "the feminine waters" (*mayin nukvin*) to speak of this unrequited longing. Regrettably, an exploration of that fascinating image lies beyond the scope of our discussion.

illusion that one has easy access to God's boundless love, can only meet with failure. This expansive, and thus by definition, "masculine" mode of being, then, must be rejected, so that a radically different awareness may develop in its stead. R. Ya'akov speaks of this new consciousness as awe or reverence (*yirah*). The inherently "feminine" valence of this reflex is already recognized as such in rabbinic thought; bound up with it are the qualities of selflessness and fecundity.[32] In relating to the divine from a position of awe, R. Ya'akov suggests, an individual expresses the willingness to be a vessel, to accept boundedness, constriction and perhaps most difficult of all, to endure the frightening sense of emptiness and abandonment that must precede any gift of plenitude.

Both of the teachings we have considered (*parashat Shemot* 20–21; 36) speak of a single encounter, an event engendering the birth of a radically new understanding for the people and for Moshe. God reveals Himself to Moshe in the name of EHYEH. By recalling the past—from the most primordial moments before Creation to the torment of the Jews here-and-now—and promising the future—historical as well as metaphysical redemption—He speaks to Moshe of the mystery of omnipresence and of transcendence. It is a difficult truth, perhaps humanly impossible to conceive of, this being both inside and outside the world. And yet Moshe learns, through the burning bush, that the same mystery is reflected in the very existence of every individual. The total interpenetration of soul and body that God shows Moshe empowers him to return to his people, allowing him to begin leading them toward wholeness. As we have seen, a most striking element in R. Ya'akov's thought is the mobility of the images he invokes. Again and again, schematic duality gives way to fluid plurality. God's chosen people is constricted within like a fetus in the womb. At "birth," divine presence comes to encompass the nation on its journey through the wilderness, yet

---

[32] Cf. *Berakhot* 61a: "Woman," R. Hisda teaches, "was created in the form of a granary/treasury (*otzar*)—narrow above and wide below to contain the fetus within her body." To become a vessel, then, is seen by the Rabbis as an essential component of human creativity. Perhaps we could read, in a similar light, R. Yehoshua ben Levi's praise for his disciple, R. Eliezer, as "a cistern that loses not a drop" (*Mishnah Avot* 2:29). The ability to remember wisdom gained and thus conserve and continually revive tradition, is vitally important in the life and continuity of a people.

remains an indwelling, guiding force as well. In speaking of the reciprocity of body and soul, vessel and contents, darkness and light, *din* and *rahamim*, the traditionally "feminine" valence gains, in each case, a radically different identity. In his teaching, rather than speaking of a feminine Other, R. Ya'akov presents the feminine as an ontological category and mode of being vital to the spiritual growth of every individual, and of the Jewish nation as a whole.

The Nation of Israel:
From Historical Process to Self-Awareness

Chana Balanson

* * *

Editorial Note

This essay was originally written in Hebrew, published in the *MaTaN Torah Journal* (*Shenaton Torani shel Matan*, Jerusalem, 1991: 21–33) and is reprinted with permission. It is translated for the first time here by Ora Wiskind Elper. Although our general policy in this volume was to publish essays originally writen in English, we made an exception in this case for several reasons. One is the extraordinary influence its author had as a Torah teacher and human being on innumerable people who knew her in Jerusalem before her untimely passing at the age of 41 in 1992. Chana Balanson *z"l* (of blessed memory), was also one of the founding teachers of MaTaN (*Machon Torani leNashim*–Sadie Rennert Women's Institute for Torah Studies), an institution in which many of the authors in this volume have studied and developed. She was a model for so many—as a scholar, as a woman, and as a Jew who lived Torah and life passionately and fully. We wanted her voice to be heard by an even wider audience, and to honor her memory.

Sarah Malka Eisen's essay in this volume portrays her from the perspective of a devoted student. This essay, despite the inevitable loss involved in translation, helps portray her through her own words as a Torah scholar. In the first part, one sees the meticulous and exacting scholarship of her traditional religious education through the prism of her own rigorous, analytical mind. In the second part, another facet opens: the associative leaps of intuitive and creative insight which equally dazzled her students. It attests, as well, to her deep engagement with the profound, personal struggles each of us faces, and concern for the intellectual issues with which modernity confronts us.

As one of her older students and friends at MaTaN wrote of her:

> *To be in her presence and hear her speak had its effect. What amazed me most about Chana was not only her greatness as a*

teacher—but as I felt from the many conversations we had—her "womanliness" was also very great. Her wants, desires, struggles and emotions were as real for her as delving into a Rambam, not once, but many times, again and again to hear what was really being said. We could speak in the elevated language of psychologists, rabbis, philosophers about the trials of life, but it was grounded: sometimes we would simply sit, saying nothing and feel the pain, because sometimes it just hurt. That is all one could do when all was said and done. To be a sphere that is able to encompass and hold all these facets was very much Chana.

For myself, I often wonder what she would say to me today; all I have is what she said to me then. I often wonder if I remember her "really," or if my memories and the essence of her have grown along with me. Of course if they have, then truly she is a great teacher of Torat imekha, *as whatever she gave me, perhaps whatever she gave to anyone who knew her, continues to be vital, to develop, to grow, to teach.*

* * *

Redemption: The *Mishkan* and Creation

The Jewish people have experienced two fundamental conditions in the course of their history: exile and redemption. The paradigm embodying both is the Egyptian bondage and Exodus from it. In the prophecy that charges Moshe with the mission to redeem the people, God makes the purpose of the Exodus explicit:

> And I will take you to me for a people, and I will be to you a God. And you shall know that I am the Lord your God, who brings you out from under the burdens of Egypt. And I will bring you into the land, which I swore to give to Abraham, to Isaac and to Jacob; and I will give it you for a heritage: I am the Lord. (Exodus 6:7–8)[1]

---

[1] An earlier prophecy appears in Exodus 3, in which Moshe is charged with the mission to bring the nation to the "Land flowing with milk and honey." In Exodus 6, the people will reach the Land only after the goal of the Exodus has been realized, when a relationship of nation-King has been established between God and Israel.

In other words, God redeemed the Jewish people from Egypt in order to create a relationship between the people and their King,[2] and this purpose was finally realized when the *Mishkan*, or "Tabernacle" was erected:

> And I will dwell among the children of Israel and will be their God. And they shall know that I am the Lord their God, who brought them out of the land of Egypt, that I may dwell among them: I am the Lord their God. (Exodus 29:45–46)[3]

If we listen closely to the Torah's words, we can discern two things. First, a linguistic parallel exists between what is conveyed to Moshe in Exodus 6, "I will be to you a God," and what is said in Exodus 29, "I will be their God." We learn, then, that God is the God of Israel because He dwells among them, and this dwelling becomes possible when the *Mishkan* is built and stands within the camp. Secondly, the purpose of the Exodus is to enable God's dwelling among the people, and becomes complete precisely when the *Mishkan* is erected in their midst.[4]

---

[2] See *Hasagot haRamban* on *Sefer haMitzvot*, S. Frankel ed. (Jerusalem, 1995) *Mitzvot Asseh* 1 (206); *Mitzvot lo ta'asseh* 5 (293–4). The notion that the relationship developed is one of kingship is found in rabbinic sources, cited there by Nahmanides (Ramban).

[3] My teacher, R. Mordechai Breuer, made me aware of these verses and their meaning. His influence, and much that I learned from him, have guided me in writing this article. My thanks for all he has taught me. Any errors are my responsibility alone.

[4] This is the inner meaning of the arrangement of the tribes around the *Mishkan*, discussed in the first ten chapters of Numbers. See Ramban's commentary at the beginning of *Terumah* (H. Chavel ed., NY: Shilo, 1973, vol. 2, 434–37) and his introduction to the book of Numbers, vol. 4, 3–4. In his introduction to the book of Exodus, Ramban writes: "The Book of *V'eileh Shemoth* was set apart for the story of the first exile, which had been clearly decreed and the redemption from it.... Now the exile was not completed until the day they returned to their place and were restored to the status of their fathers.... When they came to Mount Sinai and made the *Mishkan* and the Holy One blessed be He, caused His Divine Presence to dwell again among them, they returned to the status of their fathers when the *'sod eloka'* (counsel of God) was upon their tents. They became those who constituted the Chariot of the Holy One blessed be He and were considered redeemed. For this reason, the second book of the Torah concludes with finishing the building of the *Mishkan*, and the glory of the Eternal from it always (3–5, translation adapted)." Compare *Tanhuma*, *Naso* 22: "R. Yehoshua ben Levi said: While they were still in Egypt, God made a condition with Israel that He would bring them out only to enable them to build a *Mishkan* for Him to make His presence dwell among them."

The Bible draws another parallel between the construction of the *Mishkan* and Creation itself through the use of similar linguistic forms and ideas:

The Story of Creation:	**The Construction of the *Mishkan*:**
"Thus, the heavens and the earth were **finished** and all their host. And on the seventh day God **ended** His **work** that He had done.... And God **blessed** the seventh day...." (Genesis 2:1–3)	"Thus was all the **work** of the *Mishkan* of the Tent of Meeting **finished**.... And Moshe saw all the **work** and behold, They had done it as the Lord commanded, even so had they done it: And Moshe **blessed** them."[5] (Exodus 39:32; 43)

Two motifs arise from the parallel between Creation and the *Mishkan*: the number of days and the day following them. Firstly, in Creation, the world comes into being during six days, and on the seventh God completes His work. In the description of the *Mishkan*, a cloud covers Mount Sinai for six days and on the seventh, God calls to Moshe (Exodus 24:16) to receive the instructions for the *Mishkan* (Exodus 25–31). After the *Mishkan* is erected, Moshe works during the seven days of preparation and Aharon and his sons are trained in its service.

Secondly, God creates the world in six days and on the seventh He ceases from labor, blesses the world and sanctifies it. At the completion of the *Mishkan*, on the eighth day, Aharon works, Moshe and Aharon bless the people (Leviticus 9:23) and the *Shekhinah* appears (ibid., 9:24). This manifestation of God's presence is the divine seal approving the *Mishkan*, just like the seventh day is the divine seal completing Creation.

---

[5] The root כ.ל.ה. ("finished") is used frequently in relation to the *Mishkan*. See, for instance, Numbers 7:1.

There is an additional linguistic parallel to be found when we compare the following verses from Proverbs:

Of Creation, the Torah Says:	Of Betzalel, Who Built the *Mishkan*, the Torah Says:
"The Lord by His wisdom founded the earth, By understanding He established the heavens, By knowledge the depths were broken up...." (Proverbs 3:19–20)	"And He filled him with the spirit of God, In wisdom, in understanding and in knowledge, And in all manner of workmanship...." (Exodus 35:31)[6]

From this comparison, we can see that the same means by which God created the earth—the heavens and the depths, also inform the "spirit" with which God inspired Betzalel to build the *Mishkan*. The Rabbis, in fact, emphasize this aspect of similarity between Creation and the *Mishkan*:

> The world, at that time, was like a two-legged chair that could not stand. When the *Mishkan* was finished, the world became established, as it is written (Numbers 7:1), "And it came to pass on the day that Moshe had finished setting up the *Mishkan* (להקים את המשכן)." It does not say להקים משכן, but rather uses the word *et*, which serves to

---

[6] Compare Jeremiah's challenge of idolatry: "He has made the earth by His power, He has established the world by His wisdom, and has stretched out the heavens by His understanding" (Jeremiah 10:12). See *Yalkut Shimoni, Mishle* s. 935: "The heavens and the earth were created with these three things, and the *Mishkan* was made with them, as it is written, 'And He filled him with the spirit of God, in wisdom, in understanding and in knowledge' (Exodus 35:31). These three were used to build the first Temple as well (I Kings 7:14), and in time to come they will be used to rebuild the Temple, as it says, 'And the spirit of the Lord shall rest upon him, the spirit of wisdom and understanding...the spirit of knowledge' (Isaiah 11:2). Finally, they will be given to Israel, as it is written, 'For God will grant wisdom...'" (Proverbs 2:6). The source of this midrash is *Tanhuma, Veyak'hel* 1 (Buber ed.) 122–23. A full comparison of Creation, the *Mishkan*, the First Temple and the future Temple is beyond the bounds of this discussion.

include the creation of the world, of which it says (*Tanhuma, Naso* 19), "God created the heavens and the earth (את השמים ואת הארץ)."

In this midrashic image, before the *Mishkan* was erected, the world resembled a rickety chair, unbalanced and shaky; with its completion, a third leg was added and it stood firm.[7]

What, however, is the essence of the *Mishkan* that enables it to bring the world to its ultimate completion? The Torah itself suggests an answer in its description of the final stages of building the *Mishkan* (Exodus 29:43–46). In these verses, it is called by three names:

1. **Mishkan**. This name reflects God's causing His Presence (*shekhinato*) to dwell in this structure, and symbolizes the immanent aspect of the divine.

2. **Mikdash**. Derived from the root ק.ד.ש. (and commonly translated as "sanctuary"), this word emphasizes separation and difference, and symbolizes the transcendent aspect of God's relationship to the world (compare Exodus 25:8). These two contradictory aspects exist simultaneously in a dialectical and even paradoxical connection, expressed by the Torah in the phrase, "it shall be sanctified by My glory." The narrow bridge linking these two opposing aspects of the divine forms the very core of the Jewish faith, on all its many levels.[8]

---

[7] On this image, see Rashi on Exodus 32:13. The Jewish nation is compared to a three-legged chair, representing the three patriarchs. The source of the image is *Berakhot* 33a. Perhaps the three legs could also be understood as the three dimensions: temporal, spatial and human or, in the language of *Sefer Yezirah* [an early kabbalistic work]: world, year and soul (*olam, shanah, nefesh*). Cf. *Sefer Yetzirah* 2.6. See also R. Yehudah Halevi, *Kuzari* 4.25. This motif is further developed in hasidic thought, particularly in the teachings of R. Zadok haKohen of Lublin and the *Sefat Emet*. These three dimensions are all guises (*levushim*) of the divine. In Creation, God blessed the *temporal* dimension in His sanctification of the seventh day. At the foot of Mount Sinai, the *human* dimension was sanctified—"And you shall be to Me a kingdom of priests and a holy people" (Exodus 19:6). With the erection of the Tabernacle, the world was imbued with enduring *spatial* holiness— "Let them make Me a sanctuary" (Exodus 25:8), "and it shall be sanctified by my glory" (Exodus 29:43). When holiness is revealed in all three of these dimensions, the world becomes stable and its purpose and meaning are realized.

[8] Consider, for instance, the words of Isaiah the prophet, "Holy (*kadosh*), holy, holy is the Lord of Hosts; the whole earth is full of His glory" (Isaiah 6:3). In the parlance of the Rabbis, the word *makom* designates God Himself, the "Place" of the world. Yet another divine appellation, "The Holy One, blessed be He," similarly combines

3. *Ohel Mo'ed*. This term signifies a gathering place (היוועדות); in the Torah's poetic expression, "...at the door of the Tent of Meeting before the Lord: where I will meet you, to speak there to you. And there I will meet with the children of Israel, and it shall be sanctified by my glory" (Exodus 29:42, 44). This meeting carries a double meaning: 1) the presence of each before the other, and 2) speech. In the verse concluding the dedication of the altar by the twelve princes, we find a definition of "speech" in the Tent of Meeting: "And when Moshe was gone into the Tent of Meeting to speak with Him, then he heard the voice speaking to him from off the covering that was upon the ark of Testimony, from between the two *keruvim*: and it spoke to him" (Numbers 7:89).

To further grasp the significance of this encounter between God and humanity, and the meaning of "speech," it is important to note that the *Mishkan*, the ark, and the tablets are all spoken of in conjunction with "testimony" or "witnessing" (*edut*).[9] The word *edut* is acoustically linked to the word *mo'ed* ("meeting"),[10] which also concerns the encounter between the human and the divine. In other words, a person's meeting with the Creator engenders an instance of mutual "testimony": the individual bears witness that God is King of the world, and God bears witness that Israel is His people.[11] That is to say, when a human being stands face

---

the transcendent (*hakadosh*—"holy") with the immanent (*barukh*—"blessed"). See Maimonides' concept of negative attributes, outlined in his *Guide to the Perplexed* 1.50–60. The Kabbalists spoke of this dialectic with the expressions, "No place is void of His presence"—i.e., immanence, and "He is absolutely inconceivable"—i.e., transcendence. Elaboration of these notions is beyond the bounds of this discussion.

[9] Cf. Exodus 25:21, 22; 26:33; 31:18; 32:15; 34:29; 38:21; Numbers 1:50, etc.

[10] Cf. Isaiah 43:10—"You are my witnesses, says the Lord." The Jewish people are sometimes called the "*edah*," apparently because they bear witness for God. Cf. Ramban, Deuteronomy 32:26 (Chavel ed. vol. 5, 363–64) who suggests it is the Jewish people's mission to testify to God's kingship, and that is the purpose of Creation itself. On this point, note that witnesses are considered halakhically valid only if their testimony can be refuted with the claim, "We were there with you at the same time and place." This notion might be compared with Karl Popper's contention that for a scientific theory to be acceptable, it must be refutable. My teacher, R. Daniel Epstein, spoke of this idea; much else that I received from him underlies this essay, but I am unable to indicate it all precisely. My thanks to him for everything he taught me.

[11] For that reason it is called the "Tent of Meeting," as a testimony to all the world that the Holy One blessed be He, dwells in their sanctuary.

to face before the Divine Presence, he or she testifies that both Creation and history are the works and revelation of God. This link of "witnessing" clarifies how the *Mishkan* brought Creation to a state of completion and reinforces the parallel between the two.

God and Humanity in the Building of the *Mishkan*

To understand more deeply how this encounter is possible, we need to consider the role of each side, the divine and the human. Let's begin with the latter. In creating the world and in engendering the sanctity of time, God had no partners; He acted alone. In establishing a holy place, by contrast, human beings are God's active partners. Our example is the *Mishkan*, constructed not by God but by Betzalel, Moshe, Aharon and the people. As we have seen:

1. **Betzalel** (whose name means "in the shadow of God"—*betzel el*) built the *Mishkan* inspired by *hokhmah*, *tevunah* and *da'at* (wisdom, understanding and knowledge), all of which were "used" in the original Creation.
2. **Moshe** erected the *Mishkan*, served in it for seven days and blessed the people.
3. **Aharon** began to serve on the eighth day.
4. **The people** brought their offerings.

After the people prepared the necessary vessels, God made His presence dwell in their holy place and met with them there. What process, then, leads to the realization of this indwelling presence? The midrash suggests a rhythmic dialogue that took place between the human and divine elements:

> When God said to him, "Make a holy place for Me" (Exodus 25:8), Moshe answered: "Behold, the heaven, and heaven of heavens, cannot contain You" (I Kings 8:27). And he added, "Do I not fill the heaven and the earth? says the Lord" (Jeremiah 23:24); "Thus says the Lord, The heaven is my throne and the earth is my footstool" (Isaiah 66:1). "How can we make a holy place for Him?!" And God answered him, "I do not ask you to do all that is in My power, but rather what is in their power, as it is written, 'You shall make the *Mishkan* with ten curtains' (Exodus 26:1)." When the Israelites heard that, they began to

contribute wholeheartedly and made the *Mishkan*. When it was fin-
ished, God's glory came to fill it, as it says, "And Moshe was not able
to enter the Tent of Meeting" (Exodus 40:35). Then the princes said,
"The hour has arrived for us to bring offerings in gladness, for the
Shekhinah has come to dwell in our midst," as it says, "On the day
Moshe finished...." (*Tanhuma, Naso* 19)

This midrash recounts a dialogue between human beings and God. The
people are commanded to do what is in their own power, rather than what
is commensurate with God's power. The human response, then, is to set to
work on the *Mishkan* and the dialogue continues.

Why does God demand of Israel "only what they are able to do" (*lefi
koham*)? I believe the guiding principle here is one of mutual contraction
(*tzimtzum*).[12] The initiator of the process is God Himself. What, though,
could His motive be? One of the great hasidic masters, R. Ya'akov
Leiner, author of the commentary *Beit Ya'akov*, suggests a reason. He
teaches that the darkness in which we find ourselves is engendered
because God's divine light is so intense that no human vessels can contain
it. R. Ya'akov develops this idea in his explanation of the famous talmudic dispute between R. Eliezer and R. Yehoshua (*Rosh Hashanah* 11a)
about whether the final redemption will occur in the spring, in the month
of *Nissan* (as R. Yehoshua maintains), or in the fall, in the month of
Tishrei (as R. Eliezer maintains):

> "This month will be for you the first of all months" (Exodus 12:2). **For
> you**, because from your [human] perspective *Nissan* begins the year.
> *Nissan* is comparable to daytime, when people are awake and able to
> see, and thus to act and accomplish things.... At night, in contrast, peo-
> ple have no awareness of God's acts. Indeed, winter and summer corre-
> spond to night and day.... The rainy months allude to God's showering
> the world with more divine abundance than human beings can grasp.
> Unable to bear it, they find shelter in their homes. On a rainy day (*yom
> sagrir*—Proverbs 27:16) people are literally "closed up" (*sagur*), and in
> that sense the winter is like the night.... From God's perspective,

---

[12] The word *tzimtzum* appears explicitly in rabbinic literature. Cf. *Tanhuma,
Veyak'hel* 7: "Do not say that God contracted (*tzimtzem*) His presence (*shekhinato*)
into the *Mishkan*"; *Pesikhta de Rav Kahana* 1: "And He descends and contracts
(*metzamtzem*) His presence among them."

however, *Tishrei* begins the year, as we learn from the world's Creation. That account first says, "And it was evening" and then "it was morning" (Genesis 1:5, etc.)—nighttime comes before daytime; or, as the Sages said, "First comes darkness and then light" (*Shabbat* 77b). For God, then, the night is the beginning: He alone is master of all His creatures and for God, "darkness is as light" (Psalms 39:12).... The opposite, though, is true for human beings: we experience daytime, or *Nissan*, as the beginning, followed by night. Thus *Nissan* is, **for you**, the first of all months.[13]

In other words, a certain reality may seem to be night, due to an *excess* of light, an abundance so vast that human senses are unable to receive it. This is a paradoxical reality, in which darkness, in an absolute sense, is light. What we sense as darkness is, for God, the opposite. In another reality, by contrast, God "contracts Himself" to enable revelation to human beings commensurate with their limited abilities to contain His light. The purpose of this act of *tzimtzum*, or "divine covering and concealment," is to enable humans to stand before God and endure the experience. As we saw in the *Midrash Tanhuma*, a rhythm and dialogue take place: the first act of contraction is God's; then human beings do the same, and an infinite chain of reactions ensues. Here, too, we learn that the same reaction so vital in the building of the *Mishkan*—mutual contraction and relationship between God and human beings—informs all of Creation. There, too, the act of *tzimtzum* is central.

The Half-Shekel

This relationship between God and humanity is also the focus of R. Ya'akov Leiner's commentary on the *mitzvah* of contributing a half-shekel to the *Mishkan* (Exodus 30:13):

> When one is able to conquer one's evil tendencies, faults and masks, and raise oneself all ten levels within one's power, annulling one's own will before God's will, it becomes possible to draw close to God, up even to the tenth and final level. Then, in response, God subordinates the desires of all the accusers (*mekatregim*) to [human] will,

---

[13] *Beit Ya'akov*, vol. 2 (Exodus), *Bo* 36 (108).

humbling them level by level, even to the lowest of the ten.[14] God even "humbles Himself" to appear on the earth, drawing close to human beings. They, in turn, respond by drawing themselves yet closer, cleaving to God in intimate oneness.... Indeed, the twenty levels between God and human beings—ten from God's side and ten from the human side—allude to the stature (*komah*) of two entities. This is the meaning of God's words (Leviticus 26:13), "I have made you of two statures (*komemi'ut*) ואולך אתכם קוממיות" Thus, each person must contribute a half-shekel, the equivalent of ten *gera* of his own, and God adds ten of "His own," making a whole shekel, or twenty *gera*.[15]

R. Ya'akov here is speaking of the inner meaning of donating the shekel. A whole shekel is composed of two halves, each of them worth ten *gera*, and each of them representing the "stature" of an entity: one human, the other divine. When a person subjects his or her own ego, sense of autonomy, to the will of God, he or she causes God, as it were, to react in a counter-motion of annulment, removing a barrier that existed between them. The encounter and union between the two entities, or "statures," becomes possible when a person frees himself from all self-sufficiency— and God, in response, contracts Himself in relation to that person. Once again, a mutual state of *tzimtzum* takes place, which enables the contact and union between the human and divine.[16]

In R. Ya'akov's view, then, God contracts Himself to make a space in which human beings can act. God's ultimate object, he maintains, is suggested in the following midrashic comment: "When Moshe was told to make the *Mishkan*, he was astonished...God said to him, 'It's not [as impossible] as you suppose...indeed, I will contract my Presence (*shekhinati*) within one cubic *ama*....' In other words, although God is infinitely

---

[14] [At the beginning of this teaching, R. Ya'akov refers to a passage in the *Zohar* (3. 41a) which speaks of two systems of ten, one ascending and the other descending: "The ten *sefirot* of faith" above and their mirror image in "the ten *sefirot* of unclean sorcery" below. *Translator's note.*]

[15] *Beit Ya'akov*, vol. 2 (Exodus), *Ki tissa* 16 (404).

[16] This principle is expressed in other teachings as well. See, for instance, *Beit Ya'akov*, *Terumah* 35 (341): "To the extent that a person annuls his own will, God annuls His."

more sublime than our world, He desires heartfelt human donations, and these will rise even to His glorious throne."[17]

God, then, engages in an ongoing dialogue with human beings to enable them to recognize His presence continually. Nahmanides (Ramban) already spoke of this relationship in his commentary on the Torah:

> But R. Avraham ibn Ezra explained [the verse to mean that] the purpose of My bringing them forth from the land of Egypt was only that I might dwell in their midst, and that this was the fulfillment of [the promise to Moshe], "You shall serve God upon this mountain" (Exodus 3:12). He explained it well, and if it is so, there is a great mystery in this matter. For in the plain sense of things, it would appear that [the dwelling of] the Divine Glory in Israel was to fulfill a need below, but it is not so. It fulfilled a need above, being rather similar in thought to that which Scripture states, "Israel, in whom I will be glorified" (Isaiah 49:3). And Joshua said, "[For when the Canaanites…hear of it…and cut off our name from the earth] and what will You do for Your Great Name?" (Joshua 7:9). There are many verses which express this thought: "He has desired it [i.e., Zion] for His habitation" (Psalms 132:13); "Here I dwell, for I have desired it" (Psalms 132:13). And it is further written, "and I will remember the land." (Leviticus 26:42)[18]

The "great mystery," in Ramban's eyes, is that the *Mishkan* is "a need above" (צורך גבוה), rather than "a need below" (צורך הדיוט). "A need below" means that the commandments were given to influence the human sphere, from the individual, to the family, the tribe and the nation, and even to all of humanity. "A need above," on the other hand, implies that God needed, as it were, to reveal Himself. Of the ensuing encounter between the divine and the human, in which the two speak "face to face," human beings are charged to bear witness: it is their responsibility to testify that God is supreme King. As Ramban explains:

> God created humankind among the lower creatures in order that they acknowledge his Creator and be thankful to His Name…. I have already suggested that in the creation of humankind there is a sublime

---

[17] *Beit Ya'akov, Terumah* 10 (322), citing *Exodus Rabbah, Terumah* 34.

[18] Chavel, vol. 2, 506–7; translation adapted.

and recondite secret which requires that we be His people and He be our God. As it is written, "Every one who is called by My Name and whom I have created for My glory, I have formed him, yea, I have made him" (Isaiah 43:7).[19]

The allusion here, once again, is to God's words commanding Moshe to lead Israel out of Egypt, "And I will take you to me for a people and I will be to you a God" (Exodus 6:7), a task finally realized at the completion of the *Mishkan*: "And I will dwell among the children of Israel and will be their God" (Exodus 29: 45). The connection between the two events later becomes explicit:

> And I will set my Tabernacle among you, and my soul shall not abhor you. And I will walk among you, and will be your God and you shall be my people. I am the Lord your God, who brought you out of the land of Egypt, that you should not be their bondmen; and I have broken the bars of your yoke and made you walk upright. (Leviticus 26: 11–13)[20]

In summary, then, the process of redemption from enslavement in Egypt reaches its ultimate conclusion with the construction of the *Mishkan*, in the encounter between the people and God. And through speech, the natural world created through the Ten Utterances is brought to completion: God's kingship becomes manifest. The relationship between the divine and the human, furthermore, is expressed in mutual acts of *tzimtzum*: God contracts Himself in revelation, and human beings in doing God's will, reveal His glory in the world. Similarly, in the symbol of the half-shekel, the two halves join, eliminating the division between God and the person: the latter annuls his ego, and the former contracts Himself to become visible and revealed to human eyes. Human beings, then, must become aware of and acknowledge God, and this is the purpose of the Exodus and of redemption as well: "And I will take you to me for a people, and I will be to you a God...and you shall know that I am God." (Exodus 6:7)

---

[19] Chavel, vol. 5, 364; translation adapted.

[20] ["I have made you walk upright (*komemi'ut*)" was translated above as "I made you of two statures." *Translator's note.*]

Exile

We turn now to the second fundamental condition in the history of the Jewish people, that of exile or *galut*. The Hebrew root ‏ג.ל.ה.‎ has two meanings: the "removal of something from its place," and "revelation." The first time it is used in the sense of "removal" is in I Samuel 4:21: "And she named the child *Ikhavod*, saying, 'Honor (*khavod*) is departed (*galah*) from Israel,' because the ark of God was taken and because of her father-in-law and her husband. And she said, 'Honor is departed from Israel, for the ark of God is taken.'" What honor, though, is meant? "Honor" here seems to be an abbreviation of the expression, "God's honor" or "Glory," which is expressed in His revelation to the people of Israel.[21] This explanation becomes even more plausible when we recall the connection drawn between the verse, "the ark of God is taken," and "honor/glory is departed from Israel," for the locus of revelation was between the two *keruvim* above the ark.[22] The Rabbis have commented on the special nature of the ark made by the hand of the craftsman Betzalel: "For God's shadow (*tzel*) is upon it, as He contracts His Presence there. Hence he was called Betzalel (*betzelel*): he made the shadow of God between the two *keruvim*, as it is written, 'And I will meet with you there and I will speak with you...'" (Exodus 25:22; *Tanhuma, Veyak'hel* 7).

We see, then, that the root ‏ג.ל.ה.‎ is first used in the sense of exile in the case of the departure of Divine Presence (glory, honor) from the people. The exile or *galut* of the nation from the Land of Israel is often mentioned in the prophetic books of the Bible, but this is after God's presence (*shekhinato*) has already left. The second sense of the word—as "revelation"—appears, for instance, in prophecies of doom. Thus, "There came a man of God to Eli and said to him, 'Did I not appear (*haniglo nigleti*) to

---

[21] See, for example, Exodus 24:17, "And the sight of the Glory of the Lord was like a devouring fire on the top of the mountain in the eyes of the children of Israel." Leviticus 9:23, "And the Glory of the Lord appeared to all the people." Ezekiel 1:28, "As the appearance of the rainbow in the clouds on a rainy day, so was the appearance of the brightness round about. This was the appearance of the likeness of the Glory of the Lord."

[22] See, for instance, Leviticus 16:1–2, which speaks of the *Kohen haGadol* who enters once a year to encounter the *Shekhinah*. Also, Numbers 7:89, which speaks of the revelation to Moshe.

the house of your father, when they were in Egypt in the house of Pharaoh?'" (I Samuel 2:27). Later, when God appears before Samuel, the root ג.ל.ה. is used twice to mean revelation, first in a negative and then in a positive sense: "Now Samuel did not yet know the Lord, neither was the word of the Lord yet revealed to him…. And the Lord appeared again in Shilo, for the Lord revealed Himself to Samuel in Shilo by the word of the Lord" (I Samuel 3:7, 21).

The double meaning of the root thus seems to me to suggest a link between God's revelation in Egypt to the house of Eli, and the exile of divine "honor" or glory symbolizing the destruction of the *Mishkan* at Shilo.[23] God's revelation to Samuel, then, paves the way to kingship: he anoints a king from Binyamin and from Yehudah. In its two meanings, the root ג.ל.ה. speaks of two instances of a single phenomenon. If this is the case, we then need to clarify how there can be an essential unity between revelation of the Divine Presence and exile.

Concealment

As we saw before, the motif of speech is central in understanding the meaning of redemption. In a condition of exile, on the other hand, we would expect the opposite: speech would be absent, since human beings would then be fundamentally disconnected from their Creator. The absence of speech in exile is a prevalent theme in the hasidic teachings of R. Yehudah Aryeh Leib of Gur, the *Sefat Emet*. The Song of the Sea, for example, begins with the verse, "Then Moshe and the children of Israel sang…" which leads the *Sefat Emet* to the following reflections:

> Rashi explains that [at the parting of the sea, the song] "rose to their lips" (*ala belibam*). That is, all during the exile they longed to express those words but could not, for speech itself was in exile, as the *Zohar* teaches.[24]

---

[23] See Jeremiah 7:12 and 26:6, where the destruction of the Tabernacle at Shilo serves as a model for the destruction of the first Temple.

[24] *Sefat Emet*, Pesach 5647 (vol. 3, 84), citing Exodus 15:1 and *Zohar* 1.36a.

In other words, the Jewish people wished to express themselves and speak with God in Egypt, but their very condition of estrangement impeded them. In a later passage, the *Sefat Emet* continues:

> For the children of Israel were created in order to bear testimony for their Creator, as it is written, "I have formed this nation for myself; they shall speak my praise" (Isaiah 43:21). In Egypt, though, the people were mute, because speech, too, was exiled. That is, God's involvement in the world was invisible.

If so, the sense of God's absence among the people strikes them mute, while consciousness of His presence empowers them to speak. Why, though, does God allow this situation of hiddenness? The *Sefat Emet* addresses this question in his reading of verses in the Song of the Sea:

> "And then they believed in the Lord..." (Exodus 14:31). Earlier, we said this teaches that their faith was retrospective, reflecting on all the days of exile and darkness. Thus the Rabbis taught, "'Who is like you, O Lord, among the gods; who is like you, glorious in holiness?' (Exodus 15:11)—among the gods (*elim*), indeed, among the *mute* (*ilemim*), for He hears the curses of the wicked and remains silent." God, that is, sometimes guides the world in the aspect of concealment within nature and exile, and such is His "muteness." At other times, His presence is actively and clearly revealed, and that is the meaning of "glorious in holiness, fearful in praises, doing wonders" (Exodus 15:11). The children of Israel can, then, bear witness to the underlying unity of both these aspects: God manages the world, sometimes concealed within nature, other times in open revelation, overturning natural law...in every case, all is from Him.[25]

At issue are two modes in which God manifests His presence: one in concealment and "muteness," the other in revelation, "glorious in holiness." We must then understand and take to heart that even in a condition of concealment, God is nevertheless found in the world—He is only hidden from our eyes. Revelation, then, means the enabling of speech from within the very situation of concealment. And we must also realize that on the deepest level, good and evil are not two opposing forces embattled one with another, but rather are two expressions stemming from

---

[25] *Sefat Emet*, Pesach 5647 (vol. 3, 84–5), citing *Gittin* 56b.

a single source. The person who speaks is the one who unites these two opposites, and the concealment is ultimately for the purpose of creating this unity.

Hanukah and Purim

Yet, why is speech created through a game of hide-and-seek between God and humanity? Why is concealment needed in the building process? One key to answering these questions may be found in teachings by R. Zadok haKohen of Lublin on the meaning of Hanukah. This holiday, he remarks, comes in the middle of winter, the darkest period of the year. Its historical context is the exile of the Jewish people by the Greeks. As the Rabbis said, "Darkness symbolizes the Greek exile, for the Greeks brought darkness to the eyes of Israel" (*Genesis Rabbah* 2.4).[26] Perhaps Hanukah thus represents the desire to cause people to forget their very selves; surely that is the most profound kind of forgetting. The light of Hanukah, then, is light born out of darkness.

The events of Hanukah occurred in the period that saw the development of the Oral Torah, and the Rabbis themselves issued a ruling to commemorate those events for all generations, yet refused to permit them to be recorded as text.[27] R. Zadok's interpretation of Hanukah is based on the premise that time contains qualitative differences: the unique nature of each month of the year influences everything that occurs during it. The historical event of each month is a bringing of revelation out of concealment. *Rosh Hodesh*, the first day of the month, marked by the new moon, is called "a point of nothingness" (*nekudat ha'ayin*), since it is the hidden

---

[26] [Here the author recalls a suggestion, difficult to translate, that darkness (*hoshekh*) חשך implies that something, such as light, is withheld from being received (*hasakh*), drawing a linguistic and existential parallel to Abraham's actions at the *Akedah* (Genesis 22:16). Cf., for example, Rashi on Job 38:23 and on I Chronicles 35:25. She refers to R. Yitzhak Hutner's connection between darkness and forgetting, and of the possibility of constructing an Oral Tradition from within such a lacuna of absence. See his *Pahad Yitzhak, Hanukah* 3. *Translator's note.*]

[27] [Great significance is attached to the unique status of Hanukah in the Jewish calendar as an Oral Tradition that was not and cannot be committed to writing. This status contrasts with the Mishnah, the earliest corpus of oral rabbinic teachings, which became a written text when its contents began to fade from the collective memory of the Jewish nation. *Translator's adaptation of note by the author.*]

source containing the essence of that month. In his teachings concerning the *Rosh Hodesh* of each month, R. Zadok further refers to two separate traditions, that of *Sefer Yezirah* (an ancient mystical treatise), and that of the Geonim. According to both traditions, each month was "created" with a certain letter of the Hebrew alphabet; each has it own constellation and is represented by a specific organ of the human body.[28]

In considering the letter corresponding to each month, R. Zadok speaks of its graphic form, the etymology of its name, and its vocalization. *Sefer Yezirah* teaches that the month of *Kislev*, in which Hanukah occurred, was created with the letter *samekh* (ס). A round letter, its name suggests the word *somekh*, meaning "support." In effect, its form may be separated into two parts: the left side is a sort of shield, and the right side is a falling figure in need of protection. The "shield" is God, who stretches over and supports the fallen, *hanofel* (shaped like the letter nun–נ). This idea is developed in the Lurianic teaching of "encompassing light" (*or mekkif*). For instance, God's relationship as "supporter" and "encompasser" is His protecting and surrounding the Jewish people in the form of the "clouds of glory" during the Exodus from Egypt. The letter *samekh* also appears in the story of the creation of Woman: God causes Adam to sleep, removes his rib and closes—*vayisgor* (ויסגר)—the "incision" (Genesis 2:21). Sleep, the Rabbis taught, contains an element of death, of collapse (*Berakhot* 57b).

R. Zadok then combines all these disparate ideas to discern the essential nature of the month of *Kislev*. What kind of "support" does it give? He writes: "When physical need compels one to sleep…one should do so, and that will enable one to receive what could not be understood while awake. Then one must rise and apply oneself to learning Torah."[29] In R. Zadok's interpretation, the Oral Torah is revealed during "sleep"; that is, the Sages, in their great wisdom, are able to discover what is concealed in

---

[28] Each month is manifest in the dimensions of time, space and humanity. This echoes the principle, mentioned in note 3 above, of (constellation), year (month) and soul (bodily organ).

[29] R. Zadok haKohen, *Peri Zaddik*, vol. 1 (Genesis 73). See his wider discussion on pages 70–78, in which he develops other motifs and considers the differences between the Geonic tradition and that of *Sefer Yetzirah*.

the Written Torah. In other words, the Oral Torah can come into being only from within a reality of darkness and concealment. Darkness, on a psychological plane, is forgetting. Paradoxically, though, when one sleeps, deeper and more internal levels of the human soul may be uncovered.[30] The Rabbis commented on this phenomenon as well. Jeremiah the prophet, who foresaw the destruction of the Temple and witnessed the calamity as it was wreaked, forged the tools of reconstruction from within the ruins. That prophet said, "He [God] has set me in darkness..." (Lamentations 3:6) and the Rabbis taught: "'He has set me in darkness'—that is the Babylonian Talmud" (*Sanhedrin* 24a). The Talmud, the Oral Tradition, thus emerges out of a condition of concealment.

When, though, was the beginning of this process of discovering hidden depths of the Torah within a state of darkness, and forming them into an Oral Torah? Historically, the most immediate link is Purim. The Sages said: "In the days of Ahashverosh, that generation accepted the Torah, as it is written, 'The Jews ordained and accepted...' (Esther 9:27) what they had been given before [at Sinai]" (*Shabbat* 88a). Purim thus commemorates the nation's voluntary reception of the Oral Torah. It seems that the specific reference here to "accepting the Oral Torah" is the ascendancy of Ezra the scribe, who is described as "worthy of giving the Torah to Israel" (*Sanhedrin* 21b), and to the "firm covenant" he penned, described in Nehemiah (8–10). Ezra's was the very last of the prophetic books, and he also interpreted the Torah; hence he represents the beginning of a new period in Jewish history—the era of Oral Torah.

Ezra lived during the period in which the miracle of Purim occurred. The essential nature of that era is described via a question the Talmud poses: "What proof is there that [the story of] Esther is presaged in the [Written] Torah? From the verse, 'And I will surely hide (*haster astir*) my face on that day...' (Deuteronomy 31:18)." That is to say, the historical era of Esther is one in which God's face is concealed from the nation. (The Rabbis discern the connection between "concealment" and Esther from the doubled verb "hide" [*haster astir*] and its linguistic similarity to

---

[30] This view resembles Freud's understanding of dreams: paradoxically, while the body is dormant, dream language allows the dreamer to find access to his or her own unconscious.

"Esther.") R. Nahman of Bratslav further explains the inner dynamics of this state of concealment by remarking on the doubled verb *haster astir*:

> But when God hides Himself within hiddenness, that is, when the very truth that He is hidden is concealed from a person, then it is wholly impossible to find Him, for one is totally unaware of His existence. That is the meaning of "I will surely hide myself"—I will conceal my hiddenness, and they will not even realize that God is a concealed presence.[31]

R. Nahman is speaking here of two levels of concealment: on the first, an individual is aware of the situation; on the second, there is no consciousness at all that something is hidden. Purim occurred in this latter and more difficult state, yet it was precisely then that the period of the Oral Torah began, initiated when Ezra returned from Babylon to the Land of Israel. Perhaps this insight can help us understand the verse, "And because of all this we make a firm covenant and write it..." (Nehemiah 10:1). Despite the darkness cast by Ahashverosh, obscuring God's majesty, we have the ability to discover our innermost strengths by our own initiative. Indeed, the Jewish nation makes a covenant with God and begins a new dialogue, more profound than the previous one. As the Rabbis said, "The words of the Sages [*divrei dodeikha*; Rashi: *divrei soferim*] are more pleasing to the Holy One, blessed be He, than the wine of [the Written] Torah" (*Avodah Zarah* 35a).

The great principle here is that exile is ultimately a means that enables us to uncover and recognize an inner self through failure and concealment. Hanukah and Purim are symbols of exile, of "the hidden Face." Within the darkness, however, shines a light—the Oral Torah.

Sin and the Expulsion from the Garden of Eden

We have mapped the phenomenon of concealment through Jewish history, yet it must be understood, above all, as a human psychological condition. Its first traces may be discerned in the account of humanity in the Garden of Eden. The talmudic passage cited above, in which "Esther" is foreshadowed in the verse warning of hiddenness (*haster astir*), continues

---

[31] *Likkutei Moharan*, 56.3.

with a similar question related to the Garden of Eden: "What proof is there that Haman is presaged in the [Written] Torah? 'Have you eaten of the tree [*hamin ha'etz*], of which I commanded you not to eat?'" (Genesis 3:11; *Hullin* 139b). That is to say, Haman, the villain of the Purim tale, represents all the obstacles and concealment that came into existence when humankind ate from the Tree of Knowledge of Good and Evil. After their sin, Adam and Eve were expelled from Eden, where God Himself had been manifestly present and had spoken openly with them. No longer can they stand before God; they hide from Him and, ultimately, drive the Divine Presence away.[32]

What, in essence, is the meaning of this primal sin, and what is the purpose of the expulsion? I believe the sin represents obstacles one must overcome to reach self-awareness. Shame is also a sign of consciousness of oneself, and of the difference between oneself and others. Before their sin, Adam and Eve had no experience of individual existence. In the presence of the Garden's Keeper, autonomy was impossible. Thus the Rabbis said, "Adam could see from one end of the world to the other" (*Hagigah* 12a); the same is said of the fetus in its mother's womb (*Niddah* 31a). Before the sin, humankind was like an unborn infant: the experiential reality of both (Eden and the womb) is oceanic, a total dependence, all vitality drawn from the Mother. Before sinning, "Adam could see from one end of the world to the other"; in other words, he was the world and the world was he—with no sense of "I" and "Thou."

The expulsion from the Garden of Eden, then, parallels birth. In that "crisis," a new person comes into being. The goal of humankind is to return to the Garden of Eden, but only after a process of self-realization. Redemption is a return to that state in which God's face is present and all encompassing. Humankind will be redeemed, however, only when the most internal layers of human existence have been reached, from within a situation of absence.

Finally, then, exile and redemption are two aspects of a single essence. In redemption, a person discovers himself or herself before God, speaking with Him; exile is an essential obstacle in creating that speech and

---

[32] See *Pesikhta deRav Kahana* 1.a, b. W. Braude and I. Kapstein trans. (Philadelphia: Jewish Publication Society, 1975) 5–6.

bringing redemption. The two meanings of the root ג.ל.ה. that we noted above reflect these two aspects. They join to form a symphony of wholeness in which a person faces the Creator in testimony and witnesses to His existence. Yet they reflect more than an internal and fundamentally human experience. Redemption also reflects the existence of the Jewish people as a national unity, bearing the responsibility to encounter God and bear witness to His kingship over the world, throughout their tumultuous history.

(translated by Ora Wiskind Elper)

Torah of the Mothers: Beyond the Study Hall

Esther Sha'anan

I.

I take as my starting point the title of our anthology—*Torat imekha*, "Torah of the Mothers." As a well-trained student of Torah, I go to the sources, to the book of Proverbs, where the term appears twice, and attempt to glean some insight into its meaning. We first find the phrase in Proverbs 1:8:

> Listen, my son, to the admonishments of your father, and do not forsake the teachings of your mother.

> שמע בני מוסר אביך ואל תטש תורת אמך.

The phrase appears again in Proverbs 6:20:

> Guard, my son, the commandments of your father, and do not forsake the teachings of your mother.

> נצור בני מצות אביך ואל תטש תורך אמך.

I take the title of this anthology to mean that we are tapping a precious resource long untapped; we are at long last developing the Torah studies and novellae of women, and thus the title *"Torat imekha."* But if this phrase is rooted in Proverbs it cannot be something so new as to be divorced from these roots. I continue to dig. What is *Torat imekha*?

I find an answer as I open Rabbeinu Bahya's introduction to *Pirkei Avot*. Rabbeinu Bahya quotes the verse in Proverbs, and building on the *Talmud Bavli* in *Berakhot* 32b makes the distinction, as Kabbalists are wont to do, that *Mussar avikha* ("the admonishments of your father") pertains to the Written Torah, and *Torat imekha* ("Torah of your mother") to the Oral Tradition. He then explains:

And this is the meaning: do not abandon the Torah of your mother—
that is, the Oral Tradition, because the ways and customs of Israel are
Torah. We must also cleave to the outstanding traits of our ancestors,
that through these traits we may be elevated to the quality of *Hasidut*.
To that end, we have been given the Tractate of *Avot* and the Sages
said (*Bava Kama* 30a): "Whoever strives to attain the level of a *hasid*
should fulfill the words of *Avot*, for the highest and most refined ethics
are in this tractate, and this is the Oral Tradition which Moshe received at Sinai."

What I would like to propose, then, is that we not create a new definition of *Torat imekha*—wondrous words of Torah with a uniquely feminine bent whose time has come to be revealed in this world—while
discarding or ignoring the *Torat imekha* as described by Rabbeinu Bahya:
the Torah of *hesed* and the highest possible standards of personal ethics.
The latter is not a Torah belonging to males or females, but is the portion—and obligation—of each of us who stood at Sinai.

Nevertheless, I will let you in on a secret: I think that the world of *hesed* and caring is embodied, certainly not exclusively, but significantly, by
Jewish women. And I would venture to guess that if most of us search
back for memories or family tales of mothers, grandmothers and
great-grandmothers, the *Torat imekha* we recall is that of *hesed* with no
questions asked.

A moment, when I was seventeen years old and pondering what my
commitment to Torah should be, remains sharply engraved in my memory. It was *parashat Shoftim* (Deuteronomy 16:18–21; 9) and I sat in
synagogue, following along in the English translation. For the first time, I
began to understand that the actual study of Torah could have a very real
and concrete impact on my life. At that moment, I had the revelation that
the words printed in the book before my eyes and at my grandmother's
Shabbos table, graced by all and any who needed to be there, were not
two disparate aspects of Torah. At that moment, I understood I could learn
something from Torah so powerful that it could create something as
magnificent as my grandmother's Shabbos table. Except she had something even greater; she knew that truth without being able to read one
verse in the original Hebrew. *Torat imekha*.

And so, I think that as part of this book, we need to look back on the achievements of the Jewish women's learning movement through the prism of the *Torat imekha* of our grandmothers. Not to allow the new Torah of the Mothers to displace the old, but rather to help each complement and fertilize the other until we have a new, stronger strain.

Frequently, I do suspect we are losing the old *Torat imekha*. Sometimes in our quest to strengthen and sharpen our learning, we forget the essentials—the need to hear the cry of the oppressed, and to be sensitized to those around us who are in a position of weakness. The Torah gives us the archetypes for these persons and refers to them as the "strangers, orphans and widows." The list is not complete, but is paradigmatic of individuals who, whether by circumstance or birth, are relegated to the margins of society. I am not certain we are fulfilling the mandate of hearing the cry of the oppressed. With more caution, I would venture to suggest that in the struggle of Jewish women to grow as Torah scholars and in other ways, there is a danger we may leave the old *Torat imekha* behind. As a case in point, there was recently a Jewish women's conference in Jerusalem, but as I scanned the program, I looked for mention of the stranger, the orphan and the widow. I didn't find them. In our quest for new heights, we had cast them aside.

II.

I shall expand. We seek, at our peril, to broaden our intellectual and spiritual horizons as Jewish women, while ignoring pressing social issues growing under our feet like mushrooms in the forest after a heavy rain. Judaism is not confined to prayer, to Torah study. In Judaism, the litmus test of our real connection to holiness is ultimately our interpersonal relationships and the kind of society we build. That task is certainly not the sole domain of Jewish women. To relegate these issues to the back burner or ignore them, however, is to call into question the authenticity of our quest. To reduce this to its most basic formula: if I am worried about my ritual or liturgical place in the synagogue when I haven't considered the place of the parentless child in the synagogue, when I haven't allowed the disabled person access to the synagogue, or when I haven't kindled a warm flame in the synagogue with which to draw in those lost Jewish boys and girls exiting the synagogue in plague-like proportions, then I am losing touch with the essentials of Judaism.

In a broken world, so many kinds of people are crying for help and attention. I could speak further of Jewish children raised in exemplary homes who have fled to the streets, or of sexual abuse in the Orthodox community which often goes unacknowledged and unpunished. Unfortunately, there is no end to the list of social issues requiring our attention.

I want to take advantage of this forum, however, to speak of an issue with which my personal history has made me familiar, an issue not being addressed with enough seriousness by the Jewish community: single-mother families and their children in the Orthodox world. My apologies at the outset to those fathers raising their children alone and to my single sisters with no children. Some of what I say here is applicable to them as well, but most is unique to the experiences of the single-mother. It is simply beyond my scope here to encompass all of those who share similar burdens; my intention, however, is not to diminish their singular struggles and journeys.

Ten years ago, I embarked on an expedition into what was for me uncharted territory—the task and challenge of raising four rather young children alone as a divorced mother. Over the years, paragraphs and sentences of this article have written themselves in my mind, and finally the time has come to capture them on paper.

The time is ripe because I write from a position of strength. I have survived and grown immeasurably from the most grueling years. Along the way, I have been privileged to teach Torah for several years, fulfill a lifelong dream to study law, and have recently embarked on a busy practice of Family Law in Jerusalem. I am fortunate to have friends most people only dream of, a supportive family, and the thrill of calling Jerusalem my home. All of that is secondary to the wonder and joy of having four children who continue to blossom in ways that occasionally confound, but more frequently, amaze and delight me.

I struggle to convey what it means to raise one's children alone, especially in the Orthodox world. A divorced friend and I share a refrain: "They just don't have a clue"—"they" being anyone who is not a single-parent, not having an inkling of what our reality implies. I shall attempt to describe what this means in three frequently overlapping areas: the home, the school and the community at large.

The first question is, as always, how does this feel? There is a searing loneliness, which abates but never totally dissipates. It is a loneliness, which I prefer to call "aloneness," which means that every event in one's life is experienced alone, and every challenge is faced alone. This is not the existential loneliness of which R. Soloveitchik *z"l* (of blessed memory), speaks in his *Lonely Man of Faith*. Rather, it is a loneliness that permeates every fiber of one's being as one sits, yet again, a guest at another's Shabbos table, a loneliness that darkens the most joyous events. Personally, it means that there are days when my children have filled me with happiness and with pride, and there is no one with whom to share that. There are those magical moments every parent knows when a child's remarks fill one with laughter, or awe at the insights of the young, and that moment is yours alone. Then there are the special moments in your own life, celebrating your own achievements, when your children are with you, but they cannot share that moment in the way a spouse would.

However, this does not begin to tell the entire story. If I used the term "marginalized" to define the category of strangers, orphans and widows, it was not by accident. I do not believe there is one single-parent (or indeed any single woman) in the Orthodox community who does not feel that the term applies to her. To some, it is painful to walk into a shul or a social event; others choose to lose themselves in a flurry of activities in order to dull the pain. Some do both. I confess to leaving shul after *kedusha* of *Mussaf* so that I don't get caught in the flow of people leaving following services. It is too difficult to see all those wives rejoining their husbands, and to feel yet again that my very presence makes people awkward. So I just slip out.

A declaration from another dear friend. In frustration at the blindness of those around her, she swears that if she ever remarries, she will refuse any invitations from people in her community to herself and her new spouse to stop in for *kiddush* on a Shabbos morning. She even has a response prepared. "Where," she will ask, "Where were you all those years?" Why, she wants to know, was she invisible to them the countless times she walked out of shul alone, two young children in tow?

The single-parent deals with that aloneness in every challenge, confrontation and intense moment in life. All of the strains—physical, financial and emotional—are faced alone. A child screams with an ear infection and must be taken to the emergency room at two in the morning, while the mother knows that when the alarm rings in a few hours she will have to get up, pack the other children off to school, and make it through the rest of the day. Or, she may have to surrender her dignity and ask the financial director of a school or a synagogue for a discount, when finances are stretched well past the point that the budget can bear.

Other times, there is the urge to hang up on the teacher who calls to say that her child isn't doing his math homework. No one has ever told that math teacher that children of divorce have lower levels of concentration and motivation than children growing up in two-parent homes. More than that, in all probability, no one has ever told that math teacher that this is a child of divorce. One must then try to explain to this teacher that it is impossible to comply with a learning situation where the home is expected to review homework and check notebooks every day. There is only one parent who is working more hours than she can count, simply struggling to keep her house functional.

And then when a child is not making it in school and the system is ready to expel him, she must face the principal and beg him to take her child back, imploring him to bend the rules a little. Somehow, not all of our communities have yet acknowledged that each and every child deserves a place to learn.

It pains me to reveal that I have only once encountered a principal somewhat sensitive to the reality of single-parent families. A principal has yet to ask me what the special needs of my children are, growing up in a single-parent home.

III.

Having said all of this, the time has come to confess the most compelling reason for me to share my experiences and observations: synagogues. How can it be that a community of fine persons steeped in Torah and *mitzvot* can see an eight year old boy walk into a synagogue alone, struggle with a Yom Kippur *mahzor*, and ten men do not instantly rush to his side, ready to help him with his prayers? I allow this glimpse into a private world which I zealously guard, because a dear friend encouraged me by saying: "Perhaps if you write your article, the following week there will be just one Jewish child in the world who won't have to stand alone in synagogue." For that child I write.

Another friend who raised two children on her own, had a son who found attending synagogue a painful experience and followed the services with difficulty. All of his mother's attempts to find someone to accompany her son to synagogue failed, until in a moment of desperation she threatened the Rabbi of the synagogue that she would disguise herself as a man to be able to sit with her son. An alternate solution was swiftly found. What happens, though, to those children whose mothers are too timid to even ask someone in the community to accompany their sons?

The children of single-parent homes tend to be at once invisible and hyper-visible. They are invisible in that few want to see them as they walk to *shul* alone Friday night, or attempt to buy their *lulav* and *etrog* (used on Sukkot), wondering which one to choose. They are those children who don't show up at a father and son learning evening, or if they do, there is an awkward acknowledgment of their presence and a scramble to deal with the problem they create. (I shall never forget the kindness of a principal, when I once went to a party for my youngest son's nursery, where the grand finale of the program was for fathers to begin dancing with the children. When I realized what was happening I felt the familiar pit in my stomach, wondering where my son would be during this section of the evening. Before the music even began, that principal made sure he was holding tightly to my son's hand.) On the other hand, the absence of one active parent is highly visible. These children are often castigated, physically or verbally, by adults who are of the opinion that they are in need of a parent who is fully capable of educating her child.

Similarly, there is an irony and a paradox in the way many communities relate to the single-mother. On one hand, they often prefer not to recognize her; on the other hand, when she moves to break free of the prescribed molds, she may be reproved, either subtly or openly. Her parenting skills are subject to the scrutiny of the marketplace and her courtships, if and when they unfold, tend to be the stuff of public discussion. More than this, when she tries to change the rules, some backs bristle.

When I made the decision to attend law school, my youngest child was six and my oldest just twelve years old. There were those who confronted me with moral indignation, questioning how I could abandon my children, as it were. I have often thought that if instead of studying, I was employed long hours in a low-paying, menial job, no one would have flinched. Those filled with indignation at the fate of my children didn't offer to cook them a hot meal when my schedule became overwhelming. Those who had quietly and steadfastly encouraged me to move forward were the ones who were always there with the offers to babysit and last minute Shabbos invitations.

Apparently, this latter group divined the needs of someone struggling to get along, and had the wherewithal to act. And it is part of our identity as the Jewish people to know what it means to be marginal, and to know how to take the requisite steps. The sole intention should not just be to minimize the pain of those on the fringes of society, but to ease them into the mainstream—or better yet, to widen the stream.

In her *Studies on the Book of Exodus*, Nechama Leibowitz, *z"l* asks why the Jewish People required the experience of exile and slavery in Egypt. Why was this painful ordeal the necessary precondition for revelation at Sinai and entry into *Eretz Yisrael*? Leibowitz uses a number of prooftexts to show the purpose of the experience in Egypt. The dehumanization and suffering were meant to ensure that when we entered the world as a fully developed nation with a land of our own, we would always be certain to be sensitive to those groups in our society hovering on the periphery. In this way, she gives meaning to the juxtaposition found numerous times in the Torah of those verses admonishing us to be empathetic to the stranger, the orphan and the widow, with the verse, "For you were strangers in the Land of Egypt."

During the month of *Nissan*, all Jews expend tremendous physical and emotional energies personalizing this experience of slavery and redemption. One of the goals of this process is to impart to us the requisite sensitivity towards those marginalized members of our society. Holiday seasons are undoubtedly the most trying times of year in single-parent homes, and for single Orthodox Jews in general. Pesach is emblematic of the single-mother's experience of attempting to create a holiday, and I choose the verb "to create" consciously. It becomes her role, and her role alone, to transform the day from something mundane to a holiday in the most literal sense of the word, a day elevated to a holy and transcendent dimension.

Several months before Pesach, a single-parent begins to prepare mentally for where she will spend the *seder*—in her own home or as a guest? She will weigh the relative disadvantages of each option. The disadvantage of being a guest is the sense of still being in exile, still wandering without having found one's place. The disadvantage of staying home is that it may simply be overwhelming to organize and conduct a *seder*, and she may not be able to entice any guests to her table, as not everyone wants to be a guest in a single-mother's home. About a month before the actual holiday, she steels herself. She knows that at some point in the next four weeks, sadness and loneliness will envelop her, and her mission is to make certain that by the time she sits down at the *seder* table, there is a smile on her face—a real smile that comes from inside.

As in every Jewish home, the myriad of tasks is overwhelming, but in this case, there is only one adult directing the operation, down to every last minute detail. Some small undertakings could be done by others with minimal effort, relieving the woman facing the holiday alone. It will sound trivial to an ear unfamiliar with the single-mother's world, but the need to order *matzot* or sell her own *hametz* can sometimes feel to these women like an incredibly heavy burden. Recall that in the Orthodox community, a number of these tasks take place in a distinctly male arena, and the need to go to a Rabbi in order to sell *hametz* may be, for many women, a veritable ordeal. And at no time of the year is a phone call to a single-mother more befitting than prior to a holiday. It would take the caller a few moments, and a few simple words go a very long way in dispelling the sense of loneliness and isolation.

Finally, the home is in order, everything sparkles, the children shine at the *seder* table—and there is no other adult to share in the glow, no one who has sent her a new plant or flowers with which to greet the holiday. Ultimately, what moves all of us past these crises is an awareness that what we do has meaning and purpose. Even without being acknowledged with flowers or an appreciative remark, we have the certainty of having succeeded in our act of creation, and we derive comfort from the value of having forged another link in the chain of tradition that extends from one generation to the next.

IV.

To return, in summary, to the meaning of *Torat imekha*, of "Torah of the Mothers": the Torah study in which we engage prior to Pesach, and all our learning, should make each of us even more acutely aware of the needs around us. If it has failed to do that, then we must carefully examine our motives for learning, as well as how and what we are learning. If we can learn about the unity of the Jewish People as embodied in the four species of Sukkot, but we haven't helped a widow to build her *sukkah*, then we have learned nothing. If we can listen to the Torah reading on Shabbos morning, but be blind to the mother walking home alone with her children, we have heard nothing. To put it more boldly, it may not even be Torah study, but an academic or intellectual exercise appealing to one or another part of our being—but it is not Torah, and is certainly not *Torat imekha*.

I hope, finally, that I have been able to touch my reader, to make her or him discern some of the many hurdles that confront the single-mother and her children. I hope that having seen them, she or he will be moved to take the necessary steps and create the required mechanisms within communities, to take into account other kinds of people whose cries need to be heard, and to reach out to them. This is *Torat imekha*, the ability to hear the cry of the oppressed—and act. I have no doubt that Jewish women, once made aware of someone's plight, will take action, for I know from firsthand knowledge that "Israel is a compassionate people, the descendents of compassionate people" (ישראל רחמנים בני רחמנים). It is simply that sometimes our eyes must be opened.

Prior to the next *Yom Iyun* (intensive study day), replete with uplifting and erudite learning, before sitting down to study, we need to ask ourselves if we have made room in our lives for the stranger, the orphan and the widow, in all of their contemporary permutations. And only when we can answer in the affirmative will we be able to take the *Torat imekha* that we inherited from every Jewish woman since *Sarah imenu* ("Sarah our mother") to newer and greater heights.

CONTRIBUTORS

Rachel Adelman has a B.A. in Biology from Reed College and is completing her M.A. in Tanakh at MaTaN (*Machon Torani leNashim*– The Sadie Rennert Women's Institute for Torah Studies) in Jerusalem through Baltimore Hebrew University. She is a regular contributor to MaTaN's web page with commentaries on the weekly Bible portion. She also teaches Torah in her community in Beit Shemesh and writes poetry, much of her work inspired by biblical and midrashic sources. Her published works include "Judah's Bones" (*Commentary*), "In the Skin of a Lion," and "A Voice from the End of the World" (*European Judaism*).

Chana Balanson (Deutsch) *z"l* (1951–1992), held an M.A. in Jewish History from Touro College. She taught Bible and Jewish Thought for many years at MaTaN Women's Institute for Torah Studies, and at Michlalah Jerusalem College for Women. Additional biographical information is appended to her essay.

Miriam Birnbaum is a Ph.D. candidate in the Skirball Department of Hebrew and Judaic Studies at New York University. She holds B.A. degrees in History and English Literature, and in Jewish Education, from York University (Toronto). She was a Fellow of the Machon Gavoha Institute at Nishmat Jerusalem Center for Advanced Jewish Study for Women, has studied at Michlalah Jerusalem College for Women, and is now working as a Research Assistant at the Gruss Talmudic Civil Law and Israeli Law Collections of N.Y.U. Law School.

Erica Brown holds M.A. degrees in Religious Education and Judaic and Near Eastern Studies from Jews' College, the University of London, and Harvard University. She has served as the scholar-in-residence for the Combined Jewish Philanthropies of Boston, and has been on the faculty of numerous adult education programs in Boston, London and Jerusalem, including Jews' College, Midreshet Lindenbaum and Nishmat. She has published several articles on the study of Tanakh and education. She is currently a Jerusalem Fellow at the Mandel School for Advanced Professional Jewish Educators in Jerusalem.

Yardena Cope-Yossef holds a Law degree from Hebrew University, Jerusalem. She has studied in the Scholars Program at MaTaN Women's Institute for Torah Studies and in the Talmud Department of the Hebrew University, Jerusalem. She has taught Talmud, topics in Jewish Law, and courses on Women in Judaism at MaTaN, Pardes and an on-line course through the World Zionist Organization's Jewish University in Cyberspace. She currently serves as Director and teacher at MaTaN's Advanced Talmudic Institute.

Sarah Malka Eisen studied at the University of Toronto and Michlalah Jerusalem College for Women, and holds a B.A. in the Humanities. She has taught at Midreshet Rachel (Shapell's), She'arim, Ma'ayanot Institute of Jewish Studies in Jerusalem and various other seminaries, *yeshivot* and educational programs.

Jane Falk (Margolis) holds a Ph.D. in Linguistics from Princeton University and M.A. degrees from Princeton, Columbia University and the Sorbonne (Paris). She has also taught at the Hebrew University, City University of New York and University of California, Berkeley. She currently works as a consultant in cross-cultural communication to multinational corporations, and has taught this subject at the College of Netanya and Bar-Ilan University.

Ilana Goldstein Saks has a B.A. in Religion from Barnard College and an M.A. in Tanakh from Bar-Ilan University. She studied for a number of years in the Bruriah Scholars' program at Midreshet Lindenbaum in Jerusalem. She teaches Tanakh at Midreshet Lindenbaum and Midreshet HaRova in Jerusalem.

Tamara Goshen-Gottstein holds a B.A. degree in Education and Administration from Antioch University. She is a certified Childbirth Assistant and works as a labor companion. She studied at Yakar in Jerusalem and went on to teach in the Yakar Women's Beit Midrash. She currently works with a group of midwives exploring Jewish texts related to fertility, midwifery and birth.

Susan Handelman received her Ph.D. in Literature from the State University of New York and was Professor of English and Jewish Studies for twenty years at the University of Maryland. She is a faculty member of the Wexner Foundation for adult Jewish education, and has recently moved to Israel to join the faculty of the English Department at Bar-Ilan University. She is the author of two books, *The Slayers of Moses: The Emergence of Rabbinic Interpretation in Modern Literary Theory* (State University of New York Press, 1982) and *Fragments of Redemption: Jewish Thought and Literary Theory in Scholem, Benjamin and Levinas* (Indiana University Press, 1991). She has also co-edited with Joseph Smith, *Psychoanalysis and Religion* (Johns Hopkins University Press, 1990) and co-translated and edited *On the Essence of Chassidus* by Rabbi Menachem Schneerson, the Lubavitcher Rebbe (Kehot, 1978).

Batya Hefter has an M.A. in Rabbinic Literature from Hebrew University, Jerusalem. She has taught at Midreshet Lindenbaum and MaTaN Institute for Women's Torah Studies. She founded the Women's Beit Midrash in Cleveland, and is currently the founding director of the Women's Beit Midrash of Efrat and Gush Etzion where she teaches Rabbinic Literature and Jewish Thought.

Judy Klitsner has a B.A. in political science from Barnard College. She has taught Bible at the Pardes Institute of Jewish Studies for the past decade. She considers her formative educational experience to be the many years spent learning under the tutelage of Professor Nechama Leibowitz. She has lectured in a wide variety of adult educational forums, including Jewish Federations across the U.S., the London School of Jewish Studies, The Edah Conference, The Bat Kol Seminar and at numerous Hillel groups on university campuses in North America, such as Harvard, Brandeis and Yale.

Rella Kushelevsky received her Ph.D. in Hebrew Literature from Bar-Ilan University. She currently lectures on Midrash, Literature and Jewish Literary Thematology at the Department of the Literature of the Jewish People at Bar-Ilan University. Her publications include *Moses and the Angel of Death* (Peter Lang, 1990) and various articles on Midrash and Thematology.

Bryna Levy has a teaching degree from Michlalah Jerusalem College for Women, an M.A. in Biblical Interpretation from McGill University, and a Ph.D. in Bible from the Bernard Revel Graduate School of Yeshiva University. She has taught Bible at McGill University, Yeshiva University High School for Girls, Michlalah Jerusalem College for Women and Touro College, where she served as Assistant Professor of Bible. She currently teaches Bible at Midreshet Moriah and serves as the Director of MaTaN's Advanced Institute for Bible Studies and Graduate Program in Tanakh.

Simi Peters has an M.A. in Linguistics from the Graduate School and University Center of the City University of New York. She has taught Tanakh and Midrash at Michlalah College, Nishmat Institute and Midreshet Rachel and is involved in teacher training. She is currently at work on a book dealing with methodology in the study of Midrash. Her publications include "Rereading Midrash" (*Jewish Action*) and "Thoughts on a Metaphor" (*Wellsprings*).

Caroline Peyser holds a B.A. in Jewish Studies and a Psy.D. in Clinical Psychology from Yeshiva University. She teaches Talmud at Midreshet Lindenbaum, Jerusalem and works in private practice as a clinical psychologist.

Joy Rochwarger has a B.A. in Comparative Religion from Barnard College and an M.A. in Jewish History and Biblical Exegesis from Touro College, Jerusalem. She was the Assistant Dean at Midreshet Moriah Yeshiva for Women in Jerusalem, served the Jewish community of Poland as Community Consultant, and was a Jerusalem Fellow at the Mandel School for two years. She is currently working for the Mandel Foundation for Jewish Education in New York.

Gilla Ratzersdorfer Rosen received her B.A. from Barnard College and her M.A. in Comparative Literary Studies from Manchester University. She has lectured at Jews' College (London), Yakar, Pardes, Nishmat, and the Melton Center at the Hebrew University. She has recently become a Halakhic Consultant for Taharat Hamishpachah at Nishmat. At present, she is pursuing a doctorate and teaching Talmud and Midrash at Yakar, in Jerusalem.

Leah Rosenthal has a B.A. in Talmud and Jewish Thought from the Hebrew University, Jerusalem and a teaching degree from the Kerem Institute in Jerusalem. She teaches Talmud at the Pardes Institute of Jewish Studies, the Kerem Institute, and the graduate program at Pelech High School for Girls, all in Jerusalem.

Sara Idit (Susan) Schneider has a B.A. in Molecular, Cellular and Developmental Biology from the University of Colorado and worked as a laboratory researcher before immigrating to Israel. She is the founding director of A Still Small Voice (www.amyisrael.co.il/smallvoice), a correspondence school that provides weekly Jewish teachings to subscribers around the world. She has recently finished a book called *MoonLore: Kabbalistic Writings on the Fall and Rise of the Shekhinah* to be published by Jason Aronson. She has also published "Eating as Tikun," and two articles in *B'Or Ha'Torah*, "Evolution, Form and Consciousness," and "The Underside of Creative Expression."

Esther Sha'anan has an Ll.B. from Sha'arei Mishpat College of Law and an M.A. in Criminology from Hebrew University, Jerusalem. She has taught at She'arim College of Jewish Studies for Women and Midreshet Rachel, Jerusalem. She currently practices law in Jerusalem.

Yael Unterman has a B.A. in Psychology from Bar-Ilan University, and is completing her M.A. in Jewish History at Touro College. She teaches at MaTaN Institute for Women's Torah Studies, Michlelet Neve Daniel, and has lectured in a variety of frameworks, including the Rothberg School of the Hebrew University and the Limmud Conference in England. She also works for Shorashim as a facilitator in Jewish-Zionist identity seminars for the Israel Defense Forces. She is currently writing a biography of Nechama Leibowitz to be published by Urim Publications.

Ora Wiskind Elper has an M.A. in Comparative Literature and Ph.D. in Hebrew Literature from Hebrew University, Jerusalem. She teaches Jewish thought at Michlalah College, MaTaN Institute for Women's Torah Studies and Touro College, Jerusalem. Her publications include *Tradition and Fantasy in the Tales of Reb Nahman of Bratslav* (State University of New York Press, 1998). She has also translated works from Hebrew, French and German, including *An Introduction to the Kabbalah* by Moshe Hallamish (S.U.N.Y. Press, 1999) and *Rav Avraham Itzhak HaCohen Kook: Between Rationalism and Mysticism* by Benjamin Ish-Shalom (S.U.N.Y. Press, 1993).